# Functions of Several Variables

WENDELL H. FLEMING
*Brown University*

ADDISON-WESLEY PUBLISHING COMPANY, INC.
READING, MASSACHUSETTS · PALO ALTO · LONDON · DALLAS · ATLANTA

**ADDISON-WESLEY PUBLISHING COMPANY, INC.**

*Printed in the United States of America*



*Library of Congress Catalog Card No. 65-15697*

# Functions of Several Variables

This book is in the

**ADDISON-WESLEY SERIES IN MATHEMATICS**

LYNN H. LOOMIS, *Consulting Editor*

*To* Brown University

*on the occasion of its bicentennial*

1764–1964

# Preface

The purpose of this book is to give a systematic development of differential and integral calculus for functions of several variables. The traditional topics from advanced calculus are included: maxima and minima, chain rule, implicit function theorem, multiple integrals, divergence and Stokes' theorems, and so on. However, the treatment differs in several important respects from the traditional one. Vector notation is used throughout, and the distinction is maintained between $n$-dimensional euclidean space $E^n$ and its dual. By introducing convex and concave functions a more thorough treatment of extrema is possible. The elements of the Lebesgue theory of integrals are given. In place of the traditional vector analysis in $E^n$, we first introduce exterior algebra and the calculus of exterior differential forms. The formulas of vector analysis then become special cases of formulas about differential forms and integrals over $r$-manifolds in euclidean $E^n$, for arbitrary dimensions $r$ and $n$.

The book is suitable for a college course at the advanced undergraduate level. By omitting certain chapters, a one semester course can be based on it. For instance, if the students already have a good knowledge of partial differentiation, then Chapters 1 and 2 can be quickly reviewed, omitting those topics concerning convexity. Substantial parts of Chapters 4, 5, 6, and 7 can then be covered in a semester. There is also enough material for a more leisurely full-year course.

Some knowledge of linear algebra and elementary topology of $E^n$ is presumed. However, the results needed from linear algebra are reviewed (in some cases without proof), and the necessary topological material is given in the Appendix.

The author is indebted to many colleagues and students at Brown University. Without the stimulation they provided, this book would not have been written. Thanks are especially due Ubiratan D'Ambrosio and John Brothers, who carefully read the entire manuscript and furnished many improvements to it. Thanks are also due Fred Almgren, William Tyndall, and William Ziemer, who read various chapters; and to Joan Phillips and Lance McVay, who verified answers to the homework problems.

*Providence, Rhode Island* W. H. F.
*December 1964*

# Contents

CHAPTER 1

# Euclidean Spaces, Convexity

This book is about the differential and integral calculus of functions of several variables. For this purpose one needs first to know some basic properties of euclidean space of arbitrary finite dimension $n$. We begin in Section 1–1 with that topic. Later in the chapter, convex sets and convex functions are discussed.

Some knowledge of linear algebra and elementary topology is needed to read this book. For the reader's convenience the necessary material about topology has been included in the Appendix. An acquaintance with elementary calculus for functions of one variable is presumed. However, some of the basic theorems from elementary calculus are given at the end of the Appendix. Linear algebra is reviewed as needed in various parts of the book.

**Format.** The word *Theorem* has been reserved for what the author considers the most important results. Results of lesser depth or interest are labeled *Proposition*. The symbol ▮ indicates the end of the proof of a theorem or proposition. Occasionally part of a proof is left to the reader as a homework exercise. The sections marked with an asterisk (*) may be omitted without disrupting the organization. References and a brief historical survey are given at the end of the book.

## 1–1 EUCLIDEAN $E^n$

While calculus has been motivated in large part by problems from geometry and physics, its foundations rest upon the idea of number. Therefore a thorough treatment of calculus should begin with a study of the real numbers. The real number system satisfies a list of axioms about arithmetic and order, which express properties of numbers with which everyone is familiar from elementary mathematics. To be more precise, the real number system is what is called in algebra an ordered field. To this list of axioms must be added one further axiom which expresses the completeness of the real number system. The completeness axiom can be introduced in several different forms. Of these we shall take the property that any nonempty set of real numbers which is bounded above has a least upper bound. This axiom is more subtle than the others and is the foundation stone for some of the most important theorems in calculus. The axioms for the real number system are listed in Section 1 of the Appendix.

**Scalars and vectors.** By *scalar* we shall mean a real number. In elementary mathematics a vector is described as a quantity which has both direction and length. Vectors are illustrated by drawing arrows issuing from a given point $\mathbf{0}$. The point at the head of the arrow specifies the vector. Therefore we may (and shall) say that this point *is* the vector. Thus in two dimensions a vector is just a point $(x, y)$ of the plane $E^2$. Vectors in $E^2$ are added by the parallelogram law, which amounts to adding corresponding components. Thus

$$(x, y) + (u, v) = (x + u, y + v).$$

The product of $(x, y)$ by a scalar $c$ is the vector $(cx, cy)$. The zero vector is $(0, 0)$.

With this in mind, let us define the space $E^n$ for any positive integer $n$. The elements of $E^n$ are $n$-tuples $(x^1, \ldots, x^n)$ of real numbers. For short, we write $\mathbf{x}$ for the $n$-tuple $(x^1, \ldots, x^n)$. The notation $\mathbf{x} \in E^n$ means "$\mathbf{x}$ is an element of $E^n$." The elements of $E^n$ will be called *vectors*, and also *points*, depending on which term seems more suggestive in the context. Addition and scalar multiplication are defined in $E^n$ as follows. If

$$\mathbf{x} = (x^1, \ldots, x^n), \qquad \mathbf{y} = (y^1, \ldots, y^n)$$

are any two elements of $E^n$, then

$$\mathbf{x} + \mathbf{y} = (x^1 + y^1, \ldots, x^n + y^n).$$

If $\mathbf{x} \in E^n$ and $c$ is a scalar, then

$$c\mathbf{x} = (cx^1, \ldots, cx^n).$$

The *zero element* of $E^n$ is

$$\mathbf{0} = (0, \ldots, 0).$$

With these definitions $E^n$ satisfies the axioms for a vector space (Appendix A–2). The term "vector" will be reserved for elements of $E^n$ rather than those of any space satisfying these axioms.

The superscripts should not be confused with powers of $x$. For instance, $(x^i)^2$ means the square of the $i$th entry $x^i$ of the $n$-tuple $(x^1, \ldots, x^n)$.

If $n = 1$ we identify the 1-tuple $\mathbf{x} = (x)$ with the scalar $x$. In this case addition and scalar multiplication reduce to ordinary addition and multiplication of real numbers. If $n = 2$ or 3 we usually write $(x, y)$ or $(x, y, z)$ as is commonly done in elementary analytic geometry, rather than $(x^1, x^2)$ or $(x^1, x^2, x^3)$. Practically all of the theorems will be stated and proved for arbitrary dimension $n$. However, the special cases $n = 2, 3$ will frequently appear in the examples and homework problems.

The notions of vector sum and multiplication by scalars determine the vector space structure of $E^n$, but are not enough to define the concepts of distance and angle. These arise by introducing an inner product in $E^n$. An inner product assigns to each pair $\mathbf{x}, \mathbf{y}$ of vectors a scalar, and must have the five properties listed in Problem 2 at the end of the section. The one which we shall use is the *standard euclidean inner product*, denoted by $\cdot$ ,

$$\mathbf{x} \cdot \mathbf{y} = \sum_{i=1}^{n} x^i y^i.$$

The vector space $E^n$ with this inner product is called *euclidean n-space*. Other inner products in $E^n$ will be considered later in Section 1–6.

The *euclidean norm* (or *length*) of a vector $\mathbf{x}$ is

$$|\mathbf{x}| = \sqrt{\mathbf{x} \cdot \mathbf{x}}\,.$$

It is positive except when $\mathbf{x} = \mathbf{0}$, and satisfies the following two important inequalities: For every $\mathbf{x}, \mathbf{y} \in E^n$,

$$|\mathbf{x} \cdot \mathbf{y}| \le |\mathbf{x}|\,|\mathbf{y}| \qquad \text{(Cauchy's inequality)}, \qquad (1\text{–}1)$$

$$|\mathbf{x} + \mathbf{y}| \le |\mathbf{x}| + |\mathbf{y}| \qquad \text{(triangle inequality)}. \qquad (1\text{–}2)$$

*Proof of (1–1).* If $\mathbf{y} = \mathbf{0}$, then both sides of (1–1) are 0. Therefore let us suppose that $\mathbf{y} \neq \mathbf{0}$. For every scalar $t$,

$$(\mathbf{x} + t\mathbf{y}) \cdot (\mathbf{x} + t\mathbf{y}) = \mathbf{x} \cdot \mathbf{x} + 2t\mathbf{x} \cdot \mathbf{y} + t^2\mathbf{y} \cdot \mathbf{y},$$

since the inner product is commutative and distributive [Problem 2,* parts (a), (b), (c)]. The left-hand side is $|\mathbf{x} + t\mathbf{y}|^2$, and $\mathbf{x} \cdot \mathbf{x} = |\mathbf{x}|^2$, $\mathbf{y} \cdot \mathbf{y} = |\mathbf{y}|^2$. The right-hand side is quadratic in $t$, and has a minimum when

$$t = t_0 = -\frac{\mathbf{x} \cdot \mathbf{y}}{\mathbf{y} \cdot \mathbf{y}}.$$

Substituting this expression for $t$, we find that

$$0 \le |\mathbf{x} + t_0\mathbf{y}|^2 = |\mathbf{x}|^2 - \frac{|\mathbf{x} \cdot \mathbf{y}|^2}{|\mathbf{y}|^2},$$

or

$$|\mathbf{x} \cdot \mathbf{y}|^2 \le |\mathbf{x}|^2|\mathbf{y}|^2.$$

The last inequality is equivalent to Cauchy's inequality. ▮

From the proof we see that equality in Cauchy's inequality is equivalent to the fact that $|\mathbf{x} + t_0\mathbf{y}| = 0$, that is, that $\mathbf{x} + t_0\mathbf{y} = 0$. Thus, if $\mathbf{y} \neq 0$,

*The problem number, for example, Problem 2, refers to the end of the section in which it is cited, unless stated otherwise.

$|\mathbf{x} \cdot \mathbf{y}| = |\mathbf{x}|\,|\mathbf{y}|$ *if and only if* $\mathbf{x}$ *is a scalar multiple of* $\mathbf{y}$. If $\mathbf{x} \cdot \mathbf{y} = |\mathbf{x}|\,|\mathbf{y}|$, then $\mathbf{x}$ is a *nonnegative* scalar multiple of $\mathbf{y}$ (and conversely).

*Proof of (1–2).* We write, as before,

$$(\mathbf{x} + \mathbf{y}) \cdot (\mathbf{x} + \mathbf{y}) = \mathbf{x} \cdot \mathbf{x} + 2\mathbf{x} \cdot \mathbf{y} + \mathbf{y} \cdot \mathbf{y}.$$

From Cauchy's inequality,

$$|\mathbf{x} + \mathbf{y}|^2 \leq |\mathbf{x}|^2 + 2|\mathbf{x}|\,|\mathbf{y}| + |\mathbf{y}|^2,$$

or

$$|\mathbf{x} + \mathbf{y}|^2 \leq (|\mathbf{x}| + |\mathbf{y}|)^2.$$

This is equivalent to the triangle inequality. ∎

If $\mathbf{y} \neq \mathbf{0}$, equality holds in (1–2) if and only if $\mathbf{x}$ is a nonnegative scalar multiple of $\mathbf{y}$.

Using the fact that $|c\mathbf{x}| = |c|\,|\mathbf{x}|$, one can easily prove by induction on $m$ the following extension of the triangle inequality:

$$\left| \sum_{j=1}^{m} c^j \mathbf{x}_j \right| \leq \sum_{j=1}^{m} |c^j|\,|\mathbf{x}_j| \tag{1–3}$$

for every choice of scalars $c^1, \ldots, c^m$ and of vectors $\mathbf{x}_1, \ldots, \mathbf{x}_m$. We recall that $\sum_j c^j \mathbf{x}_j$ is called a linear combination of $\mathbf{x}_1, \ldots, \mathbf{x}_m$.

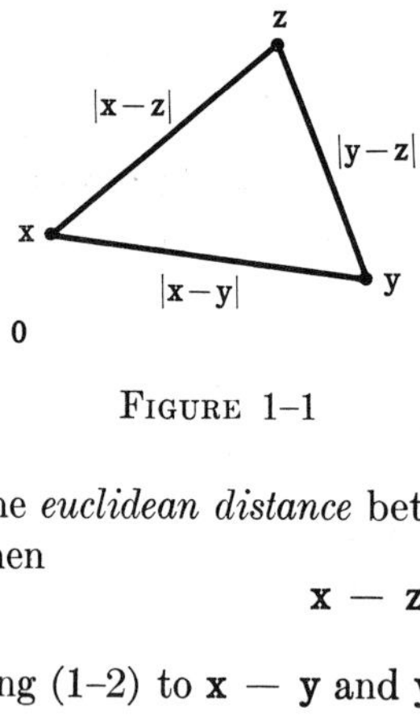


FIGURE 1–1

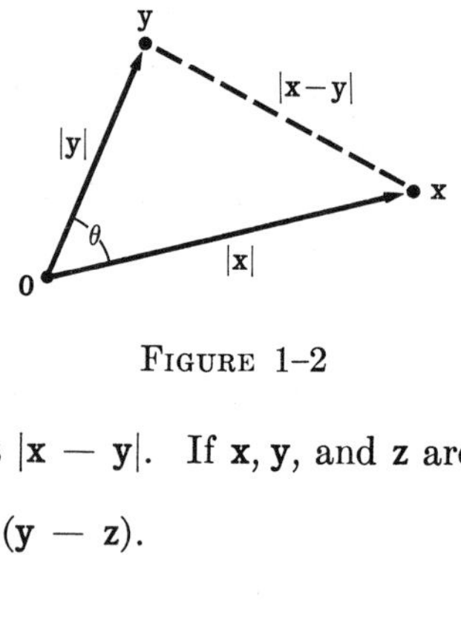


FIGURE 1–2

The *euclidean distance* between $\mathbf{x}$ and $\mathbf{y}$ is $|\mathbf{x} - \mathbf{y}|$. If $\mathbf{x}$, $\mathbf{y}$, and $\mathbf{z}$ are vectors, then

$$\mathbf{x} - \mathbf{z} = (\mathbf{x} - \mathbf{y}) + (\mathbf{y} - \mathbf{z}).$$

Applying (1–2) to $\mathbf{x} - \mathbf{y}$ and $\mathbf{y} - \mathbf{z}$, we have

$$|\mathbf{x} - \mathbf{z}| \leq |\mathbf{x} - \mathbf{y}| + |\mathbf{y} - \mathbf{z}|,$$

which justifies the name "triangle inequality." See Fig. 1–1.

If $\mathbf{x}$ and $\mathbf{y}$ are nonzero vectors, the *angle* $\theta$ between $\mathbf{x}$ and $\mathbf{y}$ is defined by the formula

$$\cos\theta = \frac{\mathbf{x} \cdot \mathbf{y}}{|\mathbf{x}|\,|\mathbf{y}|}, \qquad 0 \leq \theta \leq \pi.$$

This formula agrees in dimensions $n = 2, 3$ with the one in elementary analytic geometry. The vectors $\mathbf{x}$ and $\mathbf{y}$ are *orthogonal* if $\mathbf{x} \cdot \mathbf{y} = 0$, in other words, if $\theta$ is a right angle. We have

$$|\mathbf{x} - \mathbf{y}|^2 = |\mathbf{x}|^2 + |\mathbf{y}|^2 - 2\mathbf{x} \cdot \mathbf{y},$$

or

$$|\mathbf{x} - \mathbf{y}|^2 = |\mathbf{x}|^2 + |\mathbf{y}|^2 - 2|\mathbf{x}|\,|\mathbf{y}| \cos \theta,$$

which is the law of cosines from trigonometry (Fig. 1–2).

**Orthonormal bases.** $E^n$ is an $n$-dimensional vector space, and any linearly independent set of vectors $\{\mathbf{v}_1, \ldots, \mathbf{v}_n\}$ with $n$ elements is a basis for it.

A basis $\{\mathbf{v}_1, \ldots, \mathbf{v}_n\}$ for $E^n$ is called *orthonormal* if $\mathbf{v}_i \cdot \mathbf{v}_j = \delta_{ij}$, where

$$\delta_{ij} = \begin{cases} 0 & \text{if } i \neq j, \\ 1 & \text{if } i = j, \end{cases} \qquad i, j = 1, \ldots, n.$$

The symbol $\delta_{ij}$ was first introduced by the mathematician Kronecker, and consequently is called "Kronecker's delta." The unit coordinate vectors

$$\begin{aligned} \mathbf{e}_1 &= (1, 0, \ldots, 0), \\ \mathbf{e}_2 &= (0, 1, 0, \ldots, 0), \\ &\vdots \\ \mathbf{e}_n &= (0, 0, \ldots, 0, 1) \end{aligned}$$

form the *standard* orthonormal basis for $E^n$. We have, for each $\mathbf{x} \in E^n$,

$$\mathbf{x} = (x^1, \ldots, x^n) = \sum_{i=1}^{n} x^i \mathbf{e}_i.$$

For instance, $(2, -1, 3) = 2\mathbf{e}_1 - \mathbf{e}_2 + 3\mathbf{e}_3$.

If $\mathbf{v}$ is any unit vector ($|\mathbf{v}| = 1$), then $\mathbf{x} \cdot \mathbf{v}$ is the *component of* $\mathbf{x}$ with respect to $\mathbf{v}$. Since $\mathbf{x} \cdot \mathbf{e}_i = x^i$, the components of $\mathbf{x}$ with respect to the standard orthonormal basis vectors $\mathbf{e}_1, \ldots, \mathbf{e}_n$ are $x^1, \ldots, x^n$. If $\{\mathbf{v}_1, \ldots, \mathbf{v}_n\}$ is any orthonormal basis for $E^n$, then $\mathbf{v}_1, \ldots, \mathbf{v}_n$ are mutually orthogonal unit vectors. Each $\mathbf{x} \in E^n$ can be uniquely represented as a linear combination

$$\mathbf{x} = c^1\mathbf{v}_1 + \cdots + c^n\mathbf{v}_n. \tag{1–4}$$

Taking the inner product of each side with $\mathbf{v}_i$ and using the formula $\mathbf{v}_i \cdot \mathbf{v}_j = \delta_{ij}$, we obtain

$$\mathbf{x} \cdot \mathbf{v}_i = c^i.$$

The coefficients $c^i$ in (1–4) are just the components of $\mathbf{x}$ with respect to the orthonormal basis vectors.

**PROBLEMS**

1. Let $n = 4$, $\mathbf{x} = \mathbf{e}_1 - \mathbf{e}_2 + 2\mathbf{e}_4 = (1, -1, 0, 2)$, $\mathbf{y} = 3\mathbf{e}_1 - \mathbf{e}_2 + \mathbf{e}_3 + \mathbf{e}_4 = (3, -1, 1, 1)$. Find $\mathbf{x} + \mathbf{y}$, $\mathbf{x} - \mathbf{y}$, $|\mathbf{x} + \mathbf{y}|$, $|\mathbf{x} - \mathbf{y}|$, $|\mathbf{x}|$, $|\mathbf{y}|$, $\mathbf{x} \cdot \mathbf{y}$. Verify (1–1) and (1–2) in this example.
2. Prove that the standard euclidean inner product in $E^n$ has the following five properties:

   (a) $\mathbf{x} \cdot \mathbf{y} = \mathbf{y} \cdot \mathbf{x}$. (b) $(\mathbf{x} + \mathbf{y}) \cdot \mathbf{z} = \mathbf{x} \cdot \mathbf{z} + \mathbf{y} \cdot \mathbf{z}$.
   (c) $(c\mathbf{x}) \cdot \mathbf{y} = c(\mathbf{x} \cdot \mathbf{y})$. (d) $\mathbf{0} \cdot \mathbf{x} = 0$. (e) $\mathbf{x} \cdot \mathbf{x} > 0$ if $\mathbf{x} \neq \mathbf{0}$.
3. Using Problem 2, show that
$$(\mathbf{w} + c\mathbf{x}) \cdot (\mathbf{y} + d\mathbf{z}) = \mathbf{w} \cdot \mathbf{y} + c\mathbf{x} \cdot \mathbf{y} + d\mathbf{w} \cdot \mathbf{z} + cd\mathbf{x} \cdot \mathbf{z}.$$
4. Show that $2|\mathbf{x}|^2 + 2|\mathbf{y}|^2 = |\mathbf{x} + \mathbf{y}|^2 + |\mathbf{x} - \mathbf{y}|^2$. What does this say about parallelograms? See Fig. 1–3.

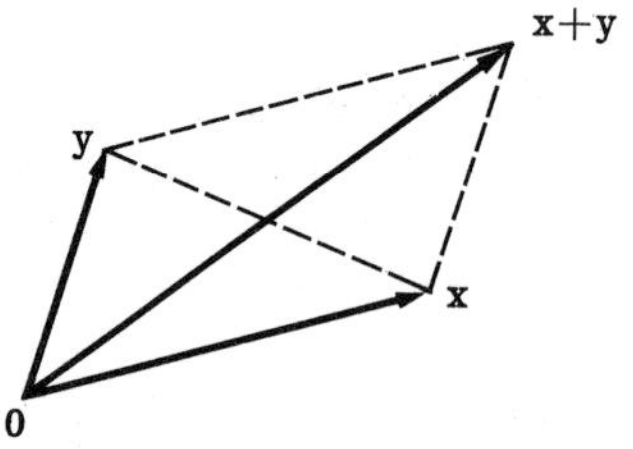


FIGURE 1–3

5. Show that $|\mathbf{x} + \mathbf{y}|\,|\mathbf{x} - \mathbf{y}| \leq |\mathbf{x}|^2 + |\mathbf{y}|^2$ with equality if and only if $\mathbf{x} \cdot \mathbf{y} = 0$. What does this say about parallelograms?
6. Prove (1–3), using (1–2) and induction on $m$.
7. Let $n = 4$, and $\mathbf{v}_1 = \frac{1}{5}(3\mathbf{e}_1 + 4\mathbf{e}_3)$, $\mathbf{v}_2 = \frac{1}{5}(4\mathbf{e}_2 - 3\mathbf{e}_4)$, $\mathbf{v}_3 = (\sqrt{2}/10)(-4\mathbf{e}_1 + 3\mathbf{e}_2 + 3\mathbf{e}_3 + 4\mathbf{e}_4)$. Show that $\mathbf{v}_1, \mathbf{v}_2, \mathbf{v}_3$ are mutually orthogonal unit vectors. Find a unit vector $\mathbf{v}_4$ such that $\mathbf{v}_1, \mathbf{v}_2, \mathbf{v}_3, \mathbf{v}_4$ form an orthonormal basis for $E^4$.
8. Show that the distance between any two elements of an orthonormal basis for $E^n$ is $\sqrt{2}$.
9. (*Gram-Schmidt process.*) Let $\{\mathbf{x}_1, \ldots, \mathbf{x}_n\}$ be a basis for $E^n$. Let $\mathbf{v}_1 = |\mathbf{x}_1|^{-1}\mathbf{x}_1$, $\mathbf{y}_2 = \mathbf{x}_2 - (\mathbf{x}_2 \cdot \mathbf{v}_1)\mathbf{v}_1$, $\mathbf{v}_2 = |\mathbf{y}_2|^{-1}\mathbf{y}_2$, $\mathbf{y}_3 = \mathbf{x}_3 - (\mathbf{x}_3 \cdot \mathbf{v}_1)\mathbf{v}_1 - (\mathbf{x}_3 \cdot \mathbf{v}_2)\mathbf{v}_2$, $\mathbf{v}_3 = |\mathbf{y}_3|^{-1}\mathbf{y}_3, \ldots, \mathbf{v}_n = |\mathbf{y}_n|^{-1}\mathbf{y}_n$. Show that $\{\mathbf{v}_1, \ldots, \mathbf{v}_n\}$ is an orthonormal basis for $E^n$.

*Note:* In this book, "Show that . . ." and "Prove that . . ." both mean "give a valid mathematical proof."

## 1–2 SETS, FUNCTIONS

In this section we have collected a number of basic definitions and some notation which will be used repeatedly. We presume that the reader is acquainted with the most elementary aspects of set theory. The symbols

$$\in, \notin, \cup, \cap, -, \subset$$

stand, respectively, for *is an element of*, *is not an element of*, *union*, *intersection*, *difference*, and *inclusion*. Sets will ordinarily be denoted by capital italicized letters. A set will be described either by listing its elements or by some property characterizing them. Thus $\{2, 5, 7\}$ is the set whose elements are the three numbers 2, 5, and 7. If $S$ is a set and $\pi$ a property pertaining to elements of $S$, then $\{p \in S : \pi\}$ denotes *the set of all* $p \in S$ *with property* $\pi$. For example, $\{(x, y) \in E^2 : x^2 + y^2 = 1\}$ is the circle with center $(0, 0)$ and radius 1. The set $\{(x, y) \in E^2 : x^2 + y^2 = -1\}$ is the empty set. The set $\{(x, y) \in E^2 : x^2 + y^2 \geq 0\}$ is all of $E^2$.

When the set $S$ in question is clear from the context, we write simply $\{p : \pi\}$.

**Topology of $E^n$.** By the *$\delta$-neighborhood* of a point $\mathbf{x}$, where $\delta > 0$, let us mean the set of all $\mathbf{y}$ distant less than $\delta$ from $\mathbf{x}$. Thus, if $U$ denotes the $\delta$-neighborhood of $\mathbf{x}$, then

$$U = \{\mathbf{y} : |\mathbf{y} - \mathbf{x}| < \delta\}.$$

A set $A \subset E^n$ is *open* if for every point $\mathbf{x} \in A$ there is a neighborhood $U$ of $\mathbf{x}$ such that $U \subset A$. A set $A$ is *closed* if its complement $A^c = E^n - A$ is open. The open sets determine what is called the *topology of* $E^n$. Such notions as limit, continuity, connected set, and compact set can be expressed in terms of open sets and are called topological notions. They are described in the Appendix.

Using the triangle inequality it can be shown that any neighborhood $U$ is an open set (see Section A–3). We shall sometimes refer to neighborhoods as *open spherical n-balls*. When $n = 1, 2, 3$, they are respectively open intervals in $E^1$, open circular disks in $E^2$, and open spherical balls in $E^3$. A set of the form $\{\mathbf{y} : |\mathbf{y} - \mathbf{x}| \leq \delta\}$, where $\delta > 0$, is closed. Such sets are called *closed spherical n-balls.*

**Cartesian product sets.** If $S$ and $T$ are sets, then the *cartesian product* set $S \times T$ is formed by taking all ordered pairs $(p, q)$ where $p \in S$ and $q \in T$. For example, if $S = \{1, 2, \ldots, n\}$ and $T = \{1, 2, \ldots, m\}$, then the elements of $S \times T$ are pairs $(i, j)$ of positive integers with $1 \leq i \leq n, i \leq j \leq m$. In the same way, the plane $E^2$ is the cartesian product $E^1 \times E^1$.

If $S_1, \ldots, S_n$ are sets, then the *n-fold cartesian product* $S_1 \times \cdots \times S_n$ is formed by taking all (ordered) $n$-tuples $(p_1, \ldots, p_n)$, where $p_i \in S_i$ for each $i = 1, \ldots, n$. In particular $E^n = E^1 \times \cdots \times E^1$.

**Functions.** A function $f$ assigns to each element $p$ of some set $S$ an element $f(p)$ of another set $T$. The element $f(p)$ is called the *value* of $f$ at $p$.

This is not a satisfactory definition of "function" because of the ambiguity of the word "assigns." A more careful definition is the following. Any subset $f$ of the cartesian product $S \times T$ is called a *relation* between $S$ and $T$. A relation $f$ is called a *function* if for every $p \in S$ there is exactly one $q \in T$ such that $(p, q) \in f$. This element $q$ is denoted by $f(p)$.

The set $S$ is the *domain* of $f$. We shall sometimes say that $f$ is a function *from S into T*. If for every $q \in T$ there is some $p \in S$ such that $q = f(p)$, then we say that $f$ is *onto* $T$. A function $f$ is *univalent* (or *one-one*) if $p_1 \neq p_2$ implies that $f(p_1) \neq f(p_2)$.

This book is about the calculus of functions whose domains are subsets of $E^n$. Such functions are frequently called by the suggestive but imprecise name, "functions of $n$ real variables." We may occasionally use this name in passages intended to motivate a more careful discussion to follow. However, we never try to make precise the phrase "$n$ real variables." It was only after such vague terms as "variable" and "quantity" were abandoned that calculus was put on a foundation acceptable by present-day standards.

A function $f$ from a set $S$ into $E^1$ is a *real-valued* function. When $S \subset E^1$, $f$ is a real-valued "function of one real variable." Among such functions are the algebraic functions and elementary transcendental functions (sin, cos, tan, log, etc.), which should be familiar from elementary calculus. The exponential function is denoted in this book by "exp." Thus $\exp x = e^x$, where $e$ is the base for natural logarithms.

Functions with values in some euclidean $E^n$, $n \geq 1$, are called *vector-valued* and will be indicated by boldface letters (say, $\mathbf{g}$). A vector-valued function $\mathbf{g}$ from a subset $\Delta$ of some euclidean $E^r$ into $E^n$ will also be called a *transformation* from $\Delta$ into $E^n$. By merely writing "transformation" in place of "vector-valued function," we have of course introduced no new mathematical idea. However, the word "transformation" is supposed to have a geometric flavor which aids intuition. Some authors say "mapping" instead of "transformation." The differential calculus of transformations is developed in Chapters 3 and 4.

If $f$ and $g$ are functions with the same domain $S$ and values in a vector space $\mathcal{V}$, then the sum $f + g$ is defined by

$$(f + g)(p) = f(p) + g(p)$$

for every $p \in S$. In particular, it makes sense to speak of sums of real-valued functions or of transformations. If $f$ has values in $\mathcal{V}$ and $\phi$ is real valued, then $\phi f$ is the $\mathcal{V}$-valued function given by

$$(\phi f)(p) = \phi(p)f(p)$$

for every $p \in S$. If $\phi$ is a constant function, $\phi(p) = c$ for every $p \in S$, then we write $cf$ instead of $\phi f$.

Often one is interested only in the values of a function $f$ for elements of some subset $A$ of its domain. The *restriction* of $f$ to $A$ is the function with domain $A$ and the same values as $f$ there. It is denoted by $f|A$. Thus

$$f|A = \{(p, f(p)) : p \in A\}.$$

For instance, if a real-valued function $f$ is integrated over an interval $I \subset E^1$, then it is only $f|I$ which is important. The values of $f$ outside $I$ do not affect the integral.

**Functions on cartesian products.** Let $S_1$ and $S_2$ be sets, and $f$ a function from the cartesian product $S_1 \times S_2$ into a set $T$. Given $p_1 \in S_1$, let $f(p_1, \ )$ denote the function from $S_2$ into $T$ whose value at each $p_2 \in S_2$ is $f(p_1, p_2)$. Given $p_2 \in S_2$, the function $f( \ , p_2)$ from $S_1$ into $T$ is similarly defined.

## 1-3 LINEAR FUNCTIONS

Let $L$ be a real-valued function whose domain is $E^n$.

**Definition.** The function $L$ is *linear* if:

(a) $L(\mathbf{x} + \mathbf{y}) = L(\mathbf{x}) + L(\mathbf{y})$ for every $\mathbf{x}, \mathbf{y} \in E^n$; and
(b) $L(c\mathbf{x}) = cL(\mathbf{x})$ for every $\mathbf{x} \in E^n$ and scalar $c$.

These two conditions are equivalent to the single condition $L(c\mathbf{x} + d\mathbf{y}) = cL(\mathbf{x}) + dL(\mathbf{y})$ for every $\mathbf{x}, \mathbf{y} \in E^n$ and scalars $c, d$. By induction, if $L$ is linear, then

$$L\left(\sum_{j=1}^{m} c^j \mathbf{x}_j\right) = \sum_{j=1}^{m} c^j L(\mathbf{x}_j) \tag{1-5}$$

for every $m, \mathbf{x}_1, \ldots, \mathbf{x}_m \in E^n$, and scalars $c^1, \ldots, c^m$. In words this states that "$L$ of a linear combination of $\mathbf{x}_1, \ldots, \mathbf{x}_m$ is the corresponding linear combination of $L(\mathbf{x}_1), \ldots, L(\mathbf{x}_m)$."

If $a_1, \ldots, a_n$ are real numbers, then the function $L$ defined by

$$L(\mathbf{x}) = a_1 x^1 + \cdots + a_n x^n, \tag{1-6}$$

for every $\mathbf{x} \in E^n$, is linear. Conversely, if $L$ is a linear function, let

$$a_i = L(\mathbf{e}_i), \qquad i = 1, \ldots, n.$$

For each $\mathbf{x}$ we have

$$\mathbf{x} = x^1\mathbf{e}_1 + \cdots + x^n\mathbf{e}_n.$$

Applying (1-5) with $c^j = x^j$, $\mathbf{x}_j = \mathbf{e}_j$, and $m = n$, we get

$$L(\mathbf{x}) = x^1 L(\mathbf{e}_1) + \cdots + x^n L(\mathbf{e}_n).$$

This has the form (1-6).

Let us denote the right-hand side of (1-6) by $\mathbf{a} \cdot \mathbf{x}$. We have proved:

**Proposition 1.** *A real-valued function $L$ is linear if and only if there exist real numbers $a_1, \ldots, a_n$ such that $L(\mathbf{x}) = \mathbf{a} \cdot \mathbf{x}$ for every $\mathbf{x} \in E^n$.* ∎

The object $\mathbf{a}$ will be called a *covector* and $a_1, \ldots, a_n$ are its components. Covectors are not elements of $E^n$, but belong to the $n$-dimensional vector space $(E^n)^*$ dual to $E^n$. This will be explained in more detail later in the section. Note that the components $x^i$ of a vector are denoted with *superscripts* and the components $a_i$ of a covector with *subscripts.* The number $\mathbf{a} \cdot \mathbf{x}$ is called the *scalar product* of the covector $\mathbf{a}$ and vector $\mathbf{x}$. The components of $\mathbf{a}$ satisfy the formula $a_i = \mathbf{a} \cdot \mathbf{e}_i$.

If $\mathbf{a}$ is a covector, then there is a vector $\mathbf{y}$ with the same components, $y^i = a_i$ for $i = 1, \ldots, n$. This vector $\mathbf{y}$ has the property that

$$\mathbf{y} \cdot \mathbf{x} = \sum_{i=1}^{n} y^i x^i = \sum_{i=1}^{n} a_i x^i = \mathbf{a} \cdot \mathbf{x}. \tag{1–7}$$

The $\cdot$ denotes the scalar product on the right-hand side and the euclidean inner product on the left-hand side.

Since covectors can be changed into vectors by this simple device, it is not immediately apparent why there is any need to distinguish between $E^n$ and its dual. In fact, by this device we shall avoid practically any mention of covectors until Chapter 2. However, they become useful there in the definition of differential (Section 2–2) and later in the statement of the chain rule (Section 4–4). The distinction between vectors and covectors is essential in the development of the last two chapters (6 and 7) of the book.

**Note about terminology.** What we call covectors are often called *covariant* vectors. What we call vectors are then called *contravariant* vectors. A vector-valued function (which we call a transformation) is often called a *contravariant vector field.* Similarly a covector-valued function (which we shall call a differential form of degree 1 in Section 2–6) is the same thing as a *covariant vector field.*

**Hyperplanes, half-spaces.** The solutions of a linear equation $\mathbf{a} \cdot \mathbf{x} = c$ form what is called a hyperplane (point for $n = 1$, line for $n = 2$, plane for $n = 3$). More precisely:

**Definition.** A *hyperplane* in $E^n$ is a set of the form $\{\mathbf{x} : \mathbf{a} \cdot \mathbf{x} = c\}$, where $\mathbf{a} \neq \mathbf{0}$.

Of course, $\mathbf{a} \neq \mathbf{0}$ means that $a_i \neq 0$ for at least one $i$. If $b$ is a scalar, then $ba_1, \ldots, ba_n$ are the components of the covector $b\mathbf{a}$. For any nonzero scalar $b$, $\{\mathbf{x} : \mathbf{a} \cdot \mathbf{x} = c\} = \{\mathbf{x} : (b\mathbf{a}) \cdot \mathbf{x} = bc\}$. Thus the covector $\mathbf{a}$ and scalar $c$ defining a hyperplane are determined only up to a scalar multiple. If $c \neq 0$, we may, for instance, always take $c = 1$.

A hyperplane $P = \{\mathbf{x} : \mathbf{a} \cdot \mathbf{x} = c\}$ is *parallel* to $\mathrm{P}_1 = \{\mathbf{x} : \mathbf{a} \cdot \mathbf{x} = c_1\}$ for any $c_1 \neq c$. If $c_1 = 0$, then $P_1$ contains $\mathbf{0}$, and $P_1$ is a vector subspace of $E^n$ of dimension $n - 1$. This last statement follows from Problem 5.

**Example.** Find the hyperplane $P$ in $E^4$ which contains the four points $\mathbf{e}_1$, $\mathbf{e}_1 + 2\mathbf{e}_2$, $\mathbf{e}_2 + 3\mathbf{e}_3$, $\mathbf{e}_3 + 4\mathbf{e}_4$. Every $\mathbf{x} \in P$ must satisfy the equation $\mathbf{a} \cdot \mathbf{x} = c$, where $\mathbf{a}$ and $c$ must be found. Taking in turn $\mathbf{x} = \mathbf{e}_1$, $\mathbf{x} = \mathbf{e}_1 + 2\mathbf{e}_2, \ldots$, we obtain

$$c = \mathbf{a} \cdot \mathbf{e}_1 = a_1, \qquad c = \mathbf{a} \cdot (\mathbf{e}_1 + 2\mathbf{e}_2) = a_1 + 2a_2,$$

$$c = \mathbf{a} \cdot (\mathbf{e}_2 + 3\mathbf{e}_3) = a_2 + 3a_3, \qquad c = \mathbf{a} \cdot (\mathbf{e}_3 + 4\mathbf{e}_4) = a_3 + 4a_4.$$

From these equations

$$a_1 = c, \qquad a_2 = 0, \qquad a_3 = c/3, \qquad a_4 = c/6.$$

Taking for convenience $c = 6$, we have

$$P = \{\mathbf{x} : 6x^1 + 2x^3 + x^4 = 6\}.$$

**Definition.** Let $\mathbf{a} \neq \mathbf{0}$. A *closed half-space* is a set of the form $\{\mathbf{x} : \mathbf{a} \cdot \mathbf{x} \geq c\}$, and an *open half-space* is a set of the form $\{\mathbf{x} : \mathbf{a} \cdot \mathbf{x} > c\}$.

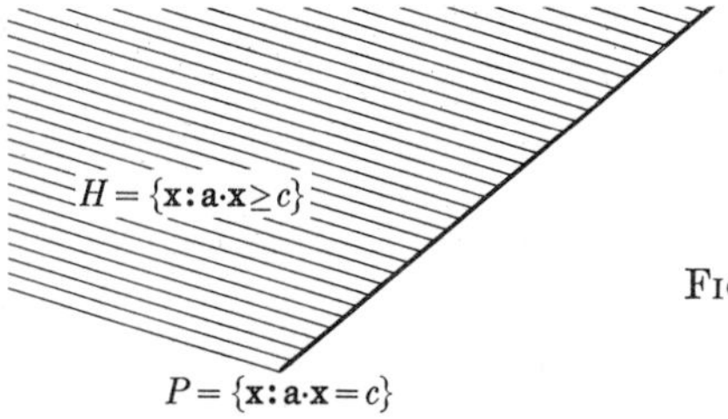


FIGURE 1-4

See Fig. 1-4. A set $H$ of the form $\{\mathbf{x}: \mathbf{a} \cdot \mathbf{x} \leq c\}$, $\mathbf{a} \neq \mathbf{0}$, is a closed half-space, since $H$ is also $\{\mathbf{x} : (-\mathbf{a}) \cdot \mathbf{x} \geq -c\}$. The same remark applies to open half-spaces. A hyperplane $P = \{\mathbf{x} : \mathbf{a} \cdot \mathbf{x} = c\}$ divides $E^n$ into two half-spaces. More precisely, $E^n - P$ is the union of the open half-spaces

$$\{\mathbf{x} : \mathbf{a} \cdot \mathbf{x} > c\} \text{ and } \{\mathbf{x} : \mathbf{a} \cdot \mathbf{x} < c\}.$$

The definition suggests that a closed half-space is a closed set. To prove this we use the fact that if $f$ is a continuous real-valued function with domain $E^n$, then $\{\mathbf{x} : f(\mathbf{x}) \geq c\}$ is a closed set. See Section A-6. Every linear function is continuous (Problem 4) and has domain $E^n$. Therefore letting $f(\mathbf{x}) = \mathbf{a} \cdot \mathbf{x}$ for every $\mathbf{x} \in E^n$, we conclude that $\{\mathbf{x} : \mathbf{a} \cdot \mathbf{x} \geq c\}$ is closed. Similarly, every open half-space is an open set.

**The dual space of $E^n$.** Let us now give a more thorough description of the space of covectors, dual to $E^n$. The reader may postpone this discussion and study it together with later chapters.

According to Section A-2 every vector space $\mathcal{V}$ has a dual $\mathcal{V}^*$, whose elements are the real-valued linear functions with domain $\mathcal{V}$. If $\mathcal{V}$ has finite dimension $n$, then $\mathcal{V}^*$ also has dimension $n$. Moreover, given any basis for $\mathcal{V}$, there is a dual basis for $\mathcal{V}^*$.

Now let $\mathcal{V} = E^n$.

**Definition.** A *covector* is an element of the space $(E^n)^*$ dual to $E^n$.

Thus a covector is just a real-valued linear function $L$. The basis dual to the standard basis $\{\mathbf{e}_1, \ldots, \mathbf{e}_n\}$ for $E^n$ is the set $\{X^1, \ldots, X^n\}$, where $X^i$ is the linear function such that $X^i(\mathbf{x}) = x^i$ for every $\mathbf{x}$. This is seen from the discussion of dual bases in A–2, setting

$$u_i = \mathbf{e}_i \qquad \text{and} \qquad c^i = x^i, \quad L^i = X^i.$$

The functions $X^1, \ldots, X^n$ are called the *standard cartesian coordinate functions.*

In order to emphasize the duality between vectors and covectors, it is desirable to change the notation for covector. From now on we shall ordinarily denote covectors by $\mathbf{a}, \mathbf{b}, \ldots$ rather than by, say, $L$. As in Proposition 1, we write $\mathbf{a} \cdot \mathbf{x}$ for $L(\mathbf{x})$, and call $\mathbf{a} \cdot \mathbf{x}$ the *scalar product.* The basis dual to $\{\mathbf{e}_1, \ldots, \mathbf{e}_n\}$ will be denoted by $\{\mathbf{e}^1, \ldots, \mathbf{e}^n\}$ rather than $\{X^1, \ldots, X^n\}$.

The notation is chosen so that for every formula about vectors there will be a corresponding formula about covectors obtained by interchanging subscripts and superscripts. For instance, the components of a vector $\mathbf{x}$ satisfy $x^i = X^i(\mathbf{x}) = \mathbf{e}^i \cdot \mathbf{x}$. The corresponding formula for the components of a covector $\mathbf{a}$ is $a_i = \mathbf{a} \cdot \mathbf{e}_i$. In $(E^n)^*$ a euclidean inner product and norm are defined in the same way as in $E^n$.

These facts are summarized in the table below.

| | Vectors | Covectors |
|---|---|---|
| Standard bases | $\mathbf{e}_1, \ldots, \mathbf{e}_n$ | $\mathbf{e}^1, \ldots, \mathbf{e}^n$ |
| | $\mathbf{x} = \sum_{i=1}^{n} x^i \mathbf{e}_i$ | $\mathbf{a} = \sum_{i=1}^{n} a_i \mathbf{e}^i$ |
| Euclidean inner product | $\mathbf{x} \cdot \mathbf{y} = \sum_{i=1}^{n} x^i y^i$ | $\mathbf{a} \cdot \mathbf{b} = \sum_{i=1}^{n} a_i b_i$ |
| Euclidean norm | $\lvert\mathbf{x}\rvert^2 = \mathbf{x} \cdot \mathbf{x}$ | $\lvert\mathbf{a}\rvert^2 = \mathbf{a} \cdot \mathbf{a}$ |
| Scalar product | $\mathbf{a} \cdot \mathbf{x} = \sum_{i=1}^{n} a_i x^i$ | |
| | $\mathbf{e}^i \cdot \mathbf{e}_j = \delta^i_j$ | |
| | $\mathbf{e}^i \cdot \mathbf{x} = x^i$ | $\mathbf{a} \cdot \mathbf{e}_i = a_i$ |

In the table, $\delta^i_j = \delta_{ij}$ is Kronecker's delta (p. 5). The scalar product of a vector and a covector involves only the vector space structure of $E^n$ and its dual. It does not depend on the fact that we chose the euclidean inner product rather than some other inner product. If $E^n$ is given a noneuclidean inner product, then the appropriate formula for changing covectors into vectors is (1–14b) in Section 1–6.

One important fact about vectors and covectors is that their components $x^i$ and $a_i$ change oppositely with respect to linear transformations. This will be seen in Section 4–2.

**PROBLEMS**

1. Let $n = 3$. Find the plane which contains the three points $\mathbf{e}_1$, $\mathbf{e}_2$, and $\mathbf{e}_3 - 3\mathbf{e}_1$. Sketch its intersection with the first octant in $E^3$.
2. (a) Find the hyperplane in $E^4$ containing the four points $\mathbf{0}$, $\mathbf{e}_1 + \mathbf{e}_2$, $\mathbf{e}_1 - \mathbf{e}_2 + 2\mathbf{e}_3$, $3\mathbf{e}_4 - \mathbf{e}_2$.
   (b) Find the value of $t$ for which $t(\mathbf{e}_1 - \mathbf{e}_2) + (1 - t)\mathbf{e}_4$ is in this hyperplane.
3. Prove that any hyperplane is a closed set.
4. Prove that any linear function is continuous. [*Hint:* $|\mathbf{a} \cdot \mathbf{x} - \mathbf{a} \cdot \mathbf{y}| = |\mathbf{a} \cdot (\mathbf{x} - \mathbf{y})|$. Use Cauchy's inequality.]
5. Let $\{\mathbf{x}_1, \ldots, \mathbf{x}_n\}$ be a basis for $E^n$. Define $L$ by the formula

$$L(c^1\mathbf{x}_1 + \cdots + c^n\mathbf{x}_n) = c^n$$

   for every $c^1, \ldots, c^n$. Show that:
   (a) $L$ is a linear function.
   (b) The set $P = \{\mathbf{x} : L(\mathbf{x}) = 0\}$ is a hyperplane containing $\mathbf{0}, \mathbf{x}_1, \ldots, \mathbf{x}_{n-1}$.
   (c) $P$ is the only hyperplane containing these $n$ points.
6. Let $\mathbf{x}_0, \mathbf{x}_1, \ldots, \mathbf{x}_{n-1}$ be such that $\mathbf{x}_1 - \mathbf{x}_0, \ldots, \mathbf{x}_{n-1} - \mathbf{x}_0$ are linearly independent. Prove that there is exactly one hyperplane containing $\mathbf{x}_0, \mathbf{x}_1, \ldots, \mathbf{x}_{n-1}$.

## 1–4 CONVEX SETS

In order to say what the term "convex set" means, let us first define the notion of line segment.

**Definition.** Let $\mathbf{x}_1, \mathbf{x}_2 \in E^n$ with $\mathbf{x}_1 \neq \mathbf{x}_2$. The *line* through $\mathbf{x}_1$ and $\mathbf{x}_2$ is

$$\{\mathbf{x} : \mathbf{x} = t\mathbf{x}_1 + (1 - t)\mathbf{x}_2,\ t \text{ any scalar}\}.$$

If we set $\mathbf{h} = \mathbf{x}_1 - \mathbf{x}_2$, then this can be rewritten as

$$\{\mathbf{x} : \mathbf{x} = \mathbf{x}_2 + t\mathbf{h},\ t \text{ any scalar}\}.$$

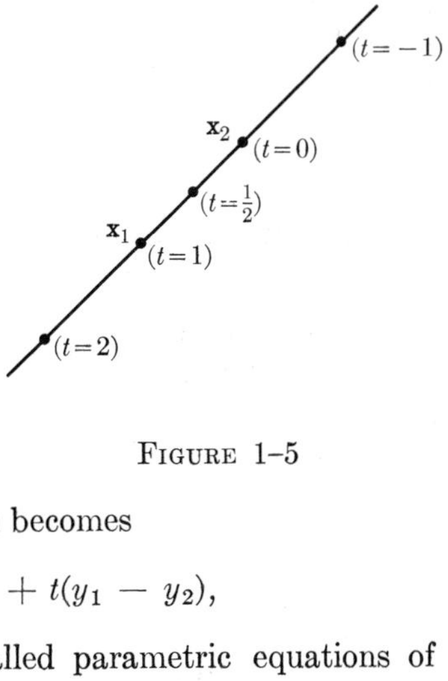


FIGURE 1–5

In the plane $E^2$ the vector equation $\mathbf{x} = \mathbf{x}_2 + t\mathbf{h}$ becomes

$$x = x_2 + t(x_1 - x_2), \qquad y = y_2 + t(y_1 - y_2),$$

which, in elementary analytic geometry, are called parametric equations of the line through $(x_1, y_1)$ and $(x_2, y_2)$.

The *line segment* joining $\mathbf{x}_1$ and $\mathbf{x}_2$ is

$$\{\mathbf{x} : \mathbf{x} = t\mathbf{x}_1 + (1 - t)\mathbf{x}_2,\ t \in [0, 1]\},$$

where $[a, b]$ denotes the set of real numbers $t$ such that $a \leq t \leq b$ (Section A–1).

For example, if $t = \frac{1}{2}$, then $\mathbf{x}$ is the midpoint of the line segment joining $\mathbf{x}_1$ and $\mathbf{x}_2$(Fig. 1–5). The points corresponding to $t = \frac{1}{3}, \frac{2}{3}$ trisect the line segment.

**Definition.** Let $K \subset E^n$. Then $K$ is a *convex* set if the line segment joining any two points of $K$ is contained in $K$ (Fig. 1–6).

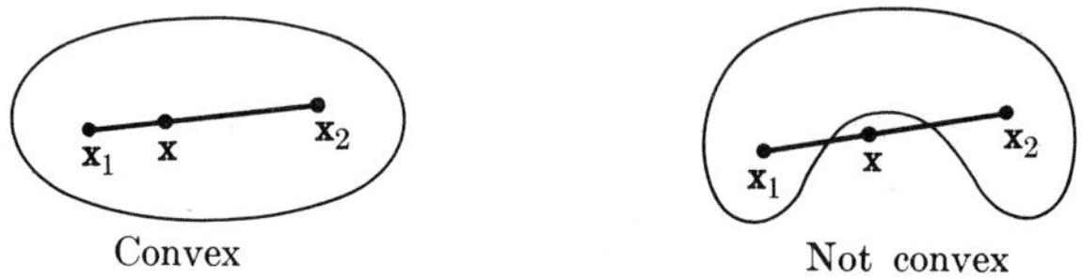


FIGURE 1–6

$E^n$ itself is a convex set. The empty set and sets with just one point trivially satisfy the definition; hence they are convex. The reader should be able to think of several kinds of geometric objects such as lines, planes, spherical balls, regular solids, and so on, which appear to be convex sets. However, geometric intuition is not always a reliable guide, especially in four or more dimensions. In any case, intuition is no substitute for a proof that the set in question is actually convex.

The convex subsets of $E^n$ have many remarkable geometric properties. There is an extensive mathematical literature devoted to them [7],* [10], [13]. However, in the present section we shall go no further than to obtain a few basic facts about convex sets which are useful in calculus. The main result (Theorem 1) will be the characterization of closed convex sets as intersections of closed half-spaces.

The definition of convex set makes sense in any vector space. During recent years the study of convexity in infinite-dimensional vector spaces has furnished powerful new tools in such diverse branches of mathematical analysis as complex function theory, differential equations, and calculus of variations.

Let us consider some familiar subsets of $E^n$ and prove that they are convex. To show that a set $K$ is convex directly from the definition, we must verify that for every $\mathbf{x}_1, \mathbf{x}_2 \in K$ and $t \in [0, 1]$, the point $\mathbf{x} = t\mathbf{x}_1 + (1 - t)\mathbf{x}_2$ also belongs to $K$. In the definition, we assumed that $\mathbf{x}_1 \neq \mathbf{x}_2$. But if $\mathbf{x}_1 = \mathbf{x}_2$, it is trivial that $\mathbf{x} \in K$, since $\mathbf{x} = \mathbf{x}_1 = \mathbf{x}_2$.

**Example 1.** Any closed half-space is a convex set. Let $H = \{\mathbf{x} : \mathbf{a} \cdot \mathbf{x} \geq c\}$, $\mathbf{a} \neq \mathbf{0}$. Let $\mathbf{x}_1, \mathbf{x}_2 \in H$ and $\mathbf{x} = t\mathbf{x}_1 + (1 - t)\mathbf{x}_2$, where $t \in [0, 1]$. Then $\mathbf{a} \cdot \mathbf{x}_1 \geq c$ and $\mathbf{a} \cdot \mathbf{x}_2 \geq c$. Since $t \geq 0$, $t\mathbf{a} \cdot \mathbf{x}_1 \geq tc$; and since $1 - t \geq 0$, $(1 - t)\mathbf{a} \cdot \mathbf{x}_2 \geq (1 - t)c$. Consequently,

$$\mathbf{a} \cdot \mathbf{x} = t\mathbf{a} \cdot \mathbf{x}_1 + (1 - t)\mathbf{a} \cdot \mathbf{x}_2 \geq tc + (1 - t)c = c.$$

This shows that $\mathbf{x} \in H$. Therefore $H$ is a convex set. Similarly, any hyperplane is a convex set (Problem 2) and any open half-space is a convex set.

**Example 2.** Let $U$ be a neighborhood, namely, $U = \{\mathbf{x} : |\mathbf{x} - \mathbf{x}_0| < \delta\}$, for some $\mathbf{x}_0$ and $\delta > 0$. To show that $U$ is a convex set, we proceed as in Example 1.

*Numbers in brackets refer to references at the end of the book.

Let $\mathbf{x}_1, \mathbf{x}_2 \in U$ and $\mathbf{x} = t\mathbf{x}_1 + (1-t)\mathbf{x}_2$, where $t \in [0, 1]$. Then

$$|\mathbf{x}_1 - \mathbf{x}_0| < \delta, \qquad |\mathbf{x}_2 - \mathbf{x}_0| < \delta,$$
$$\mathbf{x} - \mathbf{x}_0 = t(\mathbf{x}_1 - \mathbf{x}_0) + (1-t)(\mathbf{x}_2 - \mathbf{x}_0),$$
$$|\mathbf{x} - \mathbf{x}_0| \le t|\mathbf{x}_1 - \mathbf{x}_0| + (1-t)|\mathbf{x}_2 - \mathbf{x}_0| < \delta.$$

Hence $\mathbf{x} \in U$.

**Example 3.** Let $n = 1$. The nonempty convex subsets of $E^1$ are just the intervals. (See Section A–7 for the definition of interval.)

In more complicated examples it is inconvenient to verify convexity directly from the definition. Instead, it is easier to apply one of the following criteria for convexity.

**Proposition 2a.** *If $K_1, \ldots, K_m$ are convex sets, then their intersection $K_1 \cap \cdots \cap K_m$ is convex.*

*Proof.* Let $\mathbf{x}_1, \mathbf{x}_2$ be any two points of $K_1 \cap \cdots \cap K_m$, $\mathbf{x}_1 \neq \mathbf{x}_2$. Let $l$ denote the line segment joining $\mathbf{x}_1$ and $\mathbf{x}_2$. For each $j = 1, \ldots, m$, $\mathbf{x}_1, \mathbf{x}_2 \in K_j$. Since each $K_j$ is convex, $l \subset K_j$ for each $j = 1, \ldots, m$. Thus $l \subset K_1 \cap \cdots \cap K_m$. ∎

A set which is the intersection of a finite number of closed half-spaces is called a *convex polytope*. Since a half-space is a convex set, any convex polytope is a convex set by Proposition 2a.

**Example 4.** Let $T$ be a triangle in the plane $E^2$. Then $T$ is the intersection of three half-planes, bounded by the lines through the sides of $T$.

A convex polytope is the set of all points $\mathbf{x}$ which satisfy a given finite system of linear inequalities of the form $\mathbf{a}^j \cdot \mathbf{x} \ge c^j, j = 1, \ldots, m$. The theory of linear programming is concerned with the problem of maximizing or minimizing a linear function subject to such a system of linear inequalities. It has various interesting economic and engineering applications (see references [10] and [13]). In Section 2–5, it is shown that the maximum and minimum values of a linear function must occur at "extreme points" of $K$, at least if $K$ is compact.

In the proof of Proposition 2a we did not really use the fact that the number of sets $K_j$ is finite. Therefore we have:

**Proposition 2b.** *The intersection of any collection of convex sets is a convex set.* ∎

In particular, the intersection of any collection of half-spaces is convex. The intersection of any collection of closed sets is a closed set. Hence, if each of the half-spaces is closed, the intersection is a closed, convex set. An important fact about closed convex sets is that, excluding trivial cases, the converse holds. The converse can be stated in a slightly sharper form, in that only half-spaces bounded by supporting hyperplanes need be used (Theorem 1). In order to do this we first state the following.

**Definition.** Let $K$ be a closed convex set. Assume that $K$ is neither the empty set nor $E^n$. A hyperplane $P$ is called *supporting* for $K$ if $P \cap K$ is not empty and $K$ is contained in one of the two half-spaces bounded by $P$.

If $P$ is supporting for $K$, the set $P \cap K$ is convex by Proposition 2a, and contains only boundary points of $K$ (Problem 7). Moreover, given any boundary point of $K$, there is at least one supporting hyperplane containing it (Problem 8). If $K$ has interior points and the boundary fr $K$ is "sufficiently smooth," then given $\mathbf{y} \in \text{fr } K$, there is just one supporting hyperplane containing $\mathbf{y}$. It is the tangent hyperplane to fr $K$ at $\mathbf{y}$, and can be found by the methods of calculus. This will be explained in Section 4–7.

If, for example, $T$ is a triangle in $E^2$, then each vertex is contained in an infinite number of supporting lines to $T$. Each other boundary point is contained in a single supporting line, the line through the edge of $T$ containing it (Fig. 1–7).

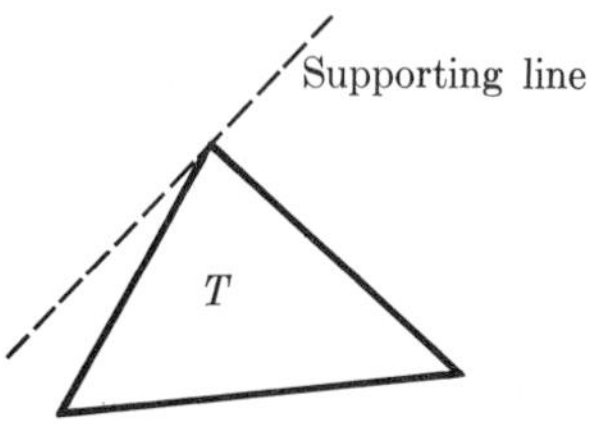

FIGURE 1–7

**Example 5.** Let $B = \{\mathbf{x} : |\mathbf{x}| \leq 1\}$, the closed unit $n$-ball. Then

$$\text{fr } B = \{\mathbf{x} : |\mathbf{x}| = 1\}.$$

Given $\mathbf{y} \in \text{fr } B$, let

$$H_{\mathbf{y}} = \{\mathbf{x} : \mathbf{y} \cdot \mathbf{x} \leq 1\},$$
$$P_{\mathbf{y}} = \{\mathbf{x} : \mathbf{y} \cdot \mathbf{x} = 1\},$$

so that $P_{\mathbf{y}}$ is the hyperplane bounding $H_{\mathbf{y}}$. By Cauchy's inequality and the fact that $|\mathbf{y}| = 1$,

$$\mathbf{y} \cdot \mathbf{x} \leq |\mathbf{y}|\,|\mathbf{x}| = |\mathbf{x}|.$$

Equality holds if and only if $\mathbf{x}$ is a positive scalar multiple of $\mathbf{y}$. Hence $B \subset H_{\mathbf{y}}$ and $B \cap P_{\mathbf{y}}$ consists only of $\mathbf{y}$. The supporting hyperplane to $B$ at $\mathbf{y}$ is $P_{\mathbf{y}}$ (Fig. 1–8).

Again let $K$ be any nonempty, closed convex set which is a proper subset of $E^n$ ($K \neq E^n$). Let $\mathcal{H}_K$ denote the collection of all closed half-spaces $H$ such that $K \subset H$ and the hyperplane $P$ bounding $H$ is supporting for $K$. For instance, the collection $\mathcal{H}_B$ in the above example consists of the various half-spaces $H_{\mathbf{y}}$ for all possible choices of $\mathbf{y} \in \text{fr } B$.

The notation

$$\bigcap_{H \in \mathcal{H}_K} H$$

stands for the intersection of all half-spaces $H \in \mathcal{H}_K$ (see Section A–3).

**Theorem 1.** $K = \displaystyle\bigcap_{H \in \mathcal{H}_K} H.$

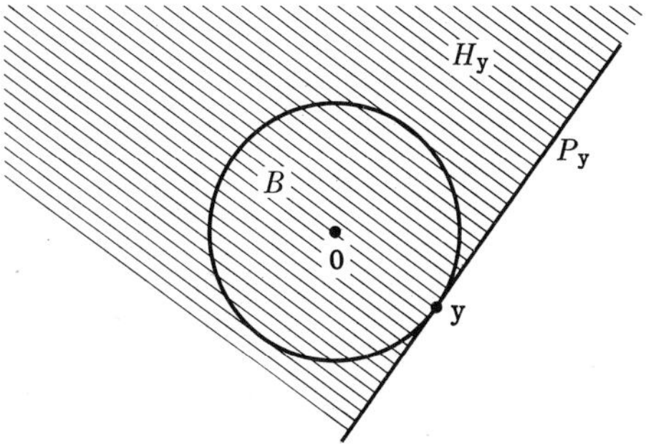


FIGURE 1–8

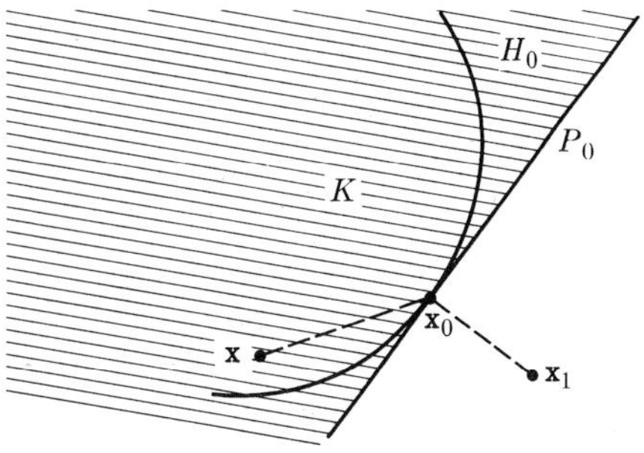


FIGURE 1–9

*Proof.* For convenience let us set

$$K_1 = \bigcup_{H \in \mathcal{H}_K} H.$$

Since $K \subset H$ for each $H \in \mathcal{H}_K$, $K \subset K_1$. Let us show that $K = K_1$.

Suppose it is not. Then there exists some $\mathbf{x}_1 \in K_1 - K$. Since $K$ is a closed set, there is a point $\mathbf{x}_0 \in K$ nearest $\mathbf{x}_1$, that is, $|\mathbf{x} - \mathbf{x}_1| \geq |\mathbf{x}_0 - \mathbf{x}_1|$ for every $\mathbf{x} \in K$ (Fig. 1–9). See Problem 5(c), Section A–8. Consider the closed half-space

$$H_0 = \{\mathbf{x} : (\mathbf{x}_0 - \mathbf{x}_1) \cdot (\mathbf{x} - \mathbf{x}_0) \geq 0\}.$$

Then $\mathbf{x}_1 \notin H_0$ since

$$(\mathbf{x}_0 - \mathbf{x}_1) \cdot (\mathbf{x}_1 - \mathbf{x}_0) = -|\mathbf{x}_0 - \mathbf{x}_1|^2 < 0.$$

To show that $K \subset H_0$ let $\mathbf{x}$ be any point of $K$. Since $K$ is convex, $t\mathbf{x} + (1 - t)\mathbf{x}_0 \in K$ for every $t \in [0, 1]$. Then

$$|t\mathbf{x} + (1 - t)\mathbf{x}_0 - \mathbf{x}_1|^2 \geq |\mathbf{x}_0 - \mathbf{x}_1|^2,$$

or

$$|(\mathbf{x}_0 - \mathbf{x}_1) + t(\mathbf{x} - \mathbf{x}_0)|^2 \geq |\mathbf{x}_0 - \mathbf{x}_1|^2,$$
$$|\mathbf{x}_0 - \mathbf{x}_1|^2 + 2t(\mathbf{x}_0 - \mathbf{x}_1) \cdot (\mathbf{x} - \mathbf{x}_0) + t^2|\mathbf{x} - \mathbf{x}_0|^2 \geq |\mathbf{x}_0 - \mathbf{x}_1|^2.$$

Subtracting $|\mathbf{x}_0 - \mathbf{x}_1|^2$ from both sides and dividing by $t$, we get for $0 < t \leq 1$

$$2(\mathbf{x}_0 - \mathbf{x}_1) \cdot (\mathbf{x} - \mathbf{x}_0) + t|\mathbf{x} - \mathbf{x}_0|^2 \geq 0.$$

Letting $t \to 0^+$ we find that $2(\mathbf{x}_0 - \mathbf{x}_1) \cdot (\mathbf{x} - \mathbf{x}_0) \geq 0$, which shows that $\mathbf{x} \in H_0$. Thus $K \subset H_0$. The boundary of $H_0$ is

$$P_0 = \{\mathbf{x} : (\mathbf{x}_0 - \mathbf{x}_1) \cdot (\mathbf{x} - \mathbf{x}_0) = 0\},$$

and $\mathbf{x}_0 \in P_0$. Hence $P_0 \cap K$ is not empty, and therefore $P_0$ is supporting for $K$. This shows that $H_0 \in \mathcal{H}_K$. Consequently, $K_1 \subset H_0$. But $\mathbf{x}_1 \in K_1$, $\mathbf{x}_1 \notin H_0$, a contradiction. Therefore $K = K_1$. ∎

We give an example to illustrate the theorem.

**Example 6.** Let $f$ be a real-valued function with domain $E^1$, which has everywhere a derivative $f'(x)$. Assume that $f'$ is an increasing function. Let

$$A = \{(x, y) : y \geq f(x)\}.$$

For each $s$ consider the closed half-space $H_s$ above the tangent line to $f$ at $(s, f(s))$, $H_s = \{(x, y) : y - f(s) \geq f'(s)(x - s)\}$. (See Fig. 1–10.) Consider $(x, y) \in A$ and suppose first that $x > s$. By the mean value theorem, $f(x) - f(s) = f'(t)(x - s)$, where $s < t < x$. Since $f'$ is increasing, $f'(t) > f'(s)$. Hence

$$y - f(s) \geq f(x) - f(s) > f'(s)(x - s),$$

which shows that $(x, y) \in H_s$. Similarly, $(x, y) \in H_s$ if $x < s$ or if $x = s$. Therefore $A \subset H_s$ for every $s \in E^1$. If $(x, y) \notin A$, then $y < f(x)$, and $(x, y) \notin H_s$ for $s = x$. Therefore $A$ is the intersection of the collection of closed half-spaces $H_s$. The tangent line at $(s, f(s))$ is supporting for $A$ at that point. The collection $\mathcal{H}_A$ consists of the half-spaces $H_s$.

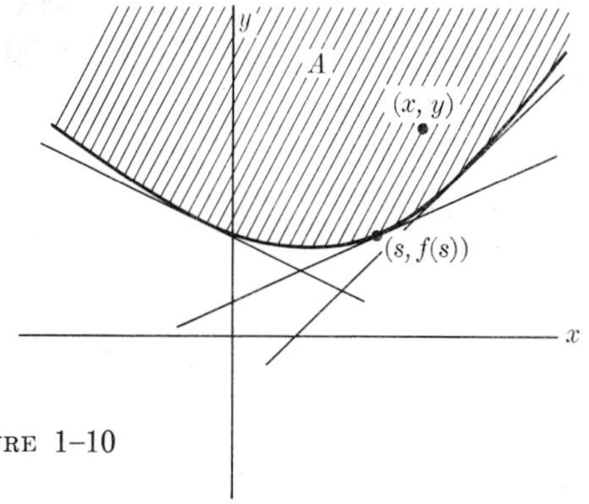


FIGURE 1–10

A sufficient condition that $f'$ be an increasing function is that $f''(x) > 0$ for every $x$. More generally, $f'$ is increasing if $f''(x) \geq 0$ for every $x$ and each point where $f''(x) = 0$ is isolated.

**Convex combinations.** The definition of convex set is expressed in terms of pairs of points. It can also be given in terms of convex combinations of any finite number $m$ of points. Let $\mathbf{x}_1, \ldots, \mathbf{x}_m$ be distinct points ($\mathbf{x}_j \neq \mathbf{x}_k$ if $j \neq k$).

**Definition.** A point $\mathbf{x}$ is a *convex combination* of $\mathbf{x}_1, \ldots, \mathbf{x}_m$ if there exist scalars $t^1, \ldots, t^m$ such that

$$\mathbf{x} = \sum_{j=1}^{m} t^j \mathbf{x}_j, \qquad 1 = \sum_{j=1}^{m} t^j, \qquad t^j \geq 0 \quad \text{for } j = 1, \ldots, m.$$

To say that $\mathbf{x}$ is a convex combination of two points of $S$ is merely to say that $\mathbf{x}$ lies on some line segment with endpoints in $S$. For instance, if $S$ is the circle with equation $x^2 + y^2 = a^2$, then every point in the circular disk

$\{(x, y) : x^2 + y^2 \leq a^2\}$ bounded by $S$ is a convex combination of two points of $S$.

On the other hand, if $S$ consists of three noncollinear points $(x_0, y_0)$, $(x_1, y_1)$, $(x_2, y_2)$, then each boundary point of the triangle with these points as vertices is a convex combination of two points of $S$, but the interior points are not. However, each interior point $(x, y)$ is a convex combination of $(x_2, y_2)$ and some point $(u, v)$ on the edge opposite $(x_2, y_2)$ (Fig. 1–11). Since $(u, v)$ is a convex combination of $(x_0, y_0)$ and $(x_1, y_1)$, we can write $(x, y)$ as a convex combination of the three points $(x_0, y_0)$, $(x_1, y_1)$, $(x_2, y_2)$ as follows. Writing $\mathbf{x} = (x, y)$, $\mathbf{x}_j = (x_j, y_j)$, there exist $s, t \in [0, 1]$ such that

$$\mathbf{x} = t[s\mathbf{x}_0 + (1 - s)\mathbf{x}_1] + (1 - t)\mathbf{x}_2 = t^0\mathbf{x}_0 + t^1\mathbf{x}_1 + t^2\mathbf{x}_2,$$

where $t^0 = ts$, $t^1 = t(1 - s)$, $t^2 = 1 - t$ are nonnegative and $t^0 + t^1 + t^2 = 1$.

**Proposition 3.** *A set $K$ is convex if and only if every convex combination of points of $K$ is a point of $K$.*

*Proof.* Let $K$ be convex. Let us prove by induction on $m$ that if $\mathbf{x}$ is any convex combination of $\mathbf{x}_1, \ldots, \mathbf{x}_m \in K$, then $\mathbf{x} \in K$. The case $m = 1$ is trivial. Assuming the result true for the integer $m \geq 1$, let $\mathbf{x}$ be a convex combination of points $\mathbf{x}_1, \ldots, \mathbf{x}_{m+1}$ of $K$,

$$\mathbf{x} = \sum_{j=1}^{m+1} t^j\mathbf{x}_j, \qquad 1 = \sum_{j=1}^{m+1} t^j, \qquad t^j \geq 0 \quad \text{for } j = 1, \ldots, m + 1.$$

If $t^{m+1} = 1$, then $t^j = 0$ for $j \leq m$ and $\mathbf{x} = \mathbf{x}_{m+1}$ is in $K$. If $t^{m+1} < 1$, let

$$t = 1 - t^{m+1}, \qquad s^j = t^j/t \quad \text{for} \quad j = 1, \ldots, m,$$

$$\mathbf{y} = \sum_{j=1}^{m} s^j\mathbf{x}_j.$$

Then $\mathbf{y}$ is a convex combination of $\mathbf{x}_1, \ldots, \mathbf{x}_m$. By the induction hypothesis, $\mathbf{y} \in K$. But

$$\mathbf{x} = t\mathbf{y} + (1 - t)\mathbf{x}_{m+1},$$

and $t \in [0, 1]$. Hence $\mathbf{x} \in K$.

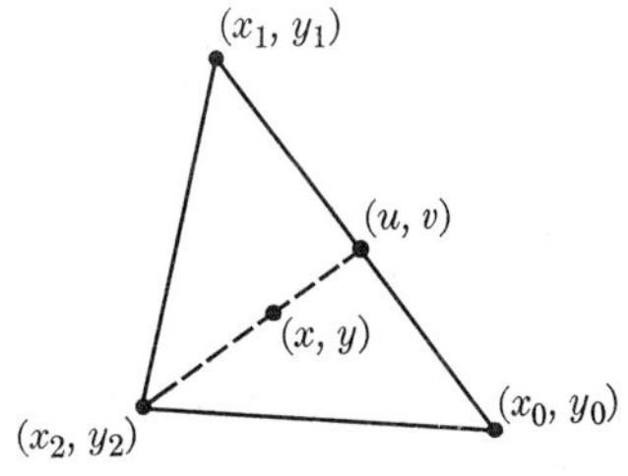


FIGURE 1–11

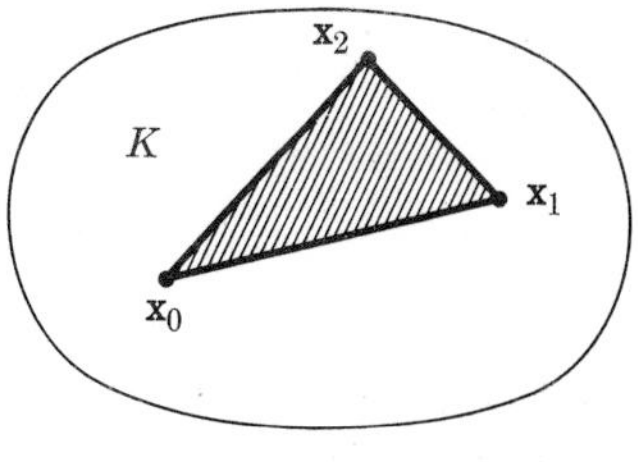


FIGURE 1–12

Conversely, assume that every convex combination of points of $K$ is a point of $K$. In particular this is true for convex combinations of any pair $\mathbf{x}_1, \mathbf{x}_2$ of points of $K$. Hence $K$ is convex. ▮

Let $\mathbf{x}_0, \mathbf{x}_1, \ldots, \mathbf{x}_r$, $r \leq n$, be distinct points of $E^n$ such that the differences $\mathbf{x}_1 - \mathbf{x}_0, \ldots, \mathbf{x}_r - \mathbf{x}_0$ form a linearly independent set. The set of all convex combinations of $\mathbf{x}_0, \mathbf{x}_1, \ldots, \mathbf{x}_r$ is called the *r-simplex with vertices* $\mathbf{x}_0, \mathbf{x}_1, \ldots, \mathbf{x}_r$. A 1-simplex is a line segment, a 2-simplex a triangle, and a 3-simplex a tetrahedron. According to Proposition 3, any simplex whose vertices lie in a convex set $K$ is contained in $K$ (Fig. 1-12).

A point $\mathbf{x}$ of an $r$-simplex can be written in a unique way as a convex combination

$$\mathbf{x} = \sum_{j=0}^{r} t^j \mathbf{x}_j$$

of the vertices $\mathbf{x}_0, \mathbf{x}_1, \ldots, \mathbf{x}_r$ (Problem 6). The numbers $t^0, t^1, \ldots, t^r$ are called the *barycentric coordinates* of $\mathbf{x}$. The $(r - 1)$-dimensional *face* opposite the vertex $\mathbf{x}_i$ is the set of points of the $r$-simplex with $t^i = 0$.

For example, the vertices $\mathbf{x}_0$, $\mathbf{x}_1$, $\mathbf{x}_2$ of a triangle have barycentric coordinates $(1, 0, 0)$, $(0, 1, 0)$, $(0, 0, 1)$, respectively. The midpoint of the face opposite $\mathbf{x}_0$ has barycentric coordinates $(0, \frac{1}{2}, \frac{1}{2})$. The interior points of the triangle have barycentric coordinates $(t^0, t^1, t^2)$, all of which are strictly positive. In each case $t^0 + t^1 + t^2 = 1$.

The simplex with vertices $\mathbf{0}, \mathbf{e}_1, \ldots, \mathbf{e}_n$ is called the *standard n-simplex*. It will be denoted by $\Sigma$, and will be of use later in Section 5-7 in connection with integration. The barycentric coordinates $(t^0, t^1, \ldots, t^n)$ of a point $\mathbf{x} \in \Sigma$ are given by $t^i = x^i$ for $i = 1, \ldots, n$, $t^0 = 1 - (x^1 + \cdots + x^n)$.

***Further results about convex combinations.** In the definition of convex combination, no upper bound was put on the positive integer $m$. However, for most purposes one need consider only $m \leq n + 1$. More precisely:

**Proposition.** *If $S \subset E^n$ and $\mathbf{x}$ is a convex combination of points of $S$, then $\mathbf{x}$ is a convex combination of $n + 1$ or fewer points of $S$.*

*Proof.* Let $\mathbf{x}$ be a convex combination with $m > n + 1$, $t^j > 0$ for $j = 1, \ldots, m$, and $\mathbf{x}_1, \ldots, \mathbf{x}_m \in S$. Let us show that $\mathbf{x}$ is a convex combination of $m - 1$ points of $S$. Since $m - 1 > n$, there exist $c^1, \ldots, c^{m-1}$ not all 0 such that

$$c^1(\mathbf{x}_1 - \mathbf{x}_m) + \cdots + c^{m-1}(\mathbf{x}_{m-1} - \mathbf{x}_m) = \mathbf{0}.$$

Let $c^m = -(c^1 + \cdots + c^{m-1})$. Then

$$\sum_{j=1}^{m} c^j \mathbf{x}_j = \mathbf{0}, \qquad \sum_{j=1}^{m} c^j = 0.$$

Let

$$s^j = t^j - \alpha c^j \quad \text{for } j = 1, \ldots, m,$$

where $\alpha$ is a positive number chosen so that $s^j \geq 0$ for each $j = 1, \ldots, m$ and $s^k = 0$ for some $k$. Explicitly,

$$\frac{1}{\alpha} = \max\left\{\frac{c^1}{t^1}, \ldots, \frac{c^m}{t^m}\right\}.$$

Then

$$\mathbf{x} = \sum_{j \neq k} s^j \mathbf{x}_j, \qquad 1 = \sum_{j \neq k} s^j,$$

and consequently $\mathbf{x}$ is a convex combination of the $m - 1$ points $\mathbf{x}_1, \ldots, \mathbf{x}_{k-1}, \mathbf{x}_{k+1}, \ldots, \mathbf{x}_m$.

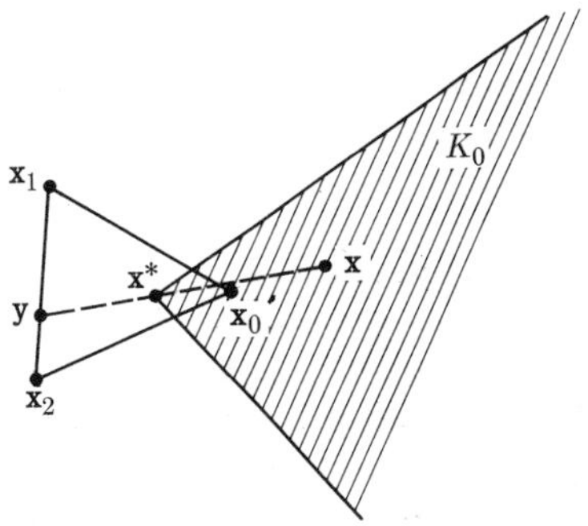


FIGURE 1–13

Either $m - 1 = n + 1$, or else the same argument shows that $\mathbf{x}$ is a convex combination of $m - 2$ points of $S$. Continuing, we find that $\mathbf{x}$ must be a convex combination of $n + 1$ or fewer points of $S$. ▮

If $S$ is the set of vertices of an $n$-simplex $T$ and each of the barycentric coordinates of $\mathbf{x}$ is positive, then $\mathbf{x}$ is not a convex combination of fewer than $n + 1$ points of $S$. Hence the number $n + 1$ is the best possible in the proposition. However, if $S$ is a connected set, then $n + 1$ can be replaced by $n$. This is proved as follows. Suppose that $\mathbf{x}^*$ is a point which is a convex combination of $n + 1$ points $\mathbf{x}_0, \mathbf{x}_1, \ldots, \mathbf{x}_n$ of a connected set $S$, but not of fewer than $n + 1$ points of $S$. The differences $\mathbf{x}_1 - \mathbf{x}_0, \ldots, \mathbf{x}_n - \mathbf{x}_0$ form a linearly independent set; for if not, the reasoning used to prove the proposition above shows that $\mathbf{x}^*$ is a convex combination of $n$ of the points $\mathbf{x}_0, \mathbf{x}_1, \ldots, \mathbf{x}_n$. Therefore $\mathbf{x}_0, \mathbf{x}_1, \ldots, \mathbf{x}_n$ are the vertices of an $n$-simplex $T$, and all the barycentric coordinates of $\mathbf{x}^*$ are positive. Let $T_0$ be the face of $T$ opposite $\mathbf{x}_0$, and

$$K_0 = \{\mathbf{x} : \mathbf{x}^* = t\mathbf{x} + (1 - t)\mathbf{y}, \text{ where } \mathbf{y} \in T_0 \text{ and } t \in [0, 1]\}.$$

$K_0$ is a convex polytope, and its boundary $\operatorname{fr} K_0$ consists of portions of the hyperplanes which contain $\mathbf{x}^*$ and the $(n - 2)$-dimensional faces of $T_0$ (we leave the verification of this to the reader). If $\operatorname{fr} K_0$ intersects $S$, then $\mathbf{x}^*$ is a convex combination of fewer than $n + 1$ points of $S$, contrary to hypothesis (Fig. 1–13). Hence $S \cap \operatorname{fr} K_0$ is empty. The interior $\operatorname{int} K_0$ and the complement $K_0^c = E^n - K_0$ are open sets, their union contains $S$, and their intersection is empty. But $\mathbf{x}_0 \in \operatorname{int} K_0$ and $\mathbf{x}_i \in K_0^c$ for $i = 1, \ldots, n$. Hence $S \cap \operatorname{int} K_0$ and $S \cap K_0^c$ are relatively open, nonempty sets, which implies that $S$ is disconnected (Section A–7). This is a contradiction.

By slightly refining the proof, an even stronger result is obtained. Suppose that $S = S_1 \cup \cdots \cup S_k$, where $k \leq n$ and $S_1, \ldots, S_k$ are connected sets. For each $i = 1, \ldots, n$ consider the corresponding convex polytope $K_i$. Then $\operatorname{int} K_i \cap \operatorname{int} K_j$ is empty whenever $i \neq j$ and $S \cap \operatorname{fr} K_i$ is empty for every $i$. Moreover, $\mathbf{x}_i \in \operatorname{int} K_i$. Since $k \leq n$, some pair of the points $\mathbf{x}_i, \mathbf{x}_j$ must belong to the same set $S_p$. Then $S_p$ is not connected, a contradiction. Hence, if $S$ is the union of $n$ or fewer connected sets, every $\mathbf{x}$ which is a convex combination of points of $S$ is a convex combination of $n$ or fewer points of $S$.

## PROBLEMS

1. Show that $K$ is a convex set by directly applying the definition. Sketch $K$ in the cases $n = 1, 2, 3$.
   (a) $K = \{\mathbf{x} : |x^1| + \cdots + |x^n| \leq 1\}$.
   (b) $K = \{\mathbf{x} = c^1\mathbf{v}_1 + \cdots + c^n\mathbf{v}_n,\ 0 \leq c^i \leq 1 \text{ for } i = 1, \ldots, n\}$, where $\{\mathbf{v}_1, \ldots, \mathbf{v}_n\}$ is a basis for $E^n$. This is the *n-parallelepiped* spanned by $\mathbf{v}_1, \ldots, \mathbf{v}_n$ with $\mathbf{0}$ as a vertex.
2. Let $P$ be a hyperplane. Prove that the line through any two points of $P$ is contained in $P$. Why does this imply that $P$ is a convex set?
3. Show that each of the following subsets of $E^2$ is closed and convex by writing it as the intersection of closed half-planes:
   (a) The regular hexagon with center $(0, 0)$ and $\mathbf{e}_1$ as one vertex.
   (b) $\{(x, y) : y \geq |x|, -1 \leq x \leq 1\}$.
   (c) $\{(x, y) : y \leq \log x, x > 0\}$. [*Hint:* Use the method of Example 6.]
   (d) $\{(x, y) : 0 \leq y \leq \sin x, 0 \leq x \leq \pi\}$.
4. Write the standard $n$-simplex as the intersection of $n + 1$ closed half-spaces. Illustrate for $n = 2$ and $n = 3$.
5. Write $\frac{1}{4}\mathbf{e}_1 + \frac{1}{2}\mathbf{e}_2$ as a convex combination of $\mathbf{e}_1$, $\frac{4}{3}\mathbf{e}_2 - \mathbf{e}_1$. Also write it as a convex combination of $\mathbf{0}$, $\mathbf{e}_2$, $\mathbf{e}_1 + \mathbf{e}_2$. Illustrate.
6. Show that if $\mathbf{x}$ can be represented in two ways as a convex combination of $\mathbf{x}_0, \mathbf{x}_1, \ldots, \mathbf{x}_r$, then $\mathbf{x}_1 - \mathbf{x}_0, \ldots, \mathbf{x}_r - \mathbf{x}_0$ form a linearly dependent set. [*Hint:* If $\mathbf{x} = t^0\mathbf{x}_0 + \cdots + t^r\mathbf{x}_r$ and $t^0 + \cdots + t^r = 1$, then $\mathbf{x} - \mathbf{x}_0 = t^1(\mathbf{x}_1 - \mathbf{x}_0) + \cdots + t^r(\mathbf{x}_r - \mathbf{x}_0)$.]
7. Prove that a supporting hyperplane for a closed convex set $K$ can contain no interior point of $K$.
8. Let $\mathbf{y}$ be any boundary point of a closed convex set $K$. Show that $K$ has a supporting hyperplane $P$ which contains $\mathbf{y}$. [*Hint:* Let $\{\mathbf{y}_m\}$ be a sequence of points exterior to $K$ such that $\mathbf{y}_m$ tends to $\mathbf{y}$ as $m \to \infty$. Let $\mathbf{x}_m$ be a point of $K$ nearest to $\mathbf{y}_m$ and $\mathbf{u}_m = (\mathbf{y}_m - \mathbf{x}_m)/|\mathbf{y}_m - \mathbf{x}_m|$. Then $|\mathbf{u}_m| = 1$ and $\mathbf{x}_m$ tends to $\mathbf{y}$ as $m \to \infty$. By the proof of Theorem 1 there is a supporting hyperplane of the form $\{\mathbf{x} : \mathbf{u}_m \cdot (\mathbf{x} - \mathbf{x}_m) = 0\}$. Let $\mathbf{u}$ be an accumulation point of the bounded set $\{\mathbf{u}_1, \mathbf{u}_2, \ldots\}$ and $P = \{\mathbf{x} : \mathbf{u} \cdot (\mathbf{x} - \mathbf{y}) = 0\}$.]
9. The *barycenter* of an $r$-simplex is the point at which the barycentric coordinates are equal, $t^0 = t^1 = \cdots = t^r$.
   (a) Show that the barycenter of a triangle is at the intersection of the medians.
   (b) State and prove a corresponding result for $r \geq 3$.
10. Let $\mathbf{x}$ be a convex combination of $\mathbf{x}_1, \ldots, \mathbf{x}_m$ and let $\mathbf{x}_j$ be a convex combination of $\mathbf{y}_{j1}, \ldots, \mathbf{y}_{jm_j}$, $j = 1, \ldots, m$. Show that $\mathbf{x}$ is a convex combination of $\mathbf{z}_1, \ldots, \mathbf{z}_p$, which are the distinct elements of the set $\{\mathbf{y}_{jk} : k = 1, \ldots, m_j, j = 1, \ldots, m\}$.

11. Let $S$ be any subset of $E^n$. The set $\hat{S}$ of all convex combinations of points of $S$ is the *convex hull* of $S$.
   (a) Using Problem 10, show that $\hat{S}$ is convex.
   (b) Using Proposition 3, show that if $K$ is convex and $S \subset K$, then $\hat{S} \subset K$. Thus the convex hull is the smallest convex set containing $S$.
12. Given $\mathbf{x}_0$ and $\delta > 0$, let $C = \{\mathbf{x} : |x^i - x_0^i| \leq \delta, i = 1, \ldots, n\}$, an *n-cube* with center $\mathbf{x}_0$ and side length $2\delta$. The *vertices* of $C$ are those $\mathbf{x}$ with $|x^i - x_0^i| = \delta$ for $i = 1, \ldots, n$. Show that $C$ is the convex hull of its set of vertices. [*Hint:* Use induction on $n$.]
13. Let $K$ be a closed subset of $E^n$ such that both $K$ and its complement $E^n - K$ are nonempty convex sets. Prove that $K$ is a half-space.
14. Let $K$ be any convex set. Prove that its interior and its closure are also convex sets.
15. Let $A$ and $B$ be convex subsets of $E^n$. The *join* of $A$ and $B$ is the set of all $\mathbf{x}$ such that $\mathbf{x}$ lies on a line segment with one endpoint in $A$ and the other in $B$. Show that the join of $A$ and $B$ is a convex set.

## 1–5 CONVEX AND CONCAVE FUNCTIONS

Functions which are either concave or convex arise naturally in connection with the study of convex sets. They also occur in a wide variety of applications of calculus. We will see in Section 2–5 that the theory of maxima and minima is much simpler for them than for functions which are neither concave nor convex.

Let $f$ be a real-valued function and $K$ a convex subset of the domain of $f$.

**Definition.** The function $f$ is *convex on* $K$ if, for every $\mathbf{x}_1, \mathbf{x}_2 \in K$ and $t \in [0, 1]$,

$$f(t\mathbf{x}_1 + (1 - t)\mathbf{x}_2) \leq tf(\mathbf{x}_1) + (1 - t)f(\mathbf{x}_2). \tag{1–8a}$$

If strict inequality holds in (1–8a) whenever $\mathbf{x}_1 \neq \mathbf{x}_2$ and $0 < t < 1$, then $f$ is *strictly convex on* $K$.

The assumption that $K$ is a convex set is needed to ensure that the point $t\mathbf{x}_1 + (1 - t)\mathbf{x}_2$ belongs to the domain of $f$. In order to see the geometric meaning of convexity let us denote points of $E^{n+1}$ by $(x^1, \ldots, x^n, z)$ or, for short, by $(\mathbf{x}, z)$. Let

$$K^+ = \{(\mathbf{x}, z) : \mathbf{x} \in K, z \geq f(\mathbf{x})\}.$$

If $\mathbf{x}_1 = \mathbf{x}_2$, then (1–8a) holds trivially. Therefore suppose that $\mathbf{x}_1 \neq \mathbf{x}_2$. Let $l$ denote the line segment in $E^{n+1}$ joining $(\mathbf{x}_1, f(\mathbf{x}_1))$ and $(\mathbf{x}_2, f(\mathbf{x}_2))$. Points of $l$ are of the form

$$(t\mathbf{x}_1 + (1 - t)\mathbf{x}_2, tf(\mathbf{x}_1) + (1 - t)f(\mathbf{x}_2)),$$

where $t \in [0, 1]$. Inequality (1–8a) says that such points belong to $K^+$. Therefore the definition says geometrically that the line segment $l$ is contained in $K^+$ for every pair of points $\mathbf{x}_1, \mathbf{x}_2 \in K$.

**Proposition 4.** *The function $f$ is convex on $K$ if and only if $K^+$ is a convex subset of $E^{n+1}$.*

*Proof.* Let $f$ be convex on $K$. Let $(\mathbf{x}_1, z_1)$, $(\mathbf{x}_2, z_2) \in K^+$, $(\mathbf{x}_1, z_1) \neq (\mathbf{x}_2, z_2)$, and $l'$ be the line segment joining them. Let $(\mathbf{x}, z)$ be any point of $l'$. Then

$$\mathbf{x} = t\mathbf{x}_1 + (1 - t)\mathbf{x}_2,$$
$$z = tz_1 + (1 - t)z_2,$$

where $0 \leq t \leq 1$. Since $z_1 \geq f(\mathbf{x}_1)$ and $z_2 \geq f(\mathbf{x}_2)$, we have (Fig. 1–14)

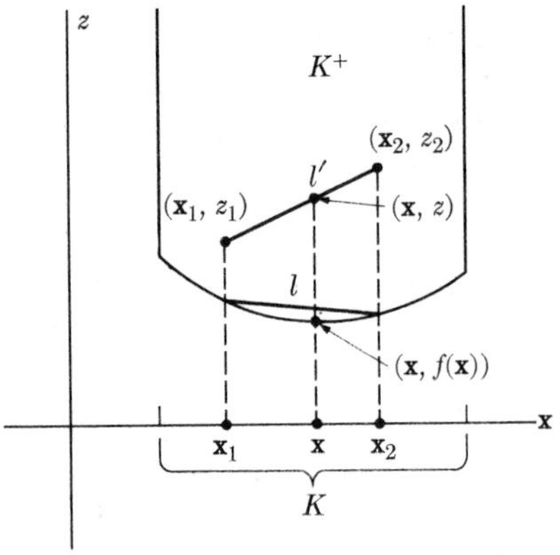


FIGURE 1–14

$$z \geq tf(\mathbf{x}_1) + (1 - t)f(\mathbf{x}_2) \geq f(\mathbf{x}).$$

Hence $(\mathbf{x}, z) \in K^+$. This proves that $K^+$ is a convex set.

Suppose, conversely, that $f$ is not convex on $K$. Then there exist $\mathbf{x}_1, \mathbf{x}_2 \in K$ and $t \in [0, 1]$ such that (1–8a) does not hold. The point $(t\mathbf{x}_1 + (1 - t)\mathbf{x}_2, tf(\mathbf{x}_1) + (1 - t)f(\mathbf{x}_2))$ belongs to the line segment $l$ joining the points $(\mathbf{x}_1, f(\mathbf{x}_1))$ and $(\mathbf{x}_2, f(\mathbf{x}_2))$, but not to $K^+$. Since $(\mathbf{x}_1, f(\mathbf{x}_1)), (\mathbf{x}_2, f(\mathbf{x}_2)) \in K^+$, the set $K^+$ is not convex. ▌

As an illustration of Proposition 4 let us return to Example 6, p. 18. If we let $K = E^1$, the set $A$ defined there is merely $K^+$. Therefore $f$ is convex on $E^1$ if $f'$ is an increasing function. Actually, the convexity is strict. This is a special case of an even stronger result.

**Proposition 5.** ($n = 1$) *Let $K \subset E^1$ be an interval, and $f$ a function which has a derivative $f'(x)$ for every $x \in K$. Then:*

(a) *$f$ is convex on $K$ if and only if $f'$ is nondecreasing on $K$.*
(b) *$f$ is strictly convex on $K$ if and only if $f'$ is increasing on $K$.*

It is convenient to postpone the proof until Section 2–4. If $f$ is convex on $K$ but not strictly convex, then $f'(x)$ is constant on some subinterval of $K$. This means that $f$ contains some line segment.

From Proposition 5 we can deduce the following useful test.

**Corollary.** *Let $f$ have a second derivative $f''(x)$ for every $x \in K$, where $K \subset E^1$ is an interval. Then:*

(a) *$f$ is convex on $K$ if and only if $f''(x) \geq 0$ for every $x \in K$.*
(b) *If $f''(x) > 0$ except at a finite number of points of $K$, then $f$ is strictly convex on $K$.*

*Proof.* Apply Proposition 5. ▌

In Section 2–4 these results are generalized to functions of $n$ variables, $n > 1$.

For any real number $c$, let

$$K_c = \{\mathbf{x} \in K : f(\mathbf{x}) \leq c\}.$$

**Proposition 6.** *If $f$ is convex on $K$, then $K_c$ is a convex set for every $c$.*

*Proof.* For every $\mathbf{x}_1, \mathbf{x}_2 \in K_c$ and $t \in [0, 1]$,

$$f(t\mathbf{x}_1 + (1 - t)\mathbf{x}_2) \leq tf(\mathbf{x}_1) + (1 - t)f(\mathbf{x}_2) \leq tc + (1 - t)c = c.$$

Hence $t\mathbf{x}_1 + (1 - t)\mathbf{x}_2 \in K_c$. ∎

The same proof shows that $\{\mathbf{x} : f(\mathbf{x}) < c\}$ is also convex. The converse to Proposition 6 is false; for example, let $f$ be any increasing function with domain $E^1$. Then $K_c$ is either all of $E^1$, a semi-infinite interval, or the empty set. In each case $K_c$ is convex. However, $f$ need not be a convex function; for instance, if $f(x) = x^3$, then $f$ is not convex on $E^1$.

**Example 1.** Let $A$ be any nonempty closed subset of $E^n$. For every $\mathbf{x}$, let $f(\mathbf{x})$ be the distance from $\mathbf{x}$ to $A$, namely,

$$f(\mathbf{x}) = \min \{|\mathbf{x} - \mathbf{y}| : \mathbf{y} \in A\}.$$

Let us show that the function $f$ so defined is convex on $E^n$ if and only if $A$ is a convex set. If $f$ is convex on $E^n$, then $K_0 = A$ and $A$ is convex by Proposition 6 with $c = 0$. Conversely, assume that $A$ is convex. Given $\mathbf{x}_1, \mathbf{x}_2 \in E^n$ and $t \in [0, 1]$, let $\mathbf{y}_1$ be a point of $A$ nearest $\mathbf{x}_1$, $\mathbf{y}_2$ a point of $A$ nearest $\mathbf{x}_2$, and

$$\mathbf{x} = t\mathbf{x}_1 + (1 - t)\mathbf{x}_2, \qquad \mathbf{y} = t\mathbf{y}_1 + (1 - t)\mathbf{y}_2.$$

(Actually, one can say "the nearest point" rather than "a nearest point" since the set $A$ is convex. This fact is not needed here.) Since $A$ is convex, $\mathbf{y} \in A$. By definition of $f$, $f(\mathbf{x}) \leq |\mathbf{x} - \mathbf{y}|$. Then

$$f(\mathbf{x}) \leq |t(\mathbf{x}_1 - \mathbf{y}_1) + (1 - t)(\mathbf{x}_2 - \mathbf{y}_2)|,$$
$$f(\mathbf{x}) \leq t|\mathbf{x}_1 - \mathbf{y}_1| + (1 - t)|\mathbf{x}_2 - \mathbf{y}_2| = tf(\mathbf{x}_1) + (1 - t)f(\mathbf{x}_2).$$

Hence $f$ is a convex function on $E^n$.

In particular, let $A$ consist of a single point $\mathbf{x}_0$. Then $f(\mathbf{x}) = |\mathbf{x} - \mathbf{x}_0|$ and this function is convex on $E^n$.

**Concave functions.** The definition of concave function is obtained by reversing the inequality sign in (1–8a) : $f$ is *concave on* $K$ if, for every $\mathbf{x}_1, \mathbf{x}_2 \in K$ and $t \in [0, 1]$,

$$f(t\mathbf{x}_1 + (1 - t)\mathbf{x}_2) \geq tf(\mathbf{x}_1) + (1 - t)f(\mathbf{x}_2). \tag{1–8b}$$

If strict inequality holds whenever $\mathbf{x}_1 \neq \mathbf{x}_2$ and $0 < t < 1$, then $f$ is *strictly concave on* $K$.

There are propositions about concave functions corresponding to Propositions 4, 5, and 6 for convex functions. In them $K^+$ must be replaced by

$$K^- = \{(\mathbf{x}, z) : \mathbf{x} \in K, z \leq f(\mathbf{x})\},$$

and $K_c$ by

$$K^c = \{\mathbf{x} \in K : f(\mathbf{x}) \geq c\}.$$

The words "increasing" and "decreasing" must be exchanged. A function $f$ is concave on $K$ if and only if $-f$ is convex on $K$. By using this fact, or by repeating the proofs of Propositions 4, 5, and 6, it is easy to prove these propositions about concave functions.

Many useful inequalities can be obtained from (1–8a) or (1–8b) by judiciously choosing the function $f$ and the number $t$.

**Example 2.** Let $p > 1$, $p$ not necessarily an integer. Let $f(x) = |x|^p$ for every $x \in E^1$. Then

$$f'(x) = \begin{cases} p|x|^{p-1} & \text{if} \quad x > 0, \\ -p|x|^{p-1} & \text{if} \quad x < 0, \end{cases}$$

and $f'(0) = 0$. The function $f'$ is increasing. Hence $f$ is strictly convex on $E^1$. Taking $t = \frac{1}{2}$, we have

$$f[\tfrac{1}{2}(x_1 + x_2)] \leq \tfrac{1}{2}f(x_1) + \tfrac{1}{2}f(x_2).$$

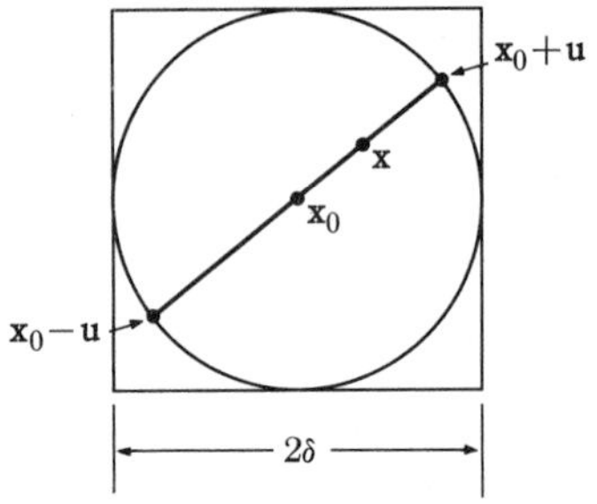


FIGURE 1–15

Multiplying both sides of the inequality by $2^p$, we get

$$|x_1 + x_2|^p \leq 2^{p-1}(|x_1|^p + |x_2|^p). \tag{1–9}$$

The inequality is strict unless $x_1 = x_2$.

### *Continuity of convex functions

**Theorem.** *Let $K$ be an open convex set and $f$ convex on $K$. Then $f$ is continuous on $K$.*

*Proof.*† Let $\mathbf{x}_0$ be any point of $K$, and $d$ the distance from $\mathbf{x}_0$ to the boundary of $K$ ($d = +\infty$ if $K = E^n$). Let $C$ be an $n$-cube with center $\mathbf{x}_0$ and side length $2\delta$, where $n^{1/2}\delta < d$. Let $V$ denote the set of vertices of $C$ (see Problem 12, Section 1–4). $V$ is a finite set. Let

$$M = \max \{f(\mathbf{x}) : \mathbf{x} \in V\}.$$

By Proposition 6, $K_M$ is a convex set. Since $C$ is the convex hull of $V$ and $V \subset K_M$, $C \subset K_M$.

† This proof was suggested by F. J. Almgren.

Let $\mathbf{x}$ be any point such that $0 < |\mathbf{x} - \mathbf{x}_0| < \delta$, and define $\mathbf{x}_0 + \mathbf{u}$, $\mathbf{x}_0 - \mathbf{u}$ on the line through $\mathbf{x}_0$ and $\mathbf{x}$ as in Fig. 1–15. Let us write $\mathbf{x}$ as a convex combination of $\mathbf{x}_0 + \mathbf{u}$ and $\mathbf{x}_0$, and $\mathbf{x}_0$ as a convex combination of $\mathbf{x}$ and $\mathbf{x}_0 - \mathbf{u}$. If $t = \delta^{-1}|\mathbf{x} - \mathbf{x}_0|$, then

$$\mathbf{x} = t(\mathbf{x}_0 + \mathbf{u}) + (1 - t)\mathbf{x}_0,$$

$$\mathbf{x}_0 = \frac{1}{1+t}\,\mathbf{x} + \frac{t}{1+t}\,(\mathbf{x}_0 - \mathbf{u}).$$

Since $f$ is convex,

$$f(\mathbf{x}) \le tf(\mathbf{x}_0 + \mathbf{u}) + (1 - t)f(\mathbf{x}_0) \le tM + (1 - t)f(\mathbf{x}_0),$$

$$f(\mathbf{x}_0) \le \frac{1}{1+t}\,f(\mathbf{x}) + \frac{t}{1+t}\,f(\mathbf{x}_0 - \mathbf{u}) \le \frac{f(\mathbf{x}) + tM}{1+t}.$$

The inequalities give

$$-t[M - f(\mathbf{x}_0)] \le f(\mathbf{x}) - f(\mathbf{x}_0) \le t[M - f(\mathbf{x}_0)],$$

or

$$|f(\mathbf{x}) - f(\mathbf{x}_0)| \le \frac{M - f(\mathbf{x}_0)}{\delta}\,|\mathbf{x} - \mathbf{x}_0|. \tag{1–10}$$

The estimate (1–10) shows that $f$ is continuous at $\mathbf{x}_0$. ▮

If $K$ is not open, then a convex function $f$ may be discontinuous at boundary points of $K$. See the example below. The interior of $K$ is an open convex set, and by the theorem $f$ is continuous at every interior point.

**Example 3.** Let $K = [0, 1]$ and $f(x) = x$ if $0 < x \le 1$, $f(0) = 1$. Then $f$ is convex on $K$ but is discontinuous at the left endpoint 0.

## PROBLEMS

1. In each case find those intervals of $E^1$ on which $f$ is convex and those on which it is concave. Illustrate with a sketch.
   (a) $f(x) = x - x^2$. (b) $f(x) = \exp(-2x)$.
   (c) $f(x) = x/(1 - |x|)$, $|x| \ne 1$. (d) $f(x) = \log(x^2 + 1)$.
2. (a) Show that no polynomial of odd degree ($\ge 3$) is a convex function on $E^1$.
   (b) Which fourth degree polynomials are convex functions on $E^1$?
   (c) Why must a polynomial (of degree $\ge 2$) which is a convex function on $E^1$ be a strictly convex function?
3. Let $f(x) = x\phi(x)$ and $g(x) = \phi(1/x)$, where $\phi$ has a second derivative $\phi''(x)$ for every $x > 0$. Show that $f$ is convex on $(0, \infty)$ if and only if $g$ is convex on $(0, \infty)$.
4. Let $x > 0$, $y > 0$, $0 \le t \le 1$. Show that $tx + (1 - t)y \ge x^t y^{1-t}$. [*Hint:* Log is an increasing, concave function.]
5. Prove by induction on $m$ that if $f$ is concave on $K$, then

$$f\left(\sum_{j=1}^{m} t^j \mathbf{x}_j\right) \ge \sum_{j=1}^{m} t^j f(\mathbf{x}_j)$$

for every $\mathbf{x}_1, \ldots, \mathbf{x}_m \in K$ and scalars $t^1, \ldots, t^m$ such that each $t^j \geq 0$ and $t^1 + \cdots + t^m = 1$. [For convex functions the sense of the inequality is reversed.]

6. (a) Generalizing Problem 4, show that if $x_1, \ldots, x_m$ are positive numbers, $0 \leq t^j$ for $j = 1, \ldots, m$, and $t^1 + \cdots + t^m = 1$, then

$$t^1 x_1 + \cdots + t^m x_m \geq x_1^{t^1} \cdots x_m^{t^m}.$$

(b) Prove that the geometric mean is no more than the arithmetic mean, namely,

$$\frac{x_1 + \cdots + x_m}{m} \geq (x_1 \cdots x_m)^{1/m}.$$

7. Show that if $f$ and $g$ are convex on $K$, then $f + g$ is convex on $K$.
8. (a) Let $f$ and $g$ be convex on $K$, and let $h(\mathbf{x}) = \max\,[f(\mathbf{x}), g(\mathbf{x})]$ for every $\mathbf{x} \in K$. Show that $h$ is convex on $K$. [*Hint:* Use Proposition 4.]
   (b) Illustrate for the case $f(x) = |x - 1|$, $g(x) = x/2$.
9. Let $f$ be strictly convex on $E^n$, with $f(\mathbf{0}) = 0$. Given $\mathbf{x} \in E^n$, $\mathbf{x} \neq \mathbf{0}$, let $\phi(t) = f(t\mathbf{x})/t$. Prove that $\phi$ is increasing on $\{t : t > 0\}$.
10. Let $K$ be compact and convex. Let $f$ be continuous and strictly convex on $K$. Let $m$ be the minimum value of $f$ on $K$. Prove that $K_m$ has precisely one element. State the corresponding result for strictly concave functions.
11. Let $f$ be both convex and concave on $E^n$. Show that there exist $\mathbf{a}$ and $b$ such that $f(\mathbf{x}) = \mathbf{a} \cdot \mathbf{x} + b$ for every $\mathbf{x} \in E^n$.
12. Let $f$ be continuous on $K$, and assume that $f(\frac{1}{2}(\mathbf{x}_1 + \mathbf{x}_2)) \leq \frac{1}{2}f(\mathbf{x}_1) + \frac{1}{2}f(\mathbf{x}_2)$ for every $\mathbf{x}_1, \mathbf{x}_2 \in K$. Show that $f$ is convex on $K$. [*Hint:* First show (1–8a) when $t = j/2^k$ where $j = 0, 1, \ldots, 2^k$ and $k$ is a positive integer.]

## *1–6 NONEUCLIDEAN NORMS

It is sometimes advantageous to consider norms on $E^n$ other than the standard euclidean norm. The distance between two points $\mathbf{x}$ and $\mathbf{y}$ defined by such a norm need not agree with the euclidean distance. As a result, such geometric notions as length, area, and spherical ball are changed when considered with respect to a noneuclidean norm. However, we shall see that any noneuclidean norm leads to the same collection of open sets as the euclidean norm. Since the collection of open sets determines all of the topological properties of $E^n$, these properties are therefore independent of the particular norm chosen.

**Definition.** A *norm* is a real-valued function $\|\ \|$ with domain $E^n$ such that:

(1) $\|\mathbf{x}\| > 0$ for every $\mathbf{x} \neq 0$,
(2) $\|c\mathbf{x}\| = |c|\,\|\mathbf{x}\|$ for every $c$ and $\mathbf{x}$, and
(3) $\|\mathbf{x} + \mathbf{y}\| \leq \|\mathbf{x}\| + \|\mathbf{y}\|$ for every $\mathbf{x}$ and $\mathbf{y}$.

This agrees with the definition of norm on any vector space $\mathcal{V}$ (Section A–6, Problem 5) if we take $\mathcal{V} = E^n$. The notation $\|\ \|$ rather than, say, $f$ is customary. From Axiom (2) with $c = 0$, $\|\mathbf{0}\| = 0$. Axiom (3) is the triangle inequality. Just as for the euclidean norm one can easily prove using (2), (3), and induction on $m$ that

$$\left\| \sum_{j=1}^{m} c^j \mathbf{x}_j \right\| \leq \sum_{j=1}^{m} |c^j| \, \|\mathbf{x}_j\| \tag{1–11}$$

for every choice of $c^1, \ldots, c^m$ and $\mathbf{x}_1, \ldots, \mathbf{x}_m$. In particular, let $m = 2$, $c^1 = t$, $c^2 = 1 - t$, where $0 \leq t \leq 1$. Then

$$\|t\mathbf{x}_1 + (1 - t)\mathbf{x}_2\| \leq t\|\mathbf{x}_1\| + (1 - t)\|\mathbf{x}_2\|.$$

This shows that $\| \;\|$ is a convex function.

The *distance* between $\mathbf{x}$ and $\mathbf{y}$ with respect to the norm $\| \;\|$ is defined as $\|\mathbf{x} - \mathbf{y}\|$. From Axiom (1) the distance between any two distinct points is positive. The *$\delta$-neighborhood* with center $\mathbf{x}_0$ with respect to the norm $\| \;\|$ is $\{\mathbf{x} : \|\mathbf{x} - \mathbf{x}_0\| < \delta\}$. The *closed $n$-ball* with center $\mathbf{x}_0$ and radius $\delta$ is

$$\{\mathbf{x} : \|\mathbf{x} - \mathbf{x}_0\| \leq \delta\}.$$

As in the euclidean case, they are convex sets.

**Example 1.** Let

$$\|\mathbf{x}\| = \sum_{i=1}^{n} |x^i|.$$

The $n$-balls with respect to this norm are convex polytopes. For example, if $n = 2$, the closed unit 2-ball $\{\mathbf{x} : \|\mathbf{x}\| \leq 1\}$ is the square with vertices $\mathbf{e}_1$, $\mathbf{e}_2$, $-\mathbf{e}_1$, $-\mathbf{e}_2$. Compare with Problem 1(a), Section 1–4.

**Example 2.** *Inner products, quadratic norms.* A real-valued function $B$ on the cartesian product $E^n \times E^n$ is *bilinear* if for each $\mathbf{x}, \mathbf{y} \in E^n$ the functions $B(\mathbf{x}, \;)$ and $B(\;, \mathbf{y})$ are linear. An *inner product* in $E^n$ is a bilinear function such that: (a) $B(\mathbf{x}, \mathbf{y}) = B(\mathbf{y}, \mathbf{x})$ for every $\mathbf{x}, \mathbf{y}$, and (b) $B(\mathbf{x}, \mathbf{x}) > 0$ for every $\mathbf{x} \neq \mathbf{0}$. With any inner product $B$ is associated a *quadratic norm* given by

$$\|\mathbf{x}\| = \sqrt{B(\mathbf{x}, \mathbf{x})}.$$

Axiom (1) follows from (b), and (2) from $B(c\mathbf{x}, c\mathbf{x}) = c^2 B(\mathbf{x}, \mathbf{x})$. The proof of the triangle inequality (3) is the same as for the standard euclidean norm (1–2).

With any bilinear function $B$ is associated an $n \times n$ matrix $(c_{ij})$ such that

$$B(\mathbf{x}, \mathbf{y}) = \sum_{i,j=1}^{n} c_{ij} x^i y^j. \tag{1–12}$$

In fact, if

$$\mathbf{x} = \sum_{i=1}^{n} x^i \mathbf{e}_i, \qquad \mathbf{y} = \sum_{j=1}^{n} y^j \mathbf{e}_j,$$

then

$$B(\mathbf{x}, \mathbf{y}) = \sum_{i=1}^{n} x^i B(\mathbf{e}_i, \mathbf{y}) = \sum_{i,j=1}^{n} x^i y^j B(\mathbf{e}_i, \mathbf{e}_j),$$

and we set $c_{ij} = B(\mathbf{e}_i, \mathbf{e}_j)$. Condition (a) states that the matrix $(c_{ij})$ is symmetric, $c_{ij} = c_{ji}$ for $i, j = 1, \ldots, n$. For the standard euclidean inner product, $c_{ij} = \delta_{ij}$ and the matrix is the identity.

The $n$-balls with respect to any quadratic norm are $n$-dimensional ellipsoids. This will be proved later (Section 4–8) by finding a new orthonormal basis for $E^n$ for which the matrix associated with $B$ is diagonal.

If $\mathbf{y}$ is a vector, then there is a covector $\mathbf{a}$ such that

$$B(\mathbf{y}, \mathbf{x}) = \mathbf{a} \cdot \mathbf{x} \tag{1–13}$$

for every vector $\mathbf{x}$. The components of $\mathbf{a}$ are

$$a_i = \sum_{j=1}^{n} c_{ij} y^j, \qquad i = 1, \ldots, n. \tag{1–14a}$$

On the other hand, given a covector $\mathbf{a}$ there is a vector $\mathbf{y}$ such that (1–13) holds. Its components are

$$y^i = \sum_{j=1}^{n} c^{ij} a_j, \qquad i = 1, \ldots, n, \tag{1–14b}$$

where $(c^{ij})$ is the inverse of the matrix $(c_{ij})$. For the standard euclidean inner product, $y^i = a_i$, and formula (1–13) becomes (1–7).

**Proposition.** *Corresponding to any norm $\| \; \|$ on $E^n$ there exist positive numbers $m$ and $M$ such that for every $\mathbf{x} \in E^n$,*

$$m|\mathbf{x}| \leq \|\mathbf{x}\| \leq M|\mathbf{x}|. \tag{1–15}$$

*Proof.* Let

$$M = n \max \{\|\mathbf{e}_1\|, \ldots, \|\mathbf{e}_n\|\}.$$

Then writing

$$\mathbf{x} = x^1\mathbf{e}_1 + \cdots + x^n\mathbf{e}_n$$

and using (1–11), we have

$$\|\mathbf{x}\| \leq \sum_{i=1}^{n} |x^i| \, \|\mathbf{e}_i\| \leq \frac{M}{n} \sum_{i=1}^{n} |x^i|.$$

But $|x^i| \leq |\mathbf{x}|$ for each $i = 1, \ldots, n$. Hence

$$\|\mathbf{x}\| \leq M|\mathbf{x}|.$$

From this $\|\mathbf{x} - \mathbf{y}\| \leq M|\mathbf{x} - \mathbf{y}|$ for every $\mathbf{x}$ and $\mathbf{y}$, which implies that $\| \; \|$ is a continuous function. Therefore it has a minimum value $m$ on the compact set $\{\mathbf{x} : |\mathbf{x}| = 1\}$,

$$m = \min \{\|\mathbf{x}\| : |\mathbf{x}| = 1\}.$$

By Axiom (1) $m > 0$. If $\mathbf{x} = \mathbf{0}$, all terms in (1–15) are 0. Given any $\mathbf{x} \neq \mathbf{0}$, let $c = |\mathbf{x}|^{-1}$. Then $|c\mathbf{x}| = c|\mathbf{x}| = 1$, and hence $\|c\mathbf{x}\| \geq m$. By Axiom (2)

$\|c\mathbf{x}\| = |c|\,\|\mathbf{x}\|$, from which

$$\|\mathbf{x}\| \geq m|\mathbf{x}|. \blacksquare$$

From the proposition,

$$m|\mathbf{x} - \mathbf{y}| \leq \|\mathbf{x} - \mathbf{y}\| \leq M|\mathbf{x} - \mathbf{y}|$$

for every $\mathbf{x}$ and $\mathbf{y}$. This says that the ratio of the $\|\ \|$-distance to the euclidean distance is bounded between $m$ and $M$. Let us call a set $D$ $\|\ \|$*-open* if every $\mathbf{x}_0 \in D$ has some neighborhood with respect to this norm which is contained in $D$. If $|\mathbf{x} - \mathbf{x}_0| < \delta/M$, then $\|\mathbf{x} - \mathbf{x}_0\| < \delta$. Therefore the $\delta$-neighborhood of $\mathbf{x}_0$ with respect to the norm $\|\ \|$ contains the ordinary euclidean $(\delta/M)$-neighborhood of $\mathbf{x}_0$. If $D$ is $\|\ \|$-open, then every $\mathbf{x}_0 \in D$ has a euclidean neighborhood contained in $D$. Hence $D$ is open in the ordinary sense. Similarly, the euclidean $\delta$-neighborhood of $\mathbf{x}_0$ contains the $(m\delta)$-neighborhood of $\mathbf{x}_0$ with respect to the norm $\|\ \|$. It follows that every set which is open in the ordinary sense is also $\|\ \|$-open. Thus a set is $\|\ \|$-open if and only if it is open in the usual sense. Since the open subsets of a topological space determine the topology (Section A–6), all norms on $E^n$ lead to the same topology of $E^n$.

The idea of norm on an infinite dimensional vector space is also very important; for instance, see [19]. In fact, it is the starting point for modern-day functional analysis. It is not true in the infinite dimensional case that any two norms on the same vector space define the same class of open sets.

The closed unit $n$-ball

$$K = \{\mathbf{x} : \|\mathbf{x}\| \leq 1\} \tag{1–16}$$

with respect to any norm has the following four properties:

(1) $K$ is compact;
(2) $K$ is convex;
(3) $K$ is symmetric about $\mathbf{0}$; and
(4) $K$ contains a euclidean neighborhood of $\mathbf{0}$.

Symmetry about $\mathbf{0}$ means that $-\mathbf{x} \in K$ for every $\mathbf{x} \in K$. By Axiom (2) with $c = -1$, $\|-\mathbf{x}\| = \|\mathbf{x}\|$, and hence $K$ has Property (3). From the proposition, $K$ has property (4) and is bounded. For any continuous function $f$, $\{\mathbf{x} : f(\mathbf{x}) \leq 1\}$ is a closed set. Since $\|\ \|$ is continuous, $K$ is closed. Hence Property (1) holds. We already noted (2), which also follows from Proposition 6 since $\|\ \|$ is a convex function.

Let us show that, conversely, any set $K$ with these four properties gives rise to a norm with respect to which $K$ is the closed unit $n$-ball.

**Theorem.** *Let $K$ be any set with Properties* (1)–(4). *Let* $\|\mathbf{0}\| = 0$, *and for every* $\mathbf{x} \neq \mathbf{0}$, *let*

$$\|\mathbf{x}\| = \frac{1}{\max\,\{t : t\mathbf{x} \in K\}}. \tag{1–17}$$

*Then* $\|\ \|$ *is a norm and* (1–16) *holds.*

*Proof.* By (1) and (4) there exist $r_1 > 0$ and $r_2 > 0$ such that $\mathbf{y} \in K$ if $|\mathbf{y}| \leq r_1$ and $\mathbf{y} \notin K$ if $|\mathbf{y}| > r_2$. Hence given $\mathbf{x} \neq \mathbf{0}$, $t\mathbf{x} \in K$ if $|t| \leq r_1/|\mathbf{x}|$, and $t\mathbf{x} \notin K$ if $|t| > r_2/|\mathbf{x}|$. (See Fig. 1–16.) Let

$$S_{\mathbf{x}} = \{t : t\mathbf{x} \in K\}.$$

Then $S_{\mathbf{x}}$ contains the $(r_1/|\mathbf{x}|)$-neighborhood of 0 and is bounded above by $r_2/|\mathbf{x}|$. Since $K$ is a closed set, $S_{\mathbf{x}}$ is also closed. Hence $S_{\mathbf{x}}$ has a largest element $\max S_{\mathbf{x}}$, which is positive. This shows that $\|\mathbf{x}\| = 1/\max S_{\mathbf{x}}$ is well-defined and is positive. Moreover, by (2) and the fact that $\mathbf{0} \in K$, the line segment between $\mathbf{0}$ and any point of $K$ is contained in $K$. Therefore $\max S_{\mathbf{x}} \geq 1$ if and only if $\mathbf{x} \in K$, which says that (1–16) holds.

It remains to verify Axioms (2) and (3) for a norm. By Property (3), $\|-\mathbf{x}\| = \|\mathbf{x}\|$. It is left to the reader to check that if $c > 0$, then

$$\max S_{c\mathbf{x}} = \frac{1}{c} \max S_{\mathbf{x}},$$

and consequently $\|c\mathbf{x}\| = c\|\mathbf{x}\|$. Then Axiom (2) holds. For (3) we may assume that $\mathbf{x} \neq \mathbf{0}$ and $\mathbf{y} \neq \mathbf{0}$. Let

$$s = \max S_{\mathbf{x}}, \qquad t = \max S_{\mathbf{y}}, \qquad u = \frac{t}{s + t}.$$

Observe that $0 < u < 1$ and

$$\frac{1}{su} = \frac{1}{s} + \frac{1}{t} = \|\mathbf{x}\| + \|\mathbf{y}\|.$$

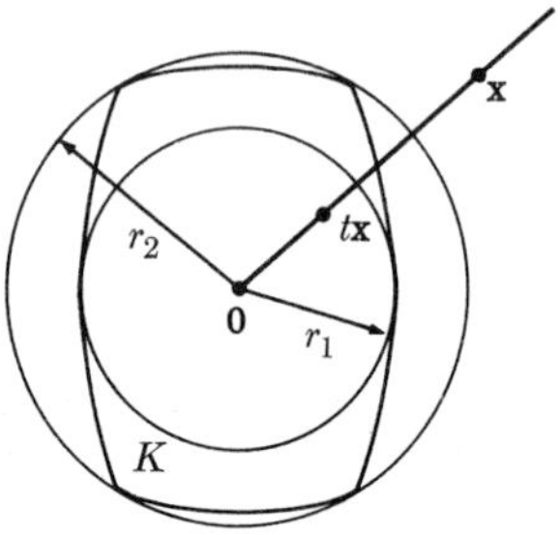


FIGURE 1–16

A little manipulation shows that $su = (1 - u)t$. Consequently,

$$su(\mathbf{x} + \mathbf{y}) = u(s\mathbf{x}) + (1 - u)t\mathbf{y}.$$

Since $s\mathbf{x}, t\mathbf{y} \in K$ and $K$ is a convex set by Property (2), $su(\mathbf{x} + \mathbf{y}) \in K$. Therefore $su \leq \max S_{\mathbf{x}+\mathbf{y}}$, and

$$\|\mathbf{x}\| + \|\mathbf{y}\| = \frac{1}{su} \geq \|\mathbf{x} + \mathbf{y}\|.$$

This verifies Axiom (3). ▮

**The dual norm.** With any norm $\| \; \|$ on $E^n$ is associated a norm on the dual space $(E^n)^*$. This norm on $(E^n)^*$ is also denoted by $\| \; \|$. It is defined, for every $\mathbf{a} \in (E^n)^*$, by

$$\|\mathbf{a}\| = \max \{\mathbf{a} \cdot \mathbf{x} : \|\mathbf{x}\| = 1\}. \qquad (1\text{–}18)$$

A linear function is continuous and has a maximum value on the compact set $\{\mathbf{x} : \|\mathbf{x}\| = 1\}$. Hence we are justified in writing max in (1–18). Let us verify

Axioms (1), (2), and (3). If $\mathbf{a} \neq \mathbf{0}$, then $\mathbf{a} \cdot \mathbf{x} \neq 0$ for some $\mathbf{x}$. We can assume that $\mathbf{a} \cdot \mathbf{x} > 0$, since if not, $\mathbf{x}$ can be replaced by $-\mathbf{x}$. If $\mathbf{y} = (1/\|\mathbf{x}\|)\mathbf{x}$, then $\mathbf{a} \cdot \mathbf{y} > 0$ and $\|\mathbf{y}\| = 1$. Thus $\{\mathbf{a} \cdot \mathbf{x} : \|\mathbf{x}\| = 1\}$ contains some positive number, and its maximum $\|\mathbf{a}\|$ is positive. The reader should verify that $\|c\mathbf{a}\| = |c|\ \|\mathbf{a}\|$. Given $\mathbf{a}, \mathbf{b} \in (E^n)^*$, we have whenever $\|\mathbf{x}\| = 1$,

$$(\mathbf{a} + \mathbf{b}) \cdot \mathbf{x} = \mathbf{a} \cdot \mathbf{x} + \mathbf{b} \cdot \mathbf{x} \leq \|\mathbf{a}\| + \|\mathbf{b}\|.$$

Hence the number $\|\mathbf{a}\| + \|\mathbf{b}\|$ is an upper bound for $\{(\mathbf{a} + \mathbf{b}) \cdot \mathbf{x} : \|\mathbf{x}\| = 1\}$. The least upper bound of this set is $\|\mathbf{a} + \mathbf{b}\|$. Thus

$$\|\mathbf{a} + \mathbf{b}\| \leq \|\mathbf{a}\| + \|\mathbf{b}\|.$$

This verifies Axioms (1), (2), and (3).

For any $\mathbf{x} \neq \mathbf{0}$, $(1/\|\mathbf{x}\|)\mathbf{x}$ has norm 1. Hence

$$\frac{1}{\|\mathbf{x}\|}\,\mathbf{a} \cdot \mathbf{x} = \mathbf{a} \cdot \left(\frac{1}{\|\mathbf{x}\|}\,\mathbf{x}\right) \leq \|\mathbf{a}\|,$$

or $\mathbf{a} \cdot \mathbf{x} \leq \|\mathbf{a}\|\ \|\mathbf{x}\|$. Replacing $\mathbf{x}$ by $-\mathbf{x}$, we find that $-\mathbf{a} \cdot \mathbf{x} \leq \|\mathbf{a}\|\ \|\mathbf{x}\|$. Therefore

$$|\mathbf{a} \cdot \mathbf{x}| \leq \|\mathbf{a}\|\ \|\mathbf{x}\|. \tag{1–19}$$

This inequality corresponds to Cauchy's inequality.

There is a formula dual to (1–18) for $\|\mathbf{x}\|$:

$$\|\mathbf{x}\| = \max\,\{\mathbf{a} \cdot \mathbf{x} : \|\mathbf{a}\| = 1\}. \tag{1–20}$$

From 1–19, $\mathbf{a} \cdot \mathbf{x} \leq \|\mathbf{x}\|$ for every covector $\mathbf{a}$ such that $\|\mathbf{a}\| = 1$. Hence

$$\|\mathbf{x}\| \geq \max\,\{\mathbf{a} \cdot \mathbf{x} : \|\mathbf{a}\| = 1\}.$$

To prove the opposite inequality, consider first any $\mathbf{y}$ with $\|\mathbf{y}\| = 1$. Then $\mathbf{y}$ is a boundary point of the closed convex set $K$ defined in (1–16). By a corollary to Theorem 1 (Problem 8, Section 1–4), $K$ has a supporting hyperplane at $\mathbf{y}$. Thus there exists a covector $\mathbf{b}$ such that

$$\mathbf{b} \cdot \mathbf{x} \leq 1 \quad \text{for every } \mathbf{x} \in K, \quad \text{and} \quad \mathbf{b} \cdot \mathbf{y} = 1.$$

By definition of the dual norm, $\|\mathbf{b}\| = 1$. Then

$$1 = \mathbf{b} \cdot \mathbf{y} \leq \max\,\{\mathbf{a} \cdot \mathbf{y} : \|\mathbf{a}\| = 1\}.$$

Thus $\|\mathbf{y}\| \leq \max\,\{\mathbf{a} \cdot \mathbf{y} : \|\mathbf{a}\| = 1\}$. We have already proved the opposite inequality. Hence (1–20) is true for elements of norm 1. Since $\|c\mathbf{y}\| = |c|\ \|\mathbf{y}\|$ and

$$\max\,\{\mathbf{a} \cdot (c\mathbf{y}) : \|\mathbf{a}\| = 1\} = |c| \max\,\{\mathbf{a} \cdot \mathbf{y} : \|\mathbf{a}\| = 1\},$$

(1–20) then follows for elements of arbitrary norm.

**PROBLEMS**

1. Let $\|\mathbf{x}\| = \max \{|x^1|, \ldots, |x^n|\}$.
   (a) Show that this is a norm.
   (b) Describe the neighborhoods with respect to it.
   (c) Show that the triangle with vertices $\mathbf{0}$, $\mathbf{e}_1$, $\mathbf{e}_2$ is equilateral with respect to the distance which it defines.
2. The ellipse $K = \{(x, y) : x^2 + xy + 4y^2 \leq 1\}$ has Properties (1)–(4). (See p. 31.)
   (a) For what (quadratic) norm is it the closed unit 2-ball?
   (b) Find $\|\mathbf{e}_1 - \mathbf{e}_2\|$.
3. Let $p \geq 1$ and let $\|\mathbf{x}\| = (\sum_{i=1}^{n} |x^i|^p)^{1/p}$. [For $p = 1$ this is Example 1 above, and for $p = 2$ this is the euclidean norm.] Show that this is a norm, in the following steps:
   (a) Let $f(\mathbf{x}) = \sum_{i=1}^{n} |x^i|^p$. Show that $f$ is convex on $E^n$. [*Hint:* In Section 1–5 we showed this for $n = 1$. Hence if $0 \leq t \leq 1$, $|tx^i + (1 - t)y^i|^p \leq t|x^i|^p + (1 - t)|y^i|^p$.]
   (b) Let $K = \{\mathbf{x} : f(\mathbf{x}) \leq 1\}$. Show that $K$ satisfies Properties (1)–(4) on p. 31.
   (c) Show that $\|\mathbf{x}\|$ is given by (1–17). [*Note:* For this norm the inequality $\|\mathbf{x} + \mathbf{y}\| \leq \|\mathbf{x}\| + \|\mathbf{y}\|$ is called *Minkowski's inequality*. There is a related inequality for integrals which we shall prove in Section 5–12.]
4. Show that if $p = 1$ in Problem 3, the dual norm is given by

$$\|\mathbf{a}\| = \max \{|a_1|, \ldots, |a_n|\}.$$

   [If $p > 1$, the dual norm will be found using calculus in Section 4–8.]
5. A *seminorm* on $E^n$ is a real-valued function $f$ satisfying: (i) $f(\mathbf{x}) \geq 0$ for every $\mathbf{x}$; (ii) $f(c\mathbf{x}) = |c|f(\mathbf{x})$ for every $c$ and $\mathbf{x}$; and (iii) $f(\mathbf{x} + \mathbf{y}) \leq f(\mathbf{x}) + f(\mathbf{y})$ for every $\mathbf{x}$ and $\mathbf{y}$.
   (a) Let $f$ be a seminorm and $K = \{\mathbf{x} : f(\mathbf{x}) \leq 1\}$. Show that $K$ is closed and satisfies Properties (2), (3), and (4), p. 31. Show that $K$ is compact if and only if $f$ is a norm.
   (b) Conversely, let $K$ be any closed set satisfying Properties (2), (3), and (4). Let $f(\mathbf{x}) = 0$ if $\mathbf{x} = \mathbf{0}$ or if the line through $\mathbf{0}$ and $\mathbf{x}$ is contained in $K$. Otherwise, let

$$f(\mathbf{x}) = \frac{1}{\max \{t : t\mathbf{x} \in K\}}$$

   as in (1–17). Show that $f$ is a seminorm.
   (c) Let $n = 3$ and $f(x, y, z) = |x| + 2|y|$. Sketch $K$ and show that $f$ is a seminorm.

CHAPTER 2

# Differentiation of Real-Valued Functions

We shall now begin the differential calculus for real-valued functions of several variables. The first step is to define the basic notions—directional derivative, differentiable function, and so on—and to prove some basic facts about differentiable functions and functions of class $C^{(q)}$. Taylor's formula is then obtained. It is applied to the characterization of convex functions of class $C^{(2)}$ and to problems of relative extrema. The chain rule for partial derivatives is postponed to Chapter 4, since it is a natural corollary of the composite function theorem for vector-valued functions to be proved there.

## 2-1 DIRECTIONAL AND PARTIAL DERIVATIVES

If $f$ is a function of one variable, then its derivative at a point $x_0$ is defined by

$$f'(x_0) = \lim_{h \to 0} \frac{f(x_0 + h) - f(x_0)}{h},$$

provided the limit exists. The corresponding expression for functions of several variables does not make sense, since $\mathbf{h}$ is then a vector and division by $\mathbf{h}$ is undefined. Therefore we must find an acceptable substitute for it. Let us first consider the derivative of $f$ in various directions.

Let us call any unit vector $\mathbf{v}$ (that is, vector with $|\mathbf{v}| = 1$) a *direction* in $E^n$. The directions are just the points of the $(n - 1)$-dimensional sphere which bounds the unit $n$-ball. If $n = 1$, the only directions are $\mathbf{e}_1$ and $-\mathbf{e}_1$, which we have identified with the scalars 1 and $-1$. If $n = 2$, every direction can be written $(\cos \theta, \sin \theta)$ where $0 \leq \theta < 2\pi$. The angle $\theta$ determines the direction. For any $n \geq 2$ the components of a direction $\mathbf{v}$ satisfy $v^i = \cos \theta_i$, $i = 1, \ldots, n$, where $\theta_i$ is the angle between $\mathbf{v}$ and $\mathbf{e}_i$.

Given $\mathbf{x}_0$ and a direction $\mathbf{v}$, the line through $\mathbf{x}_0 + \mathbf{v}$ and $\mathbf{x}_0$ is called *the line through* $\mathbf{x}_0$ *with direction* $\mathbf{v}$. According to the definition on p. 13, this line is

$$\{\mathbf{x} : \mathbf{x} = \mathbf{x}_0 + t\mathbf{v}, \quad t \text{ any scalar}\}. \tag{2–1}$$

Let $f$ be a function with domain $D \subset E^n$, and let $\mathbf{x}_0$ be an interior point of $D$.

**Definition.** The *derivative of $f$ at $\mathbf{x}_0$ in the direction $\mathbf{v}$ is*

$$\lim_{t \to 0} \frac{f(\mathbf{x}_0 + t\mathbf{v}) - f(\mathbf{x}_0)}{t} \tag{2–2}$$

*if the limit exists.*

Since $\mathbf{x}_0$ is an interior point, the $\delta$-neighborhood of $\mathbf{x}_0$ is contained in $D$ for some $\delta > 0$ (Fig. 2–1). Since

$$|(\mathbf{x}_0 + t\mathbf{v}) - \mathbf{x}_0| = |t\mathbf{v}| = |t|,$$

$\mathbf{x}_0 + t\mathbf{v} \in D$ provided $|t| < \delta$. The domain of the function $\phi$ defined by

$$\phi(t) = f(\mathbf{x}_0 + t\mathbf{v})$$

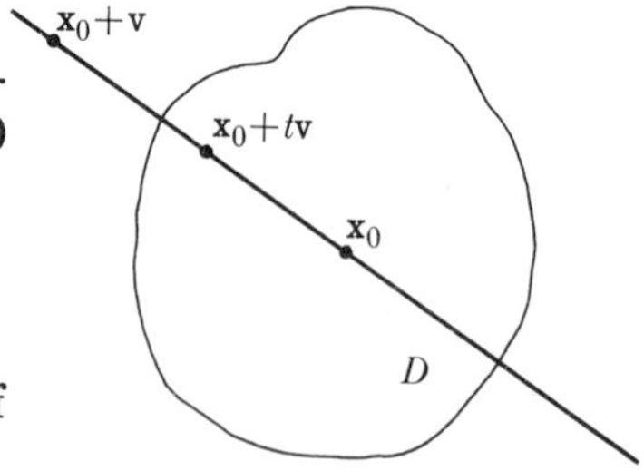


FIGURE 2–1

contains the $\delta$-neighborhood of 0. The derivative of $f$ in the direction $\mathbf{v}$ is $\phi'(0)$, if $\phi$ has a derivative at 0.

The line through $\mathbf{x}_0$ with direction $-\mathbf{v}$ is the same line as the one through $\mathbf{x}_0$ with direction $\mathbf{v}$. However, the derivative in the direction $-\mathbf{v}$ is the negative of the derivative in direction $\mathbf{v}$ (Problem 6). The direction $\mathbf{v}$ defines an *orientation* of this line, and $-\mathbf{v}$ the opposite orientation. When the orientation changes, the directional derivative changes sign. In effect, by assigning the orientation $\mathbf{v}$ we agree that the point $\mathbf{x}_0 + s\mathbf{v}$ precedes $\mathbf{x}_0 + t\mathbf{v}$ on the line if $s < t$.

**Example 1.** Let $D = E^2$ and

$$f(x, y) = \frac{2xy}{x^2 + y^2}, \quad \text{if} \quad (x, y) \neq (0, 0).$$

Since the domain $D$ is to be $E^2$ we must give $f$ some value at (0, 0). More or less arbitrarily, we let $f(0, 0) = 1$. Let us find the directional derivatives of $f$ at (0, 0). Given a direction $(\cos\theta, \sin\theta)$,

$$\phi(t) = f(t\cos\theta, t\sin\theta) = \frac{2t^2 \cos\theta \sin\theta}{t^2(\cos^2\theta + \sin^2\theta)},$$

or $\phi(t) = \sin 2\theta$, for every $t \neq 0$. But $\phi(0) = 1$. If $\sin 2\theta = 1$, then $\phi$ is the constant function with value 1 everywhere, and $\phi'(0) = 0$. Thus if $\theta = \pi/4$ or $5\pi/4$, the directional derivative exists and is 0. For all other values of $\theta$ the function $\phi$ is discontinuous at 0, and consequently $\phi'(0)$ does not exist. Thus $f$ has a directional derivative at (0, 0) only in the directions $(\sqrt{2}/2, \sqrt{2}/2)$ and $(-\sqrt{2}/2, -\sqrt{2}/2)$.

In the next section we shall see that if $f$ is differentiable at $\mathbf{x}_0$, then the derivative in every direction exists and is easily calculated. Thus the unpleasant phenomenon illustrated by the example cannot occur for differentiable functions.

The *partial derivatives* of $f$ are defined as the derivatives in the directions $\mathbf{e}_1, \ldots, \mathbf{e}_n$, if these directional derivatives exist. There are several equivalent notations in use for partial derivatives. Of these we shall adopt just two. The $i$th partial derivative of $f$ at $\mathbf{x}$, $i = 1, \ldots, n$, is denoted by

$$f_i(\mathbf{x}) \quad \text{or} \quad \frac{\partial f}{\partial x_i}(\mathbf{x}).$$

Thus

$$f_i(\mathbf{x}) = \lim_{t \to 0} \frac{f(x^1, \ldots, x^{i-1}, x^i + t, x^{i+1}, \ldots, x^n) - f(x^1, \ldots, x^n)}{t}, \tag{2-3}$$

provided the limit exists. Stated in less precise terms, $f_i(\mathbf{x})$ is the derivative taken with respect to the $i$th variable while holding all other variables fixed.

**Example 2.** Let $f(x, y, z) = x^2 + y + \cos(y^2 z)$. Then

$$\begin{aligned} f_1(x, y, z) &= 2x, \\ f_2(x, y, z) &= 1 - 2yz \sin(y^2 z), \\ f_3(x, y, z) &= -y^2 \sin(y^2 z). \end{aligned}$$

The symbol $f_i$ will denote the real-valued function whose value at $\mathbf{x}$ is $f_i(\mathbf{x})$. Its domain is the set of points where $f$ has an $i$th partial derivative.

For purposes of brevity, we shall occasionally abuse the notation by writing $f_i$ for the value $f_i(\mathbf{x})$ at some particular $\mathbf{x}$. In each such instance this abuse will be indicated either explicitly or by the context.

**Example 3.** Let $f(\mathbf{x}) = \psi[g(\mathbf{x})]$ for every $\mathbf{x} \in D$. Suppose that the $i$th partial derivative of $g$ at $\mathbf{x}_0$ and the derivative of $\psi$ at $g(\mathbf{x}_0)$ exist. By the composite function theorem for functions of one variable

$$f_i(\mathbf{x}_0) = \psi'[g(\mathbf{x}_0)] g_i(\mathbf{x}_0). \tag{2-4}$$

This theorem will be proved in Section 4-4 as a special case of the composite function theorem for transformations.

## PROBLEMS

Unless otherwise stated, the domain $D$ of $f$ is $E^n$ for the particular $n$ indicated in the problem.

1. In each case find the partial derivatives of $f$.
   (a) $f(x, y) = x \log(xy)$, $D = \{(x, y) : xy > 0\}$.
   (b) $f(x, y, z) = (x^2 + 2y^2 + z)^3$.
   (c) $f(\mathbf{x}) = \mathbf{x} \cdot \mathbf{x}$.
2. Let $f(x, y) = (x - 1)^2 - y^2$. Find the derivative of $f$ at $\mathbf{e}_2$ in any direction $\mathbf{v}$, using the definition of directional derivative.
3. Let $f(x) = x^{1/3}$. Show that $f$ has no derivative at 0.

4. Let $f(x, y) = (xy)^{1/3}$. (a) Using the definition of directional derivative, show that $f_1(0, 0) = f_2(0, 0) = 0$, and that $\pm\mathbf{e}_1$, $\pm\mathbf{e}_2$ are the only directions in which the derivative at $(0, 0)$ exists. (b) Show that $f$ is continuous at $(0, 0)$.
5. Let $f(x, y, z) = |x + y + z|$. Find those directions in which the derivative of $f$ at $\mathbf{e}_1 - \mathbf{e}_2$ exists. [*Hint:* The absolute value function, $g(t) = |t|$ for every $t \in E^1$, has no derivative at 0.]
6. Show that the derivative of $f$ at $\mathbf{x}_0$ in the direction $-\mathbf{v}$ is the negative of the derivative at $\mathbf{x}_0$ in the direction $\mathbf{v}$.

## 2–2 DIFFERENTIABLE FUNCTIONS

The existence of a derivative for a function of one variable is a fact of considerable interest. Geometrically, it says that a tangent line exists. However, the fact that a function of several variables has partial derivatives is not in itself of much interest. For one thing, the existence of derivatives in the directions of the standard basis vectors $\mathbf{e}_1, \ldots, \mathbf{e}_n$ does not imply that derivatives exist in other directions. Moreover, the function need not have a tangent hyperplane even if there is a derivative in every direction (see Example 2 below).

We shall now define a more natural notion, that of differentiability. Geometrically, differentiability means the existence of a tangent hyperplane. It will be shown that most of the basic properties of differentiable functions of one variable remain true for differentiable functions of several variables.

Let us again consider an interior point $\mathbf{x}_0$ of the domain $D$ of a real-valued function $f$.

**Definition.** The function $f$ is *differentiable at* $\mathbf{x}_0$ if there is a linear function $L$ (depending on $\mathbf{x}_0$) such that

$$\lim_{\mathbf{h}\to\mathbf{0}} \frac{f(\mathbf{x}_0 + \mathbf{h}) - f(\mathbf{x}_0) - L(\mathbf{h})}{|\mathbf{h}|} = 0. \tag{2–5}$$

Let us show that if $f$ is differentiable at $\mathbf{x}_0$, then $f$ has a derivative at $\mathbf{x}_0$ in every direction $\mathbf{v}$. Taking $\mathbf{h} = t\mathbf{v}$, (2–5) implies that

$$\lim_{t\to 0} \frac{f(\mathbf{x}_0 + t\mathbf{v}) - f(\mathbf{x}_0) - L(t\mathbf{v})}{t} = 0,$$

by Proposition A–5, and therefore

$$\lim_{t\to 0} \frac{f(\mathbf{x}_0 + t\mathbf{v}) - f(\mathbf{x}_0)}{t} - L(\mathbf{v}) = 0,$$

$$\lim_{t\to 0} \frac{f(\mathbf{x}_0 + t\mathbf{v}) - f(\mathbf{x}_0)}{t} = L(\mathbf{v}).$$

This shows that $L(\mathbf{v})$ is the derivative at $\mathbf{x}_0$ in the direction $\mathbf{v}$.

The linear function $L$ is called the *differential of $f$ at* $\mathbf{x}_0$, and will be denoted by $df(\mathbf{x}_0)$. As in Section 1–3, the linear function $df(\mathbf{x}_0)$ is also called a covector, and its value at a vector $\mathbf{h}$ is denoted by $df(\mathbf{x}_0) \cdot \mathbf{h}$ rather than $L(\mathbf{h})$. If $\mathbf{v} = \mathbf{e}_i$, then the number $a_i = L(\mathbf{e}_i)$ is the $i$th partial derivative $f_i(\mathbf{x}_0)$. Hence the components of the covector $df(\mathbf{x}_0)$ are the partial derivatives:

$$df(\mathbf{x}_0) = \sum_{i=1}^{n} f_i(\mathbf{x}_0)\mathbf{e}^i, \tag{2–6}$$

$$df(\mathbf{x}_0) \cdot \mathbf{h} = \sum_{i=1}^{n} f_i(\mathbf{x}_0)h^i. \tag{2–7}$$

If $\mathbf{x} \in D$, let us set $\mathbf{x} = \mathbf{x}_0 + \mathbf{h}$. The vector $\mathbf{h} = \mathbf{x} - \mathbf{x}_0$ is often called the "increment between $\mathbf{x}$ and $\mathbf{x}_0$," and in the time-honored notation of calculus one would write $\Delta\mathbf{x}$ for $\mathbf{h}$. The number $f(\mathbf{x}_0 + \mathbf{h}) - f(\mathbf{x}_0)$ is the corresponding "increment in $f$." However, we shall use neither the word increment nor the notation $\Delta\mathbf{x}$.

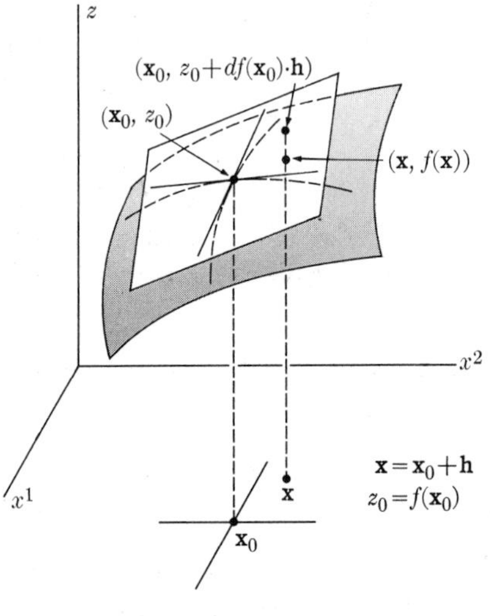


FIGURE 2–2

If $f$ is differentiable at $\mathbf{x}_0$, then the differential at $\mathbf{x}_0$ furnishes a linear approximation $df(\mathbf{x}_0) \cdot (\mathbf{x} - \mathbf{x}_0)$ to $f(\mathbf{x}) - f(\mathbf{x}_0)$ when $\mathbf{x}$ is near $\mathbf{x}_0$. The error in this approximation is $f(\mathbf{x}) - f(\mathbf{x}_0) - df(\mathbf{x}_0) \cdot (\mathbf{x} - \mathbf{x}_0)$, which is the numerator in (2–5). It is small compared to the distance $|\mathbf{x} - \mathbf{x}_0|$ when $|\mathbf{x} - \mathbf{x}_0|$ is small. Geometrically, this means that the hyperplane in $E^{n+1}$ whose equation is $z = f(\mathbf{x}_0) + df(\mathbf{x}_0) \cdot (\mathbf{x} - \mathbf{x}_0)$ is tangent to $f$ at $(\mathbf{x}_0, f(\mathbf{x}_0))$. This is illustrated by Fig. 2–2 for $n = 2$. A precise definition of tangent hyperplane will be given later in Section 4–7.

**Example 1.** Let $f(x, y) = (xy)^{1/3}$. Find the tangent plane at $(1, 1, 1)$. By elementary calculus

$$f_1(x, y) = \tfrac{1}{3}x^{-2/3}y^{1/3}, \qquad f_2(x, y) = \tfrac{1}{3}x^{1/3}y^{-2/3},$$

except at (0, 0). Moreover, $f_1$ and $f_2$ are continuous functions except at (0, 0). By Theorem 2 in the next section, $f$ is differentiable at any $(x_0, y_0) \neq (0, 0)$. The components of $df(x_0, y_0)$ are $f_1(x_0, y_0)$ and $f_2(x_0, y_0)$. The equation for the tangent plane at $(x_0, y_0, f(x_0, y_0))$ is

$$z = f(x_0, y_0) + f_1(x_0, y_0)(x - x_0) + f_2(x_0, y_0)(y - y_0).$$

Taking $x_0 = y_0 = 1$, the equation of the tangent plane at (1, 1, 1) is

$$z = 1 + \tfrac{1}{3}(x - 1) + \tfrac{1}{3}(y - 1).$$

The partial derivatives $f_1(0, 0)$ and $f_2(0, 0)$ are both 0, according to Problem 4, Section 2–1. However, there is no tangent plane at (0, 0, 0). If there were a tangent plane at (0, 0, 0), then $f$ would have to be differentiable at (0, 0). Since there is not a derivative in every direction at (0, 0), $f$ is not differentiable there.

**Proposition 7.** *If $f$ is differentiable at $\mathbf{x}_0$ then $f$ is continuous at $\mathbf{x}_0$.*

*Proof.* For any $\mathbf{h}$

$$f(\mathbf{x}_0 + \mathbf{h}) - f(\mathbf{x}_0) = [f(\mathbf{x}_0 + \mathbf{h}) - f(\mathbf{x}_0) - df(\mathbf{x}_0) \cdot \mathbf{h}] + df(\mathbf{x}_0) \cdot \mathbf{h}. \quad (*)$$

From the definition of limit (with $\epsilon = 1$) there is a positive number $\delta_0$ such that if $0 < |\mathbf{h}| < \delta_0$ the quotient in (2–5) has absolute value less than 1,

$$|f(\mathbf{x}_0 + \mathbf{h}) - f(\mathbf{x}_0) - df(\mathbf{x}_0) \cdot \mathbf{h}| < |\mathbf{h}|.$$

By Cauchy's inequality

$$|df(\mathbf{x}_0) \cdot \mathbf{h}| \leq |df(\mathbf{x}_0)|\,|\mathbf{h}|.$$

Applying the triangle inequality to the right side of (*),

$$|f(\mathbf{x}_0 + \mathbf{h}) - f(\mathbf{x}_0)| \leq |f(\mathbf{x}_0 + \mathbf{h}) - f(\mathbf{x}_0) - df(\mathbf{x}_0) \cdot \mathbf{h}| + |df(\mathbf{x}_0) \cdot \mathbf{h}|.$$

Consequently, if $0 < |\mathbf{h}| < \delta_0$,

$$|f(\mathbf{x}_0 + \mathbf{h}) - f(\mathbf{x}_0)| < C|\mathbf{h}|, \quad (2\text{–}8)$$

where $C = 1 + |df(\mathbf{x}_0)|$. Given $\epsilon > 0$, let $\delta = \min\{\delta_0, \epsilon/C\}$. Then $|f(\mathbf{x}_0 + \mathbf{h}) - f(\mathbf{x}_0)| < \epsilon$ for every $\mathbf{h}$ such that $0 < |\mathbf{h}| < \delta$. This shows that

$$\lim_{\mathbf{h} \to \mathbf{0}} f(\mathbf{x}_0 + \mathbf{h}) = f(\mathbf{x}_0),$$

in other words, that $f$ is continuous at $\mathbf{x}_0$. ∎

For $n = 1$, $f$ is differentiable at $x_0$ if and only if the derivative $f'(x_0)$ exists, since both statements are equivalent to the existence of a tangent line at $(x_0, f(x_0))$. However, for $n \geq 2$ a function $f$ may have a derivative at $\mathbf{x}_0$ in every direction yet not be differentiable or even continuous at $\mathbf{x}_0$. This is shown by the following example.

**Example 2.** Let

$$f(x, y) = \frac{2xy^2}{x^2 + y^4}, \quad \text{if} \quad (x, y) \neq (0, 0), \quad \text{and} \quad f(0, 0) = 0.$$

There are two cases to consider. If $\cos\theta \neq 0$, then the derivative at $(0, 0)$ in the direction $(\cos\theta, \sin\theta)$ is

$$\lim_{t\to 0} \frac{f(t\cos\theta, t\sin\theta) - f(0, 0)}{t} = \lim_{t\to 0} \frac{2\cos\theta\sin^2\theta}{\cos^2\theta + t^2\sin^4\theta} = \frac{2\sin^2\theta}{\cos\theta}.$$

If $\cos\theta = 0$, then $f(t\cos\theta, t\sin\theta) = 0$ for every $t$ and the directional derivative at $(0, 0)$ is 0. However, $f(y^2, y) = 1$ for every $y \neq 0$. Since $f(0, 0) = 0$, $f$ is not continuous at $(0, 0)$. By Proposition 7, $f$ is not differentiable at $(0, 0)$.

Let us next state a proposition which, although of no interest in itself, will be useful later.

**Proposition 8.** *Let* $\phi(t) = f(\mathbf{x}_0 + t\mathbf{h})$. *Then for every* $t$ *such that* $f$ *is differentiable at* $\mathbf{x}_0 + t\mathbf{h}$,

$$\phi'(t) = df(\mathbf{x}_0 + t\mathbf{h}) \cdot \mathbf{h}.$$

*Proof.* If $\mathbf{h} = \mathbf{0}$ the result is trivial. If $\mathbf{h} \neq \mathbf{0}$, then

$$0 = \lim_{\boldsymbol{\eta}\to 0} \frac{f(\mathbf{x}_0 + t\mathbf{h} + \boldsymbol{\eta}) - f(\mathbf{x}_0 + t\mathbf{h}) - df(\mathbf{x}_0 + t\mathbf{h}) \cdot \boldsymbol{\eta}}{|\boldsymbol{\eta}|}.$$

In particular, let $\boldsymbol{\eta} = \tau\mathbf{h}$. Then

$$0 = \lim_{\tau\to 0} \frac{\phi(t + \tau) - \phi(t) - \tau\, df(\mathbf{x}_0 + t\mathbf{h}) \cdot \mathbf{h}}{\tau},$$

$$0 = \lim_{\tau\to 0} \frac{\phi(t + \tau) - \phi(t)}{\tau} - df(\mathbf{x}_0 + t\mathbf{h}) \cdot \mathbf{h}. \blacksquare$$

Note that if $\mathbf{h}$ is a direction ($|\mathbf{h}| = 1$) and $t = 0$, we again obtain the formula $df(\mathbf{x}_0) \cdot \mathbf{h}$ for the directional derivative.

As a first application of Proposition 8 let us extend the mean value theorem to functions of several variables. Let $(0, 1)$ denote the open interval with endpoints 0 and 1 (as in Section A–1).

**Mean Value Theorem.** *Let* $f$ *be differentiable at every point of the line segment joining* $\mathbf{x}_0$ *and* $\mathbf{x}_0 + \mathbf{h}$. *Then there exists a number* $s \in (0, 1)$ *such that*

$$f(\mathbf{x}_0 + \mathbf{h}) - f(\mathbf{x}_0) = df(\mathbf{x}_0 + s\mathbf{h}) \cdot \mathbf{h}.$$

*Proof.* Let $\phi$ have the same meaning as in Proposition 8. By the mean value theorem for functions of one variable (Section A–8) there exists $s \in (0, 1)$ such that $\phi(1) - \phi(0) = \phi'(s)$. We apply Proposition 8. $\blacksquare$

Note that the point $\mathbf{x}_0 + s\mathbf{h}$ is on the line segment joining $\mathbf{x}_0$ and $\mathbf{x}_0 + \mathbf{h}$. The number $s$ in the mean value theorem is not unique. We have no interest in actually calculating $s$. The mean value theorem is used to obtain various estimates which are valid no matter where $s$ is in the interval $(0, 1)$. The mean value theorem is often stated in a slightly sharper form, in which $f$ is required to be differentiable at each point $\mathbf{x}_0 + t\mathbf{h}$ for $t$ in the open interval $(0, 1)$ and continuous at $\mathbf{x}_0$ and $\mathbf{x}_0 + \mathbf{h}$. The proof is the same.

**Definition.** If $f$ is differentiable at every point of a subset $A$ of its domain $D$, then we say that $f$ is *differentiable on* $A$. If $D$ is an open set and $f$ is differentiable at every point of $D$, then $f$ is called a *differentiable function.*

The mean value theorem has the following corollaries.

**Corollary 1.** *Let $f$ be differentiable on a convex set $K$ and $C \geq 0$ a number such that $|df(\mathbf{x})| \leq C$ for every $\mathbf{x} \in K$. Then for every $\mathbf{x}, \mathbf{y} \in K$,*

$$|f(\mathbf{x}) - f(\mathbf{y})| \leq C|\mathbf{x} - \mathbf{y}|.$$

*Proof.* By the mean value theorem, with $\mathbf{x}_0 = \mathbf{y}$, $\mathbf{x}_0 + \mathbf{h} = \mathbf{x}$,

$$f(\mathbf{x}) - f(\mathbf{y}) = df(\mathbf{y} + s(\mathbf{x} - \mathbf{y})) \cdot (\mathbf{x} - \mathbf{y}),$$

where $s \in (0, 1)$. By Cauchy's inequality,

$$|f(\mathbf{x}) - f(\mathbf{y})| \leq |df(\mathbf{y} + s(\mathbf{x} - \mathbf{y}))|\,|\mathbf{x} - \mathbf{y}| \leq C|\mathbf{x} - \mathbf{y}|. \blacksquare$$

**Corollary 2.** *Let $f$ be a differentiable function whose domain $D$ is an open, connected set, such that $df(\mathbf{x}) = \mathbf{0}$ for every $\mathbf{x} \in D$. Then $f$ is a constant function.*

*Proof.* Let $\mathbf{x}_0$ be some point of $D$, and let $D_1 = \{\mathbf{x} : f(\mathbf{x}) = f(\mathbf{x}_0)\}$. If $\mathbf{x} \in D_1$ then some neighborhood $U$ of $\mathbf{x}$ is contained in $D$. Every neighborhood is a convex set. By Corollary 1, with $C = 0$ and $K = U$, $f(\mathbf{y}) = f(\mathbf{x}) = f(\mathbf{x}_0)$ for every $\mathbf{y} \in U$. Hence $U \subset D_1$. This shows that $D_1$ is an open set.

Since $f$ is differentiable, $f$ is continuous by Proposition 7. Therefore $D - D_1 = \{\mathbf{x} : f(\mathbf{x}) \neq f(\mathbf{x}_0)\}$ is also open by the corollary to Proposition A–6. If $D - D_1$ is not empty, then $D$ is the union of two disjoint, nonempty open sets $D_1$ and $D - D_1$. Since $D$ is connected, this is impossible. Hence $D - D_1$ is empty, and $D = D_1$. $\blacksquare$

Corollary 2 generalizes the result that if $f'(x) = 0$ for every $x$ in an open interval, then $f$ is constant there.

*Note:* H. Whitney (*Duke Math. J.* **1** (1935), 514–517) gave an example of a connected set $A \subset E^2$ and a differentiable function $f$, such that $df(x, y) = \mathbf{0}$ for every $(x, y) \in A$ but $f(x, y)$ is not constant on $A$. The set $A$ in Whitney's example has no interior point.

If $\mathbf{x}$ is any point where $f$ is differentiable, then besides the covector

$$df(\mathbf{x}) = \sum_{i=1}^{n} f_i(\mathbf{x})\mathbf{e}^i$$

whose components are the partial derivatives $f_i(\mathbf{x})$, it is sometimes more suitable to think instead of the vector with these same components. This is called the *gradient vector* at $\mathbf{x}$ and is denoted by grad $f(\mathbf{x})$. Thus

$$\operatorname{grad} f(\mathbf{x}) = \sum_{i=1}^{n} f_i(\mathbf{x})\mathbf{e}_i.$$

Another common notation for the gradient vector is $\nabla f(\mathbf{x})$.

**Note:* This definition of the gradient vector is correct only if we use the euclidean inner product in $E^n$. If $E^n$ is given some other inner product $B$, then one should use formula (1–14b) for changing covectors into vectors. The gradient vector in that case is

$$\operatorname{grad} f(\mathbf{x}) = \sum_{i,j=1}^{n} c^{ij} f_j(\mathbf{x})\mathbf{e}_i,$$

and according to formula (1–13),

$$B(\operatorname{grad} f(\mathbf{x}), \mathbf{h}) = df(\mathbf{x}) \cdot \mathbf{h},$$

which becomes for the euclidean inner product simply grad $f(\mathbf{x}) \cdot \mathbf{h} = df(\mathbf{x}) \cdot \mathbf{h}$.

## PROBLEMS

In Problems 1, 2, 3, and 8, assume that $f$ is differentiable. In each case this follows from Theorem 2 in the next section.

1. Let $f(x, y) = 3x^2y + 2xy^2$. Find the tangent plane at $(1, -2, 2)$.
2. Using the formula $df(\mathbf{x}_0) \cdot \mathbf{v}$ for directional derivative, find the derivative of $f$ at $\mathbf{x}_0$ in the direction $\mathbf{v}$.

   (a) $f(x, y) = xy$, $\mathbf{x}_0 = (1, 3)$, $\mathbf{v} = \left(\dfrac{2}{\sqrt{5}}, -\dfrac{1}{\sqrt{5}}\right)$.

   (b) $f(x, y) = x \exp(xy)$, $\mathbf{x}_0 = \mathbf{e}_1 - \mathbf{e}_2$, $\mathbf{v} = \dfrac{1}{\sqrt{2}}(\mathbf{e}_1 + \mathbf{e}_2)$.

   (c) $f(x, y, z) = ax^2 + by^2 + cz^2$, $\mathbf{x}_0 = \mathbf{e}_1$, $\mathbf{v} = \mathbf{e}_3$.
3. Let $f(x, y) = \log(x^2 + 2y + 1) + \int_0^x \cos(t^2)\,dt$, $y > -\frac{1}{2}$.

   (a) Find $df(x, y)$.
   (b) Find approximately $f(.03, .03)$.
4. Find grad $f(\mathbf{x})$ for each of the following functions:

   (a) $f(\mathbf{x}) = \mathbf{x}_0 \cdot \mathbf{x}$. (b) $f(\mathbf{x}) = |\mathbf{x}|$, $\mathbf{x} \neq \mathbf{0}$. (c) $f(\mathbf{x}) = (\mathbf{x}_0 \cdot \mathbf{x})^2$.

5. Let $f(x, y) = 2xy^2/(x^2 + y^4)$, if $(x, y) \neq (0, 0)$, and $f(0, 0) = 0$, as in Example 2.
   (a) Show that $-1 \leq f(x, y) \leq 1$ for every $(x, y)$.
   (b) Find $\{(x, y) : f(x, y) = 1\}$ and $\{(x, y) : f(x, y) = -1\}$.
   (c) Find $\{(x, y) : \text{grad} f(x, y) = (0, 0)\}$.
   (d) Find $\{(x, y) : f(x, y) = c\}$ for any $c$, and illustrate with a sketch.
6. Let $f$ and $g$ be differentiable at $\mathbf{x}_0$. (a) Prove that the sum $f + g$ is differentiable at $\mathbf{x}_0$, and $d(f + g)(\mathbf{x}_0) = df(\mathbf{x}_0) + dg(\mathbf{x}_0)$. (b) Prove that the product $fg$ is differentiable at $\mathbf{x}_0$, and $d(fg)(\mathbf{x}_0) = f(\mathbf{x}_0)dg(\mathbf{x}_0) + g(\mathbf{x}_0)df(\mathbf{x}_0)$. [*Hint:* Recall the proof for $n = 1$.]
7. (Euler's formula). Let $p$ be a real number. A function $f$ is called *homogeneous of degree* $p$ if $f(t\mathbf{x}) = t^p f(\mathbf{x})$ for every $\mathbf{x} \neq \mathbf{0}$ and $t > 0$. Let $f$ be differentiable for all $\mathbf{x} \neq \mathbf{0}$. Show that if $f$ is homogeneous of degree $p$, then

$$df(\mathbf{x}) \cdot \mathbf{x} = pf(\mathbf{x})$$

   for every $\mathbf{x} \neq \mathbf{0}$, and conversely. [*Hint:* Let $\phi(t) = f(t\mathbf{x})$ and use Proposition 8 with $\mathbf{x}_0 = \mathbf{0}$. For the converse, show that for fixed $\mathbf{x}$, $\phi(t)t^{-p}$ is a constant.]
8. Let $Q(\mathbf{x}) = \sum_{i,j=1}^{n} C_{ij}x^i x^j$, where $C_{ij} = C_{ji}$ and $Q(\mathbf{x}) > 0$ for every $\mathbf{x} \neq \mathbf{0}$. Let $f(\mathbf{x}) = [Q(\mathbf{x})]^{p/2}$. Calculate $df(\mathbf{x})$ and verify Euler's formula for this function.

## 2-3 FUNCTIONS OF CLASS $C^{(q)}$

Let $f$ be a function whose domain is an open set $D \subset E^n$.

**Definition.** If $f$ is continuous, then $f$ is said to be a *function of class* $C^{(0)}$. If the partial derivatives $f_1(\mathbf{x}), \ldots, f_n(\mathbf{x})$ exist for every $\mathbf{x} \in D$ and $f_1, \ldots, f_n$ are continuous functions, then $f$ is a *function of class* $C^{(1)}$.

The classes $C^{(q)}$ of functions, where $q = 2, 3, \ldots$, will be defined below. We will first prove the following sufficient condition for differentiability, which is adequate for most purposes.

**Theorem 2.** *If $f$ is a function of class $C^{(1)}$, then $f$ is a differentiable function.*

*Proof.* Let us proceed by induction on the dimension $n$. If $n = 1$, differentiability means simply that $f'(x)$ exists for every $x \in D$, while if $f$ is of class $C^{(1)}$, then $f'$ is a continuous function. Let us assume that the theorem is true in dimension $n - 1$.

Let $\mathbf{x}_0$ be any point of $D$ and $\delta_0 > 0$ such that the $\delta_0$-neighborhood of $\mathbf{x}_0$ is contained in $D$. Let us write (Fig. 2-3)

$$\hat{\mathbf{x}} = (x^1, \ldots, x^{n-1}), \qquad \hat{\mathbf{x}}_0 = (x_0^1, \ldots, x_0^{n-1}),$$

$$\phi(\hat{\mathbf{x}}) = f(x^1, \ldots, x^{n-1}, x_0^n) = f(\hat{\mathbf{x}}, x_0^n),$$

provided the point $(\hat{\mathbf{x}}, x_0^n)$ is in $D$. The partial derivatives of $\phi$ are

$$\phi_i(\hat{\mathbf{x}}) = f_i(\hat{\mathbf{x}}, x_0^n), \qquad i = 1, \ldots, n - 1.$$

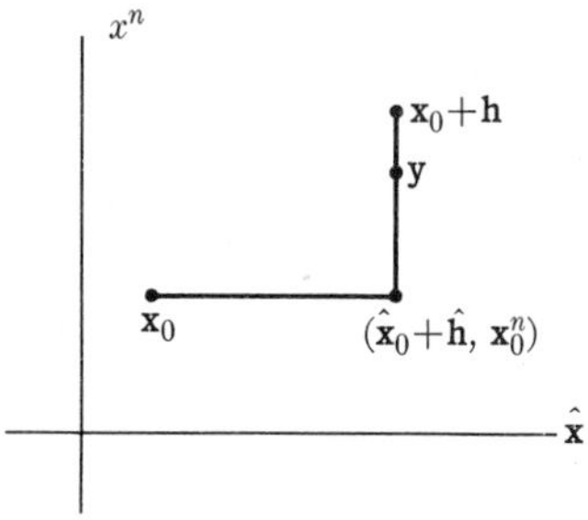


FIGURE 2-3

Since $f$ is of class $C^{(1)}$, each $f_i$ is continuous. Hence each $\phi_i$ is continuous and $\phi$ is of class $C^{(1)}$. By the induction hypothesis $\phi$ is differentiable at $\hat{\mathbf{x}}_0$. Therefore, given $\epsilon > 0$ there exists $\delta_1$, $0 < \delta_1 < \delta_0$, such that

$$|\phi(\hat{\mathbf{x}}_0 + \hat{\mathbf{h}}) - \phi(\hat{\mathbf{x}}_0) - \sum_{i=1}^{n-1} \phi_i(\hat{\mathbf{x}}_0)h^i| < \frac{\epsilon}{2}\,|\hat{\mathbf{h}}|$$

whenever $|\hat{\mathbf{h}}| < \delta_1$. Since $f_n$ is continuous, there exists $\delta_2$, $0 < \delta_2 < \delta_0$, such that $|f_n(\mathbf{y}) - f_n(\mathbf{x}_0)| < \epsilon/2$ whenever $|\mathbf{y} - \mathbf{x}_0| < \delta_2$. Let $\delta = \min\{\delta_1, \delta_2\}$ and let $|\mathbf{h}| < \delta$. By the mean value theorem,

$$\begin{aligned} f(\mathbf{x}_0 + \mathbf{h}) - \phi(\hat{\mathbf{x}}_0 + \hat{\mathbf{h}}) &= f(\hat{\mathbf{x}}_0 + \hat{\mathbf{h}}, x_0^n + h^n) - f(\hat{\mathbf{x}}_0 + \hat{\mathbf{h}}, x_0^n) \\ &= f_n(\hat{\mathbf{x}}_0 + \hat{\mathbf{h}}, x_0^n + sh^n)h^n \end{aligned}$$

for some $s \in (0, 1)$. Setting $\mathbf{y} = (\hat{\mathbf{x}}_0 + \hat{\mathbf{h}}, x_0^n + sh^n)$,

$$|\mathbf{y} - \mathbf{x}_0| = s|h^n| < |\mathbf{h}| < \delta.$$

Since $f(\mathbf{x}_0) = \phi(\hat{\mathbf{x}}_0)$,

$$\begin{aligned} f(\mathbf{x}_0 + \mathbf{h}) - f(\mathbf{x}_0) &= [f(\mathbf{x}_0 + \mathbf{h}) - \phi(\hat{\mathbf{x}}_0 + \hat{\mathbf{h}})] \\ &\quad + [\phi(\hat{\mathbf{x}}_0 + \hat{\mathbf{h}}) - \phi(\hat{\mathbf{x}}_0)], \end{aligned}$$

$$\begin{aligned} f(\mathbf{x}_0 + \mathbf{h}) - f(\mathbf{x}_0) - df(\mathbf{x}_0)\cdot\mathbf{h} &= [f_n(\mathbf{y})h^n - f_n(\mathbf{x}_0)h^n] \\ &\quad + \left[\phi(\hat{\mathbf{x}}_0 + \hat{\mathbf{h}}) - \phi(\hat{\mathbf{x}}_0) - \sum_{i=1}^{n-1} \phi_i(\hat{\mathbf{x}}_0)h^i\right]. \end{aligned}$$

Using the above inequalities, the triangle inequality, and the fact that $|h^n| \le |\mathbf{h}|$, $|\hat{\mathbf{h}}| \le |\mathbf{h}|$, we get

$$|f(\mathbf{x}_0 + \mathbf{h}) - f(\mathbf{x}_0) - df(\mathbf{x}_0)\cdot\mathbf{h}| < \frac{\epsilon}{2}\,|h^n| + \frac{\epsilon}{2}\,|\hat{\mathbf{h}}| \le \epsilon|\mathbf{h}|$$

whenever $|\mathbf{h}| < \delta$. This proves that $f$ is differentiable at $\mathbf{x}_0$. ▌

**Corollary.** *Every function of class $C^{(1)}$ is of class $C^{(0)}$.*

*Proof.* Apply Proposition 7 and Theorem 2. ▌

**Example 1.** If $f$ and $g$ are functions of class $C^{(1)}$ with the same domain $D$, then $f + g$ is of class $C^{(1)}$. Using the product rule from elementary calculus, the partial derivatives of the product are

$$(fg)_i = f_i g + f g_i, \qquad i = 1, \ldots, n.$$

Since sums and products of continuous functions are again continuous, $(fg)_i$ is continuous for each $i = 1, \ldots, n$. Hence $fg$ is of class $C^{(1)}$.

**Example 2.** The composite of two functions of class $C^{(1)}$ is also of class $C^{(1)}$. For suppose that $f = \psi \circ g$, where $\psi$ and $g$ are of class $C^{(1)}$. By formula (2–4), p. 37, $f_i = (\psi' \circ g)g_i$. Since $\psi'$ and $g$ are continuous, their composite $\psi' \circ g$ is continuous

(Proposition A-7). Since $g_i$ is continuous, the product $(\psi' \circ g)g_i$ is continuous. Thus $f$ is of class $C^{(1)}$.

**Higher-order partial derivatives.** The partial derivatives $f_1(\mathbf{x}), \ldots, f_n(\mathbf{x})$ are often called the *first-order* partial derivatives of $f$ at $\mathbf{x}$. The functions $f_1, \ldots, f_n$ may themselves possess partial derivatives. If $f_i$ has a $j$th partial derivative at $\mathbf{x}$, then this partial derivative is called a partial derivative of *order* 2, and is denoted by

$$f_{ij}(\mathbf{x}) \quad \text{or} \quad \frac{\partial^2 f}{\partial x^j \partial x^i}(\mathbf{x}).$$

For example, if $f(x, y) = x^2y^3$ then $f_1(x, y) = 2xy^3$, $f_{11}(x, y) = 2y^3$, $f_{12}(x, y) = 6xy^2$.

If all of the partial derivatives $f_{ij}(\mathbf{x})$, $i, j = 1, \ldots, n$, exist at every $\mathbf{x} \in D$ and each $f_{ij}$ is a continuous function, then $f$ is called a *function of class* $C^{(2)}$. By the corollary to Theorem 2, if $f$ is of class $C^{(2)}$ then $f_1, \ldots, f_n$ are continuous. Hence any function of class $C^{(2)}$ is also of class $C^{(1)}$.

The partial derivatives of $f$ of order $q = 3, 4, \ldots$ are defined similarly, wherever they exist. The notation for partial derivative at $\mathbf{x}$, first in the direction $\mathbf{e}_{i_1}$, second in the direction $\mathbf{e}_{i_2}$, and so on, is

$$f_{i_1 \cdots i_q}(\mathbf{x}), \qquad 1 \leq i_l \leq n, \qquad l = 1, \ldots, q.$$

**Definition.** If all of the $q$th order derivatives of $f$ exist at every $\mathbf{x} \in D$ and each $f_{i_1 \cdots i_q}$ is a continuous function, then $f$ is a *function of class* $C^{(q)}$.

By the corollary to Theorem 2, any function of class $C^{(q)}$ is also of class $C^{(q-1)}$. As $q$ increases, more and more restrictive conditions are placed on the smoothness of $f$. In many parts of differential calculus it is sufficient to assume that $f$ is of class $C^{(1)}$ or class $C^{(2)}$. However, for some purposes one needs $C^{(q)}$ for $q > 2$. For instance, in Taylor's formula it is assumed that $f$ is of class $C^{(q)}$.

The sum and product of two functions of class $C^{(q)}$ are of class $C^{(q)}$. If, in Example 2, $\psi$ and $g$ are of class $C^{(q)}$, their composite $f$ is also of class $C^{(q)}$.

**Example 3.** Let $p > 0$, $p$ not an integer, and $\psi(x) = |x|^p$ for every $x \in E^1$. Then $\psi$ is of class $C^{(q)}$ if $q < p$ but not if $q > p$. The proof of this is left to the reader (Problem 4). Thus for every $q$ there exist functions of class $C^{(q)}$ which are not of class $C^{(q+1)}$.

**Example 4.** Any polynomial in $n$ variables is a function of class $C^{(q)}$ for every $q$. If $f$ is a rational function, $f(\mathbf{x}) = P(\mathbf{x})/Q(\mathbf{x})$ where $P$ and $Q$ are polynomials, then $f$ is of class $C^{(q)}$ on any open set where $Q(\mathbf{x}) \neq 0$.

It can happen that a function $f$ has the second partial derivatives $f_{ij}$ and $f_{ji}$, $i \neq j$, but that $f_{ij} \neq f_{ji}$. See Problem 6. However, this undesirable phenomenon cannot occur if $f$ is of class $C^{(2)}$. This is even true under the slightly weaker hypotheses of the following theorem in which no assumption is made about the other second-order partial derivatives of $f$.

**Theorem 3.** *If $f$ is of class $C^{(1)}$ and both $f_{ij}$ and $f_{ji}$ are continuous, $i \neq j$, then $f_{ij} = f_{ji}$.*

*Proof.* Suppose first that $n = 2$. We need to show that $f_{12} = f_{21}$. Let $(x_0, y_0)$ be any point of $D$, and $\delta_0 > 0$ such that the $\delta_0$-neighborhood of $(x_0, y_0)$ is contained in $D$. For $0 < u < \delta_0/\sqrt{2}$ let

$$A(u) = \frac{1}{u^2}\,[f(x_0 + u, y_0 + u) - f(x_0, y_0 + u) - f(x_0 + u, y_0) + f(x_0, y_0)].$$

$A(u)$ is sometimes called the second difference quotient. Let

$$g(x) = f(x, y_0 + u) - f(x, y_0)$$

for every $x$ such that $(x, y_0 + u), (x, y_0) \in D$. The domain of $g$ is an open subset of $E^1$ which contains the closed interval $[x_0, x_0 + u]$. Moreover, $g'(x) = f_1(x, y_0 + u) - f_1(x, y_0)$. Thus $g$ is of class $C^{(1)}$ since $f_1$ is continuous, and

$$A(u) = \frac{1}{u^2}\,[g(x_0 + u) - g(x_0)].$$

Applying the mean value theorem to $g$, there exists $\xi \in (x_0, x_0 + u)$ such that

$$A(u) = \frac{1}{u}\,g'(\xi) = \frac{1}{u}\,[f_1(\xi, y_0 + u) - f_1(\xi, y_0)].$$

See Fig. 2–4. Of course the number $\xi$ depends on $u$. Let

$$h(y) = f_1(\xi, y)$$

for every $y$ such that $(\xi, y) \in D$. The domain of $h$ is open and contains $[y_0, y_0 + u]$. Moreover, $h'(y) = f_{12}(\xi, y)$, $h$ is of class $C^{(1)}$ since $f_{12}$ is continuous, and

$$A(u) = \frac{1}{u}\,[h(y_0 + u) - h(y_0)].$$

Another application of the mean value theorem gives

$$A(u) = f_{12}(\xi, \eta),$$

for some $\eta \in (y_0, y_0 + u)$, depending on $u$.

By reversing the roles of the first and second variables and repeating the proof, we find that

$$A(u) = f_{21}(\xi^*, \eta^*)$$

for some

$$\xi^* \in (x_0, x_0 + u) \text{ and } \eta^* \in (y_0, y_0 + u).$$

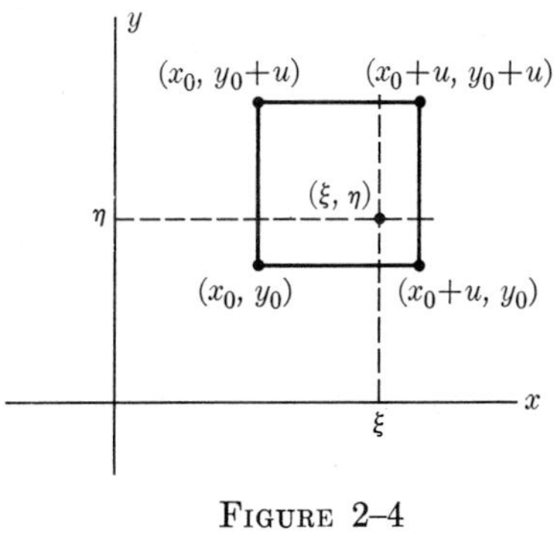


FIGURE 2–4

Since $f_{12}$ and $f_{21}$ are continuous, given $\epsilon > 0$ there exists $\delta \in (0, \delta_0)$ such that if $0 < u < \delta/\sqrt{2}$,

$$|f_{12}(\xi, \eta) - f_{12}(x_0, y_0)| < \epsilon, \qquad |f_{21}(\xi^*, \eta^*) - f_{21}(x_0, y_0)| < \epsilon.$$

This shows that

$$\lim_{u \to 0^+} A(u) = f_{12}(x_0, y_0) = f_{21}(x_0, y_0),$$

and proves the theorem if $n = 2$.

If $n > 2$ we need consider only the case $i < j$. Given $\mathbf{x}_0 = (x_0^1, \ldots, x_0^n) \in D$, let

$$\phi(x, y) = f(x_0^1, \ldots, x_0^{i-1}, x, x_0^{i+1}, \ldots, x_0^{j-1}, y, x_0^{j+1}, \ldots, x_0^n),$$

for every $(x, y)$ in some open set containing $(x_0^i, x_0^j)$. Applying the theorem to $\phi$, we find that

$$f_{ij}(\mathbf{x}_0) = \phi_{12}(x_0^i, x_0^j) = \phi_{21}(x_0^i, x_0^j) = f_{ji}(\mathbf{x}_0). \blacksquare$$

From Theorem 3 it follows that in calculating any $q$th-order partial derivative of a function of class $C^{(q)}$ it is only the number of partial differentiations with respect to each of the variables which matters, and not the order in which they are taken. Thus for functions of class $C^{(3)}$, $f_{123} = f_{132}$, $f_{112} = f_{121}$, and so on.

We are now going to prove a stronger version of the mean value theorem, which is valid for functions of class $C^{(q)}$. Let $f$ be of class $C^{(q)}$ and $\mathbf{x}, \mathbf{x}_0 \in D$ *such that the line segment joining* $\mathbf{x}$ *and* $\mathbf{x}_0$ *is contained in* $D$. In particular, if $D$ is convex then $\mathbf{x}$ and $\mathbf{x}_0$ can be any pair of points of $D$. Let $\mathbf{h} = \mathbf{x} - \mathbf{x}_0$, and define $\phi$ as in Proposition 8 by $\phi(t) = f(\mathbf{x}_0 + t\mathbf{h})$. The domain of $\phi$ is $\{t : \mathbf{x} + t\mathbf{h} \in D\}$, which is an open subset of $E^1$ containing the closed interval $[0, 1]$. By repeated application of Proposition 8 to $f, f_i, f_{ij}, \ldots$, we find that:

$$\phi'(t) = \sum_{i=1}^{n} f_i(\mathbf{x}_0 + t\mathbf{h})h^i,$$

$$\phi''(t) = \sum_{i=1}^{n} \left[ \sum_{j=1}^{n} f_{ij}(\mathbf{x}_0 + t\mathbf{h})h^j \right] h^i,$$

$$\vdots$$

$$\phi^{(q)}(t) = \sum_{i_1, \ldots, i_q = 1}^{n} f_{i_1 \ldots i_q}(\mathbf{x}_0 + t\mathbf{h})h^{i_1} \cdots h^{i_q}.$$

By Taylor's formula for functions of one variable (Section A-8) there exists $s \in (0, 1)$ such that

$$\phi(1) = \phi(0) + \phi'(0) + \frac{1}{2!}\phi''(0) + \cdots + \frac{1}{(q-1)!}\phi^{(q-1)}(0) + \frac{1}{q!}\phi^{(q)}(s).$$

But $\phi(1) = f(\mathbf{x})$, $\phi(0) = f(\mathbf{x}_0)$, and we have by substitution:

*Taylor's formula with remainder:*

$$f(\mathbf{x}) = f(\mathbf{x}_0) + \sum_{i=1}^{n} f_i(\mathbf{x}_0)(x^i - x_0^i) + \frac{1}{2!} \sum_{i,j=1}^{n} f_{ij}(\mathbf{x}_0)(x^i - x_0^i)(x^j - x_0^j) + \cdots$$

$$+ \frac{1}{(q-1)!} \sum_{i_1,\ldots,i_{q-1}=1}^{n} f_{i_1\cdots i_{q-1}}(\mathbf{x}_0) h^{i_1} \cdots h^{i_{q-1}} + R_q(\mathbf{x}), \qquad (2\text{–}9)$$

where $h^i = x^i - x_0^i$, $s \in (0, 1)$, and

$$R_q(\mathbf{x}) = \frac{1}{q!} \sum_{i_1,\ldots,i_q=1}^{n} f_{i_1\cdots i_q}(\mathbf{x}_0 + s\mathbf{h}) h^{i_1} \cdots h^{i_q}. \qquad (2\text{–}10)$$

If we ignore the remainder $R_q(\mathbf{x})$, the right-hand side is a polynomial in $h^1, \ldots, h^n$ of degree $q - 1$. If the remainder is small this polynomial furnishes an approximation to $f(\mathbf{x})$. Notice that the first terms on the right-hand side are just the first degree approximation $f(\mathbf{x}_0) + df(\mathbf{x}_0) \cdot \mathbf{h}$ to $f(\mathbf{x})$ considered in Section 2–2.

If $f$ is a polynomial of degree $q - 1$ then the Taylor approximation is exact; in other words, $R_q(\mathbf{x}) = 0$ for every $\mathbf{x}$.

**Example 5.** Let $f(x, y) = x^2y$ and $(x_0, y_0) = (1, -1)$. Then

$$f_1 = 2xy, \qquad f_2 = x^2, \qquad f_{11} = 2y,$$

$$f_{12} = f_{21} = 2x, \qquad f_{112} = f_{121} = f_{211} = 2,$$

and all other partial derivatives are 0. Here we have written $f_1$ for short in place of $f_1(x, y)$, and so on. $R_4(x, y) = 0$, and Taylor's formula becomes

$$f(x, y) = f(1, -1) + f_1(x - 1) + f_2(y + 1)$$

$$+ \frac{1}{2!}[f_{11}(x-1)^2 + 2f_{12}(x-1)(y+1)] + \frac{1}{3!}[3f_{112}(x-1)^2(y+1)],$$

where the partial derivatives on the right-hand side are evaluated at $(1, -1)$. Thus

$$x^2y = -1 - 2(x-1) + (y+1) - (x-1)^2 + 2(x-1)(y+1) + (x-1)^2(y+1).$$

**Functions of class $C^{(q)}$ on a set.** In many instances either $f$ is not of class $C^{(q)}$ on its entire domain $D$, or else one is interested only in its values on some subset of $D$.

**Definition.** Let $A$ be a nonempty subset of the domain of $f$. Then $f$ is of *class $C^{(q)}$ on $A$* if there exists an open set $D_1$ containing $A$ and a function $F$ of class $C^{(q)}$ with domain $D_1$ such that $F(\mathbf{x}) = f(\mathbf{x})$ for every $\mathbf{x} \in A$.

If $A$ is open, then we may take $D_1 = A$. In that case $F = f|A$, where $f|A$ is the restriction of $f$ to $A$. When $A$ is an open subset of $D$, $f$ is of class $C^{(q)}$ on $A$ if and only if $f|A$ is a function of class $C^{(q)}$.

The function $F$ in the definition is called an *extension of class* $C^{(q)}$ of $f|A$. It is generally not easy to determine whether there is such an extension $F$. However, if $A$ has some simple geometrical shape, there is sometimes a method for explicitly constructing extensions. Let us illustrate this only in the following case, which will be of interest in Section 3-2. Let $A$ be a closed interval $[a, b] \subset E^1$, and for simplicity let $q = 1$. Suppose that $f$ is continuous on $[a, b]$, of class $C^{(1)}$ on $(a, b)$, and that the one-sided limits (Section A-6)

$$l_1 = \lim_{x \to a^+} f'(x), \qquad l_2 = \lim_{x \to b^-} f'(x)$$

exist. Let

$$g(x) = \begin{cases} l_1 & \text{if} \quad x \leq a, \\ f'(x) & \text{if} \quad a < x < b, \\ l_2 & \text{if} \quad x \geq b. \end{cases}$$

The function $g$ is continuous on $E^1$. Let

$$F(x) = f(a) + \int_a^x g(u)\, du,$$

for every $x \in E^1$. Then $F$ is of class $C^{(1)}$, and by the fundamental theorem of calculus, $f(x) = F(x)$ for every $x \in [a, b]$. Therefore $f$ is of class $C^{(1)}$ on $[a, b]$. By induction if $f$ is continuous on $[a, b]$, of class $C^{(q)}$ on $(a, b)$, and

$$\lim_{x \to a^+} f^{(q)}(x), \qquad \lim_{x \to b^-} f^{(q)}(x)$$

exist, then $f$ is of class $C^{(q)}$ on $[a, b]$.

Some general theorems about extensions of class $C^{(q)}$ were proved by H. Whitney. Let us cite without proof a result which is a special case of a theorem of Whitney [*Ann. of Math.* **35** (1934), 485]. Let $A$ be the closure of an open set $B$, and assume either that $A$ is convex or that its boundary fr $A$ is an $(n - 1)$- manifold of class $C^{(1)}$ (see Section 4-7). Let $f$ be of class $C^{(q)}$ on $B$, and continuous on $A$. Moreover, assume that for each $i_1 \ldots i_q$ there is a function $F_{i_1 \ldots i_q}$ continuous on $A$ such that $F_{i_1 \ldots i_q}(\mathbf{x})$ equals the $q$th-order partial derivative $f_{i_1 \ldots i_q}(\mathbf{x})$ for every $\mathbf{x} \in B$. Then there exists a function $F$ of class $C^{(q)}$ on $E^n$ such that $F(\mathbf{x}) = f(\mathbf{x})$ for every $\mathbf{x} \in A$. Hence $f$ is of class $C^{(q)}$ on $A$.

Actually, what one needs to assume about $A$ to apply Whitney's theorem is the following: Every $\mathbf{x}_0 \in A$ has a neighborhood $U$ such that any pair of points $\mathbf{x}$, $\mathbf{y} \in U \cap B$ can be joined in $B$ by a polygon of length no more than $c|\mathbf{x} - \mathbf{y}|$, where $c \geq 1$ depends only on $U$. If $A$ is convex, then the line segment joining $\mathbf{x}$ and $\mathbf{y}$ lies in $B$ and one may take $c = 1$.

For other extension theorems of Whitney, see *Trans. Amer. Math. Soc.* **36** (1934), and *Bull. Amer. Math. Soc.* **50** (1944).

***Functions of class $C^{(\infty)}$; real analytic functions.** Let us say that $f$ is of *class* $C^{(\infty)}$ if $f$ is of class $C^{(q)}$ for every $q$. If $f$ is of class $C^{(\infty)}$ and $\lim_{q\to\infty} R_q(\mathbf{x}) = 0$, then in place of Taylor's formula with remainder we may put the corresponding infinite series. This infinite series is called the *Taylor series* for $f(\mathbf{x})$ at $\mathbf{x}_0$.

If $K$ is a convex subset of $D$ and $\mathbf{x}_0 \in K$, then the following is a sufficient condition that $f(\mathbf{x})$ be the sum of its Taylor series for every $\mathbf{x} \in K$. Suppose that there is a positive number $M$ whose $q$th power bounds every $q$th-order partial derivative of $f$, namely,

$$|f_{i_1,\ldots,i_q}(\mathbf{x})| \leq M^q \tag{2–11}$$

for every $\mathbf{x} \in K$, $q = 1, 2, \ldots$, and $1 \leq i_1, \ldots, i_q \leq n$. Since $K$ is convex, for each $\mathbf{x} \in K$ the estimate (2–11) also holds at $\mathbf{x}_0 + s\mathbf{h}$. Since $|h^i| \leq |\mathbf{h}|$, from (2–10) we have

$$|R_q(\mathbf{x})| \leq \frac{n^q M^q |\mathbf{h}|^q}{q!} = \frac{C^q}{q!}$$

where $C = nM|\mathbf{h}|$. Since $C^q/q! \to 0$ as $q \to \infty$,

$$\lim_{q\to\infty} R_q(\mathbf{x}) = 0$$

for every $\mathbf{x} \in K$, provided inequalities (2–11) hold.

A function $f$ is called *analytic* if every $\mathbf{x}_0 \in D$ has a neighborhood $U_{\mathbf{x}_0}$ such that the Taylor series at $\mathbf{x}_0$ converges to $f(\mathbf{x})$ for every $\mathbf{x} \in U_{\mathbf{x}_0}$. It would lead us away from our main objectives to discuss analytic functions in any detail. Therefore let us issue just one word of caution, namely, *not every function of class $C^{(\infty)}$ is analytic.* As an example, let $D = E^1$ and let

$$f(x) = \begin{cases} \exp\left(-\dfrac{1}{x^2}\right) & \text{if } x > 0, \\ 0 & \text{if } x \leq 0. \end{cases}$$

Let us show that this function is of class $C^{(\infty)}$ and that $f^{(q)}(0) = 0$ for every $q = 1, 2, \ldots$ For $x \neq 0$ the derivatives $f^{(q)}(x)$ can be computed by elementary calculus, and each $f^{(q)}$ is continuous on $E^1 - \{0\}$. It is at the point 0 where $f$ must be examined. Now

$$\lim_{u\to+\infty} u^k \exp(-u) = 0 \quad \text{for each } k = 0, 1, 2, \ldots, \tag{2–12}$$

a fact which we shall prove immediately below. If $x < 0$, then $f(x) = f'(x) = f''(x) = \cdots = 0$. Using (2–12) with $k = 0$, $\exp(-1/x^2) \to 0$ as $x \to 0^+$. Since $f(0) = 0$, $f$ is continuous. If $x > 0$

$$f'(x) = \frac{2}{x^3}\exp\left(-\frac{1}{x^2}\right) = 2x \cdot \frac{1}{x^4}\exp\left(-\frac{1}{x^2}\right).$$

Using 2–12 with $k = 2$, $f'(x) \to 0$ as $x \to 0^+$. Therefore $\lim_{x\to 0} f'(x) = 0$. By Problem 3, $f'(0) = 0$ and $f$ is of class $C^{(1)}$. For each $q = 2, 3, \ldots, f^{(q)}(x)$ is a polynomial in $1/x$ times $\exp(-1/x^2)$ for $x > 0$. Hence $\lim_{x\to 0} f^{(q)}(x) = 0$. By Problem 3 and induction on $q$, $f^{(q)}(0) = 0$ and $f \in C^{(q)}$ for every $q$. Thus $f \in C^{(\infty)}$. If we expand $f$ by Taylor's formula about 0, then $f(x) = R_q(x)$ for every $x$. If $x > 0$ the remainder $R_q(x)$ does not tend to 0 as $q \to \infty$. Hence $f$ is not an analytic function.

*Proof of (2–12).* For each $u > 0$ let $\psi(u) = u^{-k} \exp u$. Then

$$\psi'(u) = (u - k)u^{-k-1} \exp u, \qquad \psi''(u) = [u^2 - 2ku + k(k+1)]u^{-k-2} \exp u.$$

The expression in brackets has a minimum when $u = k$ and is positive there. Hence $\psi''(u) > 0$ and for each $u_0$ (p. 24)

$$\psi(u) \geq \psi(u_0) + \psi'(u_0)(u - u_0).$$

If $u_0 > k$, then $\psi'(u_0) > 0$ and the right-hand side tends to $+\infty$ as $u \to +\infty$. Hence $\psi(u) \to +\infty$ and $1/\psi(u) \to 0$ as $u \to \infty+$. ∎

## PROBLEMS

1. Expand $f(x, y, z) = xyz$ by Taylor's formula about $\mathbf{x}_0 = (1, -1, 0)$, with $q = 4$.
2. Let $f(x, y) = \psi(ax + by)$, where $a$ and $b$ are scalars and $\psi$ is of class $C^{(q)}$ in some open set containing 0. Show that Taylor's formula about $(0, 0)$ becomes

$$f(x, y) = \sum_{m=0}^{q-1} \frac{\psi^{(m)}(0)}{m!} \sum_{j=0}^{m} \binom{m}{j} (ax)^j (by)^{m-j} + R_q(x, y),$$

where $\binom{m}{j}$ is the binomial coefficient (which equals the number of $j$–element subsets of a set with $m$ elements).

3. Let $f$ be continuous on an open set $D$ and of class $C^{(1)}$ on $D - \{\mathbf{x}_0\}$. Suppose moreover that $l_i = \lim_{\mathbf{x}\to\mathbf{x}_0} f_i(\mathbf{x})$ exists for each $i = 1, \ldots, n$. Prove that $l_i = f_i(\mathbf{x}_0)$, and consequently that $f$ is of class $C^{(1)}$ on $D$. State and prove a corresponding result in case $q > 1$.
4. Prove the statement made in Example 3.
5. Let $f(x) = x^k \sin(1/x)$ if $x \neq 0$, and $f(0) = 0$. Show that:
   (a) If $k = 0$, then $f$ is discontinuous at 0.
   (b) If $k = 1$, then $f$ is of class $C^{(0)}$ but not differentiable at 0.
   (c) If $k = 2$, then $f$ is differentiable but not of class $C^{(1)}$.
   (d) What can you say for $k \geq 3$?
6. Let $f(x, y) = xy(x^2 - y^2)/(x^2 + y^2)$, if $(x, y) \neq (0, 0)$, and $f(0, 0) = 0$.
   (a) If $(x, y) \neq (0, 0)$, find $f_{12}(x, y)$ and $f_{21}(x, y)$ by elementary calculus, and verify that they are equal.
   (b) Using Problem 3 show that $f_1(0, 0) = f_2(0, 0) = 0$ and $f$ is of class $C^{(1)}$.
   (c) Using the definition of partial derivative, show that $f_{12}(0, 0)$ and $f_{21}(0, 0)$ exist but are not equal. Why does this not contradict Theorem 3?

7. Given $n$ and $q$, how many solutions of the equation $i_1 + \cdots + i_n = q$ are there with $i_1, \ldots, i_n$ nonnegative integers? With $i_1, \ldots, i_n$ positive integers? What does this say about the number of different $q$th-order partial derivatives of a function of class $C^{(q)}$?

## 2–4 CONVEX AND CONCAVE FUNCTIONS (continued)

If a function $f$ is sufficiently smooth, then $f$ can be tested for convexity or concavity by using calculus. To begin with let us assume that $f$ is differentiable. Later in the section we make the stronger assumption that $f$ is of class $C^{(2)}$ and obtain a test, in terms of the second-order partial derivatives (Theorem 4), which reduces when $n = 1$ to the second derivative test given in Section 1–5.

Figure 1–14 in Section 1–5 suggests that convexity of a differentiable function $f$ is equivalent to the fact that $f$ lies above its tangent hyperplane at each point $(\mathbf{x}_0, f(\mathbf{x}_0))$. The following proposition shows that this is indeed so.

**Proposition 9a.** *Let $f$ be differentiable on a convex set $K$. Then $f$ is convex on $K$ if and only if*

$$f(\mathbf{x}) \geq f(\mathbf{x}_0) + df(\mathbf{x}_0) \cdot (\mathbf{x} - \mathbf{x}_0) \tag{2–13a}$$

*for every $\mathbf{x}_0, \mathbf{x} \in K$.*

*Proof.* Let $f$ be convex on $K$, and let $\mathbf{x}_0, \mathbf{x}$ be any two points of $K$. Let $\mathbf{h} = \mathbf{x} - \mathbf{x}_0$ and $t \in (0, 1)$. By definition of convex function,

$$f(\mathbf{x}_0 + t\mathbf{h}) \leq tf(\mathbf{x}_0 + \mathbf{h}) + (1 - t)f(\mathbf{x}_0).$$

This inequality may be rewritten as

$$f(\mathbf{x}_0 + t\mathbf{h}) - f(\mathbf{x}_0) \leq t[f(\mathbf{x}_0 + \mathbf{h}) - f(\mathbf{x}_0)]. \tag{2–14}$$

Subtracting $tdf(\mathbf{x}_0) \cdot \mathbf{h}$ from both sides and dividing by $t$,

$$\frac{f(\mathbf{x}_0 + t\mathbf{h}) - f(\mathbf{x}_0) - tdf(\mathbf{x}_0) \cdot \mathbf{h}}{t} \leq f(\mathbf{x}_0 + \mathbf{h}) - f(\mathbf{x}_0) - df(\mathbf{x}_0) \cdot \mathbf{h}.$$

The left-hand side tends to 0 as $t \to 0^+$. Hence the right-hand side is nonnegative, which says that (2–13a) holds.

Conversely, assume that (2–13a) holds for every $\mathbf{x}_0, \mathbf{x} \in K$. Let $\mathbf{x}_1, \mathbf{x}_2 \in K$, $\mathbf{x}_1 \neq \mathbf{x}_2$, and let $t \in (0, 1)$. Let

$$\mathbf{x}_0 = t\mathbf{x}_1 + (1 - t)\mathbf{x}_2, \qquad \mathbf{h} = \mathbf{x}_1 - \mathbf{x}_0.$$

A little manipulation shows that

$$\mathbf{x}_2 = \mathbf{x}_0 - \frac{t}{1 - t}\mathbf{h}.$$

By (2–13a) we have

$$f(\mathbf{x}_1) \geq f(\mathbf{x}_0) + df(\mathbf{x}_0) \cdot \mathbf{h},$$

$$f(\mathbf{x}_2) \geq f(\mathbf{x}_0) + df(\mathbf{x}_0) \cdot \left(-\frac{t}{1-t}\mathbf{h}\right).$$

Multiplying by $t/(1 - t)$ in the first inequality and adding, we get

$$\frac{t}{1-t} f(\mathbf{x}_1) + f(\mathbf{x}_2) \geq \left(\frac{t}{1-t} + 1\right) f(\mathbf{x}_0), \quad \text{or} \quad tf(\mathbf{x}_1) + (1-t)f(\mathbf{x}_2) \geq f(\mathbf{x}_0).$$

But this is just the inequality (1–8a) in the definition of convex function. We assumed that $t \in (0, 1)$, but if $t = 0$ or 1, (1–8a) trivially holds. Therefore $f$ is convex on $K$. ▮

By sharpening the inequality in (2–13a) we get a necessary and sufficient condition for strict convexity.

**Proposition 9b.** *Let $f$ be differentiable on a convex set $K$. Then $f$ is strictly convex on $K$ if and only if*

$$f(\mathbf{x}) > f(\mathbf{x}_0) + df(\mathbf{x}_0) \cdot (\mathbf{x} - \mathbf{x}_0) \tag{2–13b}$$

*for every* $\mathbf{x}, \mathbf{x}_0 \in K$ *with* $\mathbf{x} \neq \mathbf{x}_0$.

*Proof.* Let $f$ be strictly convex on $K$. In particular, $f$ is convex on $K$ and (2–13a) holds for every $\mathbf{x}, \mathbf{x}_0 \in K$. Suppose that $\mathbf{x} \neq \mathbf{x}_0$, and let $\mathbf{h} = \mathbf{x} - \mathbf{x}_0$. For every $t \in (0, 1)$

$$df(\mathbf{x}_0) \cdot (t\mathbf{h}) \leq f(\mathbf{x}_0 + t\mathbf{h}) - f(\mathbf{x}_0),$$

by (2–13a) applied with $\mathbf{x}$ replaced by $\mathbf{x}_0 + t\mathbf{h}$. But according to (2–14), which holds strictly since $f$ is strictly convex,

$$f(\mathbf{x}_0 + t\mathbf{h}) - f(\mathbf{x}_0) < t[f(\mathbf{x}_0 + \mathbf{h}) - f(\mathbf{x}_0)].$$

Therefore

$$t\,df(\mathbf{x}_0) \cdot \mathbf{h} < t[f(\mathbf{x}_0 + \mathbf{h}) - f(\mathbf{x}_0)].$$

Upon dividing both sides by $t$ we get (2–13b).

The proof of the converse is the same as for Proposition 9a, all inequalities now being strict. ▮

For concave functions the inequality signs must be reversed in (2–13a) and (2–13b). The first of these inequalities then says geometrically that $f$ lies below its tangent hyperplane at $(\mathbf{x}_0, f(\mathbf{x}_0))$, and the second says that this is strictly true except at the point $(\mathbf{x}_0, f(\mathbf{x}_0))$ itself.

We can now easily prove Proposition 5, which was previously stated in Section 1–5.

*Proof of Proposition 5.* Let $f$ be convex on $K$, where $K \subset E^1$ is an interval. Let $x, y \in K$, $y < x$. By (2–13a) applied with $\mathbf{x}_0 = y$,

$$f(x) - f(y) \geq f'(y)(x - y).$$

By (2–13a) applied with $\mathbf{x}_0 = x$,

$$f(y) - f(x) \geq f'(x)(y - x), \qquad f(x) - f(y) \leq f'(x)(x - y).$$

Therefore $f'(y)(x - y) \leq f'(x)(x - y)$, from which $f'(y) \leq f'(x)$. This proves that $f'$ is nondecreasing on $K$. If $f$ is strictly convex, then each of these inequalities is strict. In particular, $f'(y) < f'(x)$, which shows that $f'$ is increasing on $K$.

Conversely, assume that $f'$ is nondecreasing on $K$. Let $x_0, x \in K$, and suppose first that $x_0 < x$. By the mean value theorem there exists $y \in (x_0, x)$ such that

$$f(x) - f(x_0) = f'(y)(x - x_0).$$

Since $f'$ is nondecreasing, $f'(x_0) \leq f'(y)$. Therefore

$$f(x) - f(x_0) \geq f'(x_0)(x - x_0),$$

which is equivalent to inequality (2–13a). Similarly, (2–13a) holds if $x < x_0$. By Proposition 9a, $f$ is convex on $K$. If $f'$ is increasing, then $f'(x_0) < f'(y)$, and the proof shows that (2–13b) holds. By Proposition 9b, $f$ is strictly convex on $K$. ▮

Let us next prove a theorem which provides a convenient test for concavity or convexity of a function of class $C^{(2)}$. Let $f$ be of class $C^{(2)}$ on an open set $D$. Let $Q$ be the function with domain $D \times E^n$ defined by the formula

$$Q(\mathbf{x}, \mathbf{h}) = \sum_{i,j=1}^{n} f_{ij}(\mathbf{x})h^i h^j. \tag{2–15}$$

It is the sign of $Q$ which determines whether $f$ is convex, concave, or neither. Given $\mathbf{x}$, (2–15) defines a function on $E^n$ which we denote by $Q(\mathbf{x},\ )$. The function $Q(\mathbf{x},\ )$ is a quadratic polynomial which in linear algebra is called the quadratic form corresponding to the $n \times n$ symmetric matrix $(f_{ij}(\mathbf{x}))$, of second partial derivatives. Theorem 3 guarantees that this matrix is symmetric.

Let us write $Q(\mathbf{x},\ ) \geq 0$ if $Q(\mathbf{x}, \mathbf{h}) \geq 0$ for every $\mathbf{h}$, and $Q(\mathbf{x},\ ) > 0$ if $Q(\mathbf{x}, \mathbf{h}) > 0$ for every $\mathbf{h} \neq \mathbf{0}$. Note that $Q(\mathbf{x}, \mathbf{0}) = 0$. In the theory of quadratic forms $Q(\mathbf{x},\ )$ is called *positive semidefinite* if $Q(\mathbf{x},\ ) \geq 0$, and *positive definite* if $Q(\mathbf{x},\ ) > 0$.

Similarly, we write $Q(\mathbf{x},\ ) \leq 0$ if $Q(\mathbf{x}, \mathbf{h}) \leq 0$ for every $\mathbf{h}$, and $Q(\mathbf{x},\ ) < 0$ if $Q(x, \mathbf{h}) < 0$ for every $\mathbf{h} \neq \mathbf{0}$. The corresponding terms are *negative semidefinite* and *negative definite*.

If $Q(\mathbf{x},\ )$ has values of both signs, then it is *indefinite*.

**Theorem 4.** *Let $f$ be of class $C^{(2)}$ on an open, convex set $K$. Then:*

(a) *$f$ is convex on $K$ if and only if $Q(\mathbf{x},\ ) \geq 0$ for every $\mathbf{x} \in K$.*

(a′) *If $Q(\mathbf{x},\ ) > 0$ for every $\mathbf{x} \in K$, then $f$ is strictly convex on $K$.*

(b) *$f$ is concave on $K$ if and only if $Q(\mathbf{x},\ ) \leq 0$ for every $\mathbf{x} \in K$.*

(b′) *If $Q(\mathbf{x},\ ) < 0$ for every $\mathbf{x} \in K$, then $f$ is strictly concave on $K$.*

*Proof.* Since $K$ is convex we may use Taylor's formula with $q = 2$ and any pair of points $\mathbf{x}_0, \mathbf{x} \in K$:

$$f(\mathbf{x}) = f(\mathbf{x}_0) + df(\mathbf{x}_0) \cdot \mathbf{h} + \tfrac{1}{2}Q(\mathbf{x}_0 + s\mathbf{h}, \mathbf{h}), \tag{2–16}$$

where $s \in (0, 1)$ and $\mathbf{h} = \mathbf{x} - \mathbf{x}_0$. Let us first prove (a′). By hypothesis, $Q(\mathbf{y},\ ) > 0$ for every $\mathbf{y} \in K$, and in particular for $\mathbf{y} = \mathbf{x}_0 + s\mathbf{h}$. Therefore $Q(\mathbf{x}_0 + s\mathbf{h}, \mathbf{h}) > 0$ if $\mathbf{h} \neq \mathbf{0}$, from which

$$f(\mathbf{x}) > f(\mathbf{x}_0) + df(\mathbf{x}_0) \cdot \mathbf{h}.$$

By Proposition 9b, $f$ is strictly convex on $K$.

Let us next prove (a). If $Q(\mathbf{x},\ ) \geq 0$ for every $\mathbf{x} \in K$, then the same reasoning shows that

$$f(\mathbf{x}) \geq f(\mathbf{x}_0) + df(\mathbf{x}_0) \cdot \mathbf{h}.$$

By Proposition 9a, $f$ is convex on $K$. On the other hand, if it is not true that $Q(\mathbf{x},\ ) \geq 0$ for every $\mathbf{x} \in K$, then $Q(\mathbf{x}_0, \mathbf{h}_0) < 0$ for some $\mathbf{x}_0 \in K$ and $\mathbf{h}_0 \neq \mathbf{0}$. Since $f$ is of class $C^{(2)}$, $Q(\ , \mathbf{h}_0)$ is continuous on $K$. Hence there exists $\delta > 0$ such that $Q(\mathbf{y}, \mathbf{h}_0) < 0$ for every $\mathbf{y}$ in the $\delta$-neighborhood of $\mathbf{x}_0$. Let $\mathbf{h} = c\mathbf{h}_0$, where $c > 0$ is small enough that $|\mathbf{h}| < \delta$, and let $\mathbf{x} = \mathbf{x}_0 + \mathbf{h}$. Since $Q(\mathbf{x}_0 + s\mathbf{h},\ )$ is quadratic,

$$Q(\mathbf{x}_0 + s\mathbf{h}, \mathbf{h}) = c^2 Q(\mathbf{x}_0 + s\mathbf{h}, \mathbf{h}_0) < 0.$$

From (2–16)

$$f(\mathbf{x}) < f(\mathbf{x}_0) + df(\mathbf{x}_0) \cdot \mathbf{h}.$$

By Proposition 9a, $f$ is not convex on $K$.

This proves (a) and (a′). Parts (b) and (b′) follow respectively from (a) and (a′) by considering $-f$. ∎

If $n = 1$, then $Q(x, h) = f''(x)h^2$. The sign of $f''(x)$ determines whether $Q(x,\ )$ is positive definite, negative definite, or 0. For $n = 1$, Theorem 4 restates, in a slightly weaker form, the second derivative test given in Section 1–5 (corollary to Proposition 5).

**Example 1.** Let $f$ be a homogeneous quadratic polynomial,

$$f(\mathbf{x}) = \sum_{i,j=1}^{n} c_{ij} x^i x^j,$$

for each $\mathbf{x} \in E^n$, where the $n \times n$ matrix $(c_{ij})$ is symmetric. Then $f_{ij}(\mathbf{x}) = 2c_{ij}$ and $Q(\mathbf{x}, \mathbf{h}) = 2f(\mathbf{h})$. Hence $f$ is convex on $E^n$ in case $f(\mathbf{x}) \geq 0$ for every $\mathbf{x}$, and concave in case $f(\mathbf{x}) \leq 0$ for every $\mathbf{x}$. If $f$ has values of both signs, then $f$ is neither convex nor concave.

**Example 2.** Let $f(\mathbf{x}) = \exp[g(\mathbf{x})]$, where $g$ is of class $C^{(2)}$ and convex on $K$. Then

$$f_i(\mathbf{x}) = \exp[g(\mathbf{x})]g_i(\mathbf{x}).$$

Using the product rule, we get

$$f_{ij}(\mathbf{x}) = \exp[g(\mathbf{x})]\,[g_i(\mathbf{x})g_j(\mathbf{x}) + g_{ij}(\mathbf{x})].$$

Writing for short $g_i$ for $g_i(\mathbf{x})$, and so on,

$$Q(\mathbf{x}, \mathbf{h}) = \exp[g(\mathbf{x})]\left[\sum_{i,j=1}^{n} g_i g_j h^i h^j + \sum_{i,j=1}^{n} g_{ij} h^i h^j\right].$$

The last term on the right-hand side is nonnegative since $g$ is convex. Moreover,

$$\sum_{i,j=1}^{n} g_i g_j h^i h^j = \left[\sum_{i=1}^{n} g_i h^i\right]^2 \geq 0,$$

and $\exp[g(\mathbf{x})] > 0$. Hence $Q(\mathbf{x}, \mathbf{h}) \geq 0$ for every $\mathbf{x} \in K$ and every $\mathbf{h}$. Therefore $f$ is convex on $K$. This example is a special case of Problem 4, since the exponential function is increasing and convex on $E^1$.

In both of these examples we could determine the sign of $Q(\mathbf{x},\ \ )$ by direct calculations. When this is not feasible, one of the following tests for definiteness may be applied.

I. $(n = 2)$. In this case

$$Q(x, y, h, k) = f_{11}h^2 + 2f_{12}hk + f_{22}k^2$$

where we have written $(h, k)$ for $(h^1, h^2)$ and $f_{ij}$ for $f_{ij}(x, y)$.

If the discriminant $-(f_{11}f_{22} - f_{12}^2)$ is negative, the equation $Q(x, y, h, k) = 0$ has no roots $(h, k)$ except the trivial one $(0, 0)$. The sign of $f_{11}$ and $f_{22}$ determines whether $Q(x, y,\ ,\ ) > 0$ or $Q(x, y,\ ,\ ) < 0$.

If $f_{11}f_{22} - f_{12}^2 < 0$, then $\{(h, k) : Q(x, y, h, k) = 0\}$ consists of two lines intersecting at $(0, 0)$. They divide the $(h, k)$-plane into four parts, on two of which $Q(x, y, h, k) > 0$ and on the other two of which $Q(x, y, h, k) < 0$. In this case, $Q(x, y,\ ,\ )$ is indefinite. Thus

$Q(x, y,\ ,\ ) > 0$ *if* $f_{11} > 0,\quad f_{22} > 0,\quad f_{11}f_{22} - f_{12}^2 > 0.$
$Q(x, y,\ ,\ ) < 0$ *if* $f_{11} < 0,\quad f_{22} < 0,\quad f_{11}f_{22} - f_{12}^2 > 0.$
$Q(x, y,\ ,\ )$ *is indefinite if* $f_{11}f_{22} - f_{12}^2 < 0.$

If $f_{11}f_{22} - f_{12}^2 = 0$, then

$$Q(x, y, h, k) = c(ah + bk)^2$$

where the numbers $a$, $b$, $c$ satisfy

$$ca^2 = f_{11}, \qquad cab = f_{12}, \qquad cb^2 = f_{22}.$$

If $c \geq 0$, then $Q(x, y, \ ,\ )$ is positive semidefinite but not positive definite. Similarly, if $c \leq 0$ then $Q(x, y, \ ,\ )$ is negative semidefinite.

**Example 3.** Let $f(x, y) = \frac{1}{6}(x^3 + y^3) + xy$. Then $f_{11} = x, f_{22} = y, f_{11}f_{22} - f_{12}^2 = xy - 1$. Hence $f$ is strictly convex on the part of the first quadrant above the hyperbola $xy = 1$, and strictly concave on the part of the third quadrant below this hyperbola.

II. For any $n$ let

$$d_1(\mathbf{x}) = f_{11}(\mathbf{x}), \qquad d_2(\mathbf{x}) = \det \begin{pmatrix} f_{11}(\mathbf{x}) & f_{12}(\mathbf{x}) \\ f_{21}(\mathbf{x}) & f_{22}(\mathbf{x}) \end{pmatrix}, \ldots, d_n(\mathbf{x}) = \det\left(f_{ij}(\mathbf{x})\right).$$

These are called the *principal minor determinants* of the matrix $(f_{ij}(\mathbf{x}))$. The $m$th principal minor $d_m(\mathbf{x})$ is the determinant of the matrix obtained by deleting the last $n$-$m$ rows and columns. The determinant $d_n(\mathbf{x})$ is called the *Hessian* of $f$ at $\mathbf{x}$.

Let us state without proof the following criterion:

$$Q(\mathbf{x}, \ ) > 0 \quad \textit{iff} \quad d_m(\mathbf{x}) > 0 \quad \textit{for } m = 1, \ldots, n.$$
$$Q(\mathbf{x}, \ ) < 0 \quad \textit{iff} \quad (-1)^m d_m(\mathbf{x}) > 0 \quad \textit{for } m = 1, \ldots, n.$$

For a proof of the first of these two statements, see reference [3], especially pp. 140, 147. The second follows from the first by considering $-Q$. Here *iff* is an abbreviation for "if and only if."

Criterion II is fairly convenient for small values of $n$, but becomes unwieldy for larger ones. This is because of the very large number of operations required to calculate the determinant of an $m \times m$ matrix even for moderately small $m$.

III. In linear algebra it is shown that any quadratic form can be written as a linear combination of squares by suitably choosing a new orthonormal basis for $E^n$. This fact is also proved in Section 4–8 below. Therefore

$$Q(\mathbf{x}, \mathbf{h}) = \sum_{i=1}^{n} \lambda_i(\mathbf{x})[\eta^i(\mathbf{x})]^2, \tag{2–17}$$

where for each $\mathbf{h} \in E^n$, $\eta^1(\mathbf{x}), \ldots, \eta^n(\mathbf{x})$ are the components of $\mathbf{h}$ with respect to some orthonormal basis $\{\mathbf{v}_1(\mathbf{x}), \ldots, \mathbf{v}_n(\mathbf{x})\}$ for $E^n$,

$$\mathbf{h} = \sum_{i=1}^{n} \eta^i(\mathbf{x})\mathbf{v}_i(\mathbf{x}).$$

The numbers $\lambda_1(\mathbf{x}), \ldots, \lambda_n(\mathbf{x})$ are just the characteristic values of the matrix $(f_{ij}(\mathbf{x}))$.

If $\lambda_i(\mathbf{x}) > 0$ for each $i = 1, \ldots, n$, then from (2–17) $Q(\mathbf{x}, \mathbf{h}) > 0$ unless $\eta^i(\mathbf{x}) = 0$ for each $i$ (that is, unless $\mathbf{h} = \mathbf{0}$). In this case $Q(\mathbf{x},\ )$ is positive definite. Conversely, if $\mathbf{h} = \mathbf{v}_i(\mathbf{x})$, then $Q(\mathbf{x}, \mathbf{h}) = \lambda_i(\mathbf{x})$. Therefore, if $Q(\mathbf{x},\ ) > 0$, then in particular $Q(\mathbf{x}, \mathbf{v}_i(\mathbf{x})) > 0$, and $\lambda_i(\mathbf{x}) > 0$. This proves the first of the following statements:

$$Q(\mathbf{x},\ ) > 0 \quad \textit{iff} \quad \lambda_i(\mathbf{x}) > 0 \quad \textit{for } i = 1, \ldots, n.$$
$$Q(\mathbf{x},\ ) < 0 \quad \textit{iff} \quad \lambda_i(\mathbf{x}) < 0 \quad \textit{for } i = 1, \ldots, n.$$

The second is proved in the same way. Replacing on both sides "$>0$" by "$\geq 0$" we get a criterion for nonnegative semidefiniteness, and replacing "$<0$" by "$\leq 0$," one for nonpositive semidefiniteness.

If $n$ is fairly large it is better, instead of criterion II, to try some numerical method for putting $Q(\mathbf{x},\ )$ in the form (2–17).

### PROBLEMS

1. Use Theorem 4 to determine whether $f$ is convex on $K$, concave on $K$, or neither. Unless otherwise indicated, $K = E^2$ or $E^3$.
   (a) $f(x, y, z) = x^2 + y^2 - 4z^2$.
   (b) $f(x, y, z) = x - y^2 - z^2$.
   (c) $f(x, y) = (x + y + 1)^p$, $K = \{(x, y) : x + y + 1 > 0\}$.
   (d) $f(x, y, z) = \exp(x^2 + xy + y^2 + z^2)$.
   (e) $f(x, y) = \exp(xy)$.
   In which cases is the convexity or concavity strict?
2. Let $f(x, y) = \phi(x^2 + y^2)$, where $\phi$ is of class $C^{(2)}$, increasing and concave. Show that $f$ is convex on the circular disk $x^2 + y^2 \leq a^2$ if and only if $\phi'(u) + 2u\phi''(u) \geq 0$ whenever $0 \leq u \leq a^2$.
3. Using Problem 2, find the largest $a$ such that $f$ is convex on $x^2 + y^2 \leq a^2$.
   (a) $f(x, y) = \log(1 + x^2 + y^2)$. (b) $f(x, y) = \sin(x^2 + y^2)$.
4. Let $K$ be an open, convex set, and $g$ a function which is convex and of class $C^{(2)}$ on $K$. Let $I \subset E^1$ be an interval such that $g(\mathbf{x}) \in I$ for every $\mathbf{x} \in K$. Let $\phi$ be a function which is of class $C^{(2)}$, nondecreasing, and convex on $I$. Let $f$ be the composite of $\phi$ and $g$, $f(\mathbf{x}) = \phi[g(\mathbf{x})]$ for every $\mathbf{x} \in K$.
   (a) Using Theorem 4, prove that $f$ is convex on $K$.
   (b) Prove the same result without the assumption that $\phi$ and $g$ are of class $C^{(2)}$, by using directly the definitions of convex function and nondecreasing function.
5. Using Problem 4, show that each of the following functions is convex on $E^n$:
   (a) $f(\mathbf{x}) = |\mathbf{x}|^p$, $p \geq 1$. (b) $f(\mathbf{x}) = (1 + \mathbf{x} \cdot \mathbf{x})^{\mathbf{x} \cdot \mathbf{x}}$.
   (c) $f(\mathbf{x}) = (1 + |\mathbf{x}|^2)^{p/2}$, $p \geq 1$. [*Hint:* First consider $p = 1$.]
6. Let $f$ be of class $C^{(1)}$, decreasing, and convex on a semi-infinite interval $(c, \infty)$. Prove that if $f(x) > 0$ for every $x > c$, then $\lim_{x \to +\infty} f'(x) = 0$. [*Hint:* Let $l = \sup\{f'(x) : x > c\}$. Either $l = 0$ or $l < 0$. Using the fundamental theorem of calculus, show that if $l < 0$, then $\lim_{x \to +\infty} f(x) = -\infty$.]

7. Let $K$ be a convex set with nonempty interior int $K$, and $\mathbf{x}^*$ some point of int $K$. Prove each of the following:
   (a) For every $\mathbf{x} \in K$ and $s \in (0, 1]$, $s\mathbf{x}^* + (1 - s)\mathbf{x} \in \text{int } K$.
   (b) If $f$ is continuous on $K$ and convex on int $K$, then $f$ is convex on $K$. [*Hint:* Use (a).]
   (c) Suppose that fr $K$ contains no line segment, and that $f$ is continuous on $K$ and strictly convex on int $K$. Then $f$ is strictly convex on $K$.

## 2–5 RELATIVE EXTREMA

Let $A$ be some subset of $E^n$ and $f$ a function whose domain contains $A$. Let us consider the problem of minimizing or maximizing $f(\mathbf{x})$ on $A$.

**Definitions.** If $\mathbf{x}_0$ is a point of $A$ such that $f(\mathbf{x}_0) \leq f(\mathbf{x})$ for every $\mathbf{x} \in A$, then $f$ has an *absolute minimum* at $\mathbf{x}_0$. The number

$$f(\mathbf{x}_0) = \min \{f(\mathbf{x}) : \mathbf{x} \in A\}$$

is the *minimum value* of $f$ on $A$. (Of course, there need not be any such point $\mathbf{x}_0$. However, if $A$ is a compact set, then by the corollary to Theorem A–6, any continuous function has an absolute minimum at some point of $A$.) If $f(\mathbf{x}_0) < f(\mathbf{x})$ for every $\mathbf{x} \in A$ except $\mathbf{x}_0$, then $f$ has a *strict absolute minimum at* $\mathbf{x}_0$.

We say that $f$ has a *relative minimum* at $\mathbf{x}_0$ if there is a neighborhood $U$ of $\mathbf{x}_0$ such that $f(\mathbf{x}_0) \leq f(\mathbf{x})$ for every $\mathbf{x} \in A \cap U$. If $U$ can be so chosen that $f(\mathbf{x}_0) < f(\mathbf{x})$ for every $\mathbf{x} \in A \cap U$ except $\mathbf{x}_0$, then $f$ has a *strict relative minimum* at $\mathbf{x}_0$.

The notions of absolute maximum and relative maximum are defined similarly by reversing the inequality signs. We say *extremum* for either maximum or minimum.

In some cases the extrema can be found by inspection. For example, if $A = E^n$ and $f(\mathbf{x}) = |\mathbf{x}|$, then $f(\mathbf{0}) = 0$ and $f(\mathbf{x}) > 0$ for every $\mathbf{x} \neq \mathbf{0}$. Hence $f$ has a strict absolute minimum at $\mathbf{0}$. Since this function is not differentiable at $\mathbf{0}$, the minimum could not have been found through the use of calculus.

If $f$ and $A$ are smooth enough, the relative extrema can be found by using calculus. *In the present section we assume that $A$ is an open set.* In Section 4–8 we shall learn a technique for finding the extrema when $A$ is a smooth submanifold of $E^n$.

**Definition.** A point $\mathbf{x}_0$ is a *critical point* if $df(\mathbf{x}_0) = \mathbf{0}$.

If $f$ is a differentiable function, one need look only among the critical points for relative extrema.

**Proposition 10.** *If $f$ has a relative extremum at $\mathbf{x}_0$ and $f$ is differentiable at $\mathbf{x}_0$, then $\mathbf{x}_0$ is a critical point.*

*Proof.* Given a direction $\mathbf{v}$, let $\phi(t) = f(\mathbf{x}_0 + t\mathbf{v})$ for every $t$ in some open subset of $E^1$ containing 0. Then $\phi$ has a relative extremum at 0, and consequently by elementary calculus $\phi'(0) = 0$. But $\phi'(0) = df(\mathbf{x}_0) \cdot \mathbf{v}$ is the derivative at $\mathbf{x}_0$ in the direction $\mathbf{v}$. Hence $df(\mathbf{x}_0) \cdot \mathbf{v} = 0$ for every $\mathbf{v}$, which implies that $df(\mathbf{x}_0) = \mathbf{0}$. ▌

It is illuminating to look at this result in a slightly different way. In place of the covector $df(\mathbf{x})$ let us consider the vector $\operatorname{grad} f(\mathbf{x})$ with the same components (p. 43). Suppose that $\mathbf{x}$ is not the critical point. Then $\operatorname{grad} f(\mathbf{x}) \neq \mathbf{0}$. Let us find the direction $\mathbf{v}$ for which the directional derivative at $\mathbf{x}$ is maximum.

By Cauchy's inequality,

$$\operatorname{grad} f(\mathbf{x}) \cdot \mathbf{v} \leq |\operatorname{grad} f(\mathbf{x})| \, |\mathbf{v}|;$$

and equality holds if and only if $\mathbf{v} = \mathbf{v}(\mathbf{x})$, where

$$\mathbf{v}(\mathbf{x}) = \frac{1}{|\operatorname{grad} f(\mathbf{x})|} \operatorname{grad} f(\mathbf{x}).$$

This direction is called the *direction of the gradient* at $\mathbf{x}$, and is the one which maximizes the directional derivative. The maximum value of the directional derivative is

$$\operatorname{grad} f(\mathbf{x}) \cdot \mathbf{v}(\mathbf{x}) = \frac{1}{|\operatorname{grad} f(\mathbf{x})|} \operatorname{grad} f(\mathbf{x}) \cdot \operatorname{grad} f(\mathbf{x}) = |\operatorname{grad} f(\mathbf{x})|.$$

By going a short distance from $\mathbf{x}$ in the direction $\mathbf{v}(\mathbf{x})$, $f(\mathbf{x})$ is increased. Hence $f$ cannot have a relative maximum at $\mathbf{x}$. The direction $-\mathbf{v}(\mathbf{x})$ minimizes the directional derivative at $\mathbf{x}$. In the same way, $f$ cannot have a relative minimum at $\mathbf{x}$. This confirms the conclusion of Proposition 10.

This discussion is the basis for the gradient method (or method of steepest ascent) for finding maxima. A good intuitive picture of the gradient method may be obtained by thinking of an ambitious mountain climber who always takes the steepest direction. Let us suppose that the surface of the mountain can be represented in the form $(\{x, y, f(x, y)) : (x, y) \in A\}$, where $f$ is a smooth function. In particular, no vertical cliffs, overhangs, or sharp ridges are allowed. If the mountain has the shape indicated in Fig. 2–5(a), that is, if $f$ is a strictly

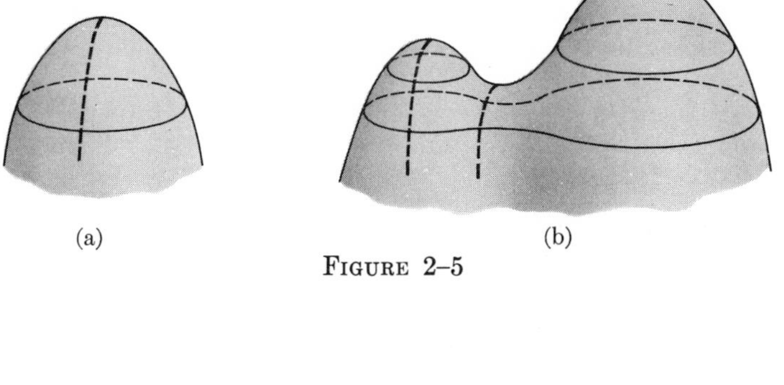

(a) (b)

FIGURE 2–5

concave function, then it appears that the summit will be reached by this technique. However, if the mountain has a more complicated shape, the climber may reach a false summit or a saddle as in Fig. 2–5(b). Once he reaches any critical point, the gradient method tells him to stay there.

The gradient method will be defined more precisely later (Section 3–4).

For functions which are convex or concave, Proposition 10 has a converse.

**Theorem 5.** *Let $f$ be differentiable and convex on an open convex set $A$ and $\mathbf{x}_0 \in A$ a critical point. Then $f$ has an absolute minimum at $\mathbf{x}_0$.*

*Proof.* Since $df(\mathbf{x}_0) = \mathbf{0}$, $f(\mathbf{x}) \geq f(\mathbf{x}_0)$ for every $\mathbf{x} \in A$ by Proposition 9a. ▮

Similarly, any differentiable concave function has an absolute maximum at any critical point.

**Corollary.** *A differentiable function which is strictly convex (or strictly concave) has at most one critical point.*

*Proof.* Let $f$ be strictly convex on $A$, and suppose that $f$ has an absolute minimum at distinct points $\mathbf{x}_0, \mathbf{x}_1 \in A$,

$$f(\mathbf{x}_0) = f(\mathbf{x}_1) \leq f(\mathbf{x})$$

for every $\mathbf{x} \in A$. Since $df(\mathbf{x}_0) = 0$, by Proposition 9b (with $\mathbf{x} = \mathbf{x}_1$), $f(\mathbf{x}_1) > f(\mathbf{x}_0)$. This is a contradiction. ▮

For functions which are neither convex nor concave, the theory of relative extrema is more complicated. We shall consider only functions of class $C^{(2)}$ on $A$. The main result is:

**Theorem 6.** *Let $f$ be of class $C^{(2)}$ on an open set $A$, and $\mathbf{x}_0 \in A$ a critical point. Then:*

(a) $Q(\mathbf{x}_0, \ ) \geq 0$ *is necessary for a relative minimum at* $\mathbf{x}_0$.

(a′) $Q(\mathbf{x}_0, \ ) > 0$ *is sufficient for a strict relative minimum at* $\mathbf{x}_0$.

(b) $Q(\mathbf{x}_0, \ ) \leq 0$ *is necessary for a relative maximum at* $\mathbf{x}_0$.

(b′) $Q(\mathbf{x}_0, \ ) < 0$ *is sufficient for a strict relative maximum at* $\mathbf{x}_0$.

*Proof.* Let $f$ have a relative minimum at $\mathbf{x}_0$. Then there exists a neighborhood $U$ of $\mathbf{x}_0$ such that

$$f(\mathbf{x}) \geq f(\mathbf{x}_0) \qquad \text{for every } \mathbf{x} \in U \cap A.$$

Since $A$ is open, we may assume that $U \subset A$. Since $df(\mathbf{x}_0) = \mathbf{0}$, Taylor's formula with $q = 2$ becomes

$$f(\mathbf{x}) = f(\mathbf{x}_0) + \tfrac{1}{2}Q(\mathbf{x}_0 + s\mathbf{h}, \mathbf{h}), \tag{2–18}$$

where $\mathbf{h} = \mathbf{x} - \mathbf{x}_0$, $\mathbf{x} \in U$. Suppose that $Q(\mathbf{x}_0, \mathbf{h}_0) < 0$ for some $\mathbf{h}_0$. The proof of Theorem 4 shows that $f(\mathbf{x}) < f(\mathbf{x}_0)$ for some $\mathbf{x} \in U$ of the form $\mathbf{x}_0 + c\mathbf{h}_0$. This is a contradiction. Therefore $Q(\mathbf{x}_0, \ ) \geq 0$, which proves (a).

To prove (a′), suppose that $Q(\mathbf{x}_0, \ ) > 0$. Using Problem 8 and the fact that the functions $f_{ij}$ are continuous at $\mathbf{x}_0$, there exists a neighborhood $U$ of $\mathbf{x}_0$ such that $U \subset A$ and $Q(\mathbf{y}, \ ) > 0$ for every $\mathbf{y} \in U$. Taking $\mathbf{y} = \mathbf{x}_0 + s\mathbf{h}$, we find from (2–18) that $f(\mathbf{x}) > f(\mathbf{x}_0)$ for every $\mathbf{x} \in U$, $\mathbf{x} \neq \mathbf{x}_0$. This proves that $f$ has a strict relative minimum at $\mathbf{x}_0$. Statements (b), (b′) follow respectively from (a), (a′) by considering $-f$. ▮

**Definition.** A critical point $\mathbf{x}$ is *nondegenerate* if the Hessian determinant $d_n(\mathbf{x}) = \det\,(f_{ij}(\mathbf{x}))$ is not 0.

A nondegenerate critical point may be tested by one of the three criteria I, II, or III at the end of Section 2–4. Note that in applying Theorem 6 we need to know the sign of $Q(\mathbf{x}_0, \ )$ at the critical point $\mathbf{x}_0$ itself, while to apply Theorem 4 one must know the sign of $Q(\mathbf{x}, \ )$ at every point of $K$.

If $n = 2$, then $f$ has a relative extremum at any critical point where $f_{11}f_{22} - f_{12}^2 > 0$. The sign of $f_{11}$ and $f_{22}$ determines whether it is a relative maximum or relative minimum. A critical point where $f_{11}f_{22} - f_{12}^2 < 0$ is called a *saddle point*. The function illustrated by Fig. 2–5(b) has one point of absolute maximum, one of relative maximum, and one saddle point.

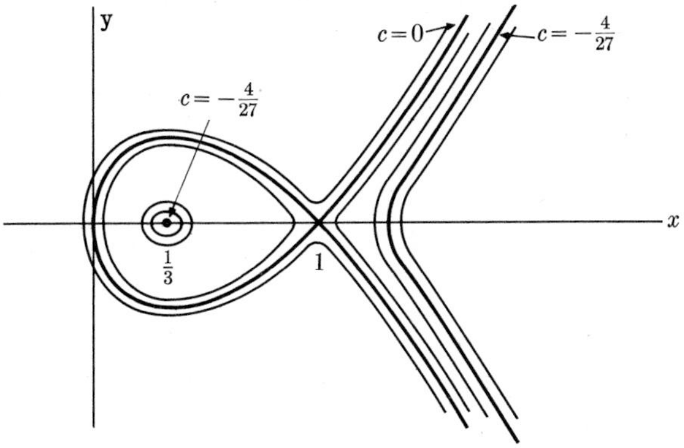


FIGURE 2–6

**Example.** Let $f(x, y) = 2y^2 - x(x-1)^2$ for every $(x, y) \in E^2$ and $A = E^2$. This function has two critical points, $(\frac{1}{3}, 0)$ and $(1, 0)$. We find that

$$f_{11} = 4 - 6x, \qquad f_{22} = 4, \qquad f_{11}f_{22} - f_{12}^2 = 16 - 24x.$$

The point $(\frac{1}{3}, 0)$ gives a relative minimum and $(1, 0)$ is a saddle point. In this example it is instructive to find the *level sets* $\{(x, y) : f(x, y) = c\}$. They are indicated in Fig. 2–6 for the critical values $-\frac{4}{27} = f(\frac{1}{3}, 0)$, $0 = f(1, 0)$, and for nearby values of $c$.

The point $(\frac{1}{3}, 0)$ of relative minimum is an isolated point of the level set containing it. For $-\frac{4}{27} < c < 0$ the level set has two parts. The one which encloses $(\frac{1}{3}, 0)$ resembles a small ellipse if $c$ is near $-\frac{4}{27}$. This can be attributed to the fact that near $(\frac{1}{3}, 0)$, $f(x, y)$ is approximated by the first two nonzero terms in its Taylor expansion about $(\frac{1}{3}, 0)$, namely,

$$f(\tfrac{1}{3}, 0) + \tfrac{1}{2}Q(\tfrac{1}{3}, 0, x - \tfrac{1}{3}, y) = -\tfrac{4}{27} + (x - \tfrac{1}{3})^2 + 2y^2.$$

The level sets of this quadratic function are ellipses with center $(\frac{1}{3}, 0)$ if $c > -\frac{4}{27}$. Similarly, $f(x, y)$ is approximated by $-(x - 1)^2 + 2y^2$ near the saddle point $(1, 0)$. The level sets $-(x - 1)^2 + 2y^2 = c$ are hyperbolas if $c \neq 0$. Near $(1, 0)$ the level sets of $f$ resemble these hyperbolas. For $c = 0$ we get the lines $\sqrt{2}y = \pm(x - 1)$ tangent to the level set of $f$ at $(1, 0)$.

If $f$ is continuous on a compact set $A$, then $f$ has absolute extrema on $A$. They may occur either at interior or at boundary points of $A$. If an absolute maximum occurs at an interior point $\mathbf{x}_0$ of $A$, then $\mathbf{x}_0$ is among the relative maxima in int $A$. We can try to find it by Theorem 6. However, Theorem 6 does not apply at boundary points of $A$.

If $\mathbf{x}_0 \in \text{fr } A$ and $\mathbf{x}_0$ gives an absolute maximum, then $f(\mathbf{x}) \leq f(\mathbf{x}_0)$ for every $\mathbf{x} \in A$, and in particular for every $\mathbf{x} \in \text{fr } A$. Therefore $\mathbf{x}_0$ also gives an absolute maximum among points of fr $A$. If fr $A$ is sufficiently smooth, the Lagrange multiplier rule (Section 4–8) can be applied.

***Extrema of linear functions.** Let $f$ be a linear function. Then calculus is of no help in finding the extrema of $f$. Since $f(\mathbf{x}) = \mathbf{a} \cdot \mathbf{x} = a_1x^1 + \cdots + a_nx^n$, the partial derivatives are $f_i(\mathbf{x}) = a_i$. If $f$ has a critical point, then $\mathbf{a} = \mathbf{0}$ and $f(\mathbf{x}) = 0$ for every $\mathbf{x}$.

Let us assume that $\mathbf{a} \neq \mathbf{0}$ and consider the problem of extremum on a convex polytope $K$ (p. 15). If $K$ is contained in $\{\mathbf{x} : x^i \geq 0, i = 1, \ldots, n\}$, this is a problem in linear programming and has various interesting applications. See [10] and [13].

For simplicity let us assume that $K$ is compact. The extrema of $f$ must occur on the boundary fr $K$. Let us show that they can be found by considering only certain points of fr $K$, called extreme points.

**Definition.** Let $K$ be a convex set. A point $\mathbf{x} \in K$ is an *extreme point* of $K$ if there do not exist distinct points $\mathbf{x}_1, \mathbf{x}_2 \in K$ and $t \in (0, 1)$ such that $\mathbf{x} = t\mathbf{x}_1 + (1 - t)\mathbf{x}_2$.

Stated geometrically, $\mathbf{x}$ is extreme if it is interior to no line segment in $K$.

**Examples.** The extreme points of a simplex are the vertices. If $K$ is a closed $n$-ball then every point of fr $K$ is extreme. A half-space has no extreme points.

**Proposition.** *Let $K$ be compact and convex. Then every point of $K$ is a convex combination of extreme points of $K$.*

*Proof.* Let us proceed by induction on the dimension $n$. If $n = 1$, then $K$ is an interval or a single point. Suppose that the proposition is true in dimension $n - 1$. Let $\mathbf{x}_0 \in K$. If $\mathbf{x}_0$ is a boundary point, then by Problem 8, Section 1–4, $K$ has a supporting hyperplane $P$ containing $\mathbf{x}_0$. By an isometry of $E^n$ (see Section 4–2), we may arrange that $\mathbf{x}_0 = \mathbf{0}$ and the equation of $P$ is $x^n = 0$. The set $K \cap P$ is compact and convex. By the induction hypothesis $\mathbf{x}_0$ is a convex combination of extreme points of $K \cap P$ and hence (Problem 11) of extreme points of $K$.

If $\mathbf{x}_0 \in \operatorname{int} K$, then any line through $\mathbf{x}_0$ intersects $K$ in a segment with endpoints $\mathbf{x}_1, \mathbf{x}_2 \in \operatorname{fr} K$. Since $\mathbf{x}_1$ and $\mathbf{x}_2$ are convex combinations of the set of extreme points, so is $\mathbf{x}_0$ (Problem 10, Section 1–4). ▮

By the proposition on p. 20, taking as $S$ the set of extreme points of $K$, each point of $K$ is a convex combination of $n + 1$ or fewer extreme points. If $S$ is connected, then $n + 1$ may be replaced by $n$.

Let $C$ be the maximum value on $K$ of the linear function $f$ and $K_1 = \{\mathbf{x} \in K : f(\mathbf{x}) = C\}$. If $K_1$ is found, the problem of maximum is solved.

**Corollary.** *$K_1$ is the convex set spanned by those extreme points of $K$ at which $f$ has an absolute maximum.*

*Proof.* Let $\mathbf{x} \in K_1$. By the proposition $\mathbf{x} = \sum t^j \mathbf{x}_j$, where $\mathbf{x}_1, \ldots, \mathbf{x}_m$ are extreme points, each $t^j > 0$, and $\sum t^j = 1$. All sums are from 1 to $m$. Since $C$ is the maximum value, $f(\mathbf{x}_j) \le C$. Since $f$ is linear,

$$f(\mathbf{x}) = \sum t^j f(\mathbf{x}_j) \le \sum t^j C = C.$$

But $f(\mathbf{x}) = C$, and since each $t^j > 0$ we must have $f(\mathbf{x}_j) = C$ for $j = 1, \ldots, m$. Thus $\mathbf{x}_1, \ldots, \mathbf{x}_m \in K_1$. Conversely, if $f(\mathbf{x}_j) = C$ for each $j$ and $\mathbf{x}$ is a convex combination of $\mathbf{x}_1, \ldots, \mathbf{x}_m$, then $f(\mathbf{x}) = C$. ▮

If $K$ is a convex polytope, then by induction on $n$ the set of extreme points is finite. The problem is no longer one of calculus, but instead that of maximizing $f$ on this finite set. Except in the simplest situations, the method of unsystematic search among the extreme points is of little value. The best known systematic method is called the simplex method of linear programming. In a sense it is an adaptation of the gradient method.

## PROBLEMS

In Problems 1 through 6 let $A = E^n$ for the indicated $n$.

1. Find the critical points, relative extrema, and saddle points. Make a sketch indicating the level sets.

   (a) $f(x, y) = x - x^2 - y^2$.
   (b) $f(x, y) = (x + 1)(y - 2)$.
   (c) $f(x, y) = \sin(xy)$.
   (d) $f(x, y) = xy(x - 1)$.

2. Find the critical points, relative extrema, and saddle points.
   (a) $f(x, y) = x^3 + x - 4xy - 2y^2$.
   (b) $f(x, y) = x(y + 1) - x^2y$.
   (c) $f(x, y) = \cos x \cosh y$.

   [*Note:* The hyperbolic functions sinh and cosh are defined by

$$\sinh x = \tfrac{1}{2}[\exp x - \exp(-x)],$$
$$\cosh x = \tfrac{1}{2}[\exp x + \exp(-x)].$$

   Their derivatives are given by the formulas $\sinh' = \cosh$, $\cosh' = \sinh$.]

3. Let $f(x, y, z) = x^2 + y^2 - z^2$. Show that $f$ has one critical point, which does not give a relative extremum. Describe the level sets.

4. Let $f(x, y, z) = x^2 + 3y^2 + 2z^2 - 2xy + 2xz$. Show that 0 is the minimum value of $f$.

5. Given $\mathbf{x}_1, \ldots, \mathbf{x}_m$, find the point $\mathbf{x}$ where $\sum_{j=1}^{m} |\mathbf{x} - \mathbf{x}_j|^2$ has an absolute minimum, and find the minimum value.

6. (a) In Problem 1(a) find the (absolute) maximum and minimum values of $f$ on the circular disk $x^2 + y^2 \leq 1$.
   (b) Do the same for 1(c).

7. (a) Show that under the hypotheses of Theorem 5, $\{\mathbf{x} \in A : df(\mathbf{x}) = \mathbf{0}\}$ is a convex set.
   (b) Illustrate this result in case $A = E^2$ and $f(x, y) = (x - y)^2$.

8. Let $g(\mathbf{h}) = \sum_{i,j=1}^{n} c_{ij}h^ih^j$. Assume that $g > 0$, that is, that $g(\mathbf{h}) > 0$ for every $\mathbf{h} \neq \mathbf{0}$.
   (a) Show that there exists a number $m > 0$ such that $g(\mathbf{h}) \geq m|\mathbf{h}|^2$ for every $\mathbf{h}$. [*Hint:* The polynomial $g$ is continuous, and has a positive minimum value $m$ on the unit $(n - 1)$-sphere.]
   (b) Suppose that $|C_{ij} - c_{ij}| < \epsilon n^{-2}$ for each $i, j = 1, \ldots, n$. Let $G(\mathbf{h}) = \sum_{i,j=1}^{n} C_{ij}h^ih^j$. Show that $G(\mathbf{h}) \geq (m - \epsilon)|\mathbf{h}|^2$ for every $\mathbf{h}$. Hence $G > 0$ if $\epsilon < m$.

9. Let $f(\mathbf{x}) = \psi(\mathbf{a} \cdot \mathbf{x})$, where $\psi$ is of class $C^{(2)}$. Show that every critical point of $f$ is degenerate.

10. Let $\mathbf{x}_0$ be a nondegenerate critical point of a function $f$ of class $C^{(2)}$. Show that $\mathbf{x}_0$ is isolated, that is, that $\mathbf{x}_0$ has a neighborhood $U$ containing no other critical points of $f$. [*Hint:* Let $\mathbf{x}$ be another critical point in $U$. Apply the mean value theorem to each of the functions $f_1, \ldots, f_n$ to find that

$$0 = \sum_{j=1}^{n} f_{ij}(\mathbf{y}_i)(x^j - x_0^j), \qquad i = 1, \ldots, n, \tag{$*$}$$

    where each $\mathbf{y}_i \in U$. Show that if $U$ is small enough, $\det(f_{ij}(\mathbf{y}_i)) \neq 0$ and consequently the system of equations (*) has only the solution $\mathbf{x} - \mathbf{x}_0 = 0$, a contradiction.]

*11. Let $K$ be closed and convex, and $P$ a supporting hyperplane for $K$. Show that any extreme point of $K \cap P$ is an extreme point of $K$.

*12. Let $K$ be a closed convex polytope (not necessarily compact) and $f$ be a linear function such that $f(\mathbf{x})$ is bounded above on $K$. Show that $f$ has an absolute maximum on $K$.

## 2–6 DIFFERENTIAL 1-FORMS

Let us first give a rough description of this notion and afterward be more precise. A differential form $\boldsymbol{\omega}$ of degree 1 is supposed to be an "expression linear in the differentials $dx^1, \ldots, dx^n$":

$$\boldsymbol{\omega} = \omega_1\, dx^1 + \cdots + \omega_n\, dx^n, \tag{2–19}$$

where the coefficients $\omega_1, \ldots, \omega_n$ are real-valued functions. In case there is a real-valued differentiable function $f$ such that $\omega_i$ is the $i$th partial derivative $f_i$ for each $i = 1, \ldots, n$, then $\boldsymbol{\omega}$ is called the differential of $f$ and is written $df$. Thus

$$df = f_1\, dx^1 + \cdots + f_n\, dx^n. \tag{2–20}$$

It is important to know whether or not a given differential form $\boldsymbol{\omega}$ is the differential of a function. A considerable part of the discussion in this section and in Section 3–3 is directed to just this question. One gets a necessary condition (2–22) from the fact that the mixed partial derivatives $f_{ij}$ and $f_{ji}$ of a function $f$ of class $C^{(2)}$ are equal. This necessary condition turns out to be sufficient if the domain is simply connected.

We recall from Section 1–3 that the elements of the space $(E^n)^*$ dual to $E^n$ are called covectors; and that the components $a_i$ of a covector $\mathbf{a}$ are written with subscripts. No matter what precise meaning we shall give to the symbols $dx^1, \ldots, dx^n$, the functions $\omega_1, \ldots, \omega_n$ must determine the differential form $\boldsymbol{\omega}$. For each $\mathbf{x}$, the numbers $\omega_1(\mathbf{x}), \ldots, \omega_n(\mathbf{x})$ are the components of a covector. This suggests that we may define a differential form as a function whose values are covectors.

To state this precisely:

**Definition.** A *differential form of degree* 1 is a function $\boldsymbol{\omega}$ with domain $D \subset E^n$ and values in $(E^n)^*$.

For short we shall usually say "1-form" instead of "differential form of degree 1." In Chapter 6 differential forms of any degree $r = 0, 1, 2, \ldots, n$ are defined.

The value of $\boldsymbol{\omega}$ at $\mathbf{x}$ is denoted by $\boldsymbol{\omega}(\mathbf{x})$. It is the covector

$$\boldsymbol{\omega}(\mathbf{x}) = \omega_1(\mathbf{x})\mathbf{e}^1 + \cdots + \omega_n(\mathbf{x})\mathbf{e}^n, \tag{2–21}$$

where, as in Section 1–3, $\mathbf{e}^1, \ldots, \mathbf{e}^n$ are the standard basis covectors.

A 1-form $\boldsymbol{\omega}$ is a constant form if there is a covector $\mathbf{a}$ such that $\boldsymbol{\omega}(\mathbf{x}) = \mathbf{a}$ for every $\mathbf{x} \in D$. In particular, for each $i = 1, \ldots, n$ let us consider the constant 1-form with value $\mathbf{e}^i$. This 1-form is denoted by $dx^i$. Since $(E^n)^*$ is a vector space, the sum $\boldsymbol{\omega} + \boldsymbol{\zeta}$ of two functions $\boldsymbol{\omega}$ and $\boldsymbol{\zeta}$ with the same domain $D$ and values in $(E^n)^*$ is defined (p. 8). Similarly, the product $f\boldsymbol{\omega}$ is defined if $f$ is a real-valued function and $\boldsymbol{\omega}$ a 1-form, with the same domain $D$. In particular, $\omega_i\, dx^i$ is the 1-form whose value at each $\mathbf{x}$ is $\omega_i(\mathbf{x})\mathbf{e}^i$. From (2–21), $\omega_1\, dx^1 + \cdots + \omega_n\, dx^n$ is the 1-form whose value at each $\mathbf{x}$ is $\boldsymbol{\omega}(\mathbf{x})$. Therefore formula (2–19) is correct.

**The differential of a function.** Let us now suppose that $D$ is an open set. Let $f$ be a real-valued differentiable function with domain $D$. The differential of $f$ at $\mathbf{x}$ is the covector $df(\mathbf{x})$ whose components are the partial derivatives $f_1(\mathbf{x}), \ldots, f_n(\mathbf{x})$.

**Definition.** The *differential* of $f$ is the differential form $df$ of degree 1 whose value at each $\mathbf{x} \in D$ is the covector $df(\mathbf{x})$.

Some authors define $df$ as the real-valued function whose domain is the cartesian product $D \times E^n$ and whose value at each pair $(\mathbf{x}, \mathbf{h})$ is the number $df(\mathbf{x}) \cdot \mathbf{h}$. Knowing $df(\mathbf{x})$, one can find $df(\mathbf{x}) \cdot \mathbf{h}$ for every $\mathbf{h} \in E^n$, and vice versa. Hence this definition is equivalent to the one which we have given.

If $f$ and $g$ are differentiable functions with the same domain $D$, then

$$d(f + g) = df + dg, \qquad d(fg) = f\, dg + g\, df.$$

These formulas follow from Problem 6, Section 2–2. Similarly, writing $c$ for the constant function with value $c$,

$$dc = \mathbf{0}$$

where $\mathbf{0}$ denotes the "zero form" whose value is $\mathbf{0}$ everywhere. If $D$ is connected, then, conversely, $df = \mathbf{0}$ implies that $f$ is a constant function. This is just a restatement of Corollary 2, Section 2–2.

If $L$ is a linear function, then $dL$ is a constant 1-form. For let $L(\mathbf{x}) = \mathbf{a} \cdot \mathbf{x}$, where $\mathbf{a}$ is just another notation for the linear function $L$ (p. 9). Then the $i$th partial derivative of $L$ is $a_i$ and $dL(\mathbf{x}) = \mathbf{a}$ for every $\mathbf{x}$.

In particular, the standard cartesian coordinate functions $X^1, \ldots, X^n$ (p. 11) are linear. In fact $X^i(\mathbf{x}) = \mathbf{e}^i \cdot \mathbf{x} = x^i$, and $dX^i(\mathbf{x}) = \mathbf{e}^i$. Hence $dX^i$ is just the constant 1-form which we have denoted by $dx^i$. The common practice of writing $dx^i$ instead of $dX^i$ arises from the habit of confusing notationally a function with its value at some particular point $\mathbf{x}$, in this case of confusing $X^i$ with $x^i = X^i(\mathbf{x})$. Nevertheless, following custom, we adhere to the notation $dx^i$.

**Definition.** A 1-form $\boldsymbol{\omega}$ is *exact* if there is a function $f$ such that $\boldsymbol{\omega} = df$.

If $df = dg$, then $d(f - g) = \mathbf{0}$. If $D$ is connected, $f - g$ is a constant function. Hence the function $f$ whose differential is a given exact 1-form $\boldsymbol{\omega}$ is determined up to the addition of a constant function, if the domain is connected.

A 1-form $\boldsymbol{\omega}$ is of *class* $C^{(q)}$ if its components $\omega_i$ are functions of class $C^{(q)}$. If $\boldsymbol{\omega} = df$, then $\omega_i = \partial f/\partial x^i$. In this case $\boldsymbol{\omega}$ is of class $C^{(q)}$ if and only if $f$ is of class $C^{(q+1)}$.

Let us look for some criteria to determine whether a 1-form $\boldsymbol{\omega}$ is exact or not. If $\boldsymbol{\omega}$ is of class $C^{(1)}$ and $\boldsymbol{\omega} = df$, then $f$ is of class $C^{(2)}$. Using Theorem 3 and the $\partial/\partial x^i$ notation for partial derivatives,

$$\frac{\partial \omega_i}{\partial x^j} = \frac{\partial^2 f}{\partial x^j \partial x^i} = \frac{\partial^2 f}{\partial x^i \partial x^j} = \frac{\partial \omega_j}{\partial x^i}.$$

Thus the conditions

$$\frac{\partial \omega_i}{\partial x^j} = \frac{\partial \omega_j}{\partial x^i}, \qquad i, j = 1, \ldots, n, \tag{2-22}$$

are necessary for exactness of $\boldsymbol{\omega}$.

**Definition.** A 1-form $\boldsymbol{\omega}$ of class $C^{(1)}$ which satisfies (2–22) is called a *closed* 1-form.

In (2–22) we may as well suppose that $i < j$. Thus the definition says in effect that $\boldsymbol{\omega}$ is a closed differential form if its components $\omega_1, \ldots, \omega_n$ satisfy these $n(n-1)/2$ conditions. For instance, if $n = 2$ let us write $dx$ and $dy$ instead of $dx^1$ and $dx^2$, and

$$M(x, y) = \omega_1(x, y), \qquad N(x, y) = \omega_2(x, y).$$

The expression for a 1-form is then

$$\boldsymbol{\omega} = M\,dx + N\,dy.$$

The condition that $\boldsymbol{\omega}$ be closed is that the components $M$ and $N$ satisfy

$$\frac{\partial M}{\partial y} = \frac{\partial N}{\partial x}.$$

We have shown that every exact 1-form is closed. The converse is false, as Example 2 below shows. It is comparatively easy to check whether conditions (2–22) are satisfied or not. Therefore it is very desirable to find some additional condition which will guarantee that the converse holds. Such a condition is that the domain $D$ be simply connected. We shall prove in Chapter 7 that if $D$ is simply connected, then every closed 1-form with domain $D$ is exact. We shall define the term "simply connected" in Section 7–7. For the present, let us merely say that any convex set, and in particular $E^n$, is simply connected. For $n = 2$, an open, connected set $D$ is simply connected if and only if, roughly speaking, $D$ has no holes.

We have been careful to distinguish notationally between functions and their values. One can scarcely attain a sound knowledge of calculus until this distinction is recognized. Nevertheless, in examples we sometimes abuse the notation for brevity. For instance, $d(x^2y) = 2xy\,dx + x^2\,dy$ is short for the statement "$df = f_1\,dx + f_2\,dy$, where $f(x, y) = x^2y$, $f_1(x, y) = 2xy$, $f_2(x, y) = x^2$ for every $(x, y) \in E^2$."

**Example 1.** Let $\boldsymbol{\omega} = 2xy\,dx + (x^2 + 2y)\,dy$, $D = E^2$. This is of course an abbreviation for $\boldsymbol{\omega} = M\,dx + N\,dy$, where $M(x, y) = 2xy$, $N(x, y) = x^2 + 2y$, for every $(x, y) \in E^2$. In this example,

$$\frac{\partial M}{\partial y}(x, y) = 2x = \frac{\partial N}{\partial x}(x, y)$$

for every $(x, y)$. Hence $\boldsymbol{\omega}$ is a closed 1-form. Since $E^2$ is connected and simply connected, $\boldsymbol{\omega} = df$ where $f$ is determined up to the addition of a constant function. The function $f$ can be found by partial integration with respect to the first variable, as follows:

$$\frac{\partial f}{\partial x}(x, y) = M(x, y) = 2xy, \qquad f(x, y) = x^2y + \phi(y),$$

where the function $\phi$ is determined from

$$\frac{\partial f}{\partial y}(x, y) = N(x, y) = x^2 + 2y, \qquad x^2 + 2y = x^2 + \phi'(y).$$

Of course these equations hold for every $(x, y) \in E^2$. Then $\phi'(y) = 2y$, and $\phi(y) = y^2 + c$ for every $y$, where the "constant of integration" $c$ is a number which may be chosen arbitrarily. Hence for every $(x, y) \in E^2$,

$$f(x, y) = x^2y + y^2 + c.$$

**Example 2.** Let $D = E^2 - \{(0, 0)\}$. By removing $(0, 0)$ we have made a hole, and $D$ is not simply connected. Let $\boldsymbol{\omega} = M\,dx + N\,dy$, where for every $(x, y) \in D$

$$M(x, y) = -\frac{y}{x^2 + y^2},$$

$$N(x, y) = \frac{x}{x^2 + y^2}.$$

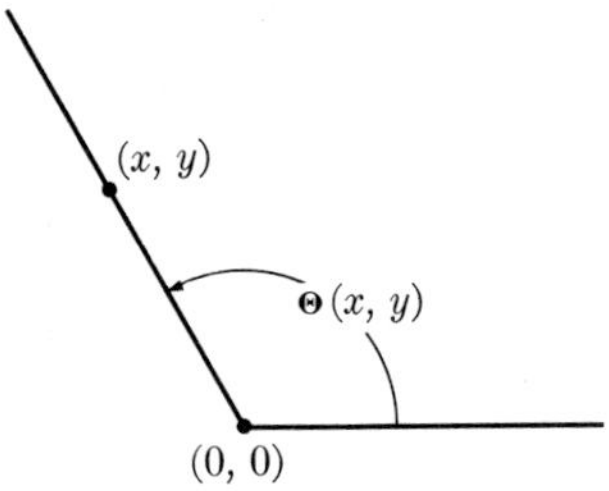


FIGURE 2–7

A computation shows that $\partial M/\partial y = \partial N/\partial x$ in $D$, hence $\boldsymbol{\omega}$ is closed. Let us show that $\boldsymbol{\omega}$ is not exact. Let $D_1$ be the open subset of $D$ obtained by deleting the positive $x$-axis. For every $(x, y) \in D_1$ let $\Theta(x, y)$ be the angle from the positive $x$-axis to $(x, y)$, $0 < \Theta(x, y) < 2\pi$ (Fig. 2–7). Using elementary calculus, we find that in $D_1$, $d\Theta = \boldsymbol{\omega}$ [Problem 6(a)]. If there were a function $f$ of class $C^{(2)}$ on $D$ such that $\boldsymbol{\omega} = df$, then upon restricting $f$ to $D_1$ we would have $d(f - \Theta) = \mathbf{0}$. Since $D_1$ is connected, $f - \Theta$ would be constant on $D_1$. This would imply that $\Theta$ can be continuously extended across the positive $x$-axis, which is false. Hence $\boldsymbol{\omega}$ is not exact.

**Example 3.** In some cases it can be seen by inspection that $\omega$ is exact. For instance, if $\omega = 2x^1 dx^1 + \cdots + 2x^n\, dx^n$ and $D = E^n$, then

$$\omega = d[(x^1)^2 + \cdots + (x^n)^2 + c] = d(\mathbf{x} \cdot \mathbf{x} + c).$$

The reader may have also discovered by inspection that the form $\omega$ in Example 1 is exact.

## PROBLEMS

1. Let $n = 1$. Give a precise interpretation of the formula $df/dx = f'$ from elementary calculus. [*Hint:* The quotient of two real-valued functions is defined wherever the denominator does not have the value 0.]

2. Let $n = 3$ and $\omega = M\,dx + N\,dy + O\,dz$. What do conditions (2–22) become in this case?

3. In each case determine whether or not $\omega$ is exact. If exact, find all functions $f$ such that $\omega = df$.

   (a) $\omega = xy\,dx + (x^2/2)\,dy,\ D = E^2$. (b) $\omega = x\,dx + xz\,dy + xy\,dz,\ D = E^3$.
   (c) $\omega = y\,dx,\ D = E^2$.
   (d) $\omega = (1/x^2 + 1/y^2)(y\,dx - x\,dy),\ D = \{(x, y) : x \neq 0 \text{ and } y \neq 0\}$.

4. Let $\omega = dy + p(x)y\,dx$ and $D$ be the vertical strip $\{(x, y) : a < x < b\}$. Let $p$ be continuous on $(a, b)$ and $P$ be an antiderivative of $p$, that is, a function such that $P'(x) = p(x)$ for every $x \in (a, b)$. Let $f(x) = \exp[P(x)]$. Show that $f\omega$ is exact.

5. Show that

   $$\text{(a)}\quad d\left[\left(\sum_{i=1}^{n} x^i\right)^2\right] = 2\sum_{i,j=1}^{n} x^i dx^j.$$

   $$\text{(b)}\quad d\left[\sum_{i\neq j} x^i x^j\right] = 2\sum_{i=1}^{n}\sum_{k\neq i} x^k dx^i.$$

   [*Hint for* (b): What is $(\sum x^i)^2 - \sum (x^i)^2$?]

6. In Example 2: (a) Show that $\Theta_1(x, y) = M(x, y)$, $\Theta_2(x, y) = N(x, y)$ for every $(x, y) \in D_1$. You may use the formulas for the derivatives of the inverse trigonometric functions.
   (b) Verify that $\partial M/\partial y = \partial N/\partial x$ by calculating these partial derivatives.

7. Let $g$ be continuous on $E^1$. Show that

   $$g(|\mathbf{x}|) \sum_{i=1}^{n} x^i dx^i$$

   is an exact 1-form. [*Hint:* Let $h(u) = ug(u)$ for every $u \in E^1$. The function $h$ has an antiderivative.]

CHAPTER 3

# Vector-Valued Functions of One Variable

In this chapter, we shall first define the derivative of a function $\mathbf{g}$ from a set $J \subset E^1$ into $E^n$. The derivative has many of the same properties as the derivative of a real-valued function in elementary calculus. When $J$ is an interval, $\mathbf{g}$ represents a curve in $E^n$, provided its derivative $\mathbf{g}'(t)$ is never $\mathbf{0}$. Any vector-valued function $\mathbf{f}$ obtained from $\mathbf{g}$ by a suitable parameter change represents the same curve as $\mathbf{g}$. The line integral of a differential 1-form $\boldsymbol{\omega}$ along a curve $\gamma$ is defined in Section 3–3. It turns out that the line integral depends just on the endpoints of $\gamma$ if and only if $\boldsymbol{\omega}$ is exact (Theorem 7). In Section 3–4 the gradient method for extrema is described.

Except for the introductory Section 3–1, this chapter may be postponed and read together with Chapter 7.

## 3–1 DERIVATIVES

Let $\mathbf{g}$ be a function from a set $J \subset E^1$ into $E^n$. Let $t$ be an interior point of $J$. Then the *derivative* of $\mathbf{g}$ at $t$ is the vector

$$\mathbf{g}'(t) = \lim_{u \to 0} \frac{1}{u} [\mathbf{g}(t + u) - \mathbf{g}(t)], \tag{3–1}$$

provided the limit exists.

The derivative of a vector-valued function has many of the same properties as in the case of real-valued functions. If $\mathbf{f}$ and $\mathbf{g}$ both have a derivative at $t$, then

$$\begin{aligned}(\mathbf{f} + \mathbf{g})'(t) &= \mathbf{f}'(t) + \mathbf{g}'(t),\\ (\mathbf{f} \cdot \mathbf{g})'(t) &= \mathbf{f}'(t) \cdot \mathbf{g}(t) + \mathbf{f}(t) \cdot \mathbf{g}'(t).\end{aligned} \tag{3–2}$$

Here $\mathbf{f} \cdot \mathbf{g}$ is the real-valued function whose value at each $t$ is the inner product $\mathbf{f}(t) \cdot \mathbf{g}(t)$. The proof of these two formulas is left to the reader (Problem 4).

The derivative has a geometric interpretation as a tangent vector. Let us suppose that $J$ is an interval. As $t$ traverses $J$ from left to right, the point

$\mathbf{g}(t)$ traverses some curve in $E^n$. A precise definition of the term "curve" is given in the next section.

Let us assume that $t_0$ is a point of $J$ at which $\mathbf{g}'(t_0) \neq \mathbf{0}$. Let

$$\mathbf{x}_0 = \mathbf{g}(t_0), \qquad \mathbf{v}_0 = \mathbf{g}'(t_0),$$
$$\mathbf{x} = \mathbf{g}(t), \qquad \mathbf{y} = \mathbf{x}_0 + u\mathbf{v}_0,$$

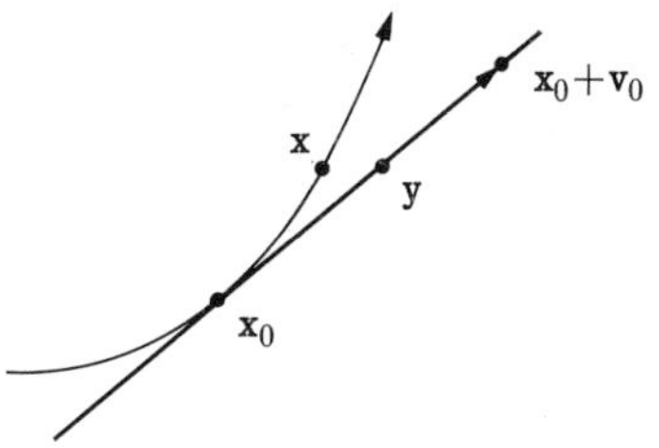


FIGURE 3–1

where $t = t_0 + u$ and $|u|$ is small enough that $t \in J$. The ratio of the distances $|\mathbf{x} - \mathbf{y}|$ and $|\mathbf{x} - \mathbf{x}_0|$ may be written, upon multiplying numerator and denominator by $1/|u|$, in the form

$$\frac{|\mathbf{x} - \mathbf{y}|}{|\mathbf{x} - \mathbf{x}_0|} = \left| \frac{1}{u} [\mathbf{g}(t) - \mathbf{g}(t_0)] - \mathbf{g}'(t_0) \right| \frac{1}{|(1/u)[\mathbf{g}(t) - \mathbf{g}(t_0)]|}.$$

Hence

$$\lim_{u \to 0} \frac{|\mathbf{x} - \mathbf{y}|}{|\mathbf{x} - \mathbf{x}_0|} = 0 \, \frac{1}{|\mathbf{g}'(t_0)|} = 0.$$

This justifies calling $\mathbf{v}_0$ a *tangent vector* at $\mathbf{x}_0$, and the line through $\mathbf{x}_0$ and $\mathbf{x}_0 + \mathbf{v}_0$ a *tangent line* at $\mathbf{x}_0$ (Fig. 3–1). Note that we have used the assumption that $\mathbf{g}'(t_0) \neq \mathbf{0}$.

The number $t$ is often called a parameter. It need not have any geometric or physical significance. However, if $n = 3$ and $t$ happens to denote time in a physical problem, then $\mathbf{g}'(t)$ is the velocity vector.

A vector-valued function $\mathbf{g}$ has components $g^1, \ldots, g^n$, which are the real-valued functions such that

$$\mathbf{g}(t) = \sum_{i=1}^{n} g^i(t)\mathbf{e}_i$$

for every $t \in J$. If $\mathbf{g}'(t)$ exists, then the $i$th component $u^{-1}[g^i(t + u) - g^i(t)]$ of the expression on the right side of (3–1) tends to $g^{i\prime}(t)$ as $u \to 0$, by Proposition A–4b, and

$$\mathbf{g}'(t) = \sum_{i=1}^{n} g^{i\prime}(t)\mathbf{e}_i. \tag{3–3}$$

Conversely, if $g^{i\prime}(t)$ exists for each $i = 1, \ldots, n$, then $\mathbf{g}'(t)$ exists and is given by (3–3).

**Example.** Let $n = 2$, $\mathbf{g}(t) = t^2\mathbf{e}_1 + (\log t)\mathbf{e}_2$. Find the tangent line at $\mathbf{e}_1$. In this example $g^1(t) = t^2$, $g^2(t) = \log t$, and $t_0 = 1$, $\mathbf{x}_0 = \mathbf{g}(1) = \mathbf{e}_1$. Then $\mathbf{g}'(t) = 2t\mathbf{e}_1 + t^{-1}\mathbf{e}_2$, and $\mathbf{v}_0 = \mathbf{g}'(1) = 2\mathbf{e}_1 + \mathbf{e}_2$. The tangent line goes through $\mathbf{e}_1$ and $3\mathbf{e}_1 + \mathbf{e}_2$. Its equation is $2y = x - 1$.

**PROBLEMS**

1. Find the tangent line at $2^{-1/2}\mathbf{e}_1 - 2^{1/2}\mathbf{e}_2$ to the ellipse represented by $\mathbf{g}(t) = (\cos t)\mathbf{e}_1 + (2\sin t)\mathbf{e}_2$, $J = [0, 2\pi]$. Illustrate with a sketch.
2. Find the tangent line at $\mathbf{e}_1 + \mathbf{e}_2 + \mathbf{e}_3$ to the curve represented by

$$\mathbf{g}(t) = t\mathbf{e}_1 + t^{1/2}\mathbf{e}_2 + t^{1/3}\mathbf{e}_3, \ \tfrac{1}{2} \leq t \leq 2.$$

3. A particle moves along the parabola $y^2 = 4x$ with constant speed 2 and so that $dy/dt = g^{2\prime}(t) > 0$. Find the velocity vector $\mathbf{g}'(t)$ at $\mathbf{e}_1 - 2\mathbf{e}_2$. [*Note:* The speed is $|\mathbf{g}'(t)|$.]
4. Give a proof of formulas (3–2):
   (a) Using the corresponding formulas for derivatives of real-valued functions and (3–3).
   (b) Directly from the definition (3–1).
5. Let $\mathbf{g}(t) = [3t/(1 + t^3)]\mathbf{e}_1 + [3t^2/(1 + t^3)]\mathbf{e}_2$, $t \neq -1$.
   (a) Sketch the curve traversed by $\mathbf{g}(t)$ on the interval $(-\infty, -1)$. On the interval $(-1, \infty)$.
   (b) Show that $\{\mathbf{g}(t) : t \neq -1\} = \{(x, y) : x^3 + y^3 = 3xy\}$. This set is called the folium of Descartes.

## 3–2 CURVES IN $E^n$

Let $\mathbf{g}$ be a function from an interval $J \subset E^1$ into $E^n$. Then $\mathbf{g}(t)$ traverses a curve in $E^n$ as the "parameter" $t$ traverses $J$. It is better not to call $\mathbf{g}$ itself a curve. Instead one should regard any vector-valued function $\mathbf{f}$ obtained from $\mathbf{g}$ by a suitable change of parameter as representing the same curve as $\mathbf{g}$. We shall define a curve as an equivalence class of equivalent parametric representations. To simplify matters we shall at first consider only curves with continuously changing tangents.

Let us now be more precise. Let us for simplicity assume that $J = [a, b]$, a closed bounded interval, and that the components $g^1, \ldots, g^n$ are of class $C^{(1)}$ on $[a, b]$. By $g^{i\prime}(a)$ and $g^{i\prime}(b)$ we mean respectively right-hand and left-hand derivatives. They are equal to the derivatives at $a$ and $b$ of any class $C^{(1)}$ extension of $g^i$ to an open set containing $[a, b]$. See p. 50.

**Definition.** If $\mathbf{g}'(t) \neq \mathbf{0}$ for every $t \in [a, b]$, then $\mathbf{g}$ is a *parametric representation of class* $C^{(1)}$ on $[a, b]$.

To motivate the definition of equivalence which we are going to make, let us first consider an example.

**Example 1.** Let $\mathbf{g}(t) = t\mathbf{e}_1 + t^2\mathbf{e}_2$, $1 \leq t \leq 2$. Then $g^1(t) = t$, $g^2(t) = t^2$, $\mathbf{g}'(t) = \mathbf{e}_1 + 2t\mathbf{e}_2 \neq \mathbf{0}$. Hence $\mathbf{g}$ is a parametric representation of class $C^{(1)}$ on the interval $[1, 2]$. In fact, it represents the arc of the parabola $y = x^2$ between $(1, 1)$ and $(2, 4)$, traversed from left to right (Fig. 3–2). If we let $\mathbf{f}(\tau) = (\exp \tau)\mathbf{e}_1 + (\exp 2\tau)\mathbf{e}_2$, $0 \leq \tau \leq \log 2$, then $\mathbf{f}$ also represents this same parabolic arc. In effect, $\mathbf{f}$ is obtained from $\mathbf{g}$ by the parameter change $t = \exp \tau$. It is reasonable to regard $\mathbf{f}$ and $\mathbf{g}$ as equivalent, and we shall do so.

Now let $\mathbf{g}$ be any parametric representation of class $C^{(1)}$ on $[a, b]$. Let $\phi$ be any real-valued function of class $C^{(1)}$ on some closed interval $[\alpha, \beta]$ such that

$$\phi'(\tau) > 0 \qquad \text{for every } \tau \in [\alpha, \beta], \qquad \phi(\alpha) = a, \qquad \phi(\beta) = b. \tag{3–4}$$

Let $\mathbf{f}$ be the composite of $\mathbf{g}$ and $\phi$, denoted by $\mathbf{f} = \mathbf{g} \circ \phi$. Then

$$\mathbf{f}(\tau) = \mathbf{g}[\phi(\tau)] \quad \text{for every } \tau \in [\alpha, \beta].$$

From the composite function theorem

$$f^{i\prime}(\tau) = g^{i\prime}[\phi(\tau)]\phi'(\tau), \quad \text{for } i = 1, \ldots, n,$$

which is the same as

$$\mathbf{f}'(\tau) = \mathbf{g}'[\phi(\tau)]\phi'(\tau). \tag{3–5}$$

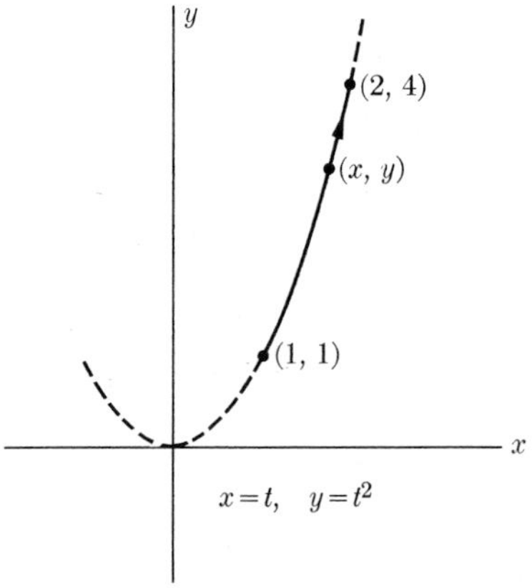


FIGURE 3–2

In particular, $\mathbf{f}'(\tau) \neq 0$ and $\mathbf{f}$ is also a parametric representation of class $C^{(1)}$. The tangent vector $\mathbf{f}'(\tau)$ differs from the tangent vector $\mathbf{g}'[\phi(\tau)]$ by the positive scalar multiple $\phi'(\tau)$. (Scalar multiplication on the right means the same thing as on the left, $\mathbf{v}c = c\mathbf{v}$.)

**Definition.** We say that $\mathbf{f}$ is *equivalent* to $\mathbf{g}$ if there exists $\phi$ satisfying the above conditions such that $\mathbf{f} = \mathbf{g} \circ \phi$.

The properties of reflexivity, symmetry, and transitivity required of an equivalence relation hold (Problem 6). By an *equivalence class* is meant the collection of all parametric representations of class $C^{(1)}$ equivalent to a given one. The reader may have encountered the notion of equivalence class elsewhere in mathematics. An example is the definition of the rational numbers starting from the integers.

**Definition.** A *curve* $\gamma$ *of class* $C^{(1)}$ is an equivalence class of parametric representations of class $C^{(1)}$.

By requiring that the components $g^1, \ldots, g^n$ be of class $C^{(q)}$, $q \geq 2$, and allowing only parameter changes $\phi$ of class $C^{(q)}$, the notion of curve of class $C^{(q)}$ can be defined in the same way. To study curvature of curves one needs to assume class $C^{(2)}$ at least. See reference [22]. However, for present purposes we need only class $C^{(1)}$. From now on we shall say "curve" instead of "curve of class $C^{(1)}$," and "representation" instead of "parametric representation of class $C^{(1)}$."

Each curve has an infinite number of representations. If $\mathbf{g}$ is one such representation, then each parameter change $\phi$ leads to another. It is often highly advantageous to make a judicious choice of parameter. In a physical problem, time (measured according to some preassigned scale) may be the preferred parameter. For certain curves one of the components $x^1, \ldots, x^n$ can be taken as the parameter. For example, if the first component $g^{1\prime}(t)$ of the tangent vector $\mathbf{g}'(t)$ is everywhere positive, then $g^1$ has an inverse (Section A–10). Let us take for $\phi$ the inverse of $g^1$. Formally this amounts simply to solving the equation $x^1 = g^1(t)$ for $t$, obtaining $t = \phi(x^1)$. Set $\tau = x^1$. Then $x^1$ is the new parameter and $f^1(x^1) = x^1$.

Figure 3–3 illustrates this situation for $n = 2$.

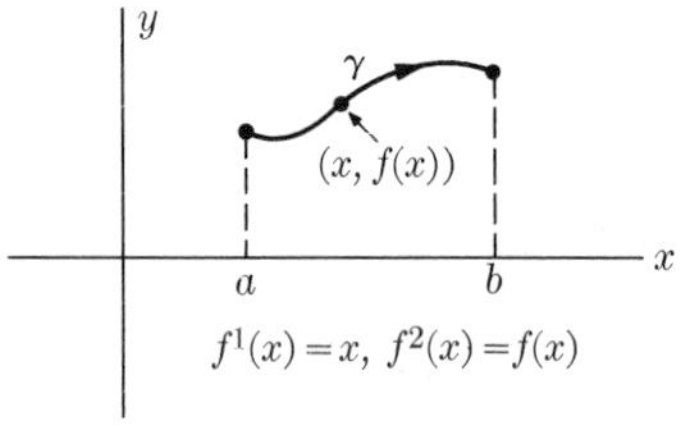


FIGURE 3–3

A curve $\gamma$ is to be regarded as the path traversed by a moving point, and we have not excluded the possibility that $\gamma$ passes through the same point several times. The *multiplicity* of a point $\mathbf{x}$ is the number of points $t \in [a, b]$ such that $\mathbf{g}(t) = \mathbf{x}$. The multiplicity does not depend on the particular representation $\mathbf{g}$ chosen for $\gamma$, since any $\phi$ satisfying (3–4) is a univalent function, namely, $\phi(\tau_1) \neq \phi(\tau_2)$ if $\tau_1 \neq \tau_2$. The *trace* of $\gamma$ is the set of points of positive multiplicity, that is, the set of points through which $\gamma$ passes at least once. If $\mathbf{x}$ has multiplicity 1, then $\mathbf{x}$ is called a *simple point.* If every point of the trace is simple, then $\gamma$ is called a *simple arc.*

The point $\mathbf{g}(a)$ is called the *initial endpoint* of $\gamma$ and $\mathbf{g}(b)$ the *final endpoint.* If $\mathbf{g}(a) = \mathbf{g}(b)$, then $\gamma$ is called a *closed curve.* A closed curve is called *simple* if every point of the trace is simple except $\mathbf{g}(a)$, which has multiplicity 2 (Fig. 3–4).

**Example 2.** Let $\mathbf{g}(t) = \mathbf{x}_0 + t(\mathbf{x}_1 - \mathbf{x}_0)$, $0 \leq t \leq 1$. Then $\gamma$ is the line segment joining $\mathbf{x}_1$ and $\mathbf{x}_0$, traversed from $\mathbf{x}_0$ to $\mathbf{x}_1$. It is a simple arc.

**Example 3.** Let $\mathbf{g}(t) = (\cos mt)\mathbf{e}_1 + (\sin mt)\mathbf{e}_2$, $0 \leq t \leq 2\pi$, where $m$ is an integer not 0. The trace is the unit circle $x^2 + y^2 = 1$. The closed curve $\gamma$ which $\mathbf{g}$ represents goes around the circle $|m|$ times, counterclockwise if $m > 0$ and clockwise if $m < 0$. If $m = \pm 1$, then $\gamma$ is a simple closed curve.

At this point we need some properties of integrals, which are reviewed in Section A–9. In the present chapter we employ the Riemann definition of integral, as is customary in calculus. The more sophisticated Lebesgue theory of integrals is developed in Chapter 5.

**Definition.** The *length* $l$ of a curve $\gamma$ is

$$l = \int_a^b |\mathbf{g}'(t)|\, dt. \tag{3–6}$$

If $\mathbf{f}$ is equivalent to $\mathbf{g}$, then

$$\int_\alpha^\beta |\mathbf{f}'(\tau)|\, d\tau = \int_\alpha^\beta |\mathbf{g}'[\phi(\tau)]|\phi'(\tau)\, d\tau = \int_a^b |\mathbf{g}'(t)| dt,$$

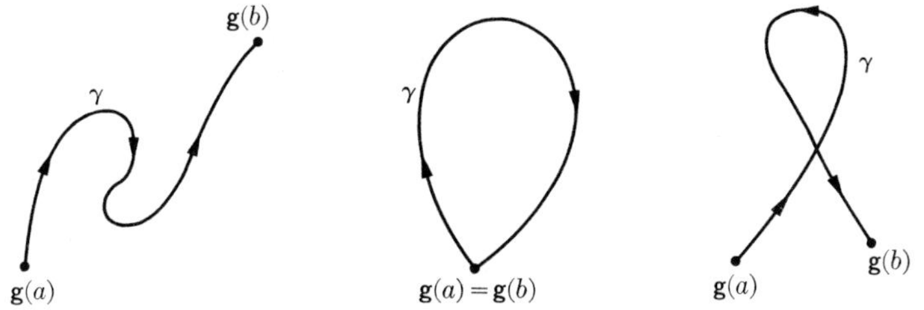


FIGURE 3–4

by (3–5) and the theorem about change of variables in integrals (Section A–9). Thus $l$ does not depend on the particular representation chosen for $\gamma$.

Formula (3–6) is suggested by considering inscribed polygons. Let $a = t_0 < t_1 < \cdots < t_{m-1} < t_m = b$, and let $\mu = \max\{t_1 - t_0, t_2 - t_1, \ldots, t_m - t_{m-1}\}$. The polygon which joins successively $\mathbf{g}(t_{j-1})$ with $\mathbf{g}(t_j)$ has elementary length

$$\sum_{j=1}^{m} |\mathbf{g}(t_j) - \mathbf{g}(t_{j-1})|. \tag{$*$}$$

The length $l$ is the limit of the elementary lengths of polygons inscribed in $\gamma$. More precisely, given $\epsilon > 0$, there exists $\delta > 0$ such that $|(*) - l| < \epsilon$ whenever $\mu < \delta$. Since we mention this fact just to motivate the definition (3–6), the proof will only be indicated. Since the derivative $\mathbf{g}'$ is continuous, $\mathbf{g}(t_j) - \mathbf{g}(t_{j-1})$ can be replaced by $\mathbf{g}'(s_j)(t_j - t_{j-1})$ and the sum $(*)$ by

$$\sum_{j=1}^{m} |\mathbf{g}'(s_j)|(t_j - t_{j-1}), \tag{$**$}$$

with error tending to 0 as $\mu \to 0$, where $s_j$ can be chosen arbitrarily in $[t_{j-1}, t_j]$. But $(**)$ is a Riemann sum for the integral (3–6), and tends to $l$ as $\mu \to 0$. The proof that $(*)$ can be replaced by $(**)$ with small error makes use of the fact that the continuous function $\mathbf{g}'$ is uniformly continuous on the compact set $[a, b]$ (Section A–8, Problem 6).

Every smooth curve $\gamma$ has a representation of particular geometric interest. It is called the standard representation, or representation with arc length $s$ as parameter, and is defined in the following way. Let $\mathbf{g}$ represent $\gamma$ on $[a, b]$, and let

$$S(t) = \int_a^t |\mathbf{g}'(u)|\, du \quad \text{for every } t \in [a, b].$$

The length of the part of $\gamma$ represented on $[a, t]$ is $S(t)$. Clearly $S(a) = 0$ and $S(b) = l$. By the fundamental theorem of calculus,

$$S'(t) = |\mathbf{g}'(t)| > 0$$

for every $t \in [a, b]$. In particular, if $t$ signifies time then $S'(t)$ is the length of the velocity vector, that is, the speed of motion.

Since $S'(t) > 0$ the equation $s = S(t)$ can be solved for $t$. More precisely, the function $S$ has an inverse $\phi$ of class $C^{(1)}$ on $[0, l]$. Let $\mathbf{G} = \mathbf{g} \circ \phi$. Then $\mathbf{G}$ is the *standard representation* of $\gamma$. From (3–5)

$$\mathbf{G}'(s) = \mathbf{g}'[\phi(s)]\phi'(s), \quad \text{for every } s \in [0, l].$$

Since

$$\phi'(s) = \frac{1}{S'[\phi(s)]} = \frac{1}{|\mathbf{g}'[\phi(s)]|},$$

we find that

$$|\mathbf{G}'(s)| = 1 \tag{3–7a}$$

for every $s \in [0, l]$. Hence $\mathbf{G}'(s)$ is a *unit tangent vector* at the point $\mathbf{G}(s)$. If we write $dx^i/ds$ for $G^{i\prime}(s)$, then (3–7a) can be rewritten

$$\left(\frac{dx^1}{ds}\right)^2 + \cdots + \left(\frac{dx^n}{ds}\right)^2 = 1. \tag{3–7b}$$

**Example 3 (continued).** Let $m > 0$. Then $|\mathbf{g}'(t)| = m$, $S(t) = mt$. Solving the equation $s = S(t)$ for $t$, we obtain the standard representation

$$\mathbf{G}(s) = (\cos s)\mathbf{e}_1 + (\sin s)\mathbf{e}_2, \qquad 0 \le s \le 2m\pi.$$

**Piecewise smooth curves.** It is not difficult to adapt the preceding discussion to curves which are of class $C^{(1)}$ except for a finite number of corners and cusps. By a parametric representation of a piecewise smooth curve is meant a continuous function $\mathbf{g}$ on an interval $[a, b]$ with the following property: There exist $t_0, t_1, \ldots, t_p$ with

$$a = t_0 < t_1 < \cdots < t_{p-1} < t_p = b$$

such that the restriction of $\mathbf{g}$ to each of the closed subintervals $[t_{j-1}, t_j]$, $j = 1, \ldots, p$, is a parametric representation of class $C^{(1)}$. In particular, $\mathbf{g}$ has at each $t_j$ interior to $[a, b]$ right- and left-hand derivatives which need not be equal. Parameter changes which are piecewise of class $C^{(1)}$ are admitted. A piecewise smooth curve is an equivalence class of parametric representations which are piecewise of class $C^{(1)}$.

**Example 4.** Let $n = 2$ and $\mathbf{g}(t) = t\mathbf{e}_1 + |t - 1|\mathbf{e}_2$, $0 \le t \le 2$. This represents the polygon from $\mathbf{e}_2$ to $\mathbf{e}_1$ to $2\mathbf{e}_1 + \mathbf{e}_2$ with a corner at $\mathbf{e}_1$. Let $\phi(\tau) = \tau^3 + 1$ and $\mathbf{f}(\tau) = \mathbf{g}(\tau^3 + 1) = (\tau^3 + 1)\mathbf{e}_1 + |\tau^3|\mathbf{e}_2$, $-1 \le \tau \le 1$. Then $f^1(\tau) = \tau^3 + 1$ and $f^2(\tau) = |\tau^3|$. The components $f^1, f^2$ are of class $C^{(1)}$, which might lead one to think that there is no corner. However, $\phi$ does not define an admissible parameter change, since $\phi'(0) = 0$ contrary to (3–4). Since $\mathbf{f}'(0) = \mathbf{0}$, $\mathbf{f}$ is not a parametric representation of class $C^{(1)}$. This example emphasizes the importance of the restriction $\phi'(\tau) > 0$ in (3–4).

**PROBLEMS**

1. Which of the following represent simple arcs? Simple closed curves? Illustrate with a sketch.
   (a) $\mathbf{g}(t) = (a \cos t)\mathbf{e}_1 + (b \sin t)\mathbf{e}_2$, $a > 0$, $b > 0$, $J = [0, 2\pi]$.
   (b) Same as (a) except $J = [-\pi, 2\pi]$.
   (c) $\mathbf{g}(t) = (-\cosh t)\mathbf{e}_1 + (\sinh t)\mathbf{e}_2$, $J = [-1, 1]$ (see p. 66 for the definition of cosh and sinh).
2. (a) Let $\gamma$ be represented by $\mathbf{f}(x) = x\mathbf{e}_1 + f(x)\mathbf{e}_2$, $a \leq x \leq b$, where $f$ is of class $C^{(1)}$ on $[a, b]$. Show that
$$l = \int_a^b \sqrt{1 + [f'(x)]^2}\, dx.$$
   (b) Find $l$ in case $f(x) = |x|^{3/2}$, $a = -b$.
3. Find the standard representation of the helical curve represented on $[0, 2\pi]$ by $\mathbf{g}(t) = (\cos t)\mathbf{e}_1 + (\sin t)\mathbf{e}_2 + t\mathbf{e}_3$. Sketch the trace.
4. Sketch the trace of the curve $\gamma$ represented on $[0, 2\pi]$ by $\mathbf{g}(t) = (\cos t)\mathbf{e}_1 + (\sin 2t)\mathbf{e}_2$. Find the tangent vectors to $\gamma$ at the double point $(0, 0)$.
5. Let $g^1(t) = \cos(1/t) \exp(-1/t)$, $g^2(t) = \sin(1/t) \exp(-1/t)$ if $0 < t \leq 1$, and $g^1(0) = g^2(0) = 0$.
   (a) Show that $g^1$ and $g^2$ are of class $C^{(1)}$ on $[0, 1]$. [*Hint:* $u^k \exp(-u) \to 0$ as $u \to +\infty$.]
   (b) Does $\mathbf{g} = g^1\mathbf{e}_1 + g^2\mathbf{e}_2$ represent a curve of class $C^{(1)}$? Illustrate with a sketch.
6. Let us write $\mathbf{f} \sim \mathbf{g}$ to mean $\mathbf{f}$ is equivalent to $\mathbf{g}$. Prove that:
   (a) $\mathbf{g} \sim \mathbf{g}$ (reflexivity).
   (b) If $\mathbf{f} \sim \mathbf{g}$, then $\mathbf{g} \sim \mathbf{f}$ (symmetry).
   (c) If $\mathbf{g}_1 \sim \mathbf{g}_2$ and $\mathbf{g}_2 \sim \mathbf{g}_3$, then $\mathbf{g}_1 \sim \mathbf{g}_3$ (transitivity).
7. Let $\gamma$ be a curve of class $C^{(1)}$. Prove that the multiplicity of any point $\mathbf{x}$ is finite.
8. Let $\gamma_0$ and $\gamma_1$ be curves represented on $[a, b]$ by $\mathbf{g}_0$ and $\mathbf{g}_1$, respectively. For every $u \in [0, 1]$ let $\gamma_u$ be the curve represented by $\mathbf{g}_u(t) = u\mathbf{g}_1(t) + (1 - u)\mathbf{g}_0(t)$, $a \leq t \leq b$. Let $l(u)$ be the length of $\gamma_u$. Prove that $l$ is a convex function on $[0, 1]$. When is the convexity strict?

## 3–3 LINE INTEGRALS

Let $D$ be an open subset of $E^n$. Let $\boldsymbol{\omega}$ be a 1-form with domain $D$, and $\gamma$ a curve whose trace is contained in $D$. We assume that $\boldsymbol{\omega}$ is continuous. Let us consider an inscribed polygon joining successively the points $\mathbf{g}(t_{j-1})$ and $\mathbf{g}(t_j)$ as in the previous section. If $s_j \in [t_{j-1}, t_j]$, then $\boldsymbol{\omega}[\mathbf{g}(s_j)]$ is a covector, and its scalar product with the vector $\mathbf{g}(t_j) - \mathbf{g}(t_{j-1})$ is a number. Let us consider the sum

$$\sum_{j=1}^{m} \boldsymbol{\omega}[\mathbf{g}(s_j)] \cdot [\mathbf{g}(t_j) - \mathbf{g}(t_{j-1})]. \tag{$*$}$$

By reasoning like that indicated on p. 77 the sum $(*)$ tends to the integral (3–8a) as $\mu \to 0$. This integral is called a line integral.

**Definition.** Let $\omega$ be continuous and $\gamma$ piecewise smooth. The *line integral* of $\omega$ along $\gamma$ is

$$\int_a^b \omega[\mathbf{g}(t)] \cdot \mathbf{g}'(t)\, dt. \tag{3–8a}$$

The line integral exists, since if $\mathbf{g}$ is piecewise of class $C^{(1)}$ the integrand in (3–8a) is bounded and has a finite number of discontinuities. If $\mathbf{f}$ is equivalent to $\mathbf{g}$, then using (3–5)

$$\int_a^b \omega[\mathbf{g}(t)] \cdot \mathbf{g}'(t)\, dt = \int_\alpha^\beta \omega[\mathbf{g}(\phi(\tau))] \cdot \mathbf{g}'[\phi(\tau)]\phi'(\tau)\, d\tau = \int_\alpha^\beta \omega[\mathbf{f}(\tau)] \cdot \mathbf{f}'(\tau)\, d\tau.$$

Hence the line integral does not depend on the particular representation $\mathbf{g}$ chosen for $\gamma$.

Line integrals have an important role in many parts of mathematical analysis, for example, in the theory of complex analytic functions. Several fundamental physical concepts are also expressed in terms of line integrals. Two of these—work and circulation of a steadily flowing fluid—will be mentioned at the end of the section.

The notation for line integral is $\int_\gamma \omega$. Writing out the scalar product in (3–8a),

$$\int_\gamma \omega = \int_a^b \left[\sum_{i=1}^n \omega_i[\mathbf{g}(t)]\, g^{i\prime}(t)\right] dt. \tag{3–8b}$$

The notation for differential form is supposed to suggest (3–8b). Let us write $\omega = \omega_1\, dx^1 + \cdots + \omega_n\, dx^n$ as in (2–19) and formally multiply and divide the right-hand side by $dt$. If we set $\mathbf{x} = \mathbf{g}(t)$ and write $dx^i/dt$ for $g^{i\prime}(t)$, then we get the integrand on the right-hand side of (3–8b).

**Example 1.** Let $\gamma$ be the semicircle with center $(0, 0)$ and endpoints $\pm a\mathbf{e}_2$, directed from $-a\mathbf{e}_2$ to $a\mathbf{e}_2$. Let us evaluate $\int_\gamma x\, dy - y\, dx$. Points $(x, y)$ of the semicircle satisfy the equations $x = a \cos \theta$, $y = a \sin \theta$, where $-\pi/2 \leq \theta \leq \pi/2$. The most convenient representation for $\gamma$ is on $[-\pi/2, \pi/2]$ with $\mathbf{g}(\theta) = (a \cos \theta)\mathbf{e}_1 + (a \sin \theta)\mathbf{e}_2$. Then

$$\int_\gamma (x\, dy - y\, dx) = \int_{-\pi/2}^{\pi/2} \left(x \frac{dy}{d\theta} - y \frac{dx}{d\theta}\right) d\theta = \int_{-\pi/2}^{\pi/2} a^2\, d\theta = a^2\pi.$$

**Elementary properties of line integrals.** From the corresponding linearity property of ordinary integrals,

$$\int_\gamma (\omega + \zeta) = \int_\gamma \omega + \int_\gamma \zeta, \qquad \int_\gamma (c\omega) = c \int_\gamma \omega, \tag{3–9}$$

for any pair of 1-forms $\omega$, $\zeta$, and scalar $c$. Let $\mathbf{g}$ represent $\gamma$ on $[a, b]$, and let $\phi$ be of class $C^{(1)}$ on $[\alpha, \beta]$ with

$$\phi'(\tau) < 0 \quad \text{for every } \tau \in [\alpha, \beta], \qquad \phi(\alpha) = b, \qquad \phi(\beta) = a.$$

The formula for change of variables in integrals still holds if we agree as usual in calculus that $\int_b^a = -\int_a^b$. The composite $\mathbf{f} = \mathbf{g} \circ \phi$ represents a curve, which is denoted by $-\gamma$ and is called the *curve obtained by reversing the sense of direction of* $\gamma$. From the change of variables formula

$$\int_{-\gamma} \omega = -\int_\gamma \omega. \tag{3–10}$$

Let $\gamma_1, \ldots, \gamma_p$ be piecewise smooth curves such that the final endpoint of $\gamma_j$ is the initial endpoint of $\gamma_{j+1}$ for $j = 1, \ldots, p - 1$. Let $\gamma$ be obtained by "joining together" the curves $\gamma_1, \ldots, \gamma_p$. More precisely, let us divide $[0, 1]$ into $p$ subintervals $[(j - 1)/p, j/p]$ of the same length. Each curve $\gamma_j$ has a representation on an interval $[a_j, b_j]$. By a linear change of parameter we may assume that $a_j = (j - 1)/p$, $b_j = j/p$. Let $\mathbf{g}_j$ be such a representation of $\gamma_j$ for each $j = 1, \ldots, p$. Then $\mathbf{g}_j(j/p) = \mathbf{g}_{j+1}(j/p)$. Let $\mathbf{g}$ be the function such that $\mathbf{g}(t) = \mathbf{g}_j(t)$ for $t \in [(j - 1)/p, j/p]$. Then $\mathbf{g}$ is a parametric representation which is piecewise of class $C^{(1)}$, and $\gamma$ is the curve which $\mathbf{g}$ represents. Let us call $\gamma$ the *sum* of these curves and write $\gamma = \gamma_1 + \cdots + \gamma_p$. Since an ordinary integral over $[a, b]$ is the sum of the integrals over the subintervals $[(j - 1)/p, j/p]$, we have

$$\int_{\gamma_1+\cdots+\gamma_p} \omega = \int_{\gamma_1} \omega + \cdots + \int_{\gamma_p} \omega. \tag{3–11}$$

**Example 2.** Let $\gamma$ be the boundary of a rectangle in $E^2$, directed counterclockwise as in Fig. 3–5. Let $\boldsymbol{\omega} = M\,dx + N\,dy$. Then

$$\int_\gamma \omega = \sum_{j=1}^{4} \int_{\gamma_j} \omega.$$

The most convenient representation for $\gamma_1$ is obtained by setting $g^1(t) = t$, $g^2(t) = c$, $a \le t \le b$. Taking similar representations for $\gamma_2, -\gamma_3, -\gamma_4$ and using (3–10), we find that

$$\int_\gamma \omega = \int_a^b M(t, c)\,dt + \int_c^d N(b, t)\,dt - \int_a^b M(t, d)\,dt - \int_c^d N(a, t)\,dt.$$

Let us now consider the case when $\boldsymbol{\omega}$ is an exact differential form, $\boldsymbol{\omega} = df$, where $f$ is of class $C^{(1)}$ on an open set $D$ containing the trace of $\gamma$. By the definition (3–8a),

$$\int_\gamma df = \int_a^b df[\mathbf{g}(t)] \cdot \mathbf{g}'(t)\,dt.$$

Let us use the formula

$$(f \circ \mathbf{g})'(t) = df[\mathbf{g}(t)] \cdot \mathbf{g}'(t).$$

This is a special case of the chain rule, which will be proved later (Section 4–4). When arc

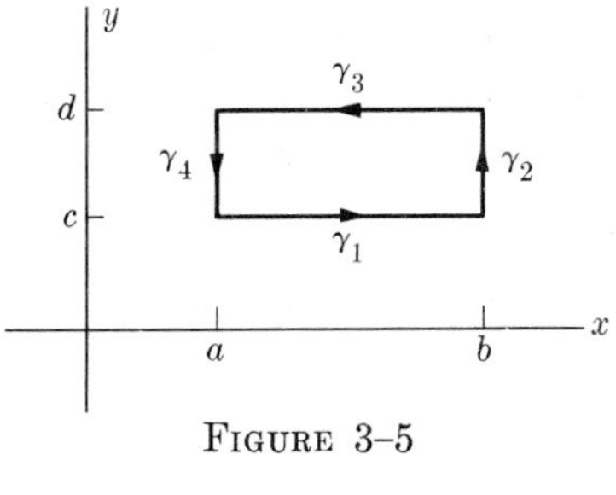


FIGURE 3–5

length is the parameter it says that the derivative at $s$ of $f \circ \mathbf{G}$ equals the derivative of $f$ in the direction of the unit tangent vector at $\mathbf{G}(\mathbf{s})$. By the fundamental theorem of calculus

$$\int_a^b (f \circ \mathbf{g})'(t)\, dt = f[\mathbf{g}(b)] - f[\mathbf{g}(a)].$$

Let $\mathbf{x}_0 = \mathbf{g}(a)$ and $\mathbf{x}_1 = \mathbf{g}(b)$ be the endpoints of $\gamma$. Then

$$\int_\gamma df = f(\mathbf{x}_1) - f(\mathbf{x}_0). \tag{3–12}$$

This is a generalization of the fundamental theorem of calculus. It shows that the line integral of an exact 1–form depends only on the endpoints of $\gamma$. In particular, if $\gamma$ is closed then the line integral is 0.

The following theorem shows that each of these properties characterizes exact 1-forms. We say that $\gamma$ *lies in* $D$ if its trace is a subset of $D$. By curve we mean here piecewise smooth curve.

**Theorem 7.** *Let $D \subset E^n$ be open, and $\boldsymbol{\omega}$ a continuous 1-form with domain $D$. The following three statements are equivalent:*

(1) *$\boldsymbol{\omega}$ is exact.*

(2) *For every closed curve $\gamma$ lying in $D$, $\int_\gamma \boldsymbol{\omega} = 0$.*

(3) *If $\gamma_1$ and $\gamma_2$ are any two curves lying in $D$ with the same initial endpoint and the same final endpoint, then $\int_{\gamma_1} \boldsymbol{\omega} = \int_{\gamma_2} \boldsymbol{\omega}$.* (See Fig. 3–6.)

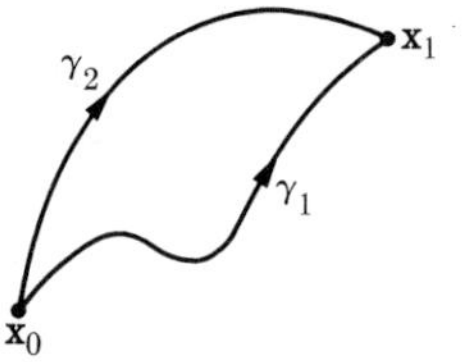


FIGURE 3–6

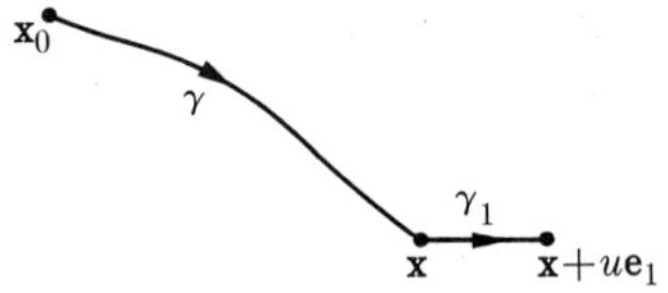


FIGURE 3–7

*Proof.* We have seen that (1) implies (2) in Theorem 7. If $\gamma_1$ and $\gamma_2$ have the same endpoints, then $\gamma_1 - \gamma_2$ is closed. If (2) holds, then

$$0 = \int_{\gamma_1 - \gamma_2} \boldsymbol{\omega} = \int_{\gamma_1} \boldsymbol{\omega} - \int_{\gamma_2} \boldsymbol{\omega}.$$

Hence (2) implies (3).

It remains to show that (3) implies (1). For simplicity let us assume that $D$ is connected. If $D$ is not connected, the construction to follow must be applied separately to each component (that is, maximal connected subset) of $D$.

Let $\mathbf{x}_0$ be some point of $D$, and define $f$ as follows. Since $D$ is open and connected, any point of $D$ can be joined to $\mathbf{x}_0$ by a curve (Section A–7). For every $\mathbf{x} \in D$ let

$$f(\mathbf{x}) = \int_\gamma \boldsymbol{\omega},$$

where $\gamma$ is any curve lying in $D$ with initial endpoint $\mathbf{x}_0$ and final endpoint $\mathbf{x}$. Since we are assuming (3) in Theorem 7, it does not matter which curve with these properties is chosen. Let us show that $df = \boldsymbol{\omega}$.

Given $\mathbf{x} \in D$, let $U$ be a neighborhood of $\mathbf{x}$ contained in $D$ and $\delta$ the radius of $U$. Let $0 < u < \delta$ and for each $i = 1, \ldots, n$ let $\gamma_i$ be the line segment from $\mathbf{x}$ to $\mathbf{x} + u\mathbf{e}_i$. (See Fig. 3–7.) Then

$$f(\mathbf{x} + u\mathbf{e}_i) - f(\mathbf{x}) = \int_{\gamma+\gamma_i} \boldsymbol{\omega} - \int_\gamma \boldsymbol{\omega} = \int_{\gamma_i} \boldsymbol{\omega}.$$

Let $\mathbf{g}_i(t) = \mathbf{x} + t\mathbf{e}_i$, $\psi_i(t) = \omega_i(\mathbf{x} + t\mathbf{e}_i)$. Then $\mathbf{g}_i$ represents $\gamma_i$ on $[0, u]$, and hence

$$\frac{1}{u}\,[f(\mathbf{x} + u\mathbf{e}_i) - f(\mathbf{x})] = \frac{1}{u}\int_{\gamma_i} \boldsymbol{\omega} = \frac{1}{u}\int_0^u \psi_i(t)\,dt.$$

Since $\omega_i$ is a continuous function, $\psi_i$ is continuous. Consequently, the right-hand side tends to $\psi_i(0) = \omega_i(\mathbf{x})$ as $u \to 0^+$ by the fundamental theorem of calculus. Similarly, $u^{-1}[f(\mathbf{x} + u\mathbf{e}_i) - f(\mathbf{x})]$ tends to $\omega_i(\mathbf{x})$ as $u \to 0^-$.

We have shown that each partial derivative of $f$ of order 1 exists at $\mathbf{x}$ and that

$$\frac{\partial f}{\partial x^i}(\mathbf{x}) = \omega_i(\mathbf{x}), \qquad i = 1, \ldots, n.$$

Therefore $df(\mathbf{x}) = \boldsymbol{\omega}(\mathbf{x})$. Since this is true for every $\mathbf{x} \in D$, $\boldsymbol{\omega} = df$. ∎

**Corollary.** *If $D$ is simply connected and $\boldsymbol{\omega}$ is of class $C^{(1)}$, then each of the statements* (1), (2), *and* (3) *of Theorem* 7 *is equivalent to the statement that $\boldsymbol{\omega}$ is closed.*

**Work.** Let $D$ be an open connected subset of $E^3$. In mechanics the idea of force field is considered. A force field assigns at each $\mathbf{x} \in D$ a linear function, which we shall call the *force covector acting at* $\mathbf{x}$ and shall denote by $\boldsymbol{\omega}(\mathbf{x})$. If $\mathbf{h}$ is a "small displacement" from $\mathbf{x}$, then the work done moving a particle along the line segment from $\mathbf{x}$ to $\mathbf{x} + \mathbf{h}$ is approximately $\boldsymbol{\omega}(\mathbf{x}) \cdot \mathbf{h}$. The force field is the differential form $\boldsymbol{\omega}$ of degree 1 whose value at each $\mathbf{x} \in D$ is the force covector $\boldsymbol{\omega}(\mathbf{x})$.

For present purposes it is simpler to regard force as a covector rather than a vector. However, one can also consider the *force vector* $\mathbf{F}(\mathbf{x}) = \omega_1(\mathbf{x})\mathbf{e}_1 + \omega_2(\mathbf{x})\mathbf{e}_2 + \omega_3(\mathbf{x})\mathbf{e}_3$ with the same components as $\boldsymbol{\omega}(\mathbf{x})$. This simple device for changing covectors into vectors is justified since we use the standard euclidean inner product. If $E^n$ is given another inner product, then the components of $\mathbf{F}(\mathbf{x})$ would be found by formula (1–14b).

Let $\gamma$ be a piecewise smooth curve lying in $D$. Using the notation on p. 79, with for sake of simplicity $s_j = t_{j-1}$, the vector $\mathbf{h}_j = \mathbf{g}(t_j) - \mathbf{g}(t_{j-1})$

is a displacement from $\mathbf{g}(t_{j-1})$, which is small if $\mu$ is small. The work done going along $\gamma$ from $\mathbf{g}(t_{j-1})$ to $\mathbf{g}(t_j)$ should be approximately $\boldsymbol{\omega}[\mathbf{g}(t_{j-1})] \cdot \mathbf{h}_j$. This suggests the following.

**Definition.** The *work* $w$ done in moving a particle along $\gamma$ is

$$w = \int_\gamma \boldsymbol{\omega}.$$

If arc length is used as parameter, then from the definition (3–8a),

$$w = \int_0^l \boldsymbol{\omega}[\mathbf{G}(s)] \cdot \mathbf{G}'(s)\, ds.$$

The expression $\boldsymbol{\omega}[\mathbf{G}(s)] \cdot \mathbf{G}'(s)$ is called the component of the field at $\mathbf{G}(s)$ in the direction of the unit tangent vector $\mathbf{G}'(s)$ to $\gamma$.

A force field $\boldsymbol{\omega}$ of class $C^{(1)}$ is called *conservative* if $\boldsymbol{\omega}$ is closed. By the corollary to Theorem 7 this is the same as saying $\boldsymbol{\omega}$ is exact if $D$ is simply connected. If $\boldsymbol{\omega}$ is exact and $\boldsymbol{\omega} = df$, then $f$ is a *potential* of the field $\boldsymbol{\omega}$. If $D$ is connected, $f$ is determined up to the addition of a constant function.

**Example 3.** Let $\boldsymbol{\omega} = -\rho^{-3}(x\,dx + y\,dy + z\,dz)$, where $\rho^2 = x^2 + y^2 + z^2$ and $D = E^3 - \{\mathbf{0}\}$. If we agree that $f(x, y, z) \to 0$ as $\rho \to \infty$, then the potential $f$ is given by $f(\mathbf{x}) = \rho^{-1}$. Except for a multiplicative constant it is the Newtonian potential due to a mass concentrated at $\mathbf{0}$.

**Steady fluid flow.** Let $\boldsymbol{\omega}(\mathbf{x})$ be interpreted as the velocity at $\mathbf{x}$ associated with a fluid flowing in $D$. It is assumed that the velocity at $\mathbf{x}$ does not vary with time. The component of the velocity in the direction of the unit tangent vector is $\boldsymbol{\omega}[\mathbf{G}(s)] \cdot \mathbf{G}'(s)$. The above expression $\int_\gamma \boldsymbol{\omega}$ is called the *circulation* along $\gamma$. The flow is called *irrotational* if $\int_\gamma \boldsymbol{\omega} = 0$ for every closed curve $\gamma$ which lies in some simply connected open subset of $D$. If $\boldsymbol{\omega}$ is of class $C^{(1)}$, this is equivalent to the fact that $\boldsymbol{\omega}$ is closed.

In Section 7–6 we shall again mention fluid flows, and shall define there the rotation covector curl $\boldsymbol{\omega}(\mathbf{x})$ which is everywhere $\mathbf{0}$ if the velocity field is irrotational.

## PROBLEMS

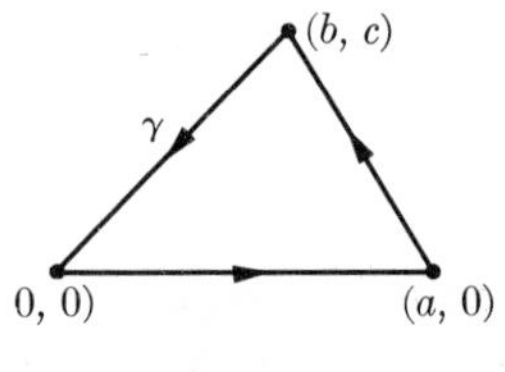

FIGURE 3–8

1. Evaluate $\frac{1}{2}\int_\gamma x\,dy - y\,dx$ in case:
   (a) $\gamma$ bounds the triangle shown in Fig. 3–8.
   (b) $\gamma$ is represented by $\mathbf{g}(t) = (a\cos t)\mathbf{e}_1 + (b\sin t)\mathbf{e}_2$, $0 \le t \le 2\pi$, where $a, b > 0$. Your answer should be the area of the set enclosed by $\gamma$. This is a very special case of Green's theorem (Section 7–6).
2. Let $\mathbf{g}_1(t) = t\mathbf{e}_1 + (2t - 1)\mathbf{e}_2$, $1 \le t \le 2$, and $\mathbf{g}_2(t) = (t + 1)\mathbf{e}_1 + (t^2 + t + 1)\mathbf{e}_2$, $0 \le t \le 1$. Evaluate $\int_{\gamma_1} \boldsymbol{\omega}$ and $\int_{\gamma_2} \boldsymbol{\omega}$ for each of the 1-forms (a), (c), and (d) in Problem 3, Section 2–6, where $\gamma_1$ and $\gamma_2$ are the curves represented by $\mathbf{g}_1$ and $\mathbf{g}_2$, respectively.

3. Let $n = 1$, $\omega = f\,dx$, and $\gamma$ be the interval $[a, b]$ directed from $a$ to $b$. Show that

$$\int_\gamma \omega = \int_a^b f(x)\,dx.$$

4. Let $D \subset E^2$ be open and simply connected, and $u, v$ functions of class $C^{(1)}$ which satisfy

$$\frac{\partial u}{\partial x} = \frac{\partial v}{\partial y}, \qquad \frac{\partial v}{\partial x} = -\frac{\partial u}{\partial y}.$$

[*Note:* These two first-order partial differential equations are called the Cauchy-Riemann equations. They are fundamental to the theory of complex analytic functions.]
Show that for any closed curve $\gamma$ lying in $D$,

$$\int_\gamma u\,dx - v\,dy = 0, \qquad \int_\gamma v\,dx + u\,dy = 0.$$

5. Show that the force field $\omega = \psi(\rho^2)(x\,dx + y\,dy + z\,dz)$ is conservative, where $\psi$ is any function of class $C^{(1)}$ on $E^1$ and $\rho^2 = x^2 + y^2 + z^2$. Find its potential $f$, if $f(\mathbf{0}) = 0$.

*Other line integrals.* The following problems deal not with integrals of 1-forms, but with some other types of line integrals which often occur.

6. If $f$ is continuous on $D$, then (by definition)

$$\int_\gamma f\,ds = \int_a^b f[\mathbf{g}(t)]|\mathbf{g}'(t)|\,dt.$$

Show that this integral does not depend on the particular representation $\mathbf{g}$ chosen for $\gamma$. In particular, if arc length is the parameter, then

$$\int_\gamma f\,ds = \int_0^l f[\mathbf{G}(s)]\,ds.$$

7. The *moment of inertia* of a curve $\gamma$ about a point $\mathbf{x}_0$ is $\int_\gamma |\mathbf{x} - \mathbf{x}_0|^2\,ds$. Find the moment of inertia about $\mathbf{0}$ of the line segment in $E^3$ joining $\mathbf{e}_1$ and $\mathbf{e}_2 + 2\mathbf{e}_3$.

8. The *centroid* $\bar{\mathbf{x}}$ of a curve $\gamma$ is the point such that

$$\bar{x}^i = \left(\int_\gamma x^i\,ds\right)/l, \qquad i = 1, \ldots, n,$$

where $l$ is the length of $\gamma$.

(a) Find the centroid of the helical curve in Problem 3, Section 3–2.

(b) Find its moment of inertia about $\pi\mathbf{e}_3$.

9. Let $W$ be continuous on $D \times E^n$ and satisfy the homogeneity condition $W(\mathbf{x}, c\mathbf{h}) = cW(\mathbf{x}, \mathbf{h})$ whenever $c \geq 0$. Then (by definition)

$$\int_\gamma W = \int_a^b W[\mathbf{g}(t), \mathbf{g}'(t)]\,dt.$$

Show that:

(a) This integral does not depend on the particular representation $\mathbf{g}$ of $\gamma$.
(b) If $W(\mathbf{x}, \mathbf{h}) = \boldsymbol{\omega}(\mathbf{x}) \cdot \mathbf{h}$, then $\int_\gamma W = \int_\gamma \boldsymbol{\omega}$; and if $W(\mathbf{x}, \mathbf{h}) = f(\mathbf{x})|\mathbf{h}|$, $\int_\gamma W = \int_\gamma f\, ds$.
(c) Let $W(\mathbf{x}, \mathbf{h}) = \|\mathbf{h}\|$, where $\|\ \|$ is any norm on $E^n$ (Section 1-6). Then $\int_\gamma W$ is called the length of $\gamma$ with respect to this norm. Show that if $\gamma$ is the line segment joining $\mathbf{x}_1$ and $\mathbf{x}_2$, then the length is $\|\mathbf{x}_1 - \mathbf{x}_2\|$.

## *3-4 GRADIENT METHOD

In Section 2-5 we found relative extrema of a function $f$ by calculating the critical points and testing them by Theorem 6. However, in practice the equation $df(\mathbf{x}) = \mathbf{0}$ for the critical points can be explicitly solved only when $f$ has some special form. On p. 61 a method for finding critical points approximately was indicated. It is called the gradient method, or method of steepest ascent, and will now be described more precisely.

Let $D$ be an open set and $\mathbf{F} = (F^1, \ldots, F^n)$ a vector-valued function whose components $F^i$ are of class $C^{(1)}$ on $D$. A function $\mathbf{g}$ from an interval $J$ into $E^n$ is called a *solution* of the system of first-order ordinary differential equations

$$\frac{dx^i}{dt} = F^i(\mathbf{x}), \qquad i = 1, \ldots, n,$$

if $\mathbf{g}'(t) = \mathbf{F}[\mathbf{g}(t)]$ for every $t \in J$. An existence theorem for such systems (see [5], Chap. 1) states that given $\mathbf{x}_1 \in D$ there is a solution $\mathbf{g}$ on some open interval $J$ containing 0 such that $\mathbf{g}(0) = \mathbf{x}_1$.

Now let $f$ be of class $C^{(2)}$ on $D$. Let $\mathbf{F}(\mathbf{x}) = \operatorname{grad} f(\mathbf{x})$ be the gradient vector of $f$ at $\mathbf{x}$. Assume that $\mathbf{x}_1$ is not a critical point of $f$. A solution $\mathbf{g}$ of

$$\mathbf{g}'(t) = \operatorname{grad} f[\mathbf{g}(t)], \qquad \mathbf{g}(0) = \mathbf{x}_1, \qquad (3\text{-}13)$$

is called a *gradient trajectory of $f$ through* $\mathbf{x}_1$. We shall prove later (Section 4-7) that grad $f(\mathbf{x})$ is a normal vector to the level set of $f$ containing $\mathbf{x}$. Therefore the gradient trajectories are normal to the level sets, as indicated in Fig. 3-9.

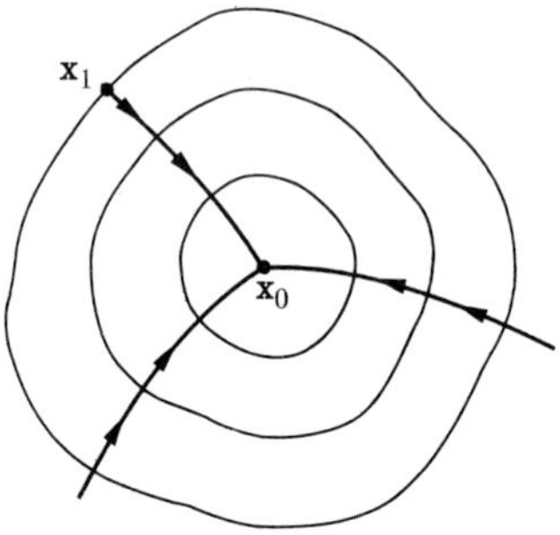

FIGURE 3-9

Let $\phi(t) = f[\mathbf{g}(t)]$. By the chain rule, which will be proved in Section 4-4,

$$\phi'(t) = \operatorname{grad} f[\mathbf{g}(t)] \cdot \mathbf{g}'(t) = |\operatorname{grad} f[\mathbf{g}(t)]|^2 > 0.$$

Hence $\phi$ is increasing. In other words, *the values of $f$ increase along each gradient trajectory as $t$ increases.*

Let us assume that there is a gradient trajectory $\mathbf{g}$ through $\mathbf{x}_1$ which is defined for every $t \geq 0$.

By the uniqueness theorem for systems of differential equations ([5], Chap. 1) $\mathbf{g}(t)$ is never a critical point. However, one may ask whether $\mathbf{g}(t)$ approaches a critical point $\mathbf{x}_0$ as $t \to +\infty$. While this is not always true, we shall prove two partial results in this direction.

**Proposition.** *If* $\mathbf{g}(t)$ *tends to a limit* $\mathbf{x}_0$ *as* $t \to +\infty$, *then* $\mathbf{x}_0$ *is a critical point of* $f$.

*Proof.* Define $\phi$ as above. Then $\phi$ is increasing and

$$f(\mathbf{x}_0) = \lim_{t \to +\infty} \phi(t).$$

Suppose that $\operatorname{grad} f(\mathbf{x}_0) \neq \mathbf{0}$. Since $\operatorname{grad} f$ is continuous there exists a neighborhood $U$ of $\mathbf{x}_0$ and $m > 0$ such that $|\operatorname{grad} f(\mathbf{x})| \geq m$ for every $\mathbf{x} \in U$. There exists $t_1$ such that $\mathbf{g}(t) \in U$ for every $t \geq t_1$. By the fundamental theorem of calculus, if $t_1 < t_2$ then

$$\phi(t_2) = \phi(t_1) + \int_{t_1}^{t_2} \phi'(t)\, dt \geq \phi(t_1) + m^2(t_2 - t_1).$$

The right-hand side tends to $+\infty$ as $t_2 \to +\infty$, but $\phi(t_2) \leq f(\mathbf{x}_0)$. This is a contradiction. Hence $\operatorname{grad} f(\mathbf{x}_0) = \mathbf{0}$. ▮

*Note:* It may happen that a trajectory $\mathbf{g}$ remains in a compact set $K \subset D$ for every $t \geq 0$, but $\mathbf{g}(t)$ does not approach a limit $\mathbf{x}_0$ as $t \to +\infty$. In that case it can be shown that $\mathbf{g}$ has a "limit set" $B$, which consists of all accumulation points of sequences $[\mathbf{g}(t_k)]$ for all possible sequences $t_1, t_2, \ldots$ tending to $+\infty$. $B$ is a compact, connected subset of the level set $\{\mathbf{x} : f(\mathbf{x}) = C\}$, where $C = \lim_{t\to\infty} \phi(t)$, and every point of $B$ is critical. If $f$ has only isolated critical points, then $B$ is a single point $\mathbf{x}_0$ and $\mathbf{g}(t) \to \mathbf{x}_0$ as $t \to \infty$. We shall not prove this.

However, let us show that if $\mathbf{x}_0$ is a nondegenerate critical point at which $f$ has a relative maximum, then any trajectory starting sufficiently near $\mathbf{x}_0$ leads to $\mathbf{x}_0$.

**Proposition.** *Let* $\mathbf{x}_0$ *be a nondegenerate critical point such that* $Q(\mathbf{x}_0, \ )$ *is negative definite. Then there is a neighborhood* $U$ *of* $\mathbf{x}_0$ *such that* $\mathbf{x}_0 = \lim_{t\to\infty} \mathbf{g}(t)$ *provided* $\mathbf{x}_1 \in U$.

*Proof.* By Problem 8, Section 2–5, there exists $m > 0$ such that $Q(\mathbf{x}_0, \mathbf{h}) \leq -m|\mathbf{h}|^2$ for every $\mathbf{h}$. Since $f$ is of class $C^{(2)}$ there is a neighborhood $U$ of $\mathbf{x}_0$ such that $|f_{ij}(\mathbf{x}_0 + s\mathbf{h}) - f_{ij}(\mathbf{x}_0)| \leq m/2n^2$ for $i, j = 1, \ldots, n$, whenever $\mathbf{x}_0 + \mathbf{h} \in U$ and $s \in (0, 1)$. Since $f_i(\mathbf{x}_0) = 0$ there is by the mean value theorem $s_i \in (0, 1)$ such that

$$f_i(\mathbf{x}_0 + \mathbf{h}) = \sum_{j=1}^{n} f_{ij}(\mathbf{x}_0 + s_i\mathbf{h})h^j.$$

If $\mathbf{x} \in U$ and $\mathbf{h} = \mathbf{x} - \mathbf{x}_0$, then

$$\text{grad}\, f(\mathbf{x}) \cdot (\mathbf{x} - \mathbf{x}_0) = \sum_{i,j=1}^{n} f_{ij}(\mathbf{x}_0 + s_i\mathbf{h})h^i h^j \leq -\frac{m}{2}|\mathbf{h}|^2.$$

Now let $\psi(t) = |\mathbf{g}(t) - \mathbf{x}_0|^2$, the square of the distance from $\mathbf{x}_0$. Taking $\mathbf{x} = \mathbf{g}(t)$, we have provided $\mathbf{g}(t) \in U$

$$\psi'(t) = 2[\mathbf{g}(t) - \mathbf{x}_0] \cdot \mathbf{g}'(t) \leq -m|\mathbf{g}(t) - \mathbf{x}_0|^2,$$

which becomes $\psi'(t) \leq -m\psi(t)$. Now $\mathbf{g}(0) = \mathbf{x}_1 \in U$, and since $\psi$ is decreasing, $\mathbf{g}(t) \in U$ for every $t \geq 0$. Dividing by $\psi(t)$ in the inequality $\psi'(t) \leq -m\psi(t)$ and integrating over $[0, t]$,

$$\log \psi(t) - \log \psi(0) \leq -mt.$$

The right-hand side tends to $-\infty$ as $t \to \infty$. Hence so does $\log \psi(t)$; and $\psi(t)$ tends to 0. ▌

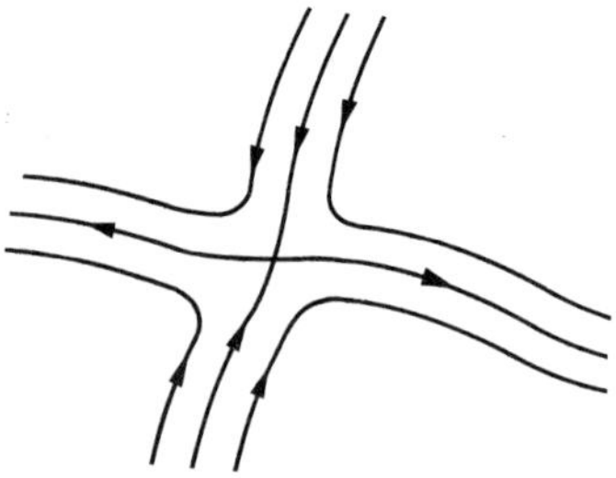

FIGURE 3–10

Figure 3–9 indicates the behavior of the level sets and gradient trajectories near a nondegenerate maximum. The situation is similar near a nondegenerate minimum. The gradient trajectories in that case are followed as $t \to -\infty$.

Near a saddle point ($n = 2$) the behavior of the trajectories is indicated in Fig. 3–10.

**Example 1.** Let $f(x, y) = x^2 - y^2$. The equations of the gradient trajectories are

$$\frac{dx}{dt} = 2x, \qquad \frac{dy}{dt} = -2y,$$

whose solutions are $g^1(t) = x_1 \exp(2t)$, $g^2(t) = y_1 \exp(-2t)$. The trajectories lie on the hyperbolas $xy = k$ orthogonal to the level sets $x^2 - y^2 = c$, and on the coordinate axes. Only trajectories starting from points $(0, y_1)$ lead to the saddle point $(0, 0)$.

## PROBLEMS

1. Sketch the level sets and gradient trajectories.

   (a) $f(x, y) = 1 - x^2 - 2y^2$.

   (b) $f(x, y) = xy + y$.

2. Let $f$ be a strictly concave function on $E^n$ which has an absolute maximum at $\mathbf{x}_0$. By Theorem 5, $f$ has no other critical points. Consider any gradient trajectory $\mathbf{g}$.

   (a) Let $\psi(t) = |\mathbf{g}(t) - \mathbf{x}_0|^2$. Show that $\psi$ is nonincreasing.

   (b) Show that $\psi(t) \to 0$, and hence $\mathbf{g}(t) \to \mathbf{x}_0$, as $t \to +\infty$.

3. Let $\mathbf{G}$ be the representation with arc length as parameter of a gradient trajectory $\mathbf{g}$. Show that $\mathbf{G}'(s)$ is the direction of the gradient at $\mathbf{G}(s)$. See pp. 61, 78.

CHAPTER 4

# Vector-Valued Functions of Several Variables

In this chapter we shall study the differential calculus of functions of several variables with values in $E^n$. Among the main results will be the theorems about composition and inverses, and the implicit function theorem. Later in the chapter, subsets of $E^n$ which are smooth manifolds are considered, and the spaces of tangent and normal vectors at a point of a smooth manifold are found. These ideas are then applied to obtain the Lagrange multiplier rule for constrained extremum problems.

Functions with values in $E^n$ will be called *transformations* rather than vector-valued functions. This term has a useful geometric connotation, and it also agrees with rather common usage. Some authors use instead the term "mapping." The differential calculus of transformations is based on local linear approximations, just as for the special case ($n = 1$) of real-valued functions already considered in Chapter 2. Consequently, it is first necessary to review some results about linear transformations. This is done in Section 4–2.

## 4–1 TRANSFORMATIONS

Let $n$ and $r$ be positive integers. Let $\mathbf{g}$ be a function with domain $\Delta \subset E^r$ and values in $E^n$. Such a vector-valued function $\mathbf{g}$ is called a *transformation* from $\Delta$ into $E^n$. Let points of $\Delta$ be denoted by $\mathbf{t} = (t^1, \ldots, t^r)$. The *image* of a set $B \subset \Delta$ is the set $\{\mathbf{g}(\mathbf{t}) : \mathbf{t} \in B\}$. It is denoted by $\mathbf{g}(B)$. The *inverse image* of a set $A \subset E^n$ is the set $\{\mathbf{t} \in \Delta : \mathbf{g}(\mathbf{t}) \in A\}$. It is denoted by $\mathbf{g}^{-1}(A)$. These ideas are indicated schematically in Fig. 4–1.

We recall that if $\mathbf{g}$ is continuous then the image of any compact set is compact and the image of any connected set is connected. Moreover, if $\mathbf{g}$ is continuous then the inverse image of any open set is open relative to $\Delta$. See Section A–6. The inverse image of a compact set under a continuous transformation need not be compact, nor the inverse image of a connected set connected. The image of an open set need not be open.

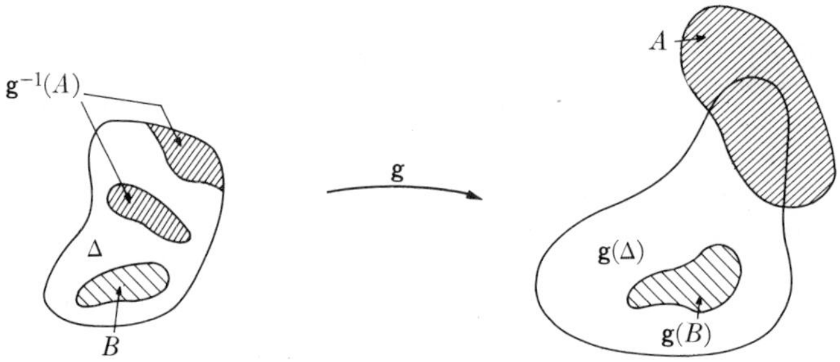


FIGURE 4-1

**Example 1.** Let $n = 1$. If we regard $E^1$ as a 1-dimensional vector space over itself, then every real-valued function is a transformation.

**Example 2.** Let $r = 1$, $\Delta = [a, b]$, and $\mathbf{g}$ be a parametric representation of a curve $\gamma$ as in Section 3-2. The image of $\Delta$ is the trace of the curve. If $A = \{\mathbf{x}\}$ is the set consisting of a single point $\mathbf{x}$ of the trace, then $\mathbf{g}^{-1}(A)$ is a finite subset of $\Delta$. The number of its elements is the multiplicity of $\mathbf{x}$.

**Example 3.** Let $n = r = 2$. Points of the domain $\Delta$ are denoted by $(s, t)$ and those of the image $\mathbf{g}(\Delta)$ by $(x, y)$. It is helpful to think of two copies of the plane $E^2$. The first contains $\Delta$ and will be called the *st*-plane. The second contains $\mathbf{g}(\Delta)$ and will be called the *xy*-plane.

In our example we let $\Delta$ be the whole *st*-plane, and

$$\mathbf{g}(s, t) = (s^2 + t^2)\mathbf{e}_1 + 2st\mathbf{e}_2$$

for every $(s, t) \in E^2$. If $(x, y) \in \mathbf{g}(\Delta)$, then $x = s^2 + t^2$, $y = 2st$ and $x + y \geq 0$, $x - y \geq 0$. Therefore $\mathbf{g}(\Delta)$ is contained in the quadrant $Q$ shown in Fig. 4-2. In fact, $\mathbf{g}(\Delta) = Q$. This is seen as follows: Let $C$ be a circle with center $(0, 0)$ and radius $a > 0$. Points of $C$ are given by $s = a \cos \phi$, $t = a \sin \phi$, where $0 \leq \phi \leq 2\pi$. The image $\mathbf{g}(C)$ is the trace of the curve represented on $[0, 2\pi]$ by

$$\mathbf{g}(a \cos \phi, a \sin \phi) = a^2\mathbf{e}_1 + (a^2 \sin 2\phi)\mathbf{e}_2.$$

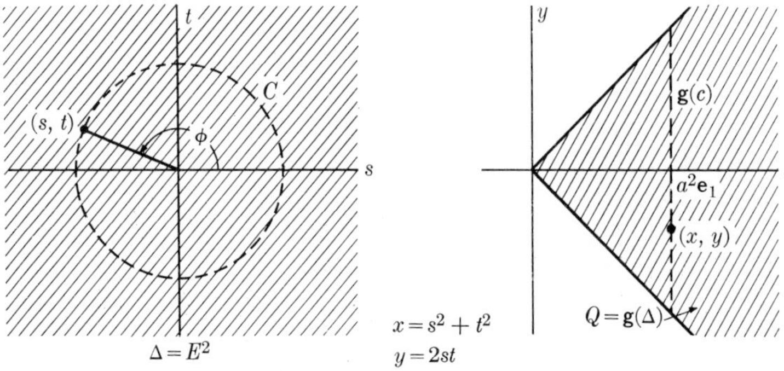


FIGURE 4-2

This trace is the vertical line segment shown in Fig. 4–2. By letting $a$ take all possible nonnegative values, one gets a collection of line segments covering $Q$. If $a = 0$, the line segment degenerates to the point $(0, 0)$. This shows that $Q = \mathbf{g}(\Delta)$.

The *components* $g^1, \ldots, g^n$ of a transformation $\mathbf{g}$ with respect to the standard basis for $E^n$ are the real-valued functions such that

$$\mathbf{g}(\mathbf{t}) = (g^1(\mathbf{t}), \ldots, g^n(\mathbf{t})) = \sum_{i=1}^{n} g^i(\mathbf{t})\mathbf{e}_i$$

for every $\mathbf{t} \in \Delta$. In Example 3,

$$g^1(s, t) = s^2 + t^2, \quad g^2(s, t) = 2st.$$

**Composition and inverses.** The composite of two transformations $\mathbf{f}$ and $\mathbf{g}$ is denoted by $\mathbf{f} \circ \mathbf{g}$. It is defined whenever $\mathbf{g}$ has its values in the domain of $\mathbf{f}$. We recall that if $\mathbf{f}$ and $\mathbf{g}$ are continuous, then the composite is also continuous (Proposition A–7). In Section 4–4 we shall prove that if $\mathbf{f}$ and $\mathbf{g}$ are differentiable, then $\mathbf{f} \circ \mathbf{g}$ is also differentiable.

A transformation $\mathbf{g}$ is *univalent* if distinct points of $\Delta$ have distinct images; that is, if $\mathbf{g}(\mathbf{t}_1) = \mathbf{g}(\mathbf{t}_2)$ implies $\mathbf{t}_1 = \mathbf{t}_2$. (The equivalent term "*one-one* transformation" is also used.) If $\mathbf{g}$ is univalent, let $\mathbf{g}^{-1}$ be the transformation whose value at each point $\mathbf{x} \in \mathbf{g}(\Delta)$ is the point $\mathbf{t} \in \Delta$ such that $\mathbf{g}(\mathbf{t}) = \mathbf{x}$. Then $\mathbf{g}^{-1}$ has domain $\mathbf{g}(\Delta)$ and

$$\mathbf{g}^{-1}[\mathbf{g}(\mathbf{t})] = \mathbf{t}, \quad \mathbf{g}[\mathbf{g}^{-1}(\mathbf{x})] = \mathbf{x}$$

for every $\mathbf{t} \in \Delta$ and $\mathbf{x} \in \mathbf{g}(\Delta)$. The transformation $\mathbf{g}^{-1}$ is called the *inverse* of $\mathbf{g}$. The notation $\mathbf{g}^{-1}(A)$ for inverse image of a set is consistent with this one. If $\mathbf{g}$ is univalent and $A \subset \mathbf{g}(\Delta)$, then $\mathbf{g}^{-1}(A)$ is the image of $A$ under $\mathbf{g}^{-1}$.

**Example 3 (continued).** This transformation $\mathbf{g}$ is not univalent. If $(x, y) = \mathbf{g}(s, t)$, then $(s + t)^2 = x + y$, $(s - t)^2 = x - y$. These equations have four solutions for $(s, t)$ if $(x, y)$ is interior to $Q$. However, if we take in each case the principal square root, then

$$s - t = \sqrt{x - y}, \quad s + t = \sqrt{x + y},$$

$$s = \frac{\sqrt{x + y} + \sqrt{x - y}}{2}, \quad t = \frac{\sqrt{x + y} - \sqrt{x - y}}{2}.$$

Such points $(s, t)$ belong to $Q$ (regarded as a subset of the $st$-plane). Let $\tilde{\mathbf{g}}$ be the restriction of $\mathbf{g}$ to $Q$. Then $\tilde{\mathbf{g}}$ is univalent and $\tilde{\mathbf{g}}(Q) = \mathbf{g}(\Delta) = Q$. The value of the inverse $\tilde{\mathbf{g}}^{-1}$ at any $(x, y) \in Q$ is

$$\tilde{\mathbf{g}}^{-1}(x, y) = \left(\frac{\sqrt{x + y} + \sqrt{x - y}}{2}, \frac{\sqrt{x + y} - \sqrt{x - y}}{2}\right).$$

The main theorem about inverses of transformations appears in Section 4–5.

**PROBLEMS**

1. Let $n = 1, \Delta = E^r$, and $g(\mathbf{t}) = \mathbf{t} \cdot \mathbf{t} - 2|\mathbf{t}|$.
   (a) Find the image $g(E^r)$.
   (b) For each $c$ find the inverse image of the semi-infinite interval $[c, \infty)$.
2. In Example 3 find:
   (a) The image of any vertical line $s = c$.
   (b) The inverse image of any line $y = mx$ through the origin.
   (c) The image of the circular disk bounded by $C$ in Fig. 4–2.
3. Let $\mathbf{g}(s, t) = |s - t|\mathbf{e}_1 + |s + t|\mathbf{e}_2$, $\Delta = E^2$. Find $\mathbf{g}(E^2)$ and answer questions (a), (b), and (c) in Problem 2 for this transformation.
4. Let $\mathbf{g}(s, t) = (t \cos 2\pi s)\mathbf{e}_1 + (t \sin 2\pi s)\mathbf{e}_2 + (1 - t)\mathbf{e}_3$, $\Delta = E^2$.
   (a) Show that $\mathbf{g}(E^2)$ is a cone with vertex $\mathbf{e}_3$.
   (b) What is the image of the square $\{(s, t): 0 \leq s \leq 1, 0 \leq t \leq 1\}$?
   (c) Find $\mathbf{g}^{-1}(\{\mathbf{e}_3\})$ and $\mathbf{g}^{-1}(\{\mathbf{e}_1\})$.
5. Let $\mathbf{g}(s, t) = 1/(s^2 + st + t^2)\mathbf{e}_1 + 1/(s^2 + st + t^2)^2\mathbf{e}_2$, $\Delta = \{(s, t) : 0 < s^2 + t^2 \leq 1\}$.
   (a) Show that $\mathbf{g}(\Delta)$ is part of the parabola $y = x^2$, and find it.
   (b) Find $\mathbf{g}^{-1}(\{(c, c^2)\})$.

## 4–2 LINEAR AND AFFINE TRANSFORMATIONS

In this section we shall collect some facts about linear transformations from one euclidean vector space into another. For those results which are stated without proof, references are given to [12]. However, the results in question are standard in linear algebra and may be found in practically any good book on the subject.

**Definition.** A set $P \subset E^n$ is a *vector subspace* of $E^n$ if:

(1) The sum $\mathbf{x} + \mathbf{y}$ of any two elements $\mathbf{x}, \mathbf{y} \in P$ is also an element of $P$; and

(2) Any scalar multiple $c\mathbf{x}$ of an element $\mathbf{x} \in P$ is also an element of $P$.

In other words, $P$ is a vector subspace of $E^n$ if $P$ provided with the addition and scalar multiplication in $E^n$ satisfies the axioms for a vector space. $P$ has a dimension $\rho$, and $0 \leq \rho \leq n$. If $\rho = 0$ then $P = \{\mathbf{0}\}$. If $\rho = 1$, then $P$ is a line containing $\mathbf{0}$; if $\rho = 2$, $P$ is a plane containing $\mathbf{0}$, and so on.

**Definition.** A transformation $\mathbf{L}$ from $E^r$ into $E^n$ is *linear* if:

(1) $\mathbf{L}(\mathbf{s} + \mathbf{t}) = \mathbf{L}(\mathbf{s}) + \mathbf{L}(\mathbf{t})$ for every $\mathbf{s}, \mathbf{t} \in E^r$; and

(2) $\mathbf{L}(c\mathbf{s}) = c\mathbf{L}(\mathbf{s})$ for every $\mathbf{s} \in E^r$ and scalar $c$.

This is a special case of the definition in Section A–2 of the Appendix.

If $\mathbf{L}$ is a linear transformation, then the set $\mathbf{L}(E^r)$ is a vector subspace of $E^n$. To prove this, let $\mathbf{x}, \mathbf{y} \in \mathbf{L}(E^r)$. Then $\mathbf{x} = \mathbf{L}(\mathbf{s})$, $\mathbf{y} = \mathbf{L}(\mathbf{t})$ for some

$\mathbf{s}, \mathbf{t} \in E^r$. But $\mathbf{x} + \mathbf{y} = \mathbf{L}(\mathbf{s}) + \mathbf{L}(\mathbf{t}) = \mathbf{L}(\mathbf{s} + \mathbf{t})$. Hence $\mathbf{x} + \mathbf{y} \in \mathbf{L}(E^r)$. Similarly, if $\mathbf{x} \in \mathbf{L}(E^r)$ then $c\mathbf{x} \in \mathbf{L}(E^r)$ for every scalar $c$. The dimension $\rho$ of the vector space $\mathbf{L}(E^r)$ is called the *rank* of $\mathbf{L}$. The *kernel* of $\mathbf{L}$ is $\{\mathbf{t} : \mathbf{L}(\mathbf{t}) = \mathbf{0}\}$. It is a vector subspace of $E^r$ (Problem 2). The dimension $\nu$ of the kernel is called the *nullity* of $\mathbf{L}$. The rank and nullity are related by (see [12], p. 66)

$$\rho + \nu = r. \tag{4–1}$$

**The matrix of *L*.** Let us denote the standard basis vectors for $E^r$ by $\boldsymbol{\epsilon}_1, \ldots, \boldsymbol{\epsilon}_r$ and those for $E^n$ by $\mathbf{e}_1, \ldots, \mathbf{e}_n$. With a linear transformation $\mathbf{L}$ and these bases is associated a matrix $(c_j^i)$ with $n$ rows and $r$ columns, in the following way. For each $j = 1, \ldots, r$ let $\mathbf{v}_j = \mathbf{L}(\boldsymbol{\epsilon}_j)$, and let $c_j^i$ be the $i$th component of the vector $\mathbf{v}_j$:

$$\mathbf{v}_j = \sum_{i=1}^{n} c_j^i \mathbf{e}_i, \qquad j = 1, \ldots, r. \tag{4–2}$$

Then $(c_j^i)$ is the *matrix* of $\mathbf{L}$, and $\mathbf{v}_1, \ldots, \mathbf{v}_r$ are the column vectors of this matrix. Note that the superscript $i$ indicates the *row*, and subscript $j$ the *column*, of the matrix.

Actually, for any pair of bases for $E^r$ and $E^n$ there is a matrix associated with $\mathbf{L}$. It is shown in linear algebra that by suitable choice of bases the associated matrix can be made to have some special form [for instance, the Jordan canonical form if $r = n$ ([12], p. 207)]. What we have called "the" matrix of $\mathbf{L}$ is the matrix corresponding to the standard bases for $E^r$ and $E^n$.

Since $\mathbf{L}$ is linear,

$$\mathbf{L}(\mathbf{t}) = \mathbf{L}\left(\sum_{j=1}^{r} t^j \boldsymbol{\epsilon}_j\right) = \sum_{j=1}^{r} t^j \mathbf{L}(\boldsymbol{\epsilon}_j).$$

Hence $\mathbf{L}(\mathbf{t})$ is a linear combination of the column vectors:

$$\mathbf{L}(\mathbf{t}) = \sum_{j=1}^{r} t^j \mathbf{v}_j. \tag{4–3a}$$

If $\mathbf{x} = \mathbf{L}(\mathbf{t})$ and we take components of each side of (4–3a), then

$$x^i = \sum_{j=1}^{r} c_j^i t^j, \qquad i = 1, \ldots, n. \tag{4–4a}$$

The components $L^1, \ldots, L^n$ of $\mathbf{L}$ are real-valued linear functions, in other words, covectors. Hence

$$x^i = L^i(\mathbf{t}) = \mathbf{w}^i \cdot \mathbf{t},$$

where $\mathbf{w}^i$ is just another notation for the covector $L^i$ (p. 12). From (4–4a) the components of $\mathbf{w}^i$ are the entries $c_1^i, \ldots, c_n^i$ of the $i$th row. For that reason

$\mathbf{w}^1, \ldots, \mathbf{w}^n$ are called the *row covectors* of the matrix $(c_j^i)$.

$$\begin{array}{c} \\ \mathbf{w}^1 \\ \mathbf{w}^2 \\ \mathbf{w}^3 \\ \vdots \\ \mathbf{w}^n \end{array} \begin{array}{c} \begin{array}{ccccc} \mathbf{v}_1 & \mathbf{v}_2 & \mathbf{v}_3 & \ldots & \mathbf{v}_r \end{array} \\ \begin{pmatrix} c_1^1 & c_2^1 & c_3^1 & \ldots & c_r^1 \\ c_1^2 & c_2^2 & \ldots & \ldots & c_r^2 \\ c_1^3 & \ldots & \ldots & \ldots & c_r^3 \\ \vdots & & & & \vdots \\ c_1^n & \ldots & \ldots & \ldots & c_r^n \end{pmatrix} \end{array}$$

By (4–3a) the column vectors $\mathbf{v}_1, \ldots, \mathbf{v}_r$ span $\mathbf{L}(E^r)$. The rank $\rho$ equals the largest number of linearly independent column vectors of the matrix. Since row rank equals column rank ([12], p. 105), $\rho$ is also the largest number of linearly independent row covectors of the matrix.

**Composition.** Let $\mathbf{L}$ be linear from $E^r$ into $E^n$, and $\mathbf{M}$ linear from $E^n$ into $E^p$. The composite $\mathbf{M} \circ \mathbf{L}$ is linear. Its matrix is the product of the matrices of $\mathbf{M}$ and $\mathbf{L}$ (Problem 4).

**The case $r = n$.** Let $\mathbf{I}$ denote the identity linear transformation, $\mathbf{I}(\mathbf{t}) = \mathbf{t}$ for every $\mathbf{t} \in E^r$. Its matrix is $(\delta_j^i)$, which has 1 for each element of the principal diagonal and 0 elsewhere. $\mathbf{L}$ is *nonsingular* if it has rank $\rho = n$, and *singular* if $\rho < n$. A nonsingular linear transformation $\mathbf{L}$ has an inverse $\mathbf{L}^{-1}$, which is also a linear transformation with

$$\mathbf{L}^{-1} \circ \mathbf{L} = \mathbf{L} \circ \mathbf{L}^{-1} = \mathbf{I}.$$

If $r = n$, then the $n \times n$ matrix $(c_j^i)$ has a determinant, denoted by $\det (c_j^i)$. This number will also be called the determinant of $\mathbf{L}$. Thus by definition

$$\det \mathbf{L} = \det (c_j^i).$$

Among the properties of determinants we recall:

$$\det (\mathbf{M} \circ \mathbf{L}) = \det \mathbf{M} \det \mathbf{L}, \qquad \text{(See Reference [12], p. 143.)}$$

$$\det \mathbf{L} = 0 \quad \text{if and only if} \quad \mathbf{L} \text{ is singular.} \qquad \text{(See Reference [12], p. 150.)}$$

By (4–1) $\mathbf{L}$ is singular if and only if $\nu > 0$. But $\nu > 0$ means that $\mathbf{L}(\mathbf{t}) = \mathbf{0}$ for some $\mathbf{t} \neq \mathbf{0}$. Therefore, from (4–4a) the system of homogeneous linear equations

$$0 = \sum_{j=1}^{n} c_j^i t^j, \qquad i = 1, \ldots, n \tag{4–5}$$

has a nontrivial solution if and only if $\det \mathbf{L} = 0$.

In later chapters we shall see that the absolute value of the determinant is the ratio of $n$-dimensional volumes, and the sign of the determinant determines an orientation.

**Example 1.** Let $n = r = p = 2$. Let $\mathbf{L}(s, t) = (2s + t)\mathbf{e}_1 + (3s - t)\mathbf{e}_2$. The matrix of $\mathbf{L}$ is

$$\begin{pmatrix} 2 & 1 \\ 3 & -1 \end{pmatrix}.$$

The row covectors are $\mathbf{w}^1 = 2\boldsymbol{\epsilon}^1 + \boldsymbol{\epsilon}^2$, $\mathbf{w}^2 = 3\boldsymbol{\epsilon}^1 - \boldsymbol{\epsilon}^2$. The column vectors are $\mathbf{v}_1 = 2\mathbf{e}_1 + 3\mathbf{e}_2$, $\mathbf{v}_2 = \mathbf{e}_1 - \mathbf{e}_2$. Since $\det \mathbf{L} = -5 \neq 0$, $\mathbf{L}$ is nonsingular. (See Fig. 4–3.)

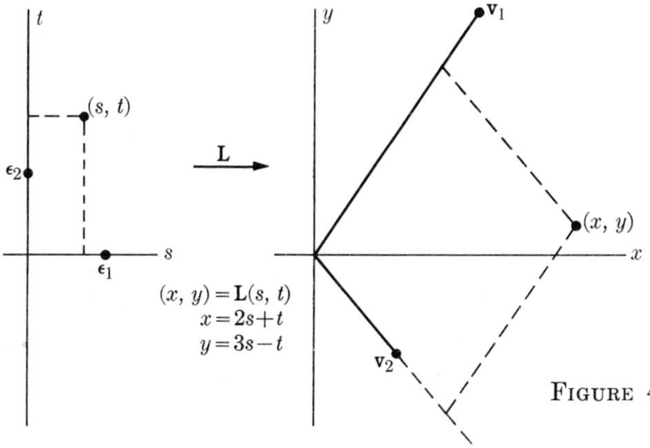


FIGURE 4–3

Let $\mathbf{M}(x, y) = (2x - 5y)\mathbf{E}_1 - x\mathbf{E}_2$, where $\mathbf{E}_1$, $\mathbf{E}_2$ denote the standard basis vectors for the plane $E^2$ in which $\mathbf{M}$ has its values. The matrix of $\mathbf{M}$ is

$$\begin{pmatrix} 2 & -5 \\ -1 & 0 \end{pmatrix}.$$

Since $\det \mathbf{M} = -5 \neq 0$, $\mathbf{M}$ is also nonsingular. The composite is found by

$$(\mathbf{M} \circ \mathbf{L})(s, t) = \mathbf{M}(2s + t, 3s - t) = [2(2s + t) - 5(3s - t)]\mathbf{E}_1 - (2s + t)\mathbf{E}_2,$$
$$(\mathbf{M} \circ \mathbf{L})(s, t) = (-11s + 7t)\mathbf{E}_1 - (2s + t)\mathbf{E}_2.$$

The matrix of $\mathbf{M} \circ \mathbf{L}$ is

$$\begin{pmatrix} -11 & 7 \\ -2 & -1 \end{pmatrix}.$$

As expected, $\det \mathbf{M} \circ \mathbf{L} = 25 = \det \mathbf{M} \det \mathbf{L}$.

**Example 2.** Let $n = r = 3$, and let $\mathbf{L}$ be the linear transformation which takes the standard basis vectors $\boldsymbol{\epsilon}_1, \boldsymbol{\epsilon}_2, \boldsymbol{\epsilon}_3$ respectively into

$$\mathbf{v}_1 = \mathbf{e}_1 + 2\mathbf{e}_2 - \mathbf{e}_3, \qquad \mathbf{v}_2 = -\mathbf{e}_1 + \mathbf{e}_2, \qquad \mathbf{v}_3 = -\mathbf{e}_1 + 4\mathbf{e}_2 - \mathbf{e}_3.$$

The matrix is

$$\begin{pmatrix} 1 & -1 & -1 \\ 2 & 1 & 4 \\ -1 & 0 & -1 \end{pmatrix},$$

which has $\mathbf{v}_1$, $\mathbf{v}_2$, $\mathbf{v}_3$ as column vectors. The determinant is 0, and therefore $\mathbf{L}$ is singular. In fact, $\mathbf{v}_3$ is a linear combination of $\mathbf{v}_1$ and $\mathbf{v}_2$, namely, $\mathbf{v}_3 = \mathbf{v}_1 + 2\mathbf{v}_2$. Since $\mathbf{v}_1$ and $\mathbf{v}_2$ are linearly independent, the rank of $\mathbf{L}$ is 2. $\mathbf{L}(E^3)$ is the plane containing $\mathbf{0}$, $\mathbf{v}_1$, $\mathbf{v}_2$. By (4–1) the kernel has dimension 1. It is found by solving the system (4–5) of homogeneous linear equations. One solution is $\mathbf{t}_1 = \boldsymbol{\epsilon}_1 + 2\boldsymbol{\epsilon}_2 - \boldsymbol{\epsilon}_3$. The kernel consists of all scalar multiples of $\mathbf{t}_1$.

**The dual $L^*$ of a linear transformation.** This is the linear transformation from the dual space $(E^n)^*$ into $(E^r)^*$, defined by the formula

$$\mathbf{a} \cdot \mathbf{L}(\mathbf{t}) = \mathbf{L}^*(\mathbf{a}) \cdot \mathbf{t}$$

for every covector $\mathbf{a} \in (E^n)^*$ and vector $\mathbf{t} \in E^r$.

$$E^r \xrightarrow{\mathbf{L}} E^n$$

$$(E^r)^* \xleftarrow{\mathbf{L}^*} (E^n)^*$$

In particular, let $\mathbf{a} = \mathbf{e}^i$. Then

$$L^i(\mathbf{t}) = \mathbf{e}^i \cdot \mathbf{L}(\mathbf{t}) = \mathbf{L}^*(\mathbf{e}^i) \cdot \mathbf{t}$$

for every $\mathbf{t} \in E^r$. Hence

$$\mathbf{L}^*(\mathbf{e}^i) = \mathbf{w}^i, \qquad i = 1, \ldots, n,$$

where $\mathbf{w}^i$ is the $i$th row covector. The formula dual to (4–3a) is

$$\mathbf{L}^*(\mathbf{a}) = \sum_{i=1}^{n} a_i \mathbf{w}^i. \tag{4–3b}$$

If $\mathbf{b} = \mathbf{L}^*(\mathbf{a})$, then its components are given by

$$b_j = \sum_{i=1}^{n} a_i c_j^i, \qquad j = 1, \ldots, r. \tag{4–4b}$$

This follows from (4–3b) since the $j$th component of $\mathbf{w}^i$ is $c_j^i$.

**Affine transformations.** If $\mathbf{L}$ is linear, then $\mathbf{L}(\mathbf{0}) = \mathbf{0}$. This fact gives $\mathbf{0}$ a special role which is somewhat unnatural from the geometric viewpoint. To avoid this it is sometimes better to deal instead with affine transformations.

**Definition.** A transformation $\mathbf{g}$ is *affine* if there exist a linear transformation $\mathbf{L}$ and $\mathbf{x}_0 \in E^n$ such that

$$\mathbf{g}(\mathbf{t}) = \mathbf{L}(\mathbf{t}) + \mathbf{x}_0 \quad \text{for every } \mathbf{t} \in E^r. \tag{4–6}$$

If $r = n$ and $\mathbf{L} = \mathbf{I}$, then $\mathbf{g}$ is a *translation*.

A translation merely takes each $\mathbf{t}$ into $\mathbf{t} + \mathbf{x}_0$. If $\mathbf{g}$ is affine, then $\mathbf{g}(\mathbf{0}) = \mathbf{x}_0$. Hence an affine transformation $\mathbf{g}$ is linear if and only if $\mathbf{g}(\mathbf{0}) = \mathbf{0}$. Every affine transformation is the composite of a translation and a linear transformation.

**Isometries of $E^n$.** Let $\mathbf{g}$ be a transformation from $E^n$ into $E^n$. If $\mathbf{g}$ preserves the distance between each pair of points, then $\mathbf{g}$ is called an isometry.

**Definition.** If $|\mathbf{g}(\mathbf{s}) - \mathbf{g}(\mathbf{t})| = |\mathbf{s} - \mathbf{t}|$ for every $\mathbf{s}, \mathbf{t} \in E^n$, then $\mathbf{g}$ is an *isometry* of $E^n$.

Let us first suppose that $\mathbf{g}$ is an isometry of $E^n$ which leaves $\mathbf{0}$ fixed, namely, $\mathbf{g}(\mathbf{0}) = \mathbf{0}$. Then taking $\mathbf{t} = \mathbf{0}$, we have $|\mathbf{g}(\mathbf{s})| = |\mathbf{s}|$ for every $\mathbf{s} \in E^n$. Using the formula $|\mathbf{x} - \mathbf{y}|^2 = |\mathbf{x}|^2 - 2\mathbf{x} \cdot \mathbf{y} + |\mathbf{y}|^2$, we have

$$|\mathbf{g}(\mathbf{s})|^2 - 2\mathbf{g}(\mathbf{s}) \cdot \mathbf{g}(\mathbf{t}) + |\mathbf{g}(\mathbf{t})|^2 = |\mathbf{s}|^2 - 2\mathbf{s} \cdot \mathbf{t} + |\mathbf{t}|^2,$$

for every $\mathbf{s}, \mathbf{t} \in E^n$. Therefore

$$\mathbf{g}(\mathbf{s}) \cdot \mathbf{g}(\mathbf{t}) = \mathbf{s} \cdot \mathbf{t}, \tag{4–7}$$

which says that $\mathbf{g}$ preserves the inner product. Let $\mathbf{v}_j = \mathbf{g}(\boldsymbol{\epsilon}_j)$, $j = 1, \ldots, n$. Then $|\mathbf{v}_j| = 1$ and from (4–7)

$$\mathbf{v}_i \cdot \mathbf{v}_j = \boldsymbol{\epsilon}_i \cdot \boldsymbol{\epsilon}_j = \delta_{ij}$$

for each $i, j = 1, \ldots, n$ where, as in Section 1–1, $\delta_{ij}$ is Kronecker's delta. Hence $\mathbf{v}_1, \ldots, \mathbf{v}_n$ form an orthonormal basis for $E^n$. Let us show that $\mathbf{g}$ is a linear transformation. For each $\mathbf{s}, \mathbf{t}$, we have from (4–7)

$$\mathbf{g}(\mathbf{s}) \cdot \mathbf{v}_j = \mathbf{s} \cdot \boldsymbol{\epsilon}_j = s^j, \qquad \mathbf{g}(\mathbf{t}) \cdot \mathbf{v}_j = t^j, \qquad \mathbf{g}(\mathbf{s} + \mathbf{t}) \cdot \mathbf{v}_j = s^j + t^j,$$

and hence

$$[\mathbf{g}(\mathbf{s} + \mathbf{t}) - \mathbf{g}(\mathbf{s}) - \mathbf{g}(\mathbf{t})] \cdot \mathbf{v}_j = 0,$$

for each $j = 1, \ldots n$. The vector $\mathbf{g}(\mathbf{s} + \mathbf{t}) - \mathbf{g}(\mathbf{s}) - \mathbf{g}(\mathbf{t})$ has component 0 with respect to each basis vector $\mathbf{v}_j$. Hence

$$\mathbf{g}(\mathbf{s} + \mathbf{t}) = \mathbf{g}(\mathbf{s}) + \mathbf{g}(\mathbf{t}).$$

Similarly $\mathbf{g}(c\mathbf{s}) = c\mathbf{g}(\mathbf{s})$ for every $\mathbf{s}$ and scalar $c$. Thus $\mathbf{g}$ is linear. The column vectors of its matrix are $\mathbf{v}_1, \ldots, \mathbf{v}_n$.

**Definition.** A linear transformation which preserves the standard euclidean inner product is an *orthogonal transformation*.

**Proposition 11.** ($r = n$). $\mathbf{L}$ *is an orthogonal transformation if and only if the column vectors* $\mathbf{v}_1, \ldots, \mathbf{v}_n$ *form an orthonormal basis for* $E^n$.

*Proof.* We have already shown that if $\mathbf{L}$ is orthogonal, then $\mathbf{v}_1, \ldots, \mathbf{v}_n$ form an orthonormal basis. To prove the converse, we see from (4–3a) that

$$\mathbf{L}(\mathbf{s}) \cdot \mathbf{L}(\mathbf{t}) = \sum_{i,j=1}^{n} s^i t^j \mathbf{v}_i \cdot \mathbf{v}_j.$$

If $\mathbf{v}_1, \ldots, \mathbf{v}_n$ is an orthonormal basis, then $\mathbf{v}_i \cdot \mathbf{v}_j = \delta_{ij}$, and

$$\mathbf{L}(\mathbf{s}) \cdot \mathbf{L}(\mathbf{t}) = \mathbf{s} \cdot \mathbf{t}$$

for every $\mathbf{s}, \mathbf{t} \in E^n$. ▮

**Theorem 8.** $(r = n)$. *A transformation* $\mathbf{g}$ *is an isometry of* $E^n$ *if and only if* $\mathbf{g}$ *is an affine transformation of the form* $\mathbf{g}(\mathbf{t}) = \mathbf{L}(\mathbf{t}) + \mathbf{x}_0$ *for every* $\mathbf{t} \in E^n$, *where* $\mathbf{L}$ *is orthogonal.*

*Proof.* Let $\mathbf{g}$ be an isometry of $E^n$. Let $\mathbf{f}(\mathbf{t}) = \mathbf{g}(\mathbf{t}) - \mathbf{x}_0$ for every $\mathbf{t} \in E^n$, where $\mathbf{x}_0 = \mathbf{g}(\mathbf{0})$. Then

$$|\mathbf{f}(\mathbf{s}) - \mathbf{f}(\mathbf{t})| = |\mathbf{g}(\mathbf{s}) - \mathbf{g}(\mathbf{t})| = |\mathbf{s} - \mathbf{t}|$$

for every $\mathbf{s}, \mathbf{t} \in E^n$. Hence $\mathbf{f}$ is an isometry. Moreover, $\mathbf{f}(\mathbf{0}) = \mathbf{0}$. We have already shown that $\mathbf{f}$ must be orthogonal.

Conversely, let $\mathbf{L}$ be orthogonal. Then $\mathbf{L}(\mathbf{s}) \cdot \mathbf{L}(\mathbf{t}) = \mathbf{s} \cdot \mathbf{t}$ for every $\mathbf{s}$, $\mathbf{t} \in E^n$. Taking $\mathbf{s} = \mathbf{t}$, we have

$$|\mathbf{L}(\mathbf{s})|^2 = \mathbf{L}(\mathbf{s}) \cdot \mathbf{L}(\mathbf{s}) = \mathbf{s} \cdot \mathbf{s} = |\mathbf{s}|^2.$$

Hence $|\mathbf{L}(\mathbf{s})| = |\mathbf{s}|$. Replacing $\mathbf{s}$ by $\mathbf{s} - \mathbf{t}$, we have

$$|\mathbf{L}(\mathbf{s}) - \mathbf{L}(\mathbf{t})| = |\mathbf{L}(\mathbf{s} - \mathbf{t})| = |\mathbf{s} - \mathbf{t}|$$

for every $\mathbf{s}, \mathbf{t} \in E^n$. Hence $\mathbf{L}$ is an isometry of $E^n$. Since $|\mathbf{g}(\mathbf{s}) - \mathbf{g}(\mathbf{t})| = |\mathbf{L}(\mathbf{s}) - \mathbf{L}(\mathbf{t})|$, $\mathbf{g}$ is also an isometry of $E^n$. ▮

Let $\mathbf{L}^t$ denote the linear transformation which is defined by the formula

$$\mathbf{y} \cdot \mathbf{L}(\mathbf{t}) = \mathbf{L}^t(\mathbf{y}) \cdot \mathbf{t} \tag{4–8}$$

for every $\mathbf{y}, \mathbf{t} \in E^n$. The $\cdot$ here denotes inner product rather than scalar product. If we did not distinguish between vectors and covectors, then $\mathbf{L}^t$ would be the same as $\mathbf{L}^*$.

The $i$th column vector $\mathbf{L}^t(\mathbf{e}_i)$ has the same components as the row covector $\mathbf{w}^i = \mathbf{L}^*(\mathbf{e}^i)$. Thus the matrix of $\mathbf{L}^t$ is the *transposed* matrix obtained by exchanging rows and columns of the matrix of $\mathbf{L}$.

Applying (4–8) with $\mathbf{y} = \mathbf{L}(\mathbf{s})$, we get

$$\mathbf{L}(\mathbf{s}) \cdot \mathbf{L}(\mathbf{t}) = (\mathbf{L}^t \circ \mathbf{L})(\mathbf{s}) \cdot \mathbf{t}.$$

From this equation, $\mathbf{L}$ is orthogonal if and only if $\mathbf{s} \cdot \mathbf{t} = (\mathbf{L}^t \circ \mathbf{L})(\mathbf{s}) \cdot \mathbf{t}$ for every $\mathbf{s}, \mathbf{t} \in E^n$. But this is equivalent to the statement that $\mathbf{s} = (\mathbf{L}^t \circ \mathbf{L})(\mathbf{s})$ for every $\mathbf{s}$, in other words, that $\mathbf{I} = \mathbf{L}^t \circ \mathbf{L}$. Hence $\mathbf{L}$ *is orthogonal if and only if*

$$\mathbf{L}^t = \mathbf{L}^{-1}.$$

If $\mathbf{L}$ is orthogonal, then

$$1 = \det \mathbf{I} = \det \mathbf{L}^t \det \mathbf{L}.$$

But $\det \mathbf{L}^t = \det \mathbf{L}$ ([12], p. 146). Hence $1 = (\det \mathbf{L})^2$, and $\det \mathbf{L} = \pm 1$. If $\mathbf{L}$ is orthogonal and $\det \mathbf{L} = 1$, then $\mathbf{L}$ is called a *rotation* of $E^n$ about $\mathbf{0}$.

**Example 3.** Any translation is an isometry of $E^n$, and $\mathbf{L} = \mathbf{I}$.

**Example 4.** Let $\mathbf{S}$ be the orthogonal transformation which takes each $\mathbf{t} = (t^1, \ldots, t^n)$ into $\mathbf{S}(\mathbf{t}) = (t^1, \ldots, t^{n-1}, -t^n)$. $\mathbf{S}$ is a reflection of $E^n$ about the hyperplane $t^n = 0$. Its matrix is

$$\begin{pmatrix} 1 & & & 0 \\ & \ddots & & \\ & & 1 & \\ 0 & & & -1 \end{pmatrix}$$

Two such reflections take each $\mathbf{t}$ into itself; that is, $\mathbf{S} \circ \mathbf{S} = \mathbf{I}$. Hence $\mathbf{S} = \mathbf{S}^{-1} = \mathbf{S}^t$. If $\mathbf{M}$ is any orthogonal transformation with $\det \mathbf{M} = -1$, then $\mathbf{L} = \mathbf{S} \circ \mathbf{M}$ is a rotation of $E^n$ about $\mathbf{0}$ and

$$\mathbf{M} = \mathbf{S}^{-1} \circ \mathbf{L} = \mathbf{S} \circ \mathbf{L}.$$

Thus any orthogonal transformation is either a rotation or the composite of $\mathbf{S}$ and a rotation.

**Example 5.** Let $n = 2$, and $\mathbf{L}$ be a rotation of the plane $E^2$ about $(0, 0)$. Since $|\mathbf{v}_1| = 1$, $\mathbf{v}_1 = (\cos \theta)\mathbf{e}_1 + (\sin \theta)\mathbf{e}_2$ for some $\theta \in [0, 2\pi)$. Since $\mathbf{L}$ is a rotation, $\mathbf{v}_2 = (-\sin \theta)\mathbf{e}_1 + (\cos \theta)\mathbf{e}_2$. The matrix is

$$\begin{pmatrix} \cos \theta & -\sin \theta \\ \sin \theta & \cos \theta \end{pmatrix}.$$

The angle of rotation is $\theta$.

## PROBLEMS

1. Let $r = 3$, $n = 2$, and $\mathbf{L}$ be the linear transformation such that $\mathbf{L}(\boldsymbol{\epsilon}_1) = \mathbf{e}_1 - 2\mathbf{e}_2$, $\mathbf{L}(\boldsymbol{\epsilon}_2) = \mathbf{e}_1$, $\mathbf{L}(\boldsymbol{\epsilon}_3) = 5\mathbf{e}_1 + \mathbf{e}_2$. Find the matrix of $\mathbf{L}$, the rank, and the kernel.
2. Show that the kernel of a linear transformation is a vector subspace of its domain.
3. Let $r = n$, and let $L^i(\mathbf{t}) = c^i t^i$ for every $\mathbf{t} \in E^n$, where $c^1, \ldots, c^n$ are scalars.
   (a) What is the matrix?
   (b) Find $\mathbf{L}^{-1}$ if it exists.

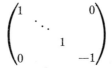

(c) If $c^1 = \cdots = c^n > 0$, then $\mathbf{L}$ is called *homothetic* about $\mathbf{0}$. Describe $\mathbf{L}$ geometrically. Show that if $\mathbf{L}$ and $\mathbf{M}$ are homothetic about $\mathbf{0}$, then $\mathbf{L}^{-1}$ and $\mathbf{M} \circ \mathbf{L}$ are also homothetic about $\mathbf{0}$.

4. (a) Show directly from the definitions that the composite of two linear transformations is also linear.
   (b) Let $(c_j^i)$, $(d_i^l)$, and $(b_j^l)$ denote respectively the matrices of $\mathbf{L}$, $\mathbf{M}$, and $\mathbf{M} \circ \mathbf{L}$. Show that

$$b_j^l = \sum_{i=1}^n d_i^l c_j^i, \quad \text{for } l = 1, \ldots, p, \qquad j = 1, \ldots, r. \tag{4-9}$$

5. Let $n = r = 2$.
   (a) Describe geometrically the linear transformation $\mathbf{L}$ with matrix $\begin{pmatrix} 0 & 1 \\ 1 & 0 \end{pmatrix}$.
   (b) Find $\mathbf{S} \circ \mathbf{L}$ and $\mathbf{L} \circ \mathbf{S}$, where $\mathbf{S}$ is the same as in Example 4. Show that both are rotations of $E^2$ about $(0, 0)$.

6. (a) Show that the vectors $\mathbf{v}_1 = (1/\sqrt{5})(\mathbf{e}_1 + 2\mathbf{e}_3)$, $\mathbf{v}_2 = (1/\sqrt{10})(-2\mathbf{e}_1 + \sqrt{5}\mathbf{e}_2 + \mathbf{e}_3)$, $\mathbf{v}_3 = (1/\sqrt{10})(2\mathbf{e}_1 + \sqrt{5}\mathbf{e}_2 - \mathbf{e}_3)$ form an orthonormal basis for $E^3$.
   (b) Let $\mathbf{L}$ be the orthogonal transformation whose matrix has $\mathbf{v}_1, \mathbf{v}_2, \mathbf{v}_3$ as column vectors. Find $\mathbf{L}^t$ and verify that $\mathbf{L}^t \circ \mathbf{L} = \mathbf{I}$. Is $\mathbf{L}$ a rotation?

7. Let $\mathbf{L}$ and $\mathbf{M}$ be rotations of $E^n$ about $\mathbf{0}$. Show that $\mathbf{L}^{-1}$ and $\mathbf{M} \circ \mathbf{L}$ are also rotations.

8. (a) Show that the composite of two affine transformations is also affine.
   (b) Which affine transformations are univalent?

## 4-3 DIFFERENTIABLE TRANSFORMATIONS

Let $\mathbf{g}$ be a transformation from $\Delta \subset E^r$ into $E^n$, and let $\mathbf{t}_0$ be an interior point of $\Delta$. We would like to find a local linear approximation for the difference $\mathbf{g}(\mathbf{t}) - \mathbf{g}(\mathbf{t}_0)$. If there is such an approximation, then $\mathbf{g}$ is said to be differentiable at $\mathbf{t}_0$. More precisely:

**Definition.** A transformation $\mathbf{g}$ is *differentiable at* $\mathbf{t}_0$ if there exists a linear transformation $\mathbf{L}$ (depending on $\mathbf{t}_0$) such that

$$\lim_{\mathbf{k} \to 0} \frac{1}{|\mathbf{k}|} [\mathbf{g}(\mathbf{t}_0 + \mathbf{k}) - \mathbf{g}(\mathbf{t}_0) - \mathbf{L}(\mathbf{k})] = \mathbf{0}. \tag{4-10a}$$

If we set $\mathbf{t} = \mathbf{t}_0 + \mathbf{k}$, then $\mathbf{L}(\mathbf{t} - \mathbf{t}_0)$ is the desired local approximation to $\mathbf{g}(\mathbf{t}) - \mathbf{g}(\mathbf{t}_0)$. If $n = 1$, the definition agrees with the one in Section 2-2, p. 38. Moreover, for $n > 1$ the expression in (4-10a) tends to $\mathbf{0}$ if and only if each of its components tends to 0 as $\mathbf{k} \to \mathbf{0}$ (see Proposition A-4b). Thus (4-10a) is equivalent to

$$\lim_{\mathbf{k} \to 0} \frac{1}{|\mathbf{k}|} [g^i(\mathbf{t}_0 + \mathbf{k}) - g^i(\mathbf{t}_0) - L^i(\mathbf{k})] = 0, \tag{4-10b}$$

for $i = 1, \ldots, n$.

The partial derivatives of the components $g^i$ are denoted by $g^i_j$ or $\partial g^i/\partial t^j$, as in Chapter 2.

**Proposition 12.** *A transformation* $\mathbf{g}$ *is differentiable at* $\mathbf{t}_0$ *if and only if each of its components* $g^1, \ldots, g^n$ *is differentiable at* $\mathbf{t}_0$.

*If* $\mathbf{g}$ *is differentiable at* $\mathbf{t}_0$, *then the matrix of the linear transformation* $\mathbf{L}$ *is the matrix of partial derivatives* $g^i_j(\mathbf{t}_0)$.

*Proof.* Since (4–10b) states that each component $g^i$ is differentiable at $\mathbf{t}_0$, the first assertion follows at once. If $\mathbf{g}$ is differentiable at $\mathbf{t}_0$, then $L^i(\mathbf{k}) = dg^i(\mathbf{t}_0) \cdot \mathbf{k}$ for every $\mathbf{k} \in E^r$. Hence the row covectors are $dg^1(\mathbf{t}_0), \ldots, dg^n(\mathbf{t}_0)$, and the elements of the matrix are the partial derivatives $g^i_j(\mathbf{t}_0)$. ▌

**Definitions.** 1. The column vectors of the matrix are called the *partial derivatives* of the transformation $\mathbf{g}$ at $\mathbf{t}_0$, and are denoted by $\mathbf{g}_j(\mathbf{t}_0)$ or $(\partial \mathbf{g}/\partial t^j)(\mathbf{t}_0)$. Thus

$$\mathbf{g}_j(\mathbf{t}_0) = \frac{\partial \mathbf{g}}{\partial t^j}(\mathbf{t}_0) = \sum_{i=1}^{n} g^i_j(\mathbf{t}_0)\mathbf{e}_i, \tag{4–11a}$$

for each $j = 1, \ldots, r$. The $j$th partial derivative $\mathbf{g}_j(\mathbf{t}_0)$ can be regarded as the derivative of $\mathbf{g}$ with respect to the $j$th variable while all of the other variables are held fixed, in the sense described in Section 3–1.

The formula, dual to (4–11a), for the row covectors is

$$dg^i(\mathbf{t}_0) = \sum_{j=1}^{n} g^i_j(\mathbf{t}_0)\mathbf{e}^j. \tag{4–11b}$$

2. If $\Delta$ is an open set and $\mathbf{g}$ is differentiable at each point of $\Delta$, then $\mathbf{g}$ is called a *differentiable transformation.*

3. The linear transformation $\mathbf{L}$ in (4–10a) is called the *differential of* $\mathbf{g}$ *at* $\mathbf{t}_0$ and is denoted by $D\mathbf{g}(\mathbf{t}_0)$. The *differential* of a differentiable transformation $\mathbf{g}$ is the function $D\mathbf{g}$ whose value at each $\mathbf{t} \in \Delta$ is $D\mathbf{g}(\mathbf{t})$.

4. In case $r = n$ the determinant of the linear transformation $D\mathbf{g}(\mathbf{t})$ is called the *Jacobian* of $\mathbf{g}$ at $\mathbf{t}$. It is denoted by $J\mathbf{g}(\mathbf{t})$. Thus

$$J\mathbf{g}(\mathbf{t}) = \det D\mathbf{g}(\mathbf{t}) = \det\left(g^i_j(\mathbf{t})\right). \tag{4–12}$$

Another common notation for the Jacobian is

$$\frac{\partial(g^1, \ldots, g^n)}{\partial(t^1, \ldots, t^n)}(\mathbf{t}).$$

We shall see that the Jacobian often plays the same role in the calculus of functions of several variables as the derivative does in the case $r = n = 1$. In particular, this is so in the theorems about inverses (Section 4–5) and transforming multiple integrals (Section 5–8). If the Jacobian is 0 at a point $\mathbf{t}_0$, then $D\mathbf{g}(\mathbf{t}_0)$ is singular. This suggests some kind of irregularity in the behavior of $\mathbf{g}$ near $\mathbf{t}_0$. In order to exclude such irregularities we shall repeatedly have to make the assumption that the Jacobian is not 0.

**Example 1.** If $n = 1$, then $Dg(\mathbf{t})$ has the single row covector $dg(\mathbf{t})$. We may identify $Dg$ with $dg$ and $Dg(\mathbf{t})$ with $dg(\mathbf{t})$. If $dg(\mathbf{t}) \neq \mathbf{0}$, the rank of $Dg(\mathbf{t})$ is 1; otherwise it is 0.

**Example 2.** If $r = 1$, then there is a single column vector. It is the derivative $\mathbf{g}'(t)$. If $\mathbf{g}'(t) \neq \mathbf{0}$, the rank is 1; otherwise it is 0.

**Example 3.** Let $n = r = 2$, $\Delta = E^2$, and

$$\mathbf{g}(s, t) = (s^2 - t^2)\mathbf{e}_1 + 2st\mathbf{e}_2.$$

The partial derivatives of $\mathbf{g}$ are the column vectors

$$\mathbf{g}_1(s, t) = 2s\mathbf{e}_1 + 2t\mathbf{e}_2,$$
$$\mathbf{g}_2(s, t) = -2t\mathbf{e}_1 + 2s\mathbf{e}_2.$$

The matrix of $D\mathbf{g}(s, t)$ is

$$\begin{pmatrix} 2s & -2t \\ 2t & 2s \end{pmatrix}.$$

The Jacobian is

$$J\mathbf{g}(s, t) = \det \begin{pmatrix} 2s & -2t \\ 2t & 2s \end{pmatrix} = 4(s^2 + t^2).$$

It is 0 only at (0, 0). If $(s, t) \neq (0, 0)$, the rank is 2. At (0, 0) the rank is 0.

**Definition.** If the components $g^1, \ldots, g^n$ are of class $C^{(q)}$, $q \geq 0$, then $\mathbf{g}$ is a *transformation of class* $C^{(q)}$. Similarly, if $g^1, \ldots, g^n$ are of class $C^{(q)}$ on $B \subset \Delta$, then $\mathbf{g}$ is *of class* $C^{(q)}$ *on* $B$.

In Section 2-3 we called a real-valued $g$ a function of class $C^{(0)}$ if $g$ is continuous. A transformation $\mathbf{g}$ is continuous if and only if $g^1, \ldots, g^n$ are continuous (Section A-5). Hence the transformations of class $C^{(0)}$ are just the continuous ones.

**Theorem 9.** *Every differentiable transformation is continuous. Every transformation of class* $C^{(1)}$ *is differentiable.*

*Proof.* Apply Propositions 7, 12, and Theorem 2. ▮

For most theorems in the differential calculus of transformations one needs to assume that $\mathbf{g}$ is of class $C^{(1)}$ at least. An exception is the composite function theorem (Section 4-4), in which only differentiability need be assumed.

In the remainder of this section we shall establish several inequalities of a rather technical nature. These inequalities will be used in the proofs of theorems to follow.

We first need to introduce a norm which measures the "size" of a linear transformation. Let

$$\|\mathbf{L}\| = \max \{|\mathbf{L}(\mathbf{t})| : |\mathbf{t}| \leq 1\}.$$

The set of all linear transformations with domain $E^r$ and values in $E^n$ forms a vector space of dimension $nr$ (see Problem 2, Section A-2). The usual properties of a norm are satisfied (Problem 3).

Let us show that

$$|\mathbf{L}(\mathbf{t})| \leq \|\mathbf{L}\| \, |\mathbf{t}| \tag{4-13}$$

for every $\mathbf{t} \in E^r$. If $\mathbf{t} = \mathbf{0}$, then both sides are 0. If $\mathbf{t} \neq \mathbf{0}$, let $c = |\mathbf{t}|^{-1}$. Since $\mathbf{L}$ is linear, $\mathbf{L}(c\mathbf{t}) = c\mathbf{L}(t)$. Since $|c\mathbf{t}| = 1$, $|\mathbf{L}(c\mathbf{t})| \leq \|\mathbf{L}\|$. Thus $|\mathbf{t}|^{-1}|\mathbf{L}(\mathbf{t})| \leq \|\mathbf{L}\|$, which is the same as (4–13).

Since $\mathbf{L}(\mathbf{s}) - \mathbf{L}(\mathbf{t}) = \mathbf{L}(\mathbf{s} - \mathbf{t})$, we have upon replacing $\mathbf{t}$ by $\mathbf{s} - \mathbf{t}$ in (4–13)

$$|\mathbf{L}(\mathbf{s}) - \mathbf{L}(\mathbf{t})| \leq \|\mathbf{L}\| \, |\mathbf{s} - \mathbf{t}|. \tag{4-14}$$

**Proposition 13a.** *Let* $\mathbf{g}$ *be differentiable at* $\mathbf{t}_0$. *Then given* $\epsilon > 0$ *there exists a neighborhood* $\Omega_0$ *of* $\mathbf{t}_0$ *such that* $\Omega_0 \subset \Delta$ *and*

$$|\mathbf{g}(\mathbf{t}) - \mathbf{g}(\mathbf{t}_0)| \leq (\|D\mathbf{g}(\mathbf{t}_0)\| + \epsilon) \, |\mathbf{t} - \mathbf{t}_0| \tag{4-15}$$

*for every* $\mathbf{t} \in \Omega_0$.

*Proof.* Let $\mathbf{L} = D\mathbf{g}(\mathbf{t}_0)$ and set $\tilde{\mathbf{g}}(\mathbf{t}) = \mathbf{g}(\mathbf{t}) - \mathbf{L}(\mathbf{t})$. Since $D\mathbf{L}(\mathbf{t}_0) = \mathbf{L}$, $D\tilde{\mathbf{g}}(\mathbf{t}_0) = \mathbf{0}$ (the zero linear transformation). By (4–10a), in which $\mathbf{g}$ is replaced by $\tilde{\mathbf{g}}$, there is a neighborhood $\Omega_0$ of $\mathbf{t}_0$ such that

$$|\tilde{\mathbf{g}}(\mathbf{t}) - \tilde{\mathbf{g}}(\mathbf{t}_0)| \leq \epsilon |\mathbf{t} - \mathbf{t}_0| \tag{$*$}$$

for every $\mathbf{t} \in \Omega_0$. But

$$\mathbf{g}(\mathbf{t}) - \mathbf{g}(\mathbf{t}_0) = [\mathbf{L}(\mathbf{t}) - \mathbf{L}(\mathbf{t}_0)] + [\tilde{\mathbf{g}}(\mathbf{t}) - \tilde{\mathbf{g}}(\mathbf{t}_0)].$$

From ($*$), (4–14), and the triangle inequality we get (4–15). ∎

If $\mathbf{g}$ is of class $C^{(1)}$, there is a stronger version of Proposition 13.

**Proposition 13b.** *Let* $\mathbf{g}$ *be of class* $C^{(1)}$ *and* $\mathbf{t}_0 \in \Delta$. *Then given* $\epsilon > 0$ *there exists a neighborhood* $\Omega$ *of* $\mathbf{t}_0$ *such that* $\Omega \subset \Delta$ *and*

$$|\mathbf{g}(\mathbf{s}) - \mathbf{g}(\mathbf{t})| \leq (\|D\mathbf{g}(\mathbf{t}_0)\| + \epsilon) \, |\mathbf{s} - \mathbf{t}| \tag{4-16}$$

*for every* $\mathbf{s}, \mathbf{t} \in \Omega$.

*Proof.* Let $\tilde{\mathbf{g}}$ be as before. The row covectors $d\tilde{g}^i(\mathbf{t}_0)$ are all $\mathbf{0}$. Since the partial derivatives of $\tilde{g}$ are continuous, given $\epsilon > 0$ there is a neighborhood $\Omega$

of $\mathbf{t}_0$ such that $|d\tilde{g}^i(\mathbf{u})| < \epsilon/n$ for every $\mathbf{u} \in \Omega$ and $i = 1, \ldots, n$. By Corollary 1, p. 42, for every $\mathbf{s}, \mathbf{t} \in \Omega$,

$$|\tilde{g}^i(\mathbf{s}) - \tilde{g}^i(\mathbf{t})| \leq \frac{\epsilon}{n} |\mathbf{s} - \mathbf{t}|,$$

$$|\tilde{\mathbf{g}}(\mathbf{s}) - \tilde{\mathbf{g}}(\mathbf{t})| \leq \sum_{i=1}^{n} |\tilde{g}^i(\mathbf{s}) - \tilde{g}^i(\mathbf{t})| \leq \epsilon |\mathbf{s} - \mathbf{t}|. \tag{**}$$

From (**) and (4–14) we obtain (4–16) in the same way as before. ▮

If $r = n$ and $\mathbf{L}$ is nonsingular, there is besides the upper estimate (4–13) a lower estimate for $|\mathbf{L}(\mathbf{t})|$. Let $\mathbf{x} = \mathbf{L}(\mathbf{t})$. Then $\mathbf{t} = \mathbf{L}^{-1}(\mathbf{x})$, and applying (4–13) to $\mathbf{L}^{-1}$, we get $|\mathbf{t}| \leq \|\mathbf{L}^{-1}\| \, |\mathbf{x}|$. Replacing $\mathbf{t}$ by $\mathbf{s} - \mathbf{t}$, we have

$$\frac{1}{\|\mathbf{L}^{-1}\|} |\mathbf{s} - \mathbf{t}| \leq |\mathbf{L}(\mathbf{s}) - \mathbf{L}(\mathbf{t})| \tag{4–17}$$

for every $\mathbf{s}, \mathbf{t} \in E^n$. From this inequality we get a lower estimate for $|\mathbf{g}(\mathbf{s}) - \mathbf{g}(\mathbf{t})|$ as follows.

**Proposition 14.** *Besides the hypotheses of Proposition* 13b, *assume that* $r = n$ *and* $D\mathbf{g}(\mathbf{t}_0)$ *is nonsingular. Let* $c = 1/\|D\mathbf{g}(\mathbf{t}_0)^{-1}\|$. *Then*

$$|\mathbf{g}(\mathbf{s}) - \mathbf{g}(\mathbf{t})| \geq (c - \epsilon)|\mathbf{s} - \mathbf{t}| \tag{4–18}$$

*for every* $\mathbf{s}, \mathbf{t} \in \Omega$.

*Proof.* We have

$$\mathbf{g}(\mathbf{s}) - \mathbf{g}(\mathbf{t}) = [\mathbf{L}(\mathbf{s}) - \mathbf{L}(\mathbf{t})] + [\tilde{\mathbf{g}}(\mathbf{s}) - \tilde{\mathbf{g}}(\mathbf{t})].$$

From the triangle inequality, $|\mathbf{x} + \mathbf{y}| \geq |\mathbf{x}| - |\mathbf{y}|$. Therefore (4–18) follows from (**) and (4–17). ▮

## PROBLEMS

1. For each of Problems 3, 4, and 5, Section 4–1, find:
   (a) Where $\mathbf{g}$ is differentiable.
   (b) The partial derivatives of $\mathbf{g}$.
   (c) The rank of $D\mathbf{g}(s, t)$.
   (d) The Jacobian $J\mathbf{g}(s, t)$, where applicable.
2. (a) Let $\mathbf{g}$ be affine, $\mathbf{g}(\mathbf{t}) = \mathbf{L}(\mathbf{t}) + \mathbf{x}_0$ for every $\mathbf{t} \in E^r$. Show that $D\mathbf{g}(\mathbf{t}) = \mathbf{L}$ for every $\mathbf{t} \in E^r$.
   (b) Let $\mathbf{g}$ be a differentiable transformation such that $D\mathbf{g}$ is a constant function and $\Delta$ is a connected open set. Show that $\mathbf{g}$ is the restriction to $\Delta$ of an affine transformation.

3. Show that:

   (a) $\|\mathbf{L}\| > 0$ unless $\mathbf{L}$ has rank 0.
   (b) $\|c\mathbf{L}\| = |c|\,\|\mathbf{L}\|$.
   (c) $\|\mathbf{L} + \mathbf{L}'\| \leq \|\mathbf{L}\| + \|\mathbf{L}'\|$.
   (d) $\|\mathbf{M} \circ \mathbf{L}\| \leq \|\mathbf{M}\|\,\|\mathbf{L}\|$.

4. Another norm for linear transformations, which we denote by $|||\ \ |||$, is defined as follows:

$$|||\mathbf{L}||| = |\mathbf{w}^1| + \cdots + |\mathbf{w}^n|,$$

where $\mathbf{w}^1, \ldots, \mathbf{w}^n$ are the row covectors. Show that properties (a)—(d) of Problem 3 hold for this norm. Show that $||\mathbf{L}|| \leq |||\mathbf{L}|||$.

5. Let $r = n$ and $\mathbf{g}$ be a differentiable transformation. Then $\mathbf{g}$ is called *conformal* if there exists a real-valued function $\mu$ such that $\mu(\mathbf{t}) > 0$ and $\mu(\mathbf{t})D\mathbf{g}(\mathbf{t})$ is a rotation of $E^n$ for every $\mathbf{t} \in \Delta$.

   (a) Using Proposition 11 show that $\mathbf{g}$ is conformal if and only if, for every $\mathbf{t} \in \Delta$, $J\mathbf{g}(\mathbf{t}) > 0$ and the partial derivatives of $\mathbf{g}$ satisfy:

$$\mathbf{g}_i(\mathbf{t}) \cdot \mathbf{g}_j(\mathbf{t}) = 0 \quad \text{if } i \neq j, \tag{1}$$

   and

$$|\mathbf{g}_1(\mathbf{t})| = |\mathbf{g}_2(\mathbf{t})| = \cdots = |\mathbf{g}_n(\mathbf{t})| = 1/\mu(\mathbf{t}). \tag{2}$$

   (b) Show that if $\mathbf{g}$ is conformal, then $\mu(\mathbf{t}) = [J\mathbf{g}(\mathbf{t})]^{-1/n}$.
   (c) Let $n = 2$. Show that $\mathbf{g}$ is conformal if and only if $J\mathbf{g}(\mathbf{t}) > 0$ and $g_1^1(\mathbf{t}) = g_2^2(\mathbf{t})$, $g_2^1(\mathbf{t}) = -g_1^2(\mathbf{t})$ for every $\mathbf{t} \in \Delta$. [*Note:* The partial differential equations $g_1^1 = g_2^2$, $g_2^1 = -g_1^2$ are the Cauchy-Riemann equations (Problem 4, Section 3-3).]

6. Show that $\mathbf{g}$ is conformal:

   (a) $\mathbf{g}$ as in Example 3, $\Delta = E^2 - \{(0, 0)\}$.
   (b) $g^1(s,t) = \exp(s^2 - t^2)\cos 2st$, $g^2(s,t) = \exp(s^2 - t^2)\sin 2st$, $\Delta = E^2 - \{(0, 0)\}$.

7. Let $\mathbf{g}$ be of class $C^{(1)}$. The maximum rank possible for $D\mathbf{g}(\mathbf{t})$ is $\min(r, n)$. Show that $\{\mathbf{t} : \text{rank } D\mathbf{g}(\mathbf{t}) = \min(r, n)\}$ is open.

## 4-4 COMPOSITION

We shall now derive a rule for differentiating the composite of two differentiable transformations. As corollaries of the basic formula (4-19) we then obtain a formula for Jacobians and the chain rule for partial derivatives.

Let $\mathbf{g}$ be a transformation from an open set $\Delta \subset E^r$ into an open set $D \subset E^n$, and let $\mathbf{f}$ be a transformation from $D$ into $E^p$.

**Composite Function Theorem.** *Let* $\mathbf{g}$ *be differentiable at* $\mathbf{t}_0$ *and* $\mathbf{f}$ *be differentiable at* $\mathbf{x}_0 = \mathbf{g}(\mathbf{t}_0)$. *Then the composite* $\mathbf{F} = \mathbf{f} \circ \mathbf{g}$ *is differentiable at* $\mathbf{t}_0$ *and*

$$D\mathbf{F}(\mathbf{t}_0) = D\mathbf{f}(\mathbf{x}_0) \circ D\mathbf{g}(\mathbf{t}_0). \tag{4-19}$$

*Proof.* Let $\mathbf{L} = D\mathbf{g}(\mathbf{t}_0)$, $\mathbf{M} = D\mathbf{f}(\mathbf{x}_0)$, and $\tilde{\mathbf{f}} = \mathbf{f} - \mathbf{M}$. Using the fact that $\mathbf{M}$ is linear, we have

$$\mathbf{F}(\mathbf{t}_0 + \mathbf{k}) - \mathbf{F}(\mathbf{t}_0) - (\mathbf{M} \circ \mathbf{L})(\mathbf{k}) = \tilde{\mathbf{f}}[\mathbf{g}(\mathbf{t}_0 + \mathbf{k})] - \tilde{\mathbf{f}}[\mathbf{g}(\mathbf{t}_0)] + \mathbf{M}[\mathbf{g}(\mathbf{t}_0 + \mathbf{k}) - \mathbf{g}(\mathbf{t}_0) - \mathbf{L}(\mathbf{k})].$$

To prove the theorem let us show that

$$\lim_{\mathbf{k}\to\mathbf{0}} \frac{1}{|\mathbf{k}|} \{\tilde{\mathbf{f}}[\mathbf{g}(\mathbf{t}_0 + \mathbf{k})] - \tilde{\mathbf{f}}[\mathbf{g}(\mathbf{t}_0)]\} = \mathbf{0}, \tag{*}$$

and

$$\lim_{\mathbf{k}\to\mathbf{0}} \frac{1}{|\mathbf{k}|} \mathbf{M}[\mathbf{g}(\mathbf{t}_0 + \mathbf{k}) - \mathbf{g}(\mathbf{t}_0) - \mathbf{L}(\mathbf{k})] = \mathbf{0}. \tag{**}$$

Let $C = \|\mathbf{L}\| + 1$. By Proposition 13a with $\epsilon = 1$, there exists $\delta_0 > 0$ such that

$$|\mathbf{g}(\mathbf{t}_0 + \mathbf{k}) - \mathbf{g}(\mathbf{t}_0)| \leq C|\mathbf{k}|$$

whenever $|\mathbf{k}| < \delta_0$. Since $D\tilde{\mathbf{f}}(\mathbf{x}_0) = \mathbf{0}$, by Proposition 13a given $\epsilon > 0$, there exists $\eta > 0$ such that

$$|\tilde{\mathbf{f}}(\mathbf{x}) - \tilde{\mathbf{f}}(\mathbf{x}_0)| \leq \frac{\epsilon}{C} |\mathbf{x} - \mathbf{x}_0|$$

whenever $|\mathbf{x} - \mathbf{x}_0| < \eta$. Let $\delta = \min\{C^{-1}\eta, \delta_0\}$. If $|\mathbf{k}| < \delta$, then taking $\mathbf{x} = \mathbf{g}(\mathbf{t}_0 + \mathbf{k})$ we get

$$|\tilde{\mathbf{f}}[\mathbf{g}(\mathbf{t}_0 + \mathbf{k}) - \tilde{\mathbf{f}}[\mathbf{g}(\mathbf{t}_0)]| \leq \frac{\epsilon}{C} C|\mathbf{k}| = \epsilon|\mathbf{k}|.$$

This proves (*).

For every $\mathbf{y}$, $|\mathbf{M}(\mathbf{y})| \leq \|\mathbf{M}\|\,|\mathbf{y}|$. Hence the norm of the expression in (**) is no more than $\|\mathbf{M}\|\,|\mathbf{k}|^{-1}|\mathbf{g}(\mathbf{t}_0 + \mathbf{k}) - \mathbf{g}(\mathbf{t}_0) - \mathbf{L}(\mathbf{k})|$, which tends to 0 as $\mathbf{k} \to \mathbf{0}$ since $\mathbf{g}$ is differentiable at $\mathbf{t}_0$. This proves (**). ▮

The matrix of $D\mathbf{F}(\mathbf{t}_0)$ is the product of the matrices of $\mathbf{M}$ and $\mathbf{L}$. Let us consider the special case $p = 1$, $f$ and $F$ now being real-valued. If we abbreviate by writing

$$F_j = F_j(\mathbf{t}_0), \qquad f_i = f_i(\mathbf{x}_0), \qquad g_j^i = g_j^i(\mathbf{t}_0)$$

and use (4–9), p. 100, with

$$b_j = F_j, \qquad d_i = f_i, \qquad c_j^i = g_j^i,$$

we obtain:

**Corollary 1.** *(Chain Rule)*

$$F_j = \sum_{i=1}^{n} f_i g_j^i, \qquad j = 1, \ldots, r. \;▮ \tag{4–20}$$

Another suggestive form for this important formula is obtained by writing it with the other notation for partial derivatives:

$$\frac{\partial F}{\partial t^j} = \frac{\partial f}{\partial x^1}\frac{\partial g^1}{\partial t^j} + \cdots + \frac{\partial f}{\partial x^n}\frac{\partial g^n}{\partial t^j}, \qquad j = 1, \ldots, r.$$

The chain rule is just a particular case of (4–4b) which describes how the components of a covector change under the dual $\mathbf{L}^*$ of a linear transformation. In the present instance $\mathbf{L} = D\mathbf{g}(\mathbf{t}_0)$, and $dF(\mathbf{t}_0) = \mathbf{L}^*[df(\mathbf{x}_0)]$.

If $r = 1$, then we may identify $D\mathbf{F}(t_0)$ with its column vector $\mathbf{F}'(t_0)$, and $D\mathbf{g}(t_0)$ with $\mathbf{g}'(t_0)$. From (4–19) we then get:

**Corollary 2.** *Let* $r = 1$. *Then* $\mathbf{F}'(t_0) = D\mathbf{f}(\mathbf{x}_0)[\mathbf{g}'(t_0)]$. ∎

Corollary 2 will be used in the discussion of tangent vectors in Section 4–7.

Again let $p = 1$, and suppose that $f$ and $\mathbf{g}$ are of class $C^{(q)}$ for some $q \geq 1$. In particular, $f$ and $\mathbf{g}$ are differentiable. Formula (4–20) applies at every point $\mathbf{t} \in \Delta$ and the corresponding point $\mathbf{x} = \mathbf{g}(\mathbf{t}) \in D$. Thus

$$F_j(\mathbf{t}) = \sum_{i=1}^{n} (f_i \circ \mathbf{g})(\mathbf{t}) g_j^i(\mathbf{t}),$$

for every $\mathbf{t} \in \Delta$ and $j = 1, \ldots, r$. Since all of the functions $f_i$, $\mathbf{g}$, $g_j^i$ are continuous, each partial derivative $F_j$ is continuous. Hence $F$ is of class $C^{(1)}$. If $q \geq 2$, then repeated application of the chain rule shows that $F$ is of class $C^{(q)}$ and gives formulas for calculating its partial derivatives of orders $1, 2, \ldots, q$.

In case $p > 1$ and $\mathbf{f}$, $\mathbf{g}$ are of class $C^{(q)}$, the preceding discussion shows that the components $F^1, \ldots, F^p$ of $\mathbf{F}$ are of class $C^{(q)}$, since $F^l = f^l \circ \mathbf{g}$ for each $l = 1, \ldots, p$. Therefore $\mathbf{F}$ is of class $C^{(q)}$. We have proved:

**Corollary 3.** *If* $\mathbf{f}$ *and* $\mathbf{g}$ *are of class* $C^{(q)}$, *then* $\mathbf{F}$ *is of class* $C^{(q)}$. ∎

**Example 1.** Let $r = 1$. The chain rule becomes

$$F'(t) = \sum_{i=1}^{n} f_i[\mathbf{g}(t)]g^{i\prime}(t),$$

which can also be written

$$F'(t) = df[\mathbf{g}(\mathbf{t})] \cdot \mathbf{g}'(t).$$

If in addition $n = 1$, it becomes $F'(t) = f'[g(t)]g'(t)$, which is the composite function rule of elementary calculus.

**Example 2.** Let $F(x) = f[x, g(x)]$, where $f$ and $g$ are of class $C^{(2)}$. In this case $g^1(x) = x$, $g^2(x) = g(x)$, and the formula in Example 1 becomes

$$F'(x) = f_1[x, g(x)] + f_2[x, g(x)]g'(x).$$

Another application of the chain rule together with the formula for the derivative of a product gives

$$F''(x) = f_{11} + 2f_{12}g'(x) + f_{22}[g'(x)]^2 + f_2 g''(x).$$

In this formula the partial derivatives of $f$ are evaluated at $(x, g(x))$.

**Example 3.** Let $f$ be of class $C^{(2)}$ and let

$$F(r, \theta) = f[r\cos\theta, r\sin\theta].$$

Let us show that

$$f_{11} + f_{22} = F_{11} + \frac{1}{r^2}F_{22} + \frac{1}{r}F_1.$$

The expression on the left-hand side is called the *Laplacian* of $f$. The partial differential equation $f_{11} + f_{22} = 0$ is called *Laplace's equation.* Its solutions are called *harmonic functions.* The formula above expresses the Laplacian in polar coordinates.

In this example

$$g^1(r, \theta) = r\cos\theta, \qquad g^2(r, \theta) = r\sin\theta.$$

Using the chain rule, we get

$$F_1 = f_1 g_1^1 + f_2 g_1^2 = f_1\cos\theta + f_2\sin\theta,$$
$$F_2 = f_1 g_2^1 + f_2 g_2^2 = f_1(-r\sin\theta) + f_2(r\cos\theta).$$

Further application of the chain rule gives

$$F_{11} = \cos\theta(f_{11}\cos\theta + f_{12}\sin\theta) + \sin\theta(f_{21}\cos\theta + f_{22}\sin\theta),$$
$$F_{22} = -r\sin\theta[f_{11}(-r\sin\theta) + f_{12}(r\cos\theta)] + r\cos\theta[f_{21}(-r\sin\theta) + f_{22}(r\cos\theta)] - f_1 r\cos\theta - f_2 r\sin\theta.$$

Combining terms and using the fact that $f_{21} = f_{12}$, we get

$$F_{11} + \frac{1}{r^2}F_{22} = f_{11} + f_{22} - \frac{1}{r}(f_1\cos\theta + f_2\sin\theta),$$

$$F_{11} + \frac{1}{r^2}F_{22} = f_{11} + f_{22} - \frac{1}{r}F_1.$$

This is what we wished to show.

**Corollary 4.** *Let $n = r = p$, and let $\mathbf{f}$ and $\mathbf{g}$ be differentiable. Then, for every $\mathbf{t} \in \Delta$,*

$$\frac{\partial(F^1, \ldots, F^n)}{\partial(t^1, \ldots, t^n)} = \frac{\partial(f^1, \ldots, f^n)}{\partial(x^1, \ldots, x^n)}\,\frac{\partial(g^1, \ldots, g^n)}{\partial(t^1, \ldots, t^n)}, \tag{4–21}$$

*the Jacobians being evaluated at $\mathbf{t}$ and at $\mathbf{x} = \mathbf{g}(\mathbf{t})$.*

*Proof.* By (4-19), $D\mathbf{F}(\mathbf{t}) = D\mathbf{f}(\mathbf{x}) \circ D\mathbf{g}(\mathbf{t})$. Hence

$$\det D\mathbf{F}(\mathbf{t}) = \det D\mathbf{f}(\mathbf{x}) \det D\mathbf{g}(\mathbf{t}). \blacksquare$$

**Example 4.** Let $n = r = p = 2$. Let $\mathbf{f}(x, y) = f^1(x, y)\mathbf{E}_1 + f^2(x, y)\mathbf{E}_2$, $\mathbf{g}(r, \theta) = (r \cos \theta)\mathbf{e}_1 + (r \sin \theta)\mathbf{e}_2$. As before, $\mathbf{E}_1$, $\mathbf{E}_2$ denote the standard basis vectors for the plane $E^2$ in which $\mathbf{f}$ takes its values. Then

$$\frac{\partial(g^1, g^2)}{\partial(r, \theta)} = \det \begin{pmatrix} \cos\theta & -r\sin\theta \\ \sin\theta & r\cos\theta \end{pmatrix} = r.$$

Hence

$$\frac{\partial(F^1, F^2)}{\partial(r, \theta)} = \frac{\partial(f^1\ f^2)}{\partial(x, y)}\, r.$$

## PROBLEMS

Assume that all functions which occur in these problems are of class $C^{(2)}$.

1. Let $F(x, y) = f(x, xy)$. Find the mixed partial derivative $F_{12}$.
2. Let $F(x, y) = f[x, y, g(x, y)]$. Express the partial derivatives of $F$ of orders 1 and 2 in terms of those of $f$ and $g$.
3. Let $n = r = p = 2$. Find the Jacobian $\partial(F^1, F^2)/\partial(s, t)$ at the indicated point by means of Corollary 4.
   (a) $\mathbf{f}(x, y) = xy\mathbf{E}_1 + x^2y\mathbf{E}_2$, $\mathbf{g}(s, t) = (s + t)\mathbf{e}_1 + (s^2 - t^2)\mathbf{e}_2$, $(s_0, t_0) = (2, 1)$.
   (b) $\mathbf{f}(x, y) = \phi(x + y)\mathbf{E}_1 + \phi(x - y)\mathbf{E}_2$, $\mathbf{g}(s, t) = (\exp t)\mathbf{e}_1 + \exp(-s)\mathbf{e}_2$, $(s_0, t_0) = (\log 2)\boldsymbol{\epsilon}_1$.
4. (a) Show that the chain rule is still true if $p > 1$, namely,

$$\frac{\partial \mathbf{F}}{\partial t^j} = \sum_{i=1}^{n} \frac{\partial g^i}{\partial t^j} \frac{\partial \mathbf{f}}{\partial x^i}, \qquad j = 1, \ldots, r.$$

   (b) Use it to find $(\partial\mathbf{F}/\partial s)(s_0, t_0)$ and $(\partial\mathbf{F}/\partial t)(s_0, t_0)$ in Problem 3(a).
5. Let $\mathbf{G}$ be the standard representation of a curve $\gamma$ of class $C^{(2)}$.
   (a) Show that $\mathbf{G}'(s) \cdot \mathbf{G}''(s) = 0$. [*Hint:* Use the fact that $|\mathbf{G}'(s)|^2 = 1$.]
   (b) Let $\mathbf{g}$ be any parametric representation of class $C^{(2)}$ of $\gamma$ and define $S(t)$ as in Section 3-2. Show that $S''(t) = \mathbf{g}'(t) \cdot \mathbf{g}''(t)/S'(t)$.
   (c) If $\mathbf{G}''(s) \neq \mathbf{0}$, then $\mathbf{G}''(s)$ is called the *principal normal vector* and $|\mathbf{G}''(s)|$ the *absolute curvature* at $\mathbf{G}(s)$. Show that

$$|\mathbf{G}''[S(t)]| = \frac{[|\mathbf{g}'(t)|^2|\mathbf{g}''(t)|^2 - (\mathbf{g}'(t) \cdot \mathbf{g}''(t))^2]^{1/2}}{|\mathbf{g}'(t)|^3}.$$

6. Let $f(x, y) = \phi(x - cy) + \psi(x + cy)$, where $c$ is a scalar. Show that $f_{22} = c^2 f_{11}$.
7. Let $n = 4$ and $\rho = [(x^1)^2 + (x^2)^2 + (x^3)^2]^{1/2}$. Let $f(\mathbf{x}) = [\phi(\rho - cx^4) + \psi(\rho + cx^4)]/\rho$. Show that $f_{44} = c^2(f_{11} + f_{22} + f_{33})$. [*Note:* The partial differential equation $f_{nn} = c^2(f_{11} + \cdots + f_{n-1,n-1})$ is called the *wave equation* in $n$ variables. Problem 6 gives D'Alembert's solution for $n = 2$. Solutions of the type in Problem 7 are called spherical waves.]

8. Suppose that $f$ satisfies the partial differential equation $f_2 = f_{11} + bf$, where $b$ is a scalar. Let $F(x, y) = \exp(-by)f(x, y)$. Show that $F_2 = F_{11}$.

9. Let $F = f \circ \mathbf{L}$, where $\mathbf{L}$ is a linear transformation with matrix $(c^i_j)$. Show that

$$F_{jl} = \sum_{i,k=1}^{n} f_{ik} c^i_j c^k_l, \qquad j, l = 1, \ldots, r.$$

10. Using Problem 9 show that if $r = n$ and $\mathbf{L}$ is orthogonal, then $F_{11} + \cdots + F_{nn} = f_{11} + \cdots + f_{nn}$. In other words, the Laplacian is invariant under orthogonal transformations of $E^n$. [*Hint:* $\mathbf{L}^t = \mathbf{L}^{-1}$.]

11. Let $n = r$. A linear transformation $\mathbf{L}$ is a *Lorentz* transformation of $E^n$ if $\mathbf{L}^{-1} = \mathbf{S} \circ \mathbf{L}^t \circ \mathbf{S}$, where $\mathbf{S}$ is as in Example 4, Section 4–2.
   (a) Show that if $\mathbf{M}$ and $\mathbf{L}$ are Lorentz, then $\mathbf{M} \circ \mathbf{L}$ and $\mathbf{L}^{-1}$ are also Lorentz. [*Hint:* $\mathbf{S}^2 = \mathbf{I}$.]
   (b) Show that $\mathbf{L}$ is Lorentz if and only if $\mathbf{S} = \mathbf{L}^t \circ \mathbf{S} \circ \mathbf{L}$.
   (c) Show that $\mathbf{L}$ is Lorentz if and only if

$$\sum_{i=1}^{n-1} [L^i(\mathbf{t})]^2 - [L^n(\mathbf{t})]^2 = \sum_{i=1}^{n-1} (t^i)^2 - (t^n)^2$$

   for every $\mathbf{t}$. [*Hint:* The right-hand side is $\mathbf{S}(\mathbf{t}) \cdot \mathbf{t}$. Use (b).]

12. Show that if $\mathbf{L}$ is Lorentz, then $F_{11} + \cdots + F_{n-1,n-1} - F_{nn} = f_{11} + \cdots + f_{n-1,n-1} - f_{nn}$. In other words, the wave operator is invariant under Lorentz transformations ($c = 1$).

## 4–5 THE INVERSE FUNCTION THEOREM

Let us assume that $r = n$. If $\mathbf{g}$ is a univalent transformation, then $\mathbf{g}$ has an inverse $\mathbf{g}^{-1}$ (and conversely). It occasionally happens that $\mathbf{g}^{-1}$ can be found explicitly by solving the system of equations $x^i = g^i(\mathbf{t})$, $i = 1, \ldots, n$, for the components $t^1, \ldots, t^n$ in terms of $\mathbf{x}$. However, the more common situation is either that these equations cannot be explicitly solved, or that it is inconvenient to solve them explicitly. One would like a criterion which guarantees that the inverse $\mathbf{g}^{-1}$ exists, and a formula for its differential, without explicitly finding $\mathbf{g}^{-1}$ itself.

If $n = 1$ and the domain is an interval, we merely have to require that $g$ is differentiable and $g'(t)$ is never 0. Then $g$ is a strictly monotone function (Section A–10) and its inverse is differentiable. The derivative of the inverse is given by

$$g^{-1\prime}(x) = 1/g'(t), \quad \text{if } x = g(t). \tag{4–22}$$

This is proved in elementary calculus. For example, see [9].

In two or more dimensions the Jacobian $J\mathbf{g}(\mathbf{t})$ takes the place of the derivative $g'(t)$. However, the situation is by no means as simple as before. First of all, we shall have to assume that $\mathbf{g}$ is at least of class $C^{(1)}$, a stronger condition than differentiability. Second, and more important, is the fact that the Jacobian's being of one sign implies only that $\mathbf{g}$ *locally* has an inverse. Any point $\mathbf{t}_0 \in \Delta$ has a neighborhood $\Omega$ such that the restriction $\mathbf{g}|\Omega$ of $\mathbf{g}$ to $\Omega$ has an inverse $\mathbf{f}$. An example given below shows that $\mathbf{g}$ itself need not have an inverse.

It is plausible that a local inverse exists. For $\mathbf{t}$ near $\mathbf{t}_0$, $\mathbf{g}(\mathbf{t})$ is approximated by $\mathbf{G}(\mathbf{t}) = \mathbf{L}(\mathbf{t} - \mathbf{t}_0) + \mathbf{x}_0$, where $\mathbf{L} = D\mathbf{g}(\mathbf{t}_0)$, $\mathbf{x}_0 = \mathbf{g}(\mathbf{t}_0)$. Since $\det \mathbf{L} = J\mathbf{g}(\mathbf{t}_0) \neq 0$, the affine transformation $\mathbf{G}$ has an inverse. This suggests, but of course does not prove, the following.

**Inverse Function Theorem.** *Let* $\mathbf{g}$ *be a transformation of class* $C^{(q)}$, $q \geq 1$, *from an open set* $\Delta \subset E^n$ *into* $E^n$. *Assume that* $J\mathbf{g}(\mathbf{t}) \neq 0$ *for every* $\mathbf{t} \in \Delta$. *Then given any* $\mathbf{t}_0 \in \Delta$ *there exists a neighborhood* $\Omega$ *of* $\mathbf{t}_0$ *such that* $\Omega \subset \Delta$ *and:*

(1) *The restriction* $\mathbf{g}|\Omega$ *is univalent.*

(2) *The set* $U = \mathbf{g}(\Omega)$ *is open.*

(3) *The inverse* $\mathbf{f}$ *of* $\mathbf{g}|\Omega$ *is of class* $C^{(q)}$. (See Fig. 4–4.)

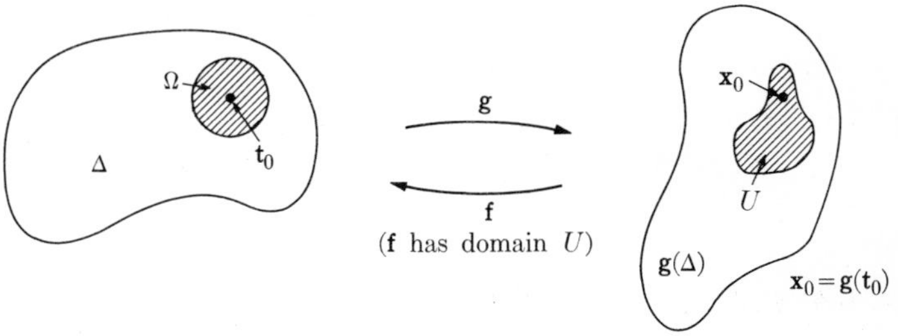


FIGURE 4–4

*Proof. Step 1.* Let $\mathbf{t}_0 \in \Delta$. Let $c$ be as in Proposition 14 (p. 104), and let $\Omega$ be as in Propositions 13b and 14, with $\epsilon = c/2$. Then

$$|\mathbf{g}(\mathbf{s}) - \mathbf{g}(\mathbf{t})| \geq \frac{c}{2} |\mathbf{s} - \mathbf{t}|$$

for every $\mathbf{s}, \mathbf{t} \in \Omega$. In particular, $\mathbf{g}(\mathbf{s}) = \mathbf{g}(\mathbf{t})$ implies that $\mathbf{s} = \mathbf{t}$. Hence the restriction of $\mathbf{g}$ to $\Omega$ is univalent.

*Step 2.* Let $U = \mathbf{g}(\Omega)$. To show that $U$ is open we shall show that any $\mathbf{x}_1 \in U$ has a neighborhood $U_1$ such that $U_1 \subset U$. From Step 1, $\mathbf{x}_1 = \mathbf{g}(\mathbf{t}_1)$ for exactly one $\mathbf{t}_1 \in \Omega$. Let $\Omega_1$ be a neighborhood of $\mathbf{t}_1$ whose closure $\operatorname{cl} \Omega_1$ is contained in $\Omega$, and let $\Gamma_1$ denote the boundary of $\Omega_1$. Since the restriction of $\mathbf{g}$ to $\Omega$ is univalent and $\mathbf{t}_1 \notin \Gamma_1$, $\mathbf{x}_1 \notin \mathbf{g}(\Gamma_1)$. (See Fig. 4–5.) Since $\mathbf{g}$ is of class $C^{(q)}$, and therefore is continuous, the image $\mathbf{g}(\Gamma_1)$ of the compact set $\Gamma_1$ is compact. Let $\sigma_1$ be one-half the distance from $\mathbf{x}_1$ to $\mathbf{g}(\Gamma_1)$, and let $U_1$ be the neighborhood of $\mathbf{x}_1$ of radius $\sigma_1$.

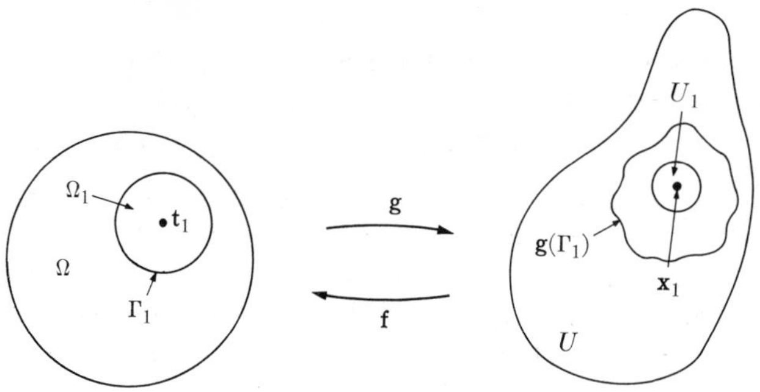


FIGURE 4-5

Let $\mathbf{x} \in U_1$. Then for every $\mathbf{t} \in \Gamma_1$,

$$\mathbf{x}_1 - \mathbf{g}(\mathbf{t}) = [\mathbf{x}_1 - \mathbf{x}] + [\mathbf{x} - \mathbf{g}(\mathbf{t})].$$

Using the triangle inequality, we get

$$2\sigma_1 \leq |\mathbf{x}_1 - \mathbf{g}(\mathbf{t})| \leq |\mathbf{x}_1 - \mathbf{x}| + |\mathbf{x} - \mathbf{g}(\mathbf{t})|.$$

Since $|\mathbf{x}_1 - \mathbf{x}| < \sigma_1$, we must have

$$\sigma_1 < |\mathbf{x} - \mathbf{g}(\mathbf{t})|$$

for every $\mathbf{t} \in \Gamma_1$. Let

$$\psi(\mathbf{t}) = |\mathbf{x} - \mathbf{g}(\mathbf{t})|^2 = \sum_{i=1}^{n} [x^i - g^i(\mathbf{t})]^2.$$

The real-valued function $\psi$ is of class $C^{(q)}$ and has a minimum on the closed $n$-ball $\text{cl}\,\Omega_1 = \Omega_1 \cup \Gamma_1$. But

$$\psi(\mathbf{t}_1) = |\mathbf{x} - \mathbf{x}_1|^2 < \sigma_1^2,$$

and

$$\psi(\mathbf{t}) > \sigma_1^2 \quad \text{for every } \mathbf{t} \in \Gamma_1.$$

Hence the minimum value is less than $\sigma_1^2$, and must be attained at some interior point $\mathbf{t}_2 \in \Omega_1$. By Proposition 10, $d\psi(\mathbf{t}_2) = \mathbf{0}$. Since

$$d\psi(\mathbf{t}) = -2 \sum_{i=1}^{n} (x^i - g^i(\mathbf{t}))\, dg^i(\mathbf{t}),$$

we have, upon setting $c^i = x^i - g^i(\mathbf{t}_2)$,

$$\mathbf{0} = \sum_{i=1}^{n} c^i\, dg^i(\mathbf{t}_2).$$

Since $J\mathbf{g}(\mathbf{t}_2) \neq 0$, the row covectors $dg^1(\mathbf{t}_2), \ldots, dg^n(\mathbf{t}_2)$ are linearly independent. Therefore $c^i = 0$, $i = 1, \ldots, n$, and $\mathbf{x} = \mathbf{g}(\mathbf{t}_2)$.

We have shown that if $\mathbf{x} \in U_1$, then $\mathbf{x} \in \mathbf{g}(\Omega_1)$. Thus $U_1 \subset \mathbf{g}(\Omega_1) \subset U$.

*Step 3.* The existence of the inverse $\mathbf{f}$ required in (3) of the theorem is immediate from (1). We must show that $\mathbf{f}$ is of class $C^{(q)}$. Let $\mathbf{x}_1 \in U$ and $\mathbf{t}_1 = \mathbf{f}(\mathbf{x}_1)$ as in Step 2. Let $\mathbf{L}_1 = D\mathbf{g}(\mathbf{t}_1)$. (The subscript on $\mathbf{L}$ does not denote a partial derivative.) Let us first show that $\mathbf{f}$ is differentiable at $\mathbf{x}_1$ and $D\mathbf{f}(\mathbf{x}_1) = \mathbf{L}_1^{-1}$. Let $c_1 = 1/\|\mathbf{L}_1^{-1}\|$. Given $\epsilon > 0$, there is a neighborhood $\Omega_2$ of $\mathbf{t}_1$, $\Omega_2 \subset \Omega$, such that

$$|\mathbf{g}(\mathbf{t}) - \mathbf{g}(\mathbf{t}_1) - \mathbf{L}_1(\mathbf{t} - \mathbf{t}_1)| \leq \frac{\epsilon c_1 c}{2} |\mathbf{t} - \mathbf{t}_1| \qquad (*)$$

for every $\mathbf{t} \in \Omega_2$ where $c$ is as in Step 1.

By (2) there is a neighborhood $U_2$ of $\mathbf{x}_1$ such that $U_2 \subset \mathbf{g}(\Omega_2)$. Let $\mathbf{x} \in U_2$. Then $\mathbf{x} = \mathbf{g}(\mathbf{t})$, where $\mathbf{t} \in \Omega_2$. Since $\mathbf{x}_1 = \mathbf{g}(\mathbf{t}_1)$, from Step 1 we have

$$\frac{c}{2} |\mathbf{t} - \mathbf{t}_1| \leq |\mathbf{x} - \mathbf{x}_1|. \qquad (**)$$

Moreover, since $\mathbf{t} = \mathbf{f}(\mathbf{x})$ and $\mathbf{t}_1 = \mathbf{f}(\mathbf{x}_1)$,

$$\mathbf{L}_1[\mathbf{f}(\mathbf{x}) - \mathbf{f}(\mathbf{x}_1) - \mathbf{L}_1^{-1}(\mathbf{x} - \mathbf{x}_1)] = -[\mathbf{g}(\mathbf{t}) - \mathbf{g}(\mathbf{t}_1) - \mathbf{L}_1(\mathbf{t} - \mathbf{t}_1)].$$

Since $c_1|\tau| \leq |\mathbf{L}_1(\tau)|$ for every $\tau$, we get

$$c_1|\mathbf{f}(\mathbf{x}) - \mathbf{f}(\mathbf{x}_1) - \mathbf{L}_1^{-1}(\mathbf{x} - \mathbf{x}_1)| \leq |\mathbf{g}(\mathbf{t}) - \mathbf{g}(\mathbf{t}_1) - \mathbf{L}_1(\mathbf{t} - \mathbf{t}_1)|.$$

Then from (*) and (**),

$$|\mathbf{f}(\mathbf{x}) - \mathbf{f}(\mathbf{x}_1) - \mathbf{L}_1^{-1}(\mathbf{x} - \mathbf{x}_1)| \leq \epsilon|\mathbf{x} - \mathbf{x}_1|,$$

for every $\mathbf{x} \in U_2$. This shows that $\mathbf{f}$ is differentiable at $\mathbf{x}_1$ and $D\mathbf{f}(\mathbf{x}_1) = \mathbf{L}_1^{-1}$.

We have shown that $\mathbf{f}$ is a differentiable function, and that

$$D\mathbf{f}(\mathbf{x}) = \{D\mathbf{g}[\mathbf{f}(\mathbf{x})]\}^{-1} \qquad (4\text{–}23)$$

for every $\mathbf{x} \in U$. By Theorem 9, $\mathbf{f}$ is continuous. Since each $g_j^i$ is a continuous function, the composite $g_j^i \circ \mathbf{f}$ is continuous. If $(y_j^i)$ is a nonsingular matrix and $(z_j^i)$ its inverse, then for each $i = 1, \ldots, n$ the elements $z_1^i, \ldots, z_n^i$ of the $i$th row satisfy the system of linear equations

$$\delta_j^i = \sum_{l=1}^{n} z_l^i y_j^l, \qquad j = 1, \ldots, n.$$

By Cramer's rule ([12], p. 151), each $z_j^i$ is a rational function (quotient of two polynomials) in $y_1^1, \ldots, y_n^n$. Applying this with $y_j^i = g_j^i[\mathbf{f}(\mathbf{x})]$, $z_j^i = f_j^i(\mathbf{x})$, we find from (4–23) that the partial derivatives $f_j^i$ are continuous. Hence $\mathbf{f}$ is of class $C^{(1)}$. If $\mathbf{g}$ is of class $C^{(2)}$, then $g_j^i$ is of class $C^{(1)}$ and by Corollary 3, Section 4–4, $g_j^i \circ \mathbf{f}$ is of class $C^{(1)}$. Hence $f_j^i$ is of class $C^{(1)}$ and $\mathbf{f}$ of class $C^{(2)}$. Repeating this argument, we find that if $\mathbf{g}$ is of class $C^{(q)}$ then $\mathbf{f}$ is also of class $C^{(q)}$. This completes the proof of the inverse function theorem. ∎

Formula (4–23) is an extension of formula (4–22). By taking the determinants, we obtain another formula which is also an extension of (4–22):

$$J\mathbf{f}(\mathbf{x}) = \frac{1}{J\mathbf{g}(\mathbf{t})}, \qquad \mathbf{t} = \mathbf{f}(\mathbf{x}). \tag{4–24}$$

The inverse function theorem has the following:

**Corollary.** *Let* $\mathbf{g}$ *satisfy the hypotheses of the inverse function theorem. Then the image of any open subset of* $\Delta$ *is open.*

*Proof.* Let $B \subset \Delta$ be open, and let $\mathbf{x}_0 \in \mathbf{g}(B)$. Then $\mathbf{x}_0 = \mathbf{g}(\mathbf{t}_0)$ for some $\mathbf{t}_0 \in B$. (There may be several possible choices for $\mathbf{t}_0$.) By the inverse function theorem, applied to $\mathbf{g}|B$, there exists a neighborhood $\Omega$ of $\mathbf{t}_0$ such that $\mathbf{g}(\Omega)$ is an open subset of $\mathbf{g}(B)$. Therefore some neighborhood of $\mathbf{x}_0$ is contained in $\mathbf{g}(B)$. This shows that $\mathbf{g}(B)$ is an open set. ∎

**Example.** Let $r = n = 2$, and

$$\mathbf{g}(s, t) = (\cosh s \cos t)\mathbf{e}_1 + (\sinh s \sin t)\mathbf{e}_2,$$

where cosh and sinh are hyperbolic functions. Then

$$g_1^1(s, t) = \sinh s \cos t, \qquad g_2^1(s, t) = -\cosh s \sin t,$$
$$g_1^2(s, t) = \cosh s \sin t, \qquad g_2^2(s, t) = \sinh s \cos t.$$

The Jacobian is $\sinh^2 s \cos^2 t + \cosh^2 s \sin^2 t$, which simplifies because $\cosh^2 s = 1 + \sinh^2 s$ and $\cos^2 t + \sin^2 t = 1$ to

$$J\mathbf{g}(s, t) = \sinh^2 s + \sin^2 t.$$

If we take for $\Delta$ the right half-plane $s > 0$, then $\sinh s > 0$ and $J\mathbf{g}(s, t) > 0$. The hypotheses of the inverse function theorem are satisfied, hence local inverses exist. Since cos and sin are periodic, $\mathbf{g}(s, t + 2\pi) = \mathbf{g}(s, t)$. The transformation $\mathbf{g}$ is not univalent, and consequently has no inverse. By the corollary, $\mathbf{g}(\Delta)$ is an open set which, as we shall soon see, is $E^2$ with a line segment removed.

Let $\tilde{\Delta} = \{(s, t) : s > 0, 0 < t < 2\pi\}$, and let $\tilde{\mathbf{g}}$ be the restriction of $\mathbf{g}$ to $\tilde{\Delta}$. Let us show that $\tilde{\mathbf{g}}$ has an inverse. It is not easy to solve the equations

$$x = g^1(s, t) = \cosh s \cos t, \qquad y = g^2(s, t) = \sinh s \sin t$$

explicitly for $s$ and $t$. However, let us consider what happens on vertical straight lines $s = c$. For each $c > 0$, $\mathbf{g}(c, t)$ represents on $[0, 2\pi]$ an ellipse with major semi-

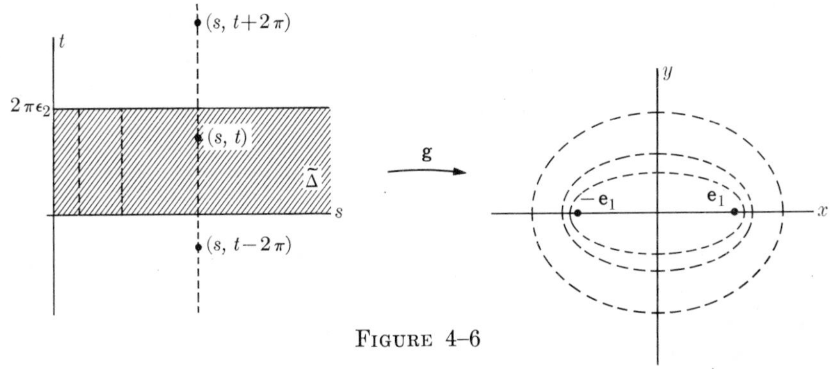


FIGURE 4–6

axis of length $\cosh c > 1$ and minor semiaxis of length $\sinh c$. Each of these ellipses has $\pm\mathbf{e}_1$ as foci, and $\mathbf{g}(c, 0) = \mathbf{g}(c, 2\pi) = (\cosh c)\mathbf{e}_1$. If $s_1 \neq s_2$, then the points $\tilde{\mathbf{g}}(s_1, t_1)$ and $\tilde{\mathbf{g}}(s_2, t_2)$ lie on different ellipses. Moreover, $\tilde{\mathbf{g}}(s, t_1) = \tilde{\mathbf{g}}(s, t_2)$ implies $t_1 = t_2$. Hence $\tilde{\mathbf{g}}(s_1, t_1) = \tilde{\mathbf{g}}(s_2, t_2)$ implies that $(s_1, t_1) = (s_2, t_2)$, and $\tilde{\mathbf{g}}$ is univalent. The image of $\tilde{\Delta}$ is $E^2$ with the semi-infinite line on the $x$-axis from $-\mathbf{e}_1$ to $\infty$ deleted. The part of the boundary of $\tilde{\Delta}$ on the $s$-axis is transformed onto the part of the line from $\mathbf{e}_1$ to $\infty$, and the vertical part of the boundary onto the part from $-\mathbf{e}_1$ to $\mathbf{e}_1$. Hence $\mathbf{g}(\operatorname{cl}\tilde{\Delta}) = E^2$. By periodicity each value which $\mathbf{g}$ takes on $\Delta$ is also taken somewhere on $\tilde{\Delta}$ or its lower boundary. Hence $\mathbf{g}(\Delta)$ is $E^2$ with the line segment joining $-\mathbf{e}_1$ and $\mathbf{e}_1$ removed. (See Fig. 4–6.)

### Regular transformations

**Definition.** $(r = n)$. A transformation $\mathbf{g}$ is *regular* if:

(1) $\mathbf{g}$ is of class $C^{(1)}$,

(2) $\mathbf{g}$ is univalent, and

(3) $J\mathbf{g}(\mathbf{t}) \neq 0$ for every $\mathbf{t} \in \Delta$.

A regular transformation $\mathbf{g}$ has an inverse $\mathbf{g}^{-1}$ which is also of class $C^{(1)}$. Regular transformations are called by many authors *diffeomorphisms of class* $C^{(1)}$. [A transformation of class $C^{(0)}$ which has an inverse of class $C^{(0)}$ is called a *homeomorphism* (Section A–6).]

One might expect naively that at worst a transformation distorts shapes, and that the image of a set has basically the same structure as the original. For instance, the image of a smooth simple arc should be a smooth simple arc, the interior of a set should transform onto the interior of the image, and so on. From various examples we know by now that this need not be the case at all. However, it is so for regular transformations. They are the ones which behave properly throughout calculus.

The notion of regular transformation is the basis for the discussion in Chapter 7 of coordinate changes on manifolds. The transformation law for multiple integrals will be proved in Chapter 5 only for regular transformations.

**PROBLEMS**

1. Determine whether $\mathbf{g}$ satisfies the hypotheses of the inverse function theorem. Find $\mathbf{g}(\Delta)$. If $\mathbf{g}$ is univalent, find $\mathbf{g}^{-1}$ explicitly.
   (a) $\mathbf{g}(\mathbf{t}) = \mathbf{t} + \mathbf{x}_0$ (a translation), $\Delta = E^n$.
   (b) $\mathbf{g}(s, t) = (s + 2t)\mathbf{e}_1 + (s - t)\mathbf{e}_2$, $\Delta = E^2$.
   (c) $\mathbf{g}(s, t) = (s^2 - s - 2)\mathbf{e}_1 + 3t\mathbf{e}_2$, $\Delta = E^2$.
   (d) $\mathbf{g}(s, t) = (s^2 - t^2)\mathbf{e}_1 + st\mathbf{e}_2$, $\Delta = E^2 - \{(0, 0)\}$.
   (e) $\mathbf{g}(s, t) = (\log st)\mathbf{e}_1 + 1/(s^2 + t^2)\mathbf{e}_2$, $\Delta = \{(s, t) : 0 < t < s\}$.
2. Let $g(t) = t^4 + 2t^2$, $\Delta = (0, \infty)$. Find $g^{-1}$.
3. Let $r = n = 3$, and $\mathbf{g}(s, t, u) = (u \cos st)\mathbf{e}_1 + (u \sin st)\mathbf{e}_2 + (s + u)\mathbf{e}_3$. Then $\mathbf{g}(\boldsymbol{\epsilon}_1 + \boldsymbol{\epsilon}_3) = \mathbf{e}_1 + 2\mathbf{e}_3$. Let $\mathbf{f}$ be a local inverse of $\mathbf{g}$ such that $\mathbf{f}(\mathbf{e}_1 + 2\mathbf{e}_3) = \boldsymbol{\epsilon}_1 + \boldsymbol{\epsilon}_3$. Find $D\mathbf{f}(\mathbf{e}_1 + 2\mathbf{e}_3)$ using (4–23).
4. In the example on p. 114, what are the images of horizontal straight lines? Show that $\mathbf{g}$ is a conformal transformation (Problem 5, Section 4–3), and hence that the images of vertical and horizontal straight lines intersect at right angles. Illustrate with a sketch.
5. Let $\mathbf{g}(s, t) = (\exp s \cos t)\mathbf{e}_1 + (\exp s \sin t)\mathbf{e}_2$ and $\Delta = E^2$.
   (a) Show that $\mathbf{g}$ satisfies the conditions of the inverse function theorem, but is not univalent.
   (b) Let $\tilde{\Delta} = \{(s, t) : 0 < t < 2\pi\}$. Show that the restriction of $\mathbf{g}$ to $\tilde{\Delta}$ is univalent, and find its inverse.
   (c) Find $\mathbf{g}(E^2)$.
   (d) Show that $\mathbf{g}$ is conformal.
6. Let $g^1(s, t) = s + f(t)$, $g^2(s, t) = t + f(s)$, where $f$ is of class $C^{(1)}$ and $|f'(s)| \leq c < 1$ for every $s \in E^1$.
   (a) Show that $\mathbf{g}(E^2) = E^2$. [*Hint:* Given $(x, y)$ define $\psi(s, t)$ as in Step 2 of the proof of the inverse function theorem. Prove that $\psi$ has a minimum at some point $(s^*, t^*)$ and that $\mathbf{g}(s^*, t^*) = (x, y)$.]
   (b) Show that $\mathbf{g}$ is univalent.
7. Let $\Delta$ be an open convex set and $\mathbf{g}$ a differentiable transformation such that $\sum_{i,j=1}^{n} g_j^i(\mathbf{t})h^ih^j > 0$ for every $\mathbf{t} \in \Delta$ and $\mathbf{h} \neq \mathbf{0}$. Show that $\mathbf{g}$ is univalent. [*Hint:* Suppose that $\mathbf{g}(\mathbf{t}_1) = \mathbf{g}(\mathbf{t}_2)$. Let $\mathbf{h} = \mathbf{t}_2 - \mathbf{t}_1$, $f(\mathbf{t}) = [\mathbf{g}(\mathbf{t}) - \mathbf{g}(\mathbf{t}_1)] \cdot \mathbf{h}$, and apply the mean value theorem to $f$.] This result is due to H. Nikaidô.

## 4–6 THE IMPLICIT FUNCTION THEOREM

There is a principle, often carelessly stated, that an equation $\Phi(\mathbf{x}) = 0$ "implicitly determines one of the variables $x^1, \ldots, x^n$ as a function of the remaining $n - 1$ variables." More generally, if $1 \leq m < n$, then $m$ equations $\Phi^1(\mathbf{x}) = \cdots = \Phi^m(\mathbf{x}) = 0$ are supposed to determine implicitly $m$ of the variables in terms of the other $n - m$.

Simple examples show that this principle is invalid unless some additional assumptions are made. Let us suppose that $\Phi^1, \ldots, \Phi^m$ are of class $C^{(q)}$, $q \geq 1$. Let

$$\boldsymbol{\Phi} = (\Phi^1, \ldots, \Phi^m).$$

The implicit function theorem guarantees the local validity of the principle near any point $\mathbf{x}_0$ such that $\mathbf{\Phi}(\mathbf{x}_0) = \mathbf{0}$ and $D\mathbf{\Phi}(\mathbf{x}_0)$ has maximum rank $m$.

Before stating and proving this theorem, let us indicate what it asserts when $n = 3$, $m = 1$. Let $\mathbf{x}_0 = (x_0, y_0, z_0)$ be a point such that $\Phi(\mathbf{x}_0) = 0$ and $d\Phi(\mathbf{x}_0) \neq \mathbf{0}$. Since the components of $d\Phi(\mathbf{x}_0)$ are the partial derivatives $\Phi_1(\mathbf{x}_0)$, $\Phi_2(\mathbf{x}_0)$, $\Phi_3(\mathbf{x}_0)$, at least one of the components is not 0. For instance, suppose that $\Phi_3(\mathbf{x}_0) \neq 0$. Then in some neighborhood $U$ of $\mathbf{x}_0$, $\Phi_3(\mathbf{x}) \neq 0$ and the equation $\Phi(\mathbf{x}) = 0$ "determines $z$ as a function of $x$ and $y$." More precisely, there is a function $\phi$ of class $C^{(q)}$ such that for $(x, y, z) \in U$, $\Phi(x, y, z) = 0$ if and only if $z = \phi(x, y)$. The domain $R$ of $\phi$ is an open subset of the $xy$–plane.

**Example 1.** Let $\Phi(x, y, z) = x^2 + y^2 - z^2 - 1$. The set $M = \{\mathbf{x} : \Phi(\mathbf{x}) = 0\}$ is a hyperboloid. Solving the equation $\Phi(\mathbf{x}) = 0$ for $z$, we get $z = \pm(x^2 + y^2 - 1)^{1/2}$. If $z_0 > 0$, then we take $\phi(x, y) = (x^2 + y^2 - 1)^{1/2}$, so that $z_0 = \phi(x_0, y_0)$. While the theorem guarantees only the existence of $\phi$ in some neighborhood of $(x_0, y_0)$, in this example $\phi$ is actually of class $C^{(\infty)}$ on the complement of the disk $x^2 + y^2 \leq 1$. If $z_0 < 0$, then one should take $\phi(x, y) = -(x^2 + y^2 - 1)^{1/2}$. If $z_0 = 0$, then $\Phi_3(\mathbf{x}_0) = 0$. In this case the equation $\Phi = 0$ determines near $\mathbf{x}_0$ one of the variables $x$ or $y$ as a function of the other two.

Returning to the general case, let $r = n - m$. If $D\mathbf{\Phi}(\mathbf{x}_0)$ has rank $m$, then some set of $m$ columns of its matrix is linearly independent. For the present let us assume that the last $m$ columns are linearly independent. This means that the square matrix obtained by deleting columns $1, 2, \ldots, r$ must have nonzero determinant. Thus

$$\frac{\partial(\Phi^1, \ldots, \Phi^m)}{\partial(x^{r+1}, \ldots, x^n)} \neq 0 \quad \text{at } \mathbf{x}_0. \tag{4–25}$$

Let us introduce the notation

$$\hat{\mathbf{x}} = (x^1, \ldots, x^r), \qquad \hat{\mathbf{x}}_0 = (x_0^1, \ldots, x_0^r)$$

for the vectors obtained by taking only the first $r$ components of $\mathbf{x}$ and $\mathbf{x}_0$.

**Implicit Function Theorem.** *Let $\Phi^1, \ldots, \Phi^m$ be of class $C^{(q)}$ on an open set $D$ containing $\mathbf{x}_0$, where $q \geq 1$ and $1 \leq m < n$. Assume that $\mathbf{\Phi}(\mathbf{x}_0) = \mathbf{0}$ and that (4–25) holds. Then there exist a neighborhood $U$ of $\mathbf{x}_0$, an open set $R \subset E^r$ containing $\hat{\mathbf{x}}_0$, and functions $\phi^1, \ldots, \phi^m$ of class $C^{(q)}$ on $R$ such that:*

$$\frac{\partial(\Phi^1, \ldots, \Phi^m)}{\partial(x^{r+1}, \ldots, x^n)} \neq 0 \quad \textit{at every } \mathbf{x} \in U; \tag{1}$$

*and*

$$\{\mathbf{x} \in U : \mathbf{\Phi}(\mathbf{x}) = \mathbf{0}\} = \{\mathbf{x} \in U : \hat{\mathbf{x}} \in R,\ x^{r+l} = \phi^l(\hat{\mathbf{x}}) \text{ for } l = 1, \ldots, m\}. \tag{2}$$

*Proof.* Since $\mathbf{\Phi}$ is at least of class $C^{(1)}$, the Jacobian in (1) is a continuous function. By assumption (4–25) it is not zero at $\mathbf{x}_0$, and therefore is not zero for $\mathbf{x}$ in some neighborhood $U_0$ of $\mathbf{x}_0$.

Let us consider the transformation $\mathbf{f}$, with domain $U_0$ and values in $E^n$, which has components $X^1, \ldots, X^r, \Phi^1, \ldots, \Phi^m$. As in Section 1–3, $X^i$ is the $i$th standard cartesian coordinate function. For every $\mathbf{x} \in U_0$,

$$\begin{aligned} f^i(\mathbf{x}) &= x^i, & i &= 1, \ldots, r, \\ f^{r+l}(\mathbf{x}) &= \Phi^l(\mathbf{x}), & l &= 1, \ldots, m. \end{aligned}$$

The transformation $\mathbf{f}$ is of class $C^{(q)}$. Its matrix of partial derivatives is

$$\begin{pmatrix} 1 & 0 & \cdots & 0 & 0 & \cdots & 0 \\ 0 & 1 & \cdots & & \cdots & \cdots & \vdots \\ \vdots & & & & & & \vdots \\ 0 & & \cdots & 1 & 0 & \cdots & 0 \\ \Phi_1^1 & & \cdots & \Phi_r^1 & \Phi_{r+1}^1 & \cdots & \Phi_n^1 \\ \vdots & & & & & & \vdots \\ \Phi_1^m & & \cdots & \Phi_r^m & \Phi_{r+1}^m & \cdots & \Phi_n^m \end{pmatrix}$$

By properties of determinants, the Jacobian $J\mathbf{f}(\mathbf{x})$ equals the determinant of the $m \times m$ block in the lower right-hand corner. Since the latter is just the Jacobian in (4–25), $J\mathbf{f}(\mathbf{x}) \neq 0$. By the inverse function theorem, there is a neighborhood $U$ of $\mathbf{x}_0$ such that $\mathbf{f}(U)$ is an open set and the restriction $\mathbf{f}|U$ has an inverse $\mathbf{g}$ of class $C^{(q)}$. Note here that the roles of the symbols $\mathbf{f}$ and $\mathbf{g}$ in Section 4–5 have been reversed.

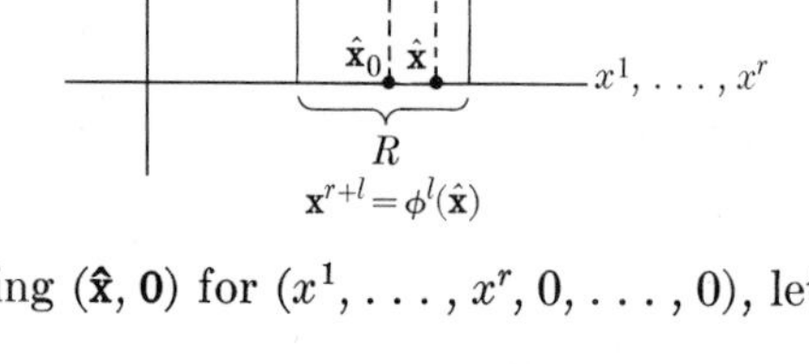

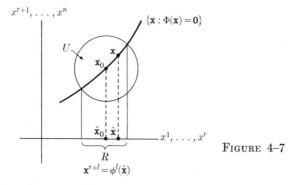

FIGURE 4–7

Writing $(\hat{\mathbf{x}}, \mathbf{0})$ for $(x^1, \ldots, x^r, 0, \ldots, 0)$, let (see Fig. 4–7)

$$R = \{\hat{\mathbf{x}} : (\hat{\mathbf{x}}, \mathbf{0}) \in \mathbf{f}(U)\}.$$

Since $\mathbf{f}(U)$ is an open set, $R$ is open. For every $\hat{\mathbf{x}} \in R$, let

$$\phi^l(\hat{\mathbf{x}}) = g^{r+l}(\hat{\mathbf{x}}, \mathbf{0}), \qquad l = 1, \ldots, m.$$

For $\mathbf{x} \in U$, $\mathbf{\Phi}(\mathbf{x}) = \mathbf{0}$ if and only if $\hat{\mathbf{x}} \in R$ and $\mathbf{f}(\mathbf{x}) = (\hat{\mathbf{x}}, \mathbf{0})$. Since $\mathbf{f}|U$ and $\mathbf{g}$ are inverses, $\mathbf{f}(\mathbf{x}) = (\hat{\mathbf{x}}, \mathbf{0})$ if and only if $\mathbf{x} = \mathbf{g}(\hat{\mathbf{x}}, \mathbf{0})$. ∎

The partial derivatives of $\phi^1, \ldots, \phi^m$ can be calculated in terms of those of $\Phi^1, \ldots, \Phi^m$ by means of the chain rule and Cramer's rule. We illustrate the technique in two special cases. Let us suppose that $q \geq 2$.

Let $n = 3$, $m = 1$ as at the beginning of the section. Then

$$\Phi[x, y, \phi(x, y)] = 0, \tag{$*$}$$

and $\Phi_3[x, y, \phi(x, y)] \neq 0$ for every $(x, y) \in R$. Applying the chain rule to $(*)$, we get

$$\begin{aligned} \Phi_1 + \Phi_3\phi_1 &= 0, & \phi_1 &= -\frac{\Phi_1}{\Phi_3}, \\ \Phi_2 + \Phi_3\phi_2 &= 0, & \phi_2 &= -\frac{\Phi_2}{\Phi_3}. \end{aligned} \tag{$**$}$$

In the formulas $(**)$ the partial derivatives of $\Phi$ are evaluated at $(x, y, \phi(x, y))$.

To calculate the second-order partial derivatives $\phi_{11}, \phi_{12}, \phi_{22}$, the chain rule is applied again. For instance, taking the partial derivative with respect to the second variable in the first of equations $(**)$, we get

$$\Phi_{12} + \Phi_{13}\phi_2 + [\Phi_{32} + \Phi_{33}\phi_2]\phi_1 + \Phi_3\phi_{12} = 0.$$

Substituting the expressions for $\phi_1$, $\phi_2$ obtained above and solving for $\phi_{12}$, we get

$$\phi_{12} = -\frac{(\Phi_3)^2\Phi_{12} - \Phi_2\Phi_3\Phi_{13} - \Phi_1\Phi_3\Phi_{32} + \Phi_1\Phi_2\Phi_{33}}{(\Phi_3)^3}.$$

Let $m = 2$, $n = 3$, $r = n - m = 1$. Writing $\mathbf{\Phi} = (\Phi, \Psi)$ rather than $(\Phi^1, \Phi^2)$, and $\phi, \psi$ rather than $\phi^1, \phi^2$, we have

$$\Phi[x, \phi(x), \psi(x)] = 0,$$
$$\Psi[x, \phi(x), \psi(x)] = 0,$$

and $\Phi_2\Psi_3 - \Phi_3\Psi_2 \neq 0$ for every $x \in R$. The partial derivatives in question are evaluated at $(x, \phi(x), \psi(x))$. By the chain rule

$$\Phi_1 + \Phi_2\phi' + \Phi_3\psi' = 0,$$
$$\Psi_1 + \Psi_2\phi' + \Psi_3\psi' = 0,$$

and by Cramer's rule

$$\phi' = \frac{\Phi_3\Psi_1 - \Phi_1\Psi_3}{\Phi_2\Psi_3 - \Phi_3\Psi_2}, \qquad \psi' = \frac{\Phi_1\Psi_2 - \Phi_2\Psi_1}{\Phi_2\Psi_3 - \Phi_3\Psi_2}.$$

The second derivatives $\phi''$, $\psi''$ can be found by another application of the chain rule.

For convenience we assumed in (4–25) that the last $m$ columns of the $m \times n$ matrix of partial derivatives $(\Phi_i^l(\mathbf{x}_0))$ were linearly independent. More generally, one need merely suppose that some set of $m$ columns is linearly independent, in other words, that the linear transformation $D\mathbf{\Phi}(\mathbf{x}_0)$ has maximum rank $m$. Let us suppose that columns $j_1, j_2, \ldots, j_m$ form a linearly independent set, where we may suppose that $j_1 < j_2 < \cdots < j_m$. Let $i_1, \ldots, i_r$ be those integers between 1 and $n$ not included among $j_1, \ldots, j_m$, with $i_1 < \cdots < i_r$. For brevity let us write $\lambda$ for the $r$-tuple of integers $(i_1, \ldots, i_r)$ and $\mathbf{x}^\lambda$ for the $r$-tuple $(x^{i_1}, \ldots, x^{i_r})$.

The implicit function theorem now states, roughly speaking, that locally the equation $\mathbf{\Phi}(\mathbf{x}) = \mathbf{0}$ determines $x^{j_1}, \ldots, x^{j_m}$ as functions of $\mathbf{x}^\lambda$. More precisely, $U$, $R$, and $\phi^1, \ldots, \phi^m$ exist as before such that

$$\frac{\partial(\Phi^1, \ldots, \Phi^m)}{\partial(x^{j_1}, \ldots, x^{j_m})} \neq 0 \quad \text{at every } \mathbf{x} \in U,$$

and

$$\{\mathbf{x} \in U : \mathbf{\Phi}(\mathbf{x}) = \mathbf{0}\} = \{\mathbf{x} : \mathbf{x}^\lambda \in R,\, x^{j_l} = \phi^l(\mathbf{x}^\lambda) \text{ for } l = 1, \ldots, m\}.$$

In the case we considered above, $j_1, \ldots, j_m$ are the integers $r + 1$, $r + 2, \ldots, n$, $\lambda = (1, 2, \ldots, r)$, and then $\mathbf{x}^\lambda = \hat{\mathbf{x}}$.

**Example 2.** Suppose that $m = 2$, $n = 5$, and

$$\frac{\partial(\Phi^1, \Phi^2)}{\partial(x^1, x^4)} \neq 0 \quad \text{at } \mathbf{x}_0.$$

Then we can take $j_1 = 1$, $j_2 = 4$, $\lambda = (2, 3, 5)$.

Let $m = 1$. Then $D\Phi(\mathbf{x}_0) = d\Phi(\mathbf{x}_0)$, and $D\Phi(\mathbf{x}_0)$ has maximum rank 1 if and only if at least one partial derivative $\Phi_j(\mathbf{x}_0)$ is not zero. If $\Phi_j(\mathbf{x}_0) \neq 0$, then we can take $j_1 = j$ and $\mathbf{x}^\lambda = (x^1, \ldots, x^{j-1}, x^{j+1}, \ldots, x^n)$.

**Example 3.** Let

$$\Phi(x, y, z) = x^2 + y^2 + z^2 - 2xz - 4.$$

Then

$$\Phi_1(x, y, z) = 2x - 2z,$$
$$\Phi_2(x, y, z) = 2y,$$
$$\Phi_3(x, y, z) = 2z - 2x.$$

If $d\Phi(x, y, z) = \mathbf{0}$, then $y = 0$, $x = z$, and $\Phi(x, y, z) = -4 \neq 0$. The implicit function theorem applies at any $(x_0, y_0, z_0)$ where $\Phi(x_0, y_0, z_0) = 0$. If $x_0 \neq z_0$, then $\Phi_3(x_0, y_0, z_0) \neq 0$. We may take $j_1 = 3$, $\lambda = (1, 2)$, and proceed as above. We may equally well take $j_1 = 1$, $\lambda = (2, 3)$. However, if $x_0 = z_0$, then we must take $j_1 = 2$, $\lambda = (1, 3)$.

## PROBLEMS

In each problem assume that $\Phi$ is of class $C^{(2)}$.

1. Let $\Phi[x, \phi(x)] = 0$ and $\Phi_2[x, \phi(x)] \neq 0$ for every $x \in R$. Find $\phi'$ and $\phi''$.
2. Let $\Phi[\phi(y, z), y, z] = 0$ and $\Phi_1[\phi(y, z), y, z] \neq 0$ for every $(y, z) \in R$. Find $\phi_{11}$.
3. Let $m = 2$, $n = 4$, $\Phi(\mathbf{x}) = (x^2)^2 + (x^4)^2 - 2x^1x^3$, $\Psi(\mathbf{x}) = (x^2)^3 + (x^4)^3 + (x^1)^3 - (x^3)^3$, and $\mathbf{\Phi} = (\Phi, \Psi)$. Let $\mathbf{x}_0 = (1, -1, 1, 1)$, $j_1 = 1$, $j_2 = 3$.
   (a) Show that the hypotheses of the implicit function theorem are satisfied.
   (b) Write $\phi^1 = \phi$, $\phi^2 = \psi$, where according to the theorem,
   $$(x^2)^2 + (x^4)^2 - 2\phi(x^2, x^4)\psi(x^2, x^4) = 0,$$
   $$(x^2)^3 + (x^4)^3 + [\phi(x^2, x^4)]^3 - [\psi(x^2, x^4)]^3 = 0$$
   for every $(x^2, x^4) \in R$. Find the first-order partial derivatives of $\phi$ and $\psi$ at $\mathbf{x}_0^\lambda = (-1, 1)$.
4. Let $\Phi(x, y, z) = x^2 + 4y^2 - 2yz - z^2$, $\mathbf{x}_0 = 2\mathbf{e}_1 + \mathbf{e}_2 - 4\mathbf{e}_3$.
   (a) Verify the hypotheses of the implicit function theorem.
   (b) Find the largest neighborhood $U$ of $\mathbf{x}_0$ such that $\Phi_3(x, y, z) \neq 0$ for every $(x, y, z) \in U$.
   (c) Find the largest neighborhood of $\mathbf{x}_0$ containing no critical point of $\Phi$.
5. Let $\Phi(x, y) = x^2 - y^2$, $\mathbf{x}_0 = (0, 0)$.
   (a) Let $U$ be any neighborhood of $(0, 0)$, of radius $a$, and $R = (-a/\sqrt{2}, a/\sqrt{2})$. Find a function $\phi$ such that $\Phi[x, \phi(x)] = 0$ for every $x \in R$.
   (b) Show that no $\phi$ exists for which Eq. (2) of the implicit function theorem holds.
6. (a) Let $m = 2$. Let $\mathbf{\Phi} = (\Phi, \Psi)$, where $\Psi(\mathbf{x}) = \theta(\mathbf{x})\Phi(\mathbf{x})$ for every $\mathbf{x} \in D$ and $\theta$ is a real-valued function. Show that $D\mathbf{\Phi}(\mathbf{x}_0)$ has rank less than 2 at any $\mathbf{x}_0$ such that $\mathbf{\Phi}(\mathbf{x}_0) = \mathbf{0}$.
   (b) State and prove a corresponding result for $m > 2$.
7. Give an alternate proof of the implicit function theorem, in case $m = 1$, $n = 2$, by carrying out the following steps. Let $\Phi$ be of class $C^{(1)}$ and suppose that $\Phi(x_0, y_0) = 0$, $\Phi_2(x_0, y_0) \neq 0$. For definiteness assume that $\Phi_2(x_0, y_0) > 0$.
   (a) Show that there exists $\epsilon > 0$ such that $\Phi(x_0, y) < 0$ if $y_0 - \epsilon \leq y < y_0$ and $\Phi(x_0, y) > 0$ if $y_0 < y \leq y_0 + \epsilon$.
   (b) Show that there exists $\delta > 0$ such that $\Phi(x, y_0 - \epsilon) < 0$ and $\Phi(x, y_0 + \epsilon) > 0$ if $|x - x_0| < \delta$.
   (c) Let $I = \{(x, y) : |x - x_0| < \delta, |y - y_0| < \epsilon\}$. The numbers $\epsilon$ and $\delta$ in (a) and (b) may be so chosen that $\Phi_2(x, y) > 0$ for every $(x, y) \in I$. Show that if $|x_1 - x_0| < \delta$ the equation $\Phi(x_1, y) = 0$ has exactly one solution $y_1$ with $(x_1, y_1) \in I$. Set $y_1 = \phi(x_1)$. This defines $\phi$ on the open interval $(x_0 - \delta, x_0 + \delta)$.
   (d) Show that $\phi$ is differentiable and that
   $$\phi'(x) = -\frac{\Phi_1[x, \phi(x)]}{\Phi_2[x, \phi(x)]}.$$

In this proof of the theorem, the rectangle $I$ replaces the circular neighborhood $U$, but this is unimportant. Can you extend this proof to the case $m = 1$, $n > 2$?

## 4–7 MANIFOLDS

The word *manifold* is used in mathematics to describe a topological space which locally is "like" euclidean $E^r$, for some $r$ called the dimension of the manifold. For instance, a circle is locally like $E^1$. Such geometric figures in $E^3$ as ellipsoids, cylinders, and tori are locally like $E^2$. A cone is not locally like $E^2$ near its vertex.

We shall approach the idea of manifold from a rather concrete viewpoint. For us, a manifold $M$ is a subset of some euclidean $E^n$ which can locally be described by an equation $\mathbf{\Phi}(\mathbf{x}) = \mathbf{0}$, where $D\mathbf{\Phi}(\mathbf{x})$ must have maximum rank. Another definition of *manifold* can be given abstractly in terms of coordinate systems. It has the advantage that one need not presuppose that $M$ is a subset of some euclidean space. This will be discussed in Chapter 7.

**Definition.** Let $1 \leq r < n$, $q \geq 1$. A nonempty set $M \subset E^n$ is a *manifold of dimension $r$ and class $C^{(q)}$* if $M$ has the following property: For every $\mathbf{x}_0 \in M$ there exist a neighborhood $U$ of $\mathbf{x}_0$ and $\mathbf{\Phi} = (\Phi^1, \cdots, \Phi^{n-r})$ of class $C^{(q)}$ on $U$, such that $D\mathbf{\Phi}(\mathbf{x})$ has rank $n - r$ for every $\mathbf{x} \in U$ and

$$M \cap U = \{\mathbf{x} \in U : \mathbf{\Phi}(\mathbf{x}) = \mathbf{0}\}.$$

Throughout the following discussion we shall take $q = 1$. For brevity we shall say *$r$-manifold* instead of "manifold of dimension $r$ and class $C^{(1)}$." If $r = n$, let us call any open subset of $E^n$ an *$n$-manifold.*

Let us indicate how an $r$-manifold $M$ is locally like $E^r$. First assume that (4–25) holds at $\mathbf{x}_0$, and define $\mathbf{f}$ as in the proof of the implicit function theorem. The neighborhood of $\mathbf{x}_0$ chosen on p. 118 need not coincide with the neighborhood $U$ in the definition of manifold. In this section let us denote the former neighborhood by $U_1$ rather than $U$, and let us denote the set $R$ on p. 118 by $R_1$. We may suppose that $U_1 \subset U$. Now $\mathbf{f}|U_1$ is a regular transformation (p. 115), and

$$\mathbf{f}(M \cap U_1) = \{(\hat{\mathbf{x}}, \mathbf{0}) : \hat{\mathbf{x}} \in R_1\}$$

is a relatively open subset of the $r$-dimensional subspace of $E^n$ spanned by $\mathbf{e}_1, \ldots, \mathbf{e}_r$. Therefore it is reasonable to say that $M \cap U_1$ is "like" $E^r$ (Fig. 4–8). In case (4–25) does not hold, one must replace the $r$-tuple of integers $1, 2, \ldots, r$ by some other $r$-tuple $\lambda$, as indicated on p. 120.

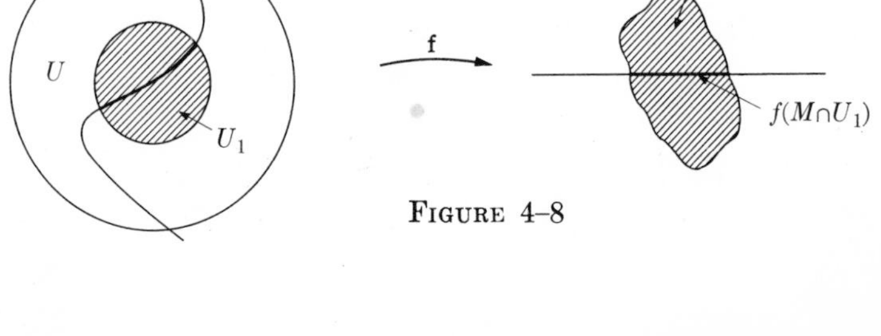


FIGURE 4–8

**Example 1.** Let $n = 2$, $r = 1$, and $H$ be the hyperbola $x^2 - y^2 = 1$. To show that $H$ is a 1-manifold, let us take $\Phi(x, y) = x^2 - y^2 - 1$. Then $D\Phi(x, y) = d\Phi(x, y) = 2x\mathbf{e}^1 - 2y\mathbf{e}^2$. If $(x, y) \neq (0, 0)$, then $d\Phi(x, y) \neq \mathbf{0}$ and the rank is 1. Given $(x_0, y_0) \in H$, let $U$ be any neighborhood of $(x_0, y_0)$ which does not contain $(0, 0)$. In this example the choice of $\Phi$ does not depend on $(x_0, y_0)$.

**Example 2.** Let $M$ be the union of $H$ and one of its asymptotes,

$$M = \{(x, y) : x^2 - y^2 = 1\} \cup \{(x, y) : y = x\}.$$

To show that $M$ is a 1-manifold we must show that given $(x_0, y_0) \in M$, there exist $U$ and $\Phi$ such that $d\Phi(x, y) \neq \mathbf{0}$ in $U$ and $M \cap U = \{(x, y) \in U : \Phi(x, y) = 0\}$. If $(x_0, y_0) \in H$, then we let $\Phi(x, y) = x^2 - y^2 - 1$ as before, and let $U$ be any neighborhood of $(x_0, y_0)$ which does not meet the asymptote $y = x$. However, if $(x_0, y_0)$ is on the asymptote, we take $\Phi(x, y) = y - x$ and $U$ any neighborhood of $(x_0, y_0)$ which does not meet $H$. In this example our choice of $\Phi$ depends on $(x_0, y_0)$.

**Example 3.** Let $M = \{(x, y) : x^2 = y^2\}$. This set consists of the two lines $y = \pm x$, and is not a 1-manifold. Roughly speaking, $M$ is not like $E^1$ near the crossing point $(0, 0)$. More precisely, if $M$ were a 1-manifold, then by the implicit function theorem the following would be true: Each $(x_0, y_0) \in M$ has a neighborhood $U_1$ such that either $M \cap U_1 = \{(x, \phi(x)) : x \in R_1\}$ or $M \cap U_1 = \{(\psi(y), y) : y \in R_2\}$, where $R_1$, $R_2$ are open. In the present example, $(0, 0)$ has no such neighborhood.

Most examples of manifolds which we shall consider are obtained in the following way. Let $\mathbf{\Phi}$ be a transformation of class $C^{(1)}$, from an open set $D \subset E^n$ into $E^m$. Let

$$M = \{\mathbf{x} : \mathbf{\Phi}(\mathbf{x}) = 0 \text{ and } D\mathbf{\Phi}(\mathbf{x}) \text{ has rank } m\}. \tag{4–26}$$

If $M$ is not empty, then it is an $r$-manifold, where $m = n - r$. To show that $M$ is an $r$-manifold, in the definition of manifold let us choose this same $\mathbf{\Phi}$ for every $\mathbf{x}_0 \in M$. By Problem 7, Section 4–3, $\{\mathbf{x} : D\mathbf{\Phi}(\mathbf{x}) \text{ has rank } m\}$ is open. Hence any $\mathbf{x}_0 \in M$ has a neighborhood $U$ such that $D\mathbf{\Phi}(\mathbf{x})$ has rank $m$ for every $\mathbf{x} \in U$, and $M \cap U = \{\mathbf{x} \in U : \mathbf{\Phi}(\mathbf{x}) = \mathbf{0}\}$.

When (4–26) holds, we say that $M$ is the *$r$-manifold determined by* $\mathbf{\Phi}$.

**Example 4.** The $(n - 1)$-sphere $\{\mathbf{x} : |\mathbf{x}| = 1\}$ is an $(n - 1)$-manifold. In fact, it is the $(n - 1)$-manifold determined by $\Phi$, where $\Phi(\mathbf{x}) = |\mathbf{x}|^2 - 1$. The only critical point of $\Phi$ is $\mathbf{0}$, which is not on the $(n - 1)$-sphere.

**Example 5.** Let $F$ be real-valued and of class $C^{(1)}$. Consider a level set

$$B_c = \{\mathbf{x} : F(\mathbf{x}) = c\}.$$

Let $\Phi(\mathbf{x}) = F(\mathbf{x}) - c$. Then $d\Phi(\mathbf{x}) = dF(\mathbf{x})$. If $B_c$ is not empty and contains no critical points of $F$, then $B_c$ is the $(n - 1)$-manifold determined by $\Phi$. If $B_c$ contains critical points, then the $(n - 1)$-manifold determined by $\Phi$ is

$$M_c = B_c - (\text{set of critical points of } F),$$

unless $M_c$ happens to be empty. We saw in Section 2–5 that $B_c$ need not resemble $E^{n-1}$ near a critical point contained in $B_c$.

**Example 6.** Let $F(x, y) = \exp(xy)$. The partial derivatives are $F_1(x, y) = y \exp(xy)$ and $F_2(x, y) = x \exp(xy)$. The only critical point is $(0, 0)$, and $F(0, 0) = 1$. If $c \leq 0$, then $B_c$ is empty. If $c > 0$, $c \neq 1$, then $B_c$ is a 1-manifold. In fact, $B_c$ is the hyperbola $xy = \log c$. The level set $B_1$ is the union of the $x$- and $y$-axes, and is not a 1-manifold. $M_1 = B_1 - \{(0, 0)\}$ is a 1-manifold.

**Example 7.** As in Example 5, if $\mathbf{F}$ is of class $C^{(1)}$ and has values in $E^m$, $m = n - r$, then

$$M_{\mathbf{c}} = \{\mathbf{x} : \mathbf{F}(\mathbf{x}) = \mathbf{c} \text{ and } D\mathbf{F}(\mathbf{x}) \text{ has rank } m\}$$

is either empty or an $r$-manifold.

**Example 8.** In particular, let $\mathbf{a}^1, \ldots, \mathbf{a}^m$ be linearly independent covectors and let $\mathbf{c} \in E^m$. The set

$$P = \{\mathbf{x} : \mathbf{a}^l \cdot \mathbf{x} = c^l \text{ for } l = 1, \ldots, m\}$$

is called an *r-dimensional plane*. Let $\mathbf{L}$ be the linear transformation with row covectors $\mathbf{a}^1, \ldots, \mathbf{a}^m$. Since $\mathbf{L}$ has rank $m$, $\mathbf{L}(E^n) = E^m$. Hence $P = \{\mathbf{x} : \mathbf{L}(\mathbf{x}) = \mathbf{c}\}$ is not empty. Moreover, $D\mathbf{L}(\mathbf{x}) = \mathbf{L}$ has rank $m$ for every $\mathbf{x}$. Thus, any $r$-dimensional plane $P$ is an $r$-manifold.

**Tangent vectors to a manifold.** Let $M$ be a manifold and $\mathbf{x}_0 \in M$.

**Definition.** A vector $\mathbf{h}$ is a *tangent vector* to $M$ at $\mathbf{x}_0$ if there exists a function $\boldsymbol{\psi}$ from an interval $(-\delta, \delta)$ into $M$ such that $\boldsymbol{\psi}(0) = \mathbf{x}_0$ and $\boldsymbol{\psi}'(0) = \mathbf{h}$.

The definition can be restated in a way which is more appealing geometrically. For brevity let us set $\mathbf{x}_t = \mathbf{x}_0 + t\mathbf{h}$. Then $\mathbf{h}$ is a tangent vector if, for some $\delta > 0$, there exists $\mathbf{y}_t \in M$ whenever $0 < |t| < \delta$, such that

$$\lim_{t \to 0} \frac{|\mathbf{y}_t - \mathbf{x}_t|}{|t|} = 0. \tag{*}$$

If we set $\boldsymbol{\psi}(t) = \mathbf{y}_t$ for $0 < |t| < \delta$, and $\boldsymbol{\psi}(0) = \mathbf{x}_0$, then (*) states that $\boldsymbol{\psi}'(0) = \mathbf{h}$. (See Fig. 4–9.)

Let $T(\mathbf{x}_0)$ denote the set of all tangent vectors at $\mathbf{x}_0$. It is called the *tangent space* to $M$ at $\mathbf{x}_0$. If $r$ is the dimension of $M$, then it is plausible that the tangent space is a vector space of dimension $r$. Let us show that this is true. Let $U$ and $\boldsymbol{\Phi}$ be the same as in the definition of manifold.

**Theorem 10.** *The tangent space $T(\mathbf{x}_0)$ is the kernel of the linear transformation $D\boldsymbol{\Phi}(\mathbf{x}_0)$.*

Since $D\boldsymbol{\Phi}(\mathbf{x}_0)$ has rank $m$, the kernel $T(\mathbf{x}_0)$ is a vector subspace of $E^n$ with dimension $r = n - m$.

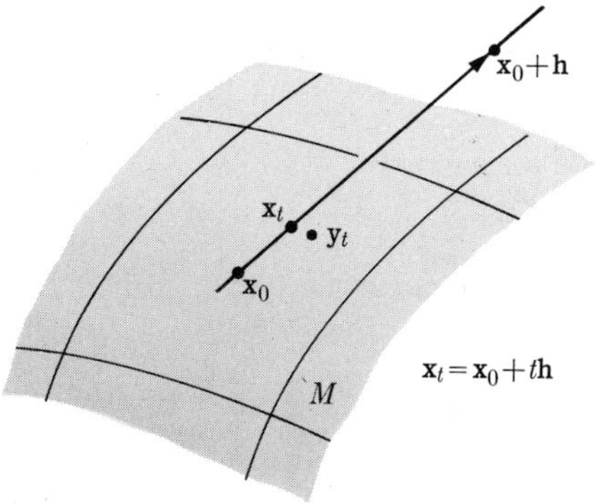


FIGURE 4-9

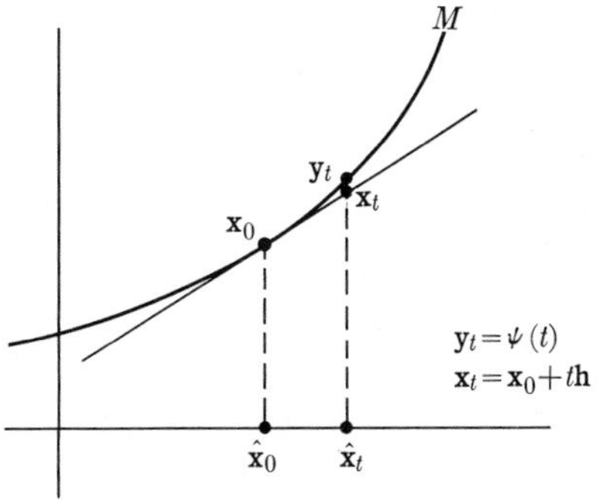


FIGURE 4-10

*Proof of Theorem* 10. Let $\mathbf{L} = D\mathbf{\Phi}(\mathbf{x}_0)$. We must show that $\mathbf{h}$ is a tangent vector if and only if $\mathbf{L}(\mathbf{h}) = \mathbf{0}$.

Let $\mathbf{h} \in T(\mathbf{x}_0)$. Let $\psi$ be as in the definition of tangent vector. Then $\mathbf{\Phi}[\psi(t)] = \mathbf{0}$ for every $t \in (-\delta, \delta)$. Calculating the derivative of $\mathbf{\Phi} \circ \psi$ by Corollary 2, Section 4–4, we have

$$\mathbf{0} = \mathbf{L}[\psi'(0)] = \mathbf{L}(\mathbf{h}).$$

Conversely, let $\mathbf{L}(\mathbf{h}) = \mathbf{0}$. For simplicity let us assume that (4–25) holds, that is, that the last $m$ columns of the matrix of $\mathbf{L}$ are linearly independent. Let $\mathbf{f} = (X^1, \ldots, X^r, \Phi^1, \ldots, \Phi^m)$, and $U_1$ be a neighborhood of $\mathbf{x}_0$ such that the restriction of $\mathbf{f}$ to $U_1$ is regular, as in the proof of the implicit function theorem. There exists $\delta > 0$ such that $\hat{\mathbf{x}}_0 + t\hat{\mathbf{h}} \in R_1$ for every $t \in (-\delta, \delta)$. Let $\mathbf{g} = (\mathbf{f}|U_1)^{-1}$ and

$$\psi(t) = \mathbf{g}(\hat{\mathbf{x}}_0 + t\hat{\mathbf{h}}, \mathbf{0}).$$

Then $\psi(t) \in M$ and $\psi$ is of class $C^{(1)}$ (Fig. 4–10). We must show that $\psi'(0) = \mathbf{h}$.

Let $\mathbf{\Lambda} = D\mathbf{f}(\mathbf{x}_0)$. By formula (4–23), $\mathbf{\Lambda}^{-1}$ is the differential of $\mathbf{g}$ at the point $(\hat{\mathbf{x}}_0, \mathbf{0}) = \mathbf{f}(\mathbf{x}_0)$. Therefore

$$\psi'(0) = \mathbf{\Lambda}^{-1}(\hat{\mathbf{h}}, \mathbf{0}).$$

By definition of $\mathbf{f}$,

$$\Lambda^i(\mathbf{h}) = h^i, \qquad i = 1, \ldots, r,$$
$$\Lambda^{l+r}(\mathbf{h}) = d\Phi^l(\mathbf{x}_0) \cdot \mathbf{h}, \qquad l = 1, \ldots, m.$$

Since $\mathbf{h}$ is in the kernel of $D\mathbf{\Phi}(\mathbf{x}_0)$, $\Lambda^{l+r}(\mathbf{h}) = 0$. Thus $\mathbf{\Lambda}(\mathbf{h}) = (\hat{\mathbf{h}}, \mathbf{0})$, and

$$\mathbf{h} = \mathbf{\Lambda}^{-1}(\hat{\mathbf{h}}, \mathbf{0}) = \psi'(0). \blacksquare$$

**Normal vectors to a manifold.** A vector $\mathbf{n}$ is called *normal* to $M$ at $\mathbf{x}_0$ if $\mathbf{n} \cdot \mathbf{h} = 0$ for every $\mathbf{h} \in T(\mathbf{x}_0)$. The normal vectors form a vector space of dimension $m = n - r$, the orthogonal complement of the tangent space $T(\mathbf{x}_0)$. The gradient grad $\Phi^l(\mathbf{x}_0)$ is the vector with the same components as the covector $d\Phi^l(\mathbf{x}_0)$. By Theorem 10

$$\text{grad}\, \Phi^l(\mathbf{x}_0) \cdot \mathbf{h} = d\Phi^l(\mathbf{x}_0) \cdot \mathbf{h} = 0$$

for every $\mathbf{h} \in T(\mathbf{x}_0)$ and $l = 1, \ldots, m$. *Hence* grad $\Phi^1(\mathbf{x}_0), \ldots,$ grad $\Phi^m(\mathbf{x}_0)$ *are normal vectors to $M$ at* $\mathbf{x}_0$. Since $D\boldsymbol{\Phi}(\mathbf{x}_0)$ has rank $m$, these vectors are linearly independent, and they form a basis for the space of normal vectors.

In particular, if $M$ is an $(n - 1)$-manifold, then $m = 1$; grad $\Phi(\mathbf{x}_0)$ is a normal vector, and all others are scalar multiples of it.

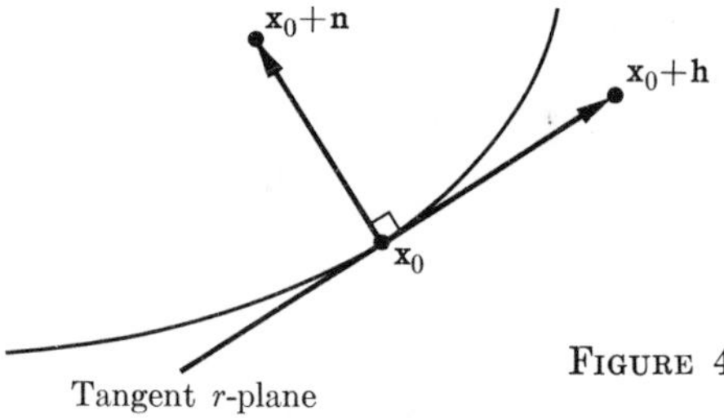


FIGURE 4–11

**Tangent *r*-planes.** The *r-plane tangent to $M$ at* $\mathbf{x}_0$ is

$$\{\mathbf{x} : \mathbf{x} = \mathbf{x}_0 + \mathbf{h}, \mathbf{h} \in T(\mathbf{x}_0)\}.$$

(See Fig. 4–11.) The terms *tangent line, tangent plane,* and *tangent hyperplane* are used when $r = 1, 2$, and $n - 1$, respectively. The tangent $r$-plane is

$$\{\mathbf{x} : d\Phi^l(\mathbf{x}_0) \cdot (\mathbf{x} - \mathbf{x}_0) = 0 \quad \text{for } l = 1, \ldots, m\}.$$

**Example 9.** Let

$$M = \{(x, y, z) : x^2 + y^2 + z^2 - 2xz - 4 = 0\}.$$

According to Example 3, Section 4–6, $M$ is the 2-manifold determined by the function $\Phi$ of that example. Then

$$d\Phi(x, y, z) = 2(x - z)\mathbf{e}^1 + 2y\mathbf{e}^2 + 2(z - x)\mathbf{e}^3.$$

Let us find the spaces of tangent and normal vectors to $M$ at $(2, \sqrt{3}, 1)$.

$$\text{grad}\, \Phi(2, \sqrt{3}, 1) = 2\mathbf{e}_1 + 2\sqrt{3}\mathbf{e}_2 - 2\mathbf{e}_3.$$

This is a normal vector, and any other is a scalar multiple of it. The tangent vectors $\mathbf{h}$ satisfy

$$0 = d\Phi(2, \sqrt{3}, 1) \cdot \mathbf{h} = 2h^1 + 2\sqrt{3}\, h^2 - 2h^3.$$

Two linearly independent solutions of this equation are $\mathbf{e}_1 + \mathbf{e}_3$ and $\sqrt{3}\mathbf{e}_1 - \mathbf{e}_2$. These vectors form a basis for $T(2, \sqrt{3}, 1)$. The equation of the tangent plane is $2(x - 2) + 2\sqrt{3}(y - \sqrt{3}) - 2(z - 1) = 0$, or $x + \sqrt{3}y - z = 4$.

**Example 10.** Let $M \subset E^3$ be a 1-manifold. Let us find the tangent space at $(x_0, y_0, z_0) \in M$. Let us write $\boldsymbol{\Phi} = (\Phi, \Psi)$. The tangent vectors satisfy

$$0 = d\Phi(x_0, y_0, z_0) \cdot \mathbf{h} = d\Psi(x_0, y_0, z_0) \cdot \mathbf{h}.$$

From Cramer's rule one solution of this pair of linear equations is the vector $\mathbf{d}$ with components (Problem 8)

$$d^1 = \Phi_2\Psi_3 - \Phi_3\Psi_2, \qquad d^2 = \Phi_3\Psi_1 - \Phi_1\Psi_3, \qquad d^3 = \Phi_1\Psi_2 - \Phi_2\Psi_1,$$

the partial derivatives being evaluated at $(x_0, y_0, z_0)$. The tangent space $T(x_0, y_0, z_0)$ consists of all scalar multiples of $\mathbf{d}$.

***Intersections of manifolds.** Let $M$ be an $r$-manifold and $N$ an $s$-manifold, with $M \cap N$ nonempty. Let us assume that $r + s > n$. Let $T_1(\mathbf{x}_0)$ denote the tangent space to $M$ at a point $\mathbf{x}_0 \in M \cap N$, and $T_2(\mathbf{x}_0)$ the tangent space to $N$ at $\mathbf{x}_0$. There exist a neighborhood $U_1$ of $\mathbf{x}_0$ and $\boldsymbol{\Phi} = (\Phi^1, \dots, \Phi^{n-r})$ such that $D\boldsymbol{\Phi}(\mathbf{x})$ has rank $n - r$ for every $\mathbf{x} \in U_1$ and

$$M \cap U_1 = \{\mathbf{x} \in U_1 : \boldsymbol{\Phi}(\mathbf{x}) = \mathbf{0}\}.$$

In the same way, there exists a neighborhood $U_2$ of $\mathbf{x}_0$ and $\boldsymbol{\Psi} = (\Psi^1, \dots, \Psi^{n-s})$ such that $D\boldsymbol{\Psi}(\mathbf{x})$ has rank $n - s$ for every $\mathbf{x} \in U_2$ and

$$N \cap U_2 = \{\mathbf{x} \in U_2 : \boldsymbol{\Psi}(\mathbf{x}) = \mathbf{0}\}.$$

Let $U = U_1 \cap U_2$, and $\boldsymbol{\Theta} = (\Phi^1, \dots, \Phi^{n-r}, \Psi^1, \dots, \Psi^{n-s})$. Then

$$(M \cap N) \cap U = \{\mathbf{x} \in U : \boldsymbol{\Theta}(\mathbf{x}) = \mathbf{0}\}.$$

The kernel of $D\boldsymbol{\Theta}(\mathbf{x}_0)$ is $T_1(\mathbf{x}_0) \cap T_2(\mathbf{x}_0)$. Hence $D\boldsymbol{\Theta}(\mathbf{x}_0)$ has the desired rank $n - (r + s - n) = (n - r) + (n - s)$. From the definition, $M \cap N$ is an $(r + s - n)$-manifold.

**Example.** Let $n = 3$, $r = s = 2$. If the tangent planes of $M$ and $N$ do not coincide at any point of $M \cap N$, then $M \cap N$ is a 1-manifold. The tangent line at $\mathbf{x}_0 \in M \cap N$ is the intersection of the tangent planes to $M$ and $N$ at $\mathbf{x}_0$.

## PROBLEMS

In Problems 1–6 and 11, one can show that the set in question is a manifold by verifying (4–26) for suitable $\boldsymbol{\Phi}$.

1. Let $F(x, y) = \exp(x^2 + 2y^2 + 2)$. Find the level sets and determine which are 1-manifolds.
2. (a) Show that if $c \neq 0$, then the hyperboloid $x^2 + y^2 - 4z^2 = c$ is a 2-manifold. Is the cone $x^2 + y^2 = 4z^2$ a 2-manifold?
   (b) Find the tangent plane at $2\mathbf{e}_1 - \mathbf{e}_2 + \mathbf{e}_3$ to the hyperboloid $x^2 + y^2 - 4z^2 = 1$.
3. Let $M = \{(x, y, z) : xy = 0,\ x^2 + y^2 + z^2 = 1,\ z \neq \pm 1\}$. Show that $M$ is a 1-manifold. Sketch $M$.

4. Let $f$ be of class $C^{(1)}$ on an open set $A \subset E^2$. Let $M = \{(x, y, f(x, y)) : (x, y) \in A\}$.
   (a) Show that $M$ is a 2-manifold.
   (b) Show that $(f_1(x, y), f_2(x, y), -1)$ is a normal vector to $M$ at $(x, y, f(x, y))$.
   (c) Show that the equation for a tangent plane agrees with the one in Section 2–2.
5. Let $A \subset E^1$ be open, and $f, g$ be real-valued functions of class $C^{(1)}$ on $A$.
   (a) Show that $M = \{(x, f(x), g(x)) : x \in A\}$ is a 1-manifold.
   (b) Show that $(1, f'(x), g'(x))$ is a tangent vector to $M$ at $(x, f(x), g(x))$.
6. Let $M = \{(x, y) : x^y = y^x, x > 0, y > 0, (x, y) \neq (e, e)\}$, where $e$ is the base for natural logarithms. Show that $M$ is a 1-manifold. Make a sketch.
7. Let $M = \{(x, y, z) : xy = xz = 0\}$. Is $M$ a 1-manifold?
8. In Example 10 show that $\mathbf{d}$ is a tangent vector, using Cramer's rule.
9. Let $M$ and $N$ be $r$-manifolds such that $(\mathrm{cl}M) \cap N$ and $M \cap \mathrm{cl}N$ are empty, $M \subset E^n$, $N \subset E^n$. Prove that $M \cup N$ is an $r$-manifold.
10. Let $M$ be an $r$-manifold and $A$ an open set such that $M \cap A$ is not empty. Prove that $M \cap A$ is an $r$-manifold.
11. Let $M = \{\mathbf{x} : \sum_{i,j=1}^{n} c_{ij} x^i x^j = 1\}$, where the matrix $(c_{ij})$ has rank $n$ and is symmetric.
    (a) Show that $M$ is an $(n - 1)$-manifold.
    (b) Show that the equation of the tangent hyperplane at $\mathbf{x}_0 \in M$ is

$$\sum_{i,j=1}^{n} c_{ij} x^i x_0^j = 1.$$

12. *Product manifolds.* Let $M \subset E^n$ be an $r$-manifold and $N \subset E^m$ an $s$-manifold. Regarding $E^{m+n}$ as the cartesian product $E^n \times E^m$, show that $M \times N$ is an $(r + s)$-manifold. Show that the tangent space at a point of $M \times N$ is the cartesian product of the tangent spaces at the corresponding points of $M$ and $N$.
13. Let points of $E^4$ be denoted by $(x, y, u, v)$. Let $C = \{\mathbf{x} : x^2 + y^2 = 1, u^2 + v^2 = 1\}$, $K = \{\mathbf{x} : x^2 + y^2 \leq 1, u^2 + v^2 \leq 1\}$, and $B = \mathrm{fr}K$ (boundary of $K$).
    (a) Show that $C$ is a 2-manifold.
    (b) Show that $B$–$C$ is a 3-manifold. [*Hint:* Use Problems 9 and 12.]
14. Let $M$, $\mathbf{\Phi}$, and $U$ be as in the definition of "manifold." For each $l = 1, \ldots, m$, let $\Psi^l(\mathbf{x}) = g^l(\mathbf{x})\Phi^l(\mathbf{x})$, where $g^l$ is of class $C^{(1)}$ and $g^l(\mathbf{x}_0) \neq 0$. Show that there is a neighborhood $U_0$ of $\mathbf{x}_0$ such that $D\mathbf{\Psi}(\mathbf{x})$ has rank $m$ for every $\mathbf{x} \in U_0$ and $M \cap U_0 = \{\mathbf{x} \in U_0 : \mathbf{\Psi}(\mathbf{x}) = \mathbf{0}\}$. [*Hint:* Show that $d\Psi^1(\mathbf{x}_0), \ldots, d\Psi^m(\mathbf{x}_0)$ are linearly independent.]
15. Let us identify $E^{n^2}$ with the set of all linear transformations from $E^n$ into itself by associating with each linear transformation $\mathbf{L}$ the vector

$$\sum_{i,j=1}^{n} c_j^i \mathbf{e}_{i+(j-1)n},$$

where $(c_j^i)$ is the matrix of $\mathbf{L}$. Let $O(n)$ be the set of orthogonal transformations of $E^n$.

(a) Show that $O(n)$ is a manifold of dimension $\frac{1}{2}n(n-1)$ and class $C^{(\infty)}$. [*Hint:* Proposition 11.]

(b) Let $\mathbf{I}$ be the identity transformation of $E^n$. Show that $\mathbf{L}$ is a tangent vector to $O(n)$ at $\mathbf{I}$ if and only if $\mathbf{L}^t = -\mathbf{L}$. (Such a linear transformation is called skew symmetric.)

(c) Let $SO(n)$ be the set of all rotations of $E^n$ about $\mathbf{0}$. Show that $SO(n)$ is a relatively open subset of $O(n)$, and hence $SO(n)$ is also a manifold of dimension $\frac{1}{2}n(n-1)$. Show that $SO(n)$ is the largest connected subset of $O(n)$ which contains $\mathbf{I}$. [*Hint:* Using induction on $n$, show that any $\mathbf{L} \in SO(n)$ can be joined with $\mathbf{I}$ by a path in $SO(n)$.]

## 4–8 THE MULTIPLIER RULE

Let $M$ be a manifold and $f$ be a real-valued function of class $C^{(1)}$ on some open set containing $M$. Let us consider the problem of finding the extrema of the function $f|M$. This is called a problem of *constrained extrema.*

If $\mathbf{x}_0$ is a point of $M$ at which $f$ has a constrained relative maximum, then $\mathbf{x}_0$ has a neighborhood $U_0$ such that

$$f(\mathbf{x}) \leq f(\mathbf{x}_0) \quad \text{for every } \mathbf{x} \in M \cap U_0.$$

(Recall the definition on p. 60.) If $f$ has a constrained relative minimum at $\mathbf{x}_0$, then the inequality sign is reversed.

Since $M$ is a manifold, there exists a neighborhood $U$ of $\mathbf{x}_0$ and $\mathbf{\Phi}$ of class $C^{(1)}$ on $U$ such that

$$M \cap U = \{\mathbf{x} \in U : \mathbf{\Phi}(\mathbf{x}) = \mathbf{0}\}$$

and $D\mathbf{\Phi}(\mathbf{x})$ has maximum rank $m$ for every $\mathbf{x} \in U$. We may assume that $U \subset U_0$.

Roughly speaking, the multiplier rule states that by introducing suitable multipliers $\sigma_1, \ldots, \sigma_m$ the constrained extremum problem can be treated as one of ordinary (unconstrained) extremum. More precisely:

**Lagrange Multiplier Rule.** *Let $f$ have a constrained relative extremum at $\mathbf{x}_0$. Then there exist real numbers $\sigma_1, \ldots, \sigma_m$ such that $\mathbf{x}_0$ is a critical point of the function*

$$F = f + \sigma_1\Phi^1 + \cdots + \sigma_m\Phi^m.$$

*Proof.* It suffices to consider the case of a constrained relative maximum. Let $\mathbf{h}$ be any tangent vector to $M$ at $\mathbf{x}_0$. Let $\phi(t) = f[\boldsymbol{\psi}(t)]$, where $\boldsymbol{\psi}$ is the same as in the definition of tangent vector. Since $\boldsymbol{\psi}(t) \in M$ and $f|M$ has a relative maximum at $\mathbf{x}_0$, $\phi$ has a relative maximum at 0. Therefore $\phi'(0) = 0$. By the chain rule,

$$\phi'(0) = df[\boldsymbol{\psi}(0)] \cdot \boldsymbol{\psi}'(0) = df(\mathbf{x}_0) \cdot \mathbf{h}.$$

Let $\mathbf{L} = D\mathbf{\Phi}(\mathbf{x}_0)$. The equation $\mathbf{b} = \mathbf{L}^*(\mathbf{a})$ has a solution $\mathbf{a}$ if $\mathbf{b} \cdot \mathbf{h} = 0$ for every $\mathbf{h}$ in the kernel of $\mathbf{L}$ ([12, p. 103]). Let $\mathbf{b} = df(\mathbf{x}_0)$. By (4–3b) and Theorem 10, the covector $df(\mathbf{x}_0)$ is a linear combination of the row covectors of $D\mathbf{\Phi}(\mathbf{x}_0)$:

$$df(\mathbf{x}_0) = a_1\, d\Phi^1(\mathbf{x}_0) + \cdots + a_m\, d\Phi^m(\mathbf{x}_0).$$

Let $\sigma_l = -a_l$ for $l = 1, \ldots, m$. Then $dF(\mathbf{x}_0) = \mathbf{0}$. ▮

**Example 1.** Let $f(x, y, z) = x - y + 2z$. Let us find the maximum and minimum values of $f$ on the ellipsoid

$$M = \{(x, y, z) : x^2 + y^2 + 2z^2 = 2\}.$$

Let $\Phi(x, y, z) = 2 - (x^2 + y^2 + 2z^2)$ and $F = f + \sigma\Phi$. The multiplier $\sigma$ is yet to be determined. From the multiplier rule we get three equations

$$\begin{aligned} F_1 &= 1 - 2\sigma x_0 = 0,\\ F_2 &= -1 - 2\sigma y_0 = 0,\\ F_3 &= 2 - 4\sigma z_0 = 0. \end{aligned}$$

From these and the fourth equation $\Phi = 0$ we get

$$x_0 = \frac{1}{2\sigma}, \qquad y_0 = -\frac{1}{2\sigma}, \qquad z_0 = \frac{1}{2\sigma}, \qquad \frac{1}{\sigma} = \pm\sqrt{2}.$$

Therefore $\mathbf{x}_0 = \pm(\sqrt{2}/2)(\mathbf{e}_1 - \mathbf{e}_2 + \mathbf{e}_3)$, depending on which of the two possible values for $\sigma$ is used. Since $f$ is continuous and $M$ is a compact set, $f$ has a maximum and a minimum value on $M$. One of the two critical points obtained by the multiplier rule must give the maximum and the other the minimum. Since $f[(\sqrt{2}/2)(\mathbf{e}_1 - \mathbf{e}_2 + \mathbf{e}_3)] = 2\sqrt{2}$ and $f[-(\sqrt{2}/2)(\mathbf{e}_1 - \mathbf{e}_2 + \mathbf{e}_3)] = -2\sqrt{2}$, these numbers are the maximum and minimum values, respectively.

**Example 2.** Let $f(\mathbf{x}) = \sum_{i=1}^n b_i (x^i)^2$, where $b_i \neq 0$ for each $i = 1, \ldots, n$. Let $M$ be the hyperplane $\{\mathbf{x} : \mathbf{a} \cdot \mathbf{x} = 1\}$, and $F(\mathbf{x}) = f(\mathbf{x}) + \sigma(1 - \mathbf{a} \cdot \mathbf{x})$. If $\mathbf{x}_0$ is a critical point of $F$, then

$$\mathbf{0} = dF(\mathbf{x}_0) = df(\mathbf{x}_0) - \sigma\mathbf{a}.$$

Thus $df(\mathbf{x}_0) = \sigma\mathbf{a}$, or

$$f_i(\mathbf{x}_0) = 2b_i x_0^i = \sigma a_i, \qquad i = 1, \ldots, n.$$

From this and the equation $\mathbf{a} \cdot \mathbf{x}_0 = 1$,

$$x_0^i = \frac{\sigma a_i}{2b_i}, \qquad \frac{1}{\sigma} = \frac{1}{2} \sum_{i=1}^n \frac{a_i^2}{b_i},$$

provided the sum is not zero. To determine whether $\mathbf{x}_0$ gives an extremum, we use the formula

$$f(\mathbf{x}_0 + \mathbf{h}) = f(\mathbf{x}_0) + df(\mathbf{x}_0) \cdot \mathbf{h} + f(\mathbf{h}),$$

which is valid for homogeneous quadratic polynomials. Points of the hyperplane $M$ are of the form $\mathbf{x}_0 + \mathbf{h}$, where $\mathbf{a} \cdot \mathbf{h} = 0$. Since $df(\mathbf{x}_0) = \sigma\mathbf{a}$, the above formula simplifies to

$$f(\mathbf{x}_0 + \mathbf{h}) = f(\mathbf{x}_0) + f(\mathbf{h}).$$

If $f(\mathbf{h}) \geq 0$ for every $\mathbf{h}$ satisfying $\mathbf{a} \cdot \mathbf{h} = 0$, then $f$ has an absolute constrained minimum at $\mathbf{x}_0$.

**The characteristic values of a symmetric matrix.** Let $(c_j^i)$ be an $n \times n$ matrix and $\mathbf{L}$ the corresponding linear transformation. A number $\lambda$ is a *characteristic value of* $\mathbf{L}$ if the linear transformation $\mathbf{L} - \lambda\mathbf{I}$ is singular. There are $n$ characteristic values $\lambda_1, \ldots, \lambda_n$, counting multiplicities. If $\mathbf{L}(\mathbf{x}) = \lambda_i\mathbf{x}$ and $\mathbf{x} \neq \mathbf{0}$, then $\mathbf{x}$ is a *characteristic vector* corresponding to the characteristic value $\lambda_i$. The numbers $\lambda_1, \ldots, \lambda_n$ may be complex, and the characteristic vectors may have complex components ([12], p. 164).

Let us suppose, however, that $(c_j^i)$ is a symmetric matrix, $c_j^i = c_i^j$ for $i, j = 1, \ldots, n$. Let us show that the characteristic values are real. In fact, $\lambda_i$ can be characterized as the value of a certain constrained maximum.

Consider the homogeneous quadratic polynomial

$$f(\mathbf{x}) = \mathbf{L}(\mathbf{x}) \cdot \mathbf{x} = \sum_{i,j=1}^{n} c_j^i x^i x^j,$$

and let $M_1$ be the unit $(n - 1)$-sphere in $E^n$, $M_1 = \{\mathbf{x} : |\mathbf{x}| = 1\}$. Let

$$\lambda_1 = \max \{f(\mathbf{x}) : \mathbf{x} \in M_1\}, \tag{4-27}$$

and let $\mathbf{v}_1$ be a point of $M_1$ at which the maximum is attained. By the multiplier rule, with

$$F(\mathbf{x}) = f(\mathbf{x}) + \sigma(1 - \mathbf{x} \cdot \mathbf{x}),$$

there is a multiplier $\sigma$ such that $\mathbf{v}_1$ is a critical point of $F$. Then $\operatorname{grad} f(\mathbf{x}) = 2\mathbf{L}(\mathbf{x})$, and hence

$$\mathbf{0} = \operatorname{grad} F(\mathbf{v}_1) = 2\mathbf{L}(\mathbf{v}_1) - 2\sigma\mathbf{v}_1.$$

Hence $\mathbf{L}(\mathbf{v}_1) = \sigma\mathbf{v}_1$, which shows that $\sigma$ is a characteristic value and $\mathbf{v}_1$ a characteristic vector. Since $f(\mathbf{x}) = \mathbf{L}(\mathbf{x}) \cdot \mathbf{x}$,

$$\lambda_1 = f(\mathbf{v}_1) = \mathbf{L}(\mathbf{v}_1) \cdot \mathbf{v}_1 = \sigma\mathbf{v}_1 \cdot \mathbf{v}_1,$$

and since $\mathbf{v}_1 \cdot \mathbf{v}_1 = 1$, $\sigma = \lambda_1$.

We next let

$$M_2 = \{\mathbf{x} : |\mathbf{x}| = 1, \mathbf{x} \cdot \mathbf{v}_1 = 0\},$$

$$\lambda_2 = \max \{f(\mathbf{x}) : \mathbf{x} \in M_2\},$$

and $\mathbf{v}_2 \in M_2$ be a point such that $f(\mathbf{v}_2) = \lambda_2$. We have added another constraint. Hence $M_2 \subset M_1$ and $\lambda_2 \leq \lambda_1$. Obviously $\mathbf{v}_2 \cdot \mathbf{v}_1 = 0$. For $k = 3, \ldots, n$ let

$$M_k = \{\mathbf{x} : |\mathbf{x}| = 1, \mathbf{x} \cdot \mathbf{v}_i = 0 \text{ for } i = 1, \ldots, k-1\},$$

$$\lambda_k = \max \{f(\mathbf{x}) : \mathbf{x} \in M_k\}, \tag{4-28}$$

and $\mathbf{v}_k \in M_k$ be such that $\lambda_k = f(\mathbf{v}_k)$. Then

$$\lambda_n \leq \lambda_{n-1} \leq \cdots \leq \lambda_1$$

and $\{\mathbf{v}_1, \ldots, \mathbf{v}_n\}$ is an orthonormal basis for $E^n$. Let us show by induction on $k$ that $\lambda_k$ is a characteristic value and $\mathbf{v}_k$ a characteristic vector. This is true if $k = 1$. Let $k \geq 2$. Applying the multiplier rule with

$$F(\mathbf{x}) = f(\mathbf{x}) + \sigma_1(1 - \mathbf{x} \cdot \mathbf{x}) + \sum_{i=1}^{k-1} \sigma_{i+1}\mathbf{x} \cdot \mathbf{v}_i,$$

we get

$$\mathbf{0} = 2\mathbf{L}(\mathbf{v}_k) - 2\sigma_1\mathbf{v}_k + \sum_{i=1}^{k-1} \sigma_{i+1}\mathbf{v}_i.$$

Since $\mathbf{v}_i \cdot \mathbf{v}_j = 0$ for $i \neq j$, we get upon taking the inner product with $\mathbf{v}_j$,

$$0 = 2\mathbf{L}(\mathbf{v}_k) \cdot \mathbf{v}_j + \sigma_{j+1}, \quad \text{if } j < k,$$
$$\sigma_1 = \mathbf{L}(\mathbf{v}_k) \cdot \mathbf{v}_k = f(\mathbf{v}_k),$$

or $\sigma_1 = \lambda_k$. Since $(c^i_j)$ is symmetric, $\mathbf{L}^t = \mathbf{L}$ (p. 98) and

$$\mathbf{L}(\mathbf{v}_k) \cdot \mathbf{v}_j = \mathbf{v}_k \cdot \mathbf{L}(\mathbf{v}_j).$$

Using the induction hypothesis, we get

$$\mathbf{L}(\mathbf{v}_k) \cdot \mathbf{v}_j = \mathbf{v}_k \cdot (\lambda_j\mathbf{v}_j) = 0 \quad \text{if } j < k.$$

Hence $\sigma_2 = \cdots = \sigma_k = 0$, and $\mathbf{L}(\mathbf{v}_k) = \lambda_k\mathbf{v}_k$.

If $k = n$, the multiplier rule does not apply. However, we used the multiplier rule only to show that $\mathbf{L}(\mathbf{v}_k)$ is a linear combination of $\mathbf{v}_1, \ldots, \mathbf{v}_k$. If $k = n$, this is clear from the fact that $\{\mathbf{v}_1, \ldots, \mathbf{v}_n\}$ is a basis for $E^n$.

**Theorem 11.** *The characteristic values of the symmetric matrix $(c^i_j)$ are $\lambda_1, \ldots, \lambda_n$. For each $i = 1, \ldots, n$, $\mathbf{v}_i$ is a characteristic vector corresponding to $\lambda_i$. If $\xi^1, \ldots, \xi^n$ denote the components of $\mathbf{x}$ with respect to the orthonormal basis $\{\mathbf{v}_1, \ldots, \mathbf{v}_n\}$, then*

$$f(\mathbf{x}) = \lambda_1(\xi^1)^2 + \cdots + \lambda_n(\xi^n)^2 \tag{4-29}$$

*for every $\mathbf{x} \in E^n$.*

*Proof.* The first two statements have already been proved. To prove the third, we have

$$\mathbf{x} = \sum_{i=1}^{n} \xi^i \mathbf{v}_i, \qquad \xi^i = \mathbf{v}_i \cdot \mathbf{x},$$

$$\mathbf{L}(\mathbf{x}) = \sum_{i=1}^{n} \xi^i \mathbf{L}(\mathbf{v}_i) = \sum_{i=1}^{n} \lambda_i \xi^i \mathbf{v}_i,$$

$$f(\mathbf{x}) = \mathbf{L}(\mathbf{x}) \cdot \mathbf{x} = \sum_{i=1}^{n} \lambda_i \xi^i \mathbf{v}_i \cdot \mathbf{x},$$

which is just (4–29). ▮

**Corollary.** *$f$ is positive definite if and only if $\lambda_i > 0$ for each $i = 1, \ldots, n$.*

*Proof.* If each $\lambda_i$ is positive, then by (4–29), $f(\mathbf{x}) > 0$ whenever $\mathbf{x} \neq \mathbf{0}$. Conversely, if $f(\mathbf{x}) > 0$ for every $\mathbf{x} \neq \mathbf{0}$, then $\lambda_i = f(\mathbf{v}_i) > 0$ for each $i$. ▮

These results have a geometric interpretation. Let

$$B = \{\mathbf{x} : f(\mathbf{x}) = 1\}.$$

If $f$ is positive definite, then $B$ is called an $(n - 1)$-*dimensional ellipsoid.* Setting $\mu_i = 1/\sqrt{\lambda_i}$, we have (Fig. 4–12)

$$B = \left\{\mathbf{x} : \sum_{i=1}^{n} (\xi^i/\mu_i)^2 = 1\right\}.$$

If $n = 2$ and $\lambda_1 > 0$, $\lambda_2 < 0$, then $B$ is a hyperbola. If $n = 3$ and $\lambda_1 > 0$, $\lambda_3 < 0$, then $B$ is a hyperboloid. It has one sheet if $\lambda_2 > 0$ and two sheets if $\lambda_2 < 0$.

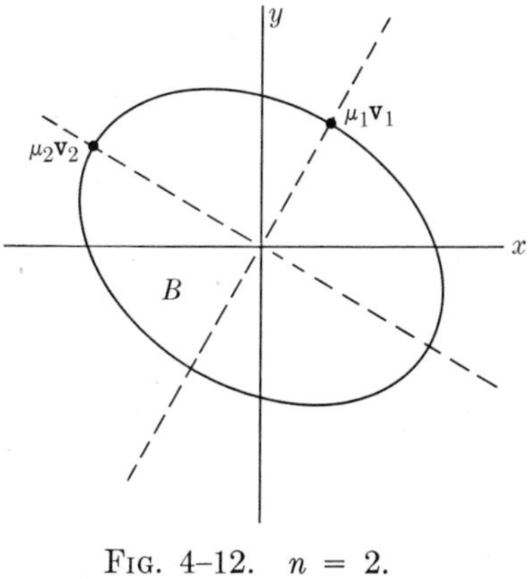


FIG. 4–12. $n = 2$.

**PROBLEMS**

1. Set $M = \{(x, y, z) : x + y + z = 1\}$ and $f(x, y, z) = 3x^2 + 3y^2 + z^2$. Show that there is a constrained absolute minimum, and find the minimum value of $f$ on $M$.
2. Use the multiplier rule to find the distance to the parabola $y^2 = x$ from the point $c\mathbf{e}_1$, $c \neq 0$. [*Hint:* Let $f(x, y) = (x - c)^2 + y^2$, which is the square of the distance.]
3. Find the distance from the point $\mathbf{e}_1 - 2\mathbf{e}_2 - \mathbf{e}_3$ to the line $\{(x, y, z) : x = y = z\}$.
4. (a) Use the multiplier rule to show that $|\mathbf{a}| = \max \{\mathbf{a} \cdot \mathbf{x} : |\mathbf{x}| = 1\}$.
   (b) Deduce the same result from Cauchy's inequality.

5. Let $M$ be a manifold, $\mathbf{x}_1 \notin M$, and suppose that $\mathbf{x}_0$ is a point of $M$ nearest $\mathbf{x}_1$. Using the multiplier rule, show that $\mathbf{x}_1 - \mathbf{x}_0$ is a normal vector to $M$ at $\mathbf{x}_0$.

6. Show that the distance from a point $\mathbf{x}_1$ to the hyperplane $\{\mathbf{x} : \mathbf{a} \cdot \mathbf{x} = b\}$ is $|\mathbf{a} \cdot \mathbf{x}_1 - b|/|\mathbf{a}|$.

7. Let $f(\mathbf{x}) = x^1 x^2 \cdots x^n$ and $M = \{\mathbf{x} : x^1 + \cdots + x^n = 1, x^i > 0 \text{ for } i = 1, \ldots, n\}$.
   (a) Show that $f(\mathbf{x}) \leq n^{-n}$ for every $\mathbf{x} \in M$, with equality if $x^1 = \cdots = x^n = n^{-1}$. [*Hint:* First show that $f$ has an absolute maximum on $M$. Apply the multiplier rule to $\log f$, which has a maximum at the same point where $f$ has one.]
   (b) Using (a), prove that the geometric mean of $n$ positive numbers is no more than their arithmetic mean. See Problem 6(b), Section 1–5.

8. Let $p > 1$ and $p'$ be the number such that $p^{-1} + (p')^{-1} = 1$. Let $\|\mathbf{x}\|$ be as in Problem 3, Section 1–6; and for each covector $\mathbf{a}$ let $\|\mathbf{a}\| = \max \{\mathbf{a} \cdot \mathbf{x} : \|\mathbf{x}\| = 1\}$. Show that
$$\|\mathbf{a}\| = \left(\sum_{i=1}^{n} |a_i|^{p'}\right)^{1/p'}.$$
[*Note:* For these norms the inequality $|\mathbf{a} \cdot \mathbf{x}| \leq \|\mathbf{a}\| \, \|\mathbf{x}\|$ [formula (1–18), p. 32] is called *Hölder's inequality*. A related inequality for integrals is given in Section 5–12].

9. Let $f(x, y, z) = 2xz + y^2$.
   (a) Find the characteristic values $\lambda_1, \lambda_2, \lambda_3$.
   (b) Sketch the surface with equation $2xz + y^2 = 1$. With equation $2xz + y^2 = 0$.

10. Let $\|\mathbf{L}\|$ be defined as in Section 4–3. Show that $\|\mathbf{L}\|^2$ is the largest characteristic value of $\mathbf{L}^t \circ \mathbf{L}$. [*Hint:* Use (4–8) with $\mathbf{y} = \mathbf{L}(\mathbf{t})$].

11. (Second derivative test for constrained relative maxima.) Let $f$ and $\mathbf{\Phi}$ be of class $C^{(2)}$, and let $Q(\mathbf{x}, \mathbf{h}) = \sum_{i,j=1}^{n} F_{ij}(\mathbf{x}) h^i h^j$ where $F$ is as in the multiplier rule. Show that:
   (a) If $f|M$ has a relative maximum at $\mathbf{x}_0$, then $Q(\mathbf{x}_0, \mathbf{h}) \geq 0$ for every $\mathbf{h} \in T(\mathbf{x}_0)$.
   (b) If $Q(\mathbf{x}_0, \mathbf{h}) > 0$ for every $\mathbf{h} \in T(\mathbf{x}_0)$, $\mathbf{h} \neq \mathbf{0}$, then $f|M$ has a strict relative maximum at $\mathbf{x}_0$. [*Hints:* See the proof of Theorem 6. Set $\mathbf{h}_t = t^{-1}(\mathbf{y}_t - \mathbf{x}_0)$, and show that $\lim_{t \to 0} Q(\mathbf{x}_0, \mathbf{h}_t) = Q(\mathbf{x}_0, \mathbf{h})$.]

# CHAPTER 5

# Integration

The integral of a real-valued function over a set is a generalization of the notion of sum. It is defined by approximating in a suitable way by certain finite sums. The first careful definition was due to Riemann (see the Historical Notes). Riemann defined the integral of a function over an interval $[a, b]$ of the real line $E^1$. In the succeeding years Riemann's idea was extended in several ways. However, the Riemann integral has several intrinsic drawbacks, and for a truly satisfactory treatment of integration a different approach had to be found.

About 1900 Lebesgue discovered a more sophisticated and flexible theory of integrals. In this chapter the elements of the Lebesgue theory are given. The first step is to define the measure of a set $A \subset E^n$. For $n = 1, 2$, or $3$, the measure is respectively the length, area, or volume of $A$. An important property of Lebesgue measure is its countable additivity [formula (5–9)]. While not every set $A$ is assigned a measure, countable additivity insures that the class of measurable sets is large enough for all applications encountered in mathematical analysis.

After measure, the integral of a bounded function $f$ over a bounded set $A$ is defined using upper and lower integrals. The integral exists under the very mild assumptions that $A$ is measurable and $f$ is measurable on $A$. Later (Sections 5–6 and 5–10), the integral is studied without those boundedness assumptions.

The definition of an integral does not furnish an effective procedure for the actual evaluation of integrals. However, the theorems on iterated integrals and transformation of integrals (Sections 5–5, 5–8), together with the fundamental theorem of calculus, provide a useful technique for this purpose.

Among the important features of the Lebesgue theory are the theorems about integration term by term in sequences of functions. Such questions are treated in Section 5–10.

**Notation.** The $n$-dimensional measure of a set $A$ will be denoted by $V_n(A)$. If the dimension $n$ is clear from the context, then we write simply "measure" rather than "$n$-dimensional measure" and $V(A)$ rather than $V_n(A)$. The integral of $f$ over $A$ is denoted by

$$\int_A f\,dV_n \qquad \text{or} \qquad \int_A f(\mathbf{x})\,dV_n(\mathbf{x}).$$

If $A = E^n$, we write simply $\int f dV_n$. The symbols $dV_n$ and $dV_n(\mathbf{x})$ are used after an integral sign merely for convenience and for traditional reasons. They will have no significance by themselves. (On the other hand, $df$ has a meaning already explained in Section 2-6. In particular, $dx^i$ stands for the differential of the $i$th standard cartesian coordinate function $X^i$.)

If $n = 1$, then we write, as is customary, $\int_A f(x)\,dx$ instead of $\int_A f(x)\,dV_1(x)$, and if $A = [a, b]$, we write $\int_a^b f(x)\,dx$.

## 5-1 INTERVALS

What is the $n$-dimensional measure of a subset $A$ of $E^n$? To start with, let us consider the simplest possible case—where $A$ is an $n$-dimensional interval.

A 2-dimensional interval is a rectangle with sides parallel to the coordinate axes (Fig. 5-1). Its area is the product of the lengths of its sides. Since $E^2$ is the cartesian product $E^1 \times E^1$, a 2-dimensional interval is just the cartesian product of 1-dimensional intervals. Similarly, a set $I \subset E^n$ is called an *$n$-dimensional interval* if $I$ is the cartesian product of 1-dimensional intervals:

$$I = J_1 \times \cdots \times J_n,$$

where each $J_i$ is a finite interval of $E^1$. The interval $I$ is *closed* if each $J_i$ is closed, and *open* if each $J_i$ is open. For instance, if $I$ is closed, then there exist

$$\mathbf{x}_0 = (x_0^1, \ldots, x_0^n), \qquad \mathbf{x}_1 = (x_1^1, \ldots, x_1^n)$$

with $x_0^i < x_1^i$ for each $i = 1, \ldots, n$, such that $J_i = [x_0^i, x_1^i]$ and

$$I = \{\mathbf{x} : x_0^i \leq x^i \leq x_1^i,\ i = 1, \ldots, n\}.$$

The *$n$-dimensional measure* $V(I)$ of $I$ is the product of the lengths of the intervals $J_1, \ldots, J_n$.

We shall next define the measure of a set which is a finite union of $n$-dimensional intervals. For this purpose the idea of grid of hyperplanes is introduced.

**Grids.** For each $i = 1, \ldots, n$ let us take a finite set of real numbers; let the elements of these sets be denoted by $x_j^i$, where

$$x_1^i < x_2^i < \cdots < x_{m_{i+1}}^i$$

and $m_{i+1}$ is the number of elements of the $i$th set. Let $P_j^i$ be the hyperplane with equation $x^i = x_j^i$, and let $\Pi$ be the union of all of these hyperplanes. Such a set $\Pi$ is called a *grid* of hyperplanes. A grid divides $E^n$ into a finite number of $n$-dimensional intervals, called *intervals of* $\Pi$, and a finite number

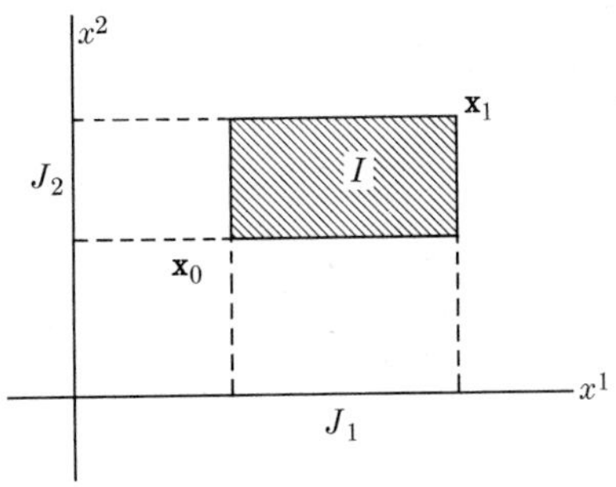


FIGURE 5–1

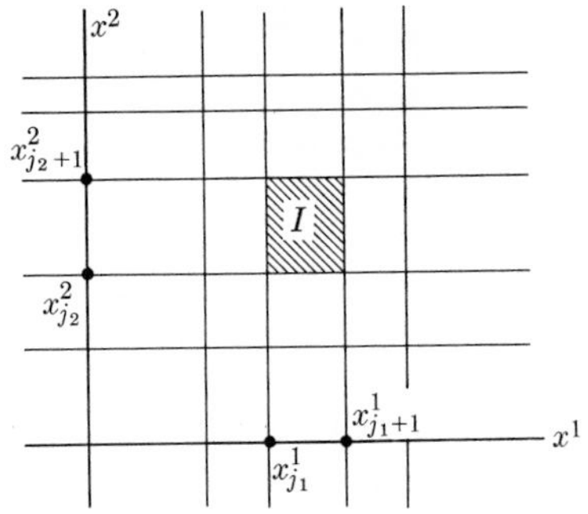


FIGURE 5–2

of unbounded sets. The latter could be called semi-infinite intervals of $\Pi$, but we shall have no occasion to do so. The intervals of $\Pi$ have the form $I = J_1 \times \cdots \times J_n$ where $J_i = [x^i_{j_i}, x^i_{j_i+1}]$ and the integers $j_1, \ldots, j_n$ may be chosen arbitrarily subject to $1 \leq j_i \leq m_{i+1}$. There are $m_1 \cdots m_n$ intervals of the grid, and for convenience we have taken them to be closed. (See Fig. 5–2.)

Let us call a set $Y$ a *figure* if $Y$ is the union of certain intervals $I_1, \ldots, I_p$ of some grid $\Pi$. The *measure* of $Y$ is

$$V(Y) = V(I_1) + \cdots + V(I_p). \tag{5–1}$$

There are many possible choices for $\Pi$. Consequently, we must show that $V(Y)$ depends only on $Y$ and not on the particular grid chosen. Let us call $\Pi'$ a refinement of $\Pi$ if $\Pi \subset \Pi'$. It is easy to show that $V(Y)$ is unchanged if $\Pi'$ is obtained by adding one hyperplane to $\Pi$, and hence by induction if $\Pi$ is replaced by any refinement of it. Now let $\Pi$ and $\Pi'$ be any two grids such that $Y$ is the union of intervals of $\Pi$ and also the union of intervals of $\Pi'$. Then $\Pi \cup \Pi'$ is a refinement of both. Consequently, $V(Y)$ is the same whether $\Pi$ or $\Pi'$ is used.

This same reasoning shows that if $Y$ and $Z$ are figures, then $Y$ and $Z$ can be written as unions of intervals of the same grid $\Pi$. Therefore $Y \cup Z$ is a figure. Moreover,

$$V(Y \cup Z) \leq V(Y) + V(Z). \tag{5–2}$$

If $Y \cap Z$ is empty, then equality holds in (5–2).

### PROBLEMS

1. Let $n = 1$ and $Y = [0, 1] \cup [2, 3]$, $Z = [1, 3] \cup [4, 5]$. Verify formula (5–2) in this example.
2. Let $n = 2$ and $Y = [0, 2] \times [0, 1] \cup [1, 3] \times [1, 2]$, $Z = [-1, 2] \times [-1, 3]$. Find a grid $\Pi$ such that both $Y$ and $Z$ are unions of intervals of $\Pi$. Find the areas of $Y, Z, Y \cup Z$, and $Y \cap Z$, and verify that $V(Y) + V(Z) - V(Y \cup Z) = V(Y \cap Z)$.

3. Let $I_1 = [0, 1] \times [0, 1] \times [0, 1]$ and $I_2 = [\frac{1}{2}, 2] \times [0, 2] \times [-1, 2]$. Find the volume of $I_1 \cup I_2$ and of $I_1 \cap I_2$.
4. Let $m$ be a positive integer, $f(x) = \exp x$, and $Y = I_1 \cup \cdots \cup I_m$, where for $k = 1, \ldots, m$

$$I_k = [(k - 1)/m, k/m] \times [0, f(k/m)].$$

Find the area $V_2(Y)$. Show that it is approximately $e - 1$ if $m$ is large.

5. (a) Let $I_1$ and $I_2$ be $n$-dimensional intervals. Show that $I_1 \cap I_2$ is also an interval provided that it has nonempty interior.
   (b) When is $I_1 \cup I_2$ an interval?

## 5-2 MEASURE

We shall now define the measure of a bounded set $A$. This is done in two stages. First, the measure of an open set $G$ is defined by approximating $G$ from within by figures, and that of a compact set $K$ by approximating $K$ from without by figures. In the second stage, $A$ is approximated from within by compact sets and from without by open sets. This two-stage approximation process is an important feature of the Lebesgue theory of measure.

There is an older theory of measure due to Jordan. In this theory $A$ is approximated simultaneously from within and without by figures. The Jordan theory is unsatisfactory for several reasons. Among them is the fact that the class of sets to which it applies is too small. For instance, there are compact sets to which the Jordan theory does not assign any measure.

Let $G$ be an open set. If $Y$ is a figure contained in $G$, then the measure of $G$ must be more than $V(Y)$. It is defined to be the least upper bound of the set of all such numbers $V(Y)$. (See Fig. 5-3.)

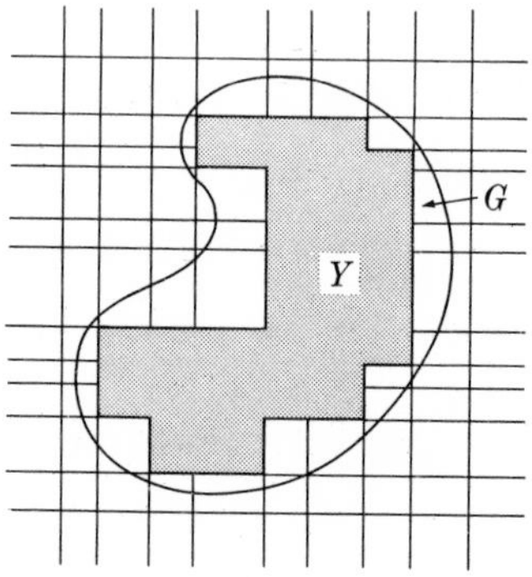


FIGURE 5-3

**Definition.** The *measure* of an open set $G$ is $V(G) = \sup \{V(Y) : Y \subset G\}$.

If the set $S = \{V(Y) : Y \subset G\}$ has no upper bound, then we set $V(G) = +\infty$. For instance, $V(E^n) = +\infty$. If $G$ is bounded, then $G$ is contained in some interval $I$, and $V(I)$ is an upper bound for $S$. In this case $V(G)$ is finite.

If $H$ is an open subset of $G$, let $T = \{V(Y) : Y \subset H\}$. Since $T \subset S$, $\sup T \leq \sup S$. Thus $V(H) \leq V(G)$.

By definition (Section A-1), the least upper bound $\sup S$ has the property that $s \leq \sup S$ for every $s \in S$, and given $\epsilon > 0$ there exists an $s \in S$ such that $\sup S < s + \epsilon$.

**Example 1.** Let $G = \text{int}\, Z$ where $Z$ is a figure (recall that any figure is a closed set). Let us show that $V(\text{int}\, Z) = V(Z)$. For any figure $Y \subset \text{int}\, Z$, $V(Y) \leq V(Z)$; and given $\epsilon > 0$ one can find such a figure $Y$ with $V(Z) < V(Y) + \epsilon$. Thus $V(Z) = \sup \{V(Y) : Y \subset \text{int}\, Z\}$.

We shall now establish a formula for the sum of the measures of two open sets. For this purpose a topological lemma is needed.

**Lemma 1.** *Let $G$ and $H$ be open sets and $K$ be a compact subset of $G \cup H$. Then there exists $d > 0$ such that the $d$-neighborhood of any $\mathbf{x} \in K$ is either contained in $G$ or in $H$.*

*Proof.* The sets $E^n - G$ and $E^n - H$ are closed. Let

$$f(\mathbf{x}) = \text{dist}\,(\mathbf{x}, E^n - G), \qquad g(\mathbf{x}) = \text{dist}\,(\mathbf{x}, E^n - H),$$

where $\text{dist}\,(\mathbf{x}, A)$ is the distance from $\mathbf{x}$ to the set $A$ (Section A-8). The functions $f$ and $g$ are continuous and $f(\mathbf{x}) + g(\mathbf{x}) > 0$ for every $\mathbf{x} \in G \cup H$. The continuous function $f + g$ has a positive minimum value $c$ on the compact set $K$. Let $d = c/2$. For every $\mathbf{x} \in K$, either $f(\mathbf{x}) \geq d$ or $g(\mathbf{x}) \geq d$. ∎

**Lemma 2a.** *Let $G$ and $H$ be open sets of finite measure. Then*

$$V(G \cup H) \leq V(G) + V(H). \tag{5-3}$$

*Proof.* Let $W$ be any figure such that $W \subset G \cup H$. Let $d$ be as in Lemma 1 with $K = W$. The figure $W$ is the union of intervals of a grid $\Pi$. By refining $\Pi$ if necessary we may suppose that each interval of $\Pi$ has diameter less than $d$. Let $Y$ be the union of those intervals of $\Pi$ which are contained in $G$, and $Z$ the union of those contained in $H$. By Lemma 1, $W \subset Y \cup Z$. Consequently,

$$V(W) \leq V(Y \cup Z) \leq V(Y) + V(Z).$$

Since $Y \subset G$, $V(Y) \leq V(G)$; similarly, $V(Z) \leq V(H)$. Hence

$$V(W) \leq V(G) + V(H).$$

The number $V(G) + V(H)$ is an upper bound for $\{V(W) : W \subset G \cup H\}$; and hence it is no less than the least upper bound $V(G \cup H)$. This proves (5-3). ∎

We next define the measure of a compact set $K$ by approximating $K$ from without by figures. For this purpose we consider those figures $Z$ such that $K$ is contained in the interior of $Z$.

**Definition.** The measure of a compact set $K$ is

$$V(K) = \inf \{V(Z) : K \subset \text{int } Z\}.$$

**Example 2.** Any figure $Y$ is a compact set. The new and old definitions of $V(Y)$ agree. The proof is like the one in Example 1.

**Lemma 3.** *Let $K$ and $L$ be compact sets such that $K \cap L$ is empty. Then*

$$V(K \cup L) \geq V(K) + V(L). \tag{5–4}$$

*Proof.* Let $f(\mathbf{x}) = \text{dist}(\mathbf{x}, L)$. Since $K \cap L$ is empty and $L$ is closed, $f(\mathbf{x}) > 0$ for every $\mathbf{x} \in K$. Since $K$ is compact and $f$ is continuous, $f$ has a positive minimum value $d$ on $K$.

Let $W$ be any figure such that $K \cup L \subset \text{int } W$. Then $W$ is the union of intervals $I_1, \ldots, I_p$ with diameters less than $d$. Let $Y$ be the union of those intervals $I_j$ such that $(\text{int } I_j) \cap K$ is not empty, and $Z$ the union of those such that $(\text{int } I_j) \cap L$ is not empty. Then $Y \cup Z \subset W$, $Y \cap Z$ is empty, and $K \subset \text{int } Y$, $L \subset \text{int } Z$. Hence

$$V(K) + V(L) \leq V(Y) + V(Z) \leq V(W).$$

This shows that $V(K) + V(L)$ is a lower bound for $\{V(W) : K \cup L \subset W\}$, and hence is no more than the greatest lower bound $V(K \cup L)$. ▮

Now let $A$ be any bounded set. Its *outer measure*, denoted by $\overline{V}(A)$, is defined by approximating from without by open sets:

$$\overline{V}(A) = \inf \{V(G) : A \subset G\}.$$

Similarly, the *inner measure* $\underline{V}(A)$ is defined by approximating from within by compact sets:

$$\underline{V}(A) = \sup \{V(K) : K \subset A\}.$$

**Lemma 4.** *Let $K$ be a compact set and $G$ an open set such that $K \subset G$. Then there is a figure $Y$ such that $K \subset \text{int } Y$ and $Y \subset G$.*

The proof is left to the reader (Problem 6).

If $K \subset A$, then by Lemma 4 $V(K) \leq V(G)$ whenever $A \subset G$. Hence $V(K)$ is a lower bound for $\{V(G) : A \subset G\}$, and $V(K) \leq \overline{V}(A)$. Thus $\overline{V}(A)$ is an upper bound for $\{V(K) : K \subset A\}$, and

$$\underline{V}(A) \leq \overline{V}(A).$$

It is easy to show that if $B \subset A$, then

$$\underline{V}(B) \leq \underline{V}(A), \qquad \overline{V}(B) \leq \overline{V}(A).$$

If $H$ is a bounded open set, then $V(H) \leq V(G)$ for any open set $G$ containing $H$, and there is equality when $G = H$. Hence $\overline{V}(H) = V(H)$. Given $\epsilon > 0$, there is a figure $Y \subset H$ with $V(H) - \epsilon < V(Y)$. Since $Y$ is a compact set, $V(Y) \leq \underline{V}(H)$, and hence $V(H) - \epsilon < \underline{V}(H)$. Since this is true for every $\epsilon > 0$, $V(H) \leq \underline{V}(H)$. But $\underline{V}(H) \leq \overline{V}(H)$, and therefore

$$\underline{V}(H) = \overline{V}(H) = V(H).$$

Similarly, if $L$ is a compact set then

$$\underline{V}(L) = \overline{V}(L) = V(L).$$

**Definition.** A bounded set $A$ is called *measurable* if its outer and inner measures are equal. If $A$ is measurable, then the number

$$V(A) = \underline{V}(A) = \overline{V}(A)$$

is called the *n-dimensional measure of* $A$.

We showed above that bounded open sets and compact sets are measurable and that the new definition of their measures agrees with the previous one. Many sets which are neither open nor compact are also measurable. In fact, the only examples of nonmeasurable sets are obtained in a quite nonconstructive way using the "axiom of choice" of set theory (see [15], p. 157).

We shall now show that finite unions, intersections, and differences of bounded measurable sets are also measurable. For this purpose let us first prove the following.

**Lemma 5.** *Let $A$ and $B$ be bounded sets. Then*

$$\overline{V}(A \cup B) \leq \overline{V}(A) + \overline{V}(B). \tag{5–5}$$

*If $A \cap B$ is empty, then*

$$\underline{V}(A \cup B) \geq \underline{V}(A) + \underline{V}(B). \tag{5–6}$$

*Proof.* Given $\epsilon > 0$, there are open sets $G \supset A$, $H \supset B$ such that

$$V(G) < \overline{V}(A) + \epsilon/2, \qquad V(H) < \overline{V}(B) + \epsilon/2.$$

Then $G \cup H$ is an open set containing $A \cup B$, and from Lemma 2a

$$\overline{V}(A \cup B) \leq V(G \cup H) \leq V(G) + V(H),$$
$$\overline{V}(A \cup B) < \overline{V}(A) + \overline{V}(B) + \epsilon.$$

Since the last inequality is true for every $\epsilon > 0$, we must have (5–5).

Similar reasoning, using Lemma 3, gives (5–6). ▌

**Proposition 15a.** *Let $A$ and $B$ be bounded measurable sets such that $A \cap B$ is empty. Then $A \cup B$ is measurable and*

$$V(A \cup B) = V(A) + V(B). \tag{5–7}$$

*Proof.* By Lemma 5,

$$V(A) + V(B) \leq \underline{V}(A \cup B) \leq \overline{V}(A \cup B) \leq V(A) + V(B).$$

Since the extreme left-hand and right-hand sides are the same, both $\underline{V}(A \cup B)$ and $\overline{V}(A \cup B)$ must equal $V(A) + V(B)$. ▮

Let us call a finite collection $\{A_1, \ldots, A_m\}$ of sets *disjoint* if $A_k \cap A_l$ is empty whenever $k \neq l$.

**Corollary 1.** *If $\{A_1, \ldots, A_m\}$ is a finite disjoint collection of bounded, measurable sets, then $A_1 \cup \cdots \cup A_m$ is measurable and*

$$V(A_1 \cup \cdots \cup A_m) = \sum_{k=1}^{m} V(A_k). \tag{5–8}$$

*Proof.* Use induction on $m$. ▮

**Corollary 2.** *Let $A$ be a bounded set. Then $A$ is measurable if and only if for every $\epsilon > 0$ there exist a compact set $K$ and an open set $G$ such that $K \subset A \subset G$ and $V(G - K) < \epsilon$.*

The proof is left to the reader (Problem 7).

**Proposition 16.** *Let $A$ and $B$ be bounded measurable sets. Then $A - B$, $A \cap B$, and $A \cup B$ are also measurable.*

*Proof.* Let us first prove that $A - B$ is measurable. Given $\epsilon > 0$, let $G$, $G'$ be open sets and $K$, $K'$ compact sets such that $K \subset A \subset G$, $K' \subset B \subset G'$, and

$$V(G - K) < \epsilon/2, \qquad V(G' - K') < \epsilon/2.$$

Let $H = G - K'$, $L = K - G'$. Then $H$ is open, $L$ is compact,

$$L \subset A - B \subset H.$$

Moreover, $H - L$ is open and

$$H - L \subset (G - K) \cup (G' - K').$$

By Lemma 2a,

$$V(H - L) \leq V(G - K) + V(G' - K') < \epsilon.$$

This shows that $A - B$ is measurable.

Now $A \cap B = A - (A - B)$. Since $A$ and $A - B$ are bounded measurable sets, by the first part of the proposition their difference $A \cap B$ is measurable. Moreover,

$$A \cup B = (A - B) \cup (B - A) \cup (A \cap B),$$

and the three sets on the right-hand side are measurable and no two of them intersect. By Corollary 1, $A \cup B$ is measurable. ▌

**Countable additivity of measure.** The result expressed by Corollary 1 is called *finite additivity* of measure. Let us now prove a stronger result.

A series $\sum_{k=1}^{\infty} a_k$ of nonnegative numbers converges if the partial sums $s_m = \sum_{k=1}^{m} a_k$ are bounded, since the partial sums then form a bounded nondecreasing sequence (see Section A-4). If the sequence of partial sums is unbounded, the series is said to diverge to $+\infty$. A sequence $A_1, A_2, \ldots$ of sets is *disjoint* if $A_k \cap A_l$ is empty whenever $k \neq l$.

**Proposition 15b.** *If $A_1, A_2, \ldots$ is a disjoint sequence of measurable sets and if $A = A_1 \cup A_2 \cup \cdots$ is bounded, then $A$ is measurable and*

$$V(A) = \sum_{k=1}^{\infty} V(A_k). \tag{5-9}$$

This property is called *countable additivity of measure*: If we let $A_k$ be empty for $k > m$, then (5-8) is a special case of (5-9).

To prove Proposition 15b we first state:

**Lemma 2b.** *Let $G_1, G_2, \ldots$ be open sets each of which has finite measure. If $G = G_1 \cup G_2 \cup \cdots$, then*

$$V(G) \leq \sum_{k=1}^{\infty} V(G_k).$$

*Proof.* Let $Y \subset G$. The figure $Y$ is a compact set and $G_1, G_2, \ldots$ form an open covering of $Y$. Hence $Y \subset G_1 \cup \cdots \cup G_m$ for some $m$, and by Lemma 2a

$$V(Y) \leq \sum_{k=1}^{m} V(G_k) \leq \sum_{k=1}^{\infty} V(G_k).$$

Since this is true for every such $Y$, the lemma follows. ▌

*Proof of Proposition 15b.* We have $A_1 \cup \cdots \cup A_m \subset A$ for every $m$. Using (5-8)

$$\sum_{k=1}^{m} V(A_k) \leq \underline{V}(A).$$

Since this is true for each $m$,

$$\sum_{k=1}^{\infty} V(A_k) \leq \underline{V}(A).$$

On the other hand, given $\epsilon > 0$ let $G_k$ be an open set such that $A_k \subset G_k$ and $V(G_k) < V(A_k) + \epsilon 2^{-k}$, $k = 1, 2, \ldots$, and let $G = G_1 \cup G_2 \cup \cdots$ Then $A \subset G$ and therefore $\overline{V}(A) \leq V(G)$. By Lemma 2

$$\overline{V}(A) < \sum_{k=1}^{\infty} V(A_k) + \epsilon \sum_{k=1}^{\infty} 2^{-k}$$

and $\sum 2^{-k} = 1$. Since this is true for any $\epsilon > 0$, $A$ is measurable and (5–9) holds. ▮

A sequence $A_1, A_2, \ldots$ of sets is called *monotone nondecreasing* if $A_1 \subset A_2 \subset \cdots$

**Theorem 12a.** *Let $A$ be a bounded set such that $A = A_1 \cup A_2 \cup \cdots$, where $A_k$ is measurable for each $k = 1, 2, \ldots$ Then $A$ is measurable, and*

$$V(A) \leq \sum_{k=1}^{\infty} V(A_k). \tag{5–10}$$

*If the sequence of sets $A_1, A_2, \ldots$ is disjoint, then equality holds in (5–10). If the sequence $A_1, A_2, \ldots$ is nondecreasing, then*

$$V(A) = \lim_{m \to \infty} V(A_m). \tag{5–11}$$

*Proof.* Let

$$B_1 = A_1, B_2 = A_2 - A_1, \ldots, B_k = A_k - (A_1 \cup \cdots \cup A_{k-1}), \ldots$$

By Proposition 16 each $B_k$ is measurable. Moreover, $B_1, B_2, \ldots$ are disjoint and their union is $A$. By Proposition 15b, $A$ is measurable and

$$V(A) = \sum_{k=1}^{\infty} V(B_k).$$

Since $B_k \subset A_k$, $V(B_k) \leq V(A_k)$, giving (5–10). If the sequence $A_1, A_2, \ldots$ is disjoint, $B_k = A_k$ and (5–10) becomes formula (5–9) which has already been proved.

If $A_1 \subset A_2 \subset \cdots$, then $B_1 \cup \cdots \cup B_m = A_m$ and

$$V(A_m) = \sum_{k=1}^{m} V(B_k).$$

Taking the limit, we get (5–11). ▮

**Unbounded sets.** Let $U_r = \{\mathbf{x} : |\mathbf{x}| < r\}$. A set $A$ is called *measurable* if $A \cap U_r$ is measurable for every $r > 0$. The *measure* of $A$ is

$$V(A) = \lim_{r \to +\infty} V(A \cap U_r). \tag{5–12}$$

If we set $\phi(r) = V(A \cap U_r)$, then $\phi$ is a nondecreasing function. Therefore the limit exists in (5–12). It may be finite or $+\infty$ (Section A–10). If $A$ is a bounded set, then $A \subset U_{r_0}$ for some $r_0$. For $r \geq r_0$, $A = A \cap U_r$. For bounded sets this definition agrees with the previous one.

It will be proved in Section 5–10 that Theorem 12a remains true without the assumption that the sets $A, A_1, A_2, \ldots$ are bounded.

Let $A_1, A_2, \ldots$ be measurable sets such that $A_1 \supset A_2 \supset \cdots$, and let $A = A_1 \cap A_2 \cap \cdots$; then formula (5–11) is still correct *provided* $V(A_1)$ *is finite.* This is also proved in Section 5–10.

**Example 3.** Let $A_m = [m, \infty)$. Then $V(A_m) = +\infty$ for each $m = 1, 2, \ldots$, but $V(A_1 \cap A_2 \cap \cdots) = 0$ since the intersection is empty.

**Example 4.** Let $G$ be an open subset of $E^1$. If $G$ is the union of a finite number of disjoint open intervals $I_1, \ldots, I_m$, then $V(G) = V(I_1) + \cdots + V(I_m)$. It can also happen that $G$ is the union of a disjoint infinite sequence $I_1, I_2, \ldots$ of open intervals, in which case

$$V(G) = \sum_{k=1}^{\infty} V(I_k).$$

The third possibility is that $G$ contains some half-line. In that case $V(G) = +\infty$.

The sets of measure 0 play a special role. They turn out to be negligible in integration theory, and for that reason we shall call them null sets.

**Definition.** If $V(A) = 0$, then $A$ is a *null set.*

**Corollary.** *If $A_1, A_2, \ldots$ are null sets, then $A_1 \cup A_2 \cup \cdots$ is a null set. If $B \subset A$ and $A$ is a null set, then $B$ is a null set.*

*Proof.* By (5–10)

$$0 \leq V(A_1 \cup A_2 \cup \cdots) \leq \sum_{k=1}^{\infty} 0 = 0,$$

which proves the first assertion. If $A$ is a bounded null set and $B \subset A$, then

$$0 \leq \underline{V}(B) \leq \overline{V}(B) \leq V(A) = 0.$$

Hence $B$ is measurable and is a null set. If $A$ is any null set, then $A \cap U_r$ is a null set for each $r$ and $B \cap U_r \subset A \cap U_r$. Hence $B \cap U_r$ is a null set, which implies that $B$ is measurable and is a null set. ▌

**Example 5.** Let $A \subset M$, where $M$ is an $(n-1)$-manifold. It is plausible that the $n$-dimensional measure of $A$ is 0, and this fact will be proved in Section 5–8. Hence any such set $A$ is a null set.

**Example 6.** A set $A$ is *countable* if either $A$ is a finite set or its elements can be arranged in an infinite sequence, $A = \{\mathbf{x}_1, \mathbf{x}_2, \ldots\}$ where $\mathbf{x}_k \neq \mathbf{x}_l$ for $k \neq l$. Any one point set is a null set. Hence, taking $A_k = \{\mathbf{x}_k\}$, we find that *any countable set is a null set.*

**Example 7.** Let $A$ be the set of rational numbers in the interval $(0, 1)$. Then $A$ is countable. For instance, one can write

$$A = \{\tfrac{1}{2}, \tfrac{1}{3}, \tfrac{2}{3}, \tfrac{1}{4}, \tfrac{3}{4}, \tfrac{1}{5}, \ldots\}.$$

Hence $A$ is a null set. Since $V_1(A) + V_1[(0, 1) - A] = V_1[(0, 1)] = 1$, the set of irrational numbers in $(0, 1)$ has measure 1 and therefore must be an uncountable set.

## PROBLEMS

In 1, 2, and 3 assume that the sets are bounded.

1. Let $A$ and $B$ be measurable. Show that:
   (a) $V(A - B) = V(A) - V(A \cap B)$.
   (b) $V(A \cup B) + V(A \cap B) = V(A) + V(B)$.
2. Show that if $A$, $B$, and $C$ are measurable, then

$$V(A \cup B \cup C) = V(A) + V(B) + V(C) - V(A \cap B) - V(A \cap C) - V(B \cap C) + V(A \cap B \cap C).$$

3. Show that if $A$ is measurable and $B$ is a null set, then

$$V(A \cup B) = V(A - B) = V(A).$$

4. Let $A = A_1 \cup A_2 \cup \cdots$, where $A_k = \{(x, y) : x = 1/k, 0 \leq y \leq 1\}$ for $k = 1, 2, \ldots$ Show that $V_2(A) = 0$.
5. Let $A_0$ be the circular disk with center $(0, 0)$ and radius 1. For $k = 1, 2, \ldots$, let $A_k$ be the circular disk with center $(1 - 4^{-k})\mathbf{e}_1$ and radius $4^{-k-1}$. Let $A = A_0 - (A_1 \cup A_2 \cup \cdots)$. Find $V_2(A)$.
6. Prove Lemma 4.
7. Prove Corollary 2 to Proposition 15a. [*Hint:* If $K \subset G$, then $G = K \cup (G - K)$. By Proposition 15a, $V(G) = V(K) + V(G - K)$.]
8. (a) Show that if $A$ and $B$ are countable sets, then $A \cup B$ is countable.
   (b) Show that if $B \subset A$ and $A$ is countable, then $B$ is countable.
   (c) Show that if $A_1, A_2, \ldots$ are countable sets, then $A_1 \cup A_2 \cup \cdots$ is countable.
9. Let $A = \{x_1, x_2, \ldots\}$ be a countable subset of $(0, 1)$. Given $0 < \epsilon < 1$, let $\epsilon_k = \epsilon 2^{-k-1}$, $I_k = (x_k - \epsilon_k, x_k + \epsilon_k)$, and $G = I_1 \cup I_2 \cup \cdots$
   (a) Show that $V_1(G) \leq \epsilon$.
   (b) In particular, let $A$ be the set of rational numbers in $(0, 1)$. Let $K = [0, 1] - G$. Then $K$ is a compact subset of the irrational numbers. Show that $V_1(K) \geq 1 - \epsilon$.
   (c) Show that $K = \operatorname{fr} K$.

10. Let $G = A_1 \cup A_2 \cup \cdots$ where $A_1 = (\frac{1}{3}, \frac{2}{3})$, $A_2 = (\frac{1}{9}, \frac{2}{9}) \cup (\frac{7}{9}, \frac{8}{9})$, $A_3 = (\frac{1}{27}, \frac{2}{27}) \cup \cdots \cup (\frac{25}{27}, \frac{26}{27})$, $\cdots$ Thus $A_j$ is the union of $2^{j-1}$ intervals of length $3^{-j}$. (See Fig. 5-4.)

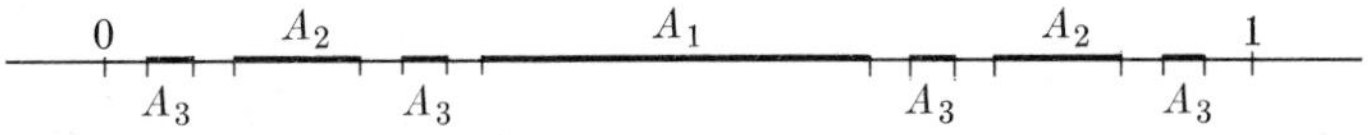


FIGURE 5-4

(a) Show that $V_1(G) = 1$. Hence the compact set $K = [0, 1] - G$ is a null set. $K$ is called the *Cantor discontinuum*.
(b) Show that no connected subset of $K$ contains more than one point.
(c) Show that $x \in K$ if and only if $x = \sum_{i=1}^{\infty} a_i 3^{-i}$ where $a_i = 0$ or $2$, $i = 1, 2, \ldots$
(d) Let $f(x) = \sum_{i=1}^{\infty} a_i 2^{-i-1}$ for $x \in K$. Show that $f(K) = [0, 1]$. Hence $K$ is uncountable.
(e) For $x$ in the $k$th interval of $A_j$ let $f(x)$ have the constant value $(2k - 1)2^{-j}$, $k = 1, 2, \ldots, 2^{j-1}$, $j = 1, 2, \ldots$ Show that $f$ is continuous and nondecreasing on $[0, 1]$. [*Note:* $f$ is called the *Cantor function.*]

11. Show that any straight line in $E^2$ has area 0.

12. Show that if $A$ is an unbounded measurable set, then

$$V(A) = \sup \{V(K) : K \subset A\}.$$

(If $V(A) = +\infty$, this means that for every $C > 0$ there is a compact set $K \subset A$ with $V(K) \geq C$.)

## 5-3 INTEGRALS OVER $E^n$

Let $f$ be real-valued with domain $E^n$. The *support* of $f$ is the smallest closed set $K$ such that $f(\mathbf{x}) = 0$ for every $\mathbf{x} \notin K$.

**Example 1.** Let $f(x) = x + 1$ if $x \in (0, 1)$ and $f(x) = 0$ if $x \notin (0, 1)$. The support of $f$ is the closed interval $[0, 1]$.

The object of this section is to define the integral $\int f\, dV$ of $f$ over $E^n$ when $f$ is bounded and has compact support. This is done first for functions taking only a finite number of values. In that case the integral is just a certain finite sum. A function $\phi$ is called a *step function* if there exists a disjoint collection $\{A_1, \ldots, A_m\}$ of bounded measurable sets such that $\phi(\mathbf{x})$ is constant on each $A_k$ and $\phi(\mathbf{x}) = 0$ for $\mathbf{x} \notin A_1 \cup \cdots \cup A_m$. If $\phi(\mathbf{x}) = c_k$ for every $\mathbf{x} \in A_k$, then the *integral of $\phi$ over $E^n$* is

$$\int \phi\, dV = \sum_{k=1}^{m} c_k V(A_k). \tag{5-13}$$

**Example 2.** Let $\phi(x) = k/m$ for $x \in [(k - 1)/m, k/m)$, $k = 1, 2, \ldots, m$, and $\phi(x) = 0$ for $x \notin [0, 1)$. Then

$$\int \phi\, dx = \frac{1}{m^2} + \frac{2}{m^2} + \cdots + \frac{m}{m^2} = \frac{m+1}{2m}.$$

We write $dx$ instead of $dV_1$ in case $n = 1$.

The collection $\{A_1, \ldots, A_m\}$ is not uniquely determined by $\phi$. However, let $\{B_1, \ldots, B_p\}$ be another disjoint collection of bounded measurable sets such that $\phi(\mathbf{x})$ is constant on each $B_l$ and $\phi(\mathbf{x}) = 0$ for $\mathbf{x} \notin B_1 \cup \cdots \cup B_l$. For each $k = 1, \ldots, m$ the collection $\{A_k \cap B_1, \ldots, A_k \cap B_p\}$ is disjoint, and applying (5–8) to it,

$$\sum_{k=1}^{m} c_k V(A_k) = \sum_{k=1}^{m} \sum_{l=1}^{p} c_k V(A_k \cap B_l).$$

In the same way, if $d_l = \phi(\mathbf{x})$ for $\mathbf{x} \in B_l$, then

$$\sum_{l=1}^{p} d_l V(B_l) = \sum_{l=1}^{p} \sum_{k=1}^{m} d_l V(B_l \cap A_k).$$

Since $d_l = c_k$ whenever $B_l \cap A_k$ is not empty, the right-hand sides are equal. This shows that $\int \phi \, dV$ does not depend on which collection is used.

Similar reasoning shows that the sum $\phi + \psi$ of two step functions is also a step function. Moreover,

$$\int (\phi + \psi) \, dV = \int \phi \, dV + \int \psi \, dV. \tag{5–14a}$$

$$\int (c\phi) \, dV = c \int \phi \, dV \text{ for any scalar } c. \tag{5–14b}$$

$$\int \psi \, dV \leq \int \phi \, dV \text{ if } \psi \leq \phi. \tag{5–14c}$$

*The notation* $\psi \leq \phi$ *means that* $\psi(\mathbf{x}) \leq \phi(\mathbf{x})$ *for every* $\mathbf{x} \in E^n$.

We are now ready to define upper and lower integrals. Let $f$ be a function which is bounded and has compact support. The upper integral of $f$ will be denoted by $\overline{\int} f \, dV$. If $\phi$ is any step function such that $\phi \geq f$, then $\int \phi \, dV$ is an upper estimate for it. We take the greatest lower bound of the set of all such numbers $\int \phi \, dV$.

**Definition.** *The upper integral of $f$ over $E^n$ is*

$$\overline{\int} f \, dV = \inf \left\{ \int \phi \, dV : \phi \geq f \right\}. \tag{5–15a}$$

We must check that there is at least one such step function, to insure that the set on the right-hand side is not empty. However, since $f$ is bounded, there is a number $C$ such that $|f(\mathbf{x})| \leq C$ for every $\mathbf{x}$. Since its support is compact there is an interval $I$ such that $f(\mathbf{x}) = 0$ for every $\mathbf{x} \notin I$. Let $\phi_0(\mathbf{x}) = C$ if $\mathbf{x} \in I$ and $\phi_0(\mathbf{x}) = 0$ if $\mathbf{x} \notin I$. Then $\phi_0 \geq f$ and $\phi_0$ is a step function.

In the same way, the *lower integral of $f$ over $E^n$* is denoted by $\underline{\int} f \, dV$. It is the least upper bound of the set of all numbers $\int \psi \, dV$, where $\psi$ is a step function and $\psi \leq f$:

$$\underline{\int} f \, dV = \sup \left\{ \int \psi \, dV : \psi \leq f \right\}. \tag{5–15b}$$

If $\psi \leq f \leq \phi$, then by (5–14c), $\int \psi \, dV \leq \int \phi \, dV$.

This implies that

$$\underline{\int} f\,dV \le \overline{\int} f\,dV.$$

If $\phi$ is a step function, then $\int \phi\,dV = \underline{\int} \phi\,dV = \overline{\int} \phi\,dV$.

**Definition.** A bounded function $f$ with compact support is *integrable* if its upper and lower integrals are equal. Its *integral over* $E^n$ is

$$\int f\,dV = \underline{\int} f\,dV = \overline{\int} f\,dV. \tag{5–16}$$

We just observed that any step function is integrable. In the next section it will be shown that every function in a much larger class is integrable.

**Proposition 17.** *Let $f$ and $g$ be integrable functions. Then $f + g$ is integrable and $cf$ is integrable for any scalar $c$. Moreover,*

$$\int (f + g)\,dV = \int f\,dV + \int g\,dV. \tag{5–17a}$$

$$\int (cf)\,dV = c\int f\,dV. \tag{5–17b}$$

$$\int f\,dV \le \int g\,dV \textit{ if } f \le g. \tag{5–17c}$$

*Proof.* Given $\epsilon > 0$ there exists a step function $\phi_1 \ge f$ such that

$$\int \phi_1\,dV < \overline{\int} f\,dV + \epsilon/2,$$

and a step function $\phi_2 \ge g$ such that

$$\int \phi_2\,dV < \overline{\int} g\,dV + \epsilon/2.$$

Then $\phi_1 + \phi_2$ is a step function and $\phi_1 + \phi_2 \ge f + g$. Consequently,

$$\overline{\int} (f + g)\,dV \le \int (\phi_1 + \phi_2)\,dV.$$

Using (5–14a), we have

$$\overline{\int} (f + g)\,dV < \overline{\int} f\,dV + \overline{\int} g\,dV + \epsilon.$$

Since this is true for every $\epsilon > 0$,

$$\overline{\int} (f + g)\,dV \le \overline{\int} f\,dV + \overline{\int} g\,dV. \tag{5–18a}$$

Similarly,

$$\underline{\int} (f + g)\,dV \ge \underline{\int} f\,dV + \underline{\int} g\,dV. \tag{5–18b}$$

If $f$ and $g$ are integrable, then the right-hand sides of (5–18a) and (5–18b) are equal. The left-hand side of (5–18b) is not greater than the left-hand side of (5–18a). Hence both upper and lower integrals of $f + g$ equal $\int f\,dV + \int g\,dV$. This proves that $f + g$ is integrable and (5–17a). The rest of the proof is left to the reader (Problem 4). ▮

An $n$-dimensional interval $I = J_1 \times \cdots \times J_n$ is *half-open to the right* if each of the 1-dimensional intervals $J_i$ is half-open *to the right.* (In the definition of figure we could equally well have used intervals half-open to the right instead of closed intervals.) Let us call a function $\phi$ an *elementary step function* if $\phi$ is constant on each interval of some grid $\Pi$ and $\phi$ has the value 0 outside the intervals of $\Pi$. To avoid ambiguity about the values of $\phi$ on the bounding faces of intervals we take the intervals of $\Pi$ half-open to the right.

***Riemann integral.** If in (5–15a) only elementary step functions $\phi$ are allowed, then the *upper Riemann integral* of $f$ is obtained. The *lower Riemann integral* of $f$ is obtained by allowing only elementary step functions $\psi$ in (5–15b). Let us denote upper and lower Riemann integrals by $\overline{S}(f)$ and $\underline{S}(f)$. Then

$$\underline{S}(f) \leq \underline{\int} f\,dV \leq \overline{\int} f\,dV \leq \overline{S}(f). \tag{5–19}$$

If $\underline{S}(f) = \overline{S}(f)$, then $f$ is called *Riemann integrable.* Their common value $S(f)$ is the *Riemann integral* of $f$. From (5–19), if $f$ is Riemann integrable, then $f$ is integrable [in the sense of (5–16)] and

$$S(f) = \int f\,dV. \tag{5–20}$$

It can be proved that a bounded function $f$ with compact support is Riemann integrable if and only if $V(\{\mathbf{x} : f \text{ is discontinuous at } \mathbf{x}\}) = 0$. See [1], pp. 230 and 260.

## PROBLEMS

1. Determine whether $f$ is bounded. Find its support.
   (a) $f(x) = x - |x|$.
   (b) $f(x, y) = x \exp(-x^2 - y^2)$.
   (c) $f(x, y) = 1$ if either $x$ or $y$ is a rational number, $f(x, y) = 0$ if both $x$ and $y$ are irrational.
   (d) $f(x, y) = (x - y)|x + y| - (x + y)|x - y|$ if $|x| + |y| < 1$, $f(x, y) = 0$ if $|x| + |y| \geq 1$. Illustrate with a sketch.
2. Let $[a]$ denote the largest integer which is no greater than $a$ (for instance, $[\pi] = 3$). Let $\phi(x, y) = [x + y]$ if $0 \leq x < r$, $0 \leq y < s$, where $r$ and $s$ are positive integers. For all other $(x, y)$ let $\phi(x, y) = 0$. Show that

$$\int \phi\,dV_2 = rs(r + s - 1)/2.$$

3. Let a unit square be divided into a small square in the center and $2m$ annular figures of equal width surrounding it, as shown in Fig. 5–5. Let $\phi(x, y) = 0$ for $(x, y)$ in the small square or outside the large square. Let $\phi(x, y) = (-1)^k k$ in the $k$th annular figure, $k = 1, \ldots, 2m$. Show that

$$\int \phi \, dV_2 = 8m(2m + 1)/(4m + 1)^2.$$

What is this approximately when $m$ is large?

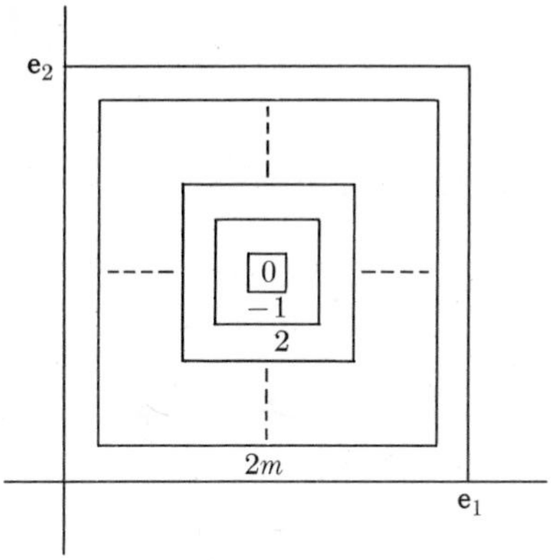


FIGURE 5–5

4. (a) Show that if $f$ is integrable, then $\int (cf) \, dV = c \int f \, dV$. [*Hint:* Show that this is true if $c \geq 0$, and that $-\underline{\int} g \, dV = \overline{\int} (-g) \, dV$ for every $g$. If $c < 0$, set $g = cf$ and $g = -cf$.]
   (b) Show that $\overline{\int} f \, dV \leq \overline{\int} g \, dV$ if $f \leq g$.

## 5–4 INTEGRALS OVER BOUNDED SETS

Let $A$ be a bounded measurable set and $f$ be a function which is bounded on $A$. More precisely, the domain of $f$ contains $A$ and there is a number $C$ such that $|f(\mathbf{x})| \leq C$ for every $\mathbf{x} \in A$. Let us consider a new function with the same values as $f$ on $A$ and the value 0 otherwise. This function will be denoted by $f_A$. Thus

$$f_A(\mathbf{x}) = \begin{cases} f(\mathbf{x}) & \text{if } \mathbf{x} \in A \\ 0 & \text{if } \mathbf{x} \notin A. \end{cases}$$

The function $f_A$ is bounded and has compact support. The values of $f$ outside $A$ should contribute nothing to the integral of $f$ over $A$.

**Definition.** The function $f$ is *integrable over* $A$ if $f_A$ is an integrable function. The *integral of $f$ over* $A$ is the number

$$\int_A f \, dV = \int f_A \, dV. \tag{5–21}$$

By Proposition 17 sums and scalar multiples of functions integrable over $A$ are again integrable over $A$.

The integral has a number of basic properties which we summarize in the next theorem.

**Theorem 13.** *If all the integrals involved exist, then:*

(1) $\int_A (f+g)\,dV = \int_A f\,dV + \int_A g\,dV.$

(2) $\int_A (cf)\,dV = c\int_A f\,dV.$

(3) $\int_A 1\,dV = V(A).$

(4) *If* $f(\mathbf{x}) \le g(\mathbf{x})$ *for every* $\mathbf{x} \in A$, *then* $\int_A f\,dV \le \int_A g\,dV.$

(5) *If* $|f(\mathbf{x})| \le C$ *for every* $\mathbf{x} \in A$, *then* $\left|\int_A f\,dV\right| \le \int_A |f|\,dV \le CV(A).$

(6) *If* $A$ *is a null set, then* $\int_A f\,dV = 0.$

(7) *If* $A \cap B$ *is a null set, then* $\int_{A\cup B} f\,dV = \int_A f\,dV + \int_B f\,dV.$

*Proof.* First of all,

$$(f+g)_A = f_A + g_A, \qquad (cf)_A = cf_A.$$

Therefore (1) and (2) follow from Proposition 17. Let $1_A$ denote the function with the value 1 on $A$ and otherwise 0. It is a step function, called the *characteristic function of* $A$, and by (5–13) with $m = 1$, $c_1 = 1$, $\int 1_A\,dV = V(A)$. This establishes (3). For (4) we have $f_A \le g_A$ and apply Proposition 17. To prove (5) we have

$$f(\mathbf{x}) \le |f(\mathbf{x})| \le C \quad \text{for every } \mathbf{x} \in A.$$

Hence from (4)

$$\int_A f\,dV \le \int_A |f|\,dV \le \int_A C\,dV,$$

and the right-hand side is $CV(A)$. Similarly, $-f(\mathbf{x}) \le |f(\mathbf{x})|$ and

$$-\int_A f\,dV \le \int_A |f|\,dV \le CV(A).$$

Since $|\int_A f\,dV|$ is either $\int_A f\,dV$ or its negative, this proves (5). Part (6) follows from (5). To prove (7), $f_{A\cup B} = f_A + f_B - f_{A\cap B}$. By Proposition 17

$$\int f_{A\cup B}\,dV = \int f_A\,dV + \int f_B\,dV - \int f_{A\cap B}\,dV,$$

and the last term is 0 by (6). ▮

From (6) and (7), the integral is unchanged if $A$ is replaced by $A \cup N$ or $A - N$, where $N$ is any null set. Similarly, if $f(\mathbf{x}) = g(\mathbf{x})$ except for $\mathbf{x}$ in some null set, then $f$ and $g$ have the same integral.

**Example.** If fr $A$ is a null set, then

$$\int_A f\,dV = \int_{\text{int}A} f\,dV = \int_{\text{cl}A} f\,dV.$$

In elementary examples fr $A$ is always a null set. If $A$ is the set of rational numbers in $[0, 1]$, then fr $A = [0, 1]$, which is not a null set. Problem 9, p. 146 furnishes an example of a compact subset of $E^1$ with frontier of positive length. There are open, connected subsets of $E^2$ with frontiers which have positive area.

Let us next show that under quite mild assumptions about $f$, the integral exists. It is for this purpose that the idea of measurable function is introduced. Let $f$ have domain $E^n$.

**Definition.** If $\{\mathbf{x} : f(\mathbf{x}) > c\}$ is a measurable set for every scalar $c$, then $f$ is a *measurable function.*

It will be shown in Section 5–10 that such operations as taking the sum of two measurable functions or the limit of a sequence of measurable functions lead again to measurable functions. Just as for nonmeasurable sets, the only examples of nonmeasurable functions are obtained in a nonconstructive way using the axiom of choice.

**Lemma.** *If $f$ is a bounded, nonnegative, measurable function with compact support, then $f$ is integrable.*

*Proof.* By replacing $f$ by $f/C$, where $C$ is an upper bound for $f(\mathbf{x})$ on $A$, we may assume that $0 \leq f(\mathbf{x}) \leq 1$ for every $\mathbf{x}$. Let $I$ be an interval containing the support of $f$. Given $\epsilon > 0$, let $m$ be a positive integer such that $V(I) < \epsilon m$. For each $k = 1, \ldots, m$ let

$$E_k = \{\mathbf{x} : f(\mathbf{x}) > (k - 1)/m\},$$

$$A_k = \{\mathbf{x} : (k - 1)/m < f(\mathbf{x}) \leq k/m\}.$$

(See Fig. 5–6.) Since $f$ is measurable, each $E_k$ is a measurable subset of $I$, hence $A_k = E_k - E_{k+1}$ is also measurable. Let $\phi$ and $\psi$ be step functions defined by

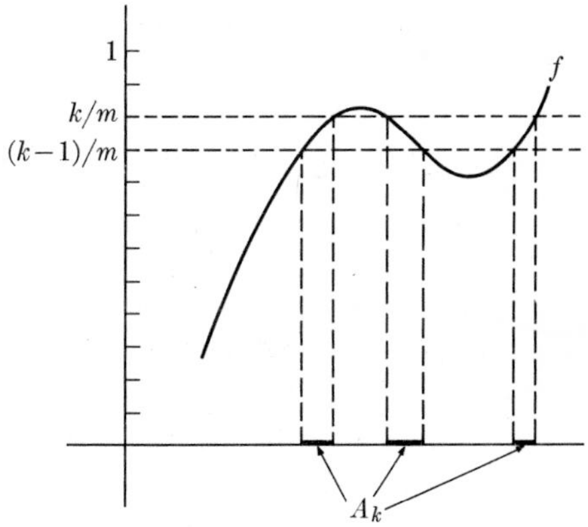


FIGURE 5–6

$$\phi(\mathbf{x}) = k/m, \qquad \psi(\mathbf{x}) = (k - 1)/m$$

for $\mathbf{x} \in A_k$, and $\phi(\mathbf{x}) = \psi(\mathbf{x}) = 0$ if $f(\mathbf{x}) = 0$. Then $\phi(\mathbf{x}) - \psi(\mathbf{x}) = 1/m$ on $E_1 = \{\mathbf{x} : f(\mathbf{x}) > 0\}$ and is 0 otherwise. Hence

$$\int \phi \, dV - \int \psi \, dV = V(E_1)/m,$$

$$V(E_1)/m \leq V(I)/m < \epsilon.$$

Moreover, $\psi \leq f \leq \phi$, from which

$$\int \psi \, dV \leq \underline{\int} f \, dV \leq \overline{\int} f \, dV \leq \int \phi \, dV.$$

Hence the upper and lower integrals differ by less than $\epsilon$. Since this is true for every positive $\epsilon$, $f$ is integrable. ▮

Now let $A$ be a bounded measurable set, and $f$ be a function whose domain contains $A$. If $\{\mathbf{x} \in A : f(\mathbf{x}) > c\}$ is measurable for every scalar $c$, then we call $f$ *measurable on* $A$.

**Theorem 14.** *If $f$ is bounded and measurable on $A$, then $f$ is integrable over $A$.*

*Proof.* Let us first assume that $f \geq 0$. If $c \geq 0$, then the set

$$\{\mathbf{x} : f_A(\mathbf{x}) > c\} = \{\mathbf{x} \in A : f(\mathbf{x}) > c\}$$

is measurable since $f$ is measurable on $A$. If $c < 0$, the left-hand side is $E^n$ which is measurable. Hence $f_A$ is measurable. By the lemma, $f_A$ is integrable.

If $f$ has negative values on $A$, let $g(\mathbf{x}) = f(\mathbf{x}) + C$ where $C$ is an upper bound for $|f(\mathbf{x})|$ on $A$. Then $g \geq 0$, and $g$ is bounded and measurable on $A$. Hence $g$ is integrable over $A$, and so is $f$. ▮

**Corollary.** *If $f$ is bounded and continuous on $A$, then $f$ is integrable over $A$.*

*Proof.* For every $c$, $\{\mathbf{x} \in A : f(\mathbf{x}) > c\}$ is open relative to $A$. In other words, it is the intersection of $A$ with an open set, and hence is measurable. ▮

In particular, if $A$ is compact, then any $f$ continuous on $A$ is bounded and therefore integrable over $A$.

Theorem 14 has a sort of converse. If a bounded function $f$ is integrable over $A$, then $f$ is measurable on $A$. We shall not prove this.

***Relation to the Riemann integral.** A function $f$ is *Riemann integrable over* $A$ if $f_A$ is Riemann integrable according to the definition on p. 150. Its *Riemann integral over* $A$ is $S(f_A)$. If $f$ is Riemann integrable over $A$, then from (5–20), $S(f_A) = \int_A f \, dV$.

A bounded set $A$ is *Jordan measurable* if its characteristic function $1_A$ is Riemann integrable. It can be shown that $A$ is Jordan measurable if and only if fr $A$ is a null set. (See [1], p. 256.)

If $A = [a, b]$, a closed interval of $E^1$, then the definition of Riemann integral given above can rather easily be shown to agree with Riemann's original definition of integral as the limit of sums (Section A–9).

## PROBLEMS

1. Let $f(x) = 2x - x^2$ if $0 \leq x \leq 2$, $f(x) = 0$ otherwise. Using the notation in the proof of the lemma, describe the sets $A_1, \ldots, A_m$. Sketch the step functions $\phi$ and $\psi$ in the case $m = 4$.
2. In each case show that $f$ is integrable over $A$.
   (a) $f(x) = x^2 \exp x$, $A = [0, a]$.
   (b) $f(x) = \sin(1/x)$ if $x \neq 0$, $f(0) = 5$, $A = [-1, 1]$.
   (c) $f(x, y) = (x^4 - y^2)/(x^2 - y)$, $A = \{(x, y) : |x| \leq 1, |y| \leq 1, x^2 \neq y\}$.
   (d) $f(x) = 0$ if $x$ is irrational, $f(x) = 1/q$ if $x = p/q$ where $p$ and $q$ are integers with no common factor, $A = (0, 1]$.
   (e) $f(x) = 1$ if $x$ is irrational, $f(x) = 0$ if $x$ is rational, $A = [a, b]$.
3. For each part of Problem 2 describe the sets $\{\mathbf{x} \in A : f(\mathbf{x}) > c\}$.
4. Show that if $f$, $g$, and $h$ are integrable over $A$ and $|f(\mathbf{x}) - g(\mathbf{x})| \leq h(\mathbf{x})$ for every $\mathbf{x} \in A$, then $|\int_A f\,dV - \int_A g\,dV| \leq \int_A h\,dV$.
5. Let $f$ be of class $C^{(2)}$ on $[0, a]$ and $b = \max\{|f''(x)| : 0 \leq x \leq a\}$. Let $g(x) = f(0) + f'(0)x$. Using Problem 4, show that $|\int_0^a f\,dx - af(0) - a^2 f'(0)/2| \leq a^3 b/6$. Use this result to estimate $\int_0^{1/2} \exp(-x^2/2)\,dx$.
6. (*Mean value theorem for integrals.*) Let $A$ be compact and connected. Let $f$ be continuous on $A$ and $g$ be integrable over $A$ with $g(\mathbf{x}) \geq 0$ for every $\mathbf{x} \in A$. Prove that there exists $\mathbf{x}^* \in A$ such that

$$\int_A fg\,dV = f(\mathbf{x}^*) \int_A g\,dV.$$

[*Hint:* Let $C$ and $c$ be the maximum and minimum values of $f$ on $A$. Then $cg \leq fg \leq Cg$. Use (2) and (4) of Theorem 13 and the intermediate value theorem.]

## 5–5 ITERATED INTEGRALS

Thus far we have given no effective procedure for the actual evaluation of integrals. One method for doing this is by writing the integral as an iterated integral and applying the fundamental theorem of calculus. Let $1 \leq s < n$. In most cases we shall take $s = 1$ or $s = n - 1$. Then $E^n$ can be regarded as the cartesian product $E^s \times E^{n-s}$. Let us write $\mathbf{x} = (\mathbf{x}', \mathbf{x}'')$, where

$$\mathbf{x}' = (x^1, \ldots, x^s) \in E^s, \qquad \mathbf{x}'' = (x^{s+1}, \ldots, x^n) \in E^{n-s}.$$

Let $A$ be a bounded set and (Fig. 5–7)

$$A(\mathbf{x}') = \{\mathbf{x}'' : (\mathbf{x}', \mathbf{x}'') \in A\},$$
$$R = \{\mathbf{x}' : A(\mathbf{x}') \text{ is not empty}\}. \tag{5–22}$$

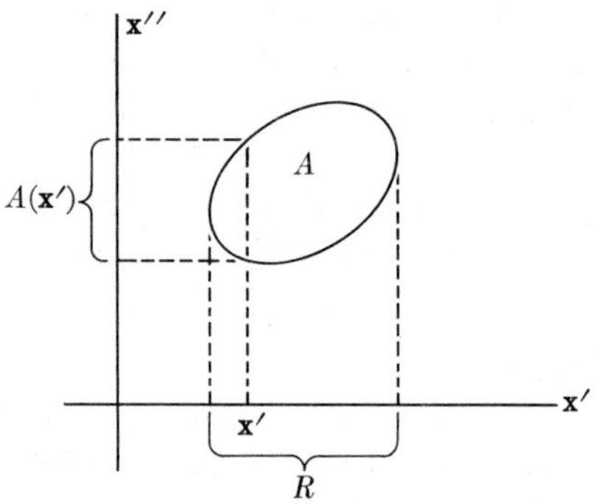


FIGURE 5–7

Let $f$ be a function whose domain contains $A$. For each fixed $\mathbf{x}' \in R$ let $f(\mathbf{x}',\ )$ denote the function whose value at each $\mathbf{x}'' \in A(\mathbf{x}')$ is $f(\mathbf{x}', \mathbf{x}'')$. Let us assume that $A$ is compact and $f$ is continuous on $A$. Then $A(\mathbf{x}')$ and $R$ are compact and $f(\mathbf{x}',\ )$ is continuous (Section A–8). In stating the theorem about iterated integrals let us use the longer notation $\int_A f(\mathbf{x})\, dV_n(\mathbf{x})$ for the integral. Let

$$g(\mathbf{x}') = \int_{A(\mathbf{x}')} f(\mathbf{x}', \mathbf{x}'')\, dV_{n-s}(\mathbf{x}'').$$

Then the integral of $f$ over $A$ equals the integral of $g$ over $R$.

**Theorem 15.** *Let $f$ be continuous on a compact set $A$. Then*

$$\int_A f(\mathbf{x})\, dV_n(\mathbf{x}) = \int_R g(\mathbf{x}')\, dV_s(\mathbf{x}'). \tag{5–23a}$$

Actually, Theorem 15 is true if $A$ is merely measurable and $f$ is integrable over $A$. In that case there may be a subset of $R$ of $s$-dimensional measure 0 for which $g(\mathbf{x}')$ is undefined. We shall not prove this general form of Theorem 15. However, in the next section the theorem will be extended to the case when $A$ is a $\sigma$-compact set.

In the proof the following fact about monotone sequences of functions will be used. For each $\nu = 1, 2, \ldots$ let $F_\nu$ be a bounded measurable function with compact support such that

$$F_1 \geq F_2 \geq \cdots \geq 0.$$

Let

$$F(\mathbf{x}) = \lim_{\nu\to\infty} F_\nu(\mathbf{x}) \quad \text{for every } \mathbf{x}.$$

Then $F$ is measurable (and of course bounded), and

$$\int F\, dV_n = \lim_{\nu\to\infty} \int F_\nu\, dV_n.$$

A proof of this fact will be given in the section on convergence theorems (Corollary 3, Section 5–10).

*Proof of Theorem 15.* The proof will proceed by observing that the theorem is true for elementary step functions, and then by constructing a monotone sequence of elementary step functions tending to $f_A$.

Let us first show that

$$\int \Phi(\mathbf{x})\, dV_n(\mathbf{x}) = \int\left\{\int \Phi(\mathbf{x}', \mathbf{x}'')\, dV_{n-s}(\mathbf{x}'')\right\} dV_s(\mathbf{x}') \tag{$*$}$$

if $\Phi$ is any elementary step function. If $I$ is any $n$-dimensional interval then $I = I' \times I''$, where $I'$ and $I''$ are $s$- and $(n - s)$-dimensional intervals. If $\Phi$ is the characteristic function $1_I$ of $I$, then $(*)$ becomes $V_n(I) = V_s(I')V_{n-s}(I'')$, which is true by definition of measure for intervals. But any elementary step function can be written as a linear combination $\Phi = c_1\Phi_1 + \cdots + c_p\Phi_p$, where each $\Phi_k$ is the characteristic function of an $n$-dimensional interval. Then

$$\int \Phi\, dV_n = \sum_{k=1}^{p} c_k \int\left\{\int \Phi_k\, dV_{n-s}\right\} dV_s = \int\left\{\int\left(\sum_{k=1}^{p} c_k\Phi_k\right) dV_{n-s}\right\} dV_s$$

which is just $(*)$.

Now let $A$ be a compact set and $f$ be continuous on $A$. For the moment, assume that $f \geq 0$. Let $F = f_A$. Let us define a monotone sequence of elementary step functions $F_1 \geq F_2 \geq \cdots$ as follows. Let $I_0$ be some interval containing $A$ and let $C$ be the maximum value of $f$ on $A$. Let $F_1(\mathbf{x}) = C$ for $\mathbf{x} \in I_0$, and $F_1(\mathbf{x}) = 0$ otherwise. Divide $I_0$ into $2^n$ congruent subintervals $I_1, \ldots, I_m$, $m = 2^n$, and let $A_k = A \cap \text{cl}\, I_k$. If $\mathbf{x} \in I_k$ and $A_k$ is not empty, let $F_2(\mathbf{x})$ be the maximum value of $f$ on $A_k$. Otherwise, let $F_2(\mathbf{x}) = 0$. Then $F_1 \geq F_2 \geq F$. The function $F_3$ is defined similarly by dividing each interval $I_k$ into $2^n$ congruent subintervals, and so on (Fig. 5-8).

Let $d_0 = \text{diam}\, I_0$. At the $\nu$th step the diameter $d_\nu$ of each interval $I$ is $2^{-\nu+1} d_0$, and $F_\nu(\mathbf{x}) = 0$ except on those intervals of diameter $d_\nu$ whose closures meet $A$. Let us show that for every $\mathbf{x}$

$$F(\mathbf{x}) = \lim_{\nu\to\infty} F_\nu(\mathbf{x}). \tag{$**$}$$

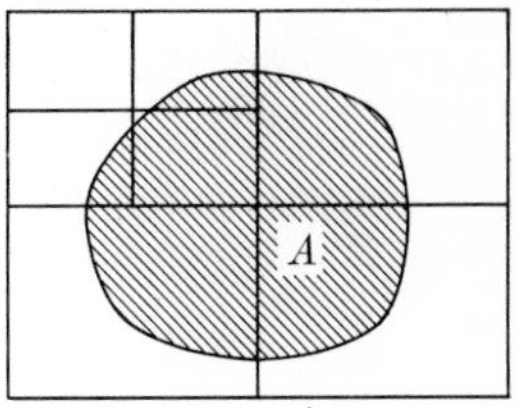


FIGURE 5-8

If $\mathbf{x} \notin A$, then since $A$ is closed there exists $\nu(\mathbf{x})$ such that $d_\nu < \text{dist}\,(\mathbf{x}, A)$ for every $\nu \geq \nu(\mathbf{x})$. In this case $0 = F(\mathbf{x}) = F_\nu(\mathbf{x})$ when $\nu \geq \nu(\mathbf{x})$. Thus $(**)$ holds for every $\mathbf{x} \notin A$. Suppose that $\mathbf{x} \in A$. Since $f$ is continuous, given $\epsilon > 0$ there exists $\delta(\mathbf{x}) > 0$ such that $|f(\mathbf{y}) - f(\mathbf{x})| < \epsilon$ for every $\mathbf{y} \in A$ such that $|\mathbf{y} - \mathbf{x}| < \delta(\mathbf{x})$. Choose $\nu(\mathbf{x})$ such that $d_\nu < \delta(\mathbf{x})$ for every $\nu \geq \nu(\mathbf{x})$. Then $F(\mathbf{x}) \leq F_\nu(\mathbf{x}) < F(\mathbf{x}) + \epsilon$ for every $\nu \geq \nu(\mathbf{x})$. Therefore $(**)$ also holds when $\mathbf{x} \in A$.

By the monotone sequences theorem

$$\int F\, dV_n = \lim_{\nu\to\infty} \int F_\nu\, dV_n.$$

For each $\mathbf{x}'$, the functions $F_\nu(\mathbf{x}', \ )$ form a monotone sequence tending to $F(\mathbf{x}', \ )$. Let

$$G_\nu(\mathbf{x}') = \int F_\nu(\mathbf{x}', \ )\, dV_{n-s}, \qquad G(\mathbf{x}') = \int F(\mathbf{x}', \ )\, dV_{n-s}.$$

Applying the monotone sequences theorem to the sequence $[F_\nu(\mathbf{x}', \ )]$,

$$\lim_{\nu \to \infty} G_\nu(\mathbf{x}') = G(\mathbf{x}')$$

for every $\mathbf{x}'$. Moreover, $G_1 \geq G_2 \geq \cdots$ Applying the monotone sequences theorem to this sequence,

$$\lim_{\nu \to \infty} \int G_\nu \, dV_s = \int G \, dV_s.$$

Since $F_\nu$ is an elementary step function, we have by (*) with $\Phi = F_\nu$,

$$\int F_\nu \, dV_n = \int G_\nu \, dV_s.$$

Therefore

$$\int F \, dV_n = \int G \, dV_s. \tag{5–23b}$$

However, $f_A = F$ and $g_R = G$. Hence (5–23b) is the same as (5–23a).

To remove the assumption $f \geq 0$, write $f = (f + C) - C$, where $C$ is the maximum value of $|f|$ on $A$. Then $f$ is the difference of nonnegative continuous functions for each of which (5–23a) holds. By subtraction, (5–23a) holds for $f$. ▮

**Corollary.**

$$V_n(A) = \int_R V_{n-s}[A(\mathbf{x}')]\, dV_s(\mathbf{x}'). \tag{5–24}$$

*Proof.* Take $f(\mathbf{x}) \equiv 1$ in (5–23a). ▮

In particular, let $s = 1$. Writing $x' = x^1 = u$, (5–24) becomes

$$V_n(A) = \int_R V_{n-1}[A(u)]\, du. \tag{5–25}$$

The set $A(u)$ is congruent to the intersection of $A$ and the hyperplane $x^1 = u$. In effect, (5–25) states that $V_n(A)$ is the integral of the $(n - 1)$-dimensional measures of these intersections. For $n = 3$, this is the method of "volumes by slices" of elementary calculus.

**Example 1.** Let $A$ be the $n$-simplex with vertices $\mathbf{0}, c\mathbf{e}_1, \ldots, c\mathbf{e}_n$, where $c > 0$. For $c = 1$ this is the standard $n$-simplex (Section 1–4). Let us show by induction on $n$ that $V_n(A) = c^n/n!$. If $n = 1$, then $A = [0, c]$ and $V_1(A) = c$. Assuming the result in dimension $n - 1$, we apply (5–25). (See Fig. 5–9.) Now

$$A = \{\mathbf{x} : x^1 + \cdots + x^n \leq c,\ x^i \geq 0 \text{ for } i = 1, \ldots, n\},$$

$$A(u) = \{\mathbf{x}'' : x^2 + \cdots + x^n \leq c - u,\ x^i \geq 0 \text{ for } i = 2, \ldots, n\},$$

and $R = [0, c]$. Therefore

$$V_n(A) = \int_0^c \frac{(c-u)^{n-1}}{(n-1)!}\,du = -\left.\frac{(c-u)^n}{n(n-1)!}\right|_0^c = \frac{c^n}{n!}.$$

To evaluate this integral we have of course used the fundamental theorem of calculus. A proof of this theorem is given in Section A–9.

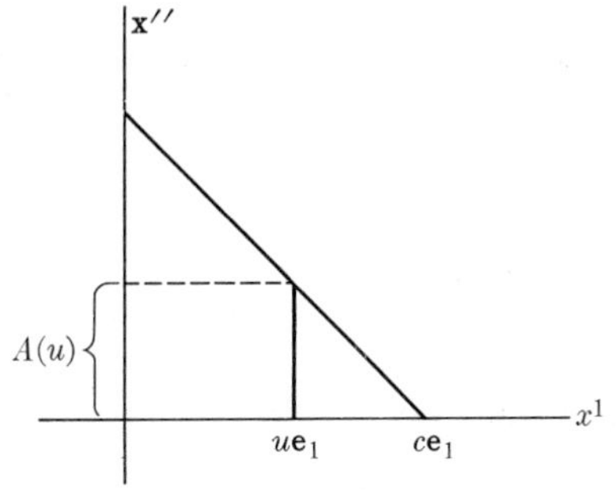


FIGURE 5–9

**Example 2.** Let $s = n - 1$. Suppose that $A$ has the particular form

$$A = \{\mathbf{x} : h(\mathbf{x}') \le x^n \le H(\mathbf{x}'), \mathbf{x}' \in R\}.$$

Then

$$A(\mathbf{x}') = [h(\mathbf{x}'), H(\mathbf{x}')]$$

and

$$V_n(A) = \int_R [H(\mathbf{x}') - h(\mathbf{x}')]\, dV_{n-1}(\mathbf{x}').$$

For instance, if $n = 3$ then $A$ is a solid bounded above by the surface with equation $z = H(x, y)$ and below by the one with equation $z = h(x, y)$, $(x, y) \in R$.

It is not essential in Theorem 15 that $\mathbf{x}' = (x^1, \ldots, x^s)$. One can equally well take integers $i_1 < \cdots < i_s$ and

$$\mathbf{x}' = (x^{i_1}, \ldots, x^{i_s}), \qquad \mathbf{x}'' = (x^{j_1}, \ldots, x^{j_{n-s}}),$$

where $j_1 < \cdots < j_{n-s}$ are those integers between 1 and $n$ not included among $i_1, \ldots, i_s$.

In particular, let $n = 2$. Then $s = 1$ and we can take either $x' = x$ or $x' = y$. To avoid writing parentheses we write $\int dx \int f\,dy$ instead of $\int \{\int f\,dy\}\,dx$. Then

$$\int_A f\,dV_2 = \int dx \int f\,dy = \int dy \int f\,dx,$$

where the iterated integrals are taken over the appropriate subsets of $E^1$. Many authors write the iterated integral as $\int\int f\,dy\,dx$, but this notation would lead to confusion when we come to the exterior differential calculus in later chapters.

The iterated integral is usually easier to evaluate when taken in one of the two possible orders than in the other order.

**Example 3.** Consider the iterated integral

$$\int_{-1}^{1} dx \int_{x^2}^{1} (x^2 + y)\, dy.$$

Then $f(x, y) = x^2 + y$ and $A$ is as shown (Fig. 5–10). Evaluating the inner integral first, we get

$$\int_{-1}^{1} \left( x^2 y + \frac{y^2}{2} \right) \Bigg|_{x^2}^{1} dx = \int_{-1}^{1} \left[ (x^2 + \tfrac{1}{2}) - \left( x^4 + \frac{x^4}{2} \right) \right] dx = \tfrac{16}{15}.$$

Writing $\int_A f\, dV_2$ as an iterated integral in the opposite order, we get

$$\int_0^1 dy \int_{-\sqrt{y}}^{\sqrt{y}} (x^2 + y)\, dx = \int_0^1 \left( \frac{x^3}{3} + xy \right) \Bigg|_{-\sqrt{y}}^{\sqrt{y}} dy = \tfrac{8}{3} \int_0^1 y^{3/2}\, dy = \tfrac{16}{15}.$$

If $n = 3$, then the integral can be written as an iterated triple integral.

**Example 4.** Let $A = \{(x, y, z) : x \geq 0, z \geq 0, 0 \leq y \leq 4 - x^2 - z^2\}$. Then

$$\int_A f\, dV_3 = \int_R \left\{ \int_{A(x,y)} f\, dz \right\} dV_2(x, y),$$

and $A(x, y)$ is the interval $[0, \sqrt{4 - x^2 - y}]$. (See Fig. 5–11.) Writing the integral over $R$ as an iterated integral, we get

$$\int_A f\, dV_3 = \int_0^2 dx \int_0^{4 - x^2} dy \int_0^{\sqrt{4 - x^2 - y}} f\, dz.$$

There are 5 other possible ways of writing $\int_A f\, dV_3$ as an iterated triple integral. For instance,

$$\int_A f\, dV_3 = \int_S \left\{ \int_0^{4 - x^2 - z^2} f\, dy \right\} dV_2(x, z)$$

$$= \int_0^2 dz \int_0^{\sqrt{4 - z^2}} dx \int_0^{4 - x^2 - z^2} f\, dy,$$

where $S = \{(x, y) : x \geq 0, z \geq 0, x^2 + z^2 \leq 4\}$.

In the same way, for any $n$ the integral can be written in $n!$ possible ways as an $n$-fold iterated integral.

**Moments.** Let $B$ be a closed set, and $A$ be a bounded measurable set. For each *even* integer $k$ the $k$th moment of a point $\mathbf{x}$ about $B$ is $[\text{dist}\,(\mathbf{x}, B)]^k$. The moment of $A$ about $B$ is

$$\int_A [\text{dist}\,(\mathbf{x}, B)]^k\, dV_n(\mathbf{x}).$$

If $k$ is odd, then we define the $k$th moment only in case $B$ is a hyperplane. Let $B = \{\mathbf{x} : \mathbf{a} \cdot \mathbf{x} = c\}$. We may suppose that $|\mathbf{a}| = 1$. This determines $\mathbf{a}$

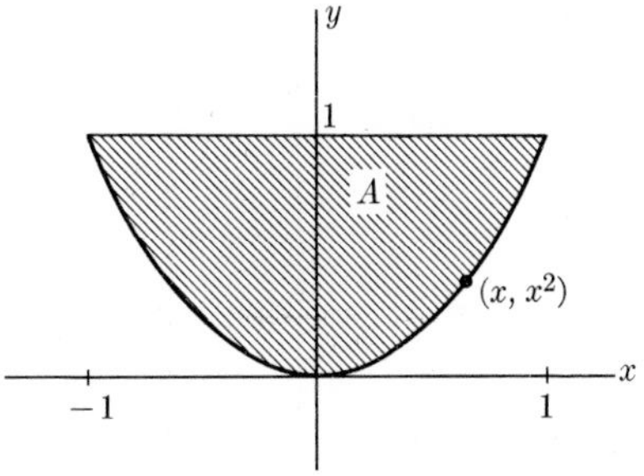


FIGURE 5–10

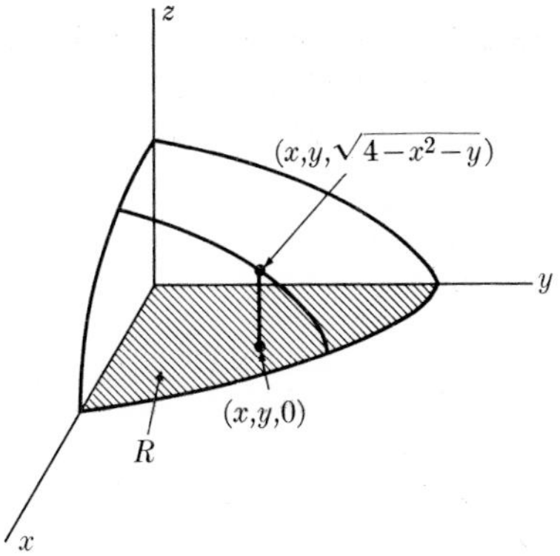


FIGURE 5–11

up to a change of sign. We make a particular choice for $\mathbf{a}$, which amounts to choosing one of the two half spaces bounded by $B$ to be "positive" and the other "negative." Then dist $(\mathbf{x}, B) = |\mathbf{a} \cdot \mathbf{x} - c|$, by Problem 6, Section 4–8. The $k$th moment of a point $\mathbf{x}$ about $B$ is defined to be $[\mathbf{a} \cdot \mathbf{x} - c]^k$, and the $k$th moment of $A$ about $B$ to be

$$\int_A [\mathbf{a} \cdot \mathbf{x} - c]^k \, dV_n(\mathbf{x}).$$

If $k$ is even, this agrees with the previous formula.

**Centroids.** Let us denote by $m^i$ the first moment of $A$ about the hyperplane $x^i = 0$, taking $\mathbf{a} = \mathbf{e}^i$, $c = 0$. Thus

$$m^i = \int_A x^i \, dV_n(\mathbf{x}), \qquad i = 1, \ldots, n.$$

Let $\mathbf{m} = (m^1, \ldots, m^n)$. The *centroid* of $A$ is the point $\bar{\mathbf{x}}$ such that $\mathbf{m} = V_n(A)\bar{\mathbf{x}}$, provided $V_n(A) > 0$. [Centroids of lower dimensional sets can be defined similarly by replacing $n$-dimensional measures and integrals by $r$-fold ones. See Section 7–3.] The first moment of $A$ about any hyperplane $B$ is then seen to be $\mathbf{a} \cdot \mathbf{m} - cV(A)$, which is $V(A)$ times the first moment of $\bar{\mathbf{x}}$ about $B$.

If $n \leq 3$, then one may think of $A$ as a body made of some material of density $\rho(\mathbf{x})$. The moments of mass are defined by inserting the factor $\rho(\mathbf{x})$ under the integral sign in each of the above formulas. The *center of mass* is the point $\bar{\bar{\mathbf{x}}}$ with

$$\bar{\bar{x}}^i = \frac{\int_A x^i \rho(\mathbf{x}) \, dV_n(\mathbf{x})}{\int_A \rho(\mathbf{x}) \, dV_n(\mathbf{x})}, \qquad i = 1, \ldots, n.$$

If $\rho$ is constant, then $\bar{\bar{\mathbf{x}}} = \bar{\mathbf{x}}$.

**Example 5.** Find the centroid of the hemispherical $n$-ball $H = \{\mathbf{x} : |\mathbf{x}| \leq 1, x^1 \geq 0\}$. (See Fig. 5–12.) Now $V_n(H) = \alpha_n/2$, where $\alpha_n$ is the measure of the unit $n$-ball (Problem 7). By symmetry, $m^i = 0$ for $i > 1$, and

$$m^1 = \int_H x^1 \, dV_n(\mathbf{x})$$

$$= \int_0^1 u \, du \int_{H(u)} 1 \, dV_{n-1}(\mathbf{x}'')$$

$$= \alpha_{n-1} \int_0^1 u(1 - u^2)^{(n-1)/2} \, du = \frac{\alpha_{n-1}}{n+1}.$$

Thus

$$\bar{\mathbf{x}} = \frac{2\alpha_{n-1}}{(n+1)\alpha_n} \mathbf{e}_1.$$

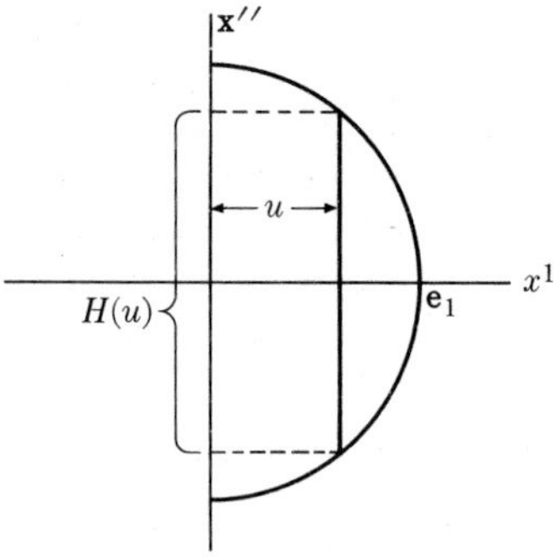


FIGURE 5–12

**PROBLEMS**

1. Find the area and also the centroid of:

   (a) $\{(x, y) : x^2 \leq y \leq x + 2\}$. (b) $\{(x, y) : |y| - 1 \leq x \leq \sqrt{1 - y^2}\}$.

2. Express the iterated integral

$$\int_0^1 dy \int_0^{f(y)} xy \, dx, \text{ where } f(y) = \min [1, \log (1/y)],$$

   as an integral over a set $A \subset E^2$, and then as an iterated integral in the opposite order. Evaluate it.

3. Express as an iterated triple integral:

$$\int_A f \, dV_3, \text{ where } A = \{(x, y, z) : x^2 + z^2 \leq y^2 \leq 8 - (x^2 + z^2)\}.$$

4. Find the volume of

$$\{(x, y, z) : |x| + |y| + |z| \leq 2, \ |x| \leq 1, \ |y| \leq 1\}.$$

5. Find the volume of

$$\{(x, y, z) : |x| + |y| + |z| \leq 2, z^2 \leq y\}.$$

6. (a) Suppose that $f(x, y) = g(x)h(y)$ for every $(x, y) \in A$ and that $A = R \times S$. Show that

$$\int_A f \, dV_2 = \left(\int_R g \, dx\right)\left(\int_S h \, dy\right).$$

   (b) Evaluate $\int_0^1 dx \int_0^1 \exp (x + y) \, dy$.

   (c) Evaluate $\int_0^{\pi} dy \int_0^{\pi/2} xy \cos (x + y) \, dx$.

7. Let $\alpha_n$ be the measure of the unit $n$-ball $\{\mathbf{x} : |\mathbf{x}| \leq 1\}$. Prove by induction that $\alpha_n r^n$ is the measure of an $n$-ball of radius $r$, and $\alpha_n = 2\alpha_{n-1} \int_0^1 (1 - u^2)^{(n-1)/2} \, du$. Show that $\alpha_4 = \pi^2/2$. [In Section 5–9 we give a general formula for $\alpha_n$.]

8. Let $\sum$ be the standard $n$-simplex.
   (a) Show that the centroid of $\sum$ is at the barycenter.
   (b) Show that the second moment of $\sum$ about the $(n-r)$-dimensional plane spanned by $\mathbf{e}_{r+1}, \ldots, \mathbf{e}_n$ is $2r/(n+2)!$
9. A sequence of functions $F_1, F_2, \ldots$ is said to converge uniformly to $F$ if given $\epsilon > 0$ there exists $\nu_0$ (depending only on $\epsilon$) such that $|F_\nu(\mathbf{x}) - F(\mathbf{x})| < \epsilon$ for every $\mathbf{x}$ and $\nu \geq \nu_0$. Show that the sequence constructed in the proof of Theorem 15 converges uniformly to $f_A$ if and only if $f(\mathbf{x}) = 0$ for every $\mathbf{x} \in \text{fr } A$. [*Hint:* $f$ is uniformly continuous on the compact set $A$. Uniform continuity of a function is defined in Problem 5, Section A–8.]

## 5–6 THE UNBOUNDED CASE

In the previous sections the integral of a bounded function $f$ over a bounded set $A$ has been considered. However, in some instances the integral can be defined without these boundedness conditions. In the present section let us make the following two simplifying assumptions:

(a) $f$ is continuous on $A$.

(b) There is a nondecreasing sequence of compact sets $K_1 \subset K_2 \subset \cdots$ such that $A = K_1 \cup K_2 \cup \cdots$

Any set $A$ with property (b) is called *$\sigma$-compact.* In Section 5–10 the integral will be considered under the weaker assumptions that $A$ is a measurable set and $f$ is measurable on $A$. However, in all elementary examples either (a) and (b) are satisfied, or else they hold as soon as $A$ is replaced by $A - N$ where $N$ is a suitable null set. Moreover, both (a) and (b) will always be satisfied in the applications made in Chapter 7 to integrals over manifolds.

The definition is given in two steps.

*Step 1.* Let us first assume that $f \geq 0$. For any compact set $K \subset A$ the integral $\int_K f\, dV$ exists in the sense of Section 5–4. The integral of $f$ over $A$ is defined as the least upper bound of such integrals:

$$\int_A f\, dV = \sup\left\{\int_K f\, dV : K \subset A\right\}. \tag{5–26}$$

If the set of numbers on the right-hand side has an upper bound, then $f$ is *integrable* over $A$. Otherwise, the integral *diverges to* $+\infty$. The definition has two immediate consequences, which we state in the following form.

**Lemma.** *Let $g$ and $h$ be continuous on $A$, with $g \geq 0$, $h \geq 0$.*

(a) *If $h \leq g$ and $g$ is integrable over $A$, then $h$ is integrable over $A$.*

(b) *If $g$ and $h$ are both integrable over $A$, then $g + h$ is integrable over $A$.*

*Proof of (a).* For every compact set $K \subset A$,

$$\int_K h\, dV \leq \int_K g\, dV \leq \int_A g\, dV.$$

Hence $\int_A g\,dV$ is an upper bound for $\{\int_K h\,dV : K \subset A\}$. ▮

*Proof of (b).* For every compact set $K \subset A$,

$$\int_K (g + h)\,dV = \int_K g\,dV + \int_K h\,dV \leq \int_A g\,dV + \int_A h\,dV.$$

Hence the right-hand side is an upper bound for $\{\int_K (g + h)\,dV : K \subset A\}$. ▮

*Step 2.* If a continuous function $f$ also has negative values, then its integral is defined by writing $f$ as the difference of two nonnegative functions. Let

$$f^+(\mathbf{x}) = \max\,\{f(\mathbf{x}), 0\},$$
$$f^-(\mathbf{x}) = \max\,\{-f(\mathbf{x}), 0\}.$$

Then $f^+$ and $f^-$ are continuous on $A$ (Problem 9) and

$$f(\mathbf{x}) = f^+(\mathbf{x}) - f^-(\mathbf{x}), \qquad |f(\mathbf{x})| = f^+(\mathbf{x}) + f^-(\mathbf{x}), \tag{5–27}$$

for every $\mathbf{x} \in A$. (See Fig. 5–13.) The function $f$ is called *integrable over* $A$ if $f^+$ and $f^-$ are integrable over $A$. Its integral is

$$\int_A f\,dV = \int_A f^+\,dV - \int_A f^-\,dV. \tag{5–28}$$

If both $f$ and $A$ are bounded, the new definition of integral agrees with the one in Section 5–4 (Problem 10).

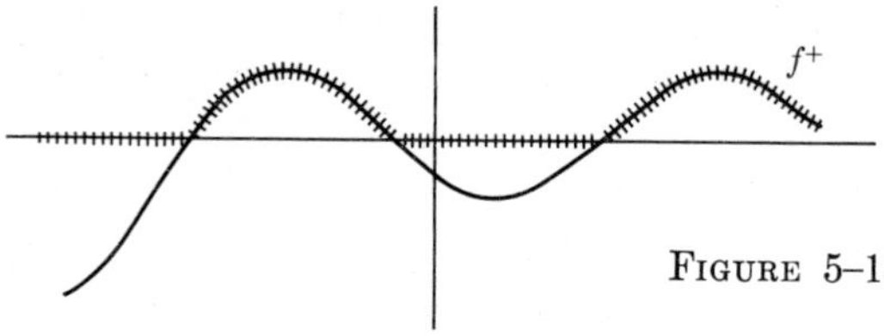


FIGURE 5–13

Some authors assign a value $+\infty$ or $-\infty$ to the integral in case at most one of the functions $f^+$ and $f^-$ has a divergent integral. However, in no case should one try to evaluate the meaningless expression $\infty - \infty$ if both $f^+$ and $f^-$ have divergent integrals.

The lemma above has two important corollaries.

**Corollary 1.** *Let $f$ be continuous on $A$. Then $f$ is integrable over $A$ if and only if $|f|$ is integrable over $A$.*

*Proof.* Let $f$ be integrable over $A$. Then $f^+$ and $f^-$ are integrable over $A$, and by (b) of the lemma so is their sum $|f| = f^+ + f^-$. Conversely, let $|f|$ be integrable over $A$. Since $0 \leq f^+ \leq |f|$, $0 \leq f^- \leq |f|$, by (a) of the lemma $f^+$ and $f^-$ are integrable over $A$. Hence $f$ is integrable over $A$. ▮

**Corollary 2.** (*Comparison test*). *Let $f$ and $g$ be continuous on $A$. If $|f| \leq g$ and $g$ is integrable over $A$, then $f$ is integrable over $A$.*

*Proof.* In (a) of the lemma, let $h = |f|$. ▮

**Corollary 3.** *Let $f$ and $g$ be continuous on $A$. If $f$ and $g$ are integrable over $A$, then $f + g$ is integrable over $A$.*

*Proof.* Note that $|f + g| \leq |f| + |g|$. By Corollary 1 and (b) of the lemma, $|f| + |g|$ is integrable over $A$. Apply the comparison test. ▮

The integral can be written as a limit. Let $K_1, K_2, \ldots$ be any nondecreasing sequence of compact sets such that $A = K_1 \cup K_2 \cup \cdots$ Then

$$\int_A f\,dV = \lim_{\nu\to\infty} \int_{K_\nu} f\,dV. \tag{5–29}$$

This will be proved later as a corollary to a theorem in Section 5–10. Notice that the limit is the same for all such sequences $K_1, K_2, \ldots$ If an additional mild assumption is made about the sequence $K_1, K_2, \ldots,$ then (5–29) can be verified directly from the definition of integral (Problem 11).

The elementary properties of integrals listed in Theorem 13 still hold. Parts (1), (2), (4), and (5) are proved by applying Theorem 13 on each set $K_\nu$ and passing to limit by means of (5–29). Of course, the right-hand estimate in (5) is meaningless if either $f$ is unbounded or $A$ has infinite measure. Part (3) is Problem 12, Section 5–2. To prove (6), let $V(A) = 0$. Since $K_\nu \subset A$, $V(K_\nu) = 0$. By Theorem 13 the integral of $f$ over each $K_\nu$ is 0, and by (5–29) the integral of $f$ over $A$ is 0.

Let us prove (7). If $A$ and $B$ are $\sigma$-compact, then

$$A = K_1 \cup K_2 \cup \cdots, \qquad B = L_1 \cup L_2 \cup \cdots,$$

where $K_\nu$ and $L_\nu$ are compact for each $\nu = 1, 2, \ldots$ and $K_1 \subset K_2 \subset \cdots$, $L_1 \subset L_2 \subset \cdots$ Then $K_\nu \cup L_\nu$ is also compact for each $\nu$, and

$$(K_1 \cup L_1) \subset (K_2 \cup L_2) \subset \cdots,$$
$$A \cup B = (K_1 \cup L_1) \cup (K_2 \cup L_2) \cup \cdots$$

Hence $A \cup B$ is $\sigma$-compact. Taking $K_\nu \cap L_\nu$ instead of $K_\nu \cup L_\nu$, the same reasoning shows that $A \cap B$ is $\sigma$-compact. If $A \cap B$ is a null set, then $K_\nu \cap L_\nu$ is a null set for each $\nu$. Hence

$$\int_{K_\nu} f\,dV + \int_{L_\nu} f\,dV = \int_{K_\nu \cup L_\nu} f\,dV.$$

Taking the limit as $\nu \to \infty$,

$$\int_A f\,dV + \int_B f\,dV = \int_{A\cup B} f\,dV.$$

*Note:* Not every measurable set is $\sigma$-compact. For instance, it can be shown that the set of irrational numbers in [0, 1] is not $\sigma$-compact. However, it turns out that any measurable set $A$ has a $\sigma$-compact subset $B$ such that $A - B$ is a null set.

Let us now consider some important particular cases.

*Case 1.* $A$ is closed. For every $r \geq 0$ let $A(r) = \{\mathbf{x} \in A : |\mathbf{x}| \leq r\}$. Each of these sets is compact. Let $r_1, r_2, \ldots$ be any nondecreasing sequence tending to $+\infty$, and $K_\nu = A(r_\nu)$. Let $f$ be integrable over $A$, and let

$$\psi(r) = \int_{A(r)} f\,dV.$$

By (5-29), $\psi(r_\nu)$ tends to the integral of $f$ over $A$ as $\nu \to \infty$. Since this is true for every such sequence $r_1, r_2, \ldots$, we have

$$\int_A f\,dV = \lim_{r \to +\infty} \int_{A(r)} f\,dV. \tag{5-30}$$

In particular, if $n = 1$ and $A = [a, \infty)$, then

$$\int_a^\infty f\,dx = \lim_{r \to +\infty} \int_a^r f\,dx.$$

**Example 1.** Let $f(x) = x^{-p}$. Then

$$\int_1^\infty x^{-p}\,dx = \frac{1}{p-1}$$

if $p > 1$. If $p \leq 1$, then the integral diverges to $+\infty$.

**Example 2.** Let $f(x) = \exp(-bx)$, $b > 0$. Then $f$ is integrable over $[a, \infty)$ for any $a$.

In these examples $f \geq 0$. When $f \geq 0$ the function $\psi$ is nondecreasing; if $\psi(r)$ is bounded, then $\psi(r)$ tends to a finite limit equal to the integral of $f$ over $A$. If $\psi(r)$ is unbounded, then the integral of $f$ over $A$ diverges to $+\infty$.

On the other hand, if $f$ has both positive and negative values on $A$, then there may be a finite limit in (5-30) while the integral of $|f|$ diverges to $+\infty$. In that case the right-hand side of (5-30) defines a conditionally convergent integral. While conditionally convergent integrals are important in some parts of mathematical analysis (for example, in the treatment of Fourier integrals), they are not within the scope of the Lebesgue theory. We treat them only in Problems 5 and 8.

*Case 2.* Let $A = K - \{\mathbf{x}_0\}$, where $K$ is compact. The function $f$ is continuous on $A$, but may be unbounded on any neighborhood of $\mathbf{x}_0$. For each $\delta > 0$ let $A'(\delta) = \{\mathbf{x} \in K : |\mathbf{x} - \mathbf{x}_0| \geq \delta\}$ (Fig. 5-14). Each of the sets $A'(\delta)$ is compact, and

$$\int_A f\,dV = \lim_{\delta \to 0+} \int_{A'(\delta)} f\,dV. \tag{5-31}$$

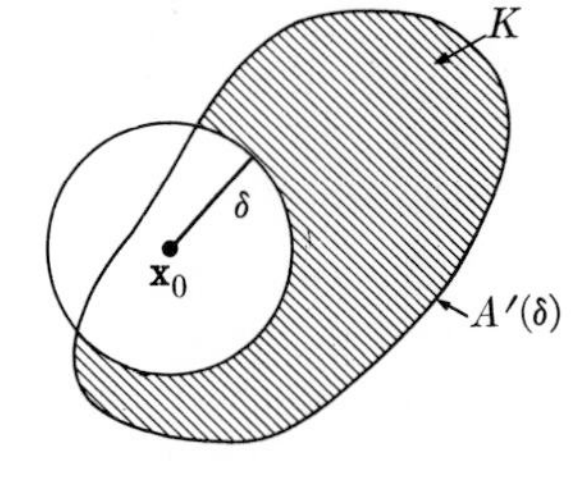


FIGURE 5-14

The same formula holds if $f$ is continuous on $A = K - L$, where $L$ is any closed set. In this case $A'(\delta)$ is the set of points of $K$ distant at least $\delta$ from $L$.

**Example 3.** Let $A = (0, 1]$ and $f(x) = x^{-p}$. Then $\int_0^1 x^{-p}\,dx = 1/(1-p)$ if $p < 1$, and the integral diverges to $+\infty$ if $p \geq 1$.

*Note:* If $A \subset [a, b]$ and $[a, b] - A$ is a null set, then we still use the notation $\int_a^b$ for $\int_A$.

*Case 3.* Let $f$ be continuous on $A = K - \{\mathbf{x}_0\}$, where $K$ is closed but not compact. Let $A_1 = \{\mathbf{x} \in K : |\mathbf{x} - \mathbf{x}_0| \geq 1\}$, $A_2 = \{\mathbf{x} \in K : 0 < |\mathbf{x} - \mathbf{x}_0| \leq 1\}$. Then $\int_{A_1} f\,dV$ and $\int_{A_2} f\,dV$ can be treated respectively as in Cases 1 and 2. Since $A_1 \cap A_2$ is a null set, if both of these integrals exist their sum is $\int_A f\,dV$. If either the integral of $f$ over $A_1$ or the integral over $A_2$ does not exist, then $f$ is not integrable over $A$. To show this, suppose for instance that $f$ is not integrable over $A_1$. By Corollary 1, $\int_{A_1} |f|\,dV$ diverges to $+\infty$. Since $A_1 \subset A$, so does $\int_A |f|\,dV$. Hence $f$ is not integrable over $A$.

**Example 3 (continued).** Let $A = (0, \infty)$ and $f(x) = x^{-p}$. Taking $A_1 = [1, \infty)$, $A_2 = (0, 1]$, the integral over $A_1$ exists only if $p > 1$, and over $A_2$ only if $p < 1$. Hence $\int_0^\infty x^{-p}\,dx$ diverges to $+\infty$ for every $p$.

*Case 4.* Any open set $A$ is $\sigma$-compact (Problem 6). In most elementary examples integrals over an open set can be treated by the methods just described, recalling that the integral is not affected by adding or removing any null set.

In many instances it can be shown that $f$ is integrable by comparing $|f|$ with a function $g$ known to be integrable (Corollary 2).

**Example 4.** Let $A = K - \{\mathbf{x}_0\}$, where $K$ is an $n$-ball with center $\mathbf{x}_0$. Then

$$\int_A |\mathbf{x} - \mathbf{x}_0|^{-p}\,dV$$

exists if $p < n$ and diverges to $+\infty$ if $p \geq n$. This is proved in Section 5–9 by introducing generalized spherical coordinates. Let $f(\mathbf{x}) = \phi(\mathbf{x})|\mathbf{x} - \mathbf{x}_0|^{-p}$, where $\phi$ is continuous and $|\phi(\mathbf{x})| \leq C$ for every $\mathbf{x} \in A$. Let $g(\mathbf{x}) = C|\mathbf{x} - \mathbf{x}_0|^{-p}$. By the comparison test, $f$ is integrable over $A$ if $p < n$. If $\phi(\mathbf{x}) \geq c > 0$ for every $\mathbf{x} \in A$, let $h(\mathbf{x}) = c|\mathbf{x} - \mathbf{x}_0|^{-p}$. If $p \geq n$, then $f \geq h$. The integral of $h$ over $A$ diverges to $+\infty$, and hence so does the integral of $f$.

In the same way

$$\int_{E^n - K} |\mathbf{x} - \mathbf{x}_0|^{-p}\,dV$$

exists if $p > n$ and diverges to $+\infty$ if $p \leq n$. A similar discussion applies.

**Example 5.** Let

$$\Gamma(u) = \int_0^\infty x^{u-1} \exp(-x)\,dx, \qquad u > 0. \tag{5–32}$$

The function $\Gamma$ is called the *gamma function.* Let $f(x) = x^{u-1}\exp(-x)$. Since $f(x) \leq x^{u-1}$ and $p = 1 - u < 1$, $f$ is integrable over $(0, 1]$ by comparison with $x^{-p}$. For any $b$, $x^b \exp(-x) \to 0$ as $x \to +\infty$ and therefore is bounded on $[1, \infty)$. Letting $b = u + 1$ we see that there is a number $C$ such that $f(x) \leq C/x^2$ for every $x \in [1, \infty)$. Thus $f$ is integrable over $[1, \infty)$ and over $(0, 1]$, therefore over $(0, \infty)$.

The gamma function generalizes the factorial. First of all,

$$\Gamma(1) = \int_0^\infty \exp(-x)\,dx = 1.$$

Integrating by parts,

$$\begin{aligned}\Gamma(u+1) &= \int_0^\infty x^u \exp(-x)\,dx \\ &= -x^u \exp(-x)\Big|_0^\infty + u\int_0^\infty x^{u-1}\exp(-x)\,dx,\end{aligned}$$

which gives

$$\Gamma(u+1) = u\Gamma(u). \tag{5-33}$$

The integration by parts over $(0, \infty)$ is justified by taking it first over intervals $[\delta, 1]$ and $[1, r]$ and letting $\delta \to 0^+$, $r \to +\infty$. In particular, if $m$ is an integer, then $\Gamma(m+1) = m\Gamma(m)$. Since $\Gamma(1) = 1$,

$$\Gamma(m+1) = m!. \tag{5-34}$$

Theorem 15 about iterated integrals can be extended as follows: Let us first consider the case $f \geq 0$. Let $F = f_A$, $F_\nu = f_{K_\nu}$, and

$$G_\nu(\mathbf{x}') = \int F_\nu(\mathbf{x}', \ )\,dV_{n-s},$$

$$G(\mathbf{x}') = \int F(\mathbf{x}', \ )\,dV_{n-s}.$$

From Section 5-5 we know that each $G_\nu$ is measurable and

$$\int F_\nu\,dV_n = \int G_\nu\,dV_s$$

for each $\nu = 1, 2, \ldots$ The sequences $F_1, F_2, \ldots$ and $G_1, G_2, \ldots$ are nondecreasing. Using the monotone sequences theorem (p. 190) three times, just as in the previous section,

$$\int F\,dV_n = \int G\,dV_s,$$

which is the formula (5-23b) for iterated integrals. If either integral in (5-23b) diverges to $+\infty$, then so does the other. Therefore, if $f \geq 0$, one way to show that $f$ is integrable over $A$ is to show that the iterated integral exists.

**Example 6.** Let $f(x, y) = |x|/(1 + x^2 + y^2)^2$, $A = E^2$. By symmetry

$$\int f\,dV_2 = 4\int_0^\infty dy \int_0^\infty \frac{x\,dx}{(1 + x^2 + y^2)^2} = 2\int_0^\infty \frac{dy}{1 + y^2} = \pi.$$

Now let $f$ be any continuous function integrable over $A$. The iterated integrals theorem applies to $f^+$ and $f^-$, and hence by subtraction to $f$. *Caution:* If $f$ has both positive and negative values on $A$, then one cannot conclude that $f$ is integrable from the fact that the iterated integral exists.

**Example 7.** Let $f(x, y) = y^{-1} \cos x$, $A = [0, \pi] \times (0, 1]$. Then

$$\int_0^1 dy \int_0^\pi y^{-1} \cos x \, dx = \int_0^1 0 \, dy = 0.$$

The iterated integral in the opposite order does not exist, hence $f$ is not integrable over $A$.

*Note:* In the discussion of iterated integrals above, the integral of $f(\mathbf{x}', \ )$ over $A(\mathbf{x}')$ is in the sense of the present section. However, the function $g$ in (5–23a) need not be continuous on $R$. In fact, $g(\mathbf{x}')$ may be $+\infty$ for certain values of $\mathbf{x}'$. If $g$ is discontinuous and unbounded on $R$, then its integral has to be taken in the sense described in Section 5–10.

## PROBLEMS

1. Determine whether the integral exists or is divergent to $+\infty$.

   (a) $\displaystyle\int_1^2 \frac{dx}{\sqrt{x^2 - 1}}$ · [*Hint:* Let $\phi(x) = 1/\sqrt{x + 1}$.]

   (b) $\displaystyle\int_{-\pi/2}^{\pi/2} |\sin x|^{-p} \, dx$. [*Hint:* $x/\sin x \to 1$ as $x \to 0$.]

   (c) $\displaystyle\int_0^\infty P(x) \exp(-cx) \, dx$, $P$ a polynomial, $c > 0$.

   (d) $\displaystyle\int_{-\infty}^\infty \frac{dx}{\sqrt[3]{x}\,(|x| + 1)}$.

   (e) $\displaystyle\int_1^\infty \frac{x^{-q}}{(x - 1)^p} \, dx$.

2. Show that $\{(x, y, z) : 0 \leq z \leq (x^2 + y^2)/xy,\ 0 < x \leq 1,\ 0 < y \leq 1\}$ has infinite volume.

3. Show that the volume of $\{(x, y, z) : 0 \leq z \leq |xy| \exp(-x^2 - y^2)\}$ is 1.

4. Show that $\int f(x, y) \, dV_2(x, y)$ exists if $f$ is bounded, continuous, and $|f(x, y)| \leq C(1 + x^2 + y^2)^{-p/2}$, $p > 2$.

5. If $\lim_{r \to \infty} \int_{-r}^{r} f(x) \, dx$ exists but $f$ is not integrable on $E^1$, then this limit is called *the Cauchy principal value.* Find the Cauchy principal value:

   (a) $f(x) = x/(1 + x^2)$.

   (b) $f(x) = x + 1/(1 + x^2)$.

   (c) Any odd function $f$, $f(-x) = -f(x)$ for every $x$.

6. Let $A$ be open. Let

$$K_\nu = \{\mathbf{x} : |\mathbf{x}| \leq r_\nu, \text{ dist } (\mathbf{x}, E^n - A) \geq \delta_\nu\},$$

where $r_1, r_2, \ldots, \delta_1, \delta_2, \ldots$ are monotone sequences tending respectively to $+\infty$ and 0. Show that each $K_\nu$ is compact and that $K_1 \subset K_2 \subset \cdots, A = K_1 \cup K_2 \cup \cdots$

7. Show that each of the following integrals over $E^n$ converges.
   (a) $\int (|\mathbf{x}|^2 + 1)^{-p/2} \, dV(\mathbf{x}), \; p > n.$
   (b) $\int |\mathbf{x}|^{-|\mathbf{x}|} \, dV(\mathbf{x}).$

8. Let $f(x) = (-1)^m/m$ if $x \in [m, m + 1), m = 1, 2, \ldots$
   (a) Show that $\lim_{r \to \infty} \int_1^r f(x) \, dx$ exists and equals $-1 + \frac{1}{2} - \frac{1}{3} + \cdots$
   (b) Let $K_\nu = (\bigcup_{k=1}^{\nu} [2k - 1, 2k]) \cup (\bigcup_{l=1}^{2\nu} [2l, 2l + 1])$. Show that

$$\lim_{\nu \to \infty} \int_{K_\nu} f(x) \, dx \neq \lim_{r \to \infty} \int_1^r f(x) \, dx.$$

9. (a) Assume that for every real number $c$, both of the sets $\{\mathbf{x} \in A : f(\mathbf{x}) < c\}$ and $\{\mathbf{x} \in A : f(\mathbf{x}) > c\}$ are open relative to $A$. Show that $f$ is continuous on $A$. [*Hint:* Show that $\{\mathbf{x} \in A : c < f(\mathbf{x}) < d\}$ is open relative to $A$.
   (b) Using (a) and the Corollary to Proposition A-6 (Section A-6), prove: if $f$ is continuous on $A$, then $f^+$ is continuous on $A$.

10. Let $A$ be a bounded, $\sigma$-compact set, and let $f$ be bounded and continuous on $A$. Show that $\int_A f \, dV$, as defined by (5-28), is the same as in Section 5-4. [*Hint:* Suppose first that $f \geq 0$. For any compact set $K \subset A$, we have, taking the integral over $A$ in the previous sense, $0 \leq \int_A f \, dV - \int_K f \, dV \leq C[V(A - K)]$ provided $f(x) \leq C$ for every $\mathbf{x} \in A$. But $V(A - K) = V(A) - V(K)$ is arbitrarily small. Apply this to $f^+, f^-$, and subtract.]

11. Let $K_1, K_2, \ldots$ be a nondecreasing sequence of compact sets, and $A = K_1 \cup K_2 \cup \cdots$ Assume that if $K$ is any compact subset of $A$, then $K \subset K_\nu$ for some $\nu$ (sufficiently large). Prove (5-29). [*Hint:* Suppose first that $f \geq 0$, the integral being then given by (5-26).]

12. (Difficult.) Let $f$ be continuous on an open set $D$. Assume that the integrals of $f^+$ and $f^-$ over $D$ both diverge to $+\infty$. Show that given any number $l$ there is a sequence of compact sets $K_1 \subset K_2 \subset \cdots$ such that $D = K_1 \cup K_2 \cup \cdots$ and $\lim_{\nu \to \infty} \int_{K_\nu} f \, dV = l$.

## 5-7 CHANGE OF MEASURE UNDER AFFINE TRANSFORMATIONS

Our next objective is to give formulas which describe how measure and integrals change under a regular transformation $\mathbf{g}$. In this section we consider the special case when $\mathbf{g}$ is affine and prove the formula for the measure of $\mathbf{g}(A)$ when $A$ is a compact set. This special result is then used in the proof of the general transformation formula (5-38).

Let $\mathbf{g}$ be an affine transformation from $E^n$ into $E^n$. According to Section 4–2, there exist $\mathbf{x}_0$ and a linear transformation $\mathbf{L}$ such that

$$\mathbf{g}(\mathbf{t}) = \mathbf{L}(\mathbf{t}) + \mathbf{x}_0$$

for every $\mathbf{t} \in E^n$.

**Theorem 16.** *For every compact set* $K$,

$$V[\mathbf{g}(K)] = |\det \mathbf{L}| V(K). \tag{5–35}$$

*Proof.* First of all, (5–35) is true for some particular kinds of affine transformations. Certain elementary details of the proofs are left to the reader (Problem 4).

(1) $\mathbf{g}$ is a translation, $\mathbf{L} = \mathbf{I}$. Then $V[\mathbf{g}(A)] = V(A)$ for any figure $A$, and hence for any compact set.

From (1) we may assume from now on that $\mathbf{x}_0 = \mathbf{0}$, $\mathbf{g} = \mathbf{L}$.

(2) For some $k$ and $l$, the transformation $\mathbf{L}$ merely interchanges the components $t^k$ and $t^l$ of $\mathbf{t}$. Then $V[\mathbf{L}(A)] = V(A)$ for every figure, and hence for every compact set.

(3) The matrix of $\mathbf{L}$ is diagonal. In this case $L^i(\mathbf{t}) = c_i^i t^i$, where $c_1^1, \ldots, c_n^n$ are the diagonal elements.

In this case $\det \mathbf{L} = c_1^1 \ldots c_n^n$. If $A$ is a figure, then $V[\mathbf{L}(A)] = |\det \mathbf{L}| V(A)$. The same is then true if $A$ is any compact set.

(4) There exist $k$ and $l$, $k \neq l$, such that

$$L^k(\mathbf{t}) = t^k + ct^l, \qquad L^i(\mathbf{t}) = t^i \quad \text{for } i \neq k.$$

Let us for notational simplicity take $l = 1$. Let $Q = \mathbf{L}(K)$, and using the notation on p. 158 let $Q(u) = \{\mathbf{x}'' : (u, \mathbf{x}'') \in Q\}$, $K(u) = \{\mathbf{t}'' : (u, \mathbf{t}'') \in K\}$. If $\mathbf{x} = \mathbf{L}(\mathbf{t})$, then $\mathbf{x}'' = ct^1\mathbf{e}_k + \mathbf{t}''$. Hence $Q(u)$ is just $K(u)$ translated by $cu\mathbf{e}_k$. Therefore

$$V_n(K) = \int V_{n-1}[K(u)]\, du = \int V_{n-1}[Q(u)]\, du = V_n(Q).$$

Since $\det \mathbf{L} = 1$, this proves (5–35) for linear transformations of type (4).

Next, we observe that if $\mathbf{M}$ and $\mathbf{N}$ are any two linear transformations for which the theorem holds, then

$$\begin{aligned} V[(\mathbf{M} \circ \mathbf{N})(K)] &= |\det \mathbf{M}| V[\mathbf{N}(K)] \\ &= |\det \mathbf{M}|\, |\det \mathbf{N}| V(K), \end{aligned}$$

and $(\det \mathbf{M})(\det \mathbf{N}) = \det \mathbf{M} \circ \mathbf{N}$. Hence the theorem also holds for their composite $\mathbf{M} \circ \mathbf{N}$.

If $\mathbf{N}$ has row covectors $\mathbf{w}^1, \ldots, \mathbf{w}^n$ and $\mathbf{M}$ is of type (4), then the $k$th row covector of $\mathbf{M} \circ \mathbf{N}$ is $\mathbf{w}^k + c\mathbf{w}^l$ and the others are unchanged. The $k$th column vector of $\mathbf{N} \circ \mathbf{M}$ is $\mathbf{v}_k + c\mathbf{v}_l$ and the others are unchanged, where $\mathbf{v}_1, \ldots, \mathbf{v}_n$ are the column vectors of $\mathbf{N}$. A transformation $\mathbf{M}$ of type (2) when applied on the left interchanges the $k$th and $l$th row covectors of $\mathbf{N}$, and when applied on the right interchanges the $k$th and $l$th column vectors. Moreover, the inverse of a transformation of type (2) or (4) is of the same type.

Now let $\mathbf{L}$ be any linear transformation. Then

$$\mathbf{L} = \mathbf{M}_p \circ \cdots \circ \mathbf{M}_1,$$

where $\mathbf{M}_1, \ldots, \mathbf{M}_p$ are of types (2), (3), and (4). Since Theorem 16 holds for each $\mathbf{M}_j$, it is true for $\mathbf{L}$. ∎

**Corollary.** *If* $\mathbf{g}$ *is an isometry of* $E^n$, *then* $V[\mathbf{g}(K)] = V(K)$.

*Proof.* For then $\det \mathbf{L} = \pm 1$. ∎

Let us apply Theorem 16 to calculate the measures of simplexes and parallelepipeds.

**Measure of an *n*-simplex.** Let $S$ be an $n$-simplex with vertices $\mathbf{x}_0, \mathbf{x}_1, \ldots, \mathbf{x}_n$ (see p. 20). Let $\mathbf{v}_i = \mathbf{x}_i - \mathbf{x}_0$. The vectors $\mathbf{v}_1, \ldots, \mathbf{v}_n$ are linearly independent. Let $\mathbf{L}$ be the linear transformation with $\mathbf{v}_1, \ldots, \mathbf{v}_n$ as column vectors, and let $\mathbf{g}(\mathbf{t}) = \mathbf{L}(\mathbf{t}) + \mathbf{x}_0$. As before, let $\Sigma$ be the standard $n$-simplex. If $\mathbf{t} = (t^1, \ldots, t^n) \in \Sigma$, let $t^0 = 1 - (t^1 + \cdots + t^n)$ and let $\mathbf{x} = \mathbf{g}(\mathbf{t})$. Then

$$\mathbf{x} = \mathbf{x}_0 + \sum_{i=1}^{n} t^i(\mathbf{x}_i - \mathbf{x}_0) = \sum_{i=0}^{n} t^i \mathbf{x}_i.$$

Hence $\mathbf{x} \in S$ and $t^0, t^1, \ldots, t^n$ are its barycentric coordinates. Conversely, every $\mathbf{x} \in S$ is obtained in this way. Thus $S = \mathbf{g}(\Sigma)$. By Example (1), Section 5–5, $V(\Sigma) = 1/n!$. Hence, from (5–35),

$$V(S) = |\det \mathbf{L}|/n!. \tag{5–36}$$

**Measure of an *n*-parallelepiped.** Given $\mathbf{x}_0$ and linearly independent vectors $\mathbf{v}_1, \ldots, \mathbf{v}_n$, let

$$P = \left\{ \mathbf{x} : \mathbf{x} = \mathbf{x}_0 + \sum_{i=1}^{n} t^i \mathbf{v}_i,\ 0 \le t^i \le 1,\ i = 1, \ldots, n \right\}.$$

Then $P$ is the $n$-parallelepiped spanned by $\mathbf{v}_1, \ldots, \mathbf{v}_n$ with $\mathbf{x}_0$ as vertex (Fig. 5–15). Let $I_0$ be the unit $n$-cube. Then $P = \mathbf{g}(I_0)$, where $\mathbf{g}$ is as before. Since $V(I_0) = 1$,

$$V(P) = |\det \mathbf{L}|. \tag{5–37}$$

If $\mathbf{v}_1, \ldots, \mathbf{v}_n$ are linearly dependent, then $P$ is called a *degenerate* $n$-parallelepiped. In that case $V(P) = 0$.

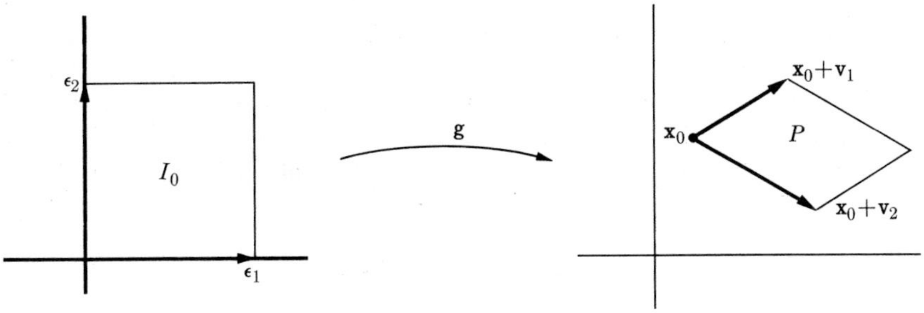


FIGURE 5–15

**PROBLEMS**

1. Find the volume of the tetrahedron with vertices $\mathbf{e}_1$, $-\mathbf{e}_2$, $\mathbf{e}_3$, $\mathbf{e}_1 + 2\mathbf{e}_2 + \mathbf{e}_3$.
2. Find the area of the parallelogram with vertices $\mathbf{e}_1 - \mathbf{e}_2$, $2\mathbf{e}_1 + \mathbf{e}_2$, $-2\mathbf{e}_1$, $-\mathbf{e}_1 + 2\mathbf{e}_2$.
3. Let $S$ be an $n$-simplex, with vertices $\mathbf{x}_0, \mathbf{x}_1, \ldots, \mathbf{x}_n$. Show that

$$V(S) = \frac{1}{n!}\left|\det\begin{pmatrix} x_0^1 & x_1^1 & \cdots & x_n^1 \\ \vdots & \vdots & & \vdots \\ x_0^n & x_1^n & \cdots & x_n^n \\ 1 & 1 & \cdots & 1 \end{pmatrix}\right|.$$

[*Hint:* Subtract the first column from each of the other columns. This does not change the determinant.]

4. Complete the details of steps (1), (2), and (3) of the proof of Theorem 16.
5. Let $(c_j^i)$ be a positive definite symmetric $n \times n$ matrix, and let $\lambda_1, \ldots, \lambda_n$ be its characteristic values. Show that

$$V\left(\left\{\mathbf{x} : \sum_{i,j=1}^{n} c_j^i x^i x^j \leq 1\right\}\right) = \alpha_n/\sqrt{\lambda_1 \cdots \lambda_n},$$

where $\alpha_n$ is the measure of the unit $n$-ball. [*Hint:* See Theorem 11.]

6. Show that if $|\mathbf{v}_i| \leq C$ for each $i = 1, \ldots, n$ and $P$ is a parallelepiped spanned by $\mathbf{v}_1, \ldots, \mathbf{v}_n$, then $V(P) \leq C^n$. [*Hint:* Use induction, a suitable rotation of $E^n$, and the method of slices.]

## 5-8 TRANSFORMATION OF INTEGRALS

Let $\mathbf{g}$ be a regular transformation with domain an open set $\Delta \subset E^n$. Regularity means that $\mathbf{g}$ is of class $C^{(1)}$ and has an inverse $\mathbf{g}^{-1}$ of class $C^{(1)}$ (p. 115). Let $f$ be continuous on the open set $D = \mathbf{g}(\Delta)$. The object of this section is to prove the formula (5–38) which expresses the integral of $f$ over a set $A \subset D$ as an integral over the corresponding subset $B = \mathbf{g}^{-1}(A)$ of $\Delta$.

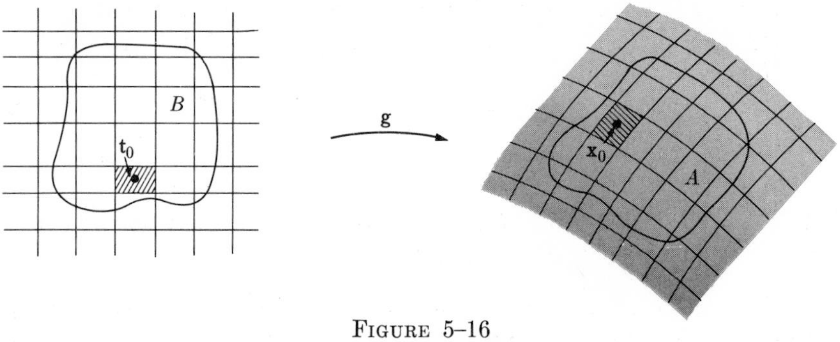


FIGURE 5–16

Let us first give an imprecise derivation of the transformation formula (5–38). (See Fig. 5–16.) For the moment, let $B$ be compact, and let $Z$ be a figure approximating $B$ from without. Let $I \subset Z$ and $\mathbf{t}_0$ be a point of $I$. Let

$$\mathbf{x}_0 = \mathbf{g}(\mathbf{t}_0), \qquad \mathbf{L} = D\mathbf{g}(\mathbf{t}_0).$$

The affine approximation $\mathbf{G}$ to $\mathbf{g}$ at $\mathbf{t}_0$ is given by

$$\mathbf{G}(\mathbf{t}) = \mathbf{x}_0 + \mathbf{L}(\mathbf{t} - \mathbf{t}_0).$$

If $I$ is small, then $\mathbf{G}(I)$ and $\mathbf{g}(I)$ nearly coincide. Hence $V[\mathbf{g}(I)]$ is nearly $V[\mathbf{G}(I)]$, which by Theorem 16 equals $|\det \mathbf{L}|V(I)$. Since $f$ is continuous, its integral over $\mathbf{g}(I)$ is approximately $f(\mathbf{x}_0)V[\mathbf{g}(I)]$, and since $\det \mathbf{L}$ is the Jacobian $J\mathbf{g}(\mathbf{t}_0)$,

$$\int_{\mathbf{g}(I)} f\, dV \sim f[\mathbf{g}(t_0)]|J\mathbf{g}(\mathbf{t}_0)|V(I).$$

Let

$$\phi(\mathbf{t}) = f[\mathbf{g}(\mathbf{t})]|J\mathbf{g}(\mathbf{t})|.$$

Since $f$ is continuous and $\mathbf{g}$ is of class $C^{(1)}$, the composite $f \circ \mathbf{g}$ is continuous and $|J\mathbf{g}|$ is continuous. Hence $\phi$ is continuous. The integral of $\phi$ over $I$ is approximately $\phi(\mathbf{t}_0)V(I)$, which is the right-hand side of the above expression.

The figure $Z$ is the union of small intervals $I_1, \ldots, I_p$. Let $\mathbf{t}_k \in \mathbf{I}_k$. We should have approximately

$$\int_{\mathbf{g}(Z)} f\, dV \sim \sum_{k=1}^{p} \phi(\mathbf{t}_k)V(I_k) \sim \int_Z \phi\, dV.$$

This suggests the formula

$$\int_A f\, dV = \int_B \phi\, dV.$$

The following theorem states that the formula is correct, and not merely for compact sets.

**Theorem 17.** *Let* $\mathbf{g}$ *be a regular transformation from* $\Delta$ *onto* $D$. *Let* $f$ *be continuous on* $D$ *and* $A$ *be any* $\sigma$*-compact subset of* $D$. *Then*

$$\int_A f(\mathbf{x})\,dV(\mathbf{x}) = \int_{\mathbf{g}^{-1}(A)} f[\mathbf{g}(\mathbf{t})]|J\mathbf{g}(\mathbf{t})|\,dV(\mathbf{t}), \tag{5-38}$$

*provided either integral exists.*

More generally, Theorem 17 is true if $A \subset D$ is measurable and $f$ is any function measurable on $D$. We shall not prove this.

*Proof of Theorem 17.* If $A$ is compact, then $\mathbf{g}^{-1}(A)$ is compact since $\mathbf{g}^{-1}$ is continuous. Since $f$ and $\phi$ are continuous, both integrals exist. The theorem states that they are equal. Suppose for the moment that the theorem is known for compact sets. If $A$ is $\sigma$-compact, then $A$ is the union of a nondecreasing sequence $K_1, K_2, \ldots$ of compact sets. Let $L_\nu = \mathbf{g}^{-1}(K_\nu)$. Then $B = \mathbf{g}^{-1}(A)$ is the union of the nondecreasing sequence $L_1, L_2, \ldots$ of compact sets. If $f \geq 0$, then $\phi \geq 0$ and

$$\int_A f\,dV = \lim_{\nu\to\infty} \int_{K_\nu} f\,dV,$$

$$\int_B \phi\,dV = \lim_{\nu\to\infty} \int_{L_\nu} \phi\,dV.$$

The right-hand sides are equal. If either integral diverges to $+\infty$, then so does the other. Thus (5-38) holds if $f \geq 0$. In the general case, write $f = f^+ - f^-$, $\phi = \phi^+ - \phi^-$. Since $|J\mathbf{g}| > 0$, we have

$$\phi^+ = (f^+ \circ \mathbf{g})|J\mathbf{g}|, \qquad \phi^- = (f^- \circ \mathbf{g})|J\mathbf{g}|.$$

If either $f$ or $\phi$ is integrable, then so is the other and (5-38) holds.

It remains to prove (5-38) in case $A$ is compact. We may assume that $f \geq 0$. An indirect proof of (5-38) will be given. For this purpose let us prove three lemmas. In these lemmas $I$ denotes an $n$-dimensional cube. It is convenient to take $I$ half-open to the right. Then $I = \text{cl } I - N$, where $N$ is a certain compact set composed of $(n-1)$-dimensional faces of $I$. Hence $\mathbf{g}(I) = \mathbf{g}(\text{cl } I) - \mathbf{g}(N)$ is the difference of compact sets, and so is measurable. Let $l$ be the side length of $I$, $d$ its diameter, and $I'$ the concentric closed $n$-cube of side length $(1 + \tau)l$. Let $\mathbf{G}$, $\mathbf{L}$, $\mathbf{x}_0$ be as defined at the beginning of the section.

**Lemma 1.** *Let* $\mathbf{t}_0 \in \Delta$ *and* $\tau > 0$ *be given. Then* $\mathbf{t}_0$ *has a neighborhood* $\Omega \subset \Delta$ *such that* $\mathbf{g}(I) \subset \mathbf{G}(I')$ *for every* $n$*-cube* $I \subset \Omega$ *with* $\mathbf{t}_0 \in \text{cl } I$. (See Fig. 5-17.)

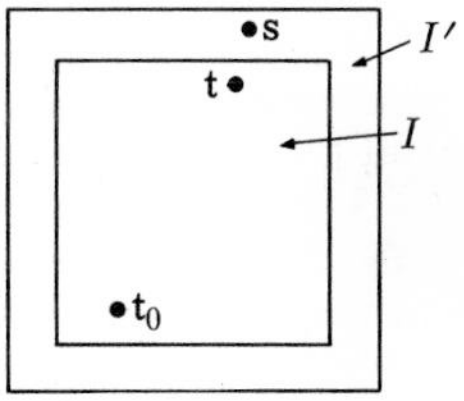


FIGURE 5-17

*Proof.* If $\mathbf{x} = \mathbf{G}(\mathbf{s})$, $\mathbf{y} = \mathbf{G}(\mathbf{t})$, then $\mathbf{x} - \mathbf{y} = \mathbf{L}(\mathbf{s} - \mathbf{t}_0) - \mathbf{L}(\mathbf{t} - \mathbf{t}_0)$. Since $\mathbf{L}$ is linear, $\mathbf{x} - \mathbf{y} =$

$\mathbf{L}(\mathrm{s} - \mathrm{t})$. Let $C = \|\mathbf{L}^{-1}\|$ (p. 103). Then $\mathrm{s} - \mathrm{t} = \mathbf{L}^{-1}(\mathbf{x} - \mathbf{y})$, and

$$|\mathrm{s} - \mathrm{t}| \leq C|\mathbf{x} - \mathbf{y}|. \tag{$*$}$$

Let $\sigma = \tau/(2\sqrt{n}\, C)$. Since $\mathbf{g}$ is differentiable, $\mathrm{t}_0$ has a neighborhood $\Omega \subset \Delta$ such that

$$|\mathbf{g}(\mathrm{t}) - \mathbf{G}(\mathrm{t})| \leq \sigma|\mathrm{t} - \mathrm{t}_0| \tag{$**$}$$

for every $\mathrm{t} \in \Omega$.

Let $\mathbf{x} \in \mathbf{g}(I)$ and $\mathrm{s} = \mathbf{G}^{-1}(\mathbf{x})$. Then $\mathbf{x} = \mathbf{G}(\mathrm{s}) = \mathbf{g}(\mathrm{t})$ for some $\mathrm{t} \in I$. By $(*)$ and $(**)$

$$|\mathrm{s} - \mathrm{t}| \leq C\sigma|\mathrm{t} - \mathrm{t}_0|.$$

Since $\mathrm{t}_0 \in I$, $|\mathrm{t} - \mathrm{t}_0| \leq d$. Since $d = \sqrt{n}\, l$,

$$|\mathrm{s} - \mathrm{t}| \leq C\sigma\sqrt{n}\, l \leq \tau l/2.$$

This implies that $\mathrm{s} \in I'$, and $\mathbf{x} \in \mathbf{G}(I')$. ▮

**Lemma 2.** *Let $\mathrm{t}_0 \in \Delta$ and $\epsilon > 0$ be given. Then $\mathrm{t}_0$ has a neighborhood $\Omega_1 \subset \Delta$ such that*

$$\int_{\mathbf{g}(I)} f\, dV < \int_I \phi\, dV + \epsilon V(I)$$

*for every n-cube $I \subset \Omega_1$ with $\mathrm{t}_0 \in \mathrm{cl}\, I$.*

*Proof.* Let

$$a = f(\mathbf{x}_0) = f[\mathbf{g}(\mathrm{t}_0)], \qquad b = |J\mathbf{g}(\mathrm{t}_0)|.$$

Let $\phi(\xi, \tau) = (a - \xi)(b - \xi) - (a + \xi)b(1 + \tau)^n$. Then $\phi(0, 0) = 0$ and $\phi$ is continuous. Hence $\phi(\xi, \tau) < \epsilon$ for every $(\xi, \tau)$ in some neighborhood $V$ of $(0, 0)$. Choose some $\xi > 0$, $\tau > 0$ small enough that $(\xi, \tau) \in V$. Then

$$(a + \xi)(1 + \tau)^n b < (a - \xi)(b - \xi) + \epsilon. \tag{$*$}$$

Since $f$ is continuous, there is a neighborhood $U$ of $\mathbf{x}_0$ such that $a - \xi < f(\mathbf{x}) < a + \xi$ for every $\mathbf{x} \in U$. Since $\mathbf{g}$ and $|J\mathbf{g}|$ are continuous, there is a neighborhood $\Omega_1$ of $\mathrm{t}_0$ such that $\mathbf{g}(\mathrm{t}) \in U$ and $b - \xi < |J\mathbf{g}(\mathrm{t})|$ for every $\mathrm{t} \in \Omega_1$. We may assume that $\Omega_1 \subset \Omega$, where $\Omega$ is as in Lemma 1.

Then

$$\int_{\mathbf{g}(I)} f\, dV \leq (a + \xi)V[\mathbf{g}(I)],$$

and by Lemma 1, $V[\mathbf{g}(I)] \leq V[\mathbf{G}(I')]$. By Theorem 16,

$$V[\mathbf{G}(I')] = bV(I') = b(1 + \tau)^n V(I).$$

Therefore

$$\int_{\mathbf{g}(I)} f\, dV \leq (a + \xi)b(1 + \tau)^n V(I).$$

On the other hand,

$$\int_I \phi \, dV \geq (a - \xi)(b - \xi)V(I).$$

These two inequalities and (*) give Lemma 2. ▮

**Lemma 3.** *Let $I \subset \Delta$ be an n-cube. Then*

$$\int_{\mathbf{g}(I)} f \, dV \leq \int_I \phi \, dV.$$

*Proof.* Suppose this is false for some $n$-cube $I^0$. Then

$$c = \int_{\mathbf{g}(I^0)} f \, dV - \int_{I^0} \phi \, dV$$

is positive. Divide $I^0$ into $m = 2^n$ congruent $n$-cubes $I_1, \ldots, I_m$, half-open to the right. Since $I_1, \ldots, I_m$ are disjoint and $\mathbf{g}$ is univalent, the sets $\mathbf{g}(I_1), \ldots, \mathbf{g}(I_m)$ are disjoint. Hence

$$\int_{I^0} \phi \, dV = \sum_{j=1}^{m} \int_{I_j} \phi \, dV,$$

$$\int_{\mathbf{g}(I^0)} f \, dV = \sum_{j=1}^{m} \int_{\mathbf{g}(I_j)} f \, dV.$$

For at least one $j$ we must have

$$\int_{\mathbf{g}(I_j)} f \, dV - \int_{I_j} \phi \, dV \geq c2^{-n}.$$

Choose some such $j$ and let $I^1 = I_j$. By dividing $I^1$ into $2^n$ congruent $n$-cubes and repeating the argument, we obtain $I^2$. Continuing, we obtain a sequence of $n$-cubes $I^1 \supset I^2 \supset \cdots$ such that

$$\int_{\mathbf{g}(I^l)} f \, dV - \int_{I^l} \phi \, dV \geq c2^{-ln}, \qquad l = 1, 2, \ldots,$$

and the diameter of $I^l$ tends to 0 as $l \to \infty$. By Theorem A-3, $(\text{cl } I^1) \cap (\text{cl } I^2) \cap \cdots$ contains just one point $\mathbf{t}_0$. Let $\epsilon < c/V(I^0)$. Then

$$\epsilon V(I^l) = \epsilon 2^{-ln} V(I^0) < c2^{-ln}.$$

If $\Omega_1$ is as in Lemma 2, then $I^l \subset \Omega_1$ for large enough $l$ and we obtain a contradiction. ▮

To complete the proof of Theorem 17, let $A$ be compact and $B = \mathbf{g}^{-1}(A)$. Let $Z_0$ be some $n$-cube, half-open to the right, containing $B$. Divide $Z_0$ into $2^n$ congruent $n$-cubes and let $Z_1$ be the union of those which meet $B$. Then divide each $n$-cube of $Z_1$ into $2^n$ congruent $n$-cubes, and let $Z_2$ be the union of those meeting $B$, and so on. Then $Z_1 \supset Z_2 \supset \cdots$ and their intersection is $B$. There exists $\nu_0$ such that $Z_\nu \subset \Delta$ for all $\nu \geq \nu_0$.

Applying Lemma 3 to each of these congruent disjoint $n$-cubes comprising $Z_\nu$, and adding, we get

$$\int_A f\, dV \leq \int_{\mathbf{g}(Z_\nu)} f\, dV \leq \int_{Z_\nu} \phi\, dV$$

for each $\nu \geq \nu_0$. Moreover,

$$\int_B \phi\, dV = \lim_{\nu \to \infty} \int_{Z_\nu} \phi\, dV.$$

This fact will be proved in the section on convergence theorems [Corollary 5(b), Section 5–10]. Thus

$$\int_A f\, dV \leq \int_B \phi\, dV.$$

But $\mathbf{g}^{-1}$ is also a regular transformation. Interchanging the roles of $A$ and $B$,

$$\int_B \phi\, dV \leq \int_A \phi \circ \mathbf{g}^{-1} |J\mathbf{g}^{-1}|\, dV.$$

But $|J\mathbf{g}^{-1}(\mathbf{x})| = |J\mathbf{g}(\mathbf{t})|^{-1}$ if $\mathbf{x} = \mathbf{g}(\mathbf{t})$, and

$$\phi[\mathbf{g}^{-1}(\mathbf{x})] |J\mathbf{g}^{-1}(\mathbf{x})| = f(\mathbf{x}).$$

Therefore

$$\int_B \phi\, dV \leq \int_A f\, dV,$$

which proves (5–38) for the case of compact sets. This completes the proof of Theorem 17. ▮

In particular, taking $f(\mathbf{x}) \equiv 1$ we have:

**Corollary 1.**

$$V(A) = \int_{\mathbf{g}^{-1}(A)} |J\mathbf{g}(\mathbf{t})|\, dV(\mathbf{t}). \tag{5–39}$$

**Corollary 2.** *If $B$ is a null set, then $\mathbf{g}(B)$ is a null set.*

**Corollary 3.** *If $A$ is a measurable subset of an $r$-manifold $M$, where $r \leq n - 1$, then $A$ is a null set.*

*Proof of Corollary 3.* By the implicit function theorem (Section 4–6), any $\mathbf{x}_0 \in M$ has a neighborhood $U$ such that $U \cap M = \mathbf{g}(R)$, where $R$ is a relatively open subset of an $r$-dimensional vector subspace. Then $R$ is a $\sigma$-compact null set. By Corollary 2, $U \cap M$ is a null set.

If $K \subset M$ and $K$ is compact, then there exist a finite number of such neighborhoods $U_1, \ldots, U_m$ such that $K \subset (U_1 \cup \cdots \cup U_m) \cap M$. Hence

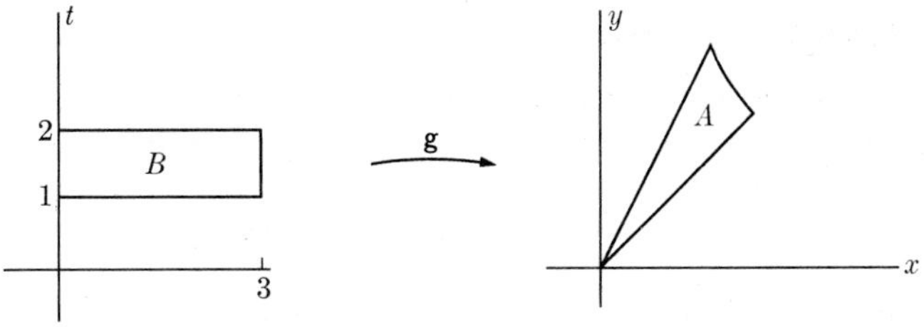


FIGURE 5–18

$K$ is a null set. If $A$ is any measurable set, then $V(A) = \sup \{V(K) : K \subset A\}$. If $A \subset M$, then $A$ is a null set. ▌

**Example 1.** Let $A = \{(x, y) : x > 0, y > 0, 0 < xy < 3, x < y < 2x\}$, $f(x, y) = y^2$, $\mathbf{g}(s, t) = \sqrt{s/t}\,\mathbf{e}_1 + \sqrt{st}\,\mathbf{e}_2$ for $s > 0, t > 0$. We show that $\mathbf{g}$ is univalent by solving the equations

$$x = \sqrt{s/t}, \qquad y = \sqrt{st}$$

explicitly, and find that $s = xy$, $t = y/x$. Since $J\mathbf{g}(s, t) = 1/2t \neq 0$, $\mathbf{g}$ is regular. Moreover, the part in $A$ of the hyperbola $xy = c$, $0 < c < 3$, corresponds to the segment $s = c$, $1 < t < 2$ in $B$. Hence $B$ is as shown in Fig. 5–18, and

$$\int_A y^2 \, dV_2(x, y) = \tfrac{1}{2}\int_1^2 dt \int_0^3 s\, ds = \tfrac{9}{4}.$$

**Example 2.** Let $P$ be an $n$-parallelepiped. Then $P = \mathbf{g}(I_0)$ where, as on p. 172, $\mathbf{g}$ is affine and $I_0$ is the unit $n$-cube. Then

$$\int_P f(\mathbf{x})\, dV(\mathbf{x}) = |\det \mathbf{L}| \int_{I_0} f[\mathbf{L}(\mathbf{t})]\, dV(\mathbf{t}).$$

**PROBLEMS**

1. Let $n = 1$, $g(t) = t^2 - 2t + 3$, $B = (0, 1)$. What does (5–38) become?
2. Let $\mathbf{g}(s, t) = (s^2 + t^2)\mathbf{e}_1 + (s^2 - t^2)\mathbf{e}_2$, $s > 0, t > 0$, and $A = \{(x, y) : 2 < x + y < 4, x - y > 0, y > 0\}$. Show that $\mathbf{g}$ is regular and evaluate $\int_A x^{-1}\, dV_2(x, y)$.
3. Find the second moment about $(0, 0)$ of the parallelogram with vertices $(0, 0)$, $\mathbf{e}_1 + \mathbf{e}_2$, $-2\mathbf{e}_1 + 3\mathbf{e}_2$, $-\mathbf{e}_1 + 4\mathbf{e}_2$. [*Hint:* Let $\mathbf{g}$ be the linear transformation $\mathbf{L}$ with column vectors $\mathbf{e}_1 + \mathbf{e}_2$, $-2\mathbf{e}_1 + 3\mathbf{e}_2$.]
4. Let $B$ be a compact set, $\bar{\mathbf{x}}$ its centroid, and $\mathbf{g}$ an affine transformation. Show that $\mathbf{g}(\bar{\mathbf{x}})$ is the centroid of $\mathbf{g}(B)$.
5. Let $A$ be symmetric about $\mathbf{0}$, that is, $\mathbf{x} \in A$ implies $-\mathbf{x} \in A$. Let $f$ be integrable over $A$ and $f(-\mathbf{x}) = -f(\mathbf{x})$ for every $\mathbf{x} \in A$. Show that $\int_A f\, dV = 0$.
6. Let $\mathbf{g}$ be of class $C^{(1)}$ on $\Delta$ and $K$ be a compact subset of $\Delta$. Show that there is a number $C$ such that $|\mathbf{g}(\mathbf{s}) - \mathbf{g}(\mathbf{t})| \leq C|\mathbf{s} - \mathbf{t}|$ for every $\mathbf{s}, \mathbf{t} \in K$. [*Hint:* Proposition 13b, Section 4–3.]
7. Let $\mathbf{g}$ be regular and $K$, $C$ as in Problem 6. Show that if $B \subset \operatorname{int} K$, then $V[\mathbf{g}(B)] \leq C^n V(B)$. [*Hint:* For $\mathbf{t} \in B$ the partial derivatives of $\mathbf{g}$ satisfy $|\mathbf{g}_i(\mathbf{t})| \leq C$. Use Problem 6, p. 173 to see that $|J\mathbf{g}(\mathbf{t})| \leq C^n$.]

## 5-9 COORDINATE SYSTEMS IN $E^n$

Let $D$ be an open subset of $E^n$. Let $f^1, \ldots, f^n$ be functions of class $C^{(1)}$ on $D$ such that the transformation $\mathbf{f} = (f^1, \ldots, f^n)$ is regular. Since a regular transformation $\mathbf{f}$ is univalent, the numbers $f^1(\mathbf{x}), \ldots, f^n(\mathbf{x})$ uniquely specify $\mathbf{x}$ and can be regarded as a set of "coordinates" for $\mathbf{x}$.

> **Definition.** A regular transformation $\mathbf{f}$ from $D$ into $E^n$ is a *coordinate system* for $D$. The numbers $f^1(\mathbf{x}), \ldots, f^n(\mathbf{x})$ are the *coordinates* of $\mathbf{x}$ in this coordinate system.

Since we have already considered regular transformations, this definition involves nothing new except a change of viewpoint. In many problems it is $D$ which has actual geometric or physical significance. The transformation $\mathbf{f}$ is introduced simply as a device for solving the problem, and the open set $\Delta = \mathbf{f}(D)$ has only an auxiliary status.

In particular, many integrals can be evaluated by introducing a suitable coordinate system. The transformation formula (5–38) is applied with $B = \mathbf{f}(A)$, $\mathbf{g} = \mathbf{f}^{-1}$. The objective usually is to choose a coordinate system for which $B$ is simpler than $A$ (for instance an interval) or $\phi$ is simpler than $f$, or both.

Let us consider some particular coordinate systems.

1. The identity transformation $\mathbf{I}$ gives the *standard cartesian coordinate* system for $E^n$. The components $x^1, \ldots, x^n$ are the standard cartesian coordinates of $\mathbf{x}$.

2. If $\mathbf{f}$ is an affine transformation, then the coordinate system is called *affine*.

3. If $M$ is an $r$-manifold, $\boldsymbol{\Phi} = (\Phi^1, \ldots, \Phi^{n-r})$ is as in Section 4–7 and

$$\partial(\Phi^1, \ldots, \Phi^{n-r})/\partial(x^{r+1}, \ldots, x^n) \neq 0$$

at $\mathbf{x}_0$, then $(X^1, \ldots, X^r, \Phi^1, \ldots, \Phi^{n-r})$ is a coordinate system for some neighborhood $U$ of $\mathbf{x}_0$. The coordinates of a point $\mathbf{x} \in M \cap U$ in this system are $(x^1, \ldots, x^r, 0, \ldots, 0)$.

4. *Polar coordinates.* Let $D$ be $E^2$ with the positive $x$-axis $N$ removed. Let $R(x, y) = \sqrt{x^2 + y^2}$ and $\Theta(x, y)$ be the angle from $N$ to the half-line from $(0, 0)$ through $(x, y)$, with $0 < \Theta(x, y) < 2\pi$. Then $(R, \Theta)$ is the *polar coordinate system* for $D$. If $r = R(x, y)$, $\theta = \Theta(x, y)$, then $(r, \theta)$ are the coordinates of $(x, y)$ and

$$x = r \cos \theta = g^1(r, \theta), \qquad y = r \sin \theta = g^2(r, \theta),$$

where $\mathbf{g} = (R, \Theta)^{-1}$. Since $J\mathbf{g}(r, \theta) = r$, the transformation formula becomes

$$\int_A f(x, y)\, dV_2(x, y) = \int_B f[r \cos \theta, r \sin \theta] r\, dV_2(r, \theta),$$

where $\mathbf{g}(B) = A - N$. Since $N$ is a null set, the integral over $A$ is the same as the integral over $A - N$.

5. *Spherical coordinates in $E^n$.* For $n = 2$, this is the polar coordinate system. Proceeding inductively, let $r = |\mathbf{x}|$, $\theta^1$ be the angle from the positive $x^1$-axis to $\mathbf{x}$ (more precisely, $\theta^1 = \cos^{-1}(x^1/r), 0 < \theta^1 < \pi$), and $(\rho, \theta^2, \ldots, \theta^{n-1})$ be spherical coordinates for $\mathbf{x}'' = (x^2, \ldots, x^n)$, where $\rho = |\mathbf{x}''| = r \sin \theta^1$. The coordinates of $\mathbf{x}$ are

$$\begin{aligned}
x^1 &= r \cos \theta^1 \\
x^2 &= r \sin \theta^1 \cos \theta^2 \\
&\vdots \\
x^{n-1} &= r \sin \theta^1 \sin \theta^2 \cdots \sin \theta^{n-2} \cos \theta^{n-1} \\
x^n &= r \sin \theta^1 \sin \theta^2 \cdots \sin \theta^{n-2} \sin \theta^{n-1}.
\end{aligned}$$

This defines the spherical coordinate system $(R, \Theta^1, \ldots, \Theta^{n-1})$ on $D = E^n - N$, where $N$ is a certain null set. The Jacobian is

$$J\mathbf{g}(r, \theta^1, \ldots, \theta^{n-1}) = r^{n-1} \sin^{n-2} \theta^1 \sin^{n-3} \theta^2 \cdots \sin \theta^{n-2}.$$

**Example 1.** Suppose that $f(\mathbf{x}) = \phi(|\mathbf{x}|)$, where $\phi$ is continuous on $(r_1, r_2)$. Then

$$\int_{r_1 < |\mathbf{x}| < r_2} f\, dV = \beta_n \int_{r_1}^{r_2} \phi(r) r^{n-1}\, dr,$$

where $\beta_n$ is a number not depending on $\phi$, $r_1$, or $r_2$. To find $\beta_n$, set $\phi \equiv 1$. Then

$$\alpha_n(r_2^n - r_1^n) = \beta_n \int_{r_1}^{r_2} r^{n-1}\, dr = \beta_n(r_2^n - r_1^n)/n,$$

where $\alpha_n$ is the measure of the unit $n$-ball. Hence $\beta_n = n\alpha_n$, which turns out to be the $(n-1)$-dimensional measure of the unit $(n-1)$-sphere.

6. *Cylindrical coordinates in $E^3$.* Let $(R, \Theta)$ be the polar coordinate system. Then $(R, \Theta, Z)$ is a coordinate system for $D = E^3 - \{(x, 0, z) : x \geq 0\}$. The equations $x = r \cos \theta$, $y = r \sin \theta$, $z = z$ relate the cylindrical and standard cartesian coordinates of a point $\mathbf{x} \in D$. In a similar way cylindrical coordinates can be introduced in $E^n$.

7. The idea of barycentric coordinates (p. 20) does not agree precisely with the definition in this section. However, let $t^0, t^1, \ldots, t^n$ be the barycentric coordinates of $\mathbf{x}$, with respect to the vertices $\mathbf{x}_0, \mathbf{x}_1, \ldots, \mathbf{x}_n$ of an $n$-simplex $S$. Let $\mathbf{g}$ be the affine transformation defined on p. 172, and let $\mathbf{f} = \mathbf{g}^{-1}$. Then $t^1, \ldots, t^n$ are the coordinates of $\mathbf{x}$ in the affine coordinate system $\mathbf{f}$, and $t^0 = 1 - (t^1 + \cdots + t^n)$.

***Gamma and beta functions.** The gamma function was defined on p. 167. If we let $x = g(s) = s^2/2$, then

$$\int_0^\infty x^{u-1} \exp(-x)\, dx = 2^{1-u} \int_0^\infty (s^2)^{u-1} \exp(-s^2/2) s\, ds,$$

and we obtain another expression for $\Gamma(u)$:

$$\Gamma(u) = 2^{1-u}\int_0^\infty s^{2u-1} \exp(-s^2/2)\, ds, \qquad u > 0. \tag{5-40}$$

Let us calculate the product $\Gamma(u)\Gamma(v)$. Now

$$\Gamma(u)\Gamma(v) = 2^{2-u-v}\int_0^\infty s^{2u-1} \exp(-s^2/2)\, ds\int_0^\infty t^{2v-1} \exp(-t^2/2)\, dt.$$

Writing the iterated integral as an integral over the first quadrant $Q$ and introducing polar coordinates,

$$\Gamma(u)\Gamma(v) = 2^{2-u-v}\int_Q s^{2u-1}t^{2v-1} \exp[-(s^2+t^2)/2]\, dV_2(s, t),$$

$$= 2^{2-u-v}\int_0^\infty r^{2(u+v)-1} \exp(-r^2/2)\, dr\int_0^{\pi/2} (\cos\theta)^{2u-1} (\sin\theta)^{2v-1}\, d\theta.$$

The first integral on the right-hand side is $2^{u+v-1}\,\Gamma(u+v)$ by (5-40). Let

$$B(u, v) = 2\int_0^{\pi/2} (\cos\theta)^{2u-1} (\sin\theta)^{2v-1}\, d\theta, \qquad u > 0, \qquad v > 0. \tag{5-41}$$

The function $B$ is called the *beta function*, and we have just shown that

$$B(u, v) = \frac{\Gamma(u)\Gamma(v)}{\Gamma(u+v)}\cdot \tag{5-42}$$

**Example 2.** Let $u = v = \frac{1}{2}$. Then $B(\frac{1}{2}, \frac{1}{2}) = 2\int_0^{\pi/2} d\theta = \pi$. Hence $[\Gamma(\frac{1}{2})]^2 = \pi\Gamma(1) = \pi$, or

$$\Gamma(\tfrac{1}{2}) = \sqrt{\pi}. \tag{5-43}$$

Using the formula

$$\Gamma(u+1) = u\Gamma(u), \tag{5-44}$$

proved earlier, $\Gamma(m + \frac{1}{2})$ can be found explicitly for any positive integer $m$. For instance,

$$\Gamma(\tfrac{5}{2}) = \tfrac{3}{2}\Gamma(\tfrac{3}{2}) = \tfrac{3}{2}\cdot\tfrac{1}{2}\Gamma(\tfrac{1}{2}) = \frac{3\sqrt{\pi}}{4}\cdot$$

If $u < 0$, then the integral defining $\Gamma(u)$ diverges. However, if $u$ is not an integer $m = 0, -1, -2, \ldots$, one can use (5-44) to define $\Gamma(u)$. For instance, if $-1 < u < 0$, then $0 < u + 1 < 1$ and by definition $\Gamma(u) = \Gamma(u+1)/u$. Next $\Gamma(u)$ is defined for $-2 < u < 1$, and so on. The gamma function can also be defined for complex values of $u$. (See [20], p. 148.)

To obtain another expression for $B(u, v)$, set $\cos^2\theta = g(\theta) = z$ and apply the transformation formula. Then $|g'(\theta)| = 2\cos\theta\sin\theta$, and

$$B(u, v) = \int_0^{\pi/2} (\cos^2\theta)^{u-1}(\sin^2\theta)^{v-1} 2\cos\theta\sin\theta\, d\theta,$$

$$B(u, v) = \int_0^1 z^{u-1}(1-z)^{v-1}\, dz. \tag{5-45}$$

A variety of integrals can be reduced to either (5–41) or (5–45) and hence can be evaluated in terms of the gamma function. See Problem 10.

**The measure $\alpha_n$ of the unit $n$-ball.** According to Problem 7, p. 162,

$$\frac{\alpha_n}{\alpha_{n-1}} = 2\int_0^1 (1 - u^2)^{(n-1)/2}\, du.$$

Setting $u = g(z) = \sqrt{z}$, then $g'(z) = \frac{1}{2} z^{-1/2}$ and

$$\frac{\alpha_n}{\alpha_{n-1}} = \int_0^1 z^{-1/2}(1 - z)^{(n-1)/2}\, dz$$

$$= B\left(\frac{1}{2}, \frac{n+1}{2}\right),$$

$$\alpha_n = \alpha_{n-1} \frac{\Gamma(\frac{1}{2})\Gamma\left(\frac{n+1}{2}\right)}{\Gamma\left(\frac{n}{2} + 1\right)}.$$

Moreover, $\alpha_1 = 2$. By induction on $n$ and formula (5–43),

$$\alpha_n = \frac{\pi^{n/2}}{(n/2)\Gamma(n/2)}, \qquad n = 1, 2, \ldots \tag{5–46}$$

If $n$ is even, $n = 2l$, then $l\Gamma(l) = l!$ and $\alpha_{2l} = \pi^l/l!$.

## PROBLEMS

1. Let $A = \{(x, y) : x^2 + y^2 \leq a^2, x \geq 0\}$. Evaluate $\int_A xy^2\, dV_2(x, y)$ by introducing polar coordinates.
2. Find the area of $\{(x, y) : x < y < 2x,\ 1 < x + 4y < 4\}$ by introducing $f^1(x, y) = y/x$, $f^2(x, y) = x + 4y$ as coordinates of $(x, y)$.
3. Let $A = \{(x, y) : 0 \leq x^2 + y^2 \leq 2, x^2 - y^2 \leq 1, x \geq 0, y \geq 0\}$. Find $\int_A x\, dV_2(x, y)$ by introducing the coordinates $f^1(x, y) = x^2 + y^2$, $f^2(x, y) = x^2 - y^2$.
4. Write the iterated integral $\int_0^1 dx \int_0^{1-x} dy \int_0^{g(x,y)} f(x, y, z)\, dz$ as an iterated integral in cylindrical coordinates.
5. Find $V_3(\{(x, y, z) : x^2 + y^2 + z^2 \leq a^2, x^2 + y^2 \geq b^2\})$ where $a > b$.
6. (Solids of revolution.) Let $S$ be a compact subset of the right half-plane and

$$A = \{(x, y, z) : (r, z) \in S\},$$

where $r^2 = x^2 + y^2$. Show that $V_3(A) = 2\pi\bar{y}V_2(S)$, where $(\bar{y}, \bar{z})$ is the centroid of $S$ (Fig. 5–19).

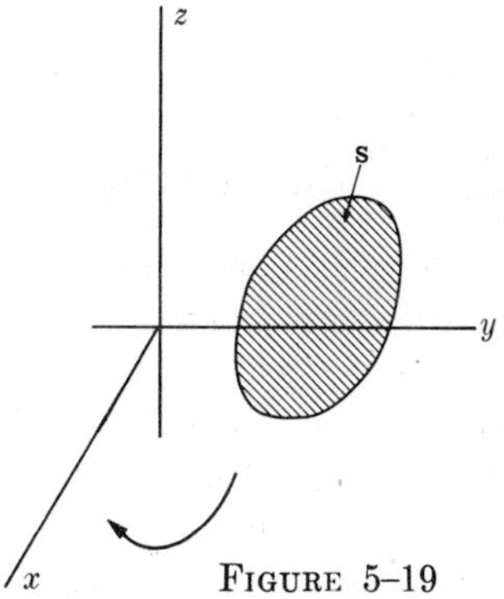


FIGURE 5–19

7. Find $V_3(\{(x, y, z) : \exp(-2x) > y^2 + z^2, x > 0\})$.
8. Let $(f^1, \ldots, f^n)$ be a coordinate system for $D_1 \subset E^n$, and $(\phi^1, \ldots, \phi^p)$ a coordinate system for $D_2 \subset E^p$. Show that $(f^1, \ldots, f^n, \phi^1, \ldots, \phi^p)$, regarded as functions on $D_1 \times D_2$, form a coordinate system for $D_1 \times D_2$.
9. (Bipolar coordinates in $E^4$). In this system the coordinates of $\mathbf{x}$ are $r \cos \theta$, $r \sin \theta$, $\rho \cos \alpha$, $\rho \sin \alpha$, where $(r, \theta)$ are polar coordinates in the $x^1x^2$-plane and $(\rho, \alpha)$ polar coordinates in the $x^3x^4$-plane. Find, using bipolar coordinates,

$$\int_{K \times K} (x^1)^2 \, dV_4(\mathbf{x})$$

where $K$ is the unit circular disk $x^2 + y^2 \leq 1$.
10. In terms of the $\Gamma$-function, find:

(a) $\displaystyle\int_0^1 \sqrt{1 - x^3} \, dx$. [*Hint:* Let $x^3 = z$.]

(b) The area of $\{(x, y) : 0 \leq y \leq \sqrt{\cos x}, -\pi/2 \leq x \leq \pi/2\}$.

(c) $\displaystyle\int_0^\infty x^a \exp(-x^b) \, dx$, $a > -1$, $b > 0$.

(d) $\displaystyle\int_1^\infty (\log x)^c x^d \, dx$, $c > -1$, $d < -1$.

(e) $\displaystyle\int_\Sigma (x^1)^k \, dV_n(\mathbf{x})$, $k = 1, 2, \ldots$, $\Sigma$ the standard $n$-simplex.

(f) $\displaystyle\int (x^1)^k \exp\left(-\sum_{i=1}^n a_i (x^i)^2\right) dV_n(\mathbf{x})$, $k = 1, 2, \ldots$, $a_i > 0$ for $i = 1, \ldots, n$.

11. Let $Q(\mathbf{x}) = \displaystyle\sum_{i,j=1}^n c_j^i x^i x^j > 0$ for every $\mathbf{x} \neq 0$, where $c_j^i = c_i^j$ for $i, j = 1, \ldots, n$.

Show that

$$\int \exp[-Q(\mathbf{x})/2] \, dV_n(\mathbf{x}) = (2\pi)^{n/2} [\det(c_j^i)]^{-1/2}.$$

[*Hint:* Make a suitable orthogonal transformation.]

## 5-10 CONVERGENCE THEOREMS

In this section we establish some properties of measurable functions. Then the Lebesgue integral is defined without the special assumptions of Section 5-6. Two important theorems about interchanging integral and limit signs are proved—the theorem about monotone sequences and Lebesgue's dominated convergence theorem.

Let us call the ordered number field $E^1$ with two "ideal points" $-\infty$ and $+\infty$ adjoined the *extended* real number system. The points $+\infty$, $-\infty$ are not numbers. However, for present purposes we agree that $-\infty < a < +\infty$ for every number $a$, and that

$$(+\infty) + (+\infty) = +\infty, \qquad (+\infty) + a = a + (+\infty) = +\infty,$$

$$(+\infty)a = a(+\infty) = \begin{cases} +\infty \text{ if } a > 0 \\ -\infty \text{ if } a < 0. \end{cases}$$

Similar conventions are made regarding $-\infty$. However, $(+\infty) + (-\infty)$ is undefined.

The extended real number system will be denoted by $\overline{E}^1$. If $S$ is a nonempty subset of $\overline{E}^1$, let $\sup S$ be the smallest $b \in \overline{E}^1$ such that $x \leq b$ for every $x \in S$. If $+\infty \in S$, then clearly $\sup S = +\infty$. Moreover, if $x < +\infty$ for every $x \in S$ but $S$ has no upper bound in $E^1$, then $\sup S = +\infty$.

The definition of $\inf S$ is similar. By neighborhood of $+\infty$ let us mean any set $\{x \in \overline{E}^1 : x > c\}$. Then convergence to $+\infty$ of sequences in $\overline{E}^1$ makes sense. Any nondecreasing sequence $x_1, x_2, \ldots$ in $\overline{E}^1$ such that $x_m > -\infty$ for some $m$ has a limit $x_0$ which is finite (that is, in $E^1$) or $+\infty$.

The following lemma about doubly indexed monotone sequences in $\overline{E}^1$ is used several times.

**Lemma 1.** *Assume that* $a_{m\nu} \geq 0$, $a_{m\nu} \leq a_{m,\nu+1}$, $a_{m\nu} \leq a_{m+1,\nu}$ *for every* $m = 1, 2, \ldots, \nu = 1, 2, \ldots$ *Then*

$$\lim_{m\to\infty} \lim_{\nu\to\infty} a_{m\nu} = \lim_{\nu\to\infty} \lim_{m\to\infty} a_{m\nu}.$$

*Proof.* Let

$$b_m = \lim_{\nu\to\infty} a_{m\nu}, \qquad c_\nu = \lim_{m\to\infty} a_{m\nu}.$$

These limits exist since $a_{m1} \leq a_{m2} \leq \cdots$ and $a_{1\nu} \leq a_{2\nu} \leq \cdots$ Moreover, $b_1 \leq b_2 \leq \cdots$ and $c_1 \leq c_2 \leq \cdots$ Let

$$b = \lim_{m\to\infty} b_m, \qquad c = \lim_{\nu\to\infty} c_\nu.$$

For every $m$ and $\nu$, $a_{m\nu} \leq c$. Hence $b_m \leq c$ for every $m$, and it follows that $b \leq c$. Similarly, $c \leq b$. ▮

**Measure.** In Section 5–2 the theory of Lebesgue measure was developed for bounded sets. For unbounded sets only the definition of measure was given there. Let us now show that Theorem 12a, which was the main result of Section 5–2, still holds without assuming boundedness.

**Theorem 12b.** *Let* $A = A_1 \cup A_2 \cup \cdots$, *where* $A_k$ *is measurable for each* $k = 1, 2, \ldots$ *Then the conclusions of Theorem* 12 *hold, providing formulas* (5–10) *and* (5–11) *are interpreted in the extended real number system* $\overline{E}^1$.

*Proof.* Let $U_r$ denote the $r$-neighborhood of $\mathbf{0}$, as on p. 145. By definition, $A_m \cap U_r$ is bounded and measurable for every $r > 0$. Moreover,

$$A \cap U_r = (A_1 \cap U_r) \cup (A_2 \cap U_r) \cup \cdots$$

By Theorem 12, $A \cap U_r$ is measurable for each $r$. Hence $A$ is measurable.

Let us next assume that $A_1 \subset A_2 \subset \cdots$ and prove (5-11). Considering only integer values of $r$, let $a_{m\nu} = V(A_m \cap U_\nu)$. The hypotheses of Lemma 1 are satisfied. Moreover, by the definition (5-12),

$$b_m = \lim_{\nu \to \infty} V(A_m \cap U_\nu) = V(A_m).$$

By (5-11) for the case of bounded nondecreasing sequences of sets,

$$c_\nu = \lim_{m \to \infty} V(A_m \cap U_\nu) = V(A \cap U_\nu).$$

By Lemma 1 and (5-12),

$$\lim_{m \to \infty} V(A_m) = \lim_{\nu \to \infty} V(A \cap U_\nu) = V(A).$$

This is (5-11).

If $A_1, A_2, \ldots$ are disjoint, let $B_m = A_1 \cup \cdots \cup A_m$. Then $B_1 \subset B_2 \subset \cdots$, $A = B_1 \cup B_2 \cup \cdots$, and by what we have just proved

$$\sum_{k=1}^{\infty} V(A_k) = \lim_{m \to \infty} V(B_m) = V(A).$$

This is (5-9). Since differences of measurable sets are measurable [Problem 1(a)], the same reasoning as on p. 144 establishes (5-10). ▮

Some additional properties of measurable sets are listed in Problem 1.

**Corollary 1.** *Let $A_1, A_2, \ldots$ be measurable sets such that $A_1 \supset A_2 \supset \cdots$ and $V(A_1)$ is finite. Then $A = A_1 \cap A_2 \cap \cdots$ is measurable and*

$$V(A) = \lim_{\nu \to \infty} V(A_\nu). \tag{5-47}$$

*Proof.* By Problem 1(c), $A$ is measurable. Let $E_\nu = A_1 - A_\nu$, $\nu = 1, 2, \ldots$, $E = A_1 - A$. By Problem 1(b), $V(E_\nu) = V(A_1) - V(A_\nu)$, and $V(E) = V(A_1) - V(A)$. Since $E_1 \subset E_2 \subset \cdots$ and $E = E_1 \cup E_2 \cup \cdots$, by Theorem 12b

$$V(A_1) - V(A) = \lim_{\nu \to \infty} [V(A_1) - V(A_\nu)].$$

Since $V(A_1)$ does not depend on $\nu$, we obtain (5-47). ▮

In the discussion of integrals to follow, it is convenient to consider functions which may have the values $-\infty$ or $+\infty$.

**Properties of measurable functions.** Let $f$ be a function with domain $E^n$ and values in the extended real number system $\overline{E}^1$. Then $f$ is *measurable* if

$$\{\mathbf{x} : f(\mathbf{x}) > c\} \tag{5–48}$$

is a measurable set for every real number $c$. Let us list and prove some properties of measurable functions.

(1) *If $f$ is measurable, then for every $c$ the sets $\{\mathbf{x} : f(\mathbf{x}) \leq c\}$, $\{\mathbf{x} : f(\mathbf{x}) \geq c\}$, and $\{\mathbf{x} : f(\mathbf{x}) < c\}$ are measurable sets.*

*Proof.* By Problem 1(a), with $A = E^n$, the complement of a measurable set is measurable. Since $\{\mathbf{x} : f(\mathbf{x}) \leq c\}$ is the complement of the set in (5–48), it is measurable. Now $\{\mathbf{x} : f(\mathbf{x}) \geq c\} = \bigcap_{m=1}^{\infty} \{\mathbf{x} : f(\mathbf{x}) > c - 1/m\}$. Each set on the right is measurable, and by Problem 1(c) their intersection is measurable. Taking complements, the third set is measurable. ▮

From the definition and (1), $f^{-1}(I)$ is measurable if $I$ is any semi-infinite interval. It can be shown that $f^{-1}(E)$ is measurable if $E$ is any open set or closed set.

In the next statement we agree that $0f = 0$ even when $f$ has extended real values.

(2) *If $f$ is measurable, then $af$ is measurable for any real number $a$.*

*Proof.* This follows from the definition and (1). ▮

(3a) *If $f$ and $g$ are measurable and*

$$h(\mathbf{x}) = \max\,\{f(\mathbf{x}), g(\mathbf{x})\} \quad \textit{for every } \mathbf{x},$$

*then $h$ is measurable.*

*Proof.* $\{\mathbf{x} : h(\mathbf{x}) > c\} = \{\mathbf{x} : f(\mathbf{x}) > c\} \cup \{\mathbf{x} : g(\mathbf{x}) > c\}$. ▮

In particular, if $f$ is measurable and

$$f^+(\mathbf{x}) = \max\,\{f(\mathbf{x}), 0\}, \qquad f^-(\mathbf{x}) = \max\,\{-f(\mathbf{x}), 0\},$$

then $f^+$ and $f^-$ are measurable.

Statement (3a) extends to the maximum of a finite number of measurable functions and, more importantly, to sequences of functions.

(3b) *If $f_1, f_2, \ldots$ are measurable and*

$$g(\mathbf{x}) = \sup\,\{f_1(\mathbf{x}), f_2(\mathbf{x}), \ldots\} \quad \textit{for every } \mathbf{x},$$

*then $g$ is measurable.*

*Proof.*

$$\{\mathbf{x} : g(\mathbf{x}) > c\} = \bigcup_{\nu=1}^{\infty} \{\mathbf{x} : f_\nu(\mathbf{x}) > c\}. \ ▮$$

In particular, if $f_1 \leq f_2 \leq \cdots$ then $g$ is the limit of this nondecreasing sequence.

Similarly, if

$$h(\mathbf{x}) = \inf \{f_1(\mathbf{x}), f_2(\mathbf{x}), \ldots\} \quad \text{for every } \mathbf{x},$$

then $h$ is measurable.

Let $y_1, y_2, \ldots$ be any sequence in $\overline{E}^1$. Let

$$z_\nu = \inf \{y_\nu, y_{\nu+1}, \ldots\}, \qquad \nu = 1, 2, \ldots$$

Then $z_1 \leq z_2 \leq \cdots$ The limit of the monotone sequence $z_1, z_2, \ldots$ is called the *lower limit* of the sequence $y_1, y_2, \ldots$, and is denoted by $\liminf_{\nu \to \infty} y_\nu$. Similarly, if

$$w_\nu = \sup \{y_\nu, y_{\nu+1}, \ldots\}, \qquad \nu = 1, 2, \ldots,$$

then $w_1 \geq w_2 \geq \cdots$ The limit of the monotone sequence $w_1, w_2, \ldots$ is the *upper limit* $\limsup_{\nu \to \infty} y_\nu$. Since $z_\nu \leq w_\nu$ for each $\nu = 1, 2, \ldots$, we must have

$$\liminf_{\nu \to \infty} y_\nu \leq \limsup_{\nu \to \infty} y_\nu.$$

Equality holds if and only if the sequence $y_1, y_2, \ldots$ has a limit.

(4) *If $f_1, f_2, \ldots$ are measurable and*

$$f(\mathbf{x}) = \liminf_{\nu \to \infty} f_\nu(\mathbf{x}) \quad \textit{for every } \mathbf{x},$$

*then $f$ is measurable.*

*Proof.* For each $\nu = 1, 2, \ldots$ let $h_\nu(\mathbf{x}) = \inf \{f_\nu(\mathbf{x}), f_{\nu+1}(\mathbf{x}), \ldots\}$. By (3b) each $h_\nu$ is measurable; $h_1 \leq h_2 \leq \cdots$, and by the definition of "lim inf," $f(\mathbf{x}) = \lim_{\nu \to \infty} h_\nu(\mathbf{x})$ for every $\mathbf{x}$. Therefore $f$ is measurable. ▮

(5) *If $f_1, f_2, \ldots$ are measurable and*

$$f(\mathbf{x}) = \lim_{\nu \to \infty} f_\nu(\mathbf{x}) \quad \textit{for every } \mathbf{x},$$

*then $f$ is measurable.*

This is a particular case of (4). ▮

In the next statement it is assumed that $f(\mathbf{x}) + g(\mathbf{x})$ is everywhere defined. In other words, for no $\mathbf{x}$ it is true that $f(\mathbf{x}) = +\infty$, $g(\mathbf{x}) = -\infty$ or vice versa.

(6) *If $f$ and $g$ are measurable, then $f + g$ is measurable.*

*Proof.* For each $\nu = 1, 2, \ldots$ let

$$f_\nu(\mathbf{x}) = \begin{cases} \nu & \text{if } f(\mathbf{x}) > \nu, \\ -\nu & \text{if } f(\mathbf{x}) \leq -\nu, \\ j/\nu & \text{if } (j-1)/\nu < f(\mathbf{x}) \leq j/\nu, \end{cases}$$

where $j$ is an integer, and $1 - \nu^2 \leq j \leq \nu^2$. This construction is like one on p. 153. Then

$$f(\mathbf{x}) = \lim_{\nu \to \infty} f_\nu(\mathbf{x})$$

for every $\mathbf{x}$. Defining $g_\nu$ in the same way,

$$g(\mathbf{x}) = \lim_{\nu \to \infty} g_\nu(\mathbf{x}).$$

For each $\nu$ the functions $f_\nu$ and $g_\nu$ are measurable and take a finite number of values. It is easy to show that their sum $f_\nu + g_\nu$ is measurable. Since for every $\mathbf{x}$

$$f(\mathbf{x}) + g(\mathbf{x}) = \lim_{\nu \to \infty} [f_\nu(\mathbf{x}) + g_\nu(\mathbf{x})],$$

$f + g$ is measurable by (5). ▮

**Definition of the integral.** The integral of a bounded measurable function with compact support was defined in Section 5–3. Let us extend the definition in three steps.

(a) Let $f$ be bounded, measurable, and $f \geq 0$. For each $r > 0$, $f$ is measurable on the $r$-neighborhood $U_r$ of $\mathbf{0}$. By Theorem 14, $f$ is integrable over $U_r$. Let $\phi(r)$ equal the integral of $f$ over $U_r$. Since $f \geq 0$, $\phi$ is nondecreasing. Hence $\phi(r)$ tends to a limit, finite or $+\infty$, as $r \to +\infty$. Let

$$\int f\, dV = \lim_{r \to +\infty} \int_{U_r} f\, dV. \tag{5–49}$$

If the limit is finite, then $f$ is *integrable* (over $E^n$). Otherwise the left-hand side of (5–49) equals $+\infty$. If $0 \leq f \leq g$, then $\int f\, dV \leq \int g\, dV$.

(b) Let $f$ be measurable and $f \geq 0$. For any $t > 0$ consider the function ${}_tf$ such that

$${}_tf(\mathbf{x}) = \min \{f(\mathbf{x}), t\} \qquad \text{for every } \mathbf{x}.$$

For each $t$, ${}_tf$ is a bounded, measurable function. It is called the *truncation* of $f$ at height $t$. If $s \leq t$, then ${}_sf \leq {}_tf$ and hence $\int {}_sf\, dV \leq \int {}_tf\, dV$. Let

$$\int f\, dV = \lim_{t \to +\infty} \int {}_tf\, dV. \tag{5–50}$$

If the limit is finite, then $f$ is *integrable*. Otherwise $\int f\, dV = +\infty$. If $0 \leq f \leq g$, then ${}_tf \leq {}_tg$ for every $t$. Consequently, $\int f\, dV \leq \int g\, dV$.

If $f$ is bounded, then ${}_tf = f$ for all sufficiently large $t$. The definitions in (a) and (b) agree. Moreover, if $f$ has compact support, then $\phi(r)$ is constant for all sufficiently large $r$ and the definition of integral in (a) agrees with the one in Section 5–3.

If $A$ is a measurable set, then its characteristic function $1_A$ (see p. 152) is bounded and measurable. From (5–12), (5–49), and (3) of Theorem 13, $V(A)$ equals the integral of $1_A$.

(c) A measurable function $f$ is integrable if $f^+$ and $f^-$ are integrable. If $f$ is integrable, then

$$\int f\,dV = \int f^+\,dV - \int f^-\,dV. \tag{5-51}$$

In case $f$ is bounded and has compact support, then the new definition agrees with the one in Section 5-3. For if the integral is taken in the sense of Section 5-3, then formula (5-51) holds. (See Proposition 17 and Theorem 14.) Since $f^+$ and $f^-$ have the same integral in the new sense as in Section 5-3, so does $f$.

Let us now give some general theorems about the validity of interchanging the symbols "$\lim_{\nu\to\infty}$" and "$\int$".

**Lemma 2.** *Let $K$ be a compact set and $\phi_1, \phi_2, \ldots$ be bounded measurable functions with supports contained in $K$ such that $\phi_1 \geq \phi_2 \geq \cdots$ and $\lim_{\nu\to\infty} \phi_\nu(\mathbf{x}) = 0$ for every $\mathbf{x}$. Then*

$$\lim_{\nu\to\infty} \int \phi_\nu\,dV = 0.$$

*Proof.* There exists $C$ such that $\phi_\nu(\mathbf{x}) \leq C$ for every $\mathbf{x}$ and $\nu = 1$, hence also for $\nu = 2, 3, \ldots$ Given $\epsilon > 0$ let $c = \epsilon/2V(K)$. Let

$$A_\nu = \{\mathbf{x} : \phi_\nu(\mathbf{x}) > c\}.$$

By hypothesis $K \supset A_1 \supset A_2 \supset \cdots$ and $A_1 \cap A_2 \cap \cdots$ is the empty set. Since $V(A_1)$ is finite, we may apply formula (5-47), obtaining

$$\lim_{\nu\to\infty} V(A_\nu) = V(A_1 \cap A_2 \cap \cdots) = 0.$$

Let $\nu_0$ be such that $V(A_\nu) < \epsilon/2C$ for every $\nu \geq \nu_0$. Then

$$\int_{A_\nu} \phi_\nu\,dV \leq CV(A_\nu) < \epsilon/2, \quad \text{if } \nu \geq \nu_0,$$

while for every $\nu$,

$$\int_{K-A_\nu} \phi_\nu\,dV \leq cV(K - A_\nu) \leq cV(K) = \epsilon/2.$$

Hence for every $\nu \geq \nu_0$,

$$\int \phi_\nu\,dV = \int_K \phi_\nu\,dV < \epsilon. \blacksquare$$

**Monotone sequences theorem.** *Let $f_1, f_2, \ldots$ be measurable functions with $0 \leq f_1 \leq f_2 \leq \cdots$, and let $f(\mathbf{x}) = \lim_{\nu\to\infty} f_\nu(\mathbf{x})$ for every $\mathbf{x}$. Then*

$$\int f\,dV = \lim_{\nu\to\infty} \int f_\nu\,dV. \tag{5-52}$$

*Proof.* We have already shown that the limit $f$ is measurable. First let us assume that $f$ is bounded and has compact support. Let $\phi_\nu = f - f_\nu$. Since $0 \leq f_\nu \leq f$, each function $f_\nu$ is also bounded and has compact support. Moreover

$$\int \phi_\nu \, dV = \int f \, dV - \int f_\nu \, dV, \qquad \nu = 1, 2, \ldots$$

From Lemma 2, we get (5–52).

Next let us suppose merely that $f$ is bounded. Let

$$a_{m\nu} = \int_{U_m} f_\nu \, dV, \qquad m, \nu = 1, 2, \ldots$$

and apply Lemma 1. Finally, if $f$ is unbounded observe that for each $m = 1, 2, \ldots,$

$$0 \leq {}_mf_1 \leq {}_mf_2 \leq \cdots, \qquad {}_mf(\mathbf{x}) = \lim_{\nu \to \infty} {}_mf_\nu(\mathbf{x}),$$

where ${}_mf_\nu$ is the truncation of $f_\nu$ at height $m$. Apply Lemma 1 again with

$$a_{m\nu} = \int {}_mf_\nu \, dV, \qquad m, \nu = 1, 2, \ldots \blacksquare$$

*Note:* The theorem states in particular that $f$ is integrable if and only if the nondecreasing sequence of numbers $\int f_1 \, dV, \int f_2 \, dV, \ldots$ has a finite limit.

The double limiting process (5–49) and (5–50) can be replaced by a single one. Let $f$ be measurable and $f \geq 0$. Let

$$f_\nu(\mathbf{x}) = \begin{cases} \nu & \text{if } f(\mathbf{x}) \geq \nu, \quad |\mathbf{x}| \leq \nu, \\ 0 & \text{if } |\mathbf{x}| > \nu, \\ f(\mathbf{x}) & \text{otherwise.} \end{cases} \tag{$*$}$$

Then $0 \leq f_1 \leq f_2 \leq \cdots$ and $f_\nu(\mathbf{x})$ tends to $f(\mathbf{x})$ for every $\mathbf{x}$. Hence by the theorem,

$$\int f \, dV = \lim_{\nu \to \infty} \int f_\nu \, dV.$$

**Corollary 2.** *If $f$ and $g$ are real-valued integrable functions, then $f + g$ is integrable and*

$$\int (f + g) \, dV = \int f \, dV + \int g \, dV. \tag{5–53}$$

*Proof.* By (6) $f + g$ is measurable. If $f \geq 0$, $g \geq 0$, define $f_\nu$ and $g_\nu$ by ($*$). For each $\nu$, $f_\nu$ and $g_\nu$ are bounded and have compact supports. By Proposition 17, Section 5–3,

$$\int (f_\nu + g_\nu) \, dV = \int f_\nu \, dV + \int g_\nu \, dV.$$

The sequences $f_1, f_2, \ldots, g_1, g_2, \ldots, f_1 + g_1, f_2 + g_2, \ldots$ are nondecreasing and tend respectively to $f, g, f + g$. By the monotone sequences theorem, the corollary is true when $f \geq 0$, $g \geq 0$.

In the general case,

$$0 \leq (f + g)^+ \leq f^+ + g^+.$$

Since $f^+$ and $g^+$ are integrable, so is $(f + g)^+$. Similarly $(f + g)^-$ is integrable. Then

$$f^+ + g^+ = (f + g)^+ + \phi,$$

$$f^- + g^- = (f + g)^- + \phi,$$

where $\phi \geq 0$. Since the corollary is true for nonnegative functions,

$$\int f^+ \, dV + \int g^+ \, dV = \int (f + g)^+ \, dV + \int \phi \, dV,$$

$$\int f^- \, dV + \int g^- \, dV = \int (f + g)^- \, dV + \int \phi \, dV.$$

Subtracting, we get (5–53). ▮

In particular, if $f$ is integrable, then $|f| = f^+ + f^-$ is integrable. It is easy to show that $cf$ is integrable if $f$ is integrable, and

$$\int (cf) \, dV = c \int f \, dV.$$

**Corollary 3.** *Let $f_1, f_2, \ldots$ be measurable, $f_1$ be integrable, $f_1 \geq f_2 \geq \cdots \geq 0$, and let $f(\mathbf{x}) = \lim_{\nu \to \infty} f_\nu(\mathbf{x})$ for every $\mathbf{x}$. Then (5–52) holds.*

*Proof.* Let $g_\nu = f_1 - f_\nu$ and apply the theorem to the nondecreasing sequence $g_1, g_2 \ldots$ which has $f_1 - f$ as limit. ▮

For sequences which are not necessarily monotone, there is a result called:

**Fatou's lemma.** *Let $f_\nu$ be measurable and $f_\nu \geq 0$ for each $\nu = 1, 2, \ldots$ Then*

$$\int (\liminf_{\nu \to \infty} f_\nu) \, dV \leq \liminf_{\nu \to \infty} \int f_\nu \, dV. \tag{5–54a}$$

*Proof.* Let $h_\nu = \inf \{f_\nu, f_{\nu+1}, \ldots\}$. Since $h_\nu \leq f_m$ whenever $\nu \leq m$,

$$\int h_\nu \, dV \leq \int f_m \, dV, \qquad m = \nu, \nu + 1, \ldots,$$

$$\int h_\nu \, dV \leq \liminf_{m \to \infty} \int f_m \, dV, \qquad \nu = 1, 2, \ldots \tag{**}$$

Let $f = \liminf_{\nu \to \infty} f_\nu$. The sequence $h_1, h_2, \ldots$ is nondecreasing and tends to $f$.

By the monotone sequences theorem,

$$\int f\,dV = \lim_{\nu\to\infty} \int h_\nu\,dV.$$

Since (**) holds for each $\nu$, the limit is no more than the right-hand side of (**). ▮

A statement about measurable functions is said to hold *almost everywhere* if it is true except for $\mathbf{x}$ in some null set.

**Proposition.** *If $f$ is integrable, then $f(\mathbf{x})$ is finite almost everywhere.*

*Proof.* If $f \geq 0$, let

$$A_m = \{\mathbf{x} : f(\mathbf{x}) \geq m\}, \qquad A_\infty = \{\mathbf{x} : f(\mathbf{x}) = +\infty\}.$$

Then $A_\infty = A_1 \cap A_2 \cap \cdots$ and $A_1 \supset A_2 \supset \cdots$ For each $m$, let $\phi_m(\mathbf{x}) = f(\mathbf{x})$ if $\mathbf{x} \in A_m$, and otherwise $\phi_m(\mathbf{x}) = 0$. Then $\phi_m \geq m1_{A_m}$, where $1_A$ is the characteristic function of $A$. Hence

$$mV(A_m) = \int m1_{A_m}\,dV \leq \int \phi_m\,dV.$$

Since $\phi_m \leq f$ we have, dividing by $m$,

$$V(A_m) \leq \frac{1}{m}\int f\,dV.$$

Since the right-hand side tends to 0 as $m \to \infty$, $V(A_\infty) = 0$.

In the general case, $f^+$ and $f^-$ are integrable and

$$\{\mathbf{x} : f(\mathbf{x}) = \pm\infty\} = \{\mathbf{x} : f^+(\mathbf{x}) = +\infty\} \cup \{\mathbf{x} : f^-(\mathbf{x}) = +\infty\}. ▮$$

If $f$ is measurable and $g(\mathbf{x}) = f(\mathbf{x})$ almost everywhere, then $g$ is measurable. Moreover, if either is integrable then so is the other and $\int f\,dV = \int g\,dV$ (Problem 3).

In Fatou's lemma the hypothesis "$f_\nu \geq 0$ for every $\nu$" can be replaced by "$f_\nu \geq \phi$ for every $\nu$, where $\phi$ is integrable." For this purpose we make the following convention. If $f \geq \phi$ and $\phi$ is integrable, then $\phi(\mathbf{x})$ is finite almost everywhere. By $f - \phi$ let us mean the function with value $f(\mathbf{x}) - \phi(\mathbf{x})$ if $\phi(\mathbf{x}) \neq +\infty$, and value 0 if $\phi(\mathbf{x}) = +\infty$. Then $\int(f - \phi)\,dV = \int f\,dV - \int\phi\,dV$ if $f - \phi$ is integrable. If the integral of $f - \phi$ diverges to $+\infty$, then we agree that the integral of $f$ also diverges to $+\infty$.

Let $g_\nu = f_\nu - \phi$. By assumption, $g_\nu \geq 0$ for each $\nu = 1, 2, \ldots$ Moreover,

$$\liminf_{\nu\to\infty} g_\nu(\mathbf{x}) = \liminf_{\nu\to\infty} f_\nu(\mathbf{x}) - \phi(\mathbf{x}),$$

provided $\phi(\mathbf{x}) \neq +\infty$, hence almost everywhere. Since for each $\nu$

$$\int g_\nu\,dV = \int f_\nu\,dV - \int \phi\,dV,$$

we have

$$\liminf_{\nu\to\infty} \int g_\nu \, dV = \liminf_{\nu\to\infty} \int f_\nu \, dV - \int \phi \, dV.$$

Applying Fatou's lemma to the sequence $g_1, g_2, \ldots$ and adding $\int \phi \, dV$ to each side, we again get (5–54a).

Similarly, if for each $\nu$, $f_\nu \leq \phi$ where $\phi$ is integrable, then

$$\int (\limsup_{\nu\to\infty} f_\nu) \, dV \geq \limsup_{\nu\to\infty} \int f_\nu \, dV. \tag{5–54b}$$

*Note:* In the monotone sequences theorem and its corollary the hypothesis $f_\nu \geq 0$ can also be replaced by $f_\nu \geq \phi$, where $\phi$ is integrable.

**Lebesgue's dominated convergence theorem.** *Let $f_1, f_2, \ldots$ be measurable functions such that:*

(a) $\lim_{\nu\to\infty} f_\nu(\mathbf{x}) = f(\mathbf{x})$ *almost everywhere.*

(b) *There is an integrable function $g$ such that $|f_\nu| \leq g$ for $\nu = 1, 2, \ldots$*
*Then*

$$\int f \, dV = \lim_{\nu\to\infty} \int f_\nu \, dV.$$

*Proof.* Since $-g \leq f_\nu \leq g$ and both $-g$ and $g$ are integrable, we can apply (5–54a) and (5–54b). But

$$\liminf_{\nu\to\infty} f_\nu(\mathbf{x}) = \limsup_{\nu\to\infty} f_\nu(\mathbf{x}) = f(\mathbf{x})$$

almost everywhere. Hence

$$\limsup_{\nu\to\infty} \int f_\nu \, dV \leq \int f \, dV \leq \liminf_{\nu\to\infty} \int f_\nu \, dV.$$

But lim inf $\leq$ lim sup, and hence $\int f_\nu \, dV$ tends to $\int f \, dV$. ▮

**Integrals over measurable sets.** Let $A$ be a measurable set. Just as in Section 5–4, a function $f$ is called *measurable on* $A$ if, for every real $c$, $\{\mathbf{x} \in A : f(\mathbf{x}) > c\}$ is measurable. If the function $f_A$ (p. 151) is integrable, then $f$ is *integrable over* $A$ and we set

$$\int_A f \, dV = \int f_A \, dV.$$

If $f$ and $g$ are integrable over $A$, then $f + g$ is integrable over $A$. This follows from Corollary 2, since $(f + g)_A = f_A + g_A$. Similarly $cf$ is integrable over $A$. The basic properties of integrals listed in Theorem 13, p. 152, remain true. The formula $V(A) = \int_A 1 \, dV$ was established above, and the remaining parts of Theorem 13 are proved exactly as before.

The monotone sequences theorem, Fatou's lemma, and Lebesgue's dominated convergence theorem remain true for integrals over $A$. In these theorems one has simply to write $\int_A$ in place of $\int$, and to replace the phrases

| | |
|---|---|
| "measurable" | by "measurable on $A$," |
| "integrable" | by "integrable over $A$," |
| "for every $\mathbf{x}$" | by "for every $\mathbf{x} \in A$," |
| "almost everywhere" | by "almost everywhere in $A$." |
| "$\lvert f_\nu \rvert \leq g$" | by "$\lvert f_\nu(\mathbf{x})\rvert \leq g(\mathbf{x})$ for every $\mathbf{x} \in A$." |

In each case let $F_\nu = (f_\nu)_A$, $F = f_A$. Then

$$\int F_\nu \, dV = \int_A f_\nu \, dV, \qquad \int F \, dV = \int_A f_A \, dV.$$

If, for every $\mathbf{x} \in A$, $0 \leq f_1(\mathbf{x}) \leq f_2(\mathbf{x}) \leq \cdots$ and $f_\nu(\mathbf{x})$ tends to $f(\mathbf{x})$ as $\nu \to \infty$, then $0 \leq F_1(\mathbf{x}) \leq F_2(\mathbf{x}) \leq \cdots$ and $F_\nu(\mathbf{x})$ tends to $F(\mathbf{x})$ for every $\mathbf{x} \in E^n$. Applying the monotone sequences theorem to the sequence $F_1, F_2, \ldots$, we get

$$\int_A f \, dV = \lim_{\nu\to\infty} \int_A f_\nu \, dV.$$

The proofs of Fatou's lemma and the dominated convergence theorem for integrals over $A$ are similar.

**Corollary 4.** *Let $A$ be a bounded measurable set of finite measure and $f_1, f_2, \ldots$ measurable on $A$. Assume that:*

(a) $\lim_{\nu\to\infty} f_\nu(\mathbf{x}) = f(\mathbf{x})$ *almost everywhere in $A$.*

(b) *There is a number $C$ such that $\lvert f_\nu(\mathbf{x})\rvert \leq C$ for every $\mathbf{x} \in A$ and $\nu = 1, 2, \ldots$ Then*

$$\int_A f \, dV = \lim_{\nu\to\infty} \int_A f_\nu \, dV.$$

*Proof.* Let $g(\mathbf{x}) = C$ for every $\mathbf{x}$. Since $V(A)$ is finite, $g$ is integrable over $A$. The corollary is then a special case of the dominated convergence theorem for integrals over $A$. ▮

**Corollary 5.** (a) *Let $A_1, A_2, \ldots$ be a nondecreasing sequence of measurable sets. Let $f$ be integrable over $A = A_1 \cup A_2 \cup \cdots$ Then*

$$\int_A f \, dV = \lim_{\nu\to\infty} \int_{A_\nu} f \, dV. \tag{5-55}$$

(b) *Let $A_1, A_2, \ldots$ be a nonincreasing sequence of measurable sets, and let $A = A_1 \cap A_2 \cap \cdots$ Then (5–55) holds provided $f$ is integrable over $A_1$.*

*Proof of* (a). Let $f_\nu = f_{A_\nu}$, $\nu = 1, 2, \ldots$ Then $\lim_{\nu\to\infty} f_\nu(\mathbf{x}) = f(\mathbf{x})$ for every $\mathbf{x} \in A$ and $\lvert f_\nu(\mathbf{x})\rvert \leq \lvert f(\mathbf{x})\rvert$. The conclusion follows from the dominated convergence theorem, with $g = \lvert f \rvert$. ▮

The proof of (b) is similar.

*Note:* If $f \geq 0$ and the sequence $A_1, A_2, \ldots$ is nondecreasing, then we could have appealed instead to the monotone sequences theorem. In that case it is unnecessary to assume that $f$ is integrable over $A$. This observation is useful in proving the next corollary.

**Corollary 6.** *Let $A$ be $\sigma$-compact, $f$ be continuous on $A$, and $f \geq 0$. Then*

$$\int_A f\,dV = \sup\left\{\int_K f\,dV : K \subset A,\ K \text{ is compact}\right\}\cdot \tag{5–56}$$

*Proof.* Let $s$ denote the right-hand side of (5–56). Since $\int_K f\,dV \leq \int_A f\,dV$ whenever $K \subset A$, we must have $s \leq \int_A f\,dV$. Let $K_1, K_2, \ldots$ be a nondecreasing sequence of compact sets such that $A = K_1 \cup K_2 \cup \cdots$ Then $\int_{K_\nu} f\,dV \leq s$ for each $\nu = 1, 2, \ldots$ Setting $A_\nu = K_\nu$ in (5–55), we find that $\int_A f\,dV \leq s$. Hence $\int_A f\,dV = s$. ▮

The right-hand side of (5–56) was taken in Section 5–6 as the definition. Corollary 6 shows that the definition there agrees with the one in the present section in case $f \geq 0$. Since the procedure for defining the integral when $f$ also has negative values was the same in both sections [see (5–28) and (5–51)], the two definitions agree in general.

## PROBLEMS

1. Show that:
   (a) If $A$ and $B$ are measurable, then $A - B$ is measurable. [*Hint:* $(A - B) \cap U_r = A \cap U_r - B \cap U_r$.]
   (b) If $B \subset A$ and $A$ has finite measure, then $V(A - B) = V(A) - V(B)$.
   (c) If $A_1, A_2, \ldots$ are measurable, then $A_1 \cap A_2 \cap \cdots$ is measurable.

   $$\textit{Hint: } E^n - \bigcap_{m=1}^{\infty} A_m = \bigcup_{m=1}^{\infty} (E^n - A_m).$$

   (d) If $A_1, A_2, \ldots$ are $\sigma$-compact, then $A_1 \cup A_2 \cup \cdots$ is $\sigma$-compact.

   *Hint: Let* $A_m = K_{m1} \cup K_{m2} \cup \cdots$, where $K_{m1} \subset K_{m2} \subset \cdots$ Let

   $$K_m = \bigcup_{j,k=1}^{m} K_{jk}.$$

   (e) If $A$ is any measurable set, then $A = B \cup N$ where $B$ is $\sigma$-compact and $N$ is a null set. [*Hint:* Show that the result is true for bounded measurable sets.]

2. Let $f$ and $g$ be measurable real-valued functions. Show that their product is measurable. [*Hint:* Show that the square of a measurable function is measurable. Then $2fg = (f + g)^2 - f^2 - g^2$.]

3. Show that:
   (a) If $A$ is measurable, $N$ is a null set, and $A - N \subset B \subset A \cup N$, then $B$ is measurable and $V(A) = V(B)$. [*Hint:* First consider the case of bounded sets.]
   (b) If $f$ is measurable and $f(\mathbf{x}) = g(\mathbf{x})$ almost everywhere, then $g$ is measurable.
   (c) Moreover, if $f$ is integrable, then $\int f\,dV = \int g\,dV$. [*Hint:* The result is known from Section 5–4 to be true if $f$ and $g$ are bounded and have compact supports.]
4. Let $f$ be measurable and $f \geq 0$. Show that if $\int f\,dV = 0$, then $f(\mathbf{x}) = 0$ almost everywhere.
5. Let $f_\nu(x) = \sin \nu\pi x$. Show that:
   (a) $\liminf_{\nu\to\infty} f_\nu(x) = -1$ and $\limsup_{\nu\to\infty} f_\nu(x) = 1$ whenever $x$ is irrational. [*Hint*: If $x$ is irrational, then every arc of the circle $s^2 + t^2 = 1$ contains $(\cos \nu\pi x, \sin \nu\pi x)$ for infinitely many $\nu$.]
   (b) $\int_0^1 (\liminf_{\nu\to\infty} f_\nu)\,dx = -1$, $\liminf_{\nu\to\infty} \int_0^1 f_\nu\,dx = 0$.
6. Let $f_\nu(x) = \nu$ if $x \in (0, \nu^{-1})$ and $f_\nu(x) = 0$ otherwise, $\nu = 1, 2, \ldots$ Show that $\lim_{\nu\to\infty} f_\nu(x) = 0$ for every $x$, but $\int f_\nu\,dx = 1$. Why does this not contradict Lebesgue's dominated convergence theorem?
7. Let $f_\nu(x) = \nu/(x^2 + \nu^2)$, $\nu = 1, 2, \ldots$ Show that $0 \leq f_\nu(x) \leq 1$, $\lim_{\nu\to\infty} f_\nu(x) = 0$ for every $x$, and $\int f_\nu\,dx = \pi$. Why does this not contradict the dominated convergence theorem?
8. (a) Let $f_1, f_2, \ldots$ be integrable over a measurable set $A$, and assume that $\sum_{k=1}^\infty \int_A |f_k|\,dV$ is finite. Let $G(\mathbf{x}) = \sum_{k=1}^\infty |f_k(\mathbf{x})|$. Since the terms of this series are nonnegative, it either converges or diverges to $+\infty$ for every $\mathbf{x} \in A$. Show that $G$ is integrable over $A$ and hence $G(\mathbf{x})$ is finite for almost every $\mathbf{x} \in A$. [*Hint:* Apply the monotone sequences theorem to the sequence $G_1, G_2, \ldots$, where $G_\nu = |(f_1)_A| + \cdots + |(f_\nu)_A|$.]
   (b) By (a) the series $\sum_{k=1}^\infty f_k(\mathbf{x})$ converges absolutely for almost every $\mathbf{x} \in A$. Let $F(\mathbf{x})$ be the sum of the series. Show that $\int_A F\,dV = \sum_{k=1}^\infty \int_A f_k\,dV$. [*Hint:* Apply the dominated convergence theorem to the sequence $F_1, F_2, \ldots$, where $F_\nu = (f_1)_A + \cdots + (f_\nu)_A$.]
9. Let $f_1, f_2, \ldots$ be integrable over $A$, where $A$ has finite measure. Assume that $|f_k(\mathbf{x})| \leq C_k$ for every $\mathbf{x} \in A$ and $k = 1, 2, \ldots$, and that the series $\sum_{k=1}^\infty C_k$ converges. Show that the series $\sum_{k=1}^\infty f_k(\mathbf{x})$ converges absolutely for almost every $\mathbf{x} \in A$; and if $F(\mathbf{x})$ is the sum of the series, then $\int_A F\,dV_n = \sum_{k=1}^\infty \int_A f_k\,dV_n$. [*Hint:* Use Problem 8.]

## 5-11 DIFFERENTIATION UNDER THE INTEGRAL SIGN

Let $A$ be a $\sigma$-compact subset of $E^n$, $B$ be an open subset of $E^l$, and $A \times B = \{(\mathbf{x}, \mathbf{t}) : \mathbf{x} \in A, \mathbf{t} \in B\}$ be their cartesian product. In this section we are concerned with the validity of the formula

$$\frac{\partial}{\partial t^j} \int_A f(\mathbf{x}, \mathbf{t})\,dV_n(\mathbf{x}) = \int_A \frac{\partial f}{\partial t^j}(\mathbf{x}, \mathbf{t})\,dV_n(\mathbf{x}), \qquad j = 1, \ldots, l. \tag{5–57}$$

**Lemma 1.** *Let $f$ be continuous on $A \times B$. Assume that there is a function $g$ integrable over $A$ such that $|f(\mathbf{x}, \mathbf{t})| \leq g(\mathbf{x})$ for every $\mathbf{x} \in A$, $\mathbf{t} \in B$. Let*

$$\phi(\mathbf{t}) = \int_A f(\mathbf{x}, \mathbf{t})\, dV_n(\mathbf{x}), \quad \mathbf{t} \in B. \tag{5-58}$$

*Then $\phi$ is continuous on $B$.*

*Proof.* Let $\mathbf{t}_0$ be any point of $B$. If $\mathbf{t}_1, \mathbf{t}_2, \ldots$ is any sequence in $B$ tending to $\mathbf{t}_0$, then since $f(\mathbf{x},\ )$ is continuous at $\mathbf{t}_0$

$$f(\mathbf{x}, \mathbf{t}_0) = \lim_{m \to \infty} f(\mathbf{x}, \mathbf{t}_m) \quad \text{for every } \mathbf{x} \in A.$$

Since $|f(\mathbf{x}, \mathbf{t}_m)| \leq g(\mathbf{x})$, by Lebesgue's dominated convergence theorem

$$\int_A f(\mathbf{x}, \mathbf{t}_0)\, dV_n(\mathbf{x}) = \lim_{m \to \infty} \int_A f(\mathbf{x}, \mathbf{t}_m)\, dV_n(\mathbf{x}).$$

Thus $\phi(\mathbf{t}_m) \to \phi(\mathbf{t}_0)$ as $m \to \infty$. Since this is true for every sequence in $B$ tending to $\mathbf{t}_0$, $\phi$ is continuous at $\mathbf{t}_0$. ∎

**Lemma 2.** *Let $l = 1$. Assume that $f$ and $\partial f/\partial t$ are continuous on $A \times B$ and satisfy*

$$|f(\mathbf{x}, t)| \leq g(\mathbf{x}), \quad \left|\frac{\partial f}{\partial t}(\mathbf{x}, t)\right| \leq h(\mathbf{x}) \quad \text{for every } \mathbf{x} \in A,\ t \in B,$$

*where $g$ and $h$ are integrable over $A$. Then*

$$\phi'(t) = \int_A \frac{\partial f}{\partial t}(\mathbf{x}, t)\, dV_n(\mathbf{x}), \quad t \in B. \tag{5-59}$$

*Proof.* Let $t_0 \in B$, and let $\delta > 0$ be such that $B$ contains the interval $(t_0 - \delta, t_0 + \delta)$. If $0 < u < \delta$, then $\partial f/\partial t$ is integrable over $A \times [t_0, t_0 + u]$. This set is $\sigma$-compact, and by the iterated integrals theorem,

$$\int_{t_0}^{t_0+u} dt \int_A \frac{\partial f}{\partial t}(\mathbf{x}, t)\, dV_n(\mathbf{x}) = \int_A \left\{\int_{t_0}^{t_0+u} \frac{\partial f}{\partial t}(\mathbf{x}, t)\, dt\right\} dV_n(\mathbf{x}). \tag{*}$$

By the fundamental theorem of calculus the inner integral on the right-hand side is $f(\mathbf{x}, t_0 + u) - f(\mathbf{x}, t_0)$. If we let $\psi(t)$ denote the right-hand side of (5-59), then (*) becomes

$$\int_{t_0}^{t_0+u} \psi(t)\, dt = \phi(t_0 + u) - \phi(t_0). \tag{**}$$

Similarly (**) is true when $-\delta < u < 0$. Lemma 1 implies that $\psi$ is continuous; hence by the fundamental theorem of calculus, $\psi(t_0) = \phi'(t_0)$. ∎

If, instead of an open set, $B$ is a closed interval $[a, b]$, then the proof of Lemma 2 shows that (5-59) is still true provided $\phi'(t)$ means the one-sided derivative at the endpoints.

**Theorem 18.** *Let $f$ and $\partial f/\partial t^j$, $j = 1, \ldots, l$, be continuous on $A \times B$ and satisfy*

$$|f(\mathbf{x}, \mathbf{t})| \leq g(\mathbf{x}), \quad \left|\frac{\partial f}{\partial t^j}(\mathbf{x}, \mathbf{t})\right| \leq h_j(\mathbf{x}) \text{ for every } \mathbf{x} \in A,\ \mathbf{t} \in B,$$

*where $g$ and $h_1, \ldots, h_l$ are integrable over $A$. Then the function $\phi$ in (5–58) is of class $C^{(1)}$ on $B$ and its partial derivatives are given by (5–57).*

*Proof.* Applying Lemma 2 with $t^1, \ldots, t^{j-1}, t^{j+1}, \ldots, t^l$ fixed, we get

$$\frac{\partial \phi}{\partial t^j}(\mathbf{t}) = \int_A \frac{\partial f}{\partial t^j}(\mathbf{x}, \mathbf{t})\, dV_n(\mathbf{x}), \qquad j = 1, \ldots, l.$$

Applying Lemma 1 to the function $\partial f/\partial t^j$, we find that $\partial \phi/\partial t^j$ is continuous on $B$ for each $j$. Hence $\phi$ is of class $C^{(1)}$. ▮

**Corollary.** *The conclusion of the theorem holds if $A$ is compact and $f$ together with $\partial f/\partial t^j$, $j = 1, \ldots, l$, are continuous on $A \times B$.*

*Proof.* Let $U$ be any neighborhood whose closure is contained in $B$. Since $A \times \text{cl}\, U$ is compact, $|f(\mathbf{x}, \mathbf{t})|$ and

$$\left|\frac{\partial f}{\partial t^j}(\mathbf{x}, \mathbf{t})\right|, \; j = 1, \ldots, l,$$

are bounded on $A \times U$ by some number $C$. Let $g = h_j = C$. By the theorem with $B$ replaced by $U$, $\phi$ is of class $C^{(1)}$ on $U$ and (5–57) holds there. Since this is true for every such $U$, $\phi$ is of class $C^{(1)}$ on $B$ and (5–57) holds for every $\mathbf{t} \in B$. ▮

**Example.** Let $\phi(t) = \int_1^\infty x^{-1} \exp(-xt)\, dx$, $t > 0$. Find $\phi'(t)$. Using (5–59)

$$\phi'(t) = -\int_1^\infty \exp(-xt)\, dx = -t^{-1} \exp(-t).$$

If $B$ is an interval $(a, \infty)$, $a > 0$, the hypotheses of Lemma 2 are satisfied with $g(x) = h(x) = \exp(-ax)$. The formula for $\phi'(t)$ is correct for all $t$ in any such interval, and hence for every $t > 0$.

**PROBLEMS**

1. Find $\phi'(t)$ if $\phi(t)$ is:

   (a) $\displaystyle\int_0^1 \log(x^2 + t^2)\, dx$, $t \neq 0$. (b) $\displaystyle\int_0^\pi x^{-1} \exp(xt) \sin x\, dx$.

2. Let $\phi(t) = \int_0^1 \log(2 - x^2t^2)\, dx$. Show that $\phi'(0) = 0$ and that $\phi$ is concave on the interval $(-1, 1)$.
3. For $x \in E^1$ let $\phi(x) = \int_0^\infty \exp(-t^2) \cos xt\, dt$. Show that $\phi'(x) = -\frac{1}{2}x\phi(x)$ and find $\phi(x)$.

4. *Leibnitz' rule.* Show that

$$\frac{d}{dt}\left[\int_{a(t)}^{b(t)} f(x, t)\, dx\right] = f[b(t), t]b'(t) - f[a(t), t]a'(t) + \int_{a(t)}^{b(t)} \frac{\partial f}{\partial t}(x, t)\, dx,$$

provided $f$ and $\partial f/\partial t$ are continuous on $[a_0, b_0] \times B$ where $B$ is open, that $a_0 \leq a(t) \leq b_0$ and $a_0 \leq b(t) \leq b_0$ for every $t \in B$, and that the functions $a, b$ are of class $C^{(1)}$. [*Hint:* Let $G(x, t) = \int_{a_0}^{x} f(s, t)\, ds$, so that $\partial G/\partial x = f$. Calculate the derivative of $G[b(t), t] - G[a(t), t]$.]

5. Let $\phi(t) = \int_{\log t}^{t} x^{-1} \exp(x^2t^2)\, dx$, $t > 1$. Find $\phi'(t)$.

6. Let $\phi(x, t) = \int_{x-ct}^{x+ct} f(s)\, ds$, where $c > 0$ and $f$ is of class $C^{(1)}$ on $E^1$. Show that $(\partial^2\phi/\partial t^2) = c^2(\partial^2\phi/\partial x^2)$.

7. Let $\phi(x, y) = \int_0^y dt \int_0^x f(s, t)\, ds$, $x > 0$, $y > 0$. Show that if $f$ is continuous on $\{(x, y) : x \geq 0, y \geq 0\}$, then $\partial^2\phi/\partial x\, \partial y = f$.

8. Let

$$\phi(x) = \int_0^{\infty} \exp\left(-t^2 - \frac{x^2}{t^2}\right) dt, \text{ for } x \in E^1.$$

(a) Show that $\phi(x) = \frac{1}{2}\sqrt{\pi} \exp(-2|x|)$ for all $x$. [*Hint:* For $x > 0$, show that $\phi'(x) = -2\phi(x)$ using the substitution $s = 1/t$.]

(b) Note that application of (5–59) gives a false result at $x = 0$. Why is this not surprising?

9. Let $\phi(t) = \int_0^{\infty} f(x, t)\, dx$, for $t > 0$, where $f(x, t) = \exp(-xt)x^{-1} \sin x$. Show that:

(a) $\phi'(t) = -1/(1 + t^2)$.

(b) $\phi(t) \to 0$ as $t \to +\infty$. [*Hint:* Apply the dominated convergence theorem with $f_\nu(x) = f(x, t_\nu)$ where $1 \leq t_1 \leq t_2 \leq \cdots$ and $t_\nu \to +\infty$ as $\nu \to \infty$.]

(c) $\displaystyle\lim_{r\to\infty} \int_0^r \frac{\sin x}{x}\, dx = \frac{\pi}{2}$. (d) $\displaystyle\int_0^{\infty} \left|\frac{\sin x}{x}\right| dx = +\infty$.

*Hints:* From (a) and (b), $\phi(t) = \pi/2 - \tan^{-1} t$. Integrate by parts to show that

$$\left|\int_r^{\infty} f(x, t)\, dx\right| \leq \frac{\exp(-rt)}{r}|\cos r| + \int_r^{\infty} \frac{dx}{x^2} \leq \frac{2}{r}.$$

By the dominated convergence theorem,

$$\lim_{t\to 0^+} \int_0^r f(x, t)\, dx = \int_0^r \frac{\sin x}{x}\, dx.$$

## *5-12 $L^p$-SPACES

Let $A$ be a measurable set of positive measure, and let $p$ be a number such that $p \geq 1$. The collection of all measurable real-valued functions $f$ with domain $A$ such that $|f|^p$ is integrable over $A$ will be denoted by $L^p(A)$. For instance, $L^1(A)$ is just the collection of all real-valued functions integrable over $A$.

By inequality (1–9),

$$|f(\mathbf{x}) + g(\mathbf{x})|^p \leq 2^{p-1}(|f(\mathbf{x})|^p + |g(\mathbf{x})|^p).$$

Hence if $|f|^p$ and $|g|^p$ are integrable over $A$, then $|f + g|^p$ is also integrable over $A$. This shows that the sum of two elements in $L^p(A)$ is also in $L^p(A)$. Clearly $cf \in L^p(A)$ if $f \in L^p(A)$ and $c$ is a real number. Thus $L^p(A)$ is a vector space over the real number field. The *p-norm* of a function $f \in L^p(A)$ is the number

$$\|f\|_p = \left(\int_A |f|^p \, dV_n\right)^{1/p}. \tag{5–60}$$

The $p$-norm has the following three properties:

(a) $\|f\|_p = 0$ if and only if $f(\mathbf{x}) = 0$ for almost all $\mathbf{x} \in A$.

(b) $\|cf\|_p = |c| \, \|f\|_p$ for every real $c$.

(c) $\|f + g\|_p \leq \|f\|_p + \|g\|_p$.

The proofs of (a) and (b) are left to the reader (Problem 4). Property (c) is called *Minkowski's inequality*. Let us defer the proof to p. 203. A finite dimensional version of Minkowski's inequality was given on p. 34.

Let us regard as equivalent any two functions whose values agree almost everywhere in $A$. Then (a), (b), and (c) state that $L^p(A)$ is a normed vector space (see Problem 6, Section A–6). The *distance* between two functions $f, g \in L^p(A)$ is $\|f - g\|_p$. It is called the distance *in mean of order p*. A sequence $f_1, f_2, \ldots$ converges to $f$ in mean of order $p$ if $\|f_m - f\|_p \to 0$ as $m \to \infty$. If for every $\epsilon > 0$ there exists $N$ such that $\|f_m - f_l\|_p < \epsilon$ for every $l, m \geq N$, then the sequence $f_1, f_2, \ldots$ is *Cauchy* in mean of order $p$.

**Theorem.** *Every Cauchy sequence $f_1, f_2, \ldots$ in $L^p(A)$ converges in mean of order $p$ to a limit $f \in L^p(A)$.*

This theorem is one of the remarkable features of the Lebesgue theory.

*Proof of Theorem.* Let $f_1, f_2, \ldots$ be a Cauchy sequence in $L^p(A)$. There is an increasing sequence of positive integers $N_1, N_2, \ldots$ such that $\|f_m - f_l\|_p < 2^{-k-k/p}$ for every $m, l \geq N_k$. Let $g_k = f_{N_k}$, and let

$$F(\mathbf{x}) = \sum_{k=1}^{\infty} 2^{kp} |g_k(\mathbf{x}) - g_{k+1}(\mathbf{x})|^p. \tag{*}$$

Since its terms are nonnegative, this series either converges or diverges to $+\infty$ for every $\mathbf{x} \in A$. But

$$\sum_{k=1}^{\infty} \int_A 2^{kp} |g_k - g_{k+1}|^p \, dV = \sum_{k=1}^{\infty} 2^{kp} (\|g_k - g_{k+1}\|_p)^p < \sum_{k=1}^{\infty} 2^{-k}.$$

Since the series on the right converges, so does the one on the left. Therefore $F$ is integrable over $A$ and $B = \{\mathbf{x} \in A : F(\mathbf{x}) = +\infty\}$ is a null set [Problem 8(a), p. 197]. Now each term of a nonnegative series is no more than the sum of the series. Applying this observation to (*), we find that for $\mathbf{x} \in A - B$

$$|g_k(\mathbf{x}) - g_{k+1}(\mathbf{x})| \leq 2^{-k}[F(\mathbf{x})]^{1/p}.$$

Therefore, for $s = 1, 2, \ldots$ and $\mathbf{x} \in A - B$,

$$|g_k(\mathbf{x}) - g_{k+s}(\mathbf{x})| \leq \sum_{r=0}^{s-1} |g_{k+r}(\mathbf{x}) - g_{k+r+1}(\mathbf{x})|$$

$$\leq [F(\mathbf{x})]^{1/p} \sum_{r=0}^{s-1} 2^{-k+r} < 2^{1-k}[F(\mathbf{x})]^{1/p}. \qquad (**)$$

Since the right-hand side approaches 0 as $k \to \infty$, the sequence of real numbers $g_1(\mathbf{x}), g_2(\mathbf{x}), \ldots$ is Cauchy. Let

$$f(\mathbf{x}) = \lim_{k \to \infty} g_k(\mathbf{x}), \quad \text{if } \mathbf{x} \in A - B,$$

and let $f(\mathbf{x}) = 0$ if $\mathbf{x} \in B$. Letting $s \to \infty$ in (**),

$$|g_k(\mathbf{x}) - f(\mathbf{x})| \leq 2^{1-k}[F(\mathbf{x})]^{1/p}$$

for $\mathbf{x} \in A - B$. Since $B$ is a null set,

$$\int_A |g_k - f|^p \, dV \leq 2^{(1-k)p} \int_A F \, dV.$$

Since $F$ is integrable over $A$, the right-hand side tends to 0. Therefore

$$\lim_{k \to \infty} \|g_k - f\|_p = 0.$$

If $m \geq N_k$, then $\|g_k - f_m\|_p < 2^{-k-k/p}$ (recall the definition of $g_k$). Using Minkowski's inequality

$$\|f_m - f\|_p \leq \|f_m - g_k\|_p + \|g_k - f\|_p.$$

Since the right-hand side tends to 0 as $k \to \infty$, this shows that

$$\lim_{m \to \infty} \|f_m - f\|_p = 0. \blacksquare$$

*Note:* The idea of convergent sequence makes sense in any metric space $S$. If every Cauchy sequence in $S$ converges, then $S$ is called a *complete* metric space. A normed vector space $\mathcal{V}$ which is complete is called a *Banach* space. The theorem above states that $L^p(A)$ is a Banach space.

If $p > 1$, then the number $p'$ such that

$$\frac{1}{p} + \frac{1}{p'} = 1$$

is called *conjugate* to $p$.

**Theorem.** *If $f \in L^p(A)$ and $g \in L^{p'}(A)$, then $fg$ is integrable over $A$ and*

$$\|fg\|_1 \leq \|f\|_p\|g\|_{p'} \qquad (\textit{Hölder's inequality}). \tag{5-61}$$

*Proof.* Let $\phi(t) = t^{1/p}$ for $t \geq 0$. Since $0 < 1/p < 1$ the function $\phi$ is concave. Hence $\phi(t) \leq \phi(1) + \phi'(1)(t - 1)$, or

$$t^{1/p} \leq 1 + \frac{1}{p}(t-1) = \frac{t}{p} + \frac{1}{p'}\cdot$$

Setting $t = u^p v^{-p'}$, where $v > 0$, we find since $1 - p' = -p'/p$ that

$$uv \leq \frac{u^p}{p} + \frac{v^{p'}}{p'}\cdot \tag{5-62}$$

Obviously this inequality also holds when $v = 0$.

If $\|f\|_p = 0$, then $f(\mathbf{x}) = 0$ almost everywhere in $A$ and both sides of Hölder's inequality are 0. Similarly both sides are 0 if $\|g\|_{p'} = 0$. Suppose that $\|f\|_p > 0$, $\|g\|_{p'} > 0$, and let

$$\tilde{f} = (1/\|f\|_p)f, \qquad \tilde{g} = (1/\|g\|_{p'})g.$$

Then

$$\int |\tilde{f}|^p\, dV = \int |\tilde{g}|^{p'}\, dV = 1,$$

and setting $u = |\tilde{f}(\mathbf{x})|$, $v = |\tilde{g}(\mathbf{x})|$ in (5-62)

$$\int_A |\tilde{f}(\mathbf{x})|\,|\tilde{g}(\mathbf{x})|\, dV_n(\mathbf{x}) \leq \frac{1}{p} + \frac{1}{p'} = 1.$$

But the left-hand side is $\|fg\|_1/\|f\|_p\|g\|_{p'}$. This proves Hölder's inequality. ∎

*Note:* The finite dimensional version of Hölder's inequality (Problem 8, p. 134) expresses the fact that the $p$-norm on $E^n$ and the $p'$-norm on the dual space $(E^n)^*$ are dually related. There is an infinite dimensional analog which we state without proof. Let $[L^p(A)]'$ denote the set of all real-valued linear functions on $L^p(A)$ which are continuous. On $[L^p(A)]'$ there is defined a dual norm, just as in the finite dimensional case. Then $[L^p(A)]'$ is isomorphic with $L^{p'}(A)$, and the dual norm is just the $p'$-norm. (See [15], p. 211.)

*Proof of Minkowski's inequality.*

$$\int_A |f+g|^p\, dV \leq \int_A |f|\,|f+g|^{p-1}\, dV + \int_A |g|\,|f+g|^{p-1}\, dV. \tag{*}$$

By Hölder's inequality,

$$\int_A |f|\,|f+g|^{p-1}\, dV \leq \left(\int_A |f|^p\, dV\right)^{1/p} \left(\int_A |f+g|^{(p-1)p'}\, dV\right)^{1/p'}.$$

But $(p-1)p' = p$. Estimating similarly the last term in (*), we get

$$\int_A |f+g|^p\,dV \leq \left(\|f\|_p + \|g\|_p\right)\left(\int_A |f+g|^p\,dV\right)^{1/p'}.$$

If $\|f+g\|_p = 0$, both sides are 0. Otherwise we divide both sides by $(\int |f+g|^p\,dV)^{1/p'}$. Since $1 - 1/p' = 1/p$, we get Minkowski's inequality. ▌

If $p = 1$, then (formally) $p' = \infty$. Let us call $f$ *essentially bounded* if $f$ is equivalent to a bounded function $g$ [equivalent means that $f(\mathbf{x}) = g(\mathbf{x})$ almost everywhere in $A$]. Let $L^\infty(A)$ be the collection of all essentially bounded measurable functions. For $f \in L^\infty(A)$ let $\|f\|_\infty = \text{ess sup } \{|f(\mathbf{x})| : \mathbf{x} \in A\}$, where the right-hand side means $\inf \{(\sup \{|g(\mathbf{x})| : \mathbf{x} \in A\}) : g$ is equivalent to $f\}$. Then Hölder's inequality is still true when $p = 1$.

If $p = 2$, then $p' = 2$. In $L^2(A)$ let us introduce an inner product $\cdot$ as follows:

$$f \cdot g = \int_A fg\,dV_n.$$

Then $f \cdot f = (\|f\|_2)^2$. Moreover $|f \cdot g| \leq \|fg\|_1$ and hence

$$|f \cdot g| \leq \|f\|_2 \|g\|_2. \tag{5-63}$$

This formula corresponds to Cauchy's inequality in $E^n$. In fact, the space $L^2(A)$ is an infinite dimensional analog of euclidean $E^n$.

An *inner product space* $H$ is a vector space with an inner product $\cdot$ satisfying a list of axioms corresponding to those on p. 6. If $H$ is infinite dimensional and complete, then $H$ is a *Hilbert space*. The preceding theorem shows that $L^2(A)$ is a Hilbert space.

## PROBLEMS

1. Let $f(\mathbf{x}) = |\mathbf{x}|^{-\alpha}$. Show that if $A$ is the unit $n$-ball, then $f \in L^p(A)$ for $p < n/\alpha$ but not for $p \geq n/\alpha$. [*Hint:* See Section 5-6, Example (4).]
2. Let $f(x) = x^{-1}(\log x)^{-2}$, $A = (0, \frac{1}{2})$. Show that $f \in L^p(A)$ only for $p = 1$.
3. Let $1 \leq q < p$. Using Hölder's inequality show that if $A$ has finite measure, then $f \in L^p(A)$ implies that $f \in L^q(A)$. Give an example to show that it is necessary to assume $A$ has finite measure. [*Hint:* Apply Hölder's inequality to the functions $|f|^q$ and 1 with $p$ replaced by $p/q$.]
4. Prove properties (a) and (b) (see p. 201) of the $p$-norm.

CHAPTER 6

# Exterior Algebra and Differential Calculus

In this chapter we shall introduce the calculus of differential forms, which also goes by the name "exterior differential calculus." We recall from Section 2–6 that a differential form of degree 1 is a covector-valued function. In order to define differential forms of higher degree $r > 1$ we first introduce multicovectors of degree $r$. For brevity, they are called $r$-covectors. An $r$-covector is an alternating, multilinear function with domain the $r$-fold cartesian product $E^n \times \cdots \times E^n$. It turns out that the $r$-covectors form a vector space of dimension $\binom{n}{r}$, which is denoted by $(E_r^n)^*$.

Dually, an alternating, multilinear function with domain the $r$-fold cartesian product $(E^n)^* \times \cdots \times (E^n)^*$ is called an $r$-vector. The $r$-vectors form a vector space $E_r^n$, whose dual space turns out to be $(E_r^n)^*$.

There is a natural product for multicovectors called the exterior product and denoted by the symbol $\wedge$. If $\boldsymbol{\omega}$ is an $r$-covector and $\boldsymbol{\zeta}$ an $s$-covector, then $\boldsymbol{\omega} \wedge \boldsymbol{\zeta}$ is a certain $(r+s)$-covector. Dually, the exterior product of an $r$-vector $\boldsymbol{\alpha}$ with an $s$-vector $\boldsymbol{\beta}$ is an $(r+s)$-vector $\boldsymbol{\alpha} \wedge \boldsymbol{\beta}$. The exterior product is associative, and it is commutative except for a possible sign change (Proposition 20).

Certain multivectors, called decomposable, have an interesting geometric interpretation. An $r$-vector $\boldsymbol{\alpha}$ is decomposable if there are 1-vectors $\mathbf{h}_1, \ldots, \mathbf{h}_r$ such that $\boldsymbol{\alpha} = \mathbf{h}_1 \wedge \cdots \wedge \mathbf{h}_r$. It turns out (Theorem 19) that if $\boldsymbol{\alpha} \neq \mathbf{0}$, then $\mathbf{h}_1, \ldots, \mathbf{h}_r$ span an $r$-dimensional vector subspace $P$ of $E^n$. With $\boldsymbol{\alpha}$ is associated an orientation of $P$. If two of the vectors $\mathbf{h}_1, \ldots, \mathbf{h}_r$ are interchanged, then $\boldsymbol{\alpha}$ changes sign and the orientation of $P$ changes. The norm $|\boldsymbol{\alpha}|$ of a decomposable $r$-vector $\boldsymbol{\alpha}$ equals the $r$-dimensional measure of a certain $r$-parallelepiped.

A differential form of degree $r$ (called for brevity an $r$-form) is defined as an $r$-covector-valued function.

Every $r$-form $\boldsymbol{\omega}$ of class $C^{(1)}$ has an exterior differential $d\boldsymbol{\omega}$, which is a form of degree $r+1$. The usual formulas for the differentials of sums and products remain true except for a possible sign change in the product rule. Another important fact is that $d(d\boldsymbol{\omega}) = \mathbf{0}$ for any form $\boldsymbol{\omega}$ of class $C^{(2)}$. Besides its differential, $\boldsymbol{\omega}$ has a codifferential $\tilde{d}\boldsymbol{\omega}$ which is a form of degree $r-1$. In the next chapter the codifferential is used only for $r = 1$, in which case it becomes the divergence. In the last section of the chapter the basic formulas of vector analysis in $E^3$ are derived.

## 6–1 ALTERNATING MULTILINEAR FUNCTIONS

Let us call a real-valued function $L$ with domain $E^n$ *1-linear* if $L$ is linear. For any integer $r > 1$ we shall now consider functions called $r$-linear. For simplicity let us first consider $r = 2$. Let $B$ be a real-valued function with domain the cartesian product $E^n \times E^n$. The elements of $E^n \times E^n$ are pairs of vectors, denoted by $(\mathbf{h}, \mathbf{k})$. We recall from p. 29 that the function $B$ is *bilinear* if $B(\mathbf{h},\ )$ and $B(\ ,\mathbf{k})$ are linear functions for every $(\mathbf{h}, \mathbf{k})$. It was shown there that if $B$ is bilinear and

$$\omega_{ij} = B(\mathbf{e}_i, \mathbf{e}_j), \qquad i, j = 1, \ldots, n, \tag{6–1a}$$

then for every $(\mathbf{h}, \mathbf{k})$

$$B(\mathbf{h}, \mathbf{k}) = \sum_{i,j=1}^{n} \omega_{ij} h^i k^j. \tag{6–2a}$$

In this chapter we are interested in a special class of $r$-linear functions, called alternating. For $r = 2$, $B$ is *alternating* if $B(\mathbf{h}, \mathbf{k}) = -B(\mathbf{k}, \mathbf{h})$ for every $(\mathbf{h}, \mathbf{k})$. If $B$ is bilinear and alternating, then $\omega_{ij} = -\omega_{ji}$, and in particular $\omega_{ii} = 0$. Formula (6–2a) can be rewritten

$$B(\mathbf{h}, \mathbf{k}) = \sum_{i<j} (\omega_{ij} h^i k^j + \omega_{ji} h^j k^i),$$

or

$$B(\mathbf{h}, \mathbf{k}) = \sum_{i<j} \omega_{ij} (h^i k^j - h^j k^i). \tag{6–3}$$

Conversely, given $n(n-1)/2$ numbers $\omega_{ij}$, $i < j$, formula (6–3) defines an alternating bilinear function.

Similarly, for any $r \geq 2$ let $M$ be a real-valued function with domain the $r$-fold cartesian product $E^n \times \cdots \times E^n$. The elements of $E^n \times \cdots \times E^n$ are $r$-tuples of vectors, denoted by $(\mathbf{h}_1, \ldots, \mathbf{h}_r)$.

**Definition.** The function $M$ is *multilinear of degree r* if for each $l = 1, \ldots, r$ and $\mathbf{h}_1, \ldots, \mathbf{h}_{l-1}, \mathbf{h}_{l+1}, \ldots, \mathbf{h}_r$ the function $M(\mathbf{h}_1, \ldots, \mathbf{h}_{l-1},\ , \mathbf{h}_{l+1}, \ldots, \mathbf{h}_r)$ is linear.

For brevity we write *r-linear* instead of multilinear of degree $r$. When $r = 2$ we wrote $\mathbf{h}_1 = \mathbf{h}$, $\mathbf{h}_2 = \mathbf{k}$. The new definition agrees for $r = 2$ with the definition of bilinear function. The formula which generalizes (6–2a) to multilinear functions is

$$M(\mathbf{h}_1, \ldots, \mathbf{h}_r) = \sum_{i_1,\ldots,i_r=1}^{n} \omega_{i_1\cdots i_r} h_1^{i_1} \cdots h_r^{i_r}, \tag{6–2b}$$

where

$$\omega_{i_1\cdots i_r} = M(\mathbf{e}_{i_1}, \ldots, \mathbf{e}_{i_r}). \tag{6–1b}$$

This is proved by induction on $r$.

**Interchanges.** Let $S$ be some set. For our purposes we shall take either $S = E^n$ or $S = \{1, 2, \ldots, n\}$. If $(p_1, \ldots, p_r)$ and $(p'_1, \ldots, p'_r)$ are $r$-tuples of elements of $S$, let us say that the second $r$-tuple is obtained from the first by interchanging $p_s$ and $p_t$ if $p'_s = p_t$, $p'_t = p_s$, and $p'_l = p_l$ for $l \neq s, t$.

**Examples.** The triple of vectors $(\mathbf{h}_3, \mathbf{h}_2, \mathbf{h}_1)$ is obtained from $(\mathbf{h}_1, \mathbf{h}_2, \mathbf{h}_3)$ by interchanging $\mathbf{h}_3$ and $\mathbf{h}_1$. The 4-tuple of integers (1, 5, 3, 7) is obtained from the 4-tuple (1, 7, 3, 5) by interchanging 5 and 7.

**Definition.** An $r$-linear function $M$ is *alternating* if $M(\mathbf{h}_1, \ldots, \mathbf{h}_r)$ changes sign whenever two vectors in an $r$-tuple $(\mathbf{h}_1, \ldots, \mathbf{h}_r)$ are interchanged.

We know that the sum of two linear functions is a linear function. From this fact and the definition of multilinear function, the sum $M + N$ of two $r$-linear functions $M$ and $N$ is $r$-linear. If $M$ and $N$ are alternating, then $M + N$ is alternating. Similarly, if $c$ is a scalar then $cM$ is $r$-linear when $M$ is $r$-linear and alternating when $M$ is alternating.

Let $(E_r^n)^*$ denote the set of all alternating, $r$-linear functions with domain $E^n \times \cdots \times E^n$. By the remarks just made, $(E_r^n)^*$ satisfies the axioms for a vector space. Let us now prove two propositions which enable us to find the dimension of $(E_r^n)^*$ and a basis for it.

An $r$-tuple $(\mathbf{h}_1, \ldots, \mathbf{h}_r)$ is called *linearly dependent* if there exist scalars $c^1, \ldots, c^r$, not all 0, such that $c^1\mathbf{h}_1 + \cdots + c^r\mathbf{h}_r = \mathbf{0}$.

**Proposition 18.** *Let $M$ be r-linear and alternating. If $(\mathbf{h}_1, \ldots, \mathbf{h}_r)$ is a linearly dependent r-tuple, then $M(\mathbf{h}_1, \ldots, \mathbf{h}_r) = 0$.*

*Proof.* First of all, the conclusion is true if some vector in the $r$-tuple is repeated. For instance, suppose that $\mathbf{h}_1 = \mathbf{h}_2$. Since $M$ is alternating,

$$M(\mathbf{h}_1, \mathbf{h}_2, \mathbf{h}_3, \ldots, \mathbf{h}_r) = -M(\mathbf{h}_2, \mathbf{h}_1, \mathbf{h}_3, \ldots, \mathbf{h}_r).$$

Then $M(\mathbf{h}_1, \mathbf{h}_1, \mathbf{h}_3, \ldots, \mathbf{h}_r)$ is its own negative, and must be 0.

Suppose for instance that $\mathbf{h}_r$ is a linear combination of the vectors preceding it,

$$\mathbf{h}_r = c^1\mathbf{h}_1 + \cdots + c^{r-1}\mathbf{h}_{r-1}.$$

Since $M(\mathbf{h}_1, \ldots, \mathbf{h}_{r-1}, \;)$ is a linear function,

$$M(\mathbf{h}_1, \ldots, \mathbf{h}_r) = \sum_{l=1}^{r-1} c^l M(\mathbf{h}_1, \ldots, \mathbf{h}_{r-1}, \mathbf{h}_l).$$

In the $l$th term on the right-hand side, the vector $\mathbf{h}_l$ is repeated, and hence each term is 0. Thus $M(\mathbf{h}_1, \ldots, \mathbf{h}_r) = 0$. ▮

For any $r \geq 2$ there is the trivial alternating $r$-linear function $\mathbf{0}$, which has the value 0 for every $r$-tuple $(\mathbf{h}_1, \ldots, \mathbf{h}_r)$. If $r > n$, then $(\mathbf{h}_1, \ldots, \mathbf{h}_r)$ must be linearly dependent and from the proposition we get the following.

**Corollary.** *If $r > n$, then $\mathbf{0}$ is the only alternating $r$-linear function.*

Therefore let us suppose that $r \leq n$. It is now convenient to introduce some more notation. The letter $\lambda$ will denote an $r$-tuple of integers,

$$\lambda = (i_1, \ldots, i_r),$$

where $1 \leq i_k \leq n$ for each $k = 1, \ldots, r$. There are $n^r$ such $r$-tuples of integers. If $i_1 < \cdots < i_r$, then $\lambda$ is called an *increasing* $r$-tuple. There are $\binom{n}{r}$ increasing $r$-tuples, where $\binom{n}{r} = n!/r!(n-r)!$ is a binomial coefficient. We write $\sum_\lambda$ for a sum over all $r$-tuples and $\sum_{[\lambda]}$ for a sum over all increasing $r$-tuples.

The following generalization of the Kronecker symbol $\delta_j^i$ will be used. Let $\lambda = (i_1, \ldots, i_r)$, $\mu = (j_1, \ldots, j_r)$ be $r$-tuples of integers. Then $\delta_{j_l}^{i_k}$ is an element of an $r \times r$ matrix; and is 1 if $i_k = j_l$, 0 otherwise. Let

$$\delta_\mu^\lambda = \det (\delta_{j_l}^{i_k}).$$

The important properties of $\delta_\mu^\lambda$ are:

(1) *If no integer is repeated in the r-tuple $\lambda$ and $\mu = \lambda$, then $\delta_\mu^\lambda = 1$.*

In this case $i_k = j_l$ if and only if $k = l$. Hence $\delta_\mu^\lambda = \det (\delta_l^k) = 1$.

(2) *If no integer is repeated in the r-tuple $\mu$ and $\lambda$ is obtained from $\mu$ by $p$ interchanges, then $\delta_\mu^\lambda = (-1)^p$.*

Each interchange of elements of $\mu$ interchanges two column vectors of the matrix $(\delta_{j_l}^{i_k})$ and changes the sign of the determinant. Therefore (2) follows from (1).

(3) *In all other cases, $\delta_\mu^\lambda = 0$.*

If some integer is repeated in $\mu$, then two column vectors of the matrix are the same and the determinant is 0. If the integers $j_1, \ldots, j_r$ are distinct and some $i_k$ does not appear among them, then the $k$th row covector of the matrix is $\mathbf{0}$ and the determinant is 0.

Now let $M$ be an alternating $r$-linear function. For brevity let us set

$$\omega_\lambda = \omega_{i_1 \cdots i_r}.$$

Sometimes we will still write $\omega_{i_1 \cdots i_r}$ rather than $\omega_\lambda$, particularly when $r \leq 3$ or $r = n$. If $\lambda$ is obtained from $\mu$ by one interchange, then $\omega_\lambda = -\omega_\mu$. In particular, $\omega_\lambda = 0$ if any integer is repeated. If $\lambda$ is obtained from $\mu$ by $p$ interchanges, then $\omega_\mu = (-1)^p \omega_\lambda = \delta^\lambda_\mu \omega_\lambda$.

If $\mu$ has no repetitions, then exactly one increasing $\lambda$ is obtained from $\mu$ by interchanges. Hence for every $\mu$,

$$\omega_\mu = \sum_{[\lambda]} \omega_\lambda \delta^\lambda_\mu, \tag{6–4}$$

where at most one term on the right-hand side is different from 0.

**Examples.** Let $n = 5$, $r = 4$. Then $\omega_{1231} = 0$ since 1 is repeated in the 4-tuple $\lambda = (1, 2, 3, 1)$. Since $(2, 3, 4, 5)$ is obtained from $(5, 4, 2, 3)$ by an odd number of interchanges, $\omega_{2345} = -\omega_{5423}$.

Let us now consider some particular elements of the space $(E^n_r)^*$. For each $r$-tuple $\lambda = (i_1, \ldots, i_r)$ let $\mathbf{e}^\lambda$ be the function such that

$$\mathbf{e}^\lambda(\mathbf{h}_1, \ldots, \mathbf{h}_r) = \det (h^{i_k}_l) \tag{6–5a}$$

for every $r$-tuple of vectors $(\mathbf{h}_1, \ldots, \mathbf{h}_r)$. Note that the $r \times r$ matrix $(h^{i_k}_l)$ is formed from rows $i_1, \ldots, i_r$ of the $n \times r$ matrix $(h^i_l)$ which has $\mathbf{h}_1, \ldots, \mathbf{h}_r$ as column vectors. By properties of determinants, $\mathbf{e}^\lambda$ is $r$-linear and alternating. Thus $\mathbf{e}^\lambda$ belongs to $(E^n_r)^*$.

Taking in particular $\mathbf{h}_1, \ldots, \mathbf{h}_r$ to be standard basis vectors, $\mathbf{h}_l = \mathbf{e}_{j_l}$ for $l = 1, \ldots, r$, we obtain in (6–5a) the matrix $(\delta^{i_k}_{j_l})$ whose determinant is $\delta^\lambda_\mu$. Thus

$$\mathbf{e}^\lambda(\mathbf{e}_{j_1}, \ldots, \mathbf{e}_{j_r}) = \delta^\lambda_\mu. \tag{6–6}$$

If $\lambda$ is obtained from $\mu$ by an interchange, then two row covectors of the matrix $(h^{i_k}_l)$ in (6–5a) are interchanged. The determinant changes sign. Hence

$$\mathbf{e}^\lambda(\mathbf{h}_1, \ldots, \mathbf{h}_r) = -\mathbf{e}^\mu(\mathbf{h}_1, \ldots, \mathbf{h}_r)$$

for every $r$-tuple $(\mathbf{h}_1, \ldots, \mathbf{h}_r)$, which means that $\mathbf{e}^\lambda = -\mathbf{e}^\mu$. In particular, $\mathbf{e}^\lambda = \mathbf{0}$ if $\lambda$ has any repetitions. If $\lambda$ is obtained from $\mu$ by $p$ interchanges, then $\mathbf{e}^\lambda = (-1)^p \mathbf{e}^\mu$.

Let us make the convention that $\mathbf{e}^\lambda = \mathbf{0}$ in case $r > n$. This is useful in defining the exterior product in the next section.

When $r = 2$ and $\lambda = (i, j)$, $\mathbf{e}^{ij}(\mathbf{h}, \mathbf{k}) = h^i k^j - h^j k^i$. If $B$ is bilinear and alternating, then

$$B = \sum_{i<j} \omega_{ij} \mathbf{e}^{ij},$$

since by formula (6–3) both sides have the same value for each pair of vectors $(\mathbf{h}, \mathbf{k})$. This is a particular case of the following.

**Proposition 19.** ($r \leq n$.) *Let $M$ be $r$-linear and alternating. Then*

$$M = \sum_{[\lambda]} \omega_\lambda \mathbf{e}^\lambda, \tag{6–7}$$

*where the numbers $\omega_\lambda$ are given by* (6–1b).

*Proof.* Let $\widetilde{M}$ equal the right-hand side of (6–7). For each $\mu = (j_1, \ldots, j_r)$,

$$\widetilde{M}(\mathbf{e}_{j_1}, \ldots, \mathbf{e}_{j_r}) = \sum_{[\lambda]} \omega_\lambda \mathbf{e}^\lambda(\mathbf{e}_{j_1}, \ldots, \mathbf{e}_{j_r}).$$

From (6–4) and (6–6),

$$\widetilde{M}(\mathbf{e}_{j_1}, \ldots, \mathbf{e}_{j_r}) = \sum_{[\lambda]} \omega_\lambda \delta^\lambda_\mu = \omega_\mu.$$

But $M$ and $\widetilde{M}$ are $r$-linear and have the same value $\omega_\mu$ at $(\mathbf{e}_{j_1}, \ldots, \mathbf{e}_{j_r})$ for each $\mu$. By (6–2b) $M = \widetilde{M}$. ▮

**PROBLEMS**

1. Let $n = 5$. Find

$$\delta^{15}_{51}, \quad \delta^{25}_{51}, \quad \delta^{142}_{214}, \quad \delta^{525}_{255}, \quad \delta^{345}_{425}.$$

2. Let $n = 4$, $r = 3$, $\omega_{123} = 2$, $\omega_{134} = -1$, and $\omega_\lambda = 0$ for every other increasing triple $\lambda$. Find $M(\mathbf{e}_4, \mathbf{e}_1 - \mathbf{e}_3, \mathbf{e}_2 + \mathbf{e}_3)$.
3. Show that:

(a) $\delta^\lambda_\mu = \delta^\mu_\lambda$. (b) $\delta^\lambda_\nu = \sum_{[\mu]} \delta^\lambda_\mu \delta^\mu_\nu = \frac{1}{r!} \sum_\mu \delta^\lambda_\mu \delta^\mu_\nu$.

(c) $\mathbf{e}^\lambda = \sum_{[\mu]} \delta^\lambda_\mu \mathbf{e}^\mu = \frac{1}{r!} \sum_\mu \delta^\lambda_\mu \mathbf{e}^\mu$.

[*Hint for* (c): Use (b) and (6–6).]

4. Let $M$ be $r$-linear, not necessarily alternating. Let $\omega_\lambda$ be as in (6–1b) and $\tilde{\omega}_\mu = (1/r!)\sum_\lambda \omega_\lambda \delta^\lambda_\mu$. The function $M_1 = \sum_{[\lambda]} \tilde{\omega}_\lambda \mathbf{e}^\lambda$ is $r$-linear and alternating.
   (a) Show that $M_1 = (1/r!)\sum_\mu \tilde{\omega}_\mu \mathbf{e}^\mu$. [*Hint:* $\tilde{\omega}_\mu = \sum_{[\lambda]} \tilde{\omega}_\lambda \delta^\lambda_\mu$; use Problem 3(c).]
   (b) Show that if $M$ is alternating, then $\tilde{\omega}_\mu = \omega_\mu$ and hence $M_1 = M$.

## 6–2 MULTICOVECTORS

Let us now introduce a different name and a different notation for alternating, multilinear functions.

**Definition.** A *multicovector of degree* $r$ is an alternating $r$-linear function with domain the $r$-fold cartesian product $E^n \times \cdots \times E^n$.

For brevity, multicovectors of degree $r$ are called *$r$-covectors*. From now on multicovectors will ordinarily be denoted by the Greek letters $\boldsymbol{\omega}$ or $\boldsymbol{\zeta}$ rather than $M$ as in the previous section.

We observed in the last section that the set $(E_r^n)^*$ of all $r$-covectors satisfies the axioms for a vector space. When $r > n$, its only element is $\mathbf{0}$ by Proposition 18. When $1 \leq r \leq n$, Proposition 19 states that if $\boldsymbol{\omega}$ is any $r$-covector, then

$$\boldsymbol{\omega} = \sum_{[\lambda]} \omega_\lambda \mathbf{e}^\lambda. \tag{6-8}$$

Therefore the $r$-covectors $\mathbf{e}^\lambda$ with $\lambda$ increasing span $(E_r^n)^*$. These $r$-covectors form a linearly independent set (Problem 7), which is therefore a basis for $(E_r^n)^*$. It is called the *standard basis*. The number $\omega_\lambda$ is the *component* of $\boldsymbol{\omega}$ with respect to the basis element $\mathbf{e}^\lambda$. Since there are $\binom{n}{r}$ increasing $r$-tuples of integers between 1 and $n$, $(E_r^n)^*$ has dimension $\binom{n}{r}$.

Every 1-linear function is alternating. Thus a 1-covector is just a covector, and $(E_1^n)^* = (E^n)^*$ is the dual space of $E^n$. If we identify the 1-tuple $(i)$ with $i$, then the standard basis 1-covectors $\mathbf{e}^1, \ldots, \mathbf{e}^n$ are just those introduced in Section 1–3. As in previous chapters we shall use the letters $\mathbf{a}, \mathbf{b}$ to denote 1-covectors.

If $r = n$, then the $n$-covector $\mathbf{e}^{1 \cdots n}$ is essentially the determinant function. Its value at $(\mathbf{h}_1, \ldots, \mathbf{h}_n)$ is $\det(h_l^k)$, which is the determinant of the $n \times n$ matrix with column vectors $\mathbf{h}_1, \ldots, \mathbf{h}_n$. Since $(E_n^n)^*$ is one-dimensional, every $n$-covector has the form $\boldsymbol{\omega} = c\mathbf{e}^{1 \cdots n}$ where $c = \omega_{1 \cdots n}$.

**Example.** Let $n = 5$, $r = 3$, and $\boldsymbol{\omega} = 6\mathbf{e}^{145} - 2\mathbf{e}^{431} - \mathbf{e}^{514}$. The increasing triple (1, 4, 5) is obtained from (5, 1, 4) by an even number of interchanges. Hence $\mathbf{e}^{514} = \mathbf{e}^{145}$. The increasing triple (1, 3, 4) is obtained from (4, 3, 1) by one interchange. Hence $\mathbf{e}^{431} = -\mathbf{e}^{134}$, and $\boldsymbol{\omega} = 2\mathbf{e}^{134} + 5\mathbf{e}^{145}$. This expresses $\boldsymbol{\omega}$ as a linear combination of the standard basis 3-covectors. The components of $\boldsymbol{\omega}$ are $\omega_{134} = 2$, $\omega_{145} = 5$, and $\omega_\lambda = 0$ for every other increasing triple $\lambda$.

**Products.** In $(E_r^n)^*$ we define the *euclidean inner product*

$$\boldsymbol{\omega} \cdot \boldsymbol{\zeta} = \sum_{[\lambda]} \omega_\lambda \zeta_\lambda$$

and set $|\boldsymbol{\omega}|^2 = \boldsymbol{\omega} \cdot \boldsymbol{\omega}$. The standard basis elements are orthonormal with respect to this inner product.

Another important product is the exterior product, denoted by the symbol $\wedge$. The exterior product of an $r$-covector and an $s$-covector is an $(r + s)$-covector, defined as follows: If

$$\lambda = (i_1, \ldots, i_r), \qquad \nu = (j_1, \ldots, j_s),$$

let us write $\lambda, \nu$ for the $(r + s)$-tuple

$$(i_1, \ldots, i_r, j_1, \ldots, j_s).$$

**Definition.** Let $1 \leq r \leq n$, $1 \leq s \leq n$. If $\lambda$ and $\nu$ are increasing, then

$$\mathbf{e}^\lambda \wedge \mathbf{e}^\nu = \mathbf{e}^{\lambda, \nu}. \tag{6-9}$$

If $\boldsymbol{\omega}$ is an $r$-covector and $\boldsymbol{\zeta}$ is an $s$-covector, with respective components $\omega_\lambda$, $\zeta_\nu$, then

$$\boldsymbol{\omega} \wedge \boldsymbol{\zeta} = \sum_{[\lambda][\nu]} \omega_\lambda \zeta_\nu \mathbf{e}^\lambda \wedge \mathbf{e}^\nu.$$

Note that if $r + s > n$ then $\boldsymbol{\omega} \wedge \boldsymbol{\zeta}$, being an $(r + s)$-covector, must be $\mathbf{0}$.

**Examples.** Let $n = 4$. Then $\mathbf{e}^{12} \wedge \mathbf{e}^{34} = \mathbf{e}^{1234}$.

$$\mathbf{e}^3 \wedge \mathbf{e}^{124} = \mathbf{e}^{3124} = \mathbf{e}^{1234}, \qquad \mathbf{e}^{14} \wedge \mathbf{e}^{24} = \mathbf{e}^{1424} = \mathbf{0},$$

since the integer 4 is repeated.

**Proposition 20.** *The exterior product has the following properties:*

(1) $(\boldsymbol{\omega} + \boldsymbol{\zeta}) \wedge \boldsymbol{\eta} = (\boldsymbol{\omega} \wedge \boldsymbol{\eta}) + (\boldsymbol{\zeta} \wedge \boldsymbol{\eta})$.

(2) $(c\boldsymbol{\omega}) \wedge \boldsymbol{\zeta} = c(\boldsymbol{\omega} \wedge \boldsymbol{\zeta})$.

(3) $\boldsymbol{\zeta} \wedge \boldsymbol{\omega} = (-1)^{rs}\boldsymbol{\omega} \wedge \boldsymbol{\zeta}$, *if* $\boldsymbol{\omega}$ *has degree* $r$ *and* $\boldsymbol{\zeta}$ *has degree* $s$.

(4) $(\boldsymbol{\zeta} \wedge \boldsymbol{\omega}) \wedge \boldsymbol{\eta} = \boldsymbol{\zeta} \wedge (\boldsymbol{\omega} \wedge \boldsymbol{\eta})$.

*Proof.* The proof of (1) and (2) is almost immediate from the definition and is left to the reader (Problem 8). To prove (3),

$$\nu, \lambda = (j_1, \ldots, j_s, i_1, \ldots, i_r).$$

By $s$ interchanges we may bring $i_1$ to the left past $j_1, \ldots, j_s$. Similarly, $s$ interchanges bring each of $i_2, \ldots, i_r$ in turn past $j_1, \ldots, j_s$. Thus $\lambda, \nu$ is obtained from $\nu, \lambda$ by $rs$ interchanges, and $\mathbf{e}^{\nu,\lambda} = (-1)^{rs}\mathbf{e}^{\lambda,\nu}$. Hence

$$\boldsymbol{\zeta} \wedge \boldsymbol{\omega} = \sum_{[\nu][\lambda]} \zeta_\nu \omega_\lambda \mathbf{e}^{\nu,\lambda} = (-1)^{rs} \sum_{[\lambda][\nu]} \omega_\lambda \zeta_\nu \mathbf{e}^{\lambda,\nu},$$

which proves (3).

Let us first prove the associative law (4) for basis elements. Let $\lambda = (i_1, \ldots, i_r)$, $\nu = (j_1, \ldots, j_s)$, and $\rho = (k_1, \ldots, k_t)$ be increasing $r$-, $s$-, and $t$-tuples, respectively. Let

$$\lambda, \nu, \rho = (i_1, \ldots, i_r, j_1, \ldots, j_s, k_1, \ldots, k_t).$$

Let us show that

$$\mathbf{e}^{\lambda,\nu,\rho} = (\mathbf{e}^\lambda \wedge \mathbf{e}^\nu) \wedge \mathbf{e}^\rho.$$

If some integer is repeated in the $(r + s)$-tuple $\lambda, \nu$, then both sides are $\mathbf{0}$. If no integer is repeated, then

$$(\mathbf{e}^\lambda \wedge \mathbf{e}^\nu) \wedge \mathbf{e}^\rho = \mathbf{e}^{\lambda,\nu} \wedge \mathbf{e}^\rho = (-1)^p \mathbf{e}^\tau \wedge \mathbf{e}^\rho = (-1)^p \mathbf{e}^{\tau,\rho},$$

where $\tau$ is an increasing $(r + s)$-tuple obtained from $\lambda, \nu$ by $p$ interchanges.

These same $p$ interchanges change the $(r + s + t)$-tuple $\lambda, \nu, \rho$ into $\tau, \rho$. Hence

$$\mathbf{e}^{\lambda,\nu,\rho} = (-1)^p \mathbf{e}^{\tau,\rho} = (\mathbf{e}^\lambda \wedge \mathbf{e}^\nu) \wedge \mathbf{e}^\rho.$$

Similarly $\mathbf{e}^{\lambda,\nu,\rho} = \mathbf{e}^\lambda \wedge (\mathbf{e}^\nu \wedge \mathbf{e}^\rho)$, and hence

$$(\mathbf{e}^\lambda \wedge \mathbf{e}^\nu) \wedge \mathbf{e}^\rho = \mathbf{e}^\lambda \wedge (\mathbf{e}^\nu \wedge \mathbf{e}^\rho). \tag{6–10}$$

From this formula it is a straightforward matter to obtain (4) (Problem 9). ▮

If either $r$ or $s$ is even, then the exterior product is commutative. If $r = s = 1$, we have $\mathbf{a} \wedge \mathbf{b} = -\mathbf{b} \wedge \mathbf{a}$.

The exterior product of any finite number of multicovectors is defined by induction. Using (6–9) repeatedly, we find that if $\lambda$ is increasing,

$$\mathbf{e}^\lambda = \mathbf{e}^{i_1} \wedge \cdots \wedge \mathbf{e}^{i_r}. \tag{6–11}$$

Since both sides of (6–9) change sign under interchanges in $\lambda$ or $\nu$, formula (6–9) is also true for nonincreasing $r$-tuples. Thus (6–11) is valid whether $\lambda$ is increasing or not.

**Examples.** Let $n = 5$. Then

$$(\mathbf{e}^1 + 3\mathbf{e}^4) \wedge (\mathbf{e}^{24} - 2\mathbf{e}^{15}) = \mathbf{e}^{124} + 3\mathbf{e}^{424} - 2\mathbf{e}^{115} - 6\mathbf{e}^{415} = \mathbf{e}^{124} + 6\mathbf{e}^{145}.$$

$$\mathbf{e}^2 \wedge (3\mathbf{e}^1 - 2\mathbf{e}^3) \wedge \mathbf{e}^5 \wedge \mathbf{e}^3 = (3\mathbf{e}^{21} - 2\mathbf{e}^{23}) \wedge \mathbf{e}^{53} = 3\mathbf{e}^{2153} = 3\mathbf{e}^{1235}.$$

***Remarks.** The exterior product has been defined in terms of the standard bases. It is not clear that it is "coordinate free," in other words, that the same exterior product would be obtained starting from different bases. However, let us add one additional property to the list (1)—(4):

(5) *If* $\omega = \mathbf{a}^1 \wedge \cdots \wedge \mathbf{a}^r$, *then* $\omega(\mathbf{h}_1, \ldots, \mathbf{h}_r) = \det(\mathbf{a}^k \cdot \mathbf{h}_l)$ *for every* $r$*-tuple* $(\mathbf{h}_1, \ldots, \mathbf{h}_r)$.

This property of the exterior product will be proved in Section 6–3 [see (6–12), (6–14)]. Formula (6–11) is a special case of (5). This is seen by taking $\mathbf{a}^k = \mathbf{e}^{i_k}$ and recalling (6–5a). Moreover, (6–9) is a consequence of (6–11) and the associative law (4). Once the product is known for basis elements, Properties (1) and (2) determine it in general. Thus $\wedge$ is the only product with Properties (1)—(5). In fact, (3) can be omitted from the list since it follows from the other four. Since none of these five properties refers to bases, the exterior product is coordinate free.

***Note about terminology.** A multilinear function $M$ of degree $r$ and domain $E^n \times \cdots \times E^n$ is often called a *covariant tensor of rank* $r$. An $r$-covector is then called an *alternating covariant tensor of rank* $r$.

The sum of an $r$-covector and an $s$-covector has been defined only when $r = s$. However, one may form the direct sum

$$(A^n)^* = (E_0^n)^* \oplus (E_1^n)^* \oplus \cdots \oplus (E_r^n)^* \oplus \cdots,$$

where we agree that $(E_0^n)^*$ is the scalar field. The exterior product induces a product in $(A^n)^*$, which is then an algebra over the real numbers. This algebra is called the *exterior algebra* of $(E^n)^*$. See reference [4]. $(A^n)^*$ is sometimes called the *covariant Grassman algebra* or the *covariant alternating tensor algebra* of $E^n$.

**PROBLEMS**

1. Write down the standard basis for $(E_r^4)^*$ for each $r = 1, 2, 3, 4$. Find all products $\mathbf{e}^\lambda \wedge \mathbf{e}^\nu$ where $\lambda = (i)$ and $\nu = (j, k, l)$ is an increasing triple.
2. Let $n = 3$. Simplify:
   (a) $(2\mathbf{e}^1 - \mathbf{e}^2) \wedge (3\mathbf{e}^2 + \mathbf{e}^3)$. (b) $\mathbf{e}^{21} \wedge \mathbf{e}^{23}$.
   (c) $(\mathbf{e}^1 - \mathbf{e}^2 + 3\mathbf{e}^3) \wedge \mathbf{e}^{21}$. (d) $(\mathbf{e}^{23} + \mathbf{e}^{31}) \wedge (5\mathbf{e}^1 - \mathbf{e}^2)$.
3. Let $n = 5$. Simplify:
   (a) $\mathbf{e}^{253} \wedge (\mathbf{e}^{14} + \mathbf{e}^{42})$. (b) $(\mathbf{e}^2 + \mathbf{e}^5) \wedge \mathbf{e}^{31} \wedge (\mathbf{e}^5 - \mathbf{e}^4)$.
4. Let $\mathbf{a}$ and $\mathbf{b}$ be 1-covectors and $\boldsymbol{\omega} = \mathbf{a} \wedge \mathbf{b}$. Show that $\omega_{ij} = a_i b_j - a_j b_i$.
5. Show that if $\mathbf{a}$, $\mathbf{b}$, $\mathbf{c}$ are 1-covectors, then
$$\mathbf{a} \wedge \mathbf{b} + \mathbf{b} \wedge \mathbf{c} + \mathbf{c} \wedge \mathbf{a} = (\mathbf{a} - \mathbf{b}) \wedge (\mathbf{b} - \mathbf{c}).$$
6. Show that if $\boldsymbol{\omega} = \mathbf{a} \wedge \mathbf{b}$, then $\omega_{ij}\omega_{kl} + \omega_{ik}\omega_{lj} + \omega_{il}\omega_{jk} = 0$ for $i, j, k, l = 1, \ldots, n$. [*Hint:* Using Problem 4,
$$\det \begin{pmatrix} \omega_{ij} & \omega_{ik} & \omega_{il} \\ a_j & a_k & a_l \\ b_j & b_k & b_l \end{pmatrix} = 0$$
since the first row is a linear combination of the second and third rows.]
7. Show that if $\sum_{[\lambda]} c_\lambda \mathbf{e}^\lambda = \mathbf{0}$, then $c_\lambda = 0$ for every increasing $\lambda$. [*Hint:* See (6–6).]
8. Prove (1) and (2) of Proposition 20.
9. Prove the associative law (4) of Proposition 20, using (1), (2), and (6–10).
10. Show that $\boldsymbol{\omega} \wedge \boldsymbol{\zeta} \wedge \boldsymbol{\eta} = -\boldsymbol{\eta} \wedge \boldsymbol{\zeta} \wedge \boldsymbol{\omega}$ if $\boldsymbol{\omega}$ has degree $r$, $\boldsymbol{\eta}$ has degree $t$, and both $r$, $t$ are odd.

## 6–3 MULTIVECTORS

If $\mathcal{V}$ is any vector space, then alternating $r$-linear functions on $\mathcal{V} \times \cdots \times \mathcal{V}$ can be defined just as in Section 6–1 where we took $\mathcal{V} = E^n$. Let us now take $\mathcal{V} = (E^n)^*$, the dual space to $E^n$.

**Definition.** A *multivector of degree* $r$ is an alternating $r$-linear function with domain the $r$-fold cartesian product $(E^n)^* \times \cdots \times (E^n)^*$.

For brevity, multivectors of degree $r$ are called *r-vectors*. They will usually be denoted by the Greek letters $\boldsymbol{\alpha}$ or $\boldsymbol{\beta}$. When $r = 1$, the 1-linear functions on $(E^n)^*$ are identified with the elements of $E^n$ in the way explained in Section A-2. Then a 1-vector is just a vector, and will be denoted as usual by $\mathbf{x}$ or $\mathbf{h}$.

For every statement about multicovectors in Sections 6-1 and 6-2, there is a dual statement about multivectors obtained by everywhere exchanging the words "vector" and "covector." For instance, if $\boldsymbol{\alpha}$ is an $r$-vector and $\lambda = (i_1, \ldots, i_r)$, let

$$\alpha^\lambda = \boldsymbol{\alpha}(\mathbf{e}^{i_1}, \ldots, \mathbf{e}^{i_r}).$$

This is dual to the formula [see (6-1b) with $M = \boldsymbol{\omega}$]

$$\omega_\lambda = \boldsymbol{\omega}(\mathbf{e}_{i_1}, \ldots, \mathbf{e}_{i_r}).$$

Let $\mathbf{e}_\lambda$ be the $r$-vector defined by the formula dual to (6-5a):

$$\mathbf{e}_\lambda(\mathbf{a}^1, \ldots, \mathbf{a}^r) = \det (a^k_{i_l}) \tag{6-5b}$$

for every $r$-tuple $(\mathbf{a}^1, \ldots, \mathbf{a}^r)$ of covectors.

Let $E^n_r$ denote the set of all $r$-vectors. Then $E^n_r$ satisfies the axioms for a vector space. It consists of $\mathbf{0}$ only if $r > n$. For $1 \leq r \leq n$ the $r$-vectors $\mathbf{e}_\lambda$ with $\lambda$ increasing form the *standard basis* for $E^n_r$. The number $\alpha^\lambda$ is the *component* of $\boldsymbol{\alpha}$ with respect to $\mathbf{e}_\lambda$.

The inner product $\boldsymbol{\alpha} \cdot \boldsymbol{\beta}$ of two $r$-vectors, and the exterior product $\boldsymbol{\alpha} \wedge \boldsymbol{\beta}$ of an $r$-vector $\boldsymbol{\alpha}$ and an $s$-vector $\boldsymbol{\beta}$ are defined by the formulas dual to those in Section 6-2. In each instance subscripts are replaced by superscripts and vice versa. The exterior product of multivectors has the same properties listed in Proposition 20. The scalar product $\boldsymbol{\omega} \cdot \boldsymbol{\alpha}$ of an $r$-covector $\boldsymbol{\omega}$ and an $r$-vector $\boldsymbol{\alpha}$ is defined in the third from last line of the Table 6-1. The last two lines of the table are particular cases of the formula for $\boldsymbol{\omega} \cdot \boldsymbol{\alpha}$.

The formulas in the second line and in the last two lines are true whether $\lambda$ and $\mu$ are increasing or not, since they are known to be true for increasing $r$-tuples, and both sides of each formula change sign under interchanges.

The reader should compare this table with the corresponding table for $r = 1$, p. 12. According to the definition (Section A-2), the dual space of $E^n_r$ consists of all real-valued linear functions $F$ with domain $E^n_r$. The dual space may be identified with $(E^n_r)^*$ in the following way. Given an $r$-covector $\boldsymbol{\omega}$, let $F(\boldsymbol{\alpha}) = \boldsymbol{\omega} \cdot \boldsymbol{\alpha}$ for every $\boldsymbol{\alpha} \in E^n_r$. This establishes an isomorphism between $(E^n_r)^*$ and the dual space of $E^n_r$. The next to last line of the table implies that the standard bases for $E^n_r$ and $(E^n_r)^*$ are dual.

***Note about terminology.** Multivectors of degree $r$ are also called *alternating contravariant tensors of rank r*. The exterior algebra $A^n$ of $E^n$ can be introduced in the way indicated at the end of Section 6-2.

TABLE 6–1

| | $r$-vectors | $r$-covectors |
|---|---|---|
| Elements of | $E_r^n$ | $(E_r^n)^*$ |
| Standard basis elements ($\lambda$ increasing) | $\mathbf{e}_\lambda = \mathbf{e}_{i_1} \wedge \cdots \wedge \mathbf{e}_{i_r}$ | $\mathbf{e}^\lambda = \mathbf{e}^{i_1} \wedge \cdots \wedge \mathbf{e}^{i_r}$ |
| | $\boldsymbol{\alpha} = \sum_{[\lambda]} \alpha^\lambda \mathbf{e}_\lambda$ | $\boldsymbol{\omega} = \sum_{[\lambda]} \omega_\lambda \mathbf{e}^\lambda$ |
| Euclidean inner product | $\boldsymbol{\alpha} \cdot \boldsymbol{\beta} = \sum_{[\lambda]} \alpha^\lambda \beta^\lambda$ | $\boldsymbol{\omega} \cdot \boldsymbol{\zeta} = \sum_{[\lambda]} \omega_\lambda \zeta_\lambda$ |
| Euclidean norm | $\lvert\boldsymbol{\alpha}\rvert^2 = \boldsymbol{\alpha} \cdot \boldsymbol{\alpha}$ | $\lvert\boldsymbol{\omega}\rvert^2 = \boldsymbol{\omega} \cdot \boldsymbol{\omega}$ |
| Scalar product | $\boldsymbol{\omega} \cdot \boldsymbol{\alpha} = \sum_{[\lambda]} \omega_\lambda \alpha^\lambda$ | |
| | $\mathbf{e}^\lambda \cdot \mathbf{e}_\mu = \delta_\mu^\lambda$ | |
| | $\mathbf{e}^\lambda \cdot \boldsymbol{\alpha} = \alpha^\lambda$ | $\mathbf{e}_\lambda \cdot \boldsymbol{\omega} = \omega_\lambda$ |

**Definition.** An $r$-covector $\boldsymbol{\omega}$ is *decomposable* if there exist covectors $\mathbf{a}^1, \ldots, \mathbf{a}^r$ such that $\boldsymbol{\omega} = \mathbf{a}^1 \wedge \cdots \wedge \mathbf{a}^r$. Similarly, an $r$-vector $\boldsymbol{\alpha}$ is decomposable if there exist vectors $\mathbf{h}_1, \ldots, \mathbf{h}_r$ such that $\boldsymbol{\alpha} = \mathbf{h}_1 \wedge \cdots \wedge \mathbf{h}_r$.

In the remainder of this section we shall mainly discuss decomposable $r$-vectors. Each statement about them has a dual which applies to decomposable $r$-covectors. Clearly every 1-vector is decomposable. If $\boldsymbol{\alpha}$ is an $n$-vector, then

$$\boldsymbol{\alpha} = c\mathbf{e}_{1\cdots n} = (c\mathbf{e}_1) \wedge \mathbf{e}_2 \wedge \cdots \wedge \mathbf{e}_n,$$

where $c = \alpha^{1\cdots n}$. Hence every $n$-vector is decomposable. In Section 6–6 it will be shown that any $(n-1)$-vector is decomposable. However, for $2 \leq r \leq n-2$ there are nondecomposable $r$-vectors; see Problem 9. Since $\mathbf{e}_\lambda = \mathbf{e}_{i_1} \wedge \cdots \wedge \mathbf{e}_{i_r}$, the standard basis $r$-vectors are decomposable.

It is not correct to identify a decomposable $r$-vector $\boldsymbol{\alpha}$ with the $r$-tuple $(\mathbf{h}_1, \ldots, \mathbf{h}_r)$ since there are many ways to write $\boldsymbol{\alpha}$ as an exterior product of vectors. The corollary to Theorem 19 below will furnish a geometric description of all possible such decompositions of $\boldsymbol{\alpha}$.

**Proposition 21.** *If* $\boldsymbol{\alpha} = \mathbf{h}_1 \wedge \cdots \wedge \mathbf{h}_r$, *then for every $r$-covector* $\boldsymbol{\omega}$,

$$\boldsymbol{\omega} \cdot \boldsymbol{\alpha} = \boldsymbol{\omega}(\mathbf{h}_1, \ldots, \mathbf{h}_r). \tag{6–12}$$

*Proof.* Let $\tilde{\boldsymbol{\omega}}(\mathbf{h}_1, \ldots, \mathbf{h}_r) = \boldsymbol{\omega} \cdot (\mathbf{h}_1 \wedge \cdots \wedge \mathbf{h}_r)$ for every $r$-tuple $(\mathbf{h}_1, \ldots, \mathbf{h}_r)$. Then $\tilde{\boldsymbol{\omega}}$ is an alternating $r$-linear function. Moreover

$$\tilde{\boldsymbol{\omega}}(\mathbf{e}_{j_1}, \ldots, \mathbf{e}_{j_r}) = \boldsymbol{\omega} \cdot \mathbf{e}_\mu = \omega_\mu$$

for every $\mu$. Hence $\tilde{\boldsymbol{\omega}} = \boldsymbol{\omega}$. ∎

**Proposition 22.** *Let* $\boldsymbol{\alpha} = \mathbf{h}_1 \wedge \cdots \wedge \mathbf{h}_r$ *and* $\boldsymbol{\omega} = \mathbf{a}^1 \wedge \cdots \wedge \mathbf{a}^r$. *Then for every r-tuple* $\lambda = (i_1, \ldots, i_r)$,

$$\alpha^\lambda = \det(h_l^{i_k}), \tag{6–13a}$$

$$\omega_\lambda = \det(a_{i_l}^k), \tag{6–13b}$$

*and*

$$\boldsymbol{\omega} \cdot \boldsymbol{\alpha} = \det(\mathbf{a}^k \cdot \mathbf{h}_l). \tag{6–14}$$

*Proof.* Taking $\boldsymbol{\omega} = \mathbf{e}^\lambda$ in formula (6–12), we get

$$\alpha^\lambda = \mathbf{e}^\lambda \cdot \boldsymbol{\alpha} = \mathbf{e}^\lambda(\mathbf{h}_1, \ldots, \mathbf{h}_r).$$

Recalling the definition (6–5a) of $\mathbf{e}^\lambda$, we get (6–13a). The formula (6–13b) dual to (6–13a) is obtained similarly. Let $\boldsymbol{\omega}'(\mathbf{h}_1, \ldots, \mathbf{h}_r) = \det(\mathbf{a}^k \cdot \mathbf{h}_l)$ for every $(\mathbf{h}_1, \ldots, \mathbf{h}_r)$. Then $\boldsymbol{\omega}'$ is multilinear and alternating and for every $\lambda$

$$\boldsymbol{\omega}'(\mathbf{e}_{i_1}, \ldots, \mathbf{e}_{i_r}) = \det(\mathbf{a}^k \cdot \mathbf{e}_{i_l}) = \det(a_{i_l}^k).$$

Using (6–13b), we get $\boldsymbol{\omega}' = \boldsymbol{\omega}$. Then (6–14) follows from (6–12). ∎

The formulas (6–13a), (6–13b), and (6–14) may not provide the easiest way to compute the components and the scalar product in numerical examples. For instance, see Examples (1) and (2) below. However, they are important for various other reasons.

**Proposition 23.** *If* $\boldsymbol{\omega} \cdot \boldsymbol{\alpha} = \boldsymbol{\omega} \cdot \boldsymbol{\beta}$ *for every decomposable r-covector* $\boldsymbol{\omega}$, *then* $\boldsymbol{\alpha} = \boldsymbol{\beta}$.

*Proof.* The standard basis $r$-covectors $\mathbf{e}^\lambda$ are decomposable. Hence for every increasing $\lambda$,

$$\alpha^\lambda = \mathbf{e}^\lambda \cdot \boldsymbol{\alpha} = \mathbf{e}^\lambda \cdot \boldsymbol{\beta} = \beta^\lambda. \ ∎$$

The decomposable $r$-vectors have an important geometric significance which will be described next.

First we recall the following results from linear algebra:

(1) Any linearly independent set $\{\mathbf{h}_1, \ldots, \mathbf{h}_r\}$ is a basis for the vector subspace $P \subset E^n$ spanned by these vectors (definition).

(2) Given any such set there exist $\mathbf{h}_{r+1}, \ldots, \mathbf{h}_n$ such that $\{\mathbf{h}_1, \ldots, \mathbf{h}_n\}$ is a basis for $E^n$.

(3) For every basis $\{\mathbf{h}_1, \ldots, \mathbf{h}_n\}$ for $E^n$ there is a dual basis $\{\mathbf{a}^1, \ldots, \mathbf{a}^n\}$ for $(E^n)^*$, $\mathbf{a}^k \cdot \mathbf{h}_l = \delta_l^k$ for $k, l = 1, \ldots, n$ (Section A–2).

**Definition.** A linearly independent $r$-tuple $(\mathbf{h}_1, \ldots, \mathbf{h}_r)$ is called a *frame* for the vector subspace $P$ spanned by $\mathbf{h}_1, \ldots, \mathbf{h}_r$.

The only difference between the notions of basis and frame is that the latter takes into account the order in which the basis vectors $\mathbf{h}_1, \ldots, \mathbf{h}_r$ are written.

**Theorem 19.** (a) *An $r$-tuple $(\mathbf{h}_1, \ldots, \mathbf{h}_r)$ is linearly dependent if and only if* $\mathbf{h}_1 \wedge \cdots \wedge \mathbf{h}_r = \mathbf{0}$.

(b) *Let $P \subset E^n$ be an $r$-dimensional vector subspace and $(\mathbf{h}_1, \ldots, \mathbf{h}_r)$, $(\mathbf{h}'_1, \ldots, \mathbf{h}'_r)$ be any two frames for $P$. Then there is a scalar $c$ such that*

$$\mathbf{h}'_1 \wedge \cdots \wedge \mathbf{h}'_r = c\mathbf{h}_1 \wedge \cdots \wedge \mathbf{h}_r. \tag{6–15}$$

(c) *Conversely, if $(\mathbf{h}_1, \ldots, \mathbf{h}_r)$ and $(\mathbf{h}'_1, \ldots, \mathbf{h}'_r)$ are frames which satisfy* (6–15) *for some scalar $c$, then they are frames for the same vector subspace $P$.* (See Fig. 6–1.)

*Proof of* (a). Let $(\mathbf{h}_1, \ldots, \mathbf{h}_r)$ be linearly dependent and $\boldsymbol{\alpha} = \mathbf{h}_1 \wedge \cdots \wedge \mathbf{h}_r$. By Propositions 18 and 21, $\boldsymbol{\omega} \cdot \boldsymbol{\alpha} = 0$ for every $\boldsymbol{\omega}$. By Proposition 23, $\boldsymbol{\alpha} = \mathbf{0}$. On the other hand, if $(\mathbf{h}_1, \ldots, \mathbf{h}_r)$ is linearly independent, let $\mathbf{a}^1, \ldots, \mathbf{a}^r$ be covectors such that $\mathbf{a}^k \cdot \mathbf{h}_l = \delta^k_l$, and let $\boldsymbol{\omega} = \mathbf{a}^1 \wedge \cdots \wedge \mathbf{a}^r$. By (6–14)

$$\boldsymbol{\omega} \cdot \boldsymbol{\alpha} = \det(\delta^k_l) = 1.$$

Hence $\boldsymbol{\alpha} \neq \mathbf{0}$.

*Proof of* (b). Each $\mathbf{h}'_l$ is a linear combination of $\mathbf{h}_1, \ldots, \mathbf{h}_r$,

$$\mathbf{h}'_l = \sum_{m=1}^{r} c^m_l \mathbf{h}_m, \qquad l = 1, \ldots, r.$$

If $\boldsymbol{\omega} = \mathbf{a}^1 \wedge \cdots \wedge \mathbf{a}^r$ is any decomposable $r$-covector, then

$$\boldsymbol{\omega} \cdot \boldsymbol{\alpha}' = \det(\mathbf{a}^k \cdot \mathbf{h}'_l) = \det\left(\sum_{m=1}^{r} (\mathbf{a}^k \cdot \mathbf{h}_m) c^m_l\right)$$

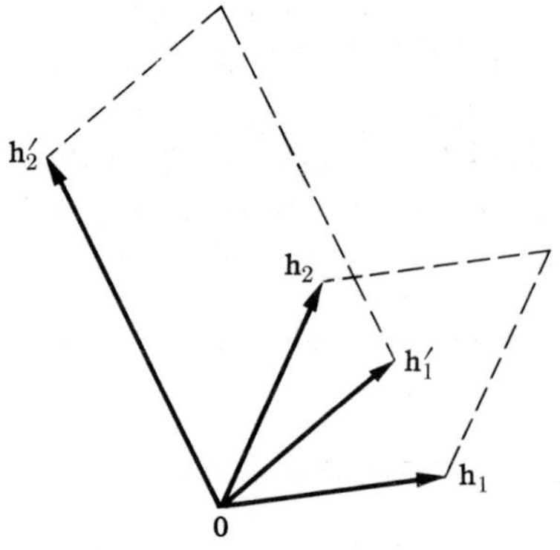


FIGURE 6–1

where $\boldsymbol{\alpha}' = \mathbf{h}'_1 \wedge \cdots \wedge \mathbf{h}'_r$. The matrix on the right is the product of the matrices $(\mathbf{a}^k \cdot \mathbf{h}_m)$ and $(c^m_l)$. Hence if $c = \det(c^m_l)$,

$$\boldsymbol{\omega} \cdot \boldsymbol{\alpha}' = c \det(\mathbf{a}^k \cdot \mathbf{h}_m) = c\boldsymbol{\omega} \cdot \boldsymbol{\alpha} = \boldsymbol{\omega} \cdot (c\boldsymbol{\alpha}).$$

This is true for every decomposable $\boldsymbol{\omega}$; hence $\boldsymbol{\alpha}' = c\boldsymbol{\alpha}$ by Proposition 23.

*Proof of* (c). Since $\boldsymbol{\alpha} = \mathbf{h}_1 \wedge \cdots \wedge \mathbf{h}_r$, $\boldsymbol{\alpha}' = \mathbf{h}'_1 \wedge \cdots \wedge \mathbf{h}'_r$ are not $\mathbf{0}$ by hypothesis, (a) implies that $\{\mathbf{h}_1, \ldots, \mathbf{h}_r\}$ and $\{\mathbf{h}'_1, \ldots, \mathbf{h}'_r\}$ are linearly independent sets. It suffices to show that each $\mathbf{h}'_l$ is a linear combination of $\mathbf{h}_1, \ldots, \mathbf{h}_r$. Suppose that this is false for some $l$, say for $l = 1$. Then $\{\mathbf{h}_1, \ldots, \mathbf{h}_r, \mathbf{h}'_1\}$ is a linearly independent set. Let $\mathbf{a}^1, \ldots, \mathbf{a}^{r+1}$ be such that $\mathbf{a}^k \cdot \mathbf{h}_m = \delta^k_m$ for $k, m = 1, \ldots, r+1$, where we have set $\mathbf{h}'_1 = \mathbf{h}_{r+1}$. Let $\boldsymbol{\omega} = \mathbf{a}^1 \wedge \cdots \wedge \mathbf{a}^r$. Then $\boldsymbol{\omega} \cdot \boldsymbol{\alpha} = 1$, but $\boldsymbol{\omega} \cdot \boldsymbol{\alpha}' = 0$ since the elements $\mathbf{a}^k \cdot \mathbf{h}'_1 = \delta^k_{r+1}$ of the first column of the $r \times r$ matrix $(\mathbf{a}^k \cdot \mathbf{h}'_l)$ are 0. This contradicts the assumption that $\boldsymbol{\alpha}' = c\boldsymbol{\alpha}$, $c \neq 0$. ▌

**Example 1.** Show that $2\mathbf{e}_1 + 3\mathbf{e}_2 - \mathbf{e}_3$, $\mathbf{e}_1 + 2\mathbf{e}_2$, $\mathbf{e}_1 - 2\mathbf{e}_3$ are linearly dependent. Their exterior product is

$$\begin{aligned}(2\mathbf{e}_1 + 3\mathbf{e}_2 - \mathbf{e}_3) &\wedge (\mathbf{e}_1 + 2\mathbf{e}_2) \wedge (\mathbf{e}_1 - 2\mathbf{e}_3) \\ &= (\mathbf{e}_{12} - \mathbf{e}_{31} - 2\mathbf{e}_{32}) \wedge (\mathbf{e}_1 - 2\mathbf{e}_3) = -2\mathbf{e}_{123} - 2\mathbf{e}_{321} = \mathbf{0}.\end{aligned}$$

**Example 2.** Show that $(\mathbf{e}_1 + 3\mathbf{e}_3, \mathbf{e}_2 - \mathbf{e}_3)$ is a frame for the same 2-dimensional vector subspace of $E^3$ as $(2\mathbf{e}_1 + \mathbf{e}_2 + 5\mathbf{e}_3, 4\mathbf{e}_1 + \mathbf{e}_2 + 11\mathbf{e}_3)$. Calculating the exterior products, we get

$$\begin{aligned}(\mathbf{e}_1 + 3\mathbf{e}_3) \wedge (\mathbf{e}_2 - \mathbf{e}_3) &= \mathbf{e}_{12} - \mathbf{e}_{13} - 3\mathbf{e}_{23}, \\ (2\mathbf{e}_1 + \mathbf{e}_2 + 5\mathbf{e}_3) \wedge (4\mathbf{e}_1 + \mathbf{e}_2 + 11\mathbf{e}_3) &= -2\mathbf{e}_{12} + 2\mathbf{e}_{13} + 6\mathbf{e}_{23}.\end{aligned}$$

The second 2-vector is $-2$ times the first.

Let $\boldsymbol{\alpha} \neq \mathbf{0}$ be a decomposable $r$-vector. Then $\boldsymbol{\alpha} = \mathbf{h}_1 \wedge \cdots \wedge \mathbf{h}_r$, and the vector subspace $P$ spanned by $\mathbf{h}_1, \ldots, \mathbf{h}_r$ is called the *r-space* of $\boldsymbol{\alpha}$. If $\boldsymbol{\alpha} = \mathbf{h}'_1 \wedge \cdots \wedge \mathbf{h}'_r$, then taking $c = 1$ in part (c) of Theorem 19, we see that $\mathbf{h}'_1, \ldots, \mathbf{h}'_r$ also span this same vector subspace $P$. Thus $P$ depends only on $\boldsymbol{\alpha}$ and not on the particular way $\boldsymbol{\alpha}$ is written as the exterior product of vectors.

If $c \neq 0$, then $(c\mathbf{h}_1, \mathbf{h}_2, \ldots, \mathbf{h}_r)$ is another frame for $P$ and $c\boldsymbol{\alpha} = (c\mathbf{h}_1) \wedge \mathbf{h}_2 \wedge \cdots \wedge \mathbf{h}_r$. Thus $\boldsymbol{\alpha}$ and $c\boldsymbol{\alpha}$ have the same $r$-space $P$. On the other hand, if $\boldsymbol{\alpha}'$ is not a scalar multiple of $\boldsymbol{\alpha}$, then $\boldsymbol{\alpha}$ and $\boldsymbol{\alpha}'$ have different $r$-spaces.

**Orientations.** Let $P$ be an $r$-dimensional vector subspace of $E^n$.

**Definition.** A decomposable $r$-vector $\boldsymbol{\alpha}_0$ is an *orientation* for $P$ if $|\boldsymbol{\alpha}_0| = 1$ and $P$ is the $r$-space of $\boldsymbol{\alpha}_0$.

If $\boldsymbol{\alpha}$ is any $r$-vector whose $r$-space is $P$, then $c\boldsymbol{\alpha}$ is an orientation for $P$ provided $|c\boldsymbol{\alpha}| = 1$. Since $|c\boldsymbol{\alpha}| = |c|\,|\boldsymbol{\alpha}|$, we must have $c = \pm|\boldsymbol{\alpha}|^{-1}$. $P$ has two orientations. If $\boldsymbol{\alpha}_0$ is one of them, then $-\boldsymbol{\alpha}_0$ is the other.

**Example 3.** Let $\lambda = (i_1, \ldots, i_r)$ have no repetitions. The $r$-space of $\mathbf{e}_\lambda$ is spanned by $\mathbf{e}_{i_1}, \ldots, \mathbf{e}_{i_r}$. Since $|\mathbf{e}_\lambda| = 1$, $\mathbf{e}_\lambda$ is an orientation for it.

If $(\mathbf{h}_1, \ldots, \mathbf{h}_r)$ is any frame for $P$ and $\boldsymbol{\alpha}_0$ is an orientation of $P$, then

$$\mathbf{h}_1 \wedge \cdots \wedge \mathbf{h}_r = c\boldsymbol{\alpha}_0, \qquad c = \pm|\mathbf{h}_1 \wedge \cdots \wedge \mathbf{h}_r| \neq 0.$$

Let us say that the frame $(\mathbf{h}_1, \ldots, \mathbf{h}_r)$ *has orientation* $\boldsymbol{\alpha}_0$ if $c > 0$, and orientation $-\boldsymbol{\alpha}_0$ if $c < 0$.

If two vectors in the frame $(\mathbf{h}_1, \ldots, \mathbf{h}_r)$ are interchanged, then the exterior product $\mathbf{h}_1 \wedge \cdots \wedge \mathbf{h}_r$ changes sign. Thus the orientation of a frame changes under interchanges.

In Example (2), $(11)^{-1/2}(\mathbf{e}_{12} - \mathbf{e}_{13} - 3\mathbf{e}_{23})$ is an orientation. The frame $(\mathbf{e}_1 + 3\mathbf{e}_3, \mathbf{e}_2 - \mathbf{e}_3)$ has this orientation.

Let $r = n$. Then $P = E^n$ and $\pm\mathbf{e}_{1\ldots n}$ are the two orientations. Let us call $\mathbf{e}_{1\ldots n}$ the *standard*, or *positive*, orientation of $E^n$ and $-\mathbf{e}_{1\ldots n}$ the *negative* orientation of $E^n$. When $r < n$ we do not attempt to call one orientation of $P$ positive and the other negative. If $(\mathbf{h}_1, \ldots, \mathbf{h}_n)$ is a frame for $E^n$, then by (6–13a)

$$\mathbf{h}_1 \wedge \cdots \wedge \mathbf{h}_n = \det (h_l^k)\mathbf{e}_{1\ldots n}.$$

The frame has positive orientation if $\det (h_l^k) > 0$ and negative orientation if $\det (h_l^k) < 0$.

**Measure for *r*-parallelepipeds.** It was shown in Section 5–7 that if $K$ is an $n$-parallelepiped spanned by $\mathbf{h}_1, \ldots, \mathbf{h}_n$ with $\mathbf{x}_0$ as vertex, then

$$V_n(K) = |\det (h_l^k)| = |\mathbf{h}_1 \wedge \cdots \wedge \mathbf{h}_n|.$$

More generally, if $\mathbf{x}_0, \mathbf{h}_1, \ldots, \mathbf{h}_r$ are vectors, then

$$K = \left\{\mathbf{x} : \mathbf{x} = \mathbf{x}_0 + \sum_{k=1}^{r} t^k\mathbf{h}_k,\ 0 \le t^k \le 1,\ k = 1, \ldots, r\right\}$$

is the *r-parallelepiped* spanned by $\mathbf{h}_1, \ldots, \mathbf{h}_r$ with $\mathbf{x}_0$ as vertex.

**Definition.** The *r-dimensional measure* of $K$ is

$$V_r(K) = |\mathbf{h}_1 \wedge \cdots \wedge \mathbf{h}_r|. \tag{6–16}$$

By part (a) of Theorem 19, $V_r(K) = 0$ if and only if $(\mathbf{h}_1, \ldots, \mathbf{h}_r)$ is linearly dependent.

We now have a criterion which shows when two frames lead to the same $r$-vector.

**Corollary.** *Let* $(\mathbf{h}_1, \ldots, \mathbf{h}_r)$, $(\mathbf{h}'_1, \ldots, \mathbf{h}'_r)$ *be frames. Then* $\mathbf{h}_1 \wedge \cdots \wedge \mathbf{h}_r = \mathbf{h}'_1 \wedge \cdots \wedge \mathbf{h}'_r$ *if and only if these frames span the same r-space P, have the same orientation, and their parallelepipeds with* **0** *as vertex have the same r-measure.*

**Measure for *r*-simplices.** Let $S$ be an $r$-simplex with vertices $\mathbf{x}_0, \ldots, \mathbf{x}_r$. Let $\mathbf{h}_k = \mathbf{x}_k - \mathbf{x}_0$, $k = 1, \ldots, r$. Reasoning as in Section 5–7, we have

$$S = \left\{\mathbf{x} : \mathbf{x} = \mathbf{x}_0 + \sum_{k=1}^{r} t^k\mathbf{h}_k,\ t^k \ge 0 \text{ for } k = 1, \ldots, r,\ \sum_{k=1}^{r} t^k \le 1\right\}.$$

The *r-dimensional measure* of $S$ is defined to be

$$V_r(S) = \frac{1}{r!}\,|\mathbf{h}_1 \wedge \cdots \wedge \mathbf{h}_r|. \tag{6–17}$$

Both (6–16) and (6–17) are very special cases of a general formula (7–5) in Chapter 7 for $r$-dimensional measure.

**Example 4.** The area of the triangle in $E^3$ with vertices $\mathbf{0}$, $3\mathbf{e}_1 + \mathbf{e}_2$, $\mathbf{e}_3 - \mathbf{e}_2$ is $\frac{1}{2}|(3\mathbf{e}_1 + \mathbf{e}_2) \wedge (\mathbf{e}_3 - \mathbf{e}_2)|$. Since

$$(3\mathbf{e}_1 + \mathbf{e}_2) \wedge (\mathbf{e}_3 - \mathbf{e}_2) = -3\mathbf{e}_{12} + 3\mathbf{e}_{13} + \mathbf{e}_{23},$$

the components are $\alpha^{12} = -3$, $\alpha^{13} = 3$, $\alpha^{23} = 1$. Since $|\boldsymbol{\alpha}|^2 = \sum_{[\lambda]} (\alpha^\lambda)^2$, the area is $\sqrt{19}/2$. The area can also be calculated from formula (6–18) below.

To show that the definition (6–16) of $r$-measure for parallelepipeds is reasonable, let us show that $V_r(K)$ is the product of the lengths of the vectors $\mathbf{h}_1, \ldots, \mathbf{h}_r$ in case these vectors are mutually orthogonal. If $\mathbf{v}_1, \ldots, \mathbf{v}_r$ are vectors, let $\mathbf{a}^k$ be the covector with the same components as the vector $\mathbf{v}_k$. Then $\mathbf{a}^1 \wedge \cdots \wedge \mathbf{a}^r$ is the $r$-covector with the same components as the $r$-vector $\mathbf{v}_1 \wedge \cdots \wedge \mathbf{v}_r$. By (6–14)

$$(\mathbf{v}_1 \wedge \cdots \wedge \mathbf{v}_r) \cdot (\mathbf{h}_1 \wedge \cdots \wedge \mathbf{h}_r) = \det(\mathbf{v}_k \cdot \mathbf{h}_l),$$

where the $\cdot$ now denotes inner product. In particular, let $\mathbf{v}_k = \mathbf{h}_k$. Then

$$|\mathbf{h}_1 \wedge \cdots \wedge \mathbf{h}_r|^2 = \det(\mathbf{h}_k \cdot \mathbf{h}_l). \tag{6–18}$$

Taking square roots, we get a formula for $V_r(K)$. If $\mathbf{h}_1, \ldots, \mathbf{h}_r$ are mutually orthogonal, then $\mathbf{h}_k \cdot \mathbf{h}_l = 0$ for $k \neq l$ and $\det(\mathbf{h}_k \cdot \mathbf{h}_l) = |\mathbf{h}_1|^2 \cdots |\mathbf{h}_r|^2$. In this case $V_r(K) = |\mathbf{h}_1| \cdots |\mathbf{h}_r|$ as required.

## PROBLEMS

1. Simplify ($n = 6$):
   (a) $\mathbf{e}_3 \wedge \mathbf{e}_5 \wedge \mathbf{e}_{24}$.
   (b) $\mathbf{e}_2 \wedge \mathbf{e}_3 \wedge \mathbf{e}_{62}$.
   (c) $\mathbf{e}_1 \wedge (\mathbf{e}_{14} + \mathbf{e}_{64})$.
   (d) $(\mathbf{e}_1 + 3\mathbf{e}_4 - \mathbf{e}_6) \wedge (2\mathbf{e}_{23} + \mathbf{e}_{36}) \wedge \mathbf{e}_{45}$.
   (e) $(\mathbf{e}_{12} + \mathbf{e}_{13}) \wedge (\mathbf{e}_{34} + \mathbf{e}_{25}) \wedge (\mathbf{e}_{56} + \mathbf{e}_{46})$.
2. Evaluate the indicated scalar products ($n = 4$), using (6–14).
   (a) $(\mathbf{e}^1 + \mathbf{e}^2) \cdot (\mathbf{e}_1 + \mathbf{e}_2)$.
   (b) $\mathbf{e}^{12} \cdot \mathbf{e}_{34}$.
   (c) $\mathbf{e}^{134} \cdot (\mathbf{e}_{431} + 3\mathbf{e}_{124})$.
   (d) $(\mathbf{e}^1 - \mathbf{e}^4) \wedge (\mathbf{e}^2 + \mathbf{e}^4) \cdot (\mathbf{e}_1 + 2\mathbf{e}_4) \wedge (\mathbf{e}_2 - 2\mathbf{e}_4)$.
3. Using Theorem 19 show that $(2\mathbf{e}_1 + \mathbf{e}_3, \mathbf{e}_2 + \mathbf{e}_4, \mathbf{e}_1 + \mathbf{e}_4, \mathbf{e}_3 + \mathbf{e}_4)$ is a frame for $E^4$. What is its orientation?

4. Do $\mathbf{e}_1 + \mathbf{e}_4$, $\mathbf{e}_2 + \mathbf{e}_5$, $\mathbf{e}_3 + \mathbf{e}_6$, $\mathbf{e}_1 + \mathbf{e}_5$, $\mathbf{e}_2 + \mathbf{e}_6$, $\mathbf{e}_3 + \mathbf{e}_4$ form a basis for $E^6$?

5. Show that $(\mathbf{e}_1 - \mathbf{e}_2, \mathbf{e}_2 - \mathbf{e}_3)$ and $(3\mathbf{e}_1 - \mathbf{e}_2 - 2\mathbf{e}_3, 2\mathbf{e}_1 - \mathbf{e}_2 - \mathbf{e}_3)$ are frames for the same vector subspace of $E^3$. Do their orientations agree?

6. Find the area of the triangle with vertices $2\mathbf{e}_3$, $\mathbf{e}_1 - \mathbf{e}_2 + 2\mathbf{e}_3$, $\mathbf{e}_1 + 3\mathbf{e}_3$.

7. Find the volume of the 3-simplex in $E^4$ with vertices $\mathbf{0}$, $\mathbf{e}_1 - \mathbf{e}_3$, $\mathbf{e}_2$, $\mathbf{e}_3 + 2\mathbf{e}_4$.

8. Let $K$ be an $r$-parallelepiped spanned by $\mathbf{h}_1, \ldots, \mathbf{h}_r$ with $\mathbf{0}$ as vertex. For each increasing $\lambda$ let $K^\lambda = \mathbf{X}^\lambda(K)$ where $\mathbf{X}^\lambda$ is the projection onto the $r$-space of $\mathbf{e}_\lambda$. ($\mathbf{X}^\lambda$ leaves the components $x^{i_1}, \ldots, x^{i_r}$ of any $\mathbf{x}$ unchanged and replaces each of the other components by 0.) Let $\boldsymbol{\alpha} = \mathbf{h}_1 \wedge \cdots \wedge \mathbf{h}_r$. Show that $|\alpha^\lambda| = V_r(K^\lambda)$ and hence $[V_r(K)]^2 = \sum_{[\lambda]} [V_r(K^\lambda)]^2$. Illustrate for $n = 3$ and $r = 1, 2$.

9. Show that:
   (a) If $\boldsymbol{\alpha}$ is decomposable, then $\boldsymbol{\alpha} \wedge \boldsymbol{\alpha} = \mathbf{0}$.
   (b) If $\boldsymbol{\alpha}$ and $\boldsymbol{\beta}$ are decomposable $r$-vectors, then $(\boldsymbol{\alpha} + \boldsymbol{\beta}) \wedge (\boldsymbol{\alpha} + \boldsymbol{\beta}) = 2\boldsymbol{\alpha} \wedge \boldsymbol{\beta}$ if $r$ is even and is $\mathbf{0}$ if $r$ is odd.
   (c) The 2-vector $\mathbf{e}_{12} + \mathbf{e}_{34}$ is not decomposable. [*Hint:* Use (a).]

10. Let $\boldsymbol{\alpha}$ and $\boldsymbol{\beta}$ be decomposable nonzero 2-vectors, and $P$, $Q$ be their respective 2-spaces. Show that if $P \cap Q = \{\mathbf{0}\}$, then $\boldsymbol{\alpha} + \boldsymbol{\beta}$ is not decomposable; and if $P \cap Q$ is a line through $\mathbf{0}$, then $\boldsymbol{\alpha} + \boldsymbol{\beta}$ is decomposable and $\boldsymbol{\alpha} \neq c\boldsymbol{\beta}$. [*Hints:* In the first instance $\boldsymbol{\alpha} = \mathbf{h} \wedge \mathbf{k}$, $\boldsymbol{\beta} = \mathbf{h}' \wedge \mathbf{k}'$, where $\{\mathbf{h}, \mathbf{k}, \mathbf{h}', \mathbf{k}'\}$ is a linearly independent set. In the second $\boldsymbol{\alpha} = \mathbf{h} \wedge \mathbf{k}$, $\boldsymbol{\beta} = \mathbf{h} \wedge \mathbf{k}'$, where $\mathbf{h} \in P \cap Q$.]

11. Let $\boldsymbol{\alpha} = \mathbf{h} \wedge \mathbf{k}$, $\boldsymbol{\alpha} \neq \mathbf{0}$. Show that the matrix $(\alpha^{ij})$ has rank 2. [*Hint:* Show that each column vector of the matrix is a linear combination of $\mathbf{h}$ and $\mathbf{k}$.]

12. Let $(\mathbf{x}_0, \mathbf{x}_1, \ldots, \mathbf{x}_r)$ be an $(r + 1)$-tuple such that the vectors $\mathbf{x}_1 - \mathbf{x}_0, \ldots, \mathbf{x}_r - \mathbf{x}_0$ are linearly independent. Such an $(r + 1)$-tuple defines an *oriented* $r$-simplex. Its *r-vector* is $1/r!(\mathbf{x}_1 - \mathbf{x}_0) \wedge \cdots \wedge (\mathbf{x}_r - \mathbf{x}_0)$. Let $\boldsymbol{\beta}_i$ be the $(r - 1)$-vector of the $i$th oriented face $(\mathbf{x}_0, \mathbf{x}_1, \ldots, \mathbf{x}_{i-1}, \mathbf{x}_{i+1}, \ldots, \mathbf{x}_r)$. Show that

$$\sum_{i=0}^{r} (-1)^i \boldsymbol{\beta}_i = \mathbf{0}.$$

## 6–4 INDUCED LINEAR TRANSFORMATIONS

Let $m$ and $n$ be positive integers. With any linear transformation $\mathbf{L}$ from $E^m$ into $E^n$ is associated for each $r = 1, 2, \ldots$ a linear transformation $\mathbf{L}_r$ from $E_r^m$ into $E_r^n$ with the following property. If $(\mathbf{k}_1, \ldots, \mathbf{k}_r)$ is any $r$-tuple of vectors in $E^m$, then we require that

$$\mathbf{L}_r(\mathbf{k}_1 \wedge \cdots \wedge \mathbf{k}_r) = \mathbf{L}(\mathbf{k}_1) \wedge \cdots \wedge \mathbf{L}(\mathbf{k}_r). \tag{6–19}$$

For $r = 2$ this is illustrated in Fig. 6–2.

With this in mind let us define $\mathbf{L}_r$ as follows. Let $\boldsymbol{\epsilon}_1, \ldots, \boldsymbol{\epsilon}_m$ be the standard basis elements of $E^m$. Then $\mathbf{v}_j = \mathbf{L}(\boldsymbol{\epsilon}_j)$ is the $j$th column vector of $\mathbf{L}$. Let $\mu = (j_1, \ldots, j_r)$ be increasing. Then $\boldsymbol{\epsilon}_\mu = \boldsymbol{\epsilon}_{j_1} \wedge \cdots \wedge \boldsymbol{\epsilon}_{j_r}$, and remembering

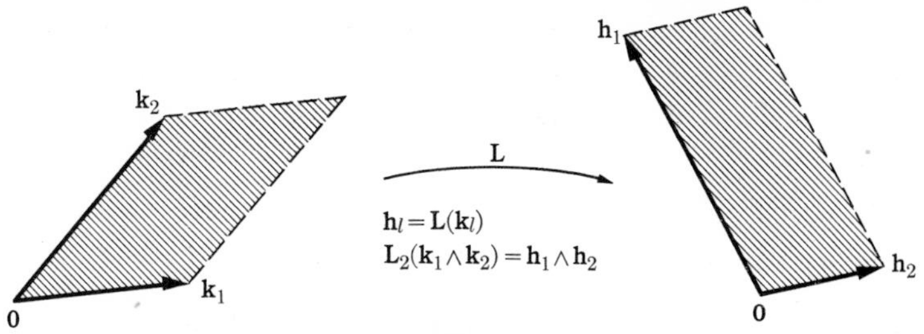


FIGURE 6–2

that we want (6–19) to be correct, we set

$$\mathbf{L}_r(\boldsymbol{\epsilon}_\mu) = \mathbf{v}_{j_1} \wedge \cdots \wedge \mathbf{v}_{j_r}. \tag{6–20a}$$

Since $\mathbf{L}_r$ is to be linear, its value at any $\boldsymbol{\beta}$ is determined once the values at the basis elements $\boldsymbol{\epsilon}_\mu$ are known. For any $\boldsymbol{\beta} = \sum_{[\mu]} \beta^\mu \boldsymbol{\epsilon}_\mu$

$$\mathbf{L}_r(\boldsymbol{\beta}) = \sum_{[\mu]} \beta^\mu \mathbf{L}_r(\boldsymbol{\epsilon}_\mu). \tag{6–21}$$

The linear transformations $\mathbf{L}_r$ are said to be *induced* by $\mathbf{L}$. Of course $\mathbf{L}_1 = \mathbf{L}$. If $r > m$, then $E_r^m$ has the single element $\mathbf{0}$ and $\mathbf{L}_r(\mathbf{0}) = \mathbf{0}$.

Let us show that for every $\boldsymbol{\beta} \in E_r^m$, $\boldsymbol{\gamma} \in E_s^m$,

$$\mathbf{L}_{r+s}(\boldsymbol{\beta} \wedge \boldsymbol{\gamma}) = \mathbf{L}_r(\boldsymbol{\beta}) \wedge \mathbf{L}_s(\boldsymbol{\gamma}). \tag{6–22a}$$

Let $\mu = (j_1, \ldots, j_r)$ and $\nu = (k_1, \ldots, k_s)$ be increasing. Then

$$\mathbf{L}_r(\boldsymbol{\epsilon}_\mu) \wedge \mathbf{L}_s(\boldsymbol{\epsilon}_\nu) = \mathbf{v}_{j_1} \wedge \cdots \wedge \mathbf{v}_{j_r} \wedge \mathbf{v}_{k_1} \wedge \cdots \wedge \mathbf{v}_{k_s}.$$

If any integer is repeated in the $(r + s)$-tuple $(\mu, \nu)$, then this is $\mathbf{0}$. Otherwise, the right-hand side is $(-1)^p \mathbf{L}_{r+s}(\boldsymbol{\epsilon}_\tau)$ where $\tau$ is the increasing $(r + s)$-tuple obtained from $(\mu, \nu)$ by $p$ interchanges. Since $\boldsymbol{\epsilon}_{\mu,\nu} = (-1)^p \boldsymbol{\epsilon}_\tau$ and $\mathbf{L}_{r+s}$ is linear, $(-1)^p \mathbf{L}_{r+s}(\boldsymbol{\epsilon}_\tau) = \mathbf{L}_{r+s}(\boldsymbol{\epsilon}_{\mu,\nu})$. Thus

$$\mathbf{L}_r(\boldsymbol{\epsilon}_\mu) \wedge \mathbf{L}_s(\boldsymbol{\epsilon}_\nu) = \mathbf{L}_{r+s}(\boldsymbol{\epsilon}_{\mu,\nu}).$$

Therefore (6–22a) is correct for basis of elements of $E_r^m$ and $E_s^m$. Since each of these transformations is linear, (6–22a) then holds in general.

By induction there is a generalization of (6–22a) for products of any number of multivectors. In particular, in this way we get the required formula (6–19) for products of vectors.

Let $\boldsymbol{\beta} \in E_r^m$ and $\boldsymbol{\alpha} = \mathbf{L}_r(\boldsymbol{\beta})$. Let us find a formula for the components $\alpha^\lambda$ in terms of the components of $\boldsymbol{\beta}$. If $\lambda = (i_1, \ldots, i_r)$, $\mu = (j_1, \ldots, j_r)$, and $(c_j^i)$ is the matrix of $\mathbf{L}$, let

$$c_\mu^\lambda = \det\,(c_{j_l}^{i_k}).$$

By (6–13a), $c_\mu^\lambda$ is the $\lambda$th component of $\mathbf{v}_{j_1} \wedge \cdots \wedge \mathbf{v}_{j_r}$. By (6–20) and (6–21)

$$\boldsymbol{\alpha} = \sum_{[\mu]} \beta^\mu \mathbf{v}_{j_1} \wedge \cdots \wedge \mathbf{v}_{j_r}.$$

Since both sides have the same components,

$$\alpha^\lambda = \sum_{[\mu]} c_\mu^\lambda \beta^\mu, \quad \text{if } \boldsymbol{\alpha} = \mathbf{L}_r(\boldsymbol{\beta}). \tag{6–23a}$$

When $r = 1$, this becomes (4–4a).

**The dual transformation.** Let $\mathbf{L}_r^*$ be the linear transformation from $(E_r^n)^*$ into $(E_r^m)^*$ which is dual to $\mathbf{L}_r$. It is defined from the formula

$$\boldsymbol{\omega} \cdot \mathbf{L}_r(\boldsymbol{\beta}) = \mathbf{L}_r^*(\boldsymbol{\omega}) \cdot \boldsymbol{\beta} \tag{6–24}$$

for every $\boldsymbol{\beta} \in E_r^m$, $\boldsymbol{\omega} \in (E_r^n)^*$. Let us prove the formula dual to (6–20a):

$$\mathbf{L}_r^*(\mathbf{e}^\lambda) = \mathbf{w}^{i_1} \wedge \cdots \wedge \mathbf{w}^{i_r}, \tag{6–20b}$$

where $\mathbf{w}^1, \ldots, \mathbf{w}^n$ are the row covectors of $\mathbf{L}$. By (6–13b) the $\mu$th component of $\mathbf{w}^{i_1} \wedge \cdots \wedge \mathbf{w}^{i_r}$ is $c_\mu^\lambda$. If in (6–24) we set $\boldsymbol{\omega} = \mathbf{e}^\lambda$, $\boldsymbol{\beta} = \boldsymbol{\epsilon}_\mu$ and recall (6–20a), then

$$\mathbf{e}^\lambda \cdot (\mathbf{v}_{j_1} \wedge \cdots \wedge \mathbf{v}_{j_r}) = \mathbf{L}_r^*(\mathbf{e}^\lambda) \cdot \boldsymbol{\epsilon}_\mu.$$

The left-hand side equals $c_\mu^\lambda$, and the right-hand side is the $\mu$th component of $\mathbf{L}_r^*(\mathbf{e}^\lambda)$. Since both sides of (6–20b) have the same components $c_\mu^\lambda$, they are equal.

From (6–20b) the formulas dual to (6–19)—(6–23a) follow in the same way as before.

## PROBLEMS

1. Let $m = 2$, $n = 3$, $\mathbf{L}(s, 2t) = (s - 2t)\mathbf{e}_1 - s\mathbf{e}_2 + (2s + 3t)\mathbf{e}_3$. Find:
   (a) $\mathbf{L}^*(\mathbf{a})$. (b) $c_{12}^{ij}$. (c) $\mathbf{L}_2(\boldsymbol{\beta})$.
   (d) $\mathbf{L}_2^*(\boldsymbol{\omega})$. (e) $\mathbf{L}_3^*(\mathbf{e}^{123})$.
2. Prove the dual of (6–22a):
$$\mathbf{L}_{r+s}^*(\boldsymbol{\omega} \wedge \boldsymbol{\zeta}) = \mathbf{L}_r^*(\boldsymbol{\omega}) \wedge \mathbf{L}_s^*(\boldsymbol{\zeta}) \tag{6–22b}$$
   if $\boldsymbol{\omega} \in (E_r^n)^*$, $\boldsymbol{\zeta} \in (E_s^n)^*$.
3. Prove the dual of (6–23a):
$$\zeta_\mu = \sum_{[\lambda]} \omega_\lambda c_\mu^\lambda, \quad \text{if } \boldsymbol{\zeta} = \mathbf{L}_r^*(\boldsymbol{\omega}). \tag{6–23b}$$
4. Let $\mathbf{L}$ be an orthogonal transformation of $E^n$. Show that $|\mathbf{L}_r(\boldsymbol{\alpha})| = |\boldsymbol{\alpha}|$:
   (a) If $\boldsymbol{\alpha}$ is decomposable. [*Hint:* (6–18).]
   (b) For any $r$-vector $\boldsymbol{\alpha}$.

## 6–5 DIFFERENTIAL FORMS

In Section 2–6 a differential form of degree 1 was defined as a covector-valued function. It was shown that any such differential form $\boldsymbol{\omega}$ is a linear combination of $dx^1, \ldots, dx^n$,

$$\boldsymbol{\omega} = \sum_{i=1}^{n} \omega_i \, dx^i,$$

where the coefficients $\omega_1, \ldots, \omega_n$ are real-valued functions. For $r > 2$ a differential form of degree $r$ is supposed to be an alternating polynomial of degree $r$ in $dx^1, \ldots, dx^n$ with coefficients $\omega_\lambda$ which are real-valued functions. This idea is expressed more precisely by the following definition.

**Definition.** A *differential form of degree* $r$ is a function $\boldsymbol{\omega}$ with domain $D \subset E^n$ and values in $(E_r^n)^*$. The value of $\boldsymbol{\omega}$ at $\mathbf{x}$ is denoted by $\boldsymbol{\omega}(\mathbf{x})$.

The values of $\boldsymbol{\omega}$ are $r$-covectors. The same Greek letters $\boldsymbol{\omega}$ and $\boldsymbol{\zeta}$ used in the last section to denote $r$-covectors are now used to denote differential forms. The context will indicate clearly which is intended.

For brevity we say "*r-form*" instead of "differential form of degree $r$." It is convenient to call any real-valued function $f$ a *0-form*. If $r > n$, then the only $r$-form is the one which has the value $\mathbf{0}$ for every $\mathbf{x} \in D$. We also use $\mathbf{0}$ to denote this $r$-form.

Let $\boldsymbol{\omega}$ be an $r$-form and $\boldsymbol{\zeta}$ be an $s$-form, with the same domain $D$. The *exterior product* $\boldsymbol{\omega} \wedge \boldsymbol{\zeta}$ is the $(r + s)$-form defined by

$$(\boldsymbol{\omega} \wedge \boldsymbol{\zeta})(\mathbf{x}) = \boldsymbol{\omega}(\mathbf{x}) \wedge \boldsymbol{\zeta}(\mathbf{x})$$

for every $\mathbf{x} \in D$. Similarly, $f\boldsymbol{\omega}$ is the $r$-form such that

$$(f\boldsymbol{\omega})(\mathbf{x}) = f(\mathbf{x})\boldsymbol{\omega}(\mathbf{x})$$

for every $\mathbf{x} \in D$. The rules for multiplication of multicovectors described in Proposition 20 hold also for products of differential forms.

We recall that $dx^i$ is the 1-form with constant value $\mathbf{e}^i$ for every $\mathbf{x}$. Then $dx^i \wedge dx^j$ is the 2-form with constant value $\mathbf{e}^i \wedge \mathbf{e}^j = \mathbf{e}^{ij}$ for every $\mathbf{x}$. Let us denote the components of the 2-covectors $\boldsymbol{\omega}(\mathbf{x})$ by $\omega_{ij}(\mathbf{x})$. By (6–8)

$$\boldsymbol{\omega}(\mathbf{x}) = \sum_{i<j} \omega_{ij}(\mathbf{x})\mathbf{e}^{ij}$$

for every $\mathbf{x} \in D$. If $\omega_{ij}$ is the real-valued function whose value at $\mathbf{x}$ is $\omega_{ij}(\mathbf{x})$, then

$$\boldsymbol{\omega} = \sum_{i<j} \omega_{ij} \, dx^i \wedge dx^j.$$

(Strictly speaking, the 2-form $dx^i \wedge dx^j$ has domain $E^n$, and we mean here its restriction to $D$.)

Similarly, for any $r$-tuple $\lambda = (i_1, \ldots, i_r)$ the $r$-form $dx^{i_1} \wedge \cdots \wedge dx^{i_r}$ has constant value $\mathbf{e}^\lambda$. Hence if $\boldsymbol{\omega}$ is an $r$-form, then

$$\boldsymbol{\omega} = \sum_{[\lambda]} \omega_\lambda \, dx^{i_1} \wedge \cdots \wedge dx^{i_r} \tag{6–25}$$

where the value of $\omega_\lambda$ at $\mathbf{x}$ is $\omega_\lambda(\mathbf{x})$. Using Problem 4, Section 6–1, one can also write

$$\boldsymbol{\omega} = \frac{1}{r!} \sum_{\lambda} \omega_\lambda \, dx^{i_1} \wedge \cdots \wedge dx^{i_r}.$$

We say that an $r$-form $\boldsymbol{\omega}$ is of *class* $C^{(q)}$ if the functions $\omega_\lambda$ in (6–25) are of class $C^{(q)}$.

We recall that if $f$ is a 0-form of class $C^{(1)}$, then $df$ is the 1-form

$$df = f_1 \, dx^1 + \cdots + f_n \, dx^n,$$

where $f_1, \ldots, f_n$ are the partial derivatives. In particular, if $\boldsymbol{\omega}$ is an $r$-form of class $C^{(1)}$, then $\omega_\lambda$ is a 0-form of class $C^{(1)}$ and $d\omega_\lambda$ is defined.

**Definition.** Let $\boldsymbol{\omega}$ be an $r$-form of class $C^{(1)}$. The *exterior differential* $d\boldsymbol{\omega}$ is the $(r + 1)$-form defined by the formula

$$d\boldsymbol{\omega} = \sum_{[\lambda]} d\omega_\lambda \wedge dx^{i_1} \wedge \cdots \wedge dx^{i_r}. \tag{6–26}$$

**Example 1.** Let $r = 1$, $\boldsymbol{\omega} = \omega_1 \, dx^1 + \cdots + \omega_n \, dx^n$. Then

$$d\boldsymbol{\omega} = \sum_{i=1}^{n} d\omega_i \wedge dx^i = \sum_{i=1}^{n} \left\{ \sum_{j=1}^{n} \frac{\partial \omega_i}{\partial x_j} dx^j \right\} \wedge dx^i.$$

From the formulas $\mathbf{e}^i \wedge \mathbf{e}^j = -\mathbf{e}^j \wedge \mathbf{e}^i$, $\mathbf{e}^i \wedge \mathbf{e}^i = 0$, we have

$$dx^i \wedge dx^j = -dx^j \wedge dx^i, \qquad dx^i \wedge dx^i = \mathbf{0}.$$

Therefore

$$d\boldsymbol{\omega} = \sum_{i<j} \left( \frac{\partial \omega_j}{\partial x^i} - \frac{\partial \omega_i}{\partial x^j} \right) dx^i \wedge dx^j. \tag{6–27}$$

In particular, if $n = 2$ and $\boldsymbol{\omega} = M \, dx + N \, dy$, then

$$d\boldsymbol{\omega} = dM \wedge dx + dN \wedge dy = \left( \frac{\partial N}{\partial x} - \frac{\partial M}{\partial y} \right) dx \wedge dy.$$

**Example 2.** If $r = n$, then

$$\boldsymbol{\omega} = f \, dx^1 \wedge \cdots \wedge dx^n$$

where $f = \omega_{1 \cdots n}$. Since $d\boldsymbol{\omega}$ is an $(n + 1)$-form, $d\boldsymbol{\omega} = \mathbf{0}$.

**Example 3.** If $n = 3$ and $\omega = 2\,dx + z^2\,dy + x^2y\,dz$, then

$$d\omega = d(2) \wedge dx + d(z^2) \wedge dy + d(x^2y) \wedge dz$$
$$= 2z\,dz \wedge dy + 2xy\,dx \wedge dz + x^2\,dy \wedge dz.$$

**Proposition 24.** *The exterior differential has the following properties:*

(1) $d(\omega + \zeta) = d\omega + d\zeta$, *if* $\omega$ *and* $\zeta$ *are r-forms of class* $C^{(1)}$.

(2) $d(\omega \wedge \zeta) = d\omega \wedge \zeta + (-1)^r\omega \wedge d\zeta$, *if* $\omega$ *is an r-form and* $\zeta$ *is an s-form, both of class* $C^{(1)}$.

(3) $d(d\omega) = 0$ *if* $\omega$ *is an r-form of class* $C^{(2)}$.

*Note:* If $r = 0$ we agree that $f \wedge \zeta = f\zeta$. Similarly, if $s = 0$ then $\omega \wedge f = f\omega$. The proposition remains true if $r = 0$ or $s = 0$.

*Proof.* The coefficients of $\omega + \zeta$ in (6–25) are $\omega_\lambda + \zeta_\lambda$ and $d(\omega_\lambda + \zeta_\lambda) = d\omega_\lambda + d\zeta_\lambda$. Therefore (1) holds. Similarly, $d(c\omega) = c\,d\omega$.

To prove (2) let us for brevity set

$$\mathbf{E}^\lambda = dx^{i_1} \wedge \cdots \wedge dx^{i_r}.$$

Let us first show that

$$d(f\mathbf{E}^\lambda \wedge \mathbf{E}^\nu) = df \wedge \mathbf{E}^\lambda \wedge \mathbf{E}^\nu. \tag{*}$$

If any integer is repeated in the $(r + s)$-tuple $\lambda, \nu$ then both sides are **0**. Otherwise, $\mathbf{E}^\lambda \wedge \mathbf{E}^\nu = (-1)^p\mathbf{E}^\tau$ where $\tau$ is increasing. By definition, $d(f\mathbf{E}^\tau) = df \wedge \mathbf{E}^\tau$. Multiplying both sides by $(-1)^p$ we get (*). Now

$$\omega \wedge \zeta = \sum_{[\lambda][\nu]} \omega_\lambda\zeta_\nu\mathbf{E}^\lambda \wedge \mathbf{E}^\nu.$$

By the ordinary product rule

$$d(\omega_\lambda\zeta_\nu) = \zeta_\nu\,d\omega_\lambda + \omega_\lambda\,d\zeta_\nu.$$

By (*) with $f = \omega_\lambda\zeta_\nu$,

$$d(\omega_\lambda\zeta_\nu\mathbf{E}^\lambda \wedge \mathbf{E}^\nu) = (\zeta_\nu\,d\omega_\lambda + \omega_\lambda\,d\zeta_\nu) \wedge \mathbf{E}^\lambda \wedge \mathbf{E}^\nu.$$

Since $d\zeta_\nu$ has degree 1 and $\mathbf{E}^\lambda$ degree $r$, by (3) of Proposition 20

$$d\zeta_\nu \wedge \mathbf{E}^\lambda = (-1)^r\mathbf{E}^\lambda \wedge d\zeta_\nu.$$

The scalar-valued function $\zeta_\nu$ commutes with any differential form. Hence

$$d(\omega_\lambda\zeta_\nu\mathbf{E}^\lambda \wedge \mathbf{E}^\nu) = (d\omega_\lambda \wedge \mathbf{E}^\lambda) \wedge (\zeta_\nu\mathbf{E}^\nu) + (-1)^r(\omega_\lambda\mathbf{E}^\lambda) \wedge (d\zeta_\nu \wedge \mathbf{E}^\nu). \tag{**}$$

Using (1),

$$d(\omega \wedge \zeta) = \sum_{[\lambda][\nu]} d(\omega_\lambda\zeta_\nu\mathbf{E}^\lambda \wedge \mathbf{E}^\nu),$$

while

$$\sum_{[\lambda][\nu]} (d\omega_\lambda \wedge \mathbf{E}^\lambda) \wedge (\zeta_\nu \mathbf{E}^\nu) = \left[\sum_{[\lambda]} d\omega_\lambda \wedge \mathbf{E}^\lambda\right] \wedge \left[\sum_{[\nu]} \zeta_\nu \mathbf{E}^\nu\right] = d\boldsymbol{\omega} \wedge \boldsymbol{\zeta}.$$

Similarly,

$$(-1)^r \sum_{[\lambda][\nu]} (\omega_\lambda \mathbf{E}^\lambda) \wedge (d\zeta_\nu \wedge \mathbf{E}^\nu) = (-1)^r \boldsymbol{\omega} \wedge d\boldsymbol{\zeta},$$

which proves (2).

If $f$ is of class $C^{(2)}$, then from (6–27)

$$d(df) = \sum_{i<j} \left(\frac{\partial^2 f}{\partial x^i\, \partial x^j} - \frac{\partial^2 f}{\partial x^j\, \partial x^i}\right) dx^i \wedge dx^j = \mathbf{0}.$$

The form $\mathbf{E}^\lambda$ has constant coefficients and hence $d\mathbf{E}^\lambda = \mathbf{0}$. Using the product rule (2), $d(df \wedge \mathbf{E}^\lambda) = \mathbf{0}$. Taking $f = \omega_\lambda$ and using (1),

$$d(d\boldsymbol{\omega}) = d\left(\sum_{[\lambda]} d\omega_\lambda \wedge \mathbf{E}^\lambda\right) = \sum_{[\lambda]} d(d\omega_\lambda \wedge \mathbf{E}^\lambda) = \mathbf{0}. \blacksquare$$

**Definition.** An $r$-form $\boldsymbol{\omega}$ is *closed* if $d\boldsymbol{\omega} = \mathbf{0}$. If $\boldsymbol{\omega} = d\boldsymbol{\zeta}$ for some $(r-1)$-form $\boldsymbol{\zeta}$, then $\boldsymbol{\omega}$ is an *exact* $r$-form.

If $r = 1$, these definitions agree with the ones given in Section 2–6. If $\boldsymbol{\omega}$ is exact and $\boldsymbol{\zeta}$ can be chosen to be of class $C^{(2)}$, then $d\boldsymbol{\omega} = d(d\boldsymbol{\zeta}) = \mathbf{0}$. Hence $\boldsymbol{\omega}$ is closed. Poincaré's lemma states that if domain $D$ is star-shaped then conversely any closed form $\boldsymbol{\omega}$ is exact. This will be proved in Section 7–7.

***Remark.** The exterior differential $d$ is uniquely determined by Properties (1), (2), (3) and the following property.

(4) *For $r = 0$, $df$ agrees with its definition in Section 2–6.*

Let $d'$ also have these four properties. Then $d'\mathbf{E}^\lambda = d'(d'x^{i_1} \wedge \mathbf{E}^\mu)$, where $\mu = (i_2, \ldots, i_r)$. But $dx^i = d'x^i$ by (4) since $dx^i$ stands for the differential of the coordinate function $X^i$. Using (2), (3), and induction on $r$, $d'\mathbf{E}^\lambda = \mathbf{0}$. Using (2) and (4), $d'(f\mathbf{E}^\lambda) = df \wedge \mathbf{E}^\lambda$. Using (1),

$$d'\boldsymbol{\omega} = d'\left(\sum_{[\lambda]} \omega_\lambda \mathbf{E}^\lambda\right) = \sum_{[\lambda]} d'(\omega_\lambda \mathbf{E}^\lambda)$$

$$= \sum_{[\lambda]} d\omega_\lambda \wedge \mathbf{E}^\lambda.$$

Thus $d'\boldsymbol{\omega} = d\boldsymbol{\omega}$ for every $\boldsymbol{\omega}$ of class $C^{(1)}$. In particular, this proves that the exterior differential $d$ is "coordinate free."

**Transformation law for differential forms.** Let $\mathbf{g}$ be a transformation of class $C^{(1)}$ from an open set $\Delta \subset E^m$ into $E^n$. Let $D$ be an open set containing

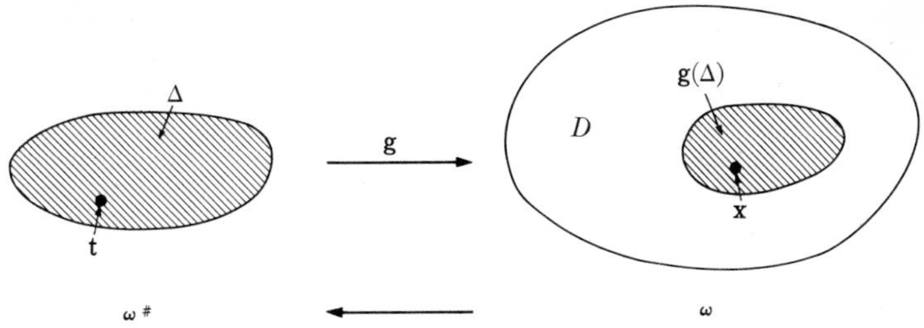


FIGURE 6–3

the image $\mathbf{g}(\Delta)$. If $\boldsymbol{\omega}$ is any $r$-form with domain $D$, then there is a corresponding $r$-form denoted by $\boldsymbol{\omega}^\#$ with domain $\Delta$. Formally, $\boldsymbol{\omega}^\#$ is obtained by merely substituting $\mathbf{g}(\mathbf{t})$ for $\mathbf{x}$ and $dg^i$ for $dx^i$. The precise definition of $\boldsymbol{\omega}^\#$ is as follows.

**Definition.** For each $\mathbf{t} \in \Delta$, the value of $\boldsymbol{\omega}^\#$ at $\mathbf{t}$ is

$$\boldsymbol{\omega}^\#(\mathbf{t}) = \mathbf{L}_r^*[\boldsymbol{\omega}(\mathbf{x})], \tag{6–28}$$

where

$$\mathbf{x} = \mathbf{g}(\mathbf{t}), \qquad \mathbf{L} = D\mathbf{g}(\mathbf{t}),$$

and $\mathbf{L}_r^*$ is the dual linear transformation induced by $\mathbf{L}$ (p. 224). In case $r = 0$ we agree that $f^\# = f \circ \mathbf{g}$. (The notation $^\#$ is used for brevity even though it does not indicate the dependence on $\mathbf{g}$ and the degree $r$.)

**Proposition 25.** *The operation $^\#$ has the following properties:*

(1) $(\boldsymbol{\omega} + \boldsymbol{\zeta})^\# = \boldsymbol{\omega}^\# + \boldsymbol{\zeta}^\#$, *if $\boldsymbol{\omega}$ and $\boldsymbol{\zeta}$ are of degree $r$.*

(2) $(\boldsymbol{\omega} \wedge \boldsymbol{\zeta})^\# = \boldsymbol{\omega}^\# \wedge \boldsymbol{\zeta}^\#$, *if $\boldsymbol{\omega}$ is of degree $r$ and $\boldsymbol{\zeta}$ of degree $s$.*

(3) $(df)^\# = d(f \circ \mathbf{g})$, *if $f$ is of class $C^{(1)}$.*

(4) $(dx^{i_1} \wedge \cdots \wedge dx^{i_r})^\# = dg^{i_1} \wedge \cdots \wedge dg^{i_r}$.

(5) $d\boldsymbol{\omega}^\# = (d\boldsymbol{\omega})^\#$, *if $\boldsymbol{\omega}$ is of class $C^{(1)}$ and $\mathbf{g}$ of class $C^{(2)}$.*

*Proof.* Since $\mathbf{L}_r^*$ is linear,

$$(\boldsymbol{\omega} + \boldsymbol{\zeta})^\#(\mathbf{t}) = \boldsymbol{\omega}^\#(\mathbf{t}) + \boldsymbol{\zeta}^\#(\mathbf{t}).$$

Since this is true for every $\mathbf{t} \in \Delta$, this proves (1). Using (6–22b), we get

$$(\boldsymbol{\omega} \wedge \boldsymbol{\zeta})^\#(\mathbf{t}) = \boldsymbol{\omega}^\#(\mathbf{t}) \wedge \boldsymbol{\zeta}^\#(\mathbf{t})$$

for every $\mathbf{t} \in \Delta$, which proves (2). By the chain rule (p. 106), $d(f \circ \mathbf{g})(\mathbf{t}) = \mathbf{L}_1^*[df(\mathbf{x})]$. By (6–28) the right-hand side is $(df)^\#(\mathbf{t})$. Thus (3) holds. Recall that $dx^i$ stands for $dX^i$, where $X^i(\mathbf{x}) = x^i$ for each $\mathbf{x}$. Then $g^i = X^i \circ \mathbf{g}$ and from (3) with $f = X^i$,

$$(dx^i)^\# = dg^i. \tag{6–29}$$

Then (4) follows from this and (2). To prove (5) we have from (1)–(4)

$$\boldsymbol{\omega}^{\#} = \sum_{[\lambda]} \omega_\lambda \circ \mathbf{g}\, dg^{i_1} \wedge \cdots \wedge dg^{i_r},$$

$$d\boldsymbol{\omega}^{\#} = \sum_{[\lambda]} d(\omega_\lambda \circ \mathbf{g}\, dg^{i_1} \wedge \cdots \wedge dg^{i_r}).$$

By (3), $(d\omega_\lambda)^{\#} = d(\omega_\lambda \circ \mathbf{g})$. Since $\mathbf{g}$ is of class $C^{(2)}$, $d(dg^i) = \mathbf{0}$. Therefore, by the product rule

$$d(dg^{i_1} \wedge \cdots \wedge dg^{i_r}) = \mathbf{0}.$$

Using the product rule again, we have

$$d\boldsymbol{\omega}^{\#} = \sum_{[\lambda]} (d\omega_\lambda)^{\#} \wedge dg^{i_1} \wedge \cdots \wedge dg^{i_r} = (d\boldsymbol{\omega})^{\#}. \blacksquare$$

As in Chapter 4 let $g_j^i$ denote the $j$th partial derivative of the component $g^i$. Let

$$g_\mu^\lambda = \det\,(g_{j_l}^{i_k}) = \frac{\partial(g^{i_1}, \ldots, g^{i_r})}{\partial(t^{j_1}, \ldots, t^{j_r})}.$$

The matrix of $D\mathbf{g}(\mathbf{t})$ is $(g_j^i(\mathbf{t}))$, and the row covectors are $dg^1(\mathbf{t}), \ldots, dg^n(\mathbf{t})$. By (6–13b) the $\mu$th component of $dg^{i_1} \wedge \cdots \wedge dg^{i_r}$ is $g_\mu^\lambda$. Therefore

$$(dx^{i_1} \wedge \cdots \wedge dx^{i_r})^{\#} = \sum_{[\mu]} g_\mu^\lambda\, dt^{j_1} \wedge \cdots \wedge dt^{j_r}. \tag{6–30}$$

In applying this formula in the next chapter we shall usually take $r = m$. In that case the only increasing $r$-tuple is $\mu = (1, 2, \ldots, r)$ and the right-hand side of (6–30) has just one term.

**Example 4.** Let $n = 3$, $r = m = 2$, $(x, y, z) = \mathbf{g}(s, t)$. Then

$$(dx \wedge dz)^{\#} = \frac{\partial(g^1, g^3)}{\partial(s, t)}\, ds \wedge dt.$$

If $\boldsymbol{\omega} = f\, dx \wedge dz$, then $\boldsymbol{\omega}^{\#} = f \circ \mathbf{g}\, (dx \wedge dz)^{\#}$.

**Example 5.** Let $m = n = r$. Then, writing $f = \omega_{1\ldots n}$, we have

$$\boldsymbol{\omega}^{\#} = (f\, dx^1 \wedge \cdots \wedge dx^n)^{\#} = f \circ \mathbf{g}(dx^1 \wedge \cdots \wedge dx^n)^{\#}$$
$$= f \circ \mathbf{g}\, \frac{\partial(g^1, \ldots, g^n)}{\partial(t^1, \ldots, t^n)}\, dt^1 \wedge \cdots \wedge dt^n.$$

**Example 6.** Let $m = r = 1$. Then $\boldsymbol{\omega}^{\#}(t) = \boldsymbol{\omega}[g(t)] \cdot \mathbf{g}'(t)$, and the definition (3–8a) of the line integral can be rewritten

$$\int_\gamma \boldsymbol{\omega} = \int_a^b \boldsymbol{\omega}^{\#}.$$

*Note. In tensor language a differential form of degree $r$, being an $r$-covector-valued function, is called a covariant alternating *tensor field* of rank $r$. From (6–23b) we obtain the transformation law for the components of such a tensor field:

$$\zeta_\mu = \sum_{[\lambda]} \omega_\lambda \circ \mathbf{g}\, g^\lambda_\mu, \quad \text{if } \zeta = \omega^\#.$$

**PROBLEMS**

Assume that all forms which appear are of class $C^{(1)}$.

1. Find the exterior differential of:
   (a) $x^2y\,dy - xy^2\,dx$.
   (b) $\cos(xy^2)\,dx \wedge dz$.
   (c) $f(x, z)\,dx$.
   (d) $x\,dy \wedge dz + y\,dz \wedge dx + z\,dx \wedge dy$.
2. Let $P, Q, R$ have domain $D \subset E^3$. Show that

$$d(P\,dy \wedge dz + Q\,dz \wedge dx + R\,dx \wedge dy) = \left(\frac{\partial P}{\partial x} + \frac{\partial Q}{\partial y} + \frac{\partial R}{\partial z}\right) dx \wedge dy \wedge dz.$$

3. (a) Find an $(n-1)$-form $\zeta$ such that $d\zeta = dx^1 \wedge \cdots \wedge dx^n$. [*Hint:* Problem 1(d).]
   (b) Find an $(r-1)$-form $\zeta^\lambda$ such that $d\zeta^\lambda = \mathbf{E}^\lambda$.
   (c) Show that if the coefficients $\omega_\lambda$ in (6–25) are constant functions, then $\omega$ is exact.
4. (a) Show that if $\omega$ and $\zeta$ are closed differential forms, then $\omega \wedge \zeta$ is closed.
   (b) Show that if $\omega$ is closed and $\zeta$ is exact, then $\omega \wedge \zeta$ is exact.
5. Find the exterior differential of:
   (a) $d\omega \wedge \zeta - \omega \wedge d\zeta$.
   (b) $d\omega \wedge \zeta \wedge \eta + \omega \wedge d\zeta \wedge \eta + \omega \wedge \zeta \wedge d\eta$, if $\omega$ and $\zeta$ are of even degree.
6. A function $f$ is an *integrating factor* for a 1-form $\omega$ if $f(\mathbf{x}) \neq 0$ for every $\mathbf{x} \in D$ and $f\omega$ is closed. Show that if $\omega$ has an integrating factor then $\omega \wedge d\omega = \mathbf{0}$.
7. Let $n = m = 2$, $r = 1$, $\omega = M\,dx + N\,dy$. Find explicitly $d\omega$ and $\omega^\#$ and verify that $(d\omega)^\# = d\omega^\#$.
8. Let $n = m = 3$, $\mathbf{g}(s, t, u) = (s\cos t)\mathbf{e}_1 + (s\sin t)\mathbf{e}_2 + u\mathbf{e}_3$. Find:
   (a) $(f\,dx \wedge dy \wedge dz)^\#$. (b) $(x\,dy \wedge dz)^\#$.
9. Show that if $\omega$ is a 2-form, then

$$d\omega = \sum_{i<j<k} \left(\frac{\partial \omega_{ij}}{\partial x^k} + \frac{\partial \omega_{ki}}{\partial x^j} + \frac{\partial \omega_{jk}}{\partial x^i}\right) dx^i \wedge dx^j \wedge dx^k.$$

10. Let $\omega^1, \ldots, \omega^p$ be 1-forms such that $\omega^i = \sum_{j=1}^p f^i_j\,dg^j$, $i = 1, \ldots, p$. Assume that the functions $f^i_j$ are of class $C^{(1)}$, the $g^j$ are of class $C^{(2)}$, and that the 1-covectors $\omega^1(\mathbf{x}), \ldots, \omega^p(\mathbf{x})$ are linearly independent for every $\mathbf{x} \in D$. Find 1-forms $\theta^i_j$ such that $d\omega^i = \sum_{j=j}^p \theta^i_j \wedge \omega^j$. [*Hint:* The $p \times p$ matrix $(f^i_j(\mathbf{x}))$ must be nonsingular.]

[*Note:* Conversely, if $d\boldsymbol{\omega}^i$ is a linear combination of $\boldsymbol{\omega}^1, \ldots, \boldsymbol{\omega}^p$ with coefficients 1-forms $\boldsymbol{\theta}^i_j$, then locally functions $f^i_j$, $g^i$ as above can be found. This result is called the *Frobenius integration theorem*, and has important applications in geometry and differential equations. See [9], p. 97.]

## 6–6 THE ADJOINT AND CODIFFERENTIAL

To each $r$-vector $\boldsymbol{\alpha}$ we shall now assign a certain $(n - r)$-vector, which is called the *adjoint* of $\boldsymbol{\alpha}$ and is denoted by $*\boldsymbol{\alpha}$. Let us begin with the special dimension $r = n - 1$, which is the only one needed in connection with the divergence theorem in the next chapter.

Let $\boldsymbol{\alpha} = \mathbf{h}_1 \wedge \cdots \wedge \mathbf{h}_{n-1}$. If $\boldsymbol{\alpha} = \mathbf{0}$, then we set $*\boldsymbol{\alpha} = \mathbf{0}$. If $\boldsymbol{\alpha} \neq \mathbf{0}$, then $*\boldsymbol{\alpha}$ will turn out to be the vector $\mathbf{h}$ with the following three properties: (1) $\mathbf{h}$ is a vector normal to the $(n - 1)$-space $P$ spanned by $\mathbf{h}_1, \ldots, \mathbf{h}_{n-1}$; (2) $(\mathbf{h}, \mathbf{h}_1, \ldots, \mathbf{h}_{n-1})$ is a positively oriented frame for $E^n$; (3) $|\mathbf{h}| = |\boldsymbol{\alpha}|$. Condition (3) says that the length of $\mathbf{h}$ equals $V_{n-1}(K)$, where $K$ is the $(n - 1)$-parallelepiped vertex $\mathbf{0}$ spanned by $\mathbf{h}_1, \ldots, \mathbf{h}_{n-1}$. (See Fig. 6–4.)

With this in mind, let us define $*$ first for the standard basis $(n - 1)$-vectors. Let $i' = (1, 2, \ldots, i - 1, i + 1, \ldots, n)$. Since $i - 1$ interchanges will change the $n$-tuple $(i, i')$ into the increasing $n$-tuple $(1, \ldots, n)$,

$$(-1)^{i-1}\mathbf{e}_i \wedge \mathbf{e}_{i'} = \mathbf{e}_{1\ldots n}.$$

Therefore we set

$$*\mathbf{e}_{i'} = (-1)^{i-1}\mathbf{e}_i. \tag{6–31}$$

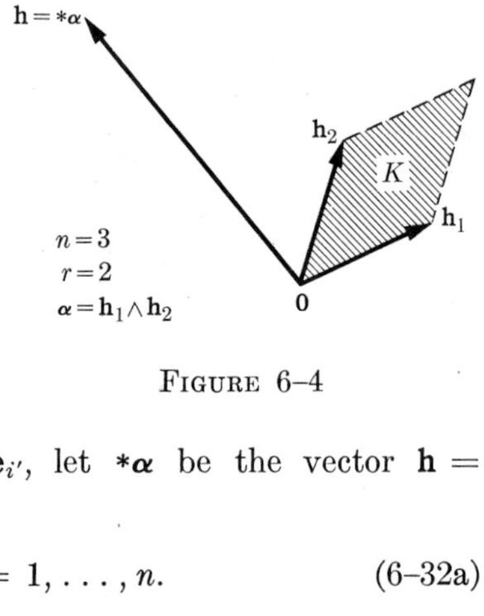


FIGURE 6–4

We want the operation $*$ to behave linearly.

For any $(n - 1)$-vector $\boldsymbol{\alpha} = \sum_{i=1}^n \alpha^{i'}\mathbf{e}_{i'}$, let $*\boldsymbol{\alpha}$ be the vector $\mathbf{h} = \sum_{i=1}^n \alpha^{i'}(*\mathbf{e}_{i'})$. Its components are

$$h^i = (-1)^{i-1}\alpha^{i'}, \qquad i = 1, \ldots, n. \tag{6–32a}$$

**Example 1.** Let $n = 3$. In this particular dimension it is useful to consider instead of the standard basis $\{\mathbf{e}_{23}, \mathbf{e}_{13}, \mathbf{e}_{12}\}$ for $E^3_2$ the basis $\{\mathbf{e}_{23}, \mathbf{e}_{31}, \mathbf{e}_{12}\}$, where $\mathbf{e}_{31} = -\mathbf{e}_{13}$. Then any 2-vector $\boldsymbol{\alpha}$ can be written $\boldsymbol{\alpha} = \alpha^{23}\mathbf{e}_{23} + \alpha^{31}\mathbf{e}_{31} + \alpha^{12}\mathbf{e}_{12}$, where $\alpha^{31} = -\alpha^{13}$; and

$$*\mathbf{e}_{23} = \mathbf{e}_1, \qquad *\mathbf{e}_{31} = \mathbf{e}_2, \qquad *\mathbf{e}_{12} = \mathbf{e}_3,$$
$$\alpha^{23} = h^1, \qquad \alpha^{31} = h^2, \qquad \alpha^{12} = h^3 \quad \text{if } \mathbf{h} = *\boldsymbol{\alpha}.$$

Let us show that $*\boldsymbol{\alpha}$ has Properties (1), (2), and (3) above. Given a frame $(\mathbf{h}_1, \ldots, \mathbf{h}_{n-1})$, these three properties determine a vector, which we denote temporarily by $\tilde{\mathbf{h}}$. Let $(\mathbf{h}'_1, \ldots, \mathbf{h}'_{n-1})$ be an orthogonal frame for $P$, $\mathbf{h}'_k \cdot \mathbf{h}'_l = 0$ if $k \neq l$. Then $\boldsymbol{\alpha}$ is a scalar multiple $b$ of $\mathbf{h}'_1 \wedge \cdots \wedge \mathbf{h}'_{n-1}$, and replacing

$\mathbf{h}_1'$ by $b\mathbf{h}_1'$ we may assume that $\boldsymbol{\alpha} = \mathbf{h}_1' \wedge \cdots \wedge \mathbf{h}_{n-1}'$. By (1), $\tilde{\mathbf{h}} \cdot \mathbf{h}_k' = 0$ for each $k = 1, \ldots, n-1$. Therefore

$$|\tilde{\mathbf{h}} \wedge \boldsymbol{\alpha}| = |\tilde{\mathbf{h}}|\,|\mathbf{h}_1'| \cdots |\mathbf{h}_{n-1}'| = |\tilde{\mathbf{h}}|\,|\boldsymbol{\alpha}|.$$

By (2), $\tilde{\mathbf{h}} \wedge \boldsymbol{\alpha} = c\mathbf{e}_{1\cdots n}$ where $c > 0$. In fact, $c = |\tilde{\mathbf{h}} \wedge \boldsymbol{\alpha}|$. Let $\mathbf{h} = *\boldsymbol{\alpha}$. From (6–32a), $|\mathbf{h}| = |\boldsymbol{\alpha}|$ and consequently $c = |\tilde{\mathbf{h}}|\,|\mathbf{h}|$.

On the other hand,

$$\tilde{\mathbf{h}} \wedge \boldsymbol{\alpha} = \left(\sum_{i=1}^{n} \tilde{h}^i \mathbf{e}_i\right) \wedge \left(\sum_{j=1}^{n} \alpha^{j'} \mathbf{e}_{j'}\right) = \left[\sum_{i=1}^{n} \tilde{h}^i \alpha^{i'} (-1)^{i-1}\right] \mathbf{e}_{1\cdots n},$$

since $\mathbf{e}_i \wedge \mathbf{e}_{j'} = \mathbf{0}$ unless $i = j$. By (6–32a)

$$\tilde{\mathbf{h}} \wedge \boldsymbol{\alpha} = (\tilde{\mathbf{h}} \cdot \mathbf{h})\mathbf{e}_{1\cdots n},$$

and hence $\tilde{\mathbf{h}} \cdot \mathbf{h} = c = |\tilde{\mathbf{h}}|\,|\mathbf{h}|$. Equality holds in Cauchy's inequality (Section 1–1) and therefore $\tilde{\mathbf{h}}$ is a positive scalar multiple of $\mathbf{h}$. By (3), $|\tilde{\mathbf{h}}| = |\mathbf{h}|$, and hence $\tilde{\mathbf{h}} = \mathbf{h}$ as required.

We can now show that every $(n-1)$-vector $\boldsymbol{\alpha}$ is decomposable. Let $\boldsymbol{\alpha} \neq \mathbf{0}$, and let $\mathbf{h} = *\boldsymbol{\alpha}$. The vector $\mathbf{h}$ is normal to an $(n-1)$-dimensional subspace $P$. Let $\tilde{\boldsymbol{\alpha}}$ be an $(n-1)$-vector of $P$ whose orientation and norm are chosen such that $\tilde{\boldsymbol{\alpha}}$ and $\mathbf{h}$ are related by (1)—(3). Then $\tilde{\boldsymbol{\alpha}}$ is decomposable and $\mathbf{h} = *\tilde{\boldsymbol{\alpha}}$. Thus $*\tilde{\boldsymbol{\alpha}} = *\boldsymbol{\alpha}$, which by (6–32a) implies that $\tilde{\boldsymbol{\alpha}} = \boldsymbol{\alpha}$.

If $\boldsymbol{\omega}$ is an $(n-1)$-covector, then $*\boldsymbol{\omega}$ is the 1-covector whose components are given by the dual to (6–32a):

$$\zeta_i = (-1)^{i-1}\omega_{i'}, \qquad i = 1, \ldots, n, \quad \text{if } \boldsymbol{\zeta} = *\boldsymbol{\omega}. \tag{6–32b}$$

If $\boldsymbol{\omega}$ is an $(n-1)$-form, then $*\boldsymbol{\omega}$ is the 1-form such that $(*\boldsymbol{\omega})(\mathbf{x}) = *\boldsymbol{\omega}(\mathbf{x})$ for each $\mathbf{x}$ in the domain $D$ of $\boldsymbol{\omega}$. The dual to (6–31) is $*\mathbf{e}^{i'} = (-1)^{i-1}\mathbf{e}^i$, and hence

$$*(dx^1 \wedge \cdots \wedge dx^{i-1} \wedge dx^{i+1} \wedge \cdots \wedge dx^n) = (-1)^{i-1}\, dx^i.$$

If $\boldsymbol{\omega}$ is an $(n-1)$-form of class $C^{(1)}$, then $d\boldsymbol{\omega}$ is an $n$-form. Consequently, $d\boldsymbol{\omega} = f\, dx^1 \wedge \cdots \wedge dx^n$, where $f$ is a scalar-valued function. To get a convenient expression for $f$, let $\boldsymbol{\zeta} = *\boldsymbol{\omega}$. Its components are given by (6–32b). Let

$$\operatorname{div} \boldsymbol{\zeta} = \frac{\partial \zeta_1}{\partial x^1} + \cdots + \frac{\partial \zeta_n}{\partial x^n}. \tag{6–33}$$

This function is called the *divergence* of the 1-form $\boldsymbol{\zeta}$. By a short calculation (Problem 2), the desired function $f$ is just $\operatorname{div} \boldsymbol{\zeta}$. Thus

$$d\boldsymbol{\omega} = \operatorname{div} \boldsymbol{\zeta}\, dx^1 \wedge \cdots \wedge dx^n, \quad \text{if } \boldsymbol{\zeta} = *\boldsymbol{\omega}. \tag{6–34}$$

When $n = 3$ the divergence has an important physical significance which will be indicated in Section 7–4.

---

The remainder of this section will not be used in Chapter 7. Let us define $*\boldsymbol{\alpha}$ for any $r$-vector $\boldsymbol{\alpha}$ when $0 \leq r \leq n$. If $r = 0$ or $n$ we set

$$*c = c\mathbf{e}_{1\cdots n}, \qquad *(c\mathbf{e}_{1\cdots n}) = c.$$

If $0 < r < n$, let $\lambda = (i_1, \ldots, i_r)$ be any increasing $r$-tuple, and let $\lambda' = (j_1, \ldots, j_{n-r})$ be the increasing $(n - r)$-tuple whose entries are those integers $j_l$ between 1 and $n$ which do not appear in $\lambda$. Let

$$\epsilon_\lambda = \delta^{1\cdots n}_{\lambda',\lambda}.$$

It is $\pm 1$, depending on whether an odd or an even number of interchanges puts $\lambda', \lambda$ in increasing order. If $\boldsymbol{\alpha}$ is any $r$-vector, then its *adjoint* is the $(n - r)$-vector $*\boldsymbol{\alpha}$ whose components satisfy

$$(*\boldsymbol{\alpha})^{\lambda'} = \alpha^\lambda \epsilon_\lambda. \tag{6–35a}$$

If $r = n - 1$ and $\lambda = i'$, then $\lambda' = (i)$, $\epsilon_\lambda = (-1)^{i-1}$, and (6–35a) agrees with (6–32a). From the definition (6–35a),

$$*(\boldsymbol{\alpha} + \boldsymbol{\beta}) = *\boldsymbol{\alpha} + *\boldsymbol{\beta}, \qquad *(c\boldsymbol{\alpha}) = c*\boldsymbol{\alpha}.$$

Moreover, $*\boldsymbol{\alpha} = \mathbf{0}$ if and only if $\boldsymbol{\alpha} = \mathbf{0}$. Thus the operation $*$ gives an isomorphism between $E^n_r$ and $E^n_{n-r}$. This isomorphism preserves inner products. In fact, if $\boldsymbol{\alpha}$ and $\boldsymbol{\beta}$ are $r$-vectors then

$$*\boldsymbol{\alpha} \cdot *\boldsymbol{\beta} = \sum_{[\lambda]} (*\boldsymbol{\alpha})^{\lambda'}(*\boldsymbol{\beta})^{\lambda'} = \sum_{[\lambda]} (\epsilon_\lambda)^2 \alpha^\lambda \beta^\lambda.$$

Since $(\epsilon_\lambda)^2 = 1$, $*\boldsymbol{\alpha} \cdot *\boldsymbol{\beta} = \boldsymbol{\alpha} \cdot \boldsymbol{\beta}$. Taking $\boldsymbol{\alpha} = \boldsymbol{\beta}$ we have in particular $|*\boldsymbol{\alpha}| = |\boldsymbol{\alpha}|$. Since $\epsilon_{\lambda'}\epsilon_\lambda = (-1)^{r(n-r)}$,

$$**\boldsymbol{\alpha} = (-1)^{r(n-r)}\boldsymbol{\alpha}.$$

Now let $\nu$ be any increasing $(n - r)$-tuple. Then

$$\mathbf{e}_\nu \wedge \mathbf{e}_\lambda = \delta^{1\cdots n}_{\nu,\lambda}\mathbf{e}_{1\cdots n},$$

which is $\mathbf{0}$ if $\nu \neq \lambda'$ and is $\epsilon_\lambda \mathbf{e}_{1\cdots n}$ if $\nu = \lambda'$. If $\boldsymbol{\beta}$ is any $(n - r)$-vector, then

$$\boldsymbol{\beta} \wedge \boldsymbol{\alpha} = \sum_{[\nu][\lambda]} \beta^\nu \alpha^\lambda \mathbf{e}_\nu \wedge \mathbf{e}_\lambda = \left(\sum_{[\lambda]} \beta^{\lambda'}\alpha^\lambda \epsilon_\lambda\right) \mathbf{e}_{1\cdots n},$$

and

$$\boldsymbol{\beta} \wedge \boldsymbol{\alpha} = (\boldsymbol{\beta} \cdot *\boldsymbol{\alpha})\mathbf{e}_{1\cdots n}. \tag{6–36}$$

If $\boldsymbol{\alpha} \neq \mathbf{0}$ is decomposable, then $*\boldsymbol{\alpha}$ has the following geometric interpretation. Let $\boldsymbol{\alpha} = \mathbf{h}_1 \wedge \cdots \wedge \mathbf{h}_r$, and let $\mathbf{h}_{r+1}, \ldots, \mathbf{h}_n$ be vectors such that: (1) $(\mathbf{h}_{r+1}, \ldots, \mathbf{h}_n)$ is a frame for the orthogonal complement of the $r$-space of $\boldsymbol{\alpha}$; (2) $(\mathbf{h}_{r+1}, \ldots, \mathbf{h}_n, \mathbf{h}_1, \ldots, \mathbf{h}_r)$ is a positively oriented frame for $E^n$; (3) $|\mathbf{h}_{r+1} \wedge \cdots \wedge \mathbf{h}_n| = |\boldsymbol{\alpha}|$. Then $*\boldsymbol{\alpha} = \mathbf{h}_{r+1} \wedge \cdots \wedge \mathbf{h}_n$. The proof is similar to the one given above for $r = n - 1$.

If $\boldsymbol{\omega}$ is an $r$-covector, then $*\boldsymbol{\omega}$ is the $(n - r)$-covector such that

$$(*\boldsymbol{\omega})_{\lambda'} = \omega_\lambda \epsilon_\lambda. \tag{6–35b}$$

If $\boldsymbol{\omega}$ is a differential form of degree $r$, then $*\boldsymbol{\omega}$ is the $(n - r)$-form such that $(*\boldsymbol{\omega})(\mathbf{x}) = *\boldsymbol{\omega}(\mathbf{x})$ for every $\mathbf{x}$ in the domain of $\boldsymbol{\omega}$.

**Example 2.** $*(f\, dx^{i_1} \wedge \cdots \wedge dx^{i_r}) = \epsilon_\lambda f\, dx^{j_1} \wedge \cdots \wedge dx^{j_{n-r}}$, where $\lambda' = (j_1, \ldots, j_{n-r})$. For $r = 0$ or $n$,

$$*f = f\, dx^1 \wedge \cdots \wedge dx^n, \quad *(f\, dx^1 \wedge \cdots \wedge dx^n) = f.$$

Let $\boldsymbol{\omega}$ be an $r$-form of class $C^{(1)}$. Then $d(*\boldsymbol{\omega})$ is an $(n - r + 1)$-form, and $*d(*\boldsymbol{\omega})$ is an $(r - 1)$-form.

**Definition.** The *codifferential* of $\boldsymbol{\omega}$ is

$$\tilde{d}\boldsymbol{\omega} = (-1)^{r(n-r)} *d(*\boldsymbol{\omega}). \tag{6–37a}$$

Since $**\boldsymbol{\omega} = (-1)^{r(n-r)}\boldsymbol{\omega}$, substituting $*\boldsymbol{\omega}$ for $\boldsymbol{\omega}$ we get

$$\tilde{d}(*\boldsymbol{\omega}) = *d\boldsymbol{\omega}. \tag{6–37b}$$

If $r = 0$, we invent a form $\mathbf{0}$ of degree $-1$ and agree that $\tilde{d}f = \mathbf{0}$. If $\boldsymbol{\zeta}$ is a 1-form, consider the $(n - 1)$-form $\boldsymbol{\omega} = (-1)^{n-1} *\boldsymbol{\zeta}$. Then $*\boldsymbol{\omega} = \boldsymbol{\zeta}$ and by (6–37b) $\tilde{d}\boldsymbol{\zeta} = *d\boldsymbol{\omega}$. By (6–34) $\tilde{d}\boldsymbol{\zeta} = \operatorname{div} \boldsymbol{\zeta}$. Thus the codifferential of a 1-form $\boldsymbol{\zeta}$ is just the 0-form div $\boldsymbol{\zeta}$.

*Notes.* Many authors define the adjoint so that in (2) above $(\mathbf{h}_1, \ldots, \mathbf{h}_r, \mathbf{h}_{r+1}, \ldots, \mathbf{h}_n)$ is a positively oriented frame for $E^n$. When $r(n - r)$ is odd, according to that definition $*\boldsymbol{\alpha}$ has opposite sign to the one here.

The definition of the adjoint involves the euclidean norm. Hence both the adjoint and the codifferential depend on the euclidean structure inherited by $E^n_r$ and $(E^n_r)^*$ from the euclidean inner product in $E^n$; while the notions of $\wedge$ and $d$ actually depend only on the vector space structure and not the inner product.

In riemannian geometry one is provided at each point $\mathbf{x}$ with an inner product $B_{\mathbf{x}}$, not necessarily the euclidean inner product. The definition of adjoint must be modified accordingly. The codifferential is again defined by (6–37a). However, the formula (6–33) for the divergence and its generalization (Problem 5) must be modified. See [9] and Chap. V of [17].

**PROBLEMS**

1. Let $n = 2$. Show that
   (a) $*\mathbf{h} = h^2\mathbf{e}_1 - h^1\mathbf{e}_2$.
   (b) $*(M\,dx + N\,dy) = N\,dx - M\,dy$.
   (c) $*d(N\,dx - M\,dy) = -(\partial M/\partial x + \partial N/\partial y)$.
2. (a) Let $n = 3$, and $\omega = P\,dy \wedge dz + Q\,dz \wedge dx + R\,dx \wedge dy$ be a 2-form. Show that

$$*\omega = P\,dx + Q\,dy + R\,dz,\quad d\omega = (\partial P/\partial x + \partial Q/\partial y + \partial R/\partial z)\,dx \wedge dy \wedge dz.$$

   (b) Let $\omega$ be an $(n-1)$-form,

$$\omega = \sum_{i=1}^{n} \omega_{i'}\,dx^1 \wedge \cdots \wedge dx^{i-1} \wedge dx^{i+1} \wedge \cdots \wedge dx^n,$$

   and let $\zeta = *\omega$. Show that $d\omega = \operatorname{div} \zeta\, dx^1 \wedge \cdots \wedge dx^n$.
3. Show that: (a) div $(df)$ is the Laplacian of $f$. (b) $\operatorname{div}(f\omega) = f \operatorname{div} \omega + df \cdot \omega$, where $(\zeta \cdot \omega)(\mathbf{x}) = \zeta(\mathbf{x}) \cdot \omega(\mathbf{x})$ for 1-forms $\zeta$, $\omega$.

---

4. Let $\boldsymbol{\alpha}$ and $\boldsymbol{\beta}$ be $r$-vectors. Show that:
   (a) $(*\boldsymbol{\alpha}) \wedge \boldsymbol{\beta} = \boldsymbol{\alpha} \cdot \boldsymbol{\beta}\,\mathbf{e}_{1\cdots n}$.
   (b) $(*\boldsymbol{\alpha}) \wedge \boldsymbol{\beta} = (-1)^{r(n-r)}\,\boldsymbol{\alpha} \wedge (*\boldsymbol{\beta})$.
   (c) $(*\omega) \cdot (*\boldsymbol{\alpha}) = \omega \cdot \boldsymbol{\alpha}$ for any $r$-covector $\omega$.
5. Show that the components of $\tilde{d}\omega$ satisfy $(\tilde{d}\omega)_\nu = \sum_{i=1}^n \partial \omega_{\nu,i}/\partial x^i$, where $(\nu, i) = (i_1, \ldots, i_{r-1}, i)$.
6. Show that the components of $d\omega$ satisfy $(d\omega)_\lambda = \sum_{j=1}^{r+1} (-1)^{j-1}\, \partial\omega_{\lambda_j}/\partial x^{i_j}$, where $\lambda_j$ is the $r$-tuple $(i_1, \ldots, i_{j-1}, i_{j+1}, \ldots, i_{r+1})$.
7. If $\zeta$ is a 1-form and $\omega$ is an $r$-form let $\zeta \cdot \omega$ be the $(r-1)$-form such that $*(\zeta \cdot \omega) = (-1)^{n-1}\zeta \wedge (*\omega)$. Show that:
   (a) $\tilde{d}(f\omega) = f\,\tilde{d}\omega + df \cdot \omega$. (b) $(\zeta \cdot \omega)_\nu = \sum_{i=1}^n \zeta_i \omega_{\nu,i}$.

## *6-7 SPECIAL RESULTS FOR $n = 3$

Vector analysis in $E^3$ is traditionally based on four operations besides the usual vector addition, scalar multiplication, and inner product. These operations are the cross product, triple scalar product, curl, and divergence. The last of these was defined in the previous section, for any dimension $n$. The other three are special to three dimensions, and can be expressed in terms of $\wedge$, $*$, and $d$ as follows.

If $\mathbf{h}_1$ and $\mathbf{h}_2$ are vectors, their cross product is denoted by $\mathbf{h}_1 \times \mathbf{h}_2$. It is the vector

$$\mathbf{h}_1 \times \mathbf{h}_2 = *(\mathbf{h}_1 \wedge \mathbf{h}_2). \tag{6-38a}$$

See Fig. 6-4. The cross product distributes with vector addition and scalar multiplication, and $\mathbf{h}_2 \times \mathbf{h}_1 = -\mathbf{h}_1 \times \mathbf{h}_2$. However, it is not associative.

The triple scalar product of three vectors is denoted by $[\mathbf{h}_1, \mathbf{h}_2, \mathbf{h}_3]$. It is given by

$$[\mathbf{h}_1, \mathbf{h}_2, \mathbf{h}_3] = *(\mathbf{h}_1 \wedge \mathbf{h}_2 \wedge \mathbf{h}_3). \tag{6–39}$$

Its absolute value equals $|\mathbf{h}_1 \wedge \mathbf{h}_2 \wedge \mathbf{h}_3|$, which is the volume of the parallelepiped spanned by $\mathbf{h}_1$, $\mathbf{h}_2$, $\mathbf{h}_3$ with vertex $\mathbf{0}$. The sign of the triple scalar product is positive if $(\mathbf{h}_1, \mathbf{h}_2, \mathbf{h}_3)$ is a positively oriented frame for $E^3$ and negative if this frame is negatively oriented.

When $n = 3$, $r(n - r)$ is always even and $(-1)^{r(n-r)} = 1$. Then $*(\mathbf{h}_1 \times \mathbf{h}_2) = \mathbf{h}_1 \wedge \mathbf{h}_2$. Using Problem 4(a), Section 6–6,

$$\mathbf{h}_1 \wedge \mathbf{h}_2 \wedge \mathbf{h}_3 = (\mathbf{h}_1 \times \mathbf{h}_2) \cdot \mathbf{h}_3 \; \mathbf{e}_{123},$$

which gives another formula for the triple scalar product:

$$[\mathbf{h}_1, \mathbf{h}_2, \mathbf{h}_3] = (\mathbf{h}_1 \times \mathbf{h}_2) \cdot \mathbf{h}_3.$$

The cross product of two covectors, or of two 1-forms, is given by

$$\boldsymbol{\omega} \times \boldsymbol{\zeta} = *(\boldsymbol{\omega} \wedge \boldsymbol{\zeta}). \tag{6–38b}$$

The curl of a 1-form $\boldsymbol{\omega}$ is the 1-form curl $\boldsymbol{\omega}$ given by

$$\text{curl}\, \boldsymbol{\omega} = *d\boldsymbol{\omega}. \tag{6–40}$$

Its physical significance will be indicated in Section 7–6 in connection with Stokes' formula.

**Example.** Show that div (curl $\boldsymbol{\omega}$) $= 0$ for every 1-form $\boldsymbol{\omega}$ of class $C^{(2)}$. Using the fact that $\tilde{d}* = *d$ (formula 6–37b),

$$\text{div}\,(\text{curl}\, \boldsymbol{\omega}) = \tilde{d}(*d\boldsymbol{\omega}) = *d(d\boldsymbol{\omega}) = *\mathbf{0} = \mathbf{0}.$$

**PROBLEMS**

Assume that all forms are of class $C^{(2)}$.

1. Show that:

   (a) $\mathbf{h} \times \mathbf{k} = -\mathbf{k} \times \mathbf{h}$. (b) $\mathbf{h} \times (\mathbf{k}_1 + \mathbf{k}_2) = \mathbf{h} \times \mathbf{k}_1 + \mathbf{h} \times \mathbf{k}_2$.

2. Let $\boldsymbol{\omega} = M\, dx + N\, dy + O\, dz$. Show that curl $\boldsymbol{\omega} = (\partial O/\partial y - \partial N/\partial z)\, dx + (\partial M/\partial z - \partial O/\partial x)\, dy + (\partial N/\partial x - \partial M/\partial y)\, dz$.

3. Find $\mathbf{e}_i \times \mathbf{e}_j$ for all pairs $i, j = 1, 2, 3$.

4. With the aid of (6–38a) and (6–40), show that:

   (a) div $(\boldsymbol{\zeta} \times \boldsymbol{\omega}) = 0$ if $\boldsymbol{\zeta}$ and $\boldsymbol{\omega}$ are closed. (b) curl $(f\boldsymbol{\omega}) = f$ curl $\boldsymbol{\omega} + df \times \boldsymbol{\omega}$.
   (c) curl $(f\, df) = \mathbf{0}$. (d) curl $(\boldsymbol{\zeta} \times \boldsymbol{\omega}) = \tilde{d}(\boldsymbol{\zeta} \wedge \boldsymbol{\omega})$.
   (e) curl (curl $\boldsymbol{\omega}$) $= d(\text{div}\, \boldsymbol{\omega})$ − Lapl $\boldsymbol{\omega}$, where Lapl $(M\, dx + N\, dy + O\, dz) =$ (Lapl $M$) $dx$ + (Lapl $N$) $dy$ + (Lapl $O$) $dz$ and Lapl $f$ is the Laplacian of the function $f$.
   (f) $\boldsymbol{\zeta} \cdot \text{curl}\, \boldsymbol{\omega} - \boldsymbol{\omega} \cdot \text{curl}\, \boldsymbol{\zeta} = \text{div}\,(\boldsymbol{\omega} \times \boldsymbol{\zeta})$. [*Hint:* By the dual to (6–36), $\boldsymbol{\zeta} \cdot *d\boldsymbol{\omega} = *(\boldsymbol{\zeta} \wedge d\boldsymbol{\omega})$.]

5. Show that:

   (a) $\mathbf{h}_1 \times (\mathbf{h}_2 \times \mathbf{h}_3) = (\mathbf{h}_1 \cdot \mathbf{h}_3)\mathbf{h}_2 - (\mathbf{h}_1 \cdot \mathbf{h}_2)\mathbf{h}_3$. [*Hint:* Since both sides are trilinear in $(\mathbf{h}_1, \mathbf{h}_2, \mathbf{h}_3)$ it suffices to prove this when $\mathbf{h}_1, \mathbf{h}_2, \mathbf{h}_3$ are standard basis vectors. Use Problem 3.]

   (b) The cross product is not associative.

   (c) $(\mathbf{h}_1 \times \mathbf{h}_2) \times (\mathbf{h}_3 \times \mathbf{h}_4) = [\mathbf{h}_1, \mathbf{h}_2, \mathbf{h}_4]\mathbf{h}_3 - [\mathbf{h}_1, \mathbf{h}_2, \mathbf{h}_3]\mathbf{h}_4$.

6. Let $\boldsymbol{\omega} = (E_1\, dx^1 + E_2\, dx^2 + E_3\, dx^3) \wedge dx^4 + B_1\, dx^2 \wedge dx^3 + B_2\, dx^3 \wedge dx^1 + B_3\, dx^1 \wedge dx^2$, where the functions $B_i$, $E_i$ are of class $C^{(1)}$ on an open subset of $E^4$. Show that $d\boldsymbol{\omega} = 0$ if and only if $\operatorname{curl} \mathbf{E} + \partial B/\partial x^4 = \mathbf{0}$, $\operatorname{div} \mathbf{B} = 0$. Here curl and div are taken in the variables $(x^1, x^2, x^3)$. [*Note:* The equation $d\boldsymbol{\omega} = 0$ represents one-half of Maxwell's equations for an electromagnetic field in free space. The functions $E_1$, $E_2$, $E_3$ represent the electrical components of the field and $B_1$, $B_2$, $B_3$ the components of a magnetic induction vector. There is a similar equation which represents the other half of Maxwell's equations. See [9], p. 45.]

CHAPTER 7

# Integration on Manifolds

The topic of this chapter is integration over subsets of an $r$-manifold $M \subset E^n$. For this purpose we first study regular transformations from one $r$-manifold into another. A regular transformation from a set $S \subset M$ into $E^r$ defines a coordinate system for $S$. It is not always possible to find a single coordinate system for all of $M$. However, from the implicit function theorem, coordinates can be introduced locally. Using this fact, together with a device called partition of unity, the integral of a continuous function $f$ over a set $A \subset M$ is defined in Section 7–3. Next, the idea of orientation on a manifold is introduced, and integrals of differential forms of degree $r$ are defined.

The divergence theorem states that the integral of an $(n - 1)$-form $\boldsymbol{\omega}$ over the boundary fr $D$ of an open set $D$ equals the integral over $D$ of $d\boldsymbol{\omega}$. The orientations on $D$ and fr $D$ must be chosen consistently, and certain regularity assumptions (p. 264) are made. When $n = 2$ and 3 the divergence theorem is equivalent to theorems in vector analysis commonly attributed to Green and to Gauss.

The divergence theorem is a special case of a result which states that the integral of the differential $d\boldsymbol{\omega}$ of an $(r - 1)$-form $\boldsymbol{\omega}$ over a portion $A$ of an oriented $r$-manifold $M$ equals the integral of $\boldsymbol{\omega}$ over the suitably oriented boundary of $A$. This is called Stokes' formula. In the final section the idea of homotopy between two transformations is introduced and is applied to give sufficient conditions in order that a closed differential form be exact.

## 7–1 REGULAR TRANSFORMATIONS

In Chapter 4 an $r$-manifold $M$ was defined as a subset of some euclidean $E^n$ which can locally be described by setting equal to 0 functions $\Phi^1, \ldots, \Phi^{n-r}$ with linearly independent differentials. For the precise definition, see Section 4–7. An $r$-manifold $M$ has at each $\mathbf{x} \in M$ a tangent space, denoted in the present section by $T_M(\mathbf{x})$.

For purposes of integration it is necessary to consider manifolds from a different point of view. We must show that a manifold can be locally described by a system of $r$ coordinate functions $F^1, \ldots, F^r$. This idea will be made precise in the next section. We need first to introduce the idea of regular transformation from one $r$-manifold into another.

Let $\mathbf{g}$ be a transformation whose domain is a set $N \subset E^m$. As in Section 2–3, we shall say that $\mathbf{g}$ is of class $C^{(q)}$ on $N$ if there exists a transformation $\mathbf{G}$ of class $C^{(q)}$ on some open set $\Delta$ containing $N$ such that $\mathbf{g} = \mathbf{G}|N$. The transformation $\mathbf{G}$ is an extension of $\mathbf{g}$ of class $C^{(q)}$.

Now let $N \subset E^m$ be an $r$-manifold, and $\mathbf{g}$ a transformation from $N$ into $E^n$, where $r \leq \min\{m, n\}$. Let $\mathbf{g}$ be of class $C^{(1)}$ on $N$. If $r = m$, $N$ is itself an open subset of $E^r$ and we shall take $N = \Delta$, $\mathbf{G} = \mathbf{g}$.

When $r < m$, different extensions of $\mathbf{g}$ may lead to different values for the differential $D\mathbf{G}(\mathbf{t})$ at a point $\mathbf{t} \in N$. However, let us now show that the restriction of $D\mathbf{G}(\mathbf{t})$ to the tangent space at $\mathbf{t}$ is the same for all extensions.

**Proposition 26.** *Let* $\mathbf{G}$ *and* $\tilde{\mathbf{G}}$ *be of class* $C^{(1)}$ *on some open set containing* $N$, *and let* $\mathbf{G}|N = \tilde{\mathbf{G}}|N$. *Then* $D\mathbf{G}(\mathbf{t})(\mathbf{k}) = D\tilde{\mathbf{G}}(\mathbf{t})(\mathbf{k})$ *for every* $\mathbf{t} \in N$ *and* $\mathbf{k} \in T_N(\mathbf{t})$.

*Proof.* Let $\mathbf{t}_0 \in N$ and $\mathbf{k} \in T_N(\mathbf{t}_0)$. By definition of tangent vector (Section 4–7), there is a function $\boldsymbol{\psi}$ from an interval $(-\delta, \delta)$ into $N$ such that $\boldsymbol{\psi}(0) = \mathbf{t}_0$, $\boldsymbol{\psi}'(0) = \mathbf{k}$. By Corollary 2, Section 4–4, the derivative of $\mathbf{G} \circ \boldsymbol{\psi}$ at 0 is $D\mathbf{G}(\mathbf{t}_0)(\mathbf{k})$. But $\mathbf{G} \circ \boldsymbol{\psi} = \tilde{\mathbf{G}} \circ \boldsymbol{\psi}$ since $\mathbf{G}|N = \tilde{\mathbf{G}}|N$. ▮

By this proposition we may set without ambiguity $D\mathbf{g}(\mathbf{t}) = D\mathbf{G}(\mathbf{t})|T_N(\mathbf{t})$, and may then write $D\mathbf{g}(\mathbf{t})(\mathbf{k})$ in place of $D\mathbf{G}(\mathbf{t})(\mathbf{k})$ if $\mathbf{k}$ is any tangent vector to $N$ at $\mathbf{t}$. Let us next show that if the values of $\mathbf{g}$ lie in an $r$-manifold $M$, then $D\mathbf{g}(\mathbf{t})$ takes the tangent space at $\mathbf{t}$ into the tangent space at $\mathbf{g}(\mathbf{t})$.

**Proposition 27.** *Let* $\mathbf{g}$ *be a transformation of class* $C^{(1)}$ *from* $N$ *into an* $r$*-manifold* $M$. *If* $\mathbf{k} \in T_N(\mathbf{t}_0)$ *and* $\mathbf{h} = D\mathbf{g}(\mathbf{t}_0)(\mathbf{k})$, *then* $\mathbf{h} \in T_M[\mathbf{g}(\mathbf{t}_0)]$.

*Proof.* Let $\mathbf{G}$ be an extension of $\mathbf{g}$ of class $C^{(1)}$. Let $\boldsymbol{\psi}$ be as in the proof of Proposition 26, and let $\boldsymbol{\theta} = \mathbf{G} \circ \boldsymbol{\psi} = \mathbf{g} \circ \boldsymbol{\psi}$. Then $\boldsymbol{\theta}'(0) = \mathbf{h}$.

Let $\mathbf{x}_0 = \mathbf{g}(\mathbf{t}_0)$, $U$ be a neighborhood of $\mathbf{x}_0$, and $\boldsymbol{\Phi} = (\Phi^1, \ldots, \Phi^{n-r})$ be the same as in the definition of manifold. Then $\boldsymbol{\Phi}[\boldsymbol{\theta}(s)] = \mathbf{0}$ for every $s$ in some interval about 0. Calculating the derivative at 0 of $\boldsymbol{\Phi} \circ \boldsymbol{\theta}$ by Corollary 2, Section 4–4,

$$D\boldsymbol{\Phi}(\mathbf{x}_0)[\boldsymbol{\theta}'(0)] = D\boldsymbol{\Phi}(\mathbf{x}_0)(\mathbf{h}) = \mathbf{0}.$$

By Theorem 10, $\mathbf{h} \in T_M(\mathbf{x}_0)$. ▮

When $r = m = n$, $\mathbf{g}$ is a transformation from an open set $\Delta \subset E^r$ into $E^r$. In this chapter we call such a transformation *flat*. A flat transformation $\mathbf{g}$ has at each $\mathbf{t} \in \Delta$ a Jacobian $J\mathbf{g}(\mathbf{t})$. We recall that the factor $|J\mathbf{g}(\mathbf{t})|$ appears in the formula (5–38) for transforming integrals.

For arbitrary $r, m$, and $n$ let us now introduce a nonnegative number $\mathcal{J}\mathbf{g}(\mathbf{t})$, which for flat transformations becomes $|J\mathbf{g}(\mathbf{t})|$. Let $\{\mathbf{k}_1, \ldots, \mathbf{k}_r\}$ be any basis for the tangent space $T_N(\mathbf{t})$. Let

$$\mathcal{J}\mathbf{g}(\mathbf{t}) = \frac{|\mathbf{h}_1 \wedge \cdots \wedge \mathbf{h}_r|}{|\mathbf{k}_1 \wedge \cdots \wedge \mathbf{k}_r|}, \tag{7-1}$$

where

$$\mathbf{h} = D\mathbf{g}(\mathbf{t})(\mathbf{k}_l), \qquad l = 1, \ldots, r.$$

By Theorem 19 the denominator is not 0. Stated geometrically, $\mathcal{J}\mathbf{g}(\mathbf{t}) = V_r(K')/V_r(K)$, where $K$ and $K'$ are $r$-parallelepipeds with $\mathbf{0}$ as vertex spanned respectively by $\mathbf{k}_1, \ldots, \mathbf{k}_r$ and by $\mathbf{h}_1, \ldots, \mathbf{h}_r$.

We must show that $\mathcal{J}\mathbf{g}(\mathbf{t})$ does not depend on the particular basis chosen for $T_N(\mathbf{t})$.

Let $\mathbf{L} = D\mathbf{g}(\mathbf{t})$, $\boldsymbol{\beta} = \mathbf{k}_1 \wedge \cdots \wedge \mathbf{k}_r$, $\boldsymbol{\alpha} = \mathbf{h}_1 \wedge \cdots \wedge \mathbf{h}_r$. Then $\boldsymbol{\alpha} = \mathbf{L}_r(\boldsymbol{\beta})$, where $\mathbf{L}_r$ is the induced linear transformation defined in Section 6–4. Let $\{\mathbf{k}_1', \ldots, \mathbf{k}_r'\}$ be another basis for $T_N(\mathbf{t})$, and consider the corresponding $\mathbf{h}_l' = \mathbf{L}(\mathbf{k}_l)$, $\boldsymbol{\beta}' = \mathbf{k}_1' \wedge \cdots \wedge \mathbf{k}_r'$, $\boldsymbol{\alpha}' = \mathbf{h}_1' \wedge \cdots \wedge \mathbf{h}_r'$. By Theorem 19 $\boldsymbol{\beta}' = c\boldsymbol{\beta}$, where $c$ is a scalar. Since $\mathbf{L}_r$ is linear, $\boldsymbol{\alpha}' = \mathbf{L}_r(c\boldsymbol{\beta}) = c\mathbf{L}_r(\boldsymbol{\beta})$. Thus $\boldsymbol{\alpha}' = c\boldsymbol{\alpha}$ and $|\boldsymbol{\alpha}'|/|\boldsymbol{\beta}'| = |\boldsymbol{\alpha}|/|\boldsymbol{\beta}|$. This shows that $\mathcal{J}\mathbf{g}(\mathbf{t})$ does not depend on the particular basis chosen for the tangent space at $\mathbf{t}$.

The condition $\mathcal{J}\mathbf{g}(\mathbf{t}) > 0$ means that $\mathbf{h}_1 \wedge \cdots \wedge \mathbf{h}_r \neq \mathbf{0}$, which by Theorem 19 is equivalent to linear independence of the set $\{\mathbf{h}_1, \ldots, \mathbf{h}_r\}$. Proposition 27 then has the following corollary.

**Corollary.** *If* $\mathcal{J}\mathbf{g}(\mathbf{t}_0) > 0$, *then* $D\mathbf{g}(\mathbf{t}_0)$ *takes* $T_N(\mathbf{t}_0)$ *onto* $T_M[\mathbf{g}(\mathbf{t}_0)]$.

*Proof.* Since $D\mathbf{g}(\mathbf{t}_0)$ is linear, it takes $T_N(\mathbf{t}_0)$ onto a vector subspace $P$ of $T_M[\mathbf{g}(\mathbf{t}_0)]$. If $\{\mathbf{k}_1, \ldots, \mathbf{k}_r\}$ is a basis for $T_N(\mathbf{t}_0)$, then the set $\{\mathbf{h}_1, \ldots, \mathbf{h}_r\}$ is linearly independent and each $\mathbf{h}_l \in P$. Since the vector spaces $P$ and $T_M[\mathbf{g}(\mathbf{t}_0)]$ have the same dimension $r$ and $P \subset T_M[\mathbf{g}(\mathbf{t}_0)]$, they are the same. ▌

If $r = m$ and $N = \Delta$ is an open subset of $E^r$, then $T_N(\mathbf{t}) = E^r$ and for $\mathbf{k}_1, \ldots, \mathbf{k}_r$ we may take the standard basis vectors $\boldsymbol{\epsilon}_1, \ldots, \boldsymbol{\epsilon}_r$. In this case, $\mathbf{h}_l = \mathbf{g}_l(\mathbf{t})$ is the $l$th partial derivative of $\mathbf{g}$ at $\mathbf{t}$. Since $|\boldsymbol{\epsilon}_1 \wedge \cdots \wedge \boldsymbol{\epsilon}_r| = |\boldsymbol{\epsilon}_{1\ldots r}| = 1$, we have

$$\mathcal{J}\mathbf{g}(\mathbf{t}) = |\mathbf{g}_1(\mathbf{t}) \wedge \cdots \wedge \mathbf{g}_r(\mathbf{t})| \qquad \text{if } r = m. \tag{7-2}$$

If $r = n = m$, then the right-hand side equals the absolute value of the determinant of $D\mathbf{g}(\mathbf{t})$; and thus $\mathcal{J}\mathbf{g}(\mathbf{t}) = |J\mathbf{g}(\mathbf{t})|$ if $\mathbf{g}$ is a flat transformation.

**Definition.** A transformation $\mathbf{g}$ from an $r$-manifold $N$ into an $r$-manifold $M$ is *regular* if:

(1) $\mathbf{g}$ is of class $C^{(1)}$ on $N$;

(2) $\mathbf{g}$ is univalent; and

(3) $\mathcal{J}\mathbf{g}(\mathbf{t}) > 0$ for every $\mathbf{t} \in N$.

A regular transformation **g** may distort shapes. However, if **g** is regular, then the image $\mathbf{g}(B)$ of any set $B \subset N$ is "qualitatively" the same as $B$. We shall prove (Theorem 20) that the inverse $\mathbf{g}^{-1}$ is regular. In particular, **g** and $\mathbf{g}^{-1}$ are continuous, which implies that $B$ and $\mathbf{g}(B)$ are the same topologically [to use the correct technical term, $B$ and $\mathbf{g}(B)$ are homeomorphic]. Conditions (1) and (3) insure that **g** is properly behaved from the viewpoint of differential calculus. For instance, we have just shown that the differential takes tangent spaces to $N$ onto the corresponding tangent spaces to $M$.

A regular transformation is called by many authors a *diffeomorphism* of class $C^{(1)}$.

Note that we have *assumed* that $\mathbf{g}(N) \subset M$ for some $r$-manifold $M$. One might guess that conditions (1), (2), and (3) imply that $\mathbf{g}(N)$ lies in an $r$-manifold; but Problem 3 shows that this is false. Later in the section we shall find some additional conditions under which the guess is correct (see Theorem 21 and its Corollary 1).

**Example 1.** Let $\Delta \subset E^1$ be an open interval, and **g** a transformation from $\Delta$ into a 1-manifold $M \subset E^n$. Let us assume (1), (2), and the condition $\mathbf{g}'(t) \neq \mathbf{0}$. Since $r = 1$, by (7–2) $\mathcal{J}\mathbf{g}(t) = |\mathbf{g}'(t)| > 0$. The vector $\mathbf{g}'(t)$ is a tangent vector to $M$ at $\mathbf{g}(t)$, and $T_M[\mathbf{g}(t)]$ consists of all scalar multiples of it. The set $\mathbf{g}(\Delta)$ is called an open simple arc. If $J \subset \Delta$ is a closed interval, then $\mathbf{g}|J$ represents a simple arc with endpoints included (see Section 3–2).

**Proposition 28.** *Let* **g** *be a regular transformation from $N$ into $M$, and $\boldsymbol{\phi}$ be a transformation of class $C^{(1)}$ from $M$ into $E^p$. Then*

$$\mathcal{J}(\boldsymbol{\phi} \circ \mathbf{g})(\mathbf{t}) = \mathcal{J}\boldsymbol{\phi}(\mathbf{x})\mathcal{J}\mathbf{g}(\mathbf{t}), \qquad \textit{if } \mathbf{x} = \mathbf{g}(\mathbf{t}). \tag{7–3}$$

*Proof.* Let $\mathbf{k}_l$, $\mathbf{h}_l$ be as above, and let $\boldsymbol{\eta}_l = D\boldsymbol{\phi}(\mathbf{x})(\mathbf{h}_l)$, $l = 1, \ldots, r$. By the composite function theorem, $\boldsymbol{\eta}_l = D(\boldsymbol{\phi} \circ \mathbf{g})(\mathbf{t})(\mathbf{k}_l)$. If $\mathcal{J}\boldsymbol{\phi}(\mathbf{x}) > 0$, then

$$\frac{|\boldsymbol{\eta}_1 \wedge \cdots \wedge \boldsymbol{\eta}_r|}{|\mathbf{k}_1 \wedge \cdots \wedge \mathbf{k}_r|} = \frac{|\boldsymbol{\eta}_1 \wedge \cdots \wedge \boldsymbol{\eta}_r|}{|\mathbf{h}_1 \wedge \cdots \wedge \mathbf{h}_r|} \, \frac{|\mathbf{h}_1 \wedge \cdots \wedge \mathbf{h}_r|}{|\mathbf{k}_1 \wedge \cdots \wedge \mathbf{k}_r|},$$

which is just (7–3). If $\mathcal{J}\boldsymbol{\phi}(\mathbf{x}) = 0$, then the set $\{\mathbf{h}_1, \ldots, \mathbf{h}_r\}$ is linearly dependent. This implies that $\{\boldsymbol{\eta}_1, \ldots, \boldsymbol{\eta}_r\}$ is linearly dependent, and therefore $\mathcal{J}(\boldsymbol{\phi} \circ \mathbf{g})(\mathbf{t}) = 0$. ▌

**Corollary.** *If $\boldsymbol{\phi}$ and* **g** *are regular, then their composite $\boldsymbol{\phi} \circ \mathbf{g}$ is regular.*

*Proof.* Since $\boldsymbol{\phi}$ and **g** are of class $C^{(1)}$ and univalent, so is $\boldsymbol{\phi} \circ \mathbf{g}$. Since $\mathcal{J}\boldsymbol{\phi}(\mathbf{x}) > 0$ and $\mathcal{J}\mathbf{g}(\mathbf{t}) > 0$, by (7–3) $\mathcal{J}(\boldsymbol{\phi} \circ \mathbf{g})(\mathbf{t}) > 0$. ▌

**Example 2.** Let $S \subset E^3$ be a set such that

$$S = \{(x, y, \phi(x, y)) : (x, y) \in R\},$$

where $R$ is an open subset of $E^2$ and $\phi$ is of class $C^{(1)}$ on $R$. The set $S$ is a 2-manifold. To see this, let $\Phi(x, y, z) = z - \phi(x, y)$, $D = \{(x, y, z) : (x, y) \in R\}$. Then $d\Phi(\mathbf{x}) \neq \mathbf{0}$ and $S = \{\mathbf{x} \in D : \Phi(\mathbf{x}) = 0\}$. Hence $S$ is the 2-manifold determined by $\Phi$.

Let $$\mathbf{g}(x, y) = x\mathbf{e}_1 + y\mathbf{e}_2 + \phi(x, y)\mathbf{e}_3.$$

Then $\mathbf{g}$ is of class $C^{(1)}$ from $R$ onto $S$ and is univalent. The vectors $\partial\mathbf{g}/\partial x$ and $\partial\mathbf{g}/\partial y$ give a basis for the tangent space $T_S[\mathbf{g}(x, y)]$. By (7–2), $\mathcal{J}\mathbf{g}(x, y) = |\partial\mathbf{g}/\partial x \wedge \partial\mathbf{g}/\partial y|$. See Fig. 7–1.

Calculating these partial derivatives, we get

$$\frac{\partial\mathbf{g}}{\partial x} = \mathbf{e}_1 + \frac{\partial\phi}{\partial x}\mathbf{e}_3, \qquad \frac{\partial\mathbf{g}}{\partial y} = \mathbf{e}_2 + \frac{\partial\phi}{\partial y}\mathbf{e}_3,$$

$$\frac{\partial\mathbf{g}}{\partial x} \wedge \frac{\partial\mathbf{g}}{\partial y} = \mathbf{e}_{12} - \frac{\partial\phi}{\partial y}\mathbf{e}_{31} - \frac{\partial\phi}{\partial x}\mathbf{e}_{23},$$

$$\left|\frac{\partial\mathbf{g}}{\partial x} \wedge \frac{\partial\mathbf{g}}{\partial y}\right| = \left[1 + \left(\frac{\partial\phi}{\partial x}\right)^2 + \left(\frac{\partial\phi}{\partial y}\right)^2\right]^{1/2}$$
$$= [1 + |d\phi|^2]^{1/2}.$$

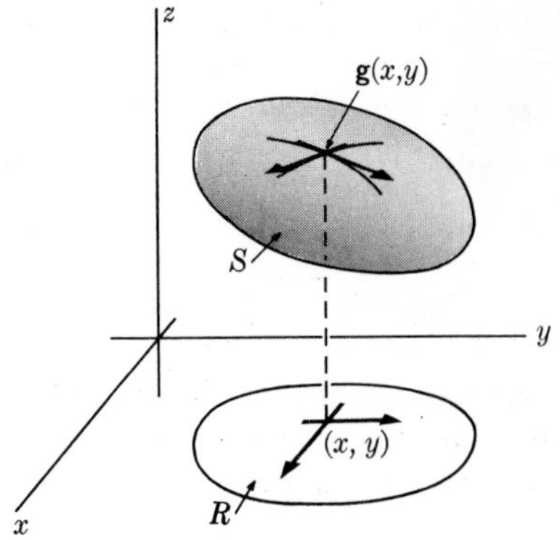


FIGURE 7–1

Since the last line is positive, $\mathcal{J}\mathbf{g}(x, y) > 0$. Thus $\mathbf{g}$ is a regular transformation.

Let $X$, $Y$, and $Z$ be the standard cartesian coordinate functions for $E^3$; and let

$$\mathbf{F} = (X|S, Y|S).$$

Since $X$ and $Y$ are of class $C^{(1)}$, $\mathbf{F}$ is of class $C^{(1)}$ on $S$. Moreover, $\mathbf{F}$ is univalent; in fact, $\mathbf{F} = \mathbf{g}^{-1}$. Since $\mathbf{F} \circ \mathbf{g}$ is the identity transformation, $\mathcal{J}(\mathbf{F} \circ \mathbf{g}) = 1$. By (7–3),

$$\mathcal{J}\mathbf{F}(\mathbf{x}) = \frac{1}{\mathcal{J}\mathbf{g}(x, y)} > 0, \qquad \text{if } \mathbf{x} = \mathbf{g}(x, y).$$

Thus $\mathbf{F}$ is also a regular transformation.

**Example 3.** Generalizing Example 2, let $\lambda = (i_1, \ldots, i_r)$ be an increasing $r$-tuple of integers, $1 \leq i_k \leq n$ for $k = 1, \ldots, r$; and let $(j_1, \ldots, j_{n-r})$ be the increasing $(n - r)$-tuple complementary to $\lambda$. Let $R$ be an open subset of $E^r$, and $\phi^1, \ldots, \phi^{n-r}$ of class $C^{(1)}$ on $R$. Let $\mathbf{g}$ be the transformation from $R$ into $E^n$ such that

$$g^{i_k}(\mathbf{x}^\lambda) = x^{i_k}, \qquad k = 1, \ldots, r$$
$$g^{j_l}(\mathbf{x}^\lambda) = \phi^l(\mathbf{x}^\lambda), \qquad l = 1, \ldots, n - r,$$

where

$$\mathbf{x}^\lambda = (x^{i_1}, \ldots, x^{i_r}).$$

Then $\mathbf{g}$ is of class $C^{(1)}$ and univalent. The explicit formula for $\mathcal{J}\mathbf{g}(\mathbf{x}^\lambda)$ is complicated. However, we can show that $\mathcal{J}\mathbf{g}(\mathbf{x}^\lambda) > 0$ as follows. Since

$$\frac{\partial\mathbf{g}}{\partial x^{i_k}} = \mathbf{e}_{i_k} + \sum_{l=1}^{n-r} \frac{\partial\phi^l}{\partial x^{i_k}}\mathbf{e}_{j_l}, \qquad \frac{\partial\mathbf{g}}{\partial x^{i_1}} \wedge \cdots \wedge \frac{\partial\mathbf{g}}{\partial x^{i_r}} = \mathbf{e}_\lambda + \text{other terms}.$$

This $r$-vector is not $\mathbf{0}$ since its $\lambda$th component (the coefficient of $\mathbf{e}_\lambda$) is 1. Hence $\mathcal{J}\mathbf{g}(\mathbf{x}_\lambda) > 0$, which shows that $\mathbf{g}$ is regular.

Let $S = \mathbf{g}(R)$ and $\mathbf{F} = \mathbf{X}^\lambda|S$, where $\mathbf{X}^\lambda = (X^{i_1}, \ldots, X^{i_r})$ and $X^1, \ldots, X^n$ are the standard cartesian coordinate functions for $E^n$. As in Example 2, $S$ is an $r$-manifold and $\mathbf{F} = \mathbf{g}^{-1}$ is regular. In the next section $\mathbf{F}$ will be called a cartesian coordinate system for $S$.

The importance of Example 3 lies in the implicit function theorem. If $M$ is an $r$-manifold, then for every $\mathbf{x}_0 \in M$ there exist an increasing $r$-tuple $\lambda$ and a neighborhood $U_1$ of $\mathbf{x}_0$ such that $S = M \cap U_1$ has a cartesian coordinate system $\mathbf{F}$ of the type just described. See p. 120.

Let us return from these examples to establish some further properties of regular transformations. We recall that a set $S \subset M$ is relatively open if $S = M \cap D$, where $D$ is an open subset of $E^n$ (Section A–6). A relatively open subset of an $r$-manifold is itself an $r$-manifold.

**Theorem 20.** *Let $\mathbf{g}$ be a regular transformation from an $r$-manifold $N$ into an $r$-manifold $M$. Then $\mathbf{g}(N)$ is a relatively open subset of $M$ and $\mathbf{g}^{-1}$ is a regular transformation.*

*Proof.* We know already that the theorem is true in the following two particular cases:

(a) If $\boldsymbol{\phi}$ is a flat regular transformation from an open set $\Delta \subset E^r$ into $E^r$, then by the inverse function theorem $\boldsymbol{\phi}(\Delta)$ is open and $\boldsymbol{\phi}^{-1}$ is regular. (b) If $\mathbf{g}$ is as in Example 3 and $S = \mathbf{g}(R) = M \cap U_1$, where $U_1$ is a neighborhood of some $\mathbf{x}_0 \in M$, then $\mathbf{g}(R)$ is open relative to $M$ and $\mathbf{F} = \mathbf{g}^{-1}$ is regular.

In the general case, let $\mathbf{g}$ be regular from $N$ into $M$. Let $\mathbf{t}_0 \in N$ and $\mathbf{x}_0 = \mathbf{g}(\mathbf{t}_0)$. By the implicit function theorem, there exist an increasing $r$-tuple $\lambda$ and a relative neighborhood $S$ of $\mathbf{x}_0$ such that $\mathbf{F} = \mathbf{X}^\lambda|S$ is regular. The set $R = \mathbf{F}(S)$ is open and $\mathbf{F}^{-1}$ is regular from $R$ onto $S$. (In Example 3, $\mathbf{F}^{-1}$ was denoted by $\mathbf{g}$.) Similarly, there exist a relative neighborhood $S'$ of $\mathbf{t}_0$ and $\mathbf{F}'$ regular from $S'$ onto an open set $R' \subset E^r$ such that $(\mathbf{F}')^{-1}$ is also regular. Since $\mathbf{g}$ is continuous, we may arrange that $\mathbf{g}(S') \subset S$. Consider the transformation $\boldsymbol{\phi} = \mathbf{F} \circ \mathbf{g} \circ (\mathbf{F}')^{-1}$ from $R'$ into $R$. By the corollary to Proposition 28, $\boldsymbol{\phi}$ is regular. Since $\boldsymbol{\phi}$ is flat, $\boldsymbol{\phi}(R')$ is open and $\boldsymbol{\phi}^{-1}$ is continuous. Let $S_1$ be a relative neighborhood of $\mathbf{x}_0$ such that $\mathbf{F}(S_1) \subset \boldsymbol{\phi}(R')$. If $\mathbf{x} \in S_1$, then $\mathbf{x} = \mathbf{g}(\mathbf{t})$ for $\mathbf{t} = \big((\mathbf{F}')^{-1} \circ \boldsymbol{\phi}^{-1} \circ \mathbf{F}\big)(\mathbf{x})$. Therefore $S_1 \subset \mathbf{g}(N)$. Moreover (see Fig. 7–2),

$$\mathbf{g}^{-1}|S_1 = (\mathbf{F}')^{-1} \circ \boldsymbol{\phi}^{-1} \circ (\mathbf{F}|S_1).$$

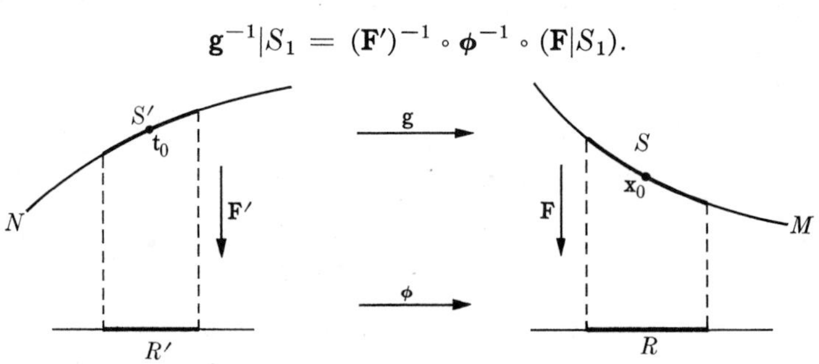


FIGURE 7–2

Since each of the three transformations on the right-hand side is regular, $\mathbf{g}^{-1}|S_1$ is regular.

Since every $\mathbf{x}_0 \in M$ has such a neighborhood $S_1$, this proves Theorem 20. ▌

In the next theorem we drop the assumption that $\mathbf{g}(N)$ is contained in an $r$-manifold. Instead we deduce it from conditions (1), (2), and (3) in the definition of regularity and the additional assumption that $\mathbf{g}$ is an open transformation.

**Definition.** A transformation $\mathbf{g}$ from a set $N \subset E^m$ into $E^n$ is *open* if $\mathbf{g}(B)$ is open relative to $\mathbf{g}(N)$ for every set $B$ open relative to $N$.

**Theorem 21.** *Let* $\mathbf{g}$ *be a transformation from an r-manifold N into* $E^n$, *such that* $\mathbf{g}$ *is open and satisfies* (1), (2), *and* (3). *Then* $\mathbf{g}(N)$ *is an r-manifold, and* $\mathbf{g}$ *is regular.*

*Proof.* We must show that $\mathbf{g}(N)$ is an $r$-manifold. Once this is proved, the regularity of $\mathbf{g}$ follows from the definition. Let us first prove the theorem in case $N$ is an open set $\Delta \subset E^r$. For each increasing $r$-tuple $\lambda = (i_1, \ldots, i_r)$ let $\mathbf{g}^\lambda$ be the flat transformation from $\Delta$ into $E^r$ with components $g^{i_1}, \ldots, g^{i_r}$. By formula (6–13a) the $\lambda$th component of the $r$-vector $\mathbf{g}_1(\mathbf{t}) \wedge \cdots \wedge \mathbf{g}_r(\mathbf{t})$ is the Jacobian $J\mathbf{g}^\lambda(\mathbf{t})$.

Let $S = \mathbf{g}(\Delta)$, and let $\mathbf{x}_0 = \mathbf{g}(\mathbf{t}_0)$ be any point of $S$. By (7–2), $\mathbf{g}_1(\mathbf{t}_0) \wedge \cdots \wedge \mathbf{g}_r(\mathbf{t}_0) \neq \mathbf{0}$. Hence there is some $\lambda$ such that $J\mathbf{g}^\lambda(\mathbf{t}_0) \neq 0$. By the inverse function theorem there is a neighborhood $\Omega$ of $\mathbf{t}_0$ such that $\mathbf{g}^\lambda|\Omega$ is regular. The set $R = \mathbf{g}^\lambda(\Omega)$ is open and contains $\mathbf{x}_0^\lambda$. Let $\boldsymbol{\phi} = (\mathbf{g}^\lambda|\Omega)^{-1}$ and $\mathbf{G} = \mathbf{g} \circ \boldsymbol{\phi}$. Since $G^{i_k}(\mathbf{x}^\lambda) = x^{i_k}$ for each $k = 1, \ldots, r$, $\mathbf{G}$ is of the type considered in Example 3. Therefore $\mathbf{G}(R)$ is an $r$-manifold. But $\mathbf{x}_0 \in \mathbf{G}(R)$ and $\mathbf{G}(R) = \mathbf{g}(\Omega)$ is a relatively open subset of $S$, since $\mathbf{g}$ is an open transformation. Since any $\mathbf{x}_0 \in S$ lies in a relatively open subset of $S$ which is an $r$-manifold, $S$ is an $r$-manifold. This proves Theorem 21 in the case $N \subset E^r$.

In the general case, let $\mathbf{t}_0 \in N$. Then $\mathbf{t}_0$ has a relative neighborhood $S'$ with which is associated by the implicit function theorem a transformation $\mathbf{F}'$ as in the proof of Theorem 20. Let $\tilde{\mathbf{g}} = \mathbf{g} \circ (\mathbf{F}')^{-1}$. Since $\mathbf{F}'$ and $(\mathbf{F}')^{-1}$ are regular, $\tilde{\mathbf{g}}$ also satisfies the hypotheses of Theorem 21. Its domain $R' = \mathbf{F}'(S')$ is an open subset of $E^r$. By what has already been proved, $\mathbf{g}(S') = \tilde{\mathbf{g}}(R')$ is an $r$-manifold. Since every $\mathbf{t}_0 \in N$ has such a neighborhood $S'$, $\mathbf{g}(N)$ is an $r$-manifold. ▌

**Corollary 1.** *If* $\mathbf{g}$ *satisfies* (1), (2), *and* (3) *and* $\mathbf{g}^{-1}$ *is continuous, then* $\mathbf{g}(N)$ *is an r-manifold and* $\mathbf{g}$ *is regular.*

*Proof.* Let $B \subset N$ be relatively open. Then $\mathbf{g}(B) = (\mathbf{g}^{-1})^{-1}(B)$ is open relative to $\mathbf{g}(N)$ by Proposition A–6. Therefore $\mathbf{g}$ is an open transformation. ▌

**Corollary 2.** *Let* $\mathbf{g}$ *be regular from an r-manifold N into an r-manifold M. If* $Q \subset N$ *is a p-manifold,* $p \leq r$, *then* $\mathbf{g}(Q)$ *is a p-manifold and* $\mathbf{g}|Q$ *is regular.*

*Proof.* Clearly the restriction $\mathbf{g}|Q$ is of class $C^{(1)}$ and univalent since $\mathbf{g}$ has these properties. If $\mathbf{t} \in Q$, then there is a basis $\{\mathbf{k}_1, \ldots, \mathbf{k}_r\}$ for $T_N(\mathbf{t})$ such that $\{\mathbf{k}_1, \ldots, \mathbf{k}_p\}$ is a basis for $T_Q(\mathbf{t})$. Since $\mathbf{g}$ is regular, the set of images $\{\mathbf{h}_1, \ldots, \mathbf{h}_r\}$ of these basis elements under $D\mathbf{g}(\mathbf{t})$ is linearly independent. Therefore $\{\mathbf{h}_1, \ldots, \mathbf{h}_p\}$ is a linearly independent set. This shows that $\mathcal{J}(\mathbf{g}|Q)(\mathbf{t}) > 0$ for every $\mathbf{t} \in Q$.

Now $(\mathbf{g}|Q)^{-1} = \mathbf{g}^{-1}|\mathbf{g}(Q)$. By Theorem 20, $\mathbf{g}^{-1}$ is regular; and in particular $\mathbf{g}^{-1}$ is continuous. Hence its restriction to $\mathbf{g}(Q)$ is continuous. The conclusion follows from Corollary 1. ▌

*Note:* If $M$ and $N$ are manifolds of class $C^{(q)}$, $q > 1$, then we may consider regular transformations of class $C^{(q)}$ from $N$ into $M$. In that case all transformations which appear in the proof of Theorem 20 are of class $C^{(q)}$, and hence $\mathbf{g}^{-1}$ is of class $C^{(q)}$. Similarly, in Theorem 21 and its corollaries, $\mathbf{g}(N)$ and $\mathbf{g}(Q)$ are of class $C^{(q)}$ if $\mathbf{g}$, $N$, and $Q$ are of class $C^{(q)}$.

All of the results of this chapter are correct if one assumes merely that $q = 1$. However, to simplify the proof of the divergence theorem and Stokes' formula, we shall later take $q = 2$.

## PROBLEMS

1. For each of the following transformations from $\Delta \subset E^2$ into $E^3$, find $\mathcal{J}\mathbf{g}(s, t)$ and $\mathbf{g}(\Delta)$. Show that $\mathbf{g}$ is univalent.
   (a) $\mathbf{g}(s, t) = (s + t)\mathbf{e}_1 + (s - 3t)\mathbf{e}_2 + (-2s + 2t + 2)\mathbf{e}_3$, $\Delta = \{(s, t) : 0 < s + t < 1, s > 0, t > 0\}$.
   (b) $\mathbf{g}(\rho, \theta) = (\rho \cos \alpha)\mathbf{e}_1 + (\rho \sin \alpha \cos \theta)\mathbf{e}_2 + (\rho \sin \alpha \sin \theta)\mathbf{e}_3$, $0 < \alpha < \pi/2$ ($\alpha$ fixed), $\Delta = (0, \infty) \times (0, 2\pi)$.
   (c) $\mathbf{g}(s, t) = st\mathbf{e}_1 + s\mathbf{e}_2 + t\mathbf{e}_3$, $\Delta = E^2$.
2. Let $\mathbf{G}(s, t, u) = as\mathbf{e}_1 + bt\mathbf{e}_2 + cu\mathbf{e}_3$, where $a$, $b$, and $c$ are positive. Let $N$ be the sphere $s^2 + t^2 + u^2 = 1$ and $M$ the ellipsoid $x^2/a^2 + y^2/b^2 + z^2/c^2 = 1$.
   (a) Find $T_N(\mathbf{t})$, $T_M[\mathbf{G}(\mathbf{t})]$, $\mathbf{t} = (s, t, u)$. Verify that the image of $T_N(\mathbf{t})$ under $D\mathbf{G}(\mathbf{t})$ is $T_M[\mathbf{G}(\mathbf{t})]$.
   (b) Let $\mathbf{g} = \mathbf{G}|N$. Calculate $\mathcal{J}\mathbf{g}(\mathbf{t})$ from (7-1) and show that $\mathbf{g}$ is regular from $N$ onto $M$.
3. Let $\mathbf{g}(t) = (\cos t)\mathbf{e}_1 + (\sin 2t)\mathbf{e}_2$, $\Delta = (0, 3\pi/2)$. Sketch $\mathbf{g}(\Delta)$. Show that $\mathbf{g}$ is univalent, and that $\mathcal{J}\mathbf{g}(t) > 0$, but that $\mathbf{g}(\Delta)$ is not a 1-manifold. Why does this not contradict Theorem 21?
4. Let $n = 4, r = 2, \lambda = (1, 2)$. Show that in Example 3, $\mathcal{J}\mathbf{g}(x^1, x^2) = [1 + |d\phi^1|^2 + |d\phi^2|^2 + (\phi_1^1\phi_2^2 - \phi_1^2\phi_2^1)^2]^{1/2}$.
5. Let $\Delta \subset E^r$ be open and bounded. Let $\mathbf{g}$ be continuous and univalent on $\mathrm{cl}\,\Delta$. Show that if $\mathbf{g}|\Delta$ is of class $C^{(1)}$ and $\mathcal{J}\mathbf{g}(\mathbf{t}) > 0$ for every $\mathbf{t} \in \Delta$, then $\mathbf{g}(\Delta)$ is an $r$-manifold and $\mathbf{g}|\Delta$ is regular. [*Hint:* Problem 8(d), Section A-8, and Corollary 1.]
6. Let $\mathbf{g}$ be of class $C^{(1)}$ from an $r$-manifold $N$ into $E^n$, and let $\mathcal{J}\mathbf{g}(\mathbf{t}_0) > 0$. Show that $\mathbf{t}_0$ has a neighborhood $\Omega$ such that $\mathbf{g}(N \cap \Omega)$ is an $r$-manifold and $\mathbf{g}|(N \cap \Omega)$ is regular. [*Hints:* First consider the case $N \subset E^r$. By generalizing Proposition 14, Section 4-3, find a neighborhood $\Omega_0$ such that $\mathbf{g}$ is univalent on $N \cap \mathrm{cl}\,\Omega_0$. Use Problem 5.]

## 7-2 COORDINATE SYSTEMS ON MANIFOLDS

Let $M$ be an $r$-manifold. Since $M$ is $r$-dimensional it should be possible to find, at least locally on $M$, $r$ functions $F^1, \ldots, F^r$ such that the numbers $F^1(\mathbf{x}), \ldots, F^r(\mathbf{x})$ will serve as coordinates of a point $\mathbf{x} \in M$. When $r = n$, $M$ is an open subset of $E^n$. In that case we saw already in Section 5-9 that any regular transformation $\mathbf{F} = (F^1, \ldots, F^n)$ will serve to coordinate $M$.

The definition of coordinate system on an $r$-manifold is similar.

**Definition.** Let $S$ be a nonempty, relatively open subset of an $r$-manifold $M \subset E^n$. Any regular transformation $\mathbf{F}$ from $S$ into $E^r$ is a *coordinate system* for $S$. The coordinates of a point $\mathbf{x} \in S$ in this system are $F^1(\mathbf{x}), \ldots, F^r(\mathbf{x})$.

By Theorem 20, the set $\Delta = \mathbf{F}(S)$ is an open subset of $E^r$ and the transformation $\mathbf{g} = \mathbf{F}^{-1}$ is regular from $\Delta$ onto $S$. It will be $\mathbf{g}$ rather than $\mathbf{F}$ which is ordinarily used for calculations in the sections to follow.

**Example 1.** Let us return to the three examples in Section 7-1. In the first of them, the function $F = \mathbf{g}^{-1}$ is a coordinate for the open simple arc $S = \mathbf{g}(\Delta)$. The coordinate of a point $\mathbf{x} = \mathbf{g}(t)$ is $t$ in this system.

In the second of those examples, $\mathbf{F}$ is a coordinate system for $S$. The coordinates of a point $(x, y, \phi(x, y)) \in S$ in this system are $x, y$. In the third example, $\mathbf{F} = \mathbf{X}^\lambda|S$. The coordinates of a point $\mathbf{x}$ in the coordinate system $\mathbf{F}$ are $x^{i_1}, \ldots, x^{i_r}$. Such a coordinate system will be called *cartesian*.

**Example 2.** Let $\mathbf{F} = (F^1, \ldots, F^r)$ be a coordinate system for $S$, and let $S_c = \{\mathbf{x} \in S : F^1(\mathbf{x}) = c\}$. Assume that $S_c$ is not empty. Then $S_c$ is an $(r - 1)$-manifold and $\mathbf{\Psi}_c = (F^2|S_c, \ldots, F^r|S_c)$ is a coordinate system for $S_c$. The proof is left to the reader (Problem 4). This is illustrated in Fig. 7-3 when $r = n$ and $S$ is an open set $D$.

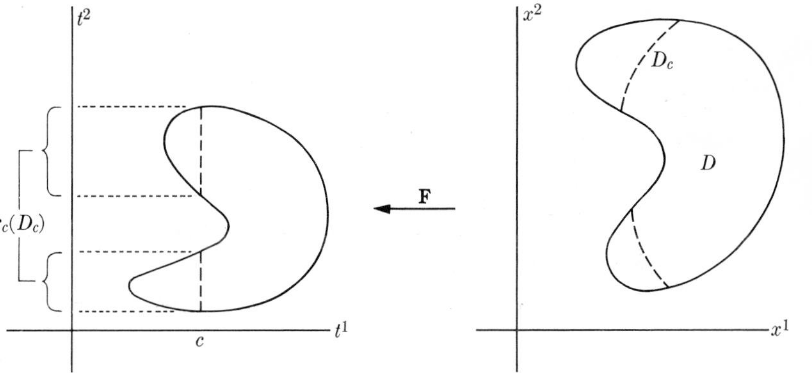


FIGURE 7-3

**Example 3.** Let $(R, \Theta^1, \ldots, \Theta^{n-1})$ be the spherical coordinate system for the open set $D$ in Example 5, p. 181. The complement of $D$ is a null set. Setting $R(\mathbf{x}) = 1$ we get, according to Example 2, a spherical coordinate system for the intersection of $D$ with the unit $(n-1)$-sphere $S^{n-1}$. It turns out that $S^{n-1} - D$ is null in dimension $n-1$, in the sense to be explained in the next section. Consequently, this coordinate system can be used to evaluate integrals over $S^{n-1}$.

It is not ordinarily possible to find a single coordinate system for all of a manifold $M$. If $S \subset M$ has a coordinate system $\mathbf{F}$, then by Theorem 20 both $\mathbf{F}$ and $\mathbf{F}^{-1}$ are continuous. Therefore $S$ is homeomorphic with an open set $\Delta \subset E^r$. Since $\Delta$ cannot be both open and compact, $S$ is not compact. In particular, a compact manifold $M$ (for instance, a sphere or torus) cannot be coordinatized by a single system.

**Definition.** A relatively open set $S \subset M$ which has a coordinate system is a *coordinate patch* on $M$.

By the implicit function theorem every point of $M$ lies in some coordinate patch $S$. Actually, each point of $M$ lies in an infinite number of coordinate patches. Let us now show how different coordinate systems are related in overlapping patches.

**Coordinate changes.** If $S$ is a coordinate patch and $\mathbf{F}$ a coordinate system for $S$, then another coordinate system $\mathbf{F}'$ for $S$ can be obtained as follows. Let $\boldsymbol{\phi}$ be a regular flat transformation from $\Delta = \mathbf{F}(S)$ into $E^r$, and let $\mathbf{F}' = \boldsymbol{\phi} \circ \mathbf{F}$. Since $\boldsymbol{\phi}$ and $\mathbf{F}$ are regular, $\mathbf{F}'$ is regular. Hence $\mathbf{F}'$ is a coordinate system for $S$.

Now let $S$ and $\tilde{S}$ be coordinate patches, $\mathbf{F}$ a coordinate system for $S$, and $\tilde{\mathbf{F}}$ a coordinate system for $\tilde{S}$. Suppose that $S \cap \tilde{S}$ is not empty. Let us show that in $S \cap \tilde{S}$, $\tilde{\mathbf{F}}$ can be obtained from $\mathbf{F}$ by a regular flat transformation $\boldsymbol{\phi}$. Let

$$\Delta_0 = \mathbf{F}(S \cap \tilde{S}), \qquad \tilde{\Delta}_0 = \tilde{\mathbf{F}}(S \cap \tilde{S}),$$

and $\mathbf{g} = \mathbf{F}^{-1}$, $\tilde{\mathbf{g}} = \tilde{\mathbf{F}}^{-1}$. By Theorem 20, $\mathbf{g}$ is regular. Its restriction to $\Delta_0$ is also regular, and hence the composite $\boldsymbol{\phi} = \tilde{\mathbf{F}} \circ (\mathbf{g}|\Delta_0)$ is regular. Moreover, $\tilde{\mathbf{F}}(\mathbf{x}) = \boldsymbol{\phi}[\mathbf{F}(\mathbf{x})]$ for every $\mathbf{x} \in S \cap \tilde{S}$. See Fig. 7–4.

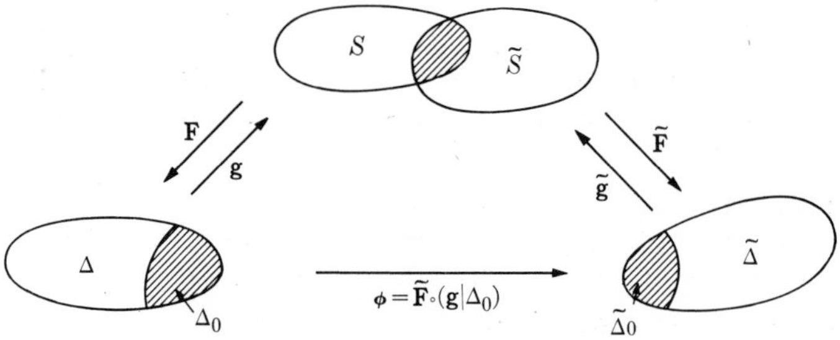


FIGURE 7–4

**Example 1 (continued).** If $r = 1$ and $\Delta \subset E^1$ is an open interval, then a coordinate change is determined by a real-valued $\phi$ such that $\phi'(t) \neq 0$. If $\phi'(t) > 0$ for every $t \in \Delta$, then $\phi$ was called in Section 3–2 a "parameter change." The condition $\phi'(t) > 0$ insures that $\phi$ does not reverse the orientation (see Section 7–4) of the 1-manifold $M$.

***Manifolds defined by coordinate systems.** We have seen that an $r$-manifold $M \subset E^n$ is covered by coordinate patches. Conversely, let $M$ be a subset of $E^n$ with the following property: There is a collection $\mathcal{S}$ of relatively open subsets of $M$ which cover $M$; and with each $S \in \mathcal{S}$ there is associated a homeomorphism $\mathbf{F}$ from $S$ onto an open set $\Delta \subset E^r$ such that $\mathbf{F}^{-1}$ is of class $C^{(1)}$ and $\mathcal{J}\mathbf{F}^{-1}(\mathbf{t}) > 0$ for each $\mathbf{t} \in \Delta$. By Corollary 1 to Theorem 21, each $S \in \mathcal{S}$ is an $r$-manifold; and hence $M$ is an $r$-manifold. This shows that instead of the approach in Section 4–7 we could have defined manifolds in terms of coordinate systems.

We have taken a rather concrete approach to the idea of manifold, considering only manifolds given as subsets of some euclidean space. However, the manifolds encountered in practice often are not given in this way. The approach via coordinate systems allows one to take a more abstract point of view. From this viewpoint the definition of manifold is as follows: An $r$-manifold of class $C^{(1)}$ is a Hausdorff topological space $Z$ provided with a collection of open subsets $S$ (called coordinate patches) covering $Z$ and for each coordinate patch a homeomorphism $\mathbf{F}$ from $S$ onto an open set $\Delta \subset E^r$. The regularity of the flat transformation $\boldsymbol{\phi}$ in Fig. 7–4 is now imposed as an axiom.

If $Z$ is an $r$-manifold according to this more abstract definition and $Z$ is separable, then $Z$ can be realized as a submanifold of some euclidean space, in fact as a submanifold of $E^{2r+1}$. See [21], Chap. IV. A result of this type is called an embedding theorem. By separable we mean that $Z$ has a covering either by finitely many coordinate patches or by a sequence of coordinate patches.

## PROBLEMS

1. Let $M = \{(x, y, z) : x^2 + 2y + z^2 = 3, z > 0, y > |x|\}$. Let $\mathbf{F} = (X|M, Y|M)$ and $\tilde{\mathbf{F}} = (X|M, Z|M)$. Describe $\Delta$, $\tilde{\Delta}$, $\mathbf{g}$, $\tilde{\mathbf{g}}$, and $\boldsymbol{\phi}$ (see Fig. 7–4).

2. Let $M = \{(y^2 + z^2, y, z) : y > 0\}$ and let $\mathbf{F}(x, y, z) = (y + z, \exp z)$ for $(x, y, z) \in M$. Show that $\mathbf{F}$ is a coordinate system for $M$ and find $\mathbf{F}(M)$. [*Hint:* First take $y$ and $z$ as coordinates on $M$ and then find a suitable coordinate change $\boldsymbol{\phi}$ giving the system $\mathbf{F}$.]

3. *Stereographic projection.* Let $M$ be the sphere $x^2 + y^2 + (z - 1)^2 = 1$. For each $\mathbf{x} = (x, y, z) \in M$ except the "north pole" $2\mathbf{e}_3$, let $(s, t, 0)$ be the point where the line through $2\mathbf{e}_3$ and $\mathbf{x}$ meets the plane $z = 0$. Let $\mathbf{F}(\mathbf{x}) = (s, t)$.
   (a) Show that $\mathbf{F}$ is a coordinate system for $M - \{2\mathbf{e}_3\}$.
   (b) Let $\mathbf{h}_1$, $\mathbf{h}_2$ be tangent vectors to $M$ at $\mathbf{x}$, and let $\mathbf{k}_l = D\mathbf{F}(\mathbf{x})(\mathbf{h}_l)$, $l = 1, 2$. Show that the angle between $\mathbf{k}_1$ and $\mathbf{k}_2$ equals the angle between $\mathbf{h}_1$ and $\mathbf{h}_2$.

4. In Example 2 prove that $S_c$ is an $(r - 1)$-manifold and $\mathbf{\Psi}_c$ is a coordinate system for it. [*Hints:* Let $\Delta = \mathbf{F}(S)$. $\mathbf{F}(S_c)$, being the intersection of $\Delta$ with the hyperplane $t^1 = c$, is an $(r - 1)$-manifold. See Corollary 2 to Theorem 21.]

5. Let $(F^1, \ldots, F^r)$ be a coordinate system for $S$. Let $s < r$ and $S_{\mathbf{c}} = \{\mathbf{x} : F^1(\mathbf{x}) = c^1, \ldots, F^s(\mathbf{x}) = c^s\}$. Show that if $S_{\mathbf{c}}$ is not empty, then $S_{\mathbf{c}}$ is an $(r - s)$-manifold and $(F^{s+1}|S_{\mathbf{c}}, \ldots, F^r|S_{\mathbf{c}})$ a coordinate system for it.

6. Let $f^1, \ldots, f^r, \Phi^1, \ldots \Phi^{n-r}$ be functions of class $C^{(1)}$ on an open set $D$. Suppose that $\mathbf{F} = (f^1|S, \ldots, f^r|S)$ is a coordinate system for $S$, that $S = \{\mathbf{x} \in D : \mathbf{\Phi}(\mathbf{x}) = \mathbf{0}\}$, and that $D\mathbf{\Phi}(\mathbf{x})$ has rank $n - r$ for every $\mathbf{x} \in D$. Show that each $\mathbf{x}_0 \in S$ has a neighborhood $U$ such that $(f^1, \ldots, f^r, \Phi^1, \ldots, \Phi^{n-r})$ restricted to $U$ is a coordinate system for $U$.

7. Let $1 \leq r < n$, and let $\mathfrak{M}(n, r) = \{\boldsymbol{\alpha} \in E_r^n : |\boldsymbol{\alpha}| = 1, \boldsymbol{\alpha} \text{ is decomposable}\}$. Identify $E_r^n$ with $E^{\binom{n}{r}}$, and show that $\mathfrak{M}(n, r)$ is a manifold of dimension $r(n - r)$. [*Hint:* Given $\boldsymbol{\alpha}_0 \in \mathfrak{M}(n, r)$ let $(\mathbf{v}_1, \ldots, \mathbf{v}_n)$ be an orthonormal frame for $E^n$ such that $\boldsymbol{\alpha}_0 = \mathbf{v}_1 \wedge \cdots \wedge \mathbf{v}_r$. Show that if $\boldsymbol{\alpha}$ is in a small enough neighborhood of $\boldsymbol{\alpha}_0$, then $\boldsymbol{\alpha}$ can be uniquely written in the form

$$\boldsymbol{\alpha} = c\left(\mathbf{v}_1 + \sum_{k=r+1}^{n} t_{1k}\mathbf{v}_k\right) \wedge \cdots \wedge \left(\mathbf{v}_r + \sum_{k=r+1}^{n} t_{rk}\mathbf{v}_k\right).$$

The $r(n - r)$ numbers $t_{jk}$ can be taken as coordinates of $\boldsymbol{\alpha}$.]

## 7-3 MEASURE AND INTEGRATION ON MANIFOLDS

Let us now define $r$-dimensional measure for subsets of an $r$-manifold $M$ and integrals with respect to it. The $r$-dimensional measure of a set $A \subset M$ will be denoted by $V_r(A)$, and the integral of a function $f$ over $A$ by $\int_A f\, dV_r$ or by $\int_A f(\mathbf{x})\, dV_r(\mathbf{x})$. When $r = n$, these turn out to have the same meaning as in Chapter 5.

For simplicity, the integral will be defined only for continuous functions. Moreover, it is assumed throughout this section that $A$ is a $\sigma$-compact set (Section 5-6). By these assumptions, we avoid some slightly tedious discussion of measurability which for present purposes is irrelevant. We recall from p. 175 that if $A$ is $\sigma$-compact and $\mathbf{F}$ is continuous on $A$, then $\mathbf{F}(A)$ is also $\sigma$-compact.

Let us first consider the case when $A$ is contained in some coordinate patch $S$. Let $\mathbf{F}$ be a coordinate system for $S$, and let $\mathbf{g} = \mathbf{F}^{-1}$. The following discussion is intended to motivate the definition of $\int_A f\, dV_r$. Let us consider a "small" $r$-cube $I$, of side length $a$ and vertex $t_0$, as indicated in Fig. 7-5.

Let us set $\mathbf{k}_l = a\boldsymbol{\epsilon}_l$, $\mathbf{h}_l = a\mathbf{g}_l(\mathbf{t}_0)$, $l = 1, \ldots, r$. Then $|\mathbf{k}_1 \wedge \cdots \wedge \mathbf{k}_r| = V_r(I)$, and by (6-16) $|\mathbf{h}_1 \wedge \cdots \wedge \mathbf{h}_r| = V_r(K)$, where $K$ is the $r$-parallelepiped with vertex $\mathbf{x}_0$ spanned by $\mathbf{h}_1, \ldots, \mathbf{h}_r$. By (7-1) the ratio of these two numbers is $\mathcal{J}\mathbf{g}(\mathbf{t}_0)$. Thus

$$V_r(K) = \mathcal{J}\mathbf{g}(\mathbf{t}_0)V_r(I).$$

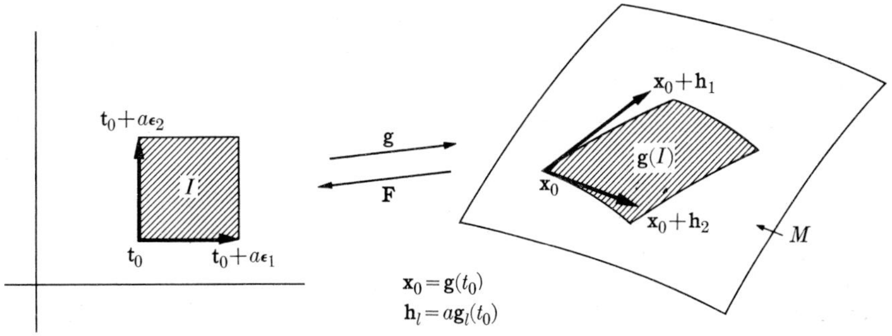


FIGURE 7–5

Moreover, $f[\mathbf{g}(\mathbf{t}_0)]V_r(K)$ should furnish a good approximation to $\int_{\mathbf{g}(I)} f\,dV_r$. If $Z$ is a figure composed of small nonoverlapping $r$-cubes $I_1, \ldots, I_m$, then $\int_{\mathbf{g}(Z)} f\,dV$ should be approximately the corresponding sum

$$\sum_{k=1}^{m} f[\mathbf{g}(\mathbf{t}_k)]\mathcal{J}\mathbf{g}(\mathbf{t}_k)V_r(I_k).$$

In the exact formula $Z$ is replaced by the set $B = \mathbf{g}^{-1}(A)$, and the sum by an integral.

**Definition.** Let $A$ be a $\sigma$-compact subset of a coordinate patch $S$, and let $f$ be continuous on $A$. Then

$$\int_A f(\mathbf{x})\,dV_r(\mathbf{x}) = \int_B f[\mathbf{g}(\mathbf{t})]\mathcal{J}\mathbf{g}(\mathbf{t})\,dV_r(\mathbf{t}), \qquad A = \mathbf{g}(B), \tag{7–4}$$

provided the function $(f \circ \mathbf{g})\mathcal{J}\mathbf{g}$ is integrable over $B$.

The integral over $B$ is taken in the sense of Section 5–6. By (7–2), $\mathcal{J}\mathbf{g}(\mathbf{t}) = |\mathbf{g}_1(\mathbf{t}) \wedge \cdots \wedge \mathbf{g}_r(\mathbf{t})|$. Since $\mathbf{g}$ is of class $C^{(1)}$, $\mathcal{J}\mathbf{g}$ is continuous. Hence $(f \circ \mathbf{g})\mathcal{J}\mathbf{g}$ is continuous. If $f \geq 0$, then the integral over $B$ either exists or diverges to $+\infty$. When the latter occurs we agree that the integral of $f$ over $A$ also diverges to $+\infty$.

We must show that the integral does not depend on the particular choice of coordinate system. Let $\tilde{S}$ be another coordinate patch such that $A \subset \tilde{S}$, and let $\tilde{\mathbf{F}}$ be a coordinate system for $\tilde{S}$. Let us adopt the notation of Fig. 7–4. Then $\mathbf{g} = \tilde{\mathbf{g}} \circ \boldsymbol{\phi}$, and by (7–3)

$$\mathcal{J}\mathbf{g}(\mathbf{t}) = \mathcal{J}\tilde{\mathbf{g}}[\boldsymbol{\phi}(\mathbf{t})]\mathcal{J}\boldsymbol{\phi}(\mathbf{t}) = \frac{\mathcal{J}\tilde{\mathbf{g}}(\boldsymbol{\tau})}{\mathcal{J}\boldsymbol{\phi}^{-1}(\boldsymbol{\tau})}, \qquad \text{if } \boldsymbol{\tau} = \boldsymbol{\phi}(\mathbf{t}).$$

Let $\tilde{B} = \tilde{\mathbf{F}}(A)$. Then $\tilde{B} = \boldsymbol{\phi}(B)$ and by the transformation formula for integrals (Theorem 17)

$$\int_B f[\mathbf{g}(\mathbf{t})]\mathcal{J}\mathbf{g}(\mathbf{t})\,dV_r(\mathbf{t}) = \int_{\tilde{B}} f[\tilde{\mathbf{g}}(\boldsymbol{\tau})]\,\frac{\mathcal{J}\tilde{\mathbf{g}}(\boldsymbol{\tau})}{\mathcal{J}\boldsymbol{\phi}^{-1}(\boldsymbol{\tau})}\,|J\boldsymbol{\phi}^{-1}(\boldsymbol{\tau})|\,dV_r(\boldsymbol{\tau}).$$

Since $\boldsymbol{\phi}^{-1}$ is a flat transformation, $|J\boldsymbol{\phi}^{-1}| = \mathcal{J}\boldsymbol{\phi}^{-1}$. Therefore

$$\int_B f[\mathbf{g}(\mathbf{t})]\mathcal{J}\mathbf{g}(\mathbf{t})\, dV_r(\mathbf{t}) = \int_{\tilde{B}} f[\tilde{\mathbf{g}}(\boldsymbol{\tau})]\mathcal{J}\tilde{\mathbf{g}}(\boldsymbol{\tau})\, dV_r(\boldsymbol{\tau}),$$

as required.

If we take $f(\mathbf{x}) = 1$, then (7–4) defines the *r-dimensional measure* of $A$:

$$V_r(A) = \int_B \mathcal{J}\mathbf{g}(\mathbf{t})\, dV_r(\mathbf{t}), \qquad A = \mathbf{g}(B). \tag{7–5}$$

**Example 1.** Let $M \subset E^3$ be a 2-manifold, and $S$ a relatively open subset of $M$ on which $x$ and $y$ can be taken as coordinates, as in Example 2, Section 7–1. Since $\mathcal{J}\mathbf{g} = [1 + |d\phi|^2]^{1/2}$, we have

$$\int_A f\, dV_2 = \int_B f[x, y, \phi(x, y)](1 + |d\phi(x, y)|^2)^{1/2}\, dV_2(x, y).$$

**Example 2.** Let $M$ be a 1-manifold and $B$ be a closed interval $[a, b]$. Using the terminology of Section 3–2, $A$ is the trace of the simple arc $\gamma$ represented on $[a, b]$ by $\mathbf{g}$. Formula (7–4) becomes

$$\int_A f(\mathbf{x})\, dV_1(\mathbf{x}) = \int_a^b f[\mathbf{g}(t)]\, |\mathbf{g}'(t)|\, dt.$$

The right-hand side is $\int_\gamma f\, ds$, as defined on p. 85.

**Note.* The line integral $\int_\gamma f\, ds$ was defined in Section 3–2 without requiring that $\gamma$ be simple. If $\gamma$ is not simple, then its trace $A = \mathbf{g}([a, b])$ need not be contained in a 1-manifold. There is a more general notion of $r$-dimensional measure and integral for sets which are not necessarily subsets of an $r$-manifold. The general formula which becomes for simple arcs the one in Example 2 is

$$\int_A f(\mathbf{x})N(\mathbf{x})\, dV_1(\mathbf{x}) = \int_a^b f[\mathbf{g}(t)]\, |\mathbf{g}'(t)|\, dt,$$

where $N(\mathbf{x})$ is the multiplicity of the point $\mathbf{x}$. For any $r \geq 1$ there is a similar formula

$$\int_A f(\mathbf{x})N(\mathbf{x})\, dV_r(\mathbf{x}) = \int_B f[\mathbf{g}(\mathbf{t})]\mathcal{J}\mathbf{g}(\mathbf{t})\, dV_r(\mathbf{t}), \tag{*}$$

where $B$ is a $\sigma$-compact subset of $E^r$, $\mathbf{g}$ is of class $C^{(1)}$ on $B$, $A = \mathbf{g}(B)$, and again $N(\mathbf{x})$ (= number of points $\mathbf{t} \in B$ such that $\mathbf{g}(\mathbf{t}) = \mathbf{x}$) is the multiplicity of $\mathbf{x}$. [See p. 144, H. Federer, "The $(\phi, k)$ rectifiable subsets of $n$ space," *Trans. Amer. Math. Soc.* **62** (1947), 114–192.]

In formula (*) it is not necessary to assume that $D\mathbf{g}(\mathbf{t})$ has maximum rank $r$. If $B' = \{\mathbf{t} \in B : \text{rank } D\mathbf{g}(\mathbf{t}) < r\}$, then $\mathcal{J}\mathbf{g}(\mathbf{t}) = 0$ for every $\mathbf{t} \in B'$. Therefore $B'$ contributes nothing to the integral on the right-hand side of (*). It turns out that $\mathbf{g}(B')$ has $r$-dimensional measure 0, and therefore contributes nothing to the integral on the left-hand side of (*).

**Example 3.** Let $H$ be the hemisphere $x^2 + y^2 + z^2 = 1$, $z > 0$. Introducing spherical coordinates on $H$, let

$$\mathbf{g}(\phi, \theta) = (\sin \phi \cos \theta)\mathbf{e}_1 + (\sin \phi \sin \theta)\mathbf{e}_2 + (\cos \phi)\mathbf{e}_3.$$

The image of a small square $[\phi, \phi + a] \times [\theta, \theta + a]$ in the $(\phi, \theta)$ plane is a small sector of the hemisphere which is approximately a rectangle of side lengths $a$ and $a \sin \phi$. Since $|\partial\mathbf{g}/\partial\phi \wedge \partial\mathbf{g}/\partial\theta| a^2$ is approximately the area of the sector, this suggests that $\mathcal{J}\mathbf{g}(\phi, \theta) = |\partial\mathbf{g}/\partial\phi \wedge \partial\mathbf{g}/\partial\theta| = \sin \phi$. The reader should check this formula (Problem 3). If we take $B = (0, \pi/2) \times (0, 2\pi)$ then $H - \mathbf{g}(B)$ is an arc of a great circle corresponding to $\theta = 0$. This arc is 2-dimensionally null in the sense defined below, and hence

$$\int_H f(\mathbf{x})\, dV_2(\mathbf{x}) = \int_{\mathbf{g}(B)} f(\mathbf{x})\, dV_2(\mathbf{x}) = \int_0^{\pi/2} d\phi \int_0^{2\pi} f[\mathbf{g}(\phi, \theta)] \sin \phi \, d\theta.$$

Let us turn to the general case when $A$ is not necessarily contained in some coordinate patch. To simplify matters let us at first assume that $M$ is a compact manifold and $f$ is continuous everywhere on $M$. The traditional way to proceed is to dissect $M$ into a finite number of nonoverlapping pieces $S_1, \ldots, S_m$ each of which has a coordinate system, with fr $S_k \cap$ fr $S_l$ contained in a finite union of $(r - 1)$-manifolds and $M = \text{cl}\, S_1 \cup \cdots \cup \text{cl}\, S_m$. Then

$$\int_A f\, dV_r = \sum_{k=1}^{m} \int_{A \cap S_k} f\, dV_r. \tag{7–6}$$

In simple examples it is easy to find such dissections of $M$. However, the theorem that every compact $r$-manifold $M$ has such a dissection is a difficult one to prove. See [21], Chap. IV. Nor is it evident that the integral is independent of the particular dissection chosen.

The same result can be achieved by a simpler device called partition of unity. The basic difficulty with dissections is that $S_k$ and $S_l$ cannot overlap. With partitions of unity this problem is avoided.

**Partition of unity.** Let us recall from Section 5–3 that the support of a function $\psi$ is the smallest closed set outside of which $\psi(\mathbf{x}) = 0$. Let us first find for every $\mathbf{x}_0$ and $r > 0$ a function $\psi$ of class $C^{(\infty)}$ on $E^n$ such that $\psi(\mathbf{x}) > 0$ on the open $r$-ball with center $\mathbf{x}_0$ and the support of $\psi$ is the closed $r$-ball with center $\mathbf{x}_0$. In fact, let

$$h(x) = \exp\left(\frac{-1}{1 - x^2}\right), \qquad -1 < x < 1,$$

$$h(x) = 0, \qquad |x| \geq 1.$$

From the example at the end of Section 2–3 and the composite function theorem, $h$ is of class $C^{(\infty)}$ on $E^1$. Let

$$\psi(\mathbf{x}) = h\left(\frac{|\mathbf{x} - \mathbf{x}_0|}{r}\right).$$

**Definition.** Let $M$ be a compact manifold. A collection of functions $\{\phi_1, \ldots, \phi_m\}$ is a *partition of unity* for $M$ if:

(1) $\phi_k$ is of class $C^{(\infty)}$ on $M$ and $\phi_k \geq 0$, $k = 1, \ldots, m$;

(2) The support of $\phi_k$ is a compact subset of some coordinate patch, $k = 1, \ldots, m$; and

(3) $\sum_{k=1}^{m} \phi_k(\mathbf{x}) = 1$ for every $\mathbf{x} \in M$.

**Proposition 29.** *Any compact manifold $M$ has a partition of unity.*

*Proof.* Every $\mathbf{x} \in M$ is contained in some coordinate patch $S$. Since $S$ is relatively open there is a neighborhood $U$ of $\mathbf{x}$ such that $M \cap \text{cl}\, U \subset S$. Since $M$ is compact, a finite collection $\{U_1, \ldots, U_m\}$ of such neighborhoods covers $M$. Let $\mathbf{x}_k$ be the center of $U_k$, $r_k$ the radius, and $\psi_k$ the function of class $C^{(\infty)}$ constructed above with $\mathbf{x}_0 = \mathbf{x}_k$, $r = r_k$. The collection of functions $\{\psi_1, \ldots, \psi_m\}$ satisfies (1) and (2) of the definition, but not necessarily (3). However, by construction $\psi_1(\mathbf{x}) + \cdots + \psi_m(\mathbf{x}) > 0$ for every $\mathbf{x} \in M$. Let

$$\phi_k(\mathbf{x}) = \frac{\psi_k(\mathbf{x})}{\psi_1(\mathbf{x}) + \cdots + \psi_m(\mathbf{x})}, \qquad k = 1, \ldots, m, \quad \mathbf{x} \in M.$$

The collection $\{\phi_1, \ldots, \phi_m\}$ is a partition of unity for $M$. ▮

Let $f$ be continuous on $M$. Since $M$ is compact, $f$ is bounded on $M$. This insures that all of the following integrals exist. If the support of $f$ is a compact subset $K$ of a coordinate patch, then we let

$$\int_A f\, dV_r = \int_{A \cap K} f\, dV_r.$$

In particular, if $\{\phi_1, \ldots, \phi_m\}$ is a partition of unity, then for any $f$ the support of $f\phi_k$ is compact and lies in some coordinate patch. Hence the integral of $f\phi_k$ is defined.

**Definition.** Let $A$ be a $\sigma$-compact subset of a compact manifold $M$, and $\{\phi_1, \ldots, \phi_m\}$ be a partition of unity for $M$. Then for any $f$ continuous on $M$

$$\int_A f\, dV_r = \sum_{k=1}^{m} \int_A f\phi_k\, dV_r. \tag{7–7}$$

In case $A$ is contained in some coordinate patch $S$, this agrees with the earlier definition (7–4), since $\sum \phi_k(\mathbf{x}) = 1$ for every $\mathbf{x} \in A$. We must show that the integral does not depend on the particular partition of unity chosen for $M$. Let $\{\chi_1, \ldots, \chi_p\}$ be another partition of unity for $M$. Then for every $\mathbf{x} \in M$

$$f(\mathbf{x})\chi_l(\mathbf{x}) = \sum_{k=1}^{m} f(\mathbf{x})\chi_l(\mathbf{x})\phi_k(\mathbf{x}), \qquad l = 1, \ldots, p.$$

Since the support of $f\chi_l$ is contained in some coordinate patch, its integral over $A$ can be written according to (7-4) as an integral over a set $B \subset E^r$. By Theorem 13, the integral over $B$ of a finite sum is the sum of the integrals. Hence

$$\int_A f\chi_l \, dV_r = \sum_{k=1}^{m} \int_A f\chi_l \phi_k \, dV_r, \qquad l = 1, \ldots, p,$$

$$\sum_{l=1}^{p} \int_A f\chi_l \, dV_r = \sum_{l=1}^{p} \sum_{k=1}^{m} \int_A f\chi_l \phi_k \, dV_r.$$

In the same way

$$\sum_{k=1}^{m} \int_A f\phi_k \, dV_r = \sum_{k=1}^{m} \sum_{l=1}^{p} \int_A f\phi_k \chi_l \, dV_r.$$

Since the right-hand sides are equal, the integral of $f$ over $A$ does not depend on which partition of unity is chosen.

If $f(\mathbf{x}) = 1$ for every $\mathbf{x} \in M$, then the integral gives the *r-dimensional measure*

$$V_r(A) = \sum_{k=1}^{m} \int_A \phi_k \, dV_r.$$

When $A$ is a subset of some coordinate patch, this agrees with the previous definition. If $V_r(A) = 0$, then $A$ is called an *r-null* set. The integral has the same elementary properties listed in Theorem 13 for $r = n$ (Problem 9). Moreover, $V_r$ is countably additive (Problem 10).

**Measure and integration on noncompact manifolds.** If $M$ is not compact then the discussion is somewhat more complicated. Partitions of unity consisting of infinite collections $\{\phi_1, \phi_2, \ldots\}$ must be considered. To (1)–(3) must be added:

(4) If $K$ is any compact subset of $M$, then the support of $\phi_k$ meets $K$ for only finitely many $k$.

The sum in (3) is now an infinite series. However, on any compact set only finitely many terms are different from 0. Every manifold has a partition of unity. This can be proved by an elaboration of the proof of Proposition 29, which we shall not give.

Let $f$ be continuous on $A$. Then $f$ is called integrable over $A$ if $\sum_{k=1}^{\infty} \int_A |f|\phi_k \, dV_r$ is finite. If $f$ is integrable over $A$, then its integral is $\sum_{k=1}^{\infty} \int_A f\phi_k \, dV_r$.

The following results are true whether $M$ is compact or not. However, we shall give the proof only for the compact case.

**Proposition 30.** *If $A$ is a subset of $M$ which is an $(r - 1)$-manifold, then $A$ is an $r$-null set.*

*Proof.* Suppose first that $A \subset S$, where $S$ is a coordinate patch. Let $\mathbf{F}$ be a coordinate system for $S$. By Theorem 21 the set $B = \mathbf{F}(A)$ is an $(r-1)$-manifold. By Corollary 3, p. 178, $V_r(B) = 0$. Therefore, from (7–5) $V_r(A) = 0$.

In the general case, let $\{\phi_1, \ldots, \phi_m\}$ be a partition of unity for $M$, and let $K_k$ be the support of $\phi_k$. Then $V_r(A \cap K_k) = 0$ and hence

$$\int_A \phi_k \, dV_r = \int_{A \cap K_k} \phi_k \, dV_r = 0.$$

Summing from 1 to $m$, $V_r(A) = 0$. ▮

**Corollary.** *If $A$ is contained in a countable union of $(r-1)$-manifolds, then $A$ is an $r$-null set.*

Formula (5–38) about change of variables in an integral by a regular flat transformation has the following generalization.

**Theorem 22.** *Let $\mathbf{g}$ be a regular transformation from an $r$-manifold $N$ into an $r$-manifold $M$. Let $f$ be continuous on $M$, and $A$ be any $\sigma$-compact subset of $M$. Then*

$$\int_A f(\mathbf{x}) \, dV_r(\mathbf{x}) = \int_{\mathbf{g}^{-1}(A)} f[\mathbf{g}(\mathbf{t})] \mathcal{J}\mathbf{g}(\mathbf{t}) \, dV_r(\mathbf{t}), \tag{7–7}$$

*provided either integral exists.*

*Proof.* By using a partition of unity, it suffices to consider the case when $f$ has compact support contained in some coordinate patch $S$ and $A \subset S$. Let $\mathbf{F}$ be a coordinate system for $S$. Then $\mathbf{F} \circ \mathbf{g}$ is a coordinate system for $S' = \mathbf{g}^{-1}(S)$. Let $\mathbf{G} = \mathbf{F}^{-1}$, $\mathbf{G}' = (\mathbf{F} \circ \mathbf{g})^{-1} = \mathbf{g}^{-1} \circ \mathbf{G}$. Let $A = \mathbf{G}(B)$. Then $\mathbf{g}^{-1}(A) = \mathbf{G}'(B)$. By (7–4) the left-hand side of (7–7) equals $\int_B (f \circ \mathbf{G}) \mathcal{J}\mathbf{G} \, dV_r$, while the right-hand side equals $\int_B [f \circ \mathbf{g} \circ \mathbf{G}'][(\mathcal{J}\mathbf{g}) \circ \mathbf{G}'] \mathcal{J}\mathbf{G}' \, dV_r$. But $\mathbf{G} = \mathbf{g} \circ \mathbf{G}'$, and by (7–3), $\mathcal{J}\mathbf{G} = (\mathcal{J}\mathbf{g}) \circ \mathbf{G}' \mathcal{J}\mathbf{G}'$. Therefore both sides of (7–7) are the same. ▮

## PROBLEMS

1. Find the area of $\{(x, y, xy) : x^2 + y^2 \leq 1\}$.
2. Let $n = 2$, $r = 3$. Show that (7–5) becomes

$$V_2(A) = \int_B \left\{ \left[ \frac{\partial(g^2, g^3)}{\partial(s, t)} \right]^2 + \left[ \frac{\partial(g^3, g^1)}{\partial(s, t)} \right]^2 + \left[ \frac{\partial(g^1, g^2)}{\partial(s, t)} \right]^2 \right\}^{1/2} dV_2(s, t).$$

3. In Example 3 calculate $\partial \mathbf{g}/\partial\phi \wedge \partial \mathbf{g}/\partial\theta$ and verify that its norm is $\sin \phi$.

*Moments, centroids.* These are defined in the same way as for $r = n$. For example, if $A$ has positive $r$-dimensional measure then the components of its centroid are

$$\bar{x}^i = \frac{1}{V_r(A)} \int_A x^i \, dV_r(\mathbf{x}), \quad i = 1, \ldots, n.$$

If $r = 2$, $n = 3$, and $A$ is thought of as a surface with continuous density $\rho(\mathbf{x})$ (mass per unit of area), then the mass is $\int_A \rho(\mathbf{x})\, dV_2(\mathbf{x})$ and the components of the center of mass are

$$\bar{x}^i = \int_A x^i \rho(\mathbf{x})\, dV_2(\mathbf{x}) \Big/ \int_A \rho(\mathbf{x})\, dV_2(\mathbf{x}), \quad i = 1, 2, 3.$$

4. Find the second moment about the $z$-axis of:
   (a) The sphere $x^2 + y^2 + z^2 = 1$.
   (b) The triangle with vertices $\mathbf{e}_1$, $\mathbf{e}_2$, $\mathbf{e}_3$.
5. Show that $\frac{1}{2}\mathbf{e}_3$ is the centroid of the hemisphere $H$ in Example 3. Use spherical coordinates on $H$.
6. (*Surfaces of revolution*). Let $\gamma$ be a simple arc (or simple closed curve) lying in the half $y > 0$ of the $(x, y)$ plane. From Section 3–2, $\gamma$ has a standard representation $\mathbf{G}$ on $[0, l]$, where $l$ is the length and $|\mathbf{G}'(s)| = 1$ for $0 \leq s \leq l$. Let $\mathbf{g}(s, t) = G^1(s)\mathbf{e}_1 + G^2(s)\,[(\cos t)\mathbf{e}_2 + (\sin t)\mathbf{e}_3]$, and let $M = \mathbf{g}((0, l) \times [0, 2\pi])$.
   (a) Prove *Pappus' theorem:* $V_2(M) = 2\pi\bar{y}l$, where $(\bar{x}, \bar{y})$ is the centroid of $\gamma$.
   (b) Find the area of a torus (doughnut) of major radius $r_1$ and minor radius $r_2$.
7. Let $S$ be the unit $(n - 1)$-sphere in $E^n$. Show that the $(n - 1)$-measure of the "zone" $\{\mathbf{x} \in S : a < x^n < b\}$ depends only on the difference $b - a$ when $n = 3$, but this is false when $n \neq 3$. Assume that $-1 \leq a < b \leq 1$.
8. Let $v(r) = \alpha_n r^n$ be the $n$-dimensional measure of a spherical $n$-ball of radius $r$. Show that $v'(r)$ is the $(n - 1)$-measure of its boundary. [*Note:* $\alpha_n$ was calculated on p. 183. If $\beta_{n-1} = V_{n-1}$ [unit $(n - 1)$-sphere], then $\beta_{n-1} = n\alpha_n$.]
9. Prove that the statements (1)–(7) obtained by replacing $n$ by $r$ everywhere in Theorem 13 are true for integrals over $\sigma$-compact subsets of a compact $r$-manifold.
10. Let $M$ be a compact $r$-manifold. Let $A = A_1 \cup A_2 \cup \cdots$, where $A_1, A_2, \ldots$ are disjoint $\sigma$-compact subsets of $M$. Show that $V_r(A) = V_r(A_1) + V_r(A_2) + \cdots$ [*Hint:* Use a partition of unity and Theorem 12.]

## 7–4 ORIENTATIONS; INTEGRALS OF $r$-FORMS

Let $M$ be an $r$-manifold. For each $\mathbf{x} \in M$ the tangent space $T(\mathbf{x})$ is an $r$-dimensional vector subspace of $E^n$. According to Section 6–3 $T(\mathbf{x})$ has two possible orientations, each of which is an $r$-vector of norm 1. If one of these orientations is denoted by $\mathbf{o}(\mathbf{x})$, then the other is $-\mathbf{o}(\mathbf{x})$. We would like to choose the orientation for $T(\mathbf{x})$ consistently on $M$; in other words we want the function $\mathbf{o}$ whose value at $\mathbf{x}$ is $\mathbf{o}(\mathbf{x})$ to be continuous on $M$.

**Definition.** $M$ is an *orientable* manifold if there exists a continuous $r$-vector-valued function $\mathbf{o}$ such that $\mathbf{o}(\mathbf{x})$ is an orientation for the tangent space $T(\mathbf{x})$ for every $\mathbf{x} \in M$. The function $\mathbf{o}$ is an *orientation* for $M$.

It can be shown that a connected manifold has at most two orientations. Let us find out what orientability means in the extreme dimensions $r = 1$, $n - 1$, $n$.

$r = 1$. If $M$ is a 1-manifold, then the two orientations for the 1-dimensional vector space $T(\mathbf{x})$ are unit tangent vectors at $\mathbf{x}$ pointing in opposite directions. $M$ is oriented by assigning a unit tangent vector $\mathbf{v}(\mathbf{x})$ continuously on $M$ (Fig. 7–6). It can be shown that every 1-manifold is orientable.

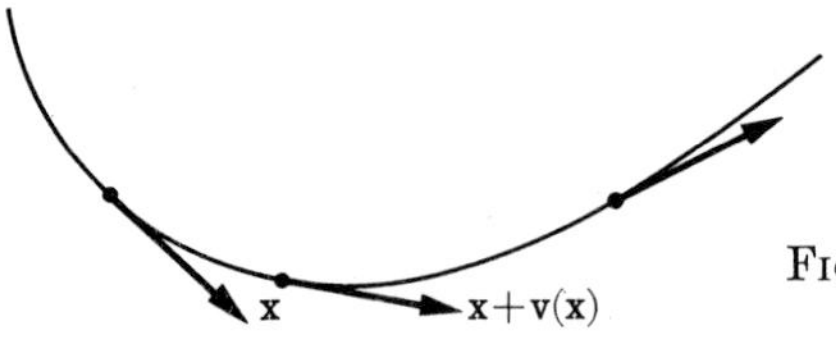


FIGURE 7–6

$r = n$. In this case the $n$-manifold $M$ is an open subset of $E^n$. The possible values for $\mathbf{o}(\mathbf{x})$ are $\pm\mathbf{e}_{1\cdots n}$. If $M$ is connected, then $\mathbf{o}(\mathbf{x})$ must be constant. If $\mathbf{o}(\mathbf{x}) = \mathbf{e}_{1\cdots n}$ for every $\mathbf{x} \in M$, then $M$ is *positively oriented;* and if $\mathbf{o}(\mathbf{x}) = -\mathbf{e}_{1\cdots n}$ for every $\mathbf{x} \in M$, then $M$ is *negatively oriented.*

$r = n - 1$. If $M$ is an $(n - 1)$-manifold in $E^n$, then the adjoint $\mathbf{n}(\mathbf{x}) = *\mathbf{o}(\mathbf{x})$ is a unit normal vector to $M$ at $\mathbf{x}$. The condition that $M$ be orientable is that a unit normal can be chosen continuously on $M$. If $D$ is an open set which is on one side of its boundary fr $D$ (see Section 7–5), then the exterior unit normal orients fr $D$. If $M$ is not the boundary of an open set, then $M$ may not be orientable. This is shown by the following famous surface.

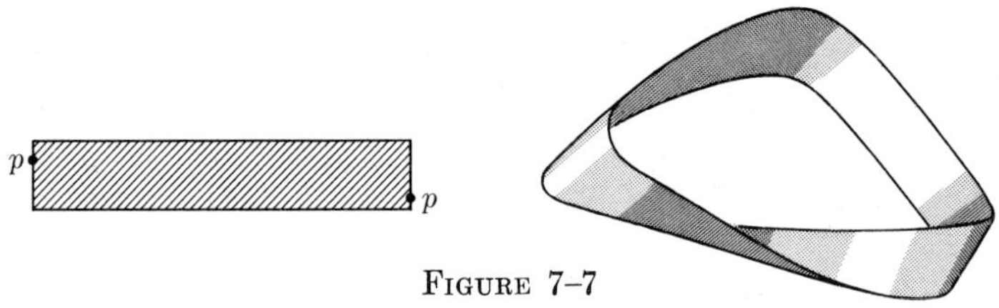


FIGURE 7–7

**Example 1.** The *Möbius strip.* This is a 2-manifold $M \subset E^3$ which is not orientable. It may be visualized by twisting a strip of paper and pasting together the ends (Fig. 7–7). The edge of the strip must be omitted in order that $M$ be locally like $E^2$. The fact that a unit normal cannot be chosen continuously may be expressed more picturesquely by saying that the Möbius strip is a surface with "only one side."

**Example 2.** The Möbius strip is not a compact 2-manifold. An example of a compact, nonorientable 2-manifold is the *Klein bottle,* or *twisted torus.* It is obtained by also joining together the lateral edges of the rectangle used to make the Möbius strip, as indicated in Fig. 7–8. The Klein bottle cannot be realized as a submanifold of $E^3$, since it can be proved that any compact $(n - 1)$-manifold $M \subset E^n$ is the boundary of an open set and hence is orientable. However, the Klein bottle can be realized as a submanifold of $E^4$.

FIGURE 7–8

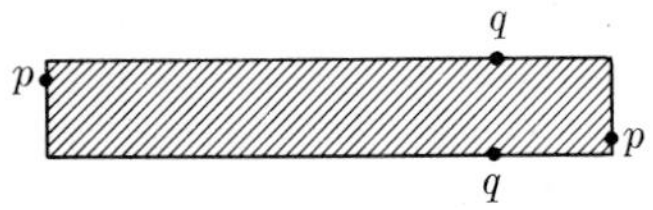

**Integrals of r-forms.** Let $M$ be an $r$-manifold with orientation $\mathbf{o}$, and $\boldsymbol{\omega}$ an $r$-form continuous on $M$. For each $\mathbf{x} \in M$ consider $\boldsymbol{\omega}(\mathbf{x}) \cdot \mathbf{o}(\mathbf{x})$, the scalar product of the $r$-covector $\boldsymbol{\omega}(\mathbf{x})$ and the $r$-vector $\mathbf{o}(\mathbf{x})$. Since $\boldsymbol{\omega}$ and $\mathbf{o}$ are continuous functions, $\boldsymbol{\omega} \cdot \mathbf{o}$ is a continuous real-valued function. Let $A$ be a $\sigma$-compact subset of $M$.

**Definition.** The integral of $\boldsymbol{\omega}$ over $A$ with the orientation $\mathbf{o}$ is

$$\int_{A^{\mathbf{o}}} \boldsymbol{\omega} = \int_A \boldsymbol{\omega}(\mathbf{x}) \cdot \mathbf{o}(\mathbf{x})\, dV_r(\mathbf{x}), \tag{7–8}$$

provided $\boldsymbol{\omega} \cdot \mathbf{o}$ is integrable over $A$.

In particular, if $M$ is compact, then $\boldsymbol{\omega} \cdot \mathbf{o}$ is continuous, bounded, and hence integrable over any $\sigma$-compact subset of $M$. The integral has the following elementary properties:

(1) $\int_{A^{\mathbf{o}}} (\boldsymbol{\omega}^1 + \boldsymbol{\omega}^2) = \int_{A^{\mathbf{o}}} \boldsymbol{\omega}^1 + \int_{A^{\mathbf{o}}} \boldsymbol{\omega}^2.$

(2) $\int_{A^{\mathbf{o}}} c\boldsymbol{\omega} = c\int_{A^{\mathbf{o}}} \boldsymbol{\omega}$, *for any scalar* $c$.

(3) $\int_{A^{-\mathbf{o}}} \boldsymbol{\omega} = -\int_{A^{\mathbf{o}}} \boldsymbol{\omega}.$

(4) *If* $|\boldsymbol{\omega}(\mathbf{x})| \leq C$ *for every* $\mathbf{x} \in A$, *then* $\left|\int_{A^{\mathbf{o}}} \boldsymbol{\omega}\right| \leq CV_r(A)$.

(5) $\int_{A^{\mathbf{o}}} \boldsymbol{\omega} = \int_{A_1^{\mathbf{o}}} \boldsymbol{\omega} + \int_{A_2^{\mathbf{o}}} \boldsymbol{\omega}$ *if* $A = A_1 \cup A_2$ *and* $A_1 \cap A_2$ *is empty.*

These follow at once from corresponding elementary properties of the right-hand side of (7–8). See Problem 9, Section 7–3.

For instance, in (3)

$$\int_A \boldsymbol{\omega}(\mathbf{x}) \cdot [-\mathbf{o}(\mathbf{x})]\, dV_r(\mathbf{x}) = -\int_A \boldsymbol{\omega}(\mathbf{x}) \cdot \mathbf{o}(\mathbf{x})\, dV_r(\mathbf{x}).$$

Since $|\mathbf{o}(\mathbf{x})| = 1$, $|\boldsymbol{\omega}(\mathbf{x}) \cdot \mathbf{o}(\mathbf{x})| \leq |\boldsymbol{\omega}(\mathbf{x})|$. Then in (4)

$$\left|\int_A \boldsymbol{\omega}(\mathbf{x}) \cdot \mathbf{o}(\mathbf{x})\, dV_r(\mathbf{x})\right| \leq \int_A |\boldsymbol{\omega}(\mathbf{x})|\, dV_r(\mathbf{x}) \leq CV_r(A).$$

In (1), one can take more generally a finite number of $r$-forms $\boldsymbol{\omega}^1, \ldots, \boldsymbol{\omega}^m$, or more generally an infinite sequence $\boldsymbol{\omega}^1, \boldsymbol{\omega}^2, \ldots$ provided $\sum_{k=1}^{\infty} \int_A |\boldsymbol{\omega}^k(\mathbf{x})|\, dV_r(\mathbf{x})$ converges. Similarly, the generalization of (5) is still true if $A = A_1 \cup A_2 \cup \cdots$, where $A_1, A_2, \ldots$ are disjoint $\sigma$-compact sets and $\sum_{k=1}^{\infty} \int_{A_k} |\boldsymbol{\omega}(\mathbf{x})|\, dV_r(\mathbf{x})$ converges.

**The case $r = n$.** Let $A^+$ denote $A$ with the positive orientation $\mathbf{e}_{1\cdots n}$ of $E^n$. Let $\boldsymbol{\omega} = f\, dx^1 \wedge \cdots \wedge dx^n$ be an $n$-form. Then

$$\boldsymbol{\omega}(\mathbf{x}) \cdot \mathbf{e}_{1\cdots n} = \omega_{1\cdots n}(\mathbf{x}) = f(\mathbf{x}),$$

and (7–8) becomes

$$\int_{A^+} f\,dx^1 \wedge \cdots \wedge dx^n = \int_A f\,dV_n. \tag{7–9}$$

The left-hand side of (7–9) changes sign if either the orientation of $A$ is reversed or two differentials $dx^i$ and $dx^j$ are interchanged. For instance, if $n = 2$ then

$$\int_{A^+} f\,dx \wedge dy = \int_A f\,dV_2,$$

$$\int_{A^-} f\,dx \wedge dy = \int_{A^+} f\,dy \wedge dx = -\int_A f\,dV_2.$$

**Orientation induced by a regular transformation.** Let $N$ be an $r$-manifold which is oriented by an orientation $\mathbf{O}$; and let $\mathbf{g}$ be regular from $N$ into $M$. Let $\mathbf{t} \in N$, and let $\mathbf{L}_r$ be the linear transformation induced by $D\mathbf{g}(\mathbf{t})$, as in the discussion on page 241. Let $\boldsymbol{\alpha}(\mathbf{x}) = \mathbf{L}_r[\mathbf{O}(\mathbf{t})]$. Since $|\mathbf{O}(\mathbf{t})| = 1$, from (7–1) we have

$$|\boldsymbol{\alpha}(\mathbf{x})| = \mathcal{J}\mathbf{g}(\mathbf{t})|\mathbf{O}(t)| = \mathcal{J}\mathbf{g}(\mathbf{t}), \quad \mathbf{x} = \mathbf{g}(\mathbf{t}).$$

Let $\mathbf{o}(\mathbf{x}) = |\boldsymbol{\alpha}(\mathbf{x})|^{-1}\boldsymbol{\alpha}(\mathbf{x})$. Then $\mathbf{o}$ is an orientation for $\mathbf{g}(N)$, called the orientation *induced* from $\mathbf{O}$ by $\mathbf{g}$.

If $N$ is a positively oriented open set $\Delta \subset E^r$, then as in the derivation of formula (7–2), $\boldsymbol{\alpha}(\mathbf{x}) = \mathbf{g}_1(\mathbf{t}) \wedge \cdots \wedge \mathbf{g}_r(\mathbf{t})$.

**Example 3.** Let $M \subset E^3$ be an orientable 2-manifold, and $\mathbf{o}$ a given orientation for $M$. Let $\mathbf{g}$ be regular from $\Delta \subset E^2$ into $M$. We must determine whether the orientation induced from the positive orientation of $E^2$ agrees with $\mathbf{o}$. If $\mathbf{x} = \mathbf{g}(s, t)$, then

$$\boldsymbol{\alpha}(\mathbf{x}) = \frac{\partial \mathbf{g}}{\partial s} \wedge \frac{\partial \mathbf{g}}{\partial t} = \alpha^{23}(\mathbf{x})\mathbf{e}_{23} + \alpha^{31}(\mathbf{x})\mathbf{e}_{31} + \alpha^{12}(\mathbf{x})\mathbf{e}_{12},$$

whereby (6–13a) $\alpha^{ij}(\mathbf{x}) = \partial(g^i, g^j)/\partial(s, t)$. Then $\mathbf{o}(\mathbf{x}) = c(\mathbf{x})\boldsymbol{\alpha}(\mathbf{x})$, where $c(\mathbf{x}) = \pm|\boldsymbol{\alpha}(\mathbf{x})|^{-1}$. The induced orientation is the given one, provided $c(\mathbf{x}) > 0$.

**Example 4.** Let $H$ be the hemisphere in Example 3, p. 253, oriented so that $\mathbf{o}^{12}(\mathbf{x}) > 0$ for every $\mathbf{x} \in H$. The vector $\mathbf{n}(\mathbf{x}) = *\mathbf{o}(\mathbf{x})$ is normal to $H$, and its third component $n^3(\mathbf{x})$ equals $o^{12}(\mathbf{x})$. We have oriented $H$ so that the normal "points upward." If $(\phi, \theta)$ are spherical coordinates of $\mathbf{x}$, and $\mathbf{g}$ is as on p. 253, then

$$\alpha^{12}(\mathbf{x}) = \frac{\partial(g^1, g^2)}{\partial(\phi, \theta)} = \sin\phi\cos\phi > 0.$$

Therefore the induced orientation is $\mathbf{o}$.

Let $\boldsymbol{\omega}$ be an $r$-form which is continuous on $M$, and let $\boldsymbol{\omega}^\#$ be the $r$-form defined in Section 6–5. It has the property that

$$\boldsymbol{\omega}^\#(\mathbf{t}) \cdot \mathbf{O}(\mathbf{t}) = \boldsymbol{\omega}(\mathbf{x}) \cdot \boldsymbol{\alpha}(\mathbf{x}), \qquad \text{if } \mathbf{x} = \mathbf{g}(\mathbf{t}).$$

Since $\mathbf{g}$ is of class $C^{(1)}$, $\boldsymbol{\omega}^\#$ is continuous on $N$.

**Proposition 31.** *Let* $A = \mathbf{g}(B)$, *where* $B$ *is a* $\sigma$*-compact subset of* $N$. *Let* $\mathbf{o}$ *be the orientation induced by* $\mathbf{g}$ *from the orientation* $\mathbf{O}$ *on* $N$. *Then*

$$\int_{A^{\mathbf{o}}} \boldsymbol{\omega} = \int_{B^{\mathbf{O}}} \boldsymbol{\omega}^{\#}, \tag{7–10}$$

*provided either integral exists.*

*Proof.* From the discussion above, $\boldsymbol{\alpha}(\mathbf{x}) = \mathcal{J}\mathbf{g}(\mathbf{t})\mathbf{o}(\mathbf{x})$ if $\mathbf{x} = \mathbf{g}(\mathbf{t})$. Dividing by $\mathcal{J}\mathbf{g}(\mathbf{t})$, we have

$$\boldsymbol{\omega}(\mathbf{x}) \cdot \mathbf{o}(\mathbf{x}) = \frac{\boldsymbol{\omega}^{\#}(\mathbf{t}) \cdot \mathbf{O}(\mathbf{t})}{\mathcal{J}\mathbf{g}(\mathbf{t})}.$$

By Theorem 22,

$$\int_A \boldsymbol{\omega}(\mathbf{x}) \cdot \mathbf{o}(\mathbf{x})\, dV_r(\mathbf{x}) = \int_B \frac{\boldsymbol{\omega}^{\#}(\mathbf{t}) \cdot \mathbf{O}(\mathbf{t})}{\mathcal{J}\mathbf{g}(\mathbf{t})} \mathcal{J}\mathbf{g}(\mathbf{t})\, dV_r(\mathbf{t}).$$

Canceling $\mathcal{J}\mathbf{g}(\mathbf{t})$ on the right-hand side, we get (7–10). ∎

An important particular case of Proposition 31 is obtained by taking for $N$ an open set $\Delta \subset E^r$. This proposition, together with a judicious choice of coordinate systems on $M$, furnishes a tool for evaluating integrals of $r$-forms.

**Example 5.** Let $r = 1$, $\Delta \subset E^1$. Then $\boldsymbol{\omega}^{\#}(t) = \boldsymbol{\omega}[\mathbf{g}(t)] \cdot \mathbf{g}'(t)$. If $B$ is an interval, then $\int_{B^+} \boldsymbol{\omega}^{\#}$ is the line integral of $\boldsymbol{\omega}$ along the curve in $E^n$ represented parametrically on $B$ by $\mathbf{g}$.

**Example 6.** Let $\boldsymbol{\omega} = f\, dx^{i_1} \wedge \cdots \wedge dx^{i_r}$, and let $\Delta \subset E^r$. From Section 6–5

$$(dx^{i_1} \wedge \cdots \wedge dx^{i_r})^{\#} = dg^{i_1} \wedge \cdots \wedge dg^{i_r}$$

$$= \frac{\partial(g^{i_1}, \ldots, g^{i_r})}{\partial(t^1, \ldots, t^r)}\, dt^1 \wedge \cdots \wedge dt^r.$$

By formulas (7–9) and (7–10),

$$\int_{A^{\mathbf{o}}} f\, dx^{i_1} \wedge \cdots \wedge dx^{i_r} = \int_B f \circ \mathbf{g}\, \frac{\partial(g^{i_1}, \ldots, g^{i_r})}{\partial(t^1, \ldots, t^r)}\, dV_r,$$

provided $\mathbf{o}$ is the orientation induced by $\mathbf{g}$.

Continuing Example 4, we have for instance

$$\int_{H^{\mathbf{o}}} f\, dx \wedge dy = \int_{B^+} f \circ \mathbf{g}\, \frac{\partial(g^1, g^2)}{\partial(\phi, \theta)}\, d\phi \wedge d\theta$$

$$= \int_B f(\sin\phi\cos\theta, \sin\phi\sin\theta, \cos\phi)\sin\phi\cos\phi\, dV_2(\phi, \theta),$$

where $B = (0, \pi/2) \times (0, 2\pi)$.

**PROBLEMS**

1. Let $\Delta \subset E^n$ have the positive orientation and let $\mathbf{g}$ be a regular flat transformation from $\Delta$ into $E^n$.
   (a) Show that $\mathbf{g}$ induces the positive orientation on $\mathbf{g}(\Delta)$ if and only if $J\mathbf{g}(\mathbf{t}) > 0$ for every $\mathbf{t} \in \Delta$.
   (b) Show that (7–10) becomes
$$\int_{A^+} f\, dx^1 \wedge \cdots \wedge dx^n = \int_{B^+} f \circ \mathbf{g}\, J\mathbf{g}\, dt^1 \wedge \cdots \wedge dt^n,$$
   provided $J\mathbf{g}(\mathbf{t}) > 0$ for every $\mathbf{t} \in \Delta$.
2. Let $A = \{(x, y, z) : y = x^2 + z^2, y \leq 4\}$, oriented so that $\mathbf{o}^{31}(\mathbf{x}) > 0$. Evaluate:
   (a) $\int_{A^{\mathbf{o}}} z\, dx \wedge dy$. (b) $\int_{A^{\mathbf{o}}} \exp y\, dz \wedge dx$.
   [*Hint:* Use polar coordinates in the $(x, z)$-plane.]
3. Let $A$ be the triangle in $E^3$ with vertices $\mathbf{e}_1$, $-\mathbf{e}_2$, $2\mathbf{e}_3$.
   (a) Show that $\mathbf{o} = \frac{1}{3}(2\mathbf{e}_{23} - 2\mathbf{e}_{31} + \mathbf{e}_{12})$ is an orientation for the plane containing $A$.
   (b) Evaluate $\int_{A^{\mathbf{o}}} x\, dy \wedge dz$. [*Hint:* Take $\mathbf{g}$ affine such that $\mathbf{g}(\Sigma) = A$, where $\Sigma$ is the standard 2-simplex.]
4. Let $A = \{(x, y, z) : x^2 + y^2 = z^2, x > 0, 0 < z < 1\}$, oriented so that $o^{12}(\mathbf{x}) < 0$. Evaluate
$$\int_{A^{\mathbf{o}}} z^2\, dy \wedge dz.$$
5. Let $n = 4$ and $M = \{\mathbf{x} : (x^1)^2 + (x^2)^2 = 1, (x^3)^2 + (x^4)^2 = 1\}$. Let $\mathbf{g}(s, t) = (\cos s)\mathbf{e}_1 + (\sin s)\mathbf{e}_2 + (\cos t)\mathbf{e}_3 + (\sin t)\mathbf{e}_4$, $0 \leq s, t \leq 2\pi$.
   (a) Find the orientation $\mathbf{o}$ induced by $\mathbf{g}$ from the positive orientation of $E^2$.
   (b) Evaluate
$$\int_{M^{\mathbf{o}}} dx^3 \wedge dx^4 + x^1x^3\, dx^2 \wedge dx^4.$$
6. Suppose that $M$ is the $r$-manifold determined by $\mathbf{\Phi}$, in the sense that $M$ satisfies (4–26), p. 123. Show that $M$ is orientable.

## 7–5 THE DIVERGENCE THEOREM

This is an $n$-dimensional generalization of the fundamental theorem of calculus and has numerous applications in geometry and in physics. We shall first state the theorem in two different ways and derive some corollaries of it. A proof is given later in the section.

The divergence theorem equates the integral of an $(n - 1)$-form $\boldsymbol{\omega}$ over the boundary of an open set $D$ and the integral of $d\boldsymbol{\omega}$ over $D$. The integral of a differential form depends on an orientation. We must assign on the boundary fr $D$ an orientation corresponding to the positive orientation on $D$.

For this purpose we must assume that $D$ lies on one side of its boundary. This is expressed precisely as follows.

**Definition.** Let $\mathbf{x}_0 \in \text{fr } D$, and let $U$ be a neighborhood of $\mathbf{x}_0$ such that $(\text{fr } D) \cap U$ is an $(n-1)$-manifold. Then *$D$ is on one side of its boundary in $U$* if there exists a function $\Phi$ of class $C^{(1)}$ on $U$ such that $d\Phi(\mathbf{x}) \neq \mathbf{0}$ for every $\mathbf{x} \in U$ and

$$(\text{fr } D) \cap U = \{\mathbf{x} \in U : \Phi(\mathbf{x}) = 0\},$$
$$D \cap U = \{\mathbf{x} \in U : \Phi(\mathbf{x}) < 0\}.$$

If fr $D$ is an $(n-1)$-manifold and every $\mathbf{x}_0 \in \text{fr } D$ has such a neighborhood $U$, then *$D$ is on one side of its boundary.*

**Example 1.** Let $D = \{\mathbf{x} : |\mathbf{x}| < 1 \text{ or } 1 < |\mathbf{x}| < 2\}$. Then fr $D$ is the union of two concentric $(n-1)$-spheres of radii 1 and 2. However, $D$ is on both sides of the inner $(n-1)$-sphere.

Actually this example is rather artificial. If $D$ is the interior of its closure, then using the implicit function theorem it can be shown that $D$ is on one side of fr $D$.

**Definition.** Let $\mathbf{x} \in \text{fr } D$, and $\mathbf{n} \neq \mathbf{0}$ be a vector normal to fr $D$ at $\mathbf{x}$. Then $\mathbf{n}$ is an *exterior normal* at $\mathbf{x}$ if there exists $\delta > 0$ such that $\mathbf{x} + t\mathbf{n} \in D$ for $-\delta < t < 0$ and $\mathbf{x} + t\mathbf{n} \in (\text{cl } D)^c$ for $0 < t < \delta$.

From the definition, all exterior normals at $\mathbf{x}$ are positive scalar multiples of any particular one. We shall be principally concerned with the unit exterior normal, which will be denoted by $\boldsymbol{\nu}(\mathbf{x})(|\boldsymbol{\nu}(\mathbf{x})| = 1)$.

Let $D$ be on one side of its boundary in $U$. The vector $\mathbf{n}(\mathbf{x}) = \text{grad } \Phi(\mathbf{x})$ is normal to fr $D$ at $\mathbf{x} \in (\text{fr } D) \cap U$.

Let $\psi(t) = \Phi(\mathbf{x} + t\mathbf{n}(\mathbf{x}))$. Then $\psi(0) = 0$ and

$$\psi'(0) = \text{grad } \Phi(\mathbf{x}) \cdot \mathbf{n}(\mathbf{x}) = |\text{grad } \Phi(\mathbf{x})|^2 > 0.$$

There exists $\delta > 0$ such that $\psi(t) < 0$ for $-\delta < t < 0$ and $\psi(t) > 0$ for $0 < t < \delta$. Therefore grad $\Phi(\mathbf{x})$ is an exterior normal at $\mathbf{x}$. The vector

$$\boldsymbol{\nu}(\mathbf{x}) = |\text{grad } \Phi(\mathbf{x})|^{-1} \text{ grad } \Phi(\mathbf{x})$$

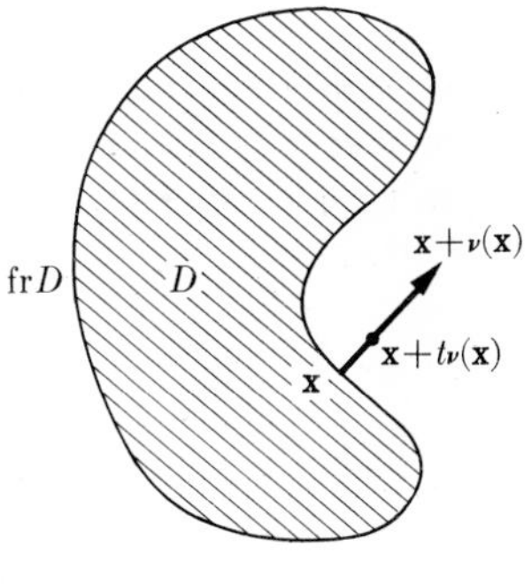


FIGURE 7–9

is the unit exterior normal to $D$ at $\mathbf{x}$. Since $\Phi$ is of class $C^{(1)}$, $\boldsymbol{\nu}$ is a continuous function on $(\text{fr } D) \cap U$. See Fig. 7–9.

Let $\mathbf{o}(\mathbf{x})$ be the $(n-1)$-vector such that $\boldsymbol{\nu}(\mathbf{x}) = *\mathbf{o}(\mathbf{x})$. The $(n-1)$-space of $\mathbf{o}(\mathbf{x})$ is the tangent space $T(\mathbf{x})$, and $|\mathbf{o}(\mathbf{x})| = |\boldsymbol{\nu}(\mathbf{x})| = 1$. Hence $\mathbf{o}(\mathbf{x})$ is an orientation for $T(\mathbf{x})$. A frame $(\mathbf{h}_1, \ldots, \mathbf{h}_{n-1})$ for $T(\mathbf{x})$ has this orientation if and only if $(\boldsymbol{\nu}(\mathbf{x}), \mathbf{h}_1, \ldots, \mathbf{h}_{n-1})$ is a positively oriented frame for $E^n$. Since $\boldsymbol{\nu}$ is continuous on $(\text{fr } D) \cap U$ and the components of $\boldsymbol{\nu}$ and $\mathbf{o}$ are related by (6–32a), the function $\mathbf{o}$ is continuous there. Thus $\mathbf{o}$ is an orientation for $(\text{fr } D) \cap U$, which we call the *positive orientation.*

The preceding discussion was local. However, let fr $D$ be an $(n - 1)$-manifold, and let $D$ lie on one side of it. There is a (unique) exterior unit normal $\boldsymbol{\nu}(\mathbf{x})$ at each $\mathbf{x} \in \text{fr } D$, and the orientation $\mathbf{o}(\mathbf{x})$ such that $*\mathbf{o}(\mathbf{x}) = \boldsymbol{\nu}(\mathbf{x})$ is defined for every $\mathbf{x} \in \text{fr } D$. Since every $\mathbf{x}_0 \in \text{fr } D$ has a relative neighborhood in which $\mathbf{o}$ is continuous, the function $\mathbf{o}$ is continuous on fr $D$.

This defines the *positive orientation* $\mathbf{o}$ on fr $D$. Let us write $\partial D^+$ instead of $(\text{fr } D)^{\mathbf{o}}$ for fr $D$ with this orientation. (The symbol $\partial$ is widely used to denote a boundary.)

Let us state and prove the divergence theorem for the following class of open sets, which will be called regular domains.

**Definition.** An open set $D \subset E^n$ is a *regular domain* if: (1) $D$ is bounded; (2) fr $D$ is an $(n - 1)$-manifold of class $C^{(2)}$; and (3) $D$ is on one side of its boundary.

**Divergence theorem.** *Let $D$ be a regular domain and $\boldsymbol{\omega}$ an $(n - 1)$-form of class $C^{(1)}$ on* cl $D$. *Then*

$$\int_{\partial D^+} \boldsymbol{\omega} = \int_{D^+} d\boldsymbol{\omega}. \tag{7–11a}$$

Let us defer the proof until later in the section. The last assumption means that $\boldsymbol{\omega}$ is the restriction to cl $D$ of a form of class $C^{(1)}$ on some open set $D_0$ containing cl $D$. The somewhat restrictive assumption (2) about fr $D$ is made to simplify the proof. The theorem is still true if fr $D$ is not a manifold but instead consists of a finite number of pieces of class $C^{(1)}$ intersecting in sets of dimension $n - 2$. For example, if $D$ is the interior of an $n$-cube then the pieces are the faces, which are cubes of dimension $n - 1$ and intersect in $(n - 2)$-dimensional cubes. This more general form of the divergence theorem will be precisely stated at the end of the section. For certain special kinds of sets $D$ there is an easy proof of the theorem (Problems 5, 6).

**The case $n = 2$.** Suppose that fr $D = C_1 \cup \cdots \cup C_m$ where each $C_k$ is the trace of a simple closed curve $\gamma_k$, and $C_1, \ldots, C_m$ are disjoint. The orientation is chosen by selecting the unit tangent vector $\mathbf{v}(x, y)$ so that $(\boldsymbol{\nu}(x, y), \mathbf{v}(x, y))$ is a positively oriented orthonormal frame for $E^2$. Intuitively speaking this means that as the boundary is traversed, $D$ is always on the left. Then

$$\int_{\partial D^+} \boldsymbol{\omega} = \int_{\gamma_1} \boldsymbol{\omega} + \cdots + \int_{\gamma_m} \boldsymbol{\omega}.$$

If we write $\boldsymbol{\omega} = M\,dx + N\,dy$, then (7–11a) becomes

$$\sum_{k=1}^{m} \int_{\gamma_k} M\,dx + N\,dy = \int_{D^+} \left(\frac{\partial N}{\partial x} - \frac{\partial M}{\partial y}\right) dx \wedge dy. \tag{7–12}$$

This is known as *Green's theorem*. (See Fig. 7–10.)

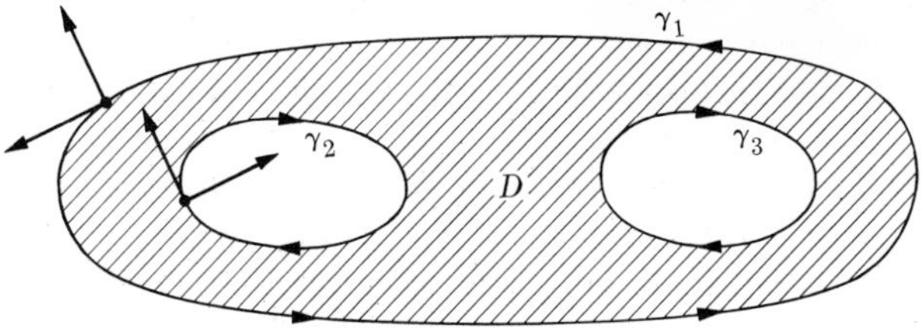


FIGURE 7–10

**Example 2.** Let $\omega = \frac{1}{2}(x\,dy - y\,dx)$. Then $d\omega = dx \wedge dy$ and $V_2(D) = \int_{D^+} dx \wedge dy$. Hence the area of $D$ can be written as an integral over the boundary:

$$V_2(D) = \tfrac{1}{2}\int_{\partial D^+} x\,dy - y\,dx.$$

The divergence theorem is often stated in a different way which does not involve integrals of differential forms. Let $\zeta$ be a 1-form of class $C^{(1)}$ on cl $D$. Its divergence

$$\operatorname{div} \zeta = \sum_{i=1}^{n} \frac{\partial \zeta_i}{\partial x^i}$$

is continuous. Let $\omega$ be the $(n-1)$-form such that $*\omega = \zeta$. By formulas (6–32) and (6–34),

$$\omega(\mathbf{x}) \cdot \mathbf{o}(\mathbf{x}) = *\omega(\mathbf{x}) \cdot *\mathbf{o}(\mathbf{x}) = \zeta(\mathbf{x}) \cdot \boldsymbol{\nu}(\mathbf{x}),$$
$$d\omega = \operatorname{div} \zeta\, dx^1 \wedge \cdots \wedge dx^n.$$

Therefore

$$\int_{\partial D^+} \omega = \int_{\operatorname{fr} D} \omega \cdot \mathbf{o}\, dV_{n-1} = \int_{\operatorname{fr} D} \zeta \cdot \boldsymbol{\nu}\, dV_{n-1},$$
$$\int_{D^+} d\omega = \int_{D^+} \operatorname{div} \zeta\, dx^1 \wedge \cdots \wedge dx^n = \int_D \operatorname{div} \zeta\, dV_n.$$

The conclusion (7–11a) of the divergence theorem can be restated as:

$$\int_{\operatorname{fr} D} \zeta(\mathbf{x}) \cdot \boldsymbol{\nu}(\mathbf{x})\, dV_{n-1}(x) = \int_D \operatorname{div} \zeta(\mathbf{x})\, dV_n(\mathbf{x}). \tag{7–11b}$$

The number $\zeta(\mathbf{x}) \cdot \boldsymbol{\nu}(\mathbf{x})$ is called the (exterior) *normal component* of the convector $\zeta(\mathbf{x})$.

*Note:* In (7–11b) the distinction between vectors and covectors which we have maintained is not customary. If the covector $\zeta(\mathbf{x})$ is replaced by the vector with the same components, then $\cdot$ means the standard euclidean inner product (see remarks in Section 3–3). In Green's formulas below, $df$ should then be replaced by grad $f$.

For $n = 3$, the divergence theorem is often called Gauss' theorem or Ostrogradsky's theorem. It has various interesting physical interpretations.

Let $\boldsymbol{\zeta}$ be a force field acting in some open set $D_0 \subset E^3$. For each $\mathbf{x} \in D_0$, $\boldsymbol{\zeta}(\mathbf{x})$ is the force covector acting at $\mathbf{x}$. For notational simplicity, let us set $M = \operatorname{fr} D$ throughout the discussion to follow. The number $\int_M \boldsymbol{\zeta}(\mathbf{x}) \cdot \boldsymbol{\nu}(\mathbf{x})\, dV_2(\mathbf{x})$ is called the *outward flux* across the boundary $M$. The divergence theorem expresses the outward flux as a volume integral over $D$. If $D$ has small diameter and contains $\mathbf{x}_0$, then the outward flux is approximately $V_3(D) \operatorname{div} \boldsymbol{\zeta}(\mathbf{x}_0)$. To make this statement more precise let us state the following.

**Lemma.** *If $f$ is continuous on an open set $D_0$ containing $\mathbf{x}_0$, then*

$$f(\mathbf{x}_0) = \lim_{\operatorname{diam} D \to 0} \frac{1}{V_n(D)} \int_D f(\mathbf{x})\, dV_n(\mathbf{x}).$$

In words, this formula says that given $\epsilon > 0$ there exists $\delta > 0$ such that if $D$ is any open set of diameter less than $\delta$ with $\mathbf{x}_0 \in D$, then

$$\left| V_n(D) f(\mathbf{x}_0) - \int_D f(\mathbf{x})\, dV_n(\mathbf{x}) \right| < \epsilon V_n(D).$$

*Proof.* Given $\epsilon > 0$ let $\delta > 0$ be such that $|f(\mathbf{x}) - f(\mathbf{x}_0)| < \epsilon$ whenever $|\mathbf{x} - \mathbf{x}_0| < \delta$. If $\mathbf{x}_0 \in D$ and $\operatorname{diam} D < \delta$, then

$$\begin{aligned} \left| V_n(D) f(\mathbf{x}_0) - \int_D f(\mathbf{x})\, dV_n \right| &= \left| \int_D [f(\mathbf{x}_0) - f(\mathbf{x})]\, dV_n(\mathbf{x}) \right| \\ &\le \int_D |f(\mathbf{x}_0) - f(\mathbf{x})|\, dV_n(\mathbf{x}) < \epsilon V_n(D). \ \blacksquare \end{aligned}$$

If in the lemma we take $D$ regular and $f = \operatorname{div} \boldsymbol{\zeta}$, then for any $n$ and $\mathbf{x}_0$ in the domain of $\boldsymbol{\zeta}$

$$\operatorname{div} \boldsymbol{\zeta}(\mathbf{x}_0) = \lim_{\operatorname{diam} D \to 0} \frac{1}{V_n(D)} \int_M \boldsymbol{\zeta}(\mathbf{x}) \cdot \boldsymbol{\nu}(\mathbf{x})\, dV_{n-1}(\mathbf{x}). \tag{7-13}$$

As another physical interpretation, consider a fluid flowing in an open set $D_0 \subset E^3$. Let $t$ denote time and $\mathbf{x} = (x, y, z)$. Let $\rho(\mathbf{x}, t)$ be the density and $\mathbf{v}(\mathbf{x}, t)$ the velocity at $\mathbf{x}$ and time $t$. Let $\boldsymbol{\zeta} = \rho\mathbf{v}$. Suppose that $D$ is regular and $\operatorname{cl} D \subset D_0$. The left-hand side of (7–11b) represents the rate at which mass is flowing out of $D$. Therefore, if $m(t)$ is the mass of the fluid in $D$ at time $t$, then from the divergence theorem

$$-\frac{dm}{dt} = \int_D \operatorname{div}(\rho\mathbf{v})\, dV_3.$$

On the other hand,

$$m(t) = \int_D \rho(\mathbf{x}, t)\, dV_3(\mathbf{x}).$$

Differentiating under the integral sign (Section 5–11),

$$\frac{dm}{dt} = \int_D \frac{\partial \rho}{\partial t}\, dV_3.$$

For each $t_0$ the functions $-\text{div}\,(\rho\mathbf{v})$ and $\partial\rho/\partial t$ have the same integral over every regular $D$ with $\text{cl}\,D \subset D_0$. By the lemma, for every $\mathbf{x}_0 \in D_0$ these functions have the same value at $(\mathbf{x}_0, t_0)$. In other words,

$$\frac{\partial\rho}{\partial t} = -\text{div}\,(\rho\mathbf{v}).$$

If the density $\rho$ is constant, then the fluid is *incompressible*. Thus for incompressible fluids $\text{div}\,\mathbf{v} = 0$ at every time $t$.

If $\text{div}\,\boldsymbol{\zeta}(\mathbf{x}) = 0$ for every $\mathbf{x}$ in its domain $D_0$, then $\boldsymbol{\zeta}$ is called *divergence free* (or *solenoidal*). The divergence theorem has the following corollary.

**Corollary.** *Let $\boldsymbol{\zeta}$ be of class $C^{(1)}$ on an open set $D_0$. Then $\boldsymbol{\zeta}$ is divergence free if and only if*

$$\int_M \boldsymbol{\zeta}(\mathbf{x}) \cdot \boldsymbol{\nu}(\mathbf{x})\, dV_{n-1}(\mathbf{x}) = 0 \tag{$*$}$$

*for every regular domain $D$ such that* $\text{cl}\,D \subset D_0$.

*Proof.* If $\boldsymbol{\zeta}$ is divergence free, then the equation $(*)$ is immediate from (7–11b). Conversely if $(*)$ holds for every such $D$, then by (7–13) $\text{div}\,\boldsymbol{\zeta}(\mathbf{x}_0) = 0$ for every $\mathbf{x}_0 \in D_0$. ▮

**Green's formulas.** Let $f$ be of class $C^{(2)}$ on $\text{cl}\,D$. Let $f_\nu(\mathbf{x})$ denote the derivative of $f$ in the direction of the exterior normal at $\mathbf{x} \in M$, namely,

$$f_{\boldsymbol{\nu}}(\mathbf{x}) = df(\mathbf{x}) \cdot \boldsymbol{\nu}(\mathbf{x}).$$

Let $\phi$ be another function of class $C^{(2)}$ on $\text{cl}\,D$, and let $\boldsymbol{\zeta}(\mathbf{x}) = \phi(\mathbf{x})\,df(\mathbf{x})$. Then

$$\boldsymbol{\zeta}(\mathbf{x}) \cdot \boldsymbol{\nu}(\mathbf{x}) = \phi(\mathbf{x})f_{\boldsymbol{\nu}}(\mathbf{x}),$$

$$\text{div}\,\boldsymbol{\zeta} = \sum_{i=1}^{n} \frac{\partial}{\partial x^i}\left(\phi\,\frac{\partial f}{\partial x^i}\right) = d\phi \cdot df + \phi\,\text{Lapl}\,f.$$

Hence we get the *first Green's formula:*

$$\int_M \phi f_{\boldsymbol{\nu}}\, dV_{n-1} = \int_D [d\phi \cdot df + \phi\,\text{Lapl}\,f]\, dV_n. \tag{7–14}$$

In the same way

$$\int_M f\phi_{\boldsymbol{\nu}}\, dV_{n-1} = \int_D [df \cdot d\phi + f\,\text{Lapl}\,\phi]\, dV_n.$$

Subtracting, we get the *second Green's formula*

$$\int_M [\phi f_{\boldsymbol{\nu}} - f\phi_{\boldsymbol{\nu}}]\, dV_{n-1} = \int_D [\phi\,\text{Lapl}\,f - f\,\text{Lapl}\,\phi]\, dV_n. \tag{7–15}$$

**Example 3.** A function $f$ is called *harmonic* if $\operatorname{Lapl} f = 0$. Let $f$ be harmonic, and apply the first Green's formula with $\phi = f$. Then

$$\int_M f f_\nu \, dV_{n-1} = \int_D |df|^2 \, dV_n. \tag{7–16}$$

When $n = 3$ the right-hand side often has (except for a suitable multiplicative constant) the physical interpretation of energy.

If $f$ is harmonic and $f(\mathbf{x}) = 0$ for every $\mathbf{x} \in M$, then from (7–16) the integral of the nonnegative continuous function $|df|^2$ is 0. Hence $df(\mathbf{x}) = 0$ for every $\mathbf{x} \in \operatorname{cl} D$. Given $\mathbf{x}_0 \in D$ let $\mathbf{x}_1$ be a point of $M$ nearest $\mathbf{x}_0$. The line joining $\mathbf{x}_0$ and $\mathbf{x}_1$ lies in cl $D$, and from the mean value theorem $f$ is constant on it. Since $f(\mathbf{x}_1) = 0$, we must have $f(\mathbf{x}_0) = 0$. Thus $f(\mathbf{x}) = 0$ for every $\mathbf{x} \in \operatorname{cl} D$.

Suppose that $f$ and $g$ are both of class $C^{(2)}$ on cl $D$ and harmonic, and that $f(\mathbf{x}) = g(\mathbf{x})$ for every $\mathbf{x} \in M$. Then $\phi(\mathbf{x}) = f(\mathbf{x}) - g(\mathbf{x}) = 0$ for $\mathbf{x} \in M$ and $\phi$ is harmonic. Hence $\phi(\mathbf{x}) = 0$, and $f(\mathbf{x}) = g(\mathbf{x})$, for every $\mathbf{x} \in \operatorname{cl} D$. This shows that there is at most one harmonic function of class $C^{(2)}$ on cl $D$ with given values on the boundary $M$. It is more difficult to show that there is in fact a harmonic function $f$ with given boundary values. This is called *Dirichlet's problem.* If the boundary data $f|M$ are merely continuous, then $f$ is continuous on cl $D$ and of class $C^{(2)}$ and harmonic on $D$. See [14], Chap. XI. If the boundary data are smooth enough, then $f$ is of class $C^{(2)}$ and harmonic on cl $D$. For instance this is true if $M$ is of class $C^{(3)}$ and $f$ is of class $C^{(3)}$ on $M$.

---

Let us now turn to the proof of the divergence theorem. The proof will proceed by first proving the theorem when $D$ is either $E^n$ or a half-space and $\omega$ has compact support. The general case will then be reduced to these two by introducing local coordinates on fr $D$ and a partition of unity. As before, we may let $\zeta = *\omega$ and may prove either of the two equivalent formulas (7–11a) and (7–11b). As in Chapter 5, $\int f \, dV_n$ denotes the integral of $f$ over all of $E^n$.

**Lemma 1.** *Let $\zeta$ be a 1-form of class $C^{(1)}$ on $E^n$ such that $\zeta$ has compact support. Then $\int \operatorname{div} \zeta \, dV_n = 0$.*

*Proof.* Let $1 \le i \le n$. By the iterated integrals theorem

$$\int \frac{\partial \zeta_i}{\partial x^i} \, dV_n = \int \left\{ \int \frac{\partial \zeta_i}{\partial x^i} \, dx^i \right\} dV_{n-1}(\mathbf{x}^{i'}),$$

where $\mathbf{x}^{i'} = (x^1, \ldots, x^{i-1}, x^{i+1}, \ldots, x^n)$. Since $\zeta_i$ has compact support, the inner integral is 0 by the fundamental theorem of calculus. Therefore $\int \partial \zeta_i / \partial x^i \, dV_n = 0$. Summing from 1 to $n$ we get the lemma. ▌

In the next lemma we write (as in Section 5–5) $\mathbf{x}' = (x^1, \ldots, x^{n-1})$ instead of $\mathbf{x}^{n'}$.

**Lemma 2.** *Let $H$ be the half-space $\{\mathbf{x} : x^n < 0\}$, and let $\boldsymbol{\zeta}$ be as in Lemma* 1. *Then*

$$\int_H \operatorname{div} \boldsymbol{\zeta}\, dV_n = \int \zeta_n(\mathbf{x}', 0)\, dV_{n-1}(\mathbf{x}').$$

*Proof.* If $i < n$, then $\int_H \partial\zeta_i/\partial x^i\, dV_n = 0$ as in the proof of Lemma 1. For $i = n$ we have

$$\int_H \frac{\partial \zeta_n}{\partial x^n}\, dV_n = \int \left\{ \int_{-\infty}^{0} \frac{\partial \zeta_n}{\partial x^n}\, dx^n \right\} dV_{n-1}(\mathbf{x}').$$

By the fundamental theorem of calculus the inner integral is $\zeta_n(\mathbf{x}', 0)$, since $\zeta_n$ has compact support. ▮

**Proposition 32.** *Let $\mathbf{f}$ be a regular flat transformation from an open set $D_1 \subset E^n$ onto an open set $\Delta_1 \subset E^n$. Let $D$ be a regular domain such that $D \cap D_1$ is not empty, and let $\Delta = \mathbf{f}(D \cap D_1)$, $S = (\text{fr } D) \cap D_1$, $N = \mathbf{f}(S)$. Then:*

(a) *$\Delta$ is open and $N = (\text{fr } \Delta) \cap \Delta_1$.*
(b) *$\Delta$ is on one side of its boundary in a neighborhood of each point of $N$.*
(c) *If $J\mathbf{f}(\mathbf{x}) > 0$ for every $\mathbf{x} \in D_1$, then the positive orientation for $D$ is induced by $\mathbf{f}^{-1}$ from the positive orientation for $\Delta$, and the positive orientation for $S$ from the positive orientation for $N$.*

*Proof.* Let $\mathbf{g} = \mathbf{f}^{-1}$. The first assertion (a) follows from the fact that a regular transformation $\mathbf{f}$ is a homeomorphism. Let $\mathbf{t}_0 \in N$, and $\mathbf{x}_0 = \mathbf{g}(\mathbf{t}_0)$. Let $U$ and $\Phi$ be as in the definition, p. 263. We may assume that $U \subset D_1$. Let $\Psi(\mathbf{t}) = \Phi[\mathbf{g}(\mathbf{t})]$ for $\mathbf{t} \in \mathbf{f}(U)$. Since $D\mathbf{g}(\mathbf{t})$ has maximum rank $n$ and $d\Phi(\mathbf{x}) \neq \mathbf{0}$, the chain rule implies that $d\Psi(\mathbf{t}) \neq \mathbf{0}$. The open set $\mathbf{f}(U)$ contains a neighborhood $\Omega$ of $\mathbf{t}_0$, and

$$(\text{fr } \Delta) \cap \Omega = \{\mathbf{t} \in \Omega : \Psi(\mathbf{t}) = 0\},$$
$$\Delta \cap \Omega = \{\mathbf{t} \in \Omega : \Psi(\mathbf{t}) < 0\}.$$

Therefore $\Delta$ is on one side of its boundary in $\Omega$. This proves (b).

Since $J\mathbf{g}(\mathbf{t}) = 1/J\mathbf{f}(\mathbf{x}) > 0$, $\mathbf{g}$ preserves the positive orientation of $E^n$. We must show that the orientation induced on $S$ from the positive orientation is positive.

Let $\mathbf{k}_0 = \text{grad } \Psi(\mathbf{t}_0)$ and $\mathbf{n}_0 = \text{grad } \Phi(\mathbf{x}_0)$. They are exterior normals to $\Delta$ and to $D$ respectively. Let $\mathbf{h}_0 = \mathbf{L}(\mathbf{k}_0)$, where $\mathbf{L} = D\mathbf{g}(\mathbf{t}_0)$. From the chain rule, $\mathbf{k}_0 = \mathbf{L}^t(\mathbf{n}_0)$ where $\mathbf{L}^t$ is the transpose of $\mathbf{L}$. By formula (4–8)

$$\mathbf{h}_0 \cdot \mathbf{n}_0 = [\mathbf{L} \circ \mathbf{L}^t(\mathbf{n}_0)] \cdot \mathbf{n}_0 = \mathbf{L}^t(\mathbf{n}_0) \cdot \mathbf{L}^t(\mathbf{n}_0),$$
$$\mathbf{h}_0 \cdot \mathbf{n}_0 = |\mathbf{L}^t(\mathbf{n}_0)|^2 > 0.$$

Let $(\mathbf{k}_1, \ldots, \mathbf{k}_{n-1})$ be a positively oriented frame for the tangent space to fr $\Delta$ at $\mathbf{t}_0$, and let $\mathbf{h}_l = \mathbf{L}(\mathbf{k}_l)$, $l = 1, \ldots, n-1$. Then $(\mathbf{h}_1, \ldots, \mathbf{h}_{n-1})$ is a frame for the tangent space $T(\mathbf{x}_0)$ to fr $D$ at $\mathbf{x}_0$. Since $(\mathbf{k}_0, \mathbf{k}_1, \ldots, \mathbf{k}_{n-1})$ is a positively oriented frame and $\mathbf{g}$ preserves the orientation of $E^n$, $(\mathbf{h}_0, \mathbf{h}_1, \ldots, \mathbf{h}_n)$ is a positively oriented frame.

Now $\mathbf{h}_0 = c\mathbf{n}_0 + \mathbf{h}$, where $c = (\mathbf{h}_0 \cdot \mathbf{n}_0)/(\mathbf{n}_0 \cdot \mathbf{n}_0)$ and $\mathbf{h} \in T(\mathbf{x}_0)$. From this,

$$\mathbf{n}_0 \wedge \mathbf{h}_1 \wedge \cdots \wedge \mathbf{h}_{n-1} = c\mathbf{h}_0 \wedge \mathbf{h}_1 \wedge \cdots \wedge \mathbf{h}_{n-1}.$$

Since $\mathbf{h}_0 \cdot \mathbf{n}_0 > 0$, $c > 0$. Therefore the frame $(\mathbf{n}_0, \mathbf{h}_1, \ldots, \mathbf{h}_{n-1})$ has positive orientation, which implies that $(\mathbf{h}_1, \ldots, \mathbf{h}_{n-1})$ orients $S$ positively at $\mathbf{x}_0$. ∎

If $Jf(\mathbf{x}) < 0$ for every $\mathbf{x} \in D_1$, then $\mathbf{f}^{-1}$ induces the negative orientation (corresponding to the interior normal) on $S$.

*Proof of divergence theorem.* Let us show that each $\mathbf{x}_0 \in \text{cl}\, D$ has a neighborhood $U_0$ such that (7–11a) holds provided $\boldsymbol{\omega}$ has compact support contained in cl $U_0$. If $\mathbf{x}_0 \in D$, let $U_0$ be a small enough neighborhood that cl $U_0 \subset D$. Then $\int_{\partial D^+} \boldsymbol{\omega} = 0$, and by Lemma 1, $\int_{\partial D^+} d\boldsymbol{\omega} = 0$.

Let $\mathbf{x}_0 \in$ fr $D$, and let $H$ be as in Lemma 2. Let us find a neighborhood $D_1$ of $\mathbf{x}_0$ and a regular transformation $\mathbf{f}$ with domain $D_1$ such that

$$\mathbf{f}(D \cap D_1) \subset H, \qquad \mathbf{f}[(\text{fr}\, D) \cap D_1] \subset \text{fr}\, H,$$

and $J\mathbf{f}(\mathbf{x}) > 0$ for every $\mathbf{x} \in D_1$. For this purpose let us first suppose that $\nu^n(\mathbf{x}_0) > 0$, where $\boldsymbol{\nu}(\mathbf{x}_0)$ is the unit exterior normal at $\mathbf{x}_0$. Let $\Phi$ be as on p. 263. Then grad $\Phi(\mathbf{x}) = c\boldsymbol{\nu}(x)$, where $c > 0$. Taking $n$th components, $\Phi_n(\mathbf{x}_0) = c\nu^n(\mathbf{x}_0)$. For $D_1$ take a neighborhood of $\mathbf{x}_0$ in which $\Phi_n(\mathbf{x}) > 0$, and let

$$f^i(\mathbf{x}) = x^i, \qquad i = 1, \ldots, n-1, \qquad f^n(\mathbf{x}) = \Phi(\mathbf{x}).$$

Then $J\mathbf{f}(\mathbf{x}) = \Phi_n(\mathbf{x}) > 0$ for every $\mathbf{x} \in D_1$. If the condition $\nu^n(\mathbf{x}_0) > 0$ is not satisfied, then for $\mathbf{f}$ we take $\tilde{\mathbf{f}} \circ \mathbf{L}$, where $\mathbf{L}$ is a rotation of $E^n$ such that $\mathbf{L}[\boldsymbol{\nu}(\mathbf{x}_0)]$ is a vector whose last component is positive and $\tilde{\mathbf{f}}$ is of the type just described.

Let $U_0$ be a neighborhood of $\mathbf{x}_0$ such that cl $U_0 \subset D_1$, and let $\boldsymbol{\omega}$ have compact support contained in $U_0$. Let $\mathbf{g} = \mathbf{f}^{-1}$. Since $\mathbf{g}$ is of class $C^{(2)}$ and preserves the positive orientation of $E^n$, by Proposition 31 and (c) of Proposition 32,

$$\int_{D^+} d\boldsymbol{\omega} = \int_{H^+} (d\boldsymbol{\omega})^{\#} = \int_{H^+} d\boldsymbol{\omega}^{\#}. \tag{*}$$

$$\int_{\partial D^+} \boldsymbol{\omega} = \int_{\partial H^+} \boldsymbol{\omega}^{\#}. \tag{**}$$

But by Lemma 2, the right-hand sides of (*) and (**) are equal.

Since cl $D$ is a compact set, a finite number of such neighborhoods $U_1, \ldots, U_m$ cover cl $D$. Let $\psi_k(\mathbf{x})$ and $\phi_k(\mathbf{x})$ be defined as in the proof of Proposition 29, for $\mathbf{x} \in \text{cl}\, D$. Since $\phi_k\boldsymbol{\omega}$ has compact support contained in cl $U_k$,

$$\int_{\partial D^+} \phi_k\boldsymbol{\omega} = \int_{D^+} d(\phi_k\boldsymbol{\omega}), \qquad k = 1, \ldots, m. \tag{*}$$

By the product rule,

$$d(\phi_k \omega) = d\phi_k \wedge \omega + \phi_k \, d\omega.$$

Since $\sum \phi_k = 1$, $\sum d\phi_k = 0$. Summing from 1 to $m$ in (*), we have

$$\int_{\partial D^+} \left( \sum_{k=1}^{m} \phi_k \right) \omega = \int_{D^+} \left( \sum_{k=1}^{m} \phi_k \right) d\omega,$$

which is precisely (7-11a). ∎

The assumption that fr $D$ is a manifold of class $C^{(2)}$ can be considerably weakened. Let us state without proof a somewhat more general version of the divergence theorem. Let $D$ be an open, bounded set. Assume that

$$\text{fr } D = A_1 \cup \cdots \cup A_p \cup B,$$

where: (a) $A_k$ is a relatively open subset of fr $D$ and cl $A_k$ is a compact subset of an $(n - 1)$-manifold $M_k$, $k = 1, \ldots, p$; and (b) $B$ is a compact set contained in a finite union of $(n - 2)$-manifolds, and $(\text{cl } A_k) \cap (\text{cl } A_l) \subset B$ whenever $k \neq l$. Moreover, assume that $D$ is on one side of its boundary in a neighborhood of each point of $(\text{fr } D) - B$. On each $A_k$ we assign the positive orientation, determined by the exterior normal. Then

$$\sum_{k=1}^{p} \int_{A_k^+} \omega = \int_{D^+} d\omega,$$

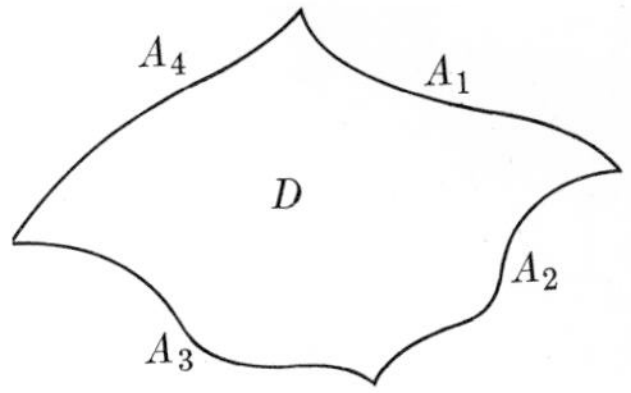

FIGURE 7-11

provided $\omega$ is of class $C^{(1)}$ on cl $D$. (See Fig. 7-11.)

Let us say that such a set $D$ has a boundary which is *piecewise of class* $C^{(1)}$.

**Example 4.** Let $D$ be an $n$-simplex. Let $A_0, \ldots, A_n$ be its (open) $(n - 1)$-dimensional faces, let $M_k$ be the hyperplane containing $A_k$, and let $B$ be the union of the $(n - 2)$-dimensional faces of $D$.

## PROBLEMS

Unless otherwise indicated, assume that $D$ is a regular domain.

1. Let $n = 2$. Show that:

   (a) $V_2(D) = -\int_{\partial D^+} y \, dx.$

   (b) $\int_D (x^2 + y^2) \, dV_2 = \frac{1}{3} \int_{\partial D^+} x^3 \, dy - y^3 \, dx.$

2. Evaluate $\int_{\partial \Sigma^+} y^2 \, dx \wedge dz$, where $\Sigma$ is the standard 3-simplex.

3. Let $D$ be the disk $x^2 + y^2 < 1$ and $\omega = (x \, dy - y \, dx)/(x^2 + y^2)$. Then $\int_{\partial D^+} \omega = 2\pi$ while $\int_{D^+} d\omega = 0$. Why does this not contradict Green's theorem?

4. Let $n = 4$ and $D = \{\mathbf{x} : (x^1)^2 + (x^2)^2 + (x^3)^2 < (x^4)^2,\ 0 < x^4 < 1\}$. Evaluate:

(a) $\int_{\partial D^+} (x^2 + x^4)\, dx^1 \wedge dx^2 \wedge dx^3$. (b) $\int_{\partial D^+} |\mathbf{x}|^2\, dx^1 \wedge dx^2 \wedge dx^3$.

5. Suppose that $D = \{(x, y) : f(x) < y < g(x),\ a < x < b\} = \{(x, y) : \phi(y) < x < \psi(y),\ c < y < d\}$. Show directly from the fundamental theorem of calculus and properties of line integrals that

$$\int_{\partial D^+} N\, dy = \int_D \frac{\partial N}{\partial x}\, dV_2,$$

$$\int_{\partial D^+} M\, dx = -\int_D \frac{\partial M}{\partial y}\, dV_2.$$

Adding, we get the Green's theorem for regular domains of this special type. (See Fig. 7-12.)

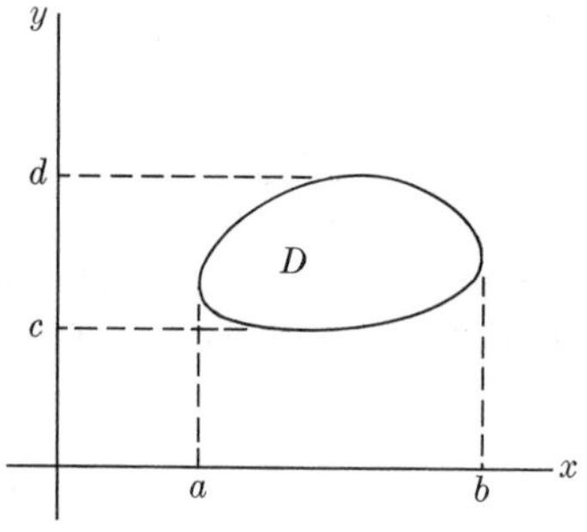


FIGURE 7-12

6. Prove the divergence theorem directly from the fundamental theorem of calculus when $D$ is:

(a) The unit $n$-cube $\{\mathbf{x} : 0 < x^i < 1,\ i = 1, \ldots, n\}$.

(b) The standard $n$-simplex.

7. For each $t$ in some interval $(-a, a)$ let $\mathbf{T}_t$ be a regular flat transformation with domain $D_0$. Assume that $\mathbf{T}_0(\mathbf{x}) = \mathbf{x}$ for every $\mathbf{x} \in D_0$ and that $\mathbf{T}$ is of class $C^{(2)}$ as a function of $(\mathbf{x}, t)$ on $D_0 \times (-a, a)$. Let $v(t) = V_n[\mathbf{T}_t(D)]$ where $\operatorname{cl} D \subset D_0$. Prove that $v'(0) = \int_D \operatorname{div} \mathbf{W}_0\, dV_n$, where $\mathbf{W}_t = \partial \mathbf{T}_t/\partial t$. [*Hint:* Show that the integrand is $(\partial/\partial t) J\mathbf{T}_t(\mathbf{x})$ evaluated at $t = 0$.]

In Problems 8 and 9 let $M = \operatorname{fr} D$.

8. Show that:

(a) $\int_M \nu^i(\mathbf{x})\, dV_{n-1}(\mathbf{x}) = 0$. (b) $\int_M \mathbf{x} \cdot \boldsymbol{\nu}(\mathbf{x})\, dV_{n-1}(\mathbf{x}) = nV_n(D)$.

(c) $\int_M f_{\boldsymbol{\nu}}(\mathbf{x})\, dV_{n-1}(\mathbf{x}) = \int_D \operatorname{Lapl} f(\mathbf{x})\, dV_n(\mathbf{x})$.

9. Let $D$ be connected, $f$ harmonic, and $f_{\boldsymbol{\nu}}(\mathbf{x}) = 0$ for every $\mathbf{x} \in M$. Show that $f(\mathbf{x})$ is constant on $D$.

10. Let $D = \{\mathbf{x} : a < |\mathbf{x}| < b\}$, where $0 < a < b$.

(a) Show that if $f(\mathbf{x}) = \psi(|\mathbf{x}|)$, then $f_{\boldsymbol{\nu}}(\mathbf{x}) = \psi'(|\mathbf{x}|)$ when $|\mathbf{x}| = b$ and $f_{\boldsymbol{\nu}}(\mathbf{x}) = -\psi'(|\mathbf{x}|)$ when $|\mathbf{x}| = a$.

(b) Let $\psi(r) = -[(n-2)\beta_{n-1}]^{-1} r^{n-2}$, where $n > 2$ and $\beta_{n-1}$ is the $(n-1)$-measure of the unit $(n-1)$-sphere. Let $f$ be as in (a). Show that $f$ is harmonic.

(c) Let $\phi$ be harmonic on the $n$-ball $B = \{\mathbf{x} : |\mathbf{x}| \leq b\}$. Show that $\phi(\mathbf{0}) = (\beta_{n-1} b^{n-1})^{-1} \int_{\operatorname{fr} B} \phi\, dV_{n-1}$. [*Hint:* Apply the second Green's formula with $D$ and $f$ as above and let $a \to 0^+$.]

## 7-6 STOKES' FORMULA

The divergence theorem is a special case of a result which is nowadays called Stokes' formula. Let $\boldsymbol{\omega}$ be an $(r-1)$-form. Stokes' formula equates the integral of $d\boldsymbol{\omega}$ over a portion $A$ of an oriented $r$-manifold $M$ and the integral of $\boldsymbol{\omega}$ over the (suitably oriented) boundary of $A$.

Let us begin with the following particular case and afterward generalize. Let $B \subset E^r$ be a regular domain, and let $A = \mathbf{g}(B)$ where $\mathbf{g}$ is a regular transformation of class $C^{(2)}$ from some open set containing $\operatorname{cl} B$ into $M$. Let $\mathbf{o}$ be the orientation induced on $A$ from the positive orientation of $E^r$. The $(r-1)$-manifold $K = \mathbf{g}(\operatorname{fr} B)$ is the boundary of $A$ relative to $M$. Let $\partial A^{\mathbf{o}}$ denote $K$ with the orientation induced from the positive orientation of $\operatorname{fr} B$.

Let $\boldsymbol{\omega}$ be an $(r-1)$-form of class $C^{(1)}$ on $\operatorname{cl} A$. Then

$$\int_{A^{\mathbf{o}}} d\boldsymbol{\omega} = \int_{B^+} (d\boldsymbol{\omega})^{\#} = \int_{B^+} d\boldsymbol{\omega}^{\#},$$

$$\int_{\partial A^{\mathbf{o}}} \boldsymbol{\omega} = \int_{\partial B^+} \boldsymbol{\omega}^{\#}$$

By the divergence theorem, the right-hand sides are equal. Therefore we have

*Stokes' formula*

$$\int_{\partial A^{\mathbf{o}}} \boldsymbol{\omega} = \int_{A^{\mathbf{o}}} d\boldsymbol{\omega}. \tag{7-17}$$

**The case $r = 1$, $n = 3$.** Then $\boldsymbol{\omega} = P\,dx + Q\,dy + R\,dz$ is a 1-form and $d\boldsymbol{\omega}$ is a 2-form. The 1-form $*d\boldsymbol{\omega}$ is called curl $\boldsymbol{\omega}$, and the vector $\mathbf{n}(\mathbf{x}) = *\mathbf{o}(\mathbf{x})$ is a unit normal to $A$. Since $d\boldsymbol{\omega}(\mathbf{x}) \cdot \mathbf{o}(\mathbf{x}) = \operatorname{curl} \boldsymbol{\omega}(\mathbf{x}) \cdot \mathbf{n}(\mathbf{x})$, formula (7-17) becomes

$$\int_{\partial A^{\mathbf{o}}} \boldsymbol{\omega} = \int_A \operatorname{curl} \boldsymbol{\omega}(\mathbf{x}) \cdot \mathbf{n}(\mathbf{x})\, dV_2(\mathbf{x}). \tag{7-18}$$

The name Stokes' formula was traditionally applied to (7-18), and not its generalization (7-17).

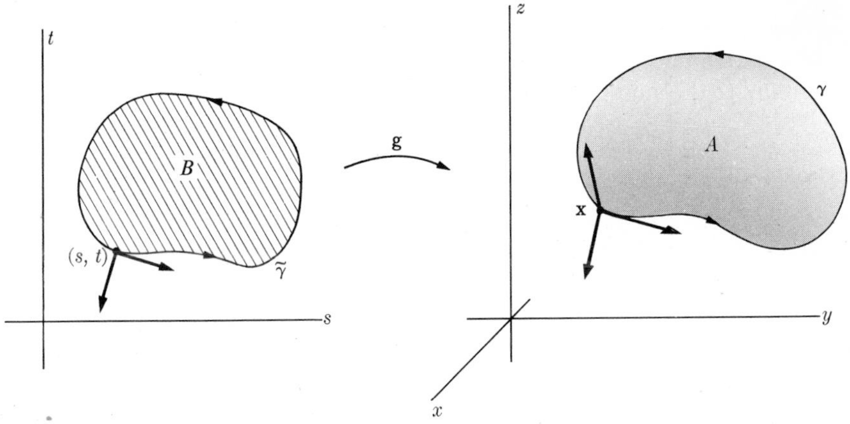


FIGURE 7-13

**Example.** Let $\partial B^+$ consist of a single simple closed curve $\tilde{\gamma}$ in $E^2$. Then $\partial A^+$ consists of a simple closed curve $\gamma$ in $E^3$.

The normal $\mathbf{n}(\mathbf{x})$ varies continuously on $A$. At a boundary point $\mathbf{x}$ of $A$, $\mathbf{n}(\mathbf{x})$ can be visualized in the following way. Let $\mathbf{x} = \mathbf{g}(s, t)$, where $(s, t) \in \text{fr } B$. Let $\boldsymbol{\nu}$ be the exterior normal and $\mathbf{v}$ the positively oriented unit tangent vector to $\tilde{\gamma}$ at $(s, t)$. The vector $\mathbf{h} = D\mathbf{g}(s, t)(\mathbf{v})$ is a tangent vector to $\gamma$ at $\mathbf{x}$. If $\mathbf{h}_0 = D\mathbf{g}(s, t)(\boldsymbol{\nu})$, then $(\mathbf{h}_0, \mathbf{h})$ is a frame for the tangent space to $M$ at $\mathbf{x}$ and has the required orientation $\mathbf{o}(\mathbf{x})$. Hence $(\mathbf{n}(\mathbf{x}), \mathbf{h}_0, \mathbf{h})$ is a positively oriented frame for $E^3$. (See Fig. 7–13.)

If $P$, $Q$, $R$ are regarded as the components of a velocity field, then $\int_\gamma \omega$ represents the circulation along the boundary $\gamma$. Stokes' formula expresses the circulation as the integral over $A$ of the normal component curl $\boldsymbol{\omega}(\mathbf{x}) \cdot \mathbf{n}(\mathbf{x})$ of the curl.

In particular, let $A$ lie in a plane $\Pi$, oriented by a unit vector $\mathbf{n}_0$ normal to $\Pi$. Then $\mathbf{n}(\mathbf{x}) = \mathbf{n}_0$ for every $\mathbf{x} \in A$. Let $\mathbf{x}_0$ be a point of the domain of $\omega$. If $A$ contains $\mathbf{x}_0$ and $A$ has small diameter, then the right-hand side of (7–18) is approximately curl $\boldsymbol{\omega}(\mathbf{x}_0) \cdot \mathbf{n}_0 V_2(A)$. More precisely,

$$\text{curl } \boldsymbol{\omega}(\mathbf{x}_0) \cdot \mathbf{n}_0 = \lim_{\text{diam} A \to 0} \frac{1}{V_2(A)} \int_\gamma \omega.$$

This is proved using a lemma similar to the one for the proof of the corresponding formula (7–12) for the divergence.

**Some generalizations.** Let $M$ be an orientable manifold of class $C^{(2)}$. We proved Stokes' formula above in case cl $A$ is contained in some coordinate patch. By using partitions of unity, this restriction can be removed.

**Proposition 33.** *Let $M$ be compact and $\mathbf{o}$ an orientation for $M$. Then*

$$\int_{M^{\mathbf{o}}} d\omega = 0$$

*for every $(r - 1)$-form of class $C^{(1)}$ on $M$.*

*Proof.* Let $\{\phi_1, \ldots, \phi_m\}$ be a partition of unity for $M$. Let $\mathbf{g}^{(k)}$ be a regular transformation of class $C^{(2)}$ from an open set $\Delta_k \subset E^r$ onto a coordinate patch $S_k$ containing the support of $\phi_k$. Then

$$\int_{M^{\mathbf{o}}} d(\phi_k \omega) = \pm \int_{\Delta_k^+} [d(\phi_k \omega)]^\# = \pm \int_{\Delta_k^+} d(\phi_k \omega)^\# = 0,$$

by Lemma 1 of the last section. Since $\sum \phi_k = 1$, $\sum d\phi_k = 0$, we get, as in the proof of the divergence theorem,

$$\int_{M^{\mathbf{o}}} d\omega = \sum_{k=1}^m \int_{M^{\mathbf{o}}} d(\phi_k \omega) = 0. \blacksquare$$

Since $M$ has empty boundary relative to itself, one would expect to obtain 0 on the left-hand side of (7–17) when $A = M$. Proposition 33 states that this is correct.

Now let $M$ be any orientable $r$-manifold of class $C^{(2)}$. Let us call a relatively open set $A \subset M$ a *regular domain on* $M$ if:

(1) cl $A$ is a compact subset of $M$;
(2) the boundary $K$ of $A$ relative to $M$ is an $(r - 1)$-manifold of class $C^{(2)}$;
(3) $A$ is on one side of $K$.

By condition (3) we mean that if $\mathbf{F}$ is any coordinate system for $S \subset M$, then $\mathbf{F}(A \cap S)$ is on one side of $\mathbf{F}(K \cap S)$ in a neighborhood of each point of $\mathbf{F}(K \cap S)$.

Let $\mathbf{o}$ be an orientation for $M$. Then $\mathbf{o}$ determines an orientation $\mathbf{o}'$ on $K$ as follows. Let $S$ be a coordinate patch and $\mathbf{F}$ a coordinate system for $S$. If the orientation induced by $\mathbf{F}^{-1}$ from the positive orientation of $E^r$ is $\mathbf{o}$, then for $\mathbf{x} \in K \cap S$, $\mathbf{o}'(\mathbf{x})$ is the orientation induced from the positive orientation of $\mathbf{F}(K \cap S)$. Otherwise, $\mathbf{o}'(\mathbf{x})$ is the orientation opposite to this one. From part (c) of Proposition 32, Section 7–5, it can be shown that $\mathbf{o}'(\mathbf{x})$ is independent of the particular coordinate system chosen (Problem 3).

Let $K$ with the orientation $\mathbf{o}'$ be denoted by $\partial A^{\mathbf{o}}$.

**Theorem 23.** *Let $A$ be a regular domain on $M$, and let $\omega$ be an $(r - 1)$-form of class $C^{(1)}$ on* cl $A$*. Then*

$$\int_{\partial A^{\mathbf{o}}} \omega = \int_{A^{\mathbf{o}}} d\omega. \tag{7–17}$$

This theorem can be proved using the divergence theorem and a partition of unity in much the same way as for Proposition 33. We shall not give the details.

We have assumed that $M$ is of class $C^{(2)}$, but Theorem 23 is still true for manifolds of class $C^{(1)}$. Moreover, the relative boundary $K$ may be piecewise of class $C^{(1)}$ in the sense explained at the end of Section 7–5. For instance, if $M$ is an $r$-plane and $A$ an $r$-simplex contained in $M$, then the boundary of $A$ relative to $M$ is piecewise of class $C^{(1)}$.

## PROBLEMS

1. Let $\omega = yz\,dx + x\,dy + dz$. Let $\gamma$ be the unit circle in the $xy$-plane, oriented in the counterclockwise direction. Calculate $\int_\gamma \omega$ and $\int_{A^{\mathbf{o}}} d\omega$ and verify that they are equal, where the orientation $\mathbf{o}$ is chosen so that $\partial A^{\mathbf{o}} = \gamma$ and:
   (a) $A$ is the disk $x^2 + y^2 < 1$ in the $xy$-plane.
   (b) $A = \{(x, y, 1 - x^2 - y^2) : x^2 + y^2 < 1\}$.
2. Let $\omega = z \exp(-y)\,dx + z\,dy + y\,dz$. Evaluate $\int_{A^{\mathbf{o}}} d\omega$ when $A$ is:
   (a) The ellipsoid $x^2/a^2 + y^2/b^2 + z^2/c^2 = 1$ oriented by the exterior normal.
   (b) The square with vertices $\mathbf{0}$, $\mathbf{e}_1 + \mathbf{e}_2$, $\sqrt{2}\,\mathbf{e}_3$, $\mathbf{e}_1 + \mathbf{e}_2 + \sqrt{2}\,\mathbf{e}_3$, oriented so that $o^{23}(\mathbf{x}) > 0$.
   (c) The paraboloid $y = x^2 + z^2$ oriented so that $o^{31}(\mathbf{x}) > 0$.
3. Show that the orientation $\mathbf{o}'$ for $K$ does not depend on the particular choice of coordinate systems for $M$ used in its definition.

4. Let $M = \text{fr } D$, where $D$ is a regular domain in $E^n$. Show that $\int_M (*d\boldsymbol{\omega}) \cdot \boldsymbol{\nu}\, dV_{n-1} = 0$ if $\boldsymbol{\omega}$ is an $(n - 2)$-form of class $C^{(1)}$ on $M$.
5. Prove the following:

$$d\boldsymbol{\omega}(\mathbf{x}_0) \cdot \boldsymbol{\alpha}_0 = \lim_{\text{diam } A \to 0} [V_r(A)]^{-1} \int_{\partial A} {}^{\boldsymbol{\alpha}_0} \boldsymbol{\omega},$$

where $\mathbf{x}_0 \in A$ and $A$ lies in an $r$-plane $\Pi$ oriented by $\boldsymbol{\alpha}_0$.

6. Let $\boldsymbol{\alpha}$ be the $r$-vector of an $r$-simplex $S_0$ and $\boldsymbol{\beta}_0, \boldsymbol{\beta}_1, \ldots, \boldsymbol{\beta}_r$ the $(r - 1)$-vectors of its oriented faces (Problem 12, Section 6–3). Show that

$$d\boldsymbol{\omega}(\mathbf{x}_0) \cdot \boldsymbol{\alpha} = \sum_{i=0}^{r} (-1)^i \boldsymbol{\omega}(\mathbf{x}_0) \cdot \boldsymbol{\beta}_i.$$

[*Hint:* Consider simplexes $S$ similar to $S_0$ and containing $\mathbf{x}_0$. Apply Problem 5 with $A = S$.]

## 7–7 CLOSED AND EXACT DIFFERENTIAL FORMS

Any exact differential form $\boldsymbol{\omega} = d\boldsymbol{\eta}$ is closed, provided $\boldsymbol{\eta}$ is of class $C^{(2)}$. This is a consequence of the formula in Section 6–5 $d(d\boldsymbol{\eta}) = \mathbf{0}$. Whether, conversely, every closed form $\boldsymbol{\omega}$ is exact depends on the topological nature of the domain $D$ of $\boldsymbol{\omega}$. In this section we shall give two sufficient conditions that every closed $r$-form with domain $D$ be exact. The first is that $D$ be simply connected and applies when $r = 1$. The second is that $D$ be star-shaped and applies for any degree $r$.

**Homotopies.** Let $\mathbf{f}$ and $\mathbf{g}$ be transformations of class $C^{(2)}$ from a set $B \subset E^m$ into a set $A \subset E^n$. We are interested in whether it is possible to smoothly interpolate in $A$ between $\mathbf{f}$ and $\mathbf{g}$. If this is possible then $\mathbf{f}$ and $\mathbf{g}$ are called homotopic in $A$. To state this more precisely, let us consider the subset $[0, 1] \times B$ of $E^{m+1}$.

**Definition.** If there is a transformation $\mathbf{H}$ of class $C^{(2)}$ on $[0, 1] \times B$ such that $\mathbf{H}(s, \mathbf{t}) \in A$ for every $(s, \mathbf{t}) \in [0, 1] \times B$ and $\mathbf{H}(0, \mathbf{t}) = \mathbf{f}(\mathbf{t}), \mathbf{H}(1, \mathbf{t}) = \mathbf{g}(\mathbf{t})$ for every $\mathbf{t} \in B$, then $\mathbf{f}$ and $\mathbf{g}$ are *homotopic in* $A$.

In the usual definition of homotopy in topology, $\mathbf{H}$ is required to be merely continuous. What we call homotopy is then called a homotopy of class $C^{(2)}$.

**Example 1.** Let $A$ be convex. Then we may take

$$\mathbf{H}(s, \mathbf{t}) = s\mathbf{g}(\mathbf{t}) + (1 - s)\mathbf{f}(\mathbf{t}).$$

Therefore any two transformations $\mathbf{f}$ and $\mathbf{g}$ of class $C^{(2)}$ with values in a convex set $A$ are homotopic in $A$. In particular, this is true when $A = E^n$.

To define simple connectedness one may take $B$ to be a circle. However, instead of a circle it is more convenient to let $B$ be an interval $[a, b]$ with the endpoints identified. Let $\mathbf{f}$ and $\mathbf{g}$ be transformations from $[a, b]$ into $A$ such that $\mathbf{f}(a) = \mathbf{f}(b)$ and $\mathbf{g}(a) = \mathbf{g}(b)$. Then $\mathbf{f}$ and $\mathbf{g}$ are *strictly homotopic in* $A$ if the homotopy $\mathbf{H}$ in the definition above can be chosen so that $\mathbf{H}(s, a) = \mathbf{H}(s, b)$ for every $s \in [0, 1]$.

If $\partial\mathbf{H}/\partial t \neq 0$, then for each $s$ the transformation $\mathbf{H}(s, \ )$ represents on $[a, b]$ a closed curve $\gamma_s$ of class $C^{(2)}$ in the sense of Section 3–2. Intuitively, one may regard a homotopy as a smooth interpolation by the curves $\gamma_s$ between the curve $\gamma_0$ represented by $\mathbf{f}$ and the curve $\gamma_1$ represented by $\mathbf{g}$. However, for technical reasons it is disadvantageous to include the conditions $\partial\mathbf{H}/\partial t \neq 0$ in the definition of homotopy.

**Definition.** If $\mathbf{g}$ is strictly homotopic in $A$ to a constant transformation $\mathbf{f}$, then $\mathbf{g}$ is *null homotopic* in $A$.

If $\mathbf{f}(t) = \mathbf{x}_0$ for every $t \in [a, b]$, then one should think intuitively that $\gamma_s$ shrinks to the point $\mathbf{x}_0$ as $s \to 0^+$. When $A$ is an open subset of $E^2$ this is possible roughly speaking provided $\gamma_s$ does not loop around any holes which may be present in $A$. In Fig. 7–14, $A$ has two holes and the curves $\gamma_s$ in the figure are not null homotopic in $A$.

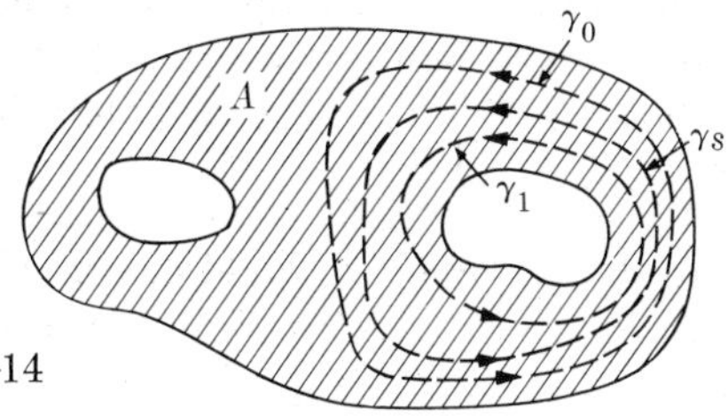


FIGURE 7–14

Let $D$ be an open set, and $\boldsymbol{\omega}$ a 1-form with domain $D$. Let us set

$$\langle \mathbf{g}, \boldsymbol{\omega} \rangle = \int_a^b \boldsymbol{\omega}[\mathbf{g}(t)] \cdot \mathbf{g}'(t)\, dt.$$

In case $\mathbf{g}'(t) \neq \mathbf{0}$, $\langle \mathbf{g}, \boldsymbol{\omega} \rangle$ is just another notation for the line integral of $\boldsymbol{\omega}$ along the curve represented by $\mathbf{g}$.

**Proposition 34.** *Let $\boldsymbol{\omega}$ be closed. If $\mathbf{f}$ and $\mathbf{g}$ are strictly homotopic in $D$, then* $\langle \mathbf{f}, \boldsymbol{\omega} \rangle = \langle \mathbf{g}, \boldsymbol{\omega} \rangle$.

*Proof.* Let $\boldsymbol{\omega}^\#$ be the 1-form on the rectangle $R = [0, 1] \times [a, b]$ induced by the transformation $\mathbf{H}$. Since $d\boldsymbol{\omega} = \mathbf{0}$, $d\boldsymbol{\omega}^\# = (d\boldsymbol{\omega})^\# = \mathbf{0}$. By Green's theorem

$$\int_{\partial R^+} \boldsymbol{\omega}^\# = \int_{R^+} d\boldsymbol{\omega}^\# = 0.$$

The integral over $\partial R^+$ is the sum of the integrals over the four segments $\lambda_1, \ldots, \lambda_4$ indicated in Fig. 7-15. Now

$$\omega^{\#} = \sum_{i=1}^{n} \omega_i \circ \mathbf{H}(dx^i)^{\#}$$

$$= \sum_{i=1}^{n} \omega_i \circ \mathbf{H}\left(\frac{\partial H^i}{\partial s}\, ds + \frac{\partial H^i}{\partial t}\, dt\right),$$

$$\int_{\lambda_2} \omega^{\#} = \sum_{i=1}^{n} \int_a^b \omega_i \circ \mathbf{H}\, \frac{\partial H^i}{\partial t}\, dt,$$

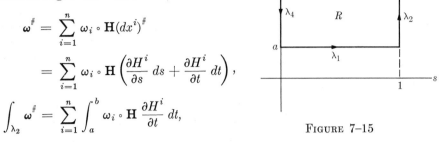

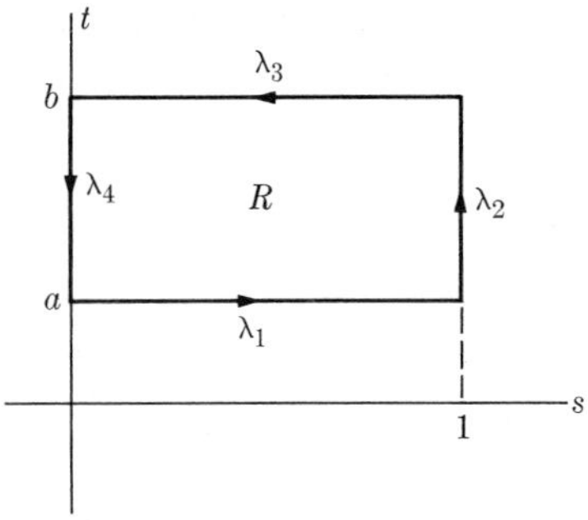


FIGURE 7-15

$\mathbf{H}$ and $\partial H^i/\partial t$ being evaluated at $(1, t)$. Since $\mathbf{H}(1, t) = \mathbf{g}(t)$, the right-hand side is just $\langle \mathbf{g}, \boldsymbol{\omega} \rangle$. Similarly, since $\mathbf{H}(0, t) = \mathbf{f}(t)$

$$\int_{\lambda_4} \omega^{\#} = -\langle \mathbf{f}, \boldsymbol{\omega} \rangle.$$

Since $\mathbf{H}(s, a) = \mathbf{H}(s, b)$,

$$\int_{\lambda_1} \omega^{\#} = -\int_{\lambda_3} \omega^{\#}. \blacksquare$$

**Example 2.** Let $n = 2$ and let $D$ be the plane with $(0, 0)$ removed. Let $\boldsymbol{\omega} = (x\,dy - y\,dx)/(x^2 + y^2)$. Formally, $\boldsymbol{\omega} = d\Theta$, where $\Theta(x, y)$ is the angle from the positive $x$-axis to $(x, y)$, $0 < \Theta(x, y) < 2\pi$. However, $\Theta$ is defined only in the plane with a slit removed even though $\boldsymbol{\omega}$ is defined and of class $C^{(\infty)}$ in $D$. For each integer $m \neq 0$ let $\mathbf{g}_m(t) = (\cos mt)\mathbf{e}_1 + (\sin mt)\mathbf{e}_2$, $0 \leq t \leq 2\pi$. Then $\langle \mathbf{g}_m, \boldsymbol{\omega} \rangle = 2m\pi$, which shows that $\mathbf{g}_m$ and $\mathbf{g}_l$ are not strictly homotopic in $D$ when $m \neq l$. The transformation $\mathbf{g}_m$ represents the unit circle traversed $|m|$ times, counterclockwise if $m > 0$ and clockwise if $m < 0$.

Proposition 34 has the following corollaries.

**Corollary 1.** *If* $\mathbf{g}$ *is null homotopic in* $D$, *then* $\langle \mathbf{g}, \boldsymbol{\omega} \rangle = 0$.

*Proof.* If $\mathbf{f}$ is constant, then $\langle \mathbf{f}, \boldsymbol{\omega} \rangle = 0$. $\blacksquare$

**Definition.** An open set $D$ is *simply connected* if every transformation $\mathbf{g}$ of class $C^{(2)}$ from an interval $[a, b]$ into $D$, satisfying $\mathbf{g}(a) = \mathbf{g}(b)$, is null homotopic in $D$.

Roughly speaking, $D$ is simply connected if every closed curve in $D$ can be shrunk in $D$ to a point. When $D \subset E^2$ this amounts to saying that $D$ "has no holes." Removal of a single point, as in Example 2, must be counted as introducing a hole.

If $D = \{\mathbf{x} \in E^3 : |\mathbf{x}| > 1\}$, then $D$ is simply connected, yet $D$ has a "hole."

**Corollary 2.** *If $D$ is a simply connected open subset of $E^n$, then every closed 1-form with domain $D$ is exact.*

*Proof.* By Theorem 7, Section 3–3, it suffices to show that $\int_\gamma \boldsymbol{\omega} = 0$ for every piecewise smooth closed curve $\gamma$ lying in $D$. Let $\mathbf{g}$ be a representation of such a curve $\gamma$ on $[0, 1]$, such that $\mathbf{g}$ is piecewise of class $C^{(1)}$. There is a sequence $\mathbf{g}_1, \mathbf{g}_2, \ldots$ of transformations of class $C^{(\infty)}$ on $[0, 1]$ such that: (1) $\mathbf{g}_m(0) = \mathbf{g}_m(1)$ for $m = 1, 2, \ldots$; (2) $\mathbf{g}_m(t) \to \mathbf{g}(t)$ for every $t \in [0, 1]$, and $\mathbf{g}'_m(t) \to \mathbf{g}'(t)$ except at the (finitely many) points of discontinuity of $\mathbf{g}'$, as $m \to \infty$; (3) $|\mathbf{g}_m(t)|$ and $|\mathbf{g}'_m(t)|$ are bounded by some number $C$. Such a sequence can be found by a standard smoothing technique (Problem 5). By Lebesgue's dominated convergence theorem, $\langle \mathbf{g}_m, \boldsymbol{\omega}\rangle \to \langle \mathbf{g}, \boldsymbol{\omega}\rangle$ as $m \to \infty$. By Corollary 1, $\langle \mathbf{g}_m, \boldsymbol{\omega}\rangle = 0$ for each $m = 1, 2, \ldots$ Therefore $\langle \mathbf{g}, \boldsymbol{\omega}\rangle = \int_\gamma \boldsymbol{\omega} = 0$. ∎

Let us turn to the question of finding a condition on $D$ which insures that any closed form of arbitrary degree $r$ is exact. For this purpose, let $B$ be an open subset of $E^m$. Let us introduce an operation which changes any $r$-form $\boldsymbol{\eta}$ of class $C^{(1)}$ on $[0, 1] \times B$ into an $(r - 1)$-form of class $C^{(1)}$ on $B$. The latter form is denoted by $\int_0^1 \boldsymbol{\eta}$. If $r = 1$, then $\boldsymbol{\eta} = f\,ds + \boldsymbol{\eta}^1$, where $\boldsymbol{\eta}^1$ involves the differentials $dt^1, \ldots, dt^m$. In this case $\int_0^1 \boldsymbol{\eta} = \int_0^1 f(s, \ )\,ds$, which is of class $C^{(1)}$ on $B$. Next, if $\boldsymbol{\eta} = ds \wedge \boldsymbol{\theta} = \sum_{[\mu]} \theta_\mu\, ds \wedge dt^{j_1} \wedge \cdots \wedge dt^{j_{r-1}}$, then we set

$$\int_0^1 \boldsymbol{\eta} = \sum_{[\mu]} \left(\int_0^1 \theta_\mu\, ds\right) dt^{j_1} \wedge \cdots \wedge dt^{j_{r-1}}. \tag{7–19}$$

Finally, any $r$-form $\boldsymbol{\eta}$ on $[0, 1] \times B$ can be written $\boldsymbol{\eta} = ds \wedge \boldsymbol{\theta} + \boldsymbol{\eta}^1$, where $\boldsymbol{\eta}^1$ involves only the differentials $dt^1, \ldots, dt^m$:

$$\boldsymbol{\eta}^1 = \sum_{[\lambda]} \eta^1_\lambda\, dt^{i_1} \wedge \cdots \wedge dt^{i_r}.$$

We set $\int_0^1 \boldsymbol{\eta} = \int_0^1 ds \wedge \boldsymbol{\theta}$. Using the rules for exterior differentiation, we find that

$$d\boldsymbol{\eta} = d(ds \wedge \boldsymbol{\theta}) + d\boldsymbol{\eta}^1 = -ds \wedge d'\boldsymbol{\theta} + ds \wedge \frac{\partial \boldsymbol{\eta}^1}{\partial s} + d'\boldsymbol{\eta}^1,$$

where $d'$ denotes the differential with respect to $\mathbf{t}$ of a form on $[0, 1] \times B$ and the components of the $r$-form $\partial\boldsymbol{\eta}^1/\partial s$ are the partial derivatives $\partial\eta^1_\lambda/\partial s$. Therefore

$$\begin{aligned}\int_0^1 d\boldsymbol{\eta} &= -\int_0^1 ds \wedge d'\boldsymbol{\theta} + \int_0^1 ds \wedge \frac{\partial \boldsymbol{\eta}^1}{\partial s} \\ &= -\int_0^1 ds \wedge d'\boldsymbol{\theta} + \boldsymbol{\eta}^1(1) - \boldsymbol{\eta}^1(0),\end{aligned} \tag{$*$}$$

where $\boldsymbol{\eta}^1(s)$ is the $r$-form on $B$ with coefficients $\eta^1_\lambda(s,\ )$. Differentiating under the integral sign,

$$\frac{\partial}{\partial t^j}\int_0^1 f\,ds = \int_0^1 \frac{\partial f}{\partial t^j}\,ds, \qquad j = 1, \ldots, m,$$

provided $f$ is of class $C^{(1)}$. Hence

$$d\int_0^1 f\,ds = \sum_{j=1}^m \left(\frac{\partial}{\partial t^j}\int_0^1 f\,ds\right) dt^j = \int_0^1 ds \wedge d'f.$$

Applying this in (7–19), if $\boldsymbol{\eta}$ is of class $C^{(1)}$ we get

$$\begin{aligned} d\int_0^1 \boldsymbol{\eta} &= \sum_{[\mu]} \int_0^1 ds \wedge d'\theta_\mu \wedge dt^{j_1} \cdots \wedge dt^{j_{r-1}} \\ &= \int_0^1 ds \wedge \left(\sum_{[\mu]} d'\theta_\mu \wedge dt^{j_1} \wedge \cdots \wedge dt^{j_{r-1}}\right) = \int_0^1 ds \wedge d'\boldsymbol{\theta}. \end{aligned} \tag{**}$$

From (*) and (**) we get

$$\int_0^1 d\boldsymbol{\eta} + d\int_0^1 \boldsymbol{\eta} = \boldsymbol{\eta}^1(1) - \boldsymbol{\eta}^1(0). \tag{7–20}$$

Now let $\boldsymbol{\omega}$ be an $r$-form of class $C^{(1)}$ on $A$. Let $\mathbf{H}$ be a homotopy between transformations $\mathbf{f}$ and $\mathbf{g}$, and let $\boldsymbol{\omega}^\#_{\mathbf{f}}$, $\boldsymbol{\omega}^\#_{\mathbf{g}}$, $\boldsymbol{\omega}^\#_{\mathbf{H}}$ denote the $r$-forms induced respectively by $\mathbf{f}$, $\mathbf{g}$, and $\mathbf{H}$. Let $\boldsymbol{\eta} = \boldsymbol{\omega}^\#_{\mathbf{H}}$. Then $\boldsymbol{\eta}^1(1) = \boldsymbol{\omega}^\#_{\mathbf{g}}$ and $\boldsymbol{\eta}^1(0) = \boldsymbol{\omega}^\#_{\mathbf{f}}$. Therefore

$$\int_0^1 d\boldsymbol{\omega}^\#_{\mathbf{H}} + d\int_0^1 \boldsymbol{\omega}^\#_{\mathbf{H}} = \boldsymbol{\omega}^\#_{\mathbf{g}} - \boldsymbol{\omega}^\#_{\mathbf{f}}. \tag{7–21}$$

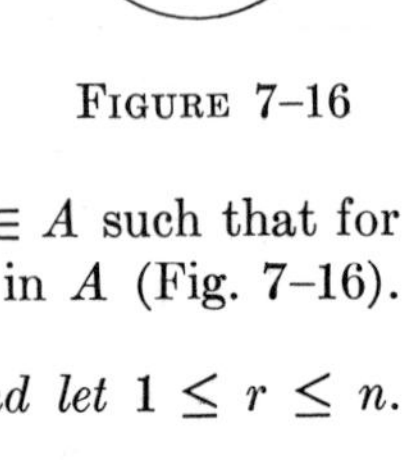

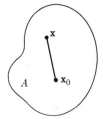

FIGURE 7–16

With this formula we can readily deduce a result about closed forms which is called Poincaré's lemma.

**Definition.** A set $A$ is *star-shaped* if there is a point $\mathbf{x}_0 \in A$ such that for every $\mathbf{x} \in A$ the line segment joining $\mathbf{x}_0$ and $\mathbf{x}$ is contained in $A$ (Fig. 7–16).

**Poincaré's lemma.** *Let $D$ be a star-shaped open set and let $1 \le r \le n$. Then every closed $r$-form with domain $D$ is exact.*

*Proof.* Let $\mathbf{x}_0$ be a point with respect to which $D$ is star-shaped. Let $\mathbf{f}(\mathbf{x}) = \mathbf{x}_0$, $\mathbf{g}(\mathbf{x}) = \mathbf{x}$, $\mathbf{H}(s, \mathbf{x}) = \mathbf{x}_0 + s(\mathbf{x} - \mathbf{x}_0)$, $B = D$. [This homotopy merely shrinks $D$ radially to the point $\mathbf{x}_0$.] Then $\boldsymbol{\omega}^\#_{\mathbf{g}} = \boldsymbol{\omega}$; and since $r > 0$ and $df^i = 0$, $\boldsymbol{\omega}^\#_{\mathbf{f}} = \mathbf{0}$. Since $\boldsymbol{\omega}$ is closed, $d\boldsymbol{\omega}^\#_{\mathbf{H}} = (d\boldsymbol{\omega})^\#_{\mathbf{H}} = \mathbf{0}$. Let $\boldsymbol{\zeta} = \int_0^1 \boldsymbol{\omega}^\#_{\mathbf{H}}$. Then by (7–21), $d\boldsymbol{\zeta} = \boldsymbol{\omega}$. ∎

**Note:* Poincaré's lemma gives only a sufficient condition on $D$ that every closed form be exact. A necessary and sufficient condition can be obtained from DeRham's theorem ([21], Chap. IV or [17], Chap. IV).

Let us state without proof the following version of the theorem. Let $\mathcal{Z}^r(D)$ denote the set of all closed $r$-forms of class $C^{(\infty)}$ on $D$. If $\omega$ and $\zeta$ are closed, then $\omega + \zeta$ is closed and $c\omega$ is closed for any scalar $c$. Thus $\mathcal{Z}^r(D)$ is a vector space over $E^1$. Similarly, let $\mathcal{E}^r(D)$ denote the vector space consisting of all exact $r$-forms of the type $\omega = d\zeta$ where $\zeta$ is of class $C^{(\infty)}$ on $D$. Then $\mathcal{E}^r(D) \subset \mathcal{Z}^r(D)$. According to DeRham's theorem, the quotient vector space $\mathcal{H}^r(D) = \mathcal{Z}^r(D)/\mathcal{E}^r(D)$ is isomorphic to the $r$-dimensional cohomology group of $D$ with real coefficients. (The homology and cohomology groups of a space are defined in algebraic topology. They contain a great deal of topological information about the space.) In particular, every closed $r$-form is exact if and only if $\mathcal{H}^r(D) = 0$.

## PROBLEMS

1. Let $D$ be the solid torus obtained by rotating the circular disk $(y - a)^2 + z^2 < b^2$, $0 < b < a$, about the $z$-axis. Let $\gamma$ be the circular path traversed by the center of the disk. Show that $\int_\gamma (x\,dy - y\,dx)/(x^2 + y^2) \neq 0$. Hence by Corollary 1, $\gamma$ is not null homotopic in $D$.
2. Let $S$ be the sphere $x^2 + y^2 + z^2 = a^2$, oriented by the unit exterior normal. Let

$$\omega = \rho^{-3}(x\,dy \wedge dz + y\,dz \wedge dx + z\,dx \wedge dy), \quad \rho^2 = x^2 + y^2 + z^2,$$

the domain of $\omega$ being $E^3 - \{\mathbf{0}\}$. Show that:

(a) $\omega$ is closed.
(b) $\int_{S^0} \omega = 4\pi$. [*Hint:* Find $*\omega(\mathbf{x}) \cdot \boldsymbol{\nu}(\mathbf{x})$, where $\boldsymbol{\nu}(\mathbf{x})$ is the exterior normal.]
(c) $E^3 - \{\mathbf{0}\}$ is simply connected.

3. Let $\tilde{D}$ be star-shaped and let $D = \mathbf{g}(\tilde{D})$, where $\mathbf{g}$ is a regular flat transformation of class $C^{(2)}$. Show that every closed form with domain $D$ is exact.
4. The *winding number* of a closed curve $\gamma$ in $E^2$ about a point $(x_0, y_0)$ not in the trace of $\gamma$ is

$$w(x_0, y_0) = \frac{1}{2\pi} \int_\gamma \frac{(x - x_0)\,dy - (y - y_0)\,dx}{(x - x_0)^2 + (y - y_0)^2}.$$

Let $\gamma$ be the positively oriented boundary of a regular domain $D$.

(a) Show that $w(x_0, y_0) = 1$ if $(x_0, y_0) \in D$. [*Hint:* Apply Green's theorem to

$$D_\epsilon = \{(x, y) \in D : (x - x_0)^2 + (y - y_0)^2 \geq \epsilon\}$$

where $\epsilon < \text{dist}\,[(x_0, y_0), \text{fr}\,D]$. Note that $m = 2$ in formula (7–12).]

(b) Show that $w(x_0, y_0) = 0$ if $(x_0, y_0) \notin \text{cl}\,D$.

5. For $m = 1, 2, \ldots$ let $h_m$ be a function of class $C^{(\infty)}$ on $E^1$ such that $h_m \geq 0$, $\int_{-\infty}^{\infty} h_m\, dx = 1$, $h_m(x) = 0$ whenever $|x| \geq 1/m$. [For instance, we may take $h_m(x) = mh(mx)$, where $h$ is as on p. 253.] Let $\psi$ be a piecewise continuous function on $E^1$ which is periodic of period 1. Let $\psi_m(x) = \int_{-\infty}^{\infty} \psi(y)h_m(x - y)\, dy = \int_{-\infty}^{\infty} \psi(x + z)h_m(z)\, dz$. Show that:
   (a) If $|\psi(x)| \leq C$ for every $x$, then $|\psi_m(\mathbf{x})| \leq C$ for every $x$ and $m = 1, 2, \ldots$
   (b) $\psi_m$ is of class $C^{(\infty)}$ and of period 1, $m = 1, 2, \ldots$
   (c) If $\int_0^1 \psi\, dx = 0$, then $\int_0^1 \psi_m\, dx = 0$, $m = 1, 2, \ldots$
   (d) At each point $x_0$ of continuity of $\psi$, $\psi_m(x_0) \to \psi(x_0)$ as $m \to \infty$. [*Hint:* $\psi_m(x_0) - \psi(x_0) = \int_{-1/m}^{1/m} [\psi(x_0 + z) - \psi(x_0)]h_m(z)\, dz$.]

   [*Note:* In the proof of Corollary 2, let $\psi$ be a periodic extension of $g^{i\prime}$, and let $g_m^i(t) = g^i(0) + \int_0^t \psi_m(x)\, dx$, $i = 1, \ldots, n$.]

# Appendix

## A–1 THE REAL NUMBER SYSTEM

Let us begin with a list of axioms which describes the real number system $E^1$.

**Axiom I.** (a) Any two real numbers have a sum $x + y$ and a product $xy$, which are also real numbers. Moreover,

| | | |
|---|---|---|
| Commutative law | $x + y = y + x,$ | $xy = yx,$ |
| Associative law | $x + (y + z) = (x + y) + z,$ | $x(yz) = (xy)z,$ |
| Distributive law | $x(y + z) = xy + xz$ | |

for every $x$, $y$, and $z$.
(b) There are two (distinct) real numbers 0 and 1 which are identity elements respectively under addition and multiplication:

$$x + 0 = x, \qquad x1 = x$$

for every $x$.
(c) Every real number $x$ has an inverse $-x$ with respect to addition, and if $x \neq 0$, an inverse $x^{-1}$ with respect to multiplication:

$$x + (-x) = 0, \qquad xx^{-1} = 1.$$

**Axiom II.** There is a relation $<$ between real numbers such that:

(a) For every pair of numbers $x$ and $y$, exactly one of the following alternatives holds: $x < y$, $x = y$, $y < x$.

(b) $w < x$ and $x < y$ imply $w < y$ (transitive law).

(c) $x < y$ implies $x + z < y + z$ for every $z$.

(d) $x < y$ implies $xz < yz$ whenever $0 < z$.

From Axioms I and II follow all of the ordinary laws of arithmetic. In algebra any set with two operations (usually called "addition" and "multiplication") having the properties listed in Axiom I is called a *field*. A field is called *ordered* if there is in it a relation $<$ satisfying Axiom II.

The real numbers form an ordered field. However, this is by no means the only ordered field. For example, the rational numbers also form an ordered field. We recall that $x$ rational means that $x = p/q$ where $p$ and $q$ are integers and $q \neq 0$. Yet another axiom is needed to characterize the real number system. This axiom can be introduced in several ways. Perhaps the simplest of these is in terms of least upper bounds.

Let $S$ be a nonempty set of real numbers. If there is a number $c$ such that $x \leq c$ for every $x \in S$, then $c$ is called an *upper bound* for $S$. If $c$ is an upper bound for $S$ and $b \geq c$, then $b$ is also an upper bound for $S$.

**Axiom IIIa.** Any set $S$ of real numbers which has an upper bound has a least upper bound.

The least upper bound for $S$ will be denoted by $\sup S$. If $S$ has no upper bound, then we set $\sup S = +\infty$.

A number $d$ is a lower bound for $S$ if $d \leq x$ for every $x \in S$. If $S$ has a lower bound, then (Problem 2) $S$ has a greatest lower bound. It is denoted by $\inf S$. If $S$ has no lower bound, then we set $\inf S = -\infty$.

**Example 1.** Let $S = \{1, 2, 3, \ldots\}$, the set of positive integers. Then $\sup S = +\infty$ and $\inf S = 1$.

**Example 2.** Let $a$ and $b$ be real numbers with $a < b$. The sets

$$[a, b] = \{x : a \leq x \leq b\}, \qquad (a, b) = \{x : a < x < b\},$$
$$[a, b) = \{x : a \leq x < b\}, \qquad (a, b] = \{x : a < x \leq b\}$$

are called *finite intervals* with endpoints $a$ and $b$. The first of these intervals is called *closed*, the second *open*, the last two *half-open*. In each instance $b$ is the least upper bound and $a$ is the greatest lower bound.

In the same way the *semi-infinite intervals*

$$[a, \infty) = \{x : x \geq a\}, \qquad (a, \infty) = \{x : x > a\}$$

are called respectively closed and open, and have $a$ as greatest lower bound. The corresponding intervals $(-\infty, b]$, $(-\infty, b)$ have $b$ as least upper bound.

Let $S$ be a set which has an upper bound. Example 2 shows that the number $\sup S$ need not belong to $S$. If $\sup S$ does happen to be an element of $S$, then it is the largest element of $S$ and we write "$\max S$" instead of "$\sup S$." Similarly, if $S$ is bounded below and $\inf S$ is an element of $S$, then we write for it "$\min S$."

**Example 3.** Let $S = \{x : x^2 < 2 \text{ and } x \text{ is a rational number}\}$. Then $\sqrt{2} = \sup S$ and $-\sqrt{2} = \inf S$. Since $\sqrt{2}$ is not a rational number, this example shows that the least upper bound axiom would no longer hold if we replaced the real number system by the rational number system.

**Example 4.** Let $S = \{\sin x : x \in [-\pi, \pi]\}$. Then $-1 = \min S$, $1 = \max S$.

For every $\epsilon > 0$, $x > 0$ there is a positive integer $m$ such that $x < m\epsilon$. This is called the *archimedean property* of the real number system. To prove it, suppose to the contrary that for some pair $\epsilon$, $x$ of positive numbers, $m\epsilon \leq x$ for every $m = 1, 2, \ldots$ Then $x$ is an upper bound for the set $S = \{\epsilon, 2\epsilon, 3\epsilon, \ldots\}$. Let $c = \sup S$. Then $(m + 1)\epsilon \leq c$ and therefore $m\epsilon \leq c - \epsilon$, for each $m = 1, 2, \ldots$ Hence $c - \epsilon$ is an upper bound for $S$ smaller than $\sup S$, a contradiction. This proves the archimedean property.

We shall not prove that there actually is a system satisfying Axioms I, II, and IIIa. There are two well-known methods of constructing the real number system, starting from the rational numbers. One of them is the method of Dedekind cuts and the other is Cantor's method of Cauchy sequences.

Axioms I, II, and IIIa characterize the real numbers; in other words, any two systems satisfying these three axioms are essentially the same. To put this more precisely in algebraic language, any two ordered fields satisfying Axiom IIIa are isomorphic.

For proofs of these facts, refer to [2], Chap. III.

**PROBLEMS**

1. Find the least upper bound and greatest lower bound of each of the following sets:
   (a) $\{x : x^2 - 3x + 2 < 0\}$.
   (b) $\{x : x^3 + x^2 - 2x \leq 2\}$.
   (c) $\{\sin x + \cos x : x \in [0, \pi]\}$.
   (d) $\{x \exp x : x < 0\}$. [*Note:* exp denotes the exponential function, $\exp x = e^x$, where $e$ is the base for natural logarithms.]
   (e) $\{1, \frac{3}{4}, \frac{5}{8}, \frac{9}{16}, \ldots\}$.
2. Let $T = \{x : -x \in S\}$. Show that $-\sup T = \inf S$.
3. Let $x$ and $y$ be real numbers with $x < y$. Show that there is a rational number $z$ such that $x < z < y$. [*Hint:* By the archimedean property there is a positive integer $q$ such that $q^{-1} < y - x$. Let $z = p/q$, where $p$ is the smallest positive integer such that $qx < p$.]

## A–2 AXIOMS FOR A VECTOR SPACE

A *vector space* over the real number field is a nonempty set $\mathcal{V}$ together with two operations called "addition" and "scalar multiplication." The sum $u + v$ of two elements $u, v \in \mathcal{V}$ is also an element of $\mathcal{V}$ and the scalar multiple $cu$ of $u \in \mathcal{V}$ by the real number $c$ is an element of $\mathcal{V}$. These operations are required to satisfy the following axioms:

(1) Addition is associative and commutative.
(2) There is a zero element $\theta$ such that $u + \theta = u$ for every $u \in \mathcal{V}$.
(3) The distributive laws hold:

$$(c + d)u = cu + du, \qquad c(u + v) = cu + cv$$

for every real $c$, $d$ and $u, v \in \mathcal{V}$.

(4) $(cd)u = c(du)$ for every real $c$, $d$, and $u \in \mathcal{V}$.
(5) $0u = \theta$, $1u = u$, for every $u \in \mathcal{V}$.

It is easy to show that $E^n$ satisfies these five axioms. However, a multitude of other important vector spaces besides $E^n$ occur in mathematics.

A subset $B$ of a vector space $\mathcal{V}$ is called a *linearly dependent set* if there exist distinct elements $u_1, \ldots u_m \in B$ and real numbers $c^1, \ldots c^m$ not all 0 such that

$$c^1 u_1 + \cdots + c^m u_m = \theta.$$

If $B$ is not linearly dependent, then $B$ is a *linearly independent set*. $\mathcal{V}$ is a *finite dimensional vector space* if some finite subset $B$ of $\mathcal{V}$ spans $\mathcal{V}$, namely, if every element $u \in \mathcal{V}$ is a linear combination $u = c^1 u_1 + \cdots + c^m u_m$ where $u_1, \ldots, u_m \in B$.

A *basis* for $\mathcal{V}$ is a linearly independent set which spans $\mathcal{V}$. If $\mathcal{V}$ is finite dimensional, then every basis $B$ has the same number $n$ of elements (see [12], p. 43). The number $n$ is the *dimension* of $\mathcal{V}$. If $n = 0$, then $\mathcal{V}$ has the single element $\theta$. If $n > 0$ and $B = \{u_1, \ldots, u_n\}$ is a basis for $\mathcal{V}$, then every $u \in \mathcal{V}$ can be uniquely written as a linear combination

$$u = c^1 u_1 + \cdots + c^n u_n.$$

Let $\mathcal{V}$ and $\mathcal{W}$ be vector spaces. Let $L$ be a function with domain $\mathcal{V}$ and values in $\mathcal{W}$. Then $L$ is *linear* if

(a) $L(u + v) = L(u) + L(v)$ for every $u, v \in \mathcal{V}$; and
(b) $L(cu) = cL(u)$ for every $u \in \mathcal{V}$ and real $c$.

Let $L$ and $M$ be linear. The sum $L + M$ is given by

$$(L + M)(u) = L(u) + M(u)$$

for every $u \in \mathcal{V}$. The function $L + M$ has properties (a) and (b), and thus is linear. If $c$ is a real number, then $cL$ is the linear function given by $(cL)(u) = cL(u)$ for every $u \in \mathcal{V}$.

Let $\mathcal{L}(\mathcal{V}, \mathcal{W})$ denote the set of all linear functions with domain $\mathcal{V}$ and values in $\mathcal{W}$, together with these operations of sum of functions and multiplication of functions by scalars. Then $\mathcal{L}(\mathcal{V}, \mathcal{W})$ satisfies Axioms (1)–(5) for a vector space. The zero element of $\mathcal{L}(\mathcal{V}, \mathcal{W})$ is the function whose value at every $u \in \mathcal{V}$ is the zero element of $\mathcal{W}$.

**The dual space of $\mathcal{V}$.** Let us now suppose that $\mathcal{W} = E^1$ and set $\mathcal{V}^* = \mathcal{L}(\mathcal{V}, E^1)$. The vector space $\mathcal{V}^*$ is called the *dual space* of $\mathcal{V}$. Let us show that if $\mathcal{V}$ has positive, finite dimension $n$, then $\mathcal{V}^*$ also has dimension $n$. Let $B = \{u_1, \ldots, u_n\}$ be a basis for $\mathcal{V}$. Let $L^1, \ldots, L^n$ be the real-valued functions such that for each $i = 1, \ldots, n$ and $u = c^1 u_1 + \cdots + c^n u_n$,

$$L^i(c^1 u_1 + \cdots + c^n u_n) = c^i.$$

These functions $L^i$ are linear, and therefore belong to $\mathcal{V}^*$. They are specified by their values at the basis elements:

$$L^i(u_j) = \delta^i_j, \qquad i, j = 1, \ldots, n, \tag{*}$$

where $\delta^i_j = 1$ if $i = j$ and $\delta^i_j = 0$ if $i \neq j$.

Let us show that $B^* = \{L^1, \ldots, L^n\}$ is a basis for $\mathcal{V}^*$. Suppose that $b_1L^1 + \cdots + b_nL^n = \theta$, where $\theta$ is the zero function. Then, for every $u \in \mathcal{V}$,

$$b_1L^1(u) + \cdots + b_nL^n(u) = \theta(u) = 0.$$

Taking $u = u_i$ and applying formula (*), $b_i = 0$ for each $i = 1, \ldots n$. Thus $B^*$ is a linearly independent set. To show that $B^*$ spans $\mathcal{V}^*$, given $L \in \mathcal{V}^*$ let $a_i = L(u_i)$. If $u = c^1u_1 + \cdots + c^nu_n$, then since $L$ is linear $L(\sum c^iu_i) = \sum c^iL(u_i)$. Therefore

$$L(u) = \sum_{i=1}^{n} a_ic^i = \sum_{i=1}^{n} a_iL^i(u).$$

Since this is true for every $u \in \mathcal{V}$,

$$L = a_1L^1 + \cdots + a_nL^n,$$

which shows that $B^*$ spans $\mathcal{V}^*$.

The basis $B^*$ is called *dual* to the basis $B$.

A function $\phi$ from a vector space $\mathcal{V}$ into a vector space $\mathcal{W}$ is an *isomorphism* if $\phi$ is linear and $\phi(u) \neq \phi(v)$ whenever $u \neq v$. If there is such an isomorphism from $\mathcal{V}$ onto $\mathcal{W}$, then $\mathcal{V}$ and $\mathcal{W}$ are *isomorphic* vector spaces. All $n$-dimensional vector spaces are isomorphic. If $\{u_1, \ldots, u_n\}$ is a basis for $\mathcal{V}$ and $\{w_1, \ldots, w_n\}$ a basis for $\mathcal{W}$, then the linear function $\phi$ such that $\phi(u_i) = w_i$ for $i = 1, \ldots, n$ is an isomorphism from $\mathcal{V}$ onto $\mathcal{W}$.

In particular, any finite-dimensional vector space $\mathcal{V}$ is isomorphic with its dual $\mathcal{V}^*$. However, this isomorphism is unnatural from several points of view. In this book we maintain the distinction between $\mathcal{V}$ and $\mathcal{V}^*$.

A more natural isomorphism is the following one from a vector space $\mathcal{V}$ into the dual $\mathcal{V}^{**}$ of $\mathcal{V}^*$. For each $u \in \mathcal{V}$ let $\phi(u) = l_u$, where $l_u \in \mathcal{V}^{**}$ is the real-valued linear function such that $l_u(L) = L(u)$ for every $L \in \mathcal{V}^*$. This isomorphism is onto $\mathcal{V}^{**}$ if $\mathcal{V}$ is finite dimensional.

## PROBLEMS

1. Let $\mathcal{V}$ be the set of all polynomials $p(x) = a_0x^m + a_1x^{m-1} + \cdots + a_{m-1}x + a_m$ of degree $\leq m$, with the usual notions of addition and scalar multiplication. Here $x^k$ denotes the $k$th power of $x$. Show that $\mathcal{V}$ is a vector space of dimension $m + 1$, and find a basis for $\mathcal{V}$.
2. Show that if $\mathcal{V}$ and $\mathcal{W}$ are vector spaces of finite positive dimensions $n$ and $r$, then $\mathcal{L}(\mathcal{V}, \mathcal{W})$ has dimension $nr$.

## A-3 BASIC TOPOLOGICAL NOTIONS IN $E^n$

Let $E^n$ be euclidean $n$-dimensional space, defined in Section 1–1. A *neighborhood* of a point $\mathbf{x}_0 \in E^n$ is a spherical ball $U = \{\mathbf{x} : |\mathbf{x} - \mathbf{x}_0| < \delta\}$, where $\delta > 0$ is called the *radius* of $U$. We also call $U$ the $\delta$-neighborhood of $\mathbf{x}_0$. Let $A$ be a subset of $E^n$. A point $\mathbf{x}$ is called *interior* to $A$ if there is some neighborhood $U$ of $\mathbf{x}$ such that $U \subset A$. If some neighborhood of $\mathbf{x}$ is contained in the complement $A^c = E^n - A$, then $\mathbf{x}$ is *exterior* to $A$. If every neighborhood of $\mathbf{x}$ contains at least one point of $A$ and at least one point of $A^c$, then $\mathbf{x}$ is a *frontier* point of $A$. An interior point of $A$ necessarily is a point of $A$, and an exterior point must be a point of $A^c$. However, a frontier point may belong either to $A$ or to $A^c$.

**Example 1.** Let $U$ be the $\delta$-neighborhood of $\mathbf{x}_0$ (Fig. A–1). Let us show that every point of $U$ is interior to $U$. Given $\mathbf{x} \in U$, let $r = \delta - |\mathbf{x} - \mathbf{x}_0|$ and let $V$ be the $r$-neighborhood of $\mathbf{x}$. If $y \in V$, then $\mathbf{y} - \mathbf{x}_0 = (\mathbf{y} - \mathbf{x}) + (\mathbf{x} - \mathbf{x}_0)$ and by the triangle inequality

$$|\mathbf{y} - \mathbf{x}_0| \leq |\mathbf{y} - \mathbf{x}| + |\mathbf{x} - \mathbf{x}_0|,$$
$$|\mathbf{y} - \mathbf{x}_0| < r + |\mathbf{x} - \mathbf{x}_0| = \delta.$$

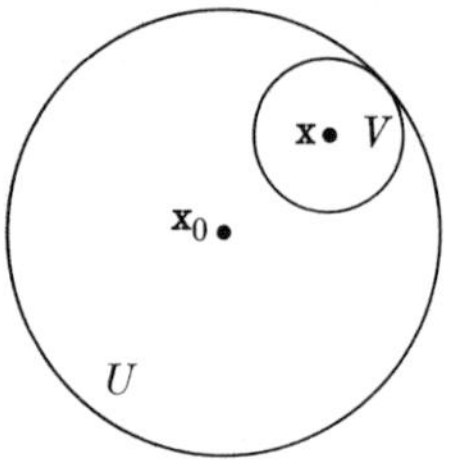


FIGURE A–1

Hence $\mathbf{y} \in U$. This shows that $V \subset U$. Similarly, every point $\mathbf{x}$ such that $|\mathbf{x} - \mathbf{x}_0| > \delta$ is exterior to $U$. If $|\mathbf{x} - \mathbf{x}_0| = \delta$, $\mathbf{x}$ is a frontier point.

**Example 2.** Let $n = 1$. Then neighborhoods are open intervals $(x_0 - \delta, x_0 + \delta)$. Let $A$ be the set of all rational numbers. Any open interval contains both rational and irrational numbers. Hence every point of $E^1$ is a frontier point of $A$.

**Definition.** The *interior* of a set $A$ is the set of all points interior to $A$. It is denoted by int $A$. The set of all frontier points of $A$ is the *boundary* (or *frontier*) of $A$, and is denoted by fr $A$. The set $A \cup$ fr $A$ is the *closure* of $A$ and is denoted by cl $A$.

In Example 1 int $U = U$ and fr $U$ is the $(n - 1)$-dimensional sphere of radius $\delta$. The set cl $U = \{\mathbf{x} : |\mathbf{x} - \mathbf{x}_0| \leq \delta\}$ is called the closed spherical $n$-ball with center $\mathbf{x}_0$ and radius $\delta$. In Example 2 int $A$ is the empty set, and fr $A$ = cl $A = E^1$.

**Example 3.** Let $A = E^n$. Then int $E^n$ = cl $E^n = E^n$ and fr $E^n$ is the empty set.

The closure of a set $A$ consists of those points not exterior to $A$. Thus

$$(\text{cl } A)^c = \text{int } (A^c).$$

It is always true that int $A \subset A$. If these two sets are the same, then $A$ is called an open set.

**Definition.** A set $A$ is *open* if every point of $A$ is interior to $A$.

From the above examples any neighborhood is an open set and $E^n$ is an open set. The empty set furnishes another example of an open set.

**Proposition A–1a.** *If $A$ and $B$ are open sets, then $A \cup B$ and $A \cap B$ are open.*

*Proof.* Let $\mathbf{x} \in A \cup B$. By the definition of the union of two sets, either $\mathbf{x} \in A$ or $\mathbf{x} \in B$. If $\mathbf{x} \in A$, then there is a neighborhood $U$ of $\mathbf{x}$ such that $U \subset A$. Since $A \subset A \cup B$, $U \subset A \cup B$. Similarly, if $\mathbf{x} \in B$ there is a neighborhood of $\mathbf{x}$ contained in $A \cup B$. This proves that $A \cup B$ is open.

If $\mathbf{x} \in A \cap B$, then $\mathbf{x}$ has neighborhoods $U_1$, $U_2$ such that $U_1 \subset A$ and $U_2 \subset B$. Let $U_3 = U_1 \cap U_2$. Then $U_3$ is a neighborhood of $\mathbf{x}$ and $U_3 \subset A \cap B$. Therefore $A \cap B$ is open. ▮

Similarly, if $A_1, \ldots, A_m$ are open sets, then their union $A_1 \cup \cdots \cup A_m$ and their intersection $A_1 \cap \cdots \cap A_m$ are open. As far as unions are concerned, the same is still true if the number of open sets is infinite. In order to make this last statement precise let us introduce some set-theoretic notation. By *indexed collection* of sets let us mean a function with domain some nonempty set $\mathcal{I}$ (called an *index set*) whose values are subsets of some set $S$. In the present instance $S = E^n$. Let $A_\mu$ denote the value of the function at $\mu \in \mathcal{I}$. Moreover, let

$$\bigcup_{\mu \in \mathcal{I}} A_\mu = \{p \in S : p \in A_\mu \text{ for some } \mu \in \mathcal{I}\},$$

$$\bigcap_{\mu \in \mathcal{I}} A_\mu = \{p \in S : p \in A_\mu \text{ for every } \mu \in \mathcal{I}\}.$$

These sets are, respectively, the *union* and *intersection* of the indexed collection. If $\mathcal{I}$ is a finite set, then the indexed collection is called finite. If $\mathcal{I} = \{1, 2, \ldots\}$, then the indexed collection is an infinite sequence of sets and is written $A_1, A_2, \ldots$, or $[A_m]$, $m = 1, 2, \ldots$ In that case the union is written $A_1 \cup A_2 \cup \cdots$ or $\bigcup_{m=1}^{\infty} A_m$, with similar notations for the intersection.

**Proposition A–1b.** *The union of any indexed collection of open sets is open.*

The proof is the same as for the first part of Proposition A–1a.

**Example 4.** Let $A_m$ be the $(1/m)$-neighborhood of a point $\mathbf{x}_0$, $m = 1, 2, \ldots$ Then

$$A_1 \cap A_2 \cap \cdots = \{\mathbf{x}_0\},$$

which is not an open set.

**Definition.** A set $A$ is *closed* if its complement $A^c$ is open.

In other words, $A$ is closed if $A$ contains all of its frontier points, which is to say $A = \text{cl}\, A$. Since

$$\Big(\bigcap_{\mu \in \mathcal{J}} A_\mu\Big)^c = \bigcup_{\mu \in \mathcal{J}} A_\mu^c, \qquad \Big(\bigcup_{\mu \in \mathcal{J}} A_\mu\Big)^c = \bigcap_{\mu \in \mathcal{J}} A_\mu^c,$$

we have the following statement from Propositions A-1a and A-1b.

**Proposition A-2.** *The intersection of any indexed collection of closed sets is closed. The union of any finite indexed collection of closed sets is closed.*

Besides indexed collections, we shall have occasion to consider unindexed collections of sets. (We use the term "collection of sets," rather than "set of sets," for a set whose elements are subsets of some given set $S$.) Let us use German script letters to denote collections of sets. For instance, the elements of a finite collection $\mathfrak{A} = \{A_1, \ldots, A_m\}$ of subsets of $E^n$ are the sets $A_i \subset E^n$, $i = 1, \ldots, m$.

The *union* and *intersection* of a collection $\mathfrak{A}$ of sets are, respectively, the sets

$$\bigcup_{A \in \mathfrak{A}} A = \{p \in S : p \in A \text{ for some } A \in \mathfrak{A}\},$$

$$\bigcap_{A \in \mathfrak{A}} A = \{p \in S : p \in A \text{ for every } A \in \mathfrak{A}\}.$$

If each set of the collection is indexed by itself (taking $\mathcal{J} = \mathfrak{A}$, $A_A = A$), then this definition of union and intersection agrees with the one for indexed collections. Propositions A-1b and A-2 remain true for unindexed collections.

## PROBLEMS

1. Find int $A$, fr $A$, cl $A$ if $A$ is:
   (a) $\{\mathbf{x} : 0 < |\mathbf{x} - \mathbf{x}_0| \leq \delta\}$, $\delta > 0$.
   (b) $\{\mathbf{x} : |\mathbf{x} - \mathbf{x}_0| = \delta\}$, $\delta > 0$.
   (c) $\{(x, y) : 0 < y < x + 1, x > -1\}$.
   (d) $\{(r \cos\theta, r \sin\theta) : 0 < r < 1, 0 < \theta < 2\pi\}$.
   (e) $\{(x, y) : x \text{ or } y \text{ is irrational}\}$.
   (f) Any finite set.
   (g) $\{1, \frac{1}{2}, \frac{1}{3}, \ldots\}$, $n = 1$.
2. In Problem 1 which sets are open? Which are closed?
3. Let $A$ be any set. Show that int $A$ is open, and that both fr $A$ and cl $A$ are closed.
4. Show that:
   (a) fr $A$ = fr $(A^c)$.
   (b) cl $A$ = cl (cl $A$).
   (c) fr $A$ = cl $A \cap$ cl $(A^c)$.
   (d) int $A$ = (cl $(A^c))^c$.
5. Show by giving examples that the following are in general *false:*
   (a) int (cl $A$) = int $A$.
   (b) fr (fr $A$) = fr $A$.
6. Let $A$ be open and $B$ closed. Show that $A - B$ is open, and that $B - A$ is closed.

## A-4 SEQUENCES IN $E^n$

An *infinite sequence* is a function whose domain is the set of positive integers. For brevity, we shall say sequence to mean infinite sequence. In this section let us consider sequences with values in $E^n$. It is customary to denote by $\mathbf{x}_m$ the value of the function at the integer $m = 1, 2, \ldots$, and to call $\mathbf{x}_m$ the $m$th *term* of the sequence. The sequence itself is denoted by $\mathbf{x}_1, \mathbf{x}_2, \ldots$, or for brevity by $[\mathbf{x}_m]$. It must not be confused with the set $\{\mathbf{x}_1, \mathbf{x}_2, \ldots\}$ whose elements are the terms of the sequence. This set may be finite or infinite. For instance if $x_m = (-1)^m$ then the sequence is $-1, 1, -1, \ldots$, and the set $\{x_1, x_2, \ldots\}$ has only two elements $-1$ and $1$.

**Definition.** Suppose that for every $\epsilon > 0$ there exists a positive integer $N$ such that $|\mathbf{x}_m - \mathbf{x}_0| < \epsilon$ for every $m \geq N$. Then $\mathbf{x}_0$ is the *limit* of the sequence $[\mathbf{x}_m]$.

The notations "$\mathbf{x}_0 = \lim_{m\to\infty} \mathbf{x}_m$" and "$\mathbf{x}_m \to \mathbf{x}_0$ as $m \to \infty$" are used to mean that $\mathbf{x}_0$ is the limit of the sequence $[\mathbf{x}_m]$. A sequence is called *convergent* if it has a limit, otherwise *divergent*. The integer $N$ in the definition depends of course on $\epsilon$. Given $\epsilon$ there is a smallest possible choice for $N$. However, for purposes of the theory of limits it is of no interest to calculate it. What matters is the fact that some $N$ exists.

**Proposition A-3a.** *Let* $\mathbf{x}_0 = \lim_{m\to\infty} \mathbf{x}_m$, $\mathbf{y}_0 = \lim_{m\to\infty} \mathbf{y}_m$. *Then:*

(a) $\mathbf{x}_0 + \mathbf{y}_0 = \lim_{m\to\infty} (\mathbf{x}_m + \mathbf{y}_m)$.

(b) $c\mathbf{x}_0 = \lim_{m\to\infty} c\mathbf{x}_m$ *for any scalar* $c$.

(c) $\mathbf{x}_0 \cdot \mathbf{y}_0 = \lim_{m\to\infty} \mathbf{x}_m \cdot \mathbf{y}_m$.

The proof of this is left to the reader (Problem 6). Only superficial changes are needed in the proof given for real-valued sequences in any careful elementary calculus text. Moreover, it is similar to the proof of Proposition A-3b in the next section.

**Proposition A-4a.** $\mathbf{x}_0 = \lim_{m\to\infty} \mathbf{x}_m$ *if and only if* $x_0^i = \lim_{m\to\infty} x_m^i$ *for each* $i = 1, \ldots, n$.

*Proof.* For any vector $\mathbf{h}$,

$$|h^i| \leq |\mathbf{h}| \leq |h^1| + \cdots + |h^n|. \tag{*}$$

In particular, this is true with $\mathbf{h} = \mathbf{x}_m - \mathbf{x}_0$. Suppose that $\mathbf{x}_m \to \mathbf{x}_0$ as $m \to \infty$. From the definition of "limit" and the fact that $|x_m^i - x_0^i| \leq |\mathbf{x}_m - \mathbf{x}_0|$, given $\epsilon > 0$ there exists $N$ such that $|x_m^i - x_0^i| < \epsilon$ for every $m \geq N$. Hence $x_m^i \to x_0^i$ as $m \to \infty$. Conversely, suppose that $x_m^i \to x_0^i$ as $m \to \infty$ for each

$i = 1, \ldots, n$. Then given $\epsilon > 0$ there exists for each $i$ an $N_i$ such that $|x_m^i - x_0^i| < \epsilon/n$ for every $m \geq N_i$. Let $N = \max\{N_1, \ldots, N_n\}$. If $m \geq N$, then

$$|\mathbf{x}_m - \mathbf{x}_0| \leq \sum_{i=1}^{n} |x_m^i - x_0^i| < n\frac{\epsilon}{n} = \epsilon.$$

Hence $\mathbf{x}_m \to \mathbf{x}_0$ as $m \to \infty$. ▮

Let us next prove three theorems which depend on the least upper bound axiom. It will be seen later that when $n = 1$ each of these theorems describes a property of the real number system which, taken together with the archimedean property, is equivalent to the least upper bound axiom.

A sequence $[x_m]$ of real numbers is called *monotone* if either $x_1 \leq x_2 \leq x_3 \leq \cdots$ or $x_1 \geq x_2 \geq x_3 \geq \cdots$ In the first instance the sequence is *nondecreasing,* in the second *nonincreasing.* A sequence $[\mathbf{x}_m]$ is *bounded* if there is a number $C$ such that $|\mathbf{x}_m| \leq C$ for every $m = 1, 2, \ldots$

**Theorem A–1.** *Every bounded monotone sequence of real numbers has a limit.*

*Proof.* Let $[x_m]$ be nondecreasing and bounded. Let $x_0 = \sup\{x_1, x_2 \ldots\}$. Given $\epsilon > 0$ there exists an $N$ such that $x_0 - x_N < \epsilon$. Otherwise $x_m \leq x_0 - \epsilon$ for every $m = 1, 2, \ldots$, and $x_0 - \epsilon$ would be a smaller upper bound than the least upper bound $x_0$. Since the sequence is nondecreasing, $x_N \leq x_m \leq x_0$ for every $m \geq N$. Hence $|x_m - x_0| = x_0 - x_m < \epsilon$ for every $m \geq N$. This shows that $x_m \to x_0$ as $m \to \infty$.

If the sequence is nonincreasing and bounded, let $x_0 = \inf\{x_1, x_2, \ldots\}$. In the same way $x_m \to x_0$ as $m \to \infty$. ▮

**Example 1.** Let $0 < a < 1$. The sequence $a, a^2, a^3, \ldots$ of its powers is decreasing, and is bounded below by 0. The limit of the sequence is $b = \inf\{a, a^2, a^3, \ldots\}$. Since $b \leq a^{m+1}$, $a^{-1}b \leq a^m$ for $m = 1, 2, \ldots$ Therefore $a^{-1}b \leq b$. However, $a^{-1}b \geq b$ since $0 < a < 1$; and hence $a^{-1}b = b$. This implies that $b = 0$.

Let us next obtain a criterion for convergence due to Cauchy.

**Definition.** If for every $\epsilon > 0$ there exists a positive integer $N$ such that $|\mathbf{x}_l - \mathbf{x}_m| < \epsilon$ for every $l, m \geq N$, then $[\mathbf{x}_m]$ is a *Cauchy sequence.*

**Theorem A–2.** (*Cauchy convergence criterion.*) *A sequence* $[\mathbf{x}_m]$ *is convergent if and only if it is a Cauchy sequence.*

*Proof.* Let $[\mathbf{x}_m]$ be convergent, and $\mathbf{x}_0$ be its limit. Then given $\epsilon > 0$ there exists $N$ such that $|\mathbf{x}_m - \mathbf{x}_0| < \epsilon/2$ for every $m \geq N$. Now

$$\mathbf{x}_l - \mathbf{x}_m = (\mathbf{x}_l - \mathbf{x}_0) + (\mathbf{x}_0 - \mathbf{x}_m).$$

If $l, m \geq N$, then by the triangle inequality

$$|\mathbf{x}_l - \mathbf{x}_m| \leq |\mathbf{x}_l - \mathbf{x}_0| + |\mathbf{x}_0 - \mathbf{x}_m| < \frac{\epsilon}{2} + \frac{\epsilon}{2} = \epsilon.$$

Therefore $[\mathbf{x}_m]$ is a Cauchy sequence.

The proof of the converse is more difficult. Let us first show that every Cauchy sequence is bounded. If $[\mathbf{x}_m]$ is Cauchy, then taking $\epsilon = 1$ in the definition there is an $N$ such that $|\mathbf{x}_l - \mathbf{x}_m| < 1$ for every $l, m \geq N$. In particular let $l = N$ and let $C = \max \{|\mathbf{x}_1|, \ldots, |\mathbf{x}_{N-1}|, |\mathbf{x}_N| + 1\}$. Then by the triangle inequality and the fact that $\mathbf{x}_m = \mathbf{x}_N + (\mathbf{x}_m - \mathbf{x}_N)$,

$$|\mathbf{x}_m| \leq |\mathbf{x}_N| + |\mathbf{x}_m - \mathbf{x}_N| < |\mathbf{x}_N| + 1$$

if $m \geq N$. Therefore $|\mathbf{x}_m| \leq C$ for every $m = 1, 2, \ldots$

Next, let $[x_m]$ be a Cauchy sequence of real numbers, and $C$ be a number such that $|x_m| \leq C$ for every $m$. For each $m = 1, 2, \ldots$ let

$$y_m = \inf \{x_m, x_{m+1}, \ldots\}.$$

Since $\{x_{m+1}, x_{m+2}, \ldots\} \subset \{x_m, x_{m+1}, \ldots\}$, we must have $y_m \leq y_{m+1}$. Since $x_m \leq C$ for every $m$, $y_m \leq C$ for every $m$. The sequence $[y_m]$ is nondecreasing and bounded. By Theorem A–1 the sequence $[y_m]$ has a limit $y_0$. Let us show that $x_m \to y_0$ as $m \to \infty$. Given $\epsilon > 0$ there exists $N$ such that for every $m \geq N$, $|x_N - x_m| < \epsilon/2$, and hence

$$x_N - \frac{\epsilon}{2} < x_m < x_N + \frac{\epsilon}{2}.$$

If $m \geq N$, then $x_N - \epsilon/2$ is a lower bound and $x_N + \epsilon/2$ an upper bound for $\{x_m, x_{m+1}, \ldots\}$. Therefore when $m \geq N$

$$x_N - \frac{\epsilon}{2} \leq y_m \leq y_0 \leq x_N + \frac{\epsilon}{2},$$

$$|x_m - y_0| \leq |x_m - x_N| + |x_N - y_0| < \frac{\epsilon}{2} + \frac{\epsilon}{2} = \epsilon.$$

This proves that $x_m \to y_0$ as $m \to \infty$.

Finally, if $[\mathbf{x}_m]$ is a Cauchy sequence in $E^n$, then for each $i = 1, \ldots, n$ the components form a Cauchy sequence $[x_m^i]$ of real numbers (Problem 4). Each of these sequences has a limit $y_0^i$. By Proposition A–4a, $\mathbf{x}_m \to \mathbf{y}_0$ as $m \to \infty$. ∎

A nonempty set is called *bounded* if it is contained in some spherical $n$-ball. The *diameter* of a nonempty set $A$ is

$$\operatorname{diam} A = \sup \{|\mathbf{x} - \mathbf{y}| : \mathbf{x}, \mathbf{y} \in A\}.$$

$A$ is bounded if and only if $\operatorname{diam} A$ is finite.

**Theorem A–3.** (*Cantor*). *Let $[A_m]$ be a sequence of closed sets such that $A_1 \supset A_2 \supset \cdots$ and $0 = \lim_{m\to\infty} \operatorname{diam} A_m$. Then $A_1 \cap A_2 \cap \cdots$ contains a single point.*

*Proof.* For each $m = 1, 2, \ldots$ let $\mathbf{x}_m$ be a point of $A_m$. Let us show that $[\mathbf{x}_m]$ is a Cauchy sequence. Given $\epsilon > 0$, there exists $N$ such that diam $A_N < \epsilon$. If $l, m > N$, then $\mathbf{x}_l, \mathbf{x}_m \in A_N$ since $A_l \subset A_N$, $A_m \subset A_N$. Therefore

$$|\mathbf{x}_l - \mathbf{x}_m| \leq \operatorname{diam} A_N < \epsilon.$$

By Theorem A–2 the sequence $[\mathbf{x}_m]$ has a limit $\mathbf{x}_0$. For each $l = 1, 2, \ldots$, $\mathbf{x}_m \in A_l$ for every $m \geq l$ since $A_m \subset A_l$. Since $A_l$ is closed, $\mathbf{x}_0 \in A_l$ (Problem 5). Since this is true for each $l$, $\mathbf{x}_0 \in A_1 \cap A_2 \cap \cdots$

If $\mathbf{x} \in A_1 \cap A_2 \cap \cdots$, then $\mathbf{x} \in A_m$ and

$$0 \leq |\mathbf{x} - \mathbf{x}_0| \leq \operatorname{diam} A_m, \qquad m = 1, 2, \ldots$$

Since diam $A_m \to 0$ as $m \to \infty$, $|\mathbf{x} - \mathbf{x}_0| = 0$ and $\mathbf{x} = \mathbf{x}_0$. ∎

If in Theorem A–3 it is not assumed that the diameter of $A_m$ tends to 0, then it is still true that $A_1 \cap A_2 \cap \cdots$ is not empty, provided some set $A_m$ is bounded. (See Problem 4, Section A–8.)

**Example 2.** Let $n = 1$, $A_m = \{m, m+1, m+2, \ldots\}$. Then each $A_m$ is closed, unbounded, and $A_1 \supset A_2 \supset \cdots$ The intersection $A_1 \cap A_2 \cap \cdots$ is empty.

**Note.* Let $n = 1$. Suppose that we took instead of the least upper bound property of $E^1$ (Axiom IIIa, Section A–1) the following.

**Axiom IIIb.** (a) $E^1$ has the archimedean property.

(b) Every Cauchy sequence of real numbers is convergent.

Then the least upper bound property becomes a theorem. To prove this, let $S$ be any subset of $E^1$ which is bounded above, and let $c$ be some upper bound for $S$. Let us define a sequence of closed intervals $I_1, I_2, \ldots$ as follows: Let $a$ be some point of $S$, and $I_1 = [a, c]$. Divide $I_1$ at the midpoint $(a + c)/2$ into two congruent closed intervals. If $(a + c)/2$ is an upper bound for $S$, let $I_2$ be the left-hand interval, otherwise let $I_2$ be the right-hand interval. In general, suppose $m \geq 1$ and $I_m$ has been defined. If the midpoint of $I_m$ is an upper bound for $S$, let $I_{m+1}$ be the left half of $I_m$, otherwise the right half. The archimedean property implies that for any $x \geq 0$, the sequence $[m^{-1}x]$ tends to 0 as $m \to \infty$. Since $0 \leq 2^{-m} \leq m^{-1}$, the sequence $[2^{-m}x]$ also tends to 0. Let $x = 2(c - a)$. Now $I_1 \supset I_2 \supset \cdots$ and the length of $I_m$ is $2^{-m}x$. By the proof of Theorem A–3, $I_1 \cap I_2 \cap \cdots$ contains a single point $x_0$. By the construction, $x_0 = \sup S$. (See Fig. A–2.)

This shows that (in the presence of Axioms I and II) Axioms IIIa and IIIb are equivalent. The endpoints of the intervals $I_m$ form monotone sequences. If we took as an axiom the archimedean property and Theorem A–1,

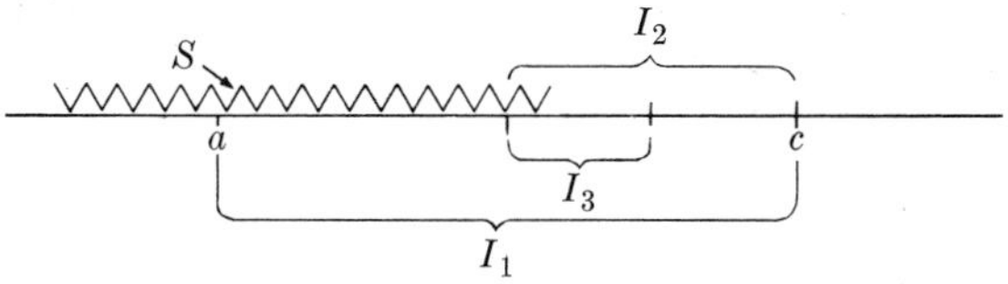


FIGURE A-2

then similar reasoning shows that these sequences must converge to a common limit $x_0$ and $x_0 = \sup S$. Again, this is equivalent to Axiom IIIa.

**Infinite series.** Formally, an infinite series is an expression written $\sum_{k=1}^{\infty} \mathbf{x}_k$ or $\mathbf{x}_1 + \mathbf{x}_2 + \cdots$ To be more precise, with any sequence $[\mathbf{x}_k]$ is associated another sequence $[\mathbf{s}_m]$, where $\mathbf{s}_m = \mathbf{x}_1 + \cdots + \mathbf{x}_m$ is called the $m$th *partial sum*. This pair of sequences defines an *infinite series*. If the sequence of partial sums has a limit $\mathbf{s}$, then the series is *convergent* and $\mathbf{s}$ is its *sum*. This is denoted by $\mathbf{s} = \mathbf{x}_1 + \mathbf{x}_2 + \cdots$ If the sequence of partial sums has no limit, then the series is *divergent*.

If $\mathbf{s} = \mathbf{x}_1 + \mathbf{x}_2 + \cdots$, $\mathbf{t} = \mathbf{y}_1 + \mathbf{y}_2 + \cdots$, then $\mathbf{s} + \mathbf{t} = (\mathbf{x}_1 + \mathbf{y}_1) + (\mathbf{x}_2 + \mathbf{y}_2) + \cdots$ and $c\mathbf{s} = (c\mathbf{x}_1) + (c\mathbf{x}_2) + \cdots$ for any scalar $c$. This follows from the definition and Proposition A-3a. Some further elementary properties are given in Problems 7(c) and 8.

## PROBLEMS

In Problems 1 and 2 you may use the results of Problems 9 and 10.

1. Find the limit if it exists.
   (a) $x_m = (2^m - 2^{-m})/(3^m + 3^{-m})$.
   (b) $x_m = \sin (m\pi/2)$.
   (c) $x_m = \sin m\pi$.
   (d) $x_m = ((m + 1)/(m - 1))^m$. [*Hint:* $(1 + 1/m)^m \to e$ as $m \to \infty$.]
   (e) $x_m = ((m^2 + 1)/(m^2 - 1))^m$.
2. Find the limit if it exists, using Proposition A-4a.
   (a) $(x_m, y_m) = ((1 + m)/(1 - 2m), 1/(1 + m))$.
   (b) $(x_m, y_m) = (2^{-m}, 1 + m)$.
   (c) $(x_m, y_m) = (1 - 2^{-m}, (m^2 + 3^m)/m!)$.
3. Show that a sequence $[\mathbf{x}_m]$ has at most one limit $\mathbf{x}_0$. [*Hint:* If $\mathbf{y}_0$ were another limit, let $\epsilon = |\mathbf{x}_0 - \mathbf{y}_0|/2$.]
4. Show that $[\mathbf{x}_m]$ is a Cauchy sequence if and only if $[x_m^i]$ is a Cauchy sequence for each $i = 1, \ldots, n$.
5. Show that if $\mathbf{x}_m \in A$ for every $m \geq l$ and $\mathbf{x}_0 = \lim_{m\to\infty} \mathbf{x}_m$, then $\mathbf{x}_0 \in \text{cl } A$.
6. Prove Proposition A-3a.
7. (*Comparison tests.*) Show that:
   (a) If $0 \leq x_m \leq y_m$ for every $m \geq l$ and $y_m \to 0$ as $m \to \infty$, then $x_m \to 0$ as $m \to \infty$.

(b) If $[x_m]$, $[y_m]$ are nondecreasing sequences such that $x_m \le y_m$ for each $m = 1, 2, \ldots$ and $y_m \to y$ as $m \to \infty$, then $[x_m]$ has a limit $x \le y$.
(c) If $0 \le x_m \le y_m$ for every $m = 1, 2, \ldots$ and $t = y_1 + y_2 + \cdots$, then the series $x_1 + x_2 + \cdots$ converges with sum $s \le t$.

8. An infinite series $\mathbf{x}_1 + \mathbf{x}_2 + \cdots$ converges *absolutely* if the series of nonnegative numbers $|\mathbf{x}_1| + |\mathbf{x}_2| + \cdots$ converges. Prove that any absolutely convergent infinite series is convergent. [*Hint:* Show that the sequence $[\mathbf{s}_m]$ of partial sums is Cauchy.]

9. Show that if $a > 0$, then

(a) $\lim_{m\to\infty} a^{1/m} = 1$. (b) $\lim_{m\to\infty} a^m/m! = 0$.

(c) $\lim_{m\to\infty} (x_m)^{1/m} = 1$ provided $\lim_{m\to\infty} x_m = a$.

[*Hints:* For part (a) reduce to the case $0 < a < 1$. By Example 1, if $b < 1$ then $a \le b^m$ for only finitely many $m$. For part (b), compare with the sequence $[c/m]$ for suitable $c$ and suitable $l$ in Problem 7(a).]

10. Let $x_0 = \lim_{m\to\infty} x_m$, $y_0 = \lim_{m\to\infty} y_m$, and assume that $y_m \ne 0$ for $m = 0, 1, 2, \ldots$ Show that $x_0/y_0 = \lim_{m\to\infty} x_m/y_m$. [*Hint:* By (c) of Proposition A-3a it suffices to show that $y_0^{-1} = \lim_{m\to\infty} x_m^{-1}$.]

## A-5 LIMITS AND CONTINUITY OF TRANSFORMATIONS

In discussing continuity of functions it is convenient to introduce the following terminology. Let $f$ be a function from a set $S$ into a set $T$. The *image* under $f$ of a set $A \subset S$ is the set $f(A) = \{f(p) : p \in A\}$. It is a subset of $T$, and in fact the restriction $f|A$ (Section 1–2) is a function from $A$ onto $f(A)$. The *inverse image* of a set $B \subset T$ is the set $f^{-1}(B) = \{p : f(p) \in B\}$. It is a subset of $S$. See Section 4–1 for illustrations and examples.

Let us now suppose that $\mathbf{f}$ is a function from a set $D \subset E^n$ into $E^m$, where $n$ and $m$ are positive integers. Such functions are called *transformations* in this book.

The definition of "limit" for transformations is patterned after the one encountered in elementary calculus for real-valued functions of one variable. A *punctured* neighborhood of $\mathbf{x}_0$ is a neighborhood with the center $\mathbf{x}_0$ removed. Let us assume that $D$ contains some punctured neighborhood of $\mathbf{x}_0$. For the definition of "limit", $\mathbf{x}_0$ itself need not be in $D$. If $\mathbf{x}_0 \in D$, the value of $f$ at $\mathbf{x}_0$ is irrelevant.

**Definition.** If for every neighborhood $V$ of $\mathbf{y}_0$ there is a punctured neighborhood $U$ of $\mathbf{x}_0$ such that $\mathbf{f}(U) \subset V$, then $\mathbf{y}_0$ is the *limit* of the transformation $\mathbf{f}$ at $\mathbf{x}_0$ (Fig. A–3).

In the definition it is understood that the radius of $U$ is small enough so that $U \subset D$. The notations $\mathbf{y}_0 = \lim_{\mathbf{x}\to\mathbf{x}_0} \mathbf{f}(\mathbf{x})$ and $\mathbf{f}(\mathbf{x}) \to \mathbf{y}_0$ as $\mathbf{x} \to \mathbf{x}_0$ are used to mean that $\mathbf{y}_0$ is the limit of $\mathbf{f}$ at $\mathbf{x}_0$.

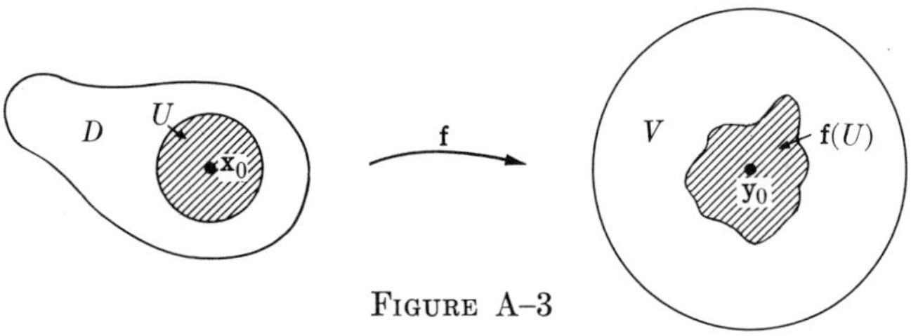


FIGURE A-3

If we let $\epsilon$ and $\delta$ denote respectively the radii of $V$ and $U$, then the definition may be rephrased as follows: $\mathbf{f}(\mathbf{x}) \to \mathbf{y}_0$ as $\mathbf{x} \to \mathbf{x}_0$ if for every $\epsilon > 0$ there exists $\delta > 0$ such that $|\mathbf{f}(\mathbf{x}) - \mathbf{y}_0| < \epsilon$ whenever $0 < |\mathbf{x} - \mathbf{x}_0| < \delta$. The number $\delta$ depends of course on $\epsilon$ and may also depend on $\mathbf{x}_0$. Given $\epsilon$ and $\mathbf{x}_0$, there is a largest possible $\delta$. However, there is ordinarily no reason to try to calculate it.

Let us first show that limits behave properly with respect to sums and products. Let $\mathbf{f}$ and $\mathbf{g}$ have the same domain and values in the same euclidean $E^n$.

**Proposition A-3b.** *If* $\mathbf{y}_0 = \lim_{\mathbf{x}\to\mathbf{x}_0} \mathbf{f}(\mathbf{x})$ *and* $\mathbf{z}_0 = \lim_{\mathbf{x}\to\mathbf{x}_0} \mathbf{g}(\mathbf{x})$, *then*

(1) $\mathbf{y}_0 + \mathbf{z}_0 = \lim_{\mathbf{x}\to\mathbf{x}_0} [\mathbf{f}(\mathbf{x}) + \mathbf{g}(\mathbf{x})]$.

(2) $c\mathbf{y}_0 = \lim_{\mathbf{x}\to\mathbf{x}_0} c\mathbf{f}(\mathbf{x})$, *for any scalar c.*

(3) $\mathbf{y}_0 \cdot \mathbf{z}_0 = \lim_{\mathbf{x}\to\mathbf{x}_0} \mathbf{f}(\mathbf{x}) \cdot \mathbf{g}(\mathbf{x})$.

*Proof.* Let $V$ be any neighborhood of $\mathbf{y}_0 + \mathbf{z}_0$ and let $\epsilon$ be its radius. Let $V_1$, $V_2$ be the neighborhoods of radius $\epsilon/2$ of $\mathbf{y}_0$, $\mathbf{z}_0$ respectively. If $\mathbf{y} \in V_1$ and $\mathbf{z} \in V_2$, then by the triangle inequality

$$|(\mathbf{y} + \mathbf{z}) - (\mathbf{y}_0 + \mathbf{z}_0)| \leq |\mathbf{y} - \mathbf{y}_0| + |\mathbf{z} - \mathbf{z}_0| < \frac{\epsilon}{2} + \frac{\epsilon}{2} = \epsilon.$$

Hence $\mathbf{y} + \mathbf{z} \in V$. By hypothesis there exist punctured neighborhoods $U_1$, $U_2$ of $\mathbf{x}_0$ such that $\mathbf{f}(U_1) \subset V_1$ and $\mathbf{g}(U_2) \subset V_2$. Let $U = U_1 \cap U_2$, which is also a punctured neighborhood of $\mathbf{x}_0$. If $\mathbf{x} \in U$, then $\mathbf{f}(\mathbf{x}) \in V_1$, $\mathbf{g}(\mathbf{x}) \in V_2$. Consequently, $\mathbf{f}(\mathbf{x}) + \mathbf{g}(\mathbf{x}) \in V$, which shows that $(\mathbf{f} + \mathbf{g})(U) \subset V$. This proves (1). The proof of (2) is left to the reader (Problem 2).

To prove (3) let $V_0$ be the neighborhood of $\mathbf{y}_0$ of radius 1, and $U_0$ be a punctured neighborhood of $\mathbf{x}_0$ such that $\mathbf{f}(U_0) \subset V_0$. Let

$$C = \max\{|\mathbf{y}_0| + 1, |\mathbf{z}_0|\}.$$

If $\mathbf{y} \in V_0$, then

$$|\mathbf{y}| \leq |\mathbf{y}_0| + |\mathbf{y} - \mathbf{y}_0| < |\mathbf{y}_0| + 1,$$

and hence $|\mathbf{y}| < C$.

Now

$$\mathbf{f}(\mathbf{x}) \cdot \mathbf{g}(\mathbf{x}) - \mathbf{y}_0 \cdot \mathbf{z}_0 = \mathbf{f}(\mathbf{x}) \cdot [\mathbf{g}(\mathbf{x}) - \mathbf{z}_0] + \mathbf{z}_0 \cdot [\mathbf{f}(\mathbf{x}) - \mathbf{y}_0].$$

From the triangle inequality and Cauchy's inequality,

$$|\mathbf{f}(\mathbf{x}) \cdot \mathbf{g}(\mathbf{x}) - \mathbf{y}_0 \cdot \mathbf{z}_0| \leq |\mathbf{f}(\mathbf{x})|\,|\mathbf{g}(\mathbf{x}) - \mathbf{z}_0| + |\mathbf{z}_0|\,|\mathbf{f}(\mathbf{x}) - \mathbf{y}_0|. \qquad (*)$$

Given $\epsilon > 0$, let $V_1$, $V_2$ be the neighborhoods of radius $\epsilon/2C$ of $\mathbf{y}_0$, $\mathbf{z}_0$ respectively, and let $V_1' = V_0 \cap V_1$. If $\epsilon \leq 2C$, then $V_1' = V_1$. By hypothesis there are punctured neighborhoods $U_1$, $U_2$ of $\mathbf{x}_0$ such that $\mathbf{f}(U_1) \subset V_2'$, $\mathbf{g}(U_2) \subset V_2$. Let $U = U_1 \cap U_2$. For every $\mathbf{x} \in U$, $\mathbf{f}(\mathbf{x}) \in V_0$ and hence $|\mathbf{f}(\mathbf{x})| < C$. From $(*)$,

$$|\mathbf{f}(\mathbf{x}) \cdot \mathbf{g}(\mathbf{x}) - \mathbf{y}_0 \cdot \mathbf{z}_0| < C\,\frac{\epsilon}{2C} + C\,\frac{\epsilon}{2C} = \epsilon$$

for every $\mathbf{x} \in U$. This proves (3). ▮

A transformation $\mathbf{f}$ is called *bounded* on a set $A$ if there exists $C$ such that $|\mathbf{f}(\mathbf{x})| \leq C$ for every $\mathbf{x} \in A$. In the course of the proof we showed that if $\mathbf{f}$ has a limit at $\mathbf{x}_0$, then $\mathbf{f}$ is bounded on some punctured neighborhood $U_0$ of $\mathbf{x}_0$.

**Proposition A–4b.** $\mathbf{y}_0 = \lim_{\mathbf{x}\to\mathbf{x}_0} \mathbf{f}(\mathbf{x})$ *if and only if* $y_0^i = \lim_{\mathbf{x}\to\mathbf{x}_0} f^i(\mathbf{x})$ *for each* $i = 1, \ldots, m$.

The proof is like that for Proposition A–4a.

**Proposition A–5.** *If* $\mathbf{y}_0 = \lim_{\mathbf{x}\to\mathbf{x}_0} \mathbf{f}(\mathbf{x})$, *then for any* $\mathbf{v} \neq \mathbf{0}$,

$$\mathbf{y}_0 = \lim_{t\to 0} \mathbf{f}(\mathbf{x}_0 + t\mathbf{v}).$$

*Proof.* Let $V$ be any neighborhood of $\mathbf{y}_0$. There exists $\delta > 0$ such that $\mathbf{f}(\mathbf{x}) \in V$ whenever $0 < |\mathbf{x} - \mathbf{x}_0| < \delta$. If $0 < |t| < \delta/|\mathbf{v}|$, then

$$|(\mathbf{x}_0 + t\mathbf{v}) - \mathbf{x}_0| = |t|\,|\mathbf{v}| < \delta.$$

Hence $\mathbf{f}(\mathbf{x}_0 + t\mathbf{v}) \in V$ for every $t$ in the punctured $\delta/|\mathbf{v}|$-neighborhood of 0. ▮

The points $\mathbf{x}_0 + t\mathbf{v}$ lie on the line through $\mathbf{x}_0$ and $\mathbf{x}_0 + \mathbf{v}$. Roughly speaking, Proposition A–5 states that if $\mathbf{f}$ has a limit $\mathbf{y}_0$ at $\mathbf{x}_0$, then $\mathbf{y}_0$ is also the limit as $\mathbf{x}_0$ is approached along any line containing $\mathbf{x}_0$. When $\mathbf{f}$ fails to have a limit at $\mathbf{x}_0$ this fact can often be discovered by testing $\mathbf{f}$ along various lines.

**Example 1.** Let $f(x, y) = x^2/(x^2 + y^2)$, $(x, y) \neq (0, 0)$, and let $\mathbf{x}_0 = (0, 0)$. Taking $\mathbf{v} = \mathbf{e}_1 = (1, 0)$, $f(t, 0) = 1$ for every $t \neq 0$. Hence $f(t, 0) \to 1$ as $t \to 0$. Similarly, taking $\mathbf{v} = \mathbf{e}_2 = (0, 1)$, $f(0, t) = 0$ for every $t \neq 0$ and $f(0, t) \to 0$ as $t \to 0$. Since these limits are different, $f$ has no limit at $(0, 0)$.

The converse to Proposition A-5 is false, as the following example shows.

**Example 2.** Let $f(x, y) = (y^2 - x)^2/(y^4 + x^2)$, $(x, y) \neq (0, 0)$, and again let $\mathbf{x}_0 = (0, 0)$. Consider any $\mathbf{v} = (h, k) \neq (0, 0)$. Then

$$f(th, tk) = \frac{(tk^2 - h)^2}{t^2k^4 + h^2}$$

which tends to 1 as $t \to 0$. However, every punctured neighborhood of $(0, 0)$ contains part of the parabola $y^2 = x$, and $f(y^2, y) = 0$. Hence $f$ does not have a limit at $(0, 0)$.

**Continuity.** It often happens that $\mathbf{x}_0 \in D$ and the limit at $\mathbf{x}_0$ is just $\mathbf{f}(\mathbf{x}_0)$.

**Definition.** A transformation $\mathbf{f}$ is *continuous* at $\mathbf{x}_0$ if $\mathbf{f}(\mathbf{x}_0) = \lim_{\mathbf{x}\to\mathbf{x}_0} \mathbf{f}(\mathbf{x})$.

When $\mathbf{f}$ is continuous at $\mathbf{x}_0$, punctured neighborhoods may be replaced by neighborhoods. The definition may be restated: $\mathbf{f}$ is continuous at $\mathbf{x}_0$ if for every neighborhood $V$ of $\mathbf{f}(\mathbf{x}_0)$ there is a neighborhood $U$ of $\mathbf{x}_0$ such that $\mathbf{f}(U) \subset V$.

From Proposition A–3b, sums and products of transformations continuous at $\mathbf{x}_0$ are also continuous at $\mathbf{x}_0$. From Proposition A–4b, $\mathbf{f}$ is continuous at $\mathbf{x}_0$ if and only if its components $f^1, \ldots, f^m$ are continuous at $\mathbf{x}_0$.

**Example 3.** Let $\mathbf{I}(\mathbf{x}) = \mathbf{x}$, the identity transformation. Then $\mathbf{I}$ is everywhere continuous (take $U = V$ above). Therefore the components of $\mathbf{I}$ are everywhere continuous. In this book these components are called the standard cartesian coordinate functions, and are denoted by $X^1, \ldots, X^n$. For each $\mathbf{x}$, $X^i(\mathbf{x}) = x^i$. See Section 1–3.

**Example 4.** Any polynomial in $n$ variables is everywhere continuous. This is proved by induction on the degree of the polynomial using the continuity of the coordinate functions $X^i$ and of constant functions.

**Example 5.** A rational function $f(\mathbf{x}) = P(\mathbf{x})/Q(\mathbf{x})$, where $P$ and $Q$ are polynomials, is continuous at each point where $Q(\mathbf{x}) \neq 0$ (see Problem 4). For instance, in Examples 1 and 2, $f$ is continuous at each $(x, y) \neq (0, 0)$.

It will be shown later (Proposition A–7) that the composite of two continuous transformations is continuous. In Section 4–4 it is shown that any differentiable transformation is continuous.

**Limits at $\infty$.** Let us call a set of the form $\{\mathbf{x} : |\mathbf{x}| > b\}$ a *punctured neighborhood* of $\infty$. The definition of "limit at $\infty$" then reads: $\mathbf{y}_0 = \lim_{|\mathbf{x}|\to\infty} \mathbf{f}(\mathbf{x})$ if for every neighborhood $V$ of $\mathbf{y}_0$ there exists a punctured neighborhood $U$ of $\infty$ such that $\mathbf{f}(U) \subset V$.

When $f$ is real valued we say that $\lim_{\mathbf{x}\to\mathbf{x}_0} f(\mathbf{x}) = +\infty$ if for every $C > 0$ there is a punctured neighborhood $U$ of $\mathbf{x}_0$ such that $f(\mathbf{x}) > C$ whenever $\mathbf{x} \in U$. The definition of "$\lim_{\mathbf{x}\to\mathbf{x}_0} f(\mathbf{x}) = -\infty$" is similar.

**PROBLEMS**

1. Find the limit at $\mathbf{x}_0$ if it exists.

   (a) $f(x, y) = xy/(x^2 + y^2)$, $\mathbf{x}_0 = \mathbf{e}_1 + \mathbf{e}_2$.
   (b) $f(x, y) = xy/(x^2 + y^2)$, $\mathbf{x}_0 = (0, 0)$.
   (c) $f(x) = (1 - \cos x)/x^2$, $x_0 = 0$. [*Hint:* $\lim_{x\to 0} (\sin x)/x = 1$.]
   (d) $\mathbf{f}(x) = |x - 2|\mathbf{e}_1 + |x + 2|\mathbf{e}_2$, $x_0 = 3$.
   (e) $\mathbf{f}(x, y) = y\mathbf{e}_1 + (xy)^2/[(xy)^2 + (x - y)^2]\mathbf{e}_2$, $\mathbf{x}_0 = (0, 0)$.

   At which points is each of these functions continuous?

2. Prove (2) of Proposition A–3b.

3. Show that if $\mathbf{y}_0 = \lim_{\mathbf{x}\to\mathbf{x}_0} \mathbf{f}(\mathbf{x})$, then $|\mathbf{y}_0| = \lim_{\mathbf{x}\to\mathbf{x}_0} |\mathbf{f}(\mathbf{x})|$. By an example, show that the converse is false.

4. Let $y_0 = \lim_{\mathbf{x}\to\mathbf{x}_0} f(\mathbf{x})$, $z_0 = \lim_{\mathbf{x}\to\mathbf{x}_0} g(\mathbf{x})$. Show that if $z_0 \neq 0$ then

$$\lim_{\mathbf{x}\to\mathbf{x}_0} \frac{f(\mathbf{x})}{g(\mathbf{x})} = \frac{y_0}{z_0}.$$

5. Show that $\lim_{\mathbf{x}\to\mathbf{x}_0} f(\mathbf{x}) = +\infty$ if and only if $\lim_{\mathbf{x}\to\mathbf{x}_0} [f(\mathbf{x})]^{-1} = 0$ and $f(\mathbf{x}) > 0$ for every $\mathbf{x}$ in some punctured neighborhood of $\mathbf{x}_0$.

6. Find the limit if it exists.

   (a) $\displaystyle\lim_{(x,y)\to(0,0)} \frac{x^4 + y^4}{x^2 + y^2}$.  (b) $\displaystyle\lim_{(x,y)\to(0,0)} \frac{xy^2}{x^2 + y^4}$.

   (c) $\displaystyle\lim_{|\mathbf{x}|\to\infty} \frac{(\mathbf{x}\cdot\mathbf{x}_1)(\mathbf{x}\cdot\mathbf{x}_2)}{\mathbf{x}\cdot\mathbf{x}}$, where $\mathbf{x}_1$ and $\mathbf{x}_2$ are given vectors not $\mathbf{0}$.

   (d) $\displaystyle\lim_{|\mathbf{x}|\to\infty} \frac{|\mathbf{x} - \mathbf{x}_1|}{|\mathbf{x} - \mathbf{x}_2|}$.

7. Show that $\mathbf{f}$ is continuous at $\mathbf{x}_0$ if and only if $\mathbf{f}(\mathbf{x}_0) = \lim_{m\to\infty} \mathbf{f}(\mathbf{x}_m)$ for every sequence $[\mathbf{x}_m]$ such that $\mathbf{x}_m \in D$ for $m = 1, 2, \ldots$ and $\mathbf{x}_m \to \mathbf{x}_0$ as $m \to \infty$.

## A–6 TOPOLOGICAL SPACES

The notion of topological space occurs in practically all branches of mathematics. There are several equivalent definitions; of these, we shall give the one in terms of neighborhoods.

**Definition.** Let $S$ be a nonempty set. For every $p \in S$ let $\mathfrak{U}_p$ be a collection of subsets of $S$ called *neighborhoods* of $p$ such that:

(1) Every point $p$ has at least one neighborhood.
(2) Every neighborhood of $p$ contains $p$.
(3) If $U_1$ and $U_2$ are neighborhoods of $p$, then there is a neighborhood $U_3$ of $p$ such that $U_3 \subset U_1 \cap U_2$.
(4) If $U$ is a neighborhood of $p$ and $q \in U$, then there is a neighborhood $V$ of $q$ such that $V \subset U$.

Then $S$ is a *topological space*.

More precisely, the topological space is $S$ together with the collections $\mathcal{U}_p$ of neighborhoods. However, it is common practice to omit explicit reference to the collections of neighborhoods when no ambiguity can arise.

For our purposes, the following two examples of topological spaces are of primary importance.

**Example 1.** Let $S = E^n$, and as in Section A–3 let $\mathcal{U}_{\mathbf{x}}$ be the collection of all open spherical $n$-balls with center $\mathbf{x}$. Clearly, Axioms (1) and (2) of the definition above are satisfied, and in (3) we may take $U_3 = U_1 \cap U_2$. Axiom (4) was verified in Example 1, Section A–3. Thus $E^n$ is a topological space.

**Example 2.** Let $S \subset E^n$. Let neighborhoods of $\mathbf{x} \in S$ be all sets $S \cap U$ where $U$ is a neighborhood of $\mathbf{x}$ in $E^n$ (Fig. A–4). These are called *relative neighborhoods* of $\mathbf{x}$ and the topology on $S$ defined by the collections of relative neighborhoods is the *relative topology*. It is discussed further later in the section. Roughly speaking, the relative topology is the one obtained by simply ignoring the complementary set $S^c = E^n - S$.

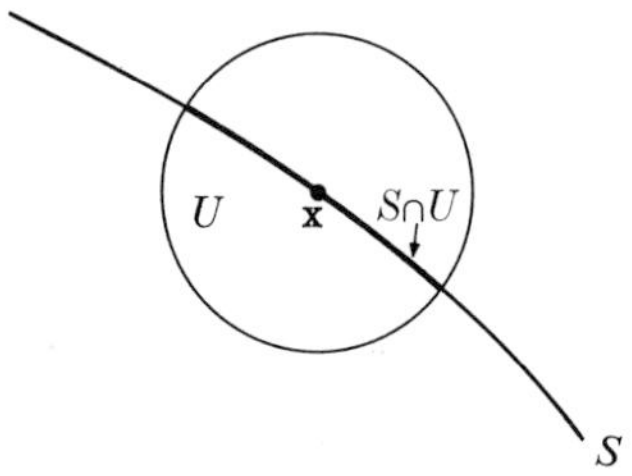


FIGURE A–4

In any topological space $S$ the basic notions of interior, frontier, and closure are defined just as in Section A–3 for the topological space $E^n$. For instance, $p$ is interior to a set $A \subset S$ if some neighborhood of $p$ is contained in $A$. An open subset of the topological space $S$ is a subset $A$ each point of which is interior to $A$. If $S - A$ is open, then $A$ is a *closed* subset of $S$. Axiom (4) guarantees that any neighborhood is an open set. Propositions A–1a, A–1b, and A–2 are still true, and the proofs are almost the same as before.

It often happens that two different collections of neighborhoods $\mathcal{U}_p$, $\mathcal{U}'_p$ lead to the same collection of open subsets of $S$. In $E^n$ we need not have started with spherical neighborhoods. For instance, the neighborhoods obtained from any noneuclidean norm on $E^n$ lead to the same open sets as in Section A–3. See Section 1–6.

The open sets, and not the particular kinds of neighborhoods from which they were obtained, determine all of the topological properties of $S$. Thus we say that the collections $\mathcal{U}_p$, $\mathcal{U}'_p$ define the same topology on $S$ if they have the same collection of open sets.

To give some idea of the breadth of the notion of topological space, let us give a few more examples.

**Example 3.** Let $S$ be any set, and let every $p \in S$ have exactly one neighborhood, namely $S$ itself. The only open sets are $S$ and the empty set.

**Example 4.** Let $S$ be any set, and let the sole neighborhood of $p$ be the set $\{p\}$ with the one element $p$. Then every subset of $S$ is open.

These examples represent opposite extremes. In Example 3, $S$ is called an *indiscrete space,* in Example 4 a *discrete space.*

**Example 5.** Let $\mathfrak{F}$ be the set whose elements are all bounded real-valued functions on the interval $[0, 1]$. Let us call the *distance* between functions $f$ and $g$ the number

$$d(f, g) = \sup \{|f(x) - g(x)| : x \in [0, 1]\}.$$

Let neighborhoods of $f$ be all sets of the form $\{g \in \mathfrak{F} : d(f, g) < \epsilon\}$. (See Fig. A-5.)

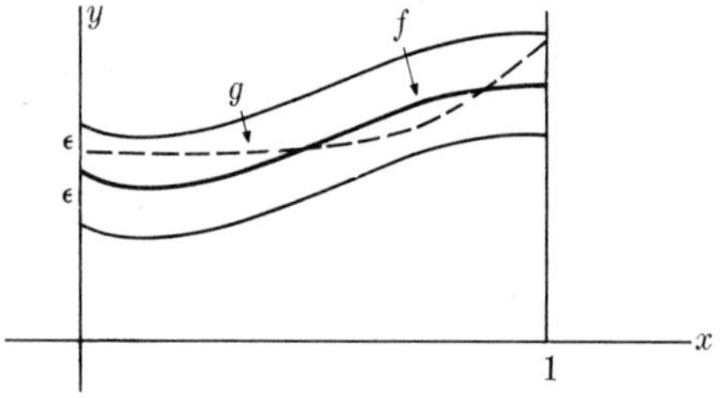


FIGURE A-5

**Continuous functions.** Let $f$ be a function from a topological space $S$ into a topological space $T$.

**Definition.** The function $f$ is *continuous at* $p_0$ if for every neighborhood $V$ of $f(p_0)$ there exists a neighborhood $U$ of $p_0$ such that $f(U) \subset V$. If $f$ is continuous at every point of $S$, then $f$ is *continuous on* $S$.

In this book the following cases will be of interest: (a) $S$ is an open subset of $E^n$ and $T = E^m$. In that case the definition of continuity agrees with the one in Section A-5. (b) $S \subset E^n$ and $T \subset E^m$. The sets $S$ and $T$ are given the relative topology, defined below. (c) $S$ is an open subset of $E^n$, and $T$ is some other finite-dimensional vector space. Specifically, for $T$ we shall take either the dual space $(E^n)^*$, the space $E_r^n$ of multivectors of degree $r$, or its dual $(E_r^n)^*$. Each of these spaces has a euclidean norm. Just as for $E^n$, neighborhoods of a point $p$ in each of them are of the form $\{q : |q - p| < \delta, \delta > 0\}$. Case (c) could be reduced to (a), since there is a norm preserving isomorphism between each of these vector spaces and euclidean $E^m$ of the appropriate dimension $m$.

**Proposition A-6.** *$f$ is continuous on $S$ if and only if the inverse image $f^{-1}(B)$ of any open set $B$ is open.*

*Proof.* Let $f$ be continuous on $S$ and $B \subset T$ be open. Let $p$ be any point of $f^{-1}(B)$ and $V$ be a neighborhood of $f(p)$ such that $V \subset B$. Since $f$ is continuous, there is a neighborhood $U$ of $p$ such that $f(U) \subset V$. Then $U \subset f^{-1}(B)$, which shows that $f^{-1}(B)$ is open.

Conversely, let $f^{-1}(B)$ be open for each open set $B$. Let $p$ be any point of $S$, and $V$ be any neighborhood of $f(p)$. Since $V$ is open, $f^{-1}(V)$ is open and contains $p$. Let $U$ be a neighborhood of $p$ such that $U \subset f^{-1}(V)$. Then $f(U) \subset V$, which shows that $f$ is continuous at $p$. Since this is true for every $p \in S$, $f$ is continuous on $S$. ▮

**Corollary.** *If $f$ is real valued and continuous on $S$, then*

$$\{p : f(p) > c\}, \quad \{p : f(p) < c\} \quad \textit{are open sets,}$$
$$\{p : f(p) \geq c\}, \quad \{p : f(p) \leq c\} \quad \textit{are closed sets.}$$

*Proof.* In this case $T = E^1$. The semi-infinite interval $(c, \infty)$ is open and $\{p : f(p) > c\} = f^{-1}[(c, \infty)]$. Similarly, $\{p : f(p) < c\} = f^{-1}[(-\infty, c)]$. The last two sets are complements of the first two. ▮

**Composites.** Let $f$ be a function from $S$ into $T$, and $g$ from $R$ into $S$. The composite $f \circ g$ is defined by

$$(f \circ g)(r) = f\,[g(r)] \quad \text{for every } r \in R.$$

**Proposition A–7.** *If $g$ is continuous at $r_0$ and $f$ is continuous at $p_0 = g(r_0)$, then $f \circ g$ is continuous at $r_0$.*

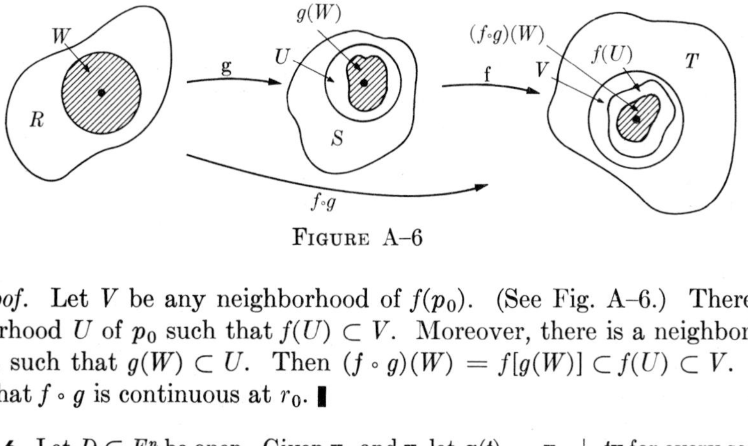


FIGURE A–6

*Proof.* Let $V$ be any neighborhood of $f(p_0)$. (See Fig. A–6.) There is a neighborhood $U$ of $p_0$ such that $f(U) \subset V$. Moreover, there is a neighborhood $W$ of $r_0$ such that $g(W) \subset U$. Then $(f \circ g)(W) = f[g(W)] \subset f(U) \subset V$. This shows that $f \circ g$ is continuous at $r_0$. ▮

**Example 6.** Let $D \subset E^n$ be open. Given $\mathbf{x}_0$ and $\mathbf{v}$, let $\mathbf{g}(t) = \mathbf{x}_0 + t\mathbf{v}$ for every scalar $t$. Then $\mathbf{g}$ is continuous from $E^1$ into $E^n$. By Proposition A–6, $\Delta = \{t : \mathbf{x}_0 + t\mathbf{v} \in D\}$ is open. Let $f$ be continuous on $D$ and let $\phi(t) = f(\mathbf{x}_0 + t\mathbf{v})$ for $t \in \Delta$. Then $\phi = f \circ (\mathbf{g}|\Delta)$, and by Proposition A–7 $\phi$ is continuous on $\Delta$. This result is similar to Proposition A–5.

**Example 7.** Let $1 \leq s \leq n - 1$. Let us regard $E^n$ as the cartesian product $E^s \times E^{n-s}$, and write $\mathbf{x} = (\mathbf{x}', \mathbf{x}'')$, where $\mathbf{x}' = (x^1, \ldots, x^s)$, $\mathbf{x}'' = (x^{s+1}, \ldots, x^n)$.

Given $\mathbf{x}_0' \in E^s$, let $\mathbf{g}$ be the function from $E^{n-s}$ into $E^n$ such that $\mathbf{g}(\mathbf{x}'') = (\mathbf{x}_0', \mathbf{x}'')$ for every $\mathbf{x}'' \in E^{n-s}$. Such a function $\mathbf{g}$ is called an *injection*. Since $|\mathbf{g}(\mathbf{x}'') - \mathbf{g}(\mathbf{y}'')| = |\mathbf{x}'' - \mathbf{y}''|$, $\mathbf{g}$ is continuous. Let $D \subset E^n$ be open, and let $D(\mathbf{x}_0') = \{\mathbf{x}'' : (\mathbf{x}_0', \mathbf{x}'') \in D\}$. Since $D(\mathbf{x}_0') = \mathbf{g}^{-1}(D)$, by Proposition A–6 $D(\mathbf{x}_0')$ is an open subset of $E^{n-s}$. Let $f$ be continuous on $D$. The function $f(\mathbf{x}_0', \ )$ whose value at each $\mathbf{x}'' \in D(\mathbf{x}_0')$ is $f(\mathbf{x}_0', \mathbf{x}'')$ is the composite of $f$ and $\mathbf{g}|D(\mathbf{x}_0')$. By Proposition A–7, $f(\mathbf{x}_0', \ )$ is continuous. Similarly, given $\mathbf{x}_0''$, the set $\{\mathbf{x}' : (\mathbf{x}', \mathbf{x}_0'') \in D\}$ is open and the function $f( \ , \mathbf{x}_0'')$ is continuous.

**Subspaces.** Let $S_0$ be a topological space and $S$ a nonempty subset of $S_0$. By disregarding the complement $S_0 - S$, $S$ becomes a topological space in the following way. If $p \in S$, then a *neighborhood of $p$ relative to $S$* is a set $S \cap U$ where $U$ is a neighborhood in $S_0$ of $p$. Axioms (1)–(4) are satisfied. For instance, to prove (3) let $V_1$ and $V_2$ be relative neighborhoods of $p$. Then $V_1 = S \cap U_1$, $V_2 = S \cap U_2$, where $U_1$ and $U_2$ are neighborhoods in $S_0$ of $p$. Since $S_0$ is a topological space, there is a neighborhood $U_3$ in $S_0$ of $p$ with $U_3 \subset U_1 \cap U_2$. Then $V_3 = S \cap U_3$ is a relative neighborhood of $p$ and $V_3 \subset V_1 \cap V_2$. This topology is called the *relative topology* induced on $S$ by the topology of $S_0$, and $S$ is a *topological subspace* of $S_0$. In particular, if $S_0 = E^n$ this is the relative topology on $S$ mentioned in Example 2.

**Proposition A–8.** *A set $A$ is open relative to $S$ if and only if $A = S \cap D$, where $D$ is an open subset of $S_0$.*

*Proof.* Let $A = S \cap D$, where $D$ is open in $S_0$. If $p \in A$, then there is a neighborhood $U$ in $S_0$ such that $U \subset D$. Then $V = S \cap U$ is a relative neighborhood of $p$ and $V \subset A$. Hence $A$ is relatively open.

Conversely, let $A$ be relatively open. For each $p \in A$, let $V_p$ be some relative neighborhood of $p$ with $V_p \subset A$. Then $V_p = S \cap U_p$, where $U_p$ is a neighborhood in $S_0$ of $p$. Let $D = \bigcup_{p \in A} U_p$. Then $D$ is open and $A = S \cap D$. ▮

Taking complements we find that *the relatively closed sets are those of the form $S \cap E$ where $E$ is a closed subset of $S_0$.*

If $A \subset S$ and $A$ is an open subset of $S_0$, then $A$ is relatively open (take $D = A$ in Proposition A–8). On the other hand, there are generally many sets which are relatively open but not open.

**Example 8.** Let $S_0 = E^1$, $S = [a, b]$. If $a < x < b$, then the interval $[a, x)$ is open relative to $S$ but is not an open subset of $E^1$. A function $f$ is said to have *right-hand limit* $y_0$ at $a$ if for every $\epsilon > 0$ there exists $\delta > 0$ such that $|f(x) - y_0| < \epsilon$ whenever $a < x < a + \delta$. The idea of left-hand limit at the other endpoint $b$ is defined similarly. A function $f$ is continuous on $[a, b]$ if and only if $f$ is continuous on the open interval $(a, b)$ and

$$f(a) = \lim_{x \to a^+} f(x), \qquad f(b) = \lim_{x \to b^-} f(x),$$

whee thre limits are respectively right- and left-hand.

**Example 9.** Let $S_0 = E^1$, $S$ be the set of rational numbers, $A = S \cap (-\infty, \sqrt{2}) = S \cap (-\infty, \sqrt{2}]$. Then $A$ is both open and closed relative to $S$. However, $A$ is neither an open nor a closed subset of $E^1$.

**Homeomorphisms.** Let $f$ be a univalent function from a topological space $S$ into a topological space $T$. Then $f$ has an inverse $f^{-1}$, whose domain is $f(S)$. For each $q \in f(S)$ its value $f^{-1}(q)$ is the unique $p \in S$ such that $f(p) = q$. If both $f$ and its inverse $f^{-1}$ are continuous functions, then $f$ is a *homeomorphism*. If there is a homeomorphism from $S$ onto $T$, then $S$ and $T$ are *homeomorphic* topological spaces.

In topology, homeomorphic spaces $S$ and $T$ may be regarded as indistinguishable. Every topological property enjoyed by $S$ is also enjoyed by $T$.

## PROBLEMS

1. Show that:
   (a) In Example 3 any real-valued function continuous on $S$ is constant.
   (b) In Example 4 every function with domain $S$ is continuous.
2. Let $S$ be an open subset of $S_0$. Show that the relatively open sets are just those open subsets of $S_0$ contained in $S$.
3. Consider the following nonstandard topology on the plane $E^2$: In this topology the "$\delta$-neighborhood" of $(x_0, y_0)$ is the set $\{(x, y) : x_0 - \delta < x < x_0 + \delta, y = y_0\}$.
   (a) Verify that Axioms (1)–(4) are satisfied.
   (b) Show that if $D \subset E^2$ is open in the usual sense, then $D$ is open in this topology, but not conversely.
   (c) Let $f(x, y) = g(x)h(y)$, where $g$ and $h$ have domain $E^1$ and $g$ is continuous in the usual topology of $E^1$. Show that $f$ is continuous in this topology.
4. Let $S_0$ be a topological space, and let $f$ be continuous on $S_0$. Let $S \subset S_0$ have the relative topology. Show that $f|S$ is continuous on $S$.
5. A *metric space* is a nonempty set $S$ together with a real-valued function $d$ with domain the cartesian product $S \times S$, such that:
   (i) $d(p, q) \geq 0$ for every $p, q \in S$, $d(p, q) = 0$ if and only if $p = q$;
   (ii) $d(p, q) = d(q, p)$ for every $p, q \in S$;
   (iii) $d(p, q) \leq d(p, r) + d(r, q)$ for every $p, q, r \in S$.

   Let the collection $\mathfrak{U}_p$ consist of all sets $\{q : d(p, q) < \delta\}$, where $\delta > 0$.
   (a) Verify Axioms (1)–(4) for a topological space.
   (b) Show that $\{q : d(p, q) < \delta\}$ is open and that $\{q : d(p, q) \leq \delta\}$ is closed.
6. A *normed vector space* is a vector space $\mathcal{V}$ together with a real-valued function $\| \ \|$ with domain $\mathcal{V}$ such that: (a) $\|u\| > 0$ for every $u \in \mathcal{V}$, $u \neq 0$, (b) $\|cu\| = |c| \, \|u\|$ for every $c$ and $u \in \mathcal{V}$, and (c) $\|u + v\| \leq \|u\| + \|v\|$ for every $u, v \in \mathcal{V}$. Let $d(u, v) = \|u - v\|$. Verify the axioms (i), (ii), and (iii) for a metric space in Problem 5. [*Note:* If $\mathcal{V} = E^n$, then it was shown in Section 1–6 that every norm on $E^n$ leads to the same topology. In Example 5 above $\mathfrak{F}$ is a normed vector space. The norm is $\|f\| = \sup\{|f(x)| : x \in [0, 1]\}$. The $L^p$-spaces (Section 5–12) furnish other examples of normed vector spaces.]

## A–7 CONNECTED SPACES

From the intuitive point of view a set should be regarded as connected if it consists of one piece. Thus an interval on the real line $E^1$ is connected, while the set $[0, 1] \cup [2, 3]$ is disconnected. For more complicated sets, intuition is not a reliable guide.

**Definition.** A topological space $S$ is *disconnected* if there exist nonempty open sets $A$ and $B$ such that $S = A \cup B$ and $A \cap B$ is empty. If $S$ is not disconnected, then $S$ is a *connected space*.
A subset $S$ of a topological space $S_0$ is *connected* if $S$ is a connected space in the relative topology.

**Example 1.** Let $S = [0, 1] \cup [2, 3]$. Let $A = [0, 1]$, $B = [2, 3]$. Then $A = S \cap (-1, \frac{3}{2})$, which shows that $A$ is open relative to $S$. Similarly, $B$ is open relative to $S$. Since $S = A \cup B$ and $A \cap B$ is empty, $S$ is disconnected.

**Definition.** A nonempty set $J \subset E^1$ is an *interval* if for every $x, y \in J$, $x < y$, the set $[x, y]$ is contained in $J$ (Fig. A–7).

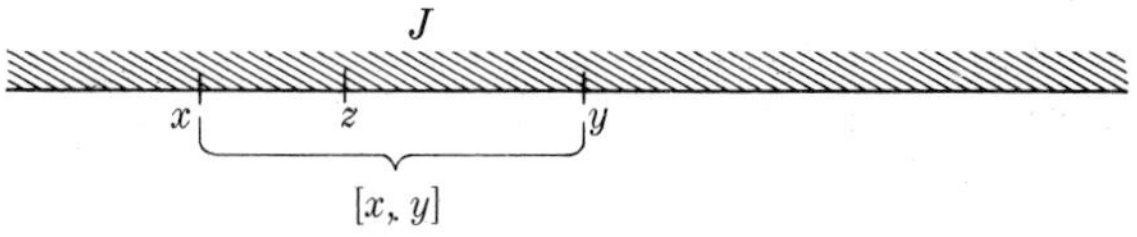


FIGURE A–7

The intervals can be classified into 10 types (Problem 4).

**Proposition A–9.** *A set $S \subset E^1$ is connected if and only if $S$ is an interval.*

*Proof.* If $S$ is not an interval, then there exist $x, y \in S$, $x < y$, and $z \notin S$ such that $x < z < y$. Let $A = S \cap (-\infty, z)$, $B = S \cap (z, \infty)$. Then $A$ and $B$ are nonempty and relatively open, $A \cup B = S$, and $A \cap B$ is empty. Therefore $S$ is disconnected.

Conversely, suppose that some interval $J$ is disconnected. Then $J = A \cup B$ where $A$ and $B$ are not empty and open relative to $J$, and $A \cap B$ is empty. Let $x_1 \in A$ and $x_2 \in B$. The notation $A$, $B$ may be chosen so that $x_1 < x_2$. Since $J$ is an interval, $[x_1, x_2] \subset J$; hence the fact that $A$ is relatively open implies that there exists $\delta_1 > 0$ such that $[x_1, x_1 + \delta_1) \subset A$. Similarly, there exists $\delta_2 > 0$ such that $(x_2 - \delta_2, x_2] \subset B$. Letting $B_1 = \{x \in B : x > x_1\}$ and $y = \inf B_1$, we have $x_1 < y < x_2$. Since $J$ is an interval, $y \in J$. If $y \in A$, then some interval $(y - \delta, y + \delta)$ is contained in $A$ and $y + \delta$ is a lower bound for $B_1$, contrary to the fact that $y$ is the greatest lower bound. Similarly, if $y \in B$, then some interval $(y - \delta, y + \delta)$ is contained in $B_1$, and $y$ is not a lower bound. This is a contradiction. ∎

Let $f$ be a function from a topological space $S$ into a topological space $T$. In the definition of continuity in the last section we may as well assume that $T = f(S)$. For if $V$ is a neighborhood of $f(p_0)$, then $f(U) \subset V$ if and only if $f(U) \subset V \cap f(S)$. The sets $V \cap f(S)$ are just the relative neighborhoods of $f(p_0)$ in the topological subspace $f(S)$.

**Theorem A–4.** *If $S$ is a connected space and $f$ is continuous on $S$, then $f(S)$ is connected.*

*Proof.* Suppose that $f(S)$ is disconnected. Then $f(S) = P \cup Q$ where $P$ and $Q$ are open relative to $f(S)$, nonempty, and $P \cap Q$ is empty. By Proposition A–6, taking $T = f(S)$, the nonempty sets $A = f^{-1}(P)$, $B = f^{-1}(Q)$ are open. Moreover, $S = A \cup B$ and $A \cap B$ is empty. Hence $S$ is disconnected, contrary to hypothesis. ▌

**Corollary.** (*Intermediate value theorem*). *If $S$ is a connected space and $f$ is real-valued and continuous on $S$, then $f(S)$ is an interval.*

*Proof.* By Proposition A–9 every connected subset of $E^1$ is an interval. ▌

***Pathwise connectedness.** Let $p$ and $q$ be points of a topological space $S$. A *path in $S$ from $p$ to $q$* is a continuous function $g$ from $[0, 1]$ into $S$ with $g(0) = p$, $g(1) = q$. If every such pair of points can be joined by a path in $S$, then $S$ is called *pathwise connected.*

**Proposition A–10.** *If $S$ is pathwise connected, then $S$ is connected.*

*Proof.* If $S$ is disconnected, then $S = A \cup B$ as in the definition of disconnected space. Let $p \in A$, $q \in B$, and $g$ be a path in $S$ joining $p$ and $q$. Since $g$ is continuous, $g^{-1}(A)$ and $g^{-1}(B)$ are open relative to $[0, 1]$, their union is $[0, 1]$, and their intersection is empty. This contradicts the fact that $[0, 1]$ is connected. ▌

**Example 2.** Let $S = S_1 \cup S_2$, where

$$S_1 = \{(0, y) : -1 \leq y \leq 1\},$$
$$S_2 = \{(x, \sin 1/x) : x > 0\}.$$

Then it can be shown that $S$ is connected but not pathwise connected.

On the other hand, any *open* connected subset of $E^n$ is pathwise connected. In fact, any two points of $D$ can be connected by a polygonal path (Problem 9).

**PROBLEMS**

1. Show from the definition that the following are disconnected subsets of the plane $E^2$:
   (a) The hyperbola $x^2 - y^2 = 1$.
   (b) Any finite subset of $E^2$ with at least two elements.
   (c) $\{(x, y) : x^2 < y^2\}$.

2. Show that each of the following sets is pathwise connected.
   (a) Any convex set (See Section 1-4).
   (b) The unit circle $x^2 + y^2 = 1$ in $E^2$.
   (c) The unit sphere $x^2 + y^2 + z^2 = 1$ in $E^3$.
3. Show that a space $S$ is disconnected if and only if $S$ has a nonempty proper subset $A$ which is both open and closed. (Proper subset means $A \neq S$.)
4. Show that:
   (a) Each interval of the eight types described in Section A-1 is an interval according to the definition in the present section.
   (b) Every interval is either one of these types, a point, or $E^1$.
5. Let $S$ be as in Example 2. Show that:
   (a) $S$ is a closed set.
   (b) There is no path in $S$ joining (0, 0) and any point of $S_2$.
   (c) $S$ is a connected set.
6. Instead of Axiom IIIa (least upper bound property) about the real numbers, take as an axiom the property that $E^1$ is connected. Prove Axiom IIIa as a theorem. [*Hint:* Let $A = \{$all upper bounds of $S\}$ and $B = A^c$. Show that $B$ is open; and if $S$ has no least upper bound, then $A$ is open.]
7. Let $g_1$ be a path from $p_1$ to $p_2$ and $g_2$ a path from $p_2$ to $p_3$. Let $h(t) = g_1(2t)$ if $0 \leq t \leq \frac{1}{2}$, and $h(t) = g_2(2t - 1)$ if $\frac{1}{2} \leq t \leq 1$. Show that $h$ is a path from $p_1$ to $p_3$.
8. Let $D \subset E^n$ be open. By *polygonal path* in $D$ from $\mathbf{x}$ to $\mathbf{y}$ let us mean a path $\mathbf{g}$ in $D$ from $\mathbf{x}$ to $\mathbf{y}$ with the following property: There exist $t_0, t_1, \ldots, t_m$ such that $0 = t_0 < t_1 < \cdots < t_{m-1} < t_m = 1$ and $\mathbf{g}(t) = \mathbf{g}(t_k) + (t - t_k)\mathbf{v}_k$ if $t_k \leq t \leq t_{k+1}$, where $\mathbf{v}_k = (t_{k+1} - t_k)^{-1}[\mathbf{g}(t_{k+1}) - \mathbf{g}(t_k)]$, $k = 0, 1, \ldots m - 1$.

   Let $\mathbf{g}$ be a polygonal path in $D$ from $\mathbf{x}$ to $\mathbf{y}$, and $U$ be any convex set (Section 1-4) such that $\mathbf{y} \in U$ and $U \subset D$. Using Problem 7, find a polygonal path in $D$ from $\mathbf{x}$ to any point $\mathbf{z} \in U$.
9. Let $D \subset E^n$ be open. Given $\mathbf{x} \in D$, let $A = \{\mathbf{y}:$ there is a polygonal path in $D$ from $\mathbf{x}$ to $\mathbf{y}\}$ and let $B = D - A$. Using Problem 8, show that $A$ and $B$ are open sets and $A$ is not empty. [*Hint:* Any neighborhood is convex.] If $B$ is not empty, then $D$ is disconnected.

## A-8 COMPACT SPACES

Let us begin the discussion of compact spaces by considering subsets of $E^n$.

**Definition.** A point $\mathbf{x}_0$ is an *accumulation point* of a set $A \subset E^n$ if every neighborhood of $\mathbf{x}_0$ contains an infinite number of points of $A$.

For instance every point of the closed interval $[a, b]$ is an accumulation point of the open interval $(a, b)$. The set $\{1, \frac{1}{2}, \frac{1}{3}, \ldots\}$ has the single accumulation point 0. The set of positive integers has no accumulation point.

We recall from Section A-4 that a set $A \subset E^n$ is called bounded if $A$ has finite diameter. It is plausible that if a bounded set has an infinite number of points, then its points must accumulate somewhere. The truth of this is expressed by the following.

**Bolzano-Weierstrass theorem.** *Every bounded infinite subset of $E^n$ has at least one accumulation point.*

*Proof.* Let $A$ be a bounded infinite set and $I_1$ be some closed $n$-cube containing $A$. A closed $n$-cube has the form $\{\mathbf{x} : |x^i - x_0^i| \leq a/2,\ i = 1, \ldots, n\}$, where $\mathbf{x}_0$ is the center and $a$ is the side length. Divide $I_1$ into $m = 2^n$ closed congruent $n$-cubes $I_{11}, \ldots, I_{1m}$ as indicated in Fig. A–8. Since $A$ is an infinite set, $A \cap I_{1k}$ must be infinite for at least one $k = 1, \ldots, m$. Choose some such $k$ and let $I_{1k} = I_2$. In the same way divide $I_2$ into $2^n$ closed congruent $n$-cubes $I_{21}, \ldots, I_{2m}$. As before, $A \cap I_{2k}$ is infinite for at least one $k$. Choose such a $k$ and let $I_{2k} = I_3$. Continuing, we obtain closed $n$-cubes $I_1 \supset I_2 \supset I_3 \supset \cdots$ such that $A \cap I_l$ is infinite for each $l = 1, 2, \ldots$ and diam $I_l \to 0$ as $l \to \infty$. By Theorem A–3, $I_1 \cap I_2 \cap \cdots$ has a single point $\mathbf{x}_0$. If $U$ is any neighborhood of $\mathbf{x}_0$, then $I_l \subset U$ for large enough $l$. Since $A \cap I_l \subset A \cap U$, $A \cap U$ is an infinite set. Therefore $\mathbf{x}_0$ is an accumulation point of $A$. ∎

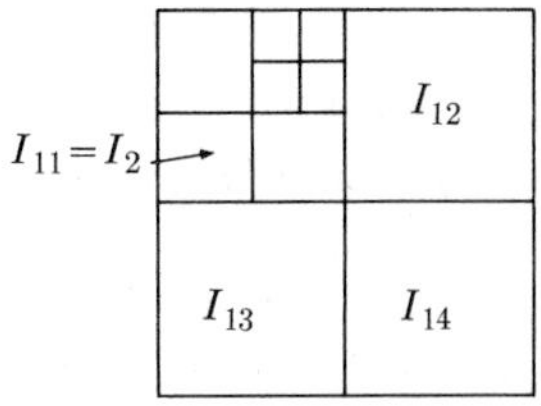


FIGURE A–8

**Definition.** A set $S \subset E^n$ is *compact* if every infinite set $A \subset S$ has at least one accumulation point $\mathbf{x}_0 \in S$.

**Theorem A–5.** *A subset $S$ of $E^n$ is compact if and only if $S$ is bounded and closed.*

*Proof.* Let $S$ be bounded and closed, and let $A$ be any infinite subset of $S$. Since $S$ is bounded, $A$ is bounded. By the Bolzano-Weierstrass theorem $A$ has an accumulation point $\mathbf{x}_0$. If $\mathbf{x}_0 \notin S$, then $\mathbf{x}_0$ is exterior to $S$ since $S$ is closed. Thus $\mathbf{x}_0$ has a neighborhood $U$ which does not intersect $S$. Since $A \cap U$ is not empty, this is impossible. Therefore $\mathbf{x}_0 \in S$, which shows that $S$ is compact.

To prove the converse, suppose that $S$ is unbounded. Then for each $m = 1, 2, \ldots$ there exists $\mathbf{x}_m \in S$ such that $|\mathbf{x}_m| \geq m$. The set $A = \{\mathbf{x}_1, \mathbf{x}_2, \ldots\}$ is infinite and has no accumulation point. Hence $S$ is not compact. If $S$ is not closed, then there exists a point $\mathbf{x}_0 \in \text{fr } S - S$. For $m = 1, 2, \ldots$ there exists $\mathbf{x}_m \in S$ such that $|\mathbf{x}_m - \mathbf{x}_0| < 1/m$. The set $A = \{\mathbf{x}_1, \mathbf{x}_2, \ldots\}$ is infinite and has the single accumulation point $\mathbf{x}_0$. But $\mathbf{x}_0 \notin S$. Hence $S$ is not compact. ∎

Let us next give another description of compactness, in terms of open coverings. Let $S$ be a subset of a topological space $S_0$. A collection $\mathfrak{A}$ of sets is a *covering* of $S$ if every point of $S$ belongs to some set $A \in \mathfrak{A}$, that is, if

$S \subset \bigcup_{A \in \mathfrak{A}} A$. If $\mathfrak{A}' \subset \mathfrak{A}$ and $\mathfrak{A}'$ is also a covering of $S$, then $\mathfrak{A}'$ is called a *subcovering*. If every $A \in \mathfrak{A}$ is open, then $\mathfrak{A}$ is an *open covering* of $S$.

In the following theorem $S_0 = E^n$.

**Heine-Borel theorem.** *If $S$ is a compact subset of $E^n$, then every open covering of $S$ contains a finite subcovering.*

*Proof.* Let $\mathfrak{A}$ be an open covering of $S$. Suppose that no finite collection $\mathfrak{A}' \subset \mathfrak{A}$ covers $S$. Let us define a sequence of compact sets $S_1 \supset S_2 \supset \cdots$ such that $\operatorname{diam} S_k \to 0$ as $k \to \infty$ and no finite subcollection of $\mathfrak{A}$ covers any $S_k$. Let $S_1 = S$. Since $S_1$ is bounded, some closed $n$-cube $I_1$ contains $S_1$. Divide $I_1$ into $n$-cubes $I_{11}, \ldots, I_{1m}$ as in the proof of the Bolzano-Weierstrass theorem, and let $S_{1k} = S_1 \cap I_{1k}$. Since $S_1$ and $I_{1k}$ are closed, so is $S_{1k}$. If for every $k = 1, \ldots, m$ some finite collection $\mathfrak{A}_k \subset \mathfrak{A}$ covered $S_{1k}$, then $\mathfrak{A}_1 \cup \cdots \cup \mathfrak{A}_m$ would be a finite subcovering of $S$, contrary to assumption. Choose some $k$ for which no finite subcollection of $\mathfrak{A}$ covers $S_{1k}$, and let $S_{1k} = S_2$. Repeating this process, we obtain the desired sequence of compact sets.

By Theorem A–3, $S_1 \cap S_2 \cap \cdots$ contains a single point $\mathbf{x}_0$. Since $\mathfrak{A}$ covers $S$, $\mathbf{x}_0$ belongs to some set $A \in \mathfrak{A}$; and since $\mathfrak{A}$ is an open covering, $A$ is an open set. Therefore there is a neighborhood $U$ of $\mathbf{x}_0$ such that $U \subset A$. Since $\operatorname{diam} S_k \to 0$ as $k \to \infty$, $S_k \subset U$ for large enough $k$. For such $k$, $S_k$ is covered by the subcollection of $\mathfrak{A}$ consisting of the single set $A$. Since by construction no finite subcollection of $\mathfrak{A}$ covers any $S_k$, this is a contradiction. ▮

**Example 1.** Let $D$ be open and $S$ be a compact subset of $D$. Each $\mathbf{x} \in S$ has a neighborhood $U_{\mathbf{x}}$ such that $U_{\mathbf{x}} \subset D$. Let $\mathfrak{A}$ be the collection of these neighborhoods $U_{\mathbf{x}}$. Then there is a finite subset $\{\mathbf{x}_1, \ldots, \mathbf{x}_p\}$ of $S$ such that $S \subset U_{\mathbf{x}_1} \cup \cdots \cup U_{\mathbf{x}_p} \subset D$.

The *converse* to the Heine-Borel theorem is true. To prove it, suppose that $S$ is not compact. Then either $S$ is unbounded or $S$ is not closed. If $S$ is unbounded, let $A_m$ be the neighborhood of $\mathbf{0}$ of radius $m = 1, 2, \ldots$ Then $\{A_1, A_2, \ldots\}$ is an open covering of $S$ which has no finite subcovering. If $S$ is not closed, let $\mathbf{x}_0 \in \operatorname{fr} S - S$ and $A_m = \{\mathbf{x} : |\mathbf{x} - \mathbf{x}_0| > 1/m\}$. Then $\{A_1, A_2, \ldots\}$ is an open covering of $S$ with no finite subcovering. This proves the converse.

The definition of compactness in terms of accumulation points was the first historically. The characterization in terms of open coverings has less intuitive appeal but is more useful for proving theorems. Moreover, it is the appropriate notion of compactness in general topological spaces.

**Definition.** A subset $S$ of a topological space $S_0$ is *compact* if every open covering of $S$ contains a finite subcovering.

From the Heine-Borel theorem and its converse, if $S_0 = E^n$ this definition is equivalent to the previous one.

If $S_0$, considered as a subset of itself, is compact, then $S_0$ is called a *compact topological space.*

**Theorem A–6.** *If $S$ is a compact space and $f$ is continuous on $S$, then $f(S)$ is compact.*

*Proof.* Let $\mathcal{B}$ be any open covering of $f(S)$. Since $f$ is continuous, $f^{-1}(B)$ is open for every $B \in \mathcal{B}$. The collection of sets $f^{-1}(B)$ is an open covering of $S$. Since $S$ is compact, a finite subcollection $\{f^{-1}(B_1), \ldots, f^{-1}(B_m)\}$ covers $S$. Then $\{B_1, \ldots, B_m\}$ is a finite subcollection of $\mathcal{B}$ which covers $f(S)$. Hence $f(S)$ is compact. ▮

**Example 2.** Let $A \subset E^n$ be compact. Using the notation of Example 7, p. 303, the set $A(\mathbf{x}_0')$ is closed since its complement is open. Since $A$ is bounded, $A(\mathbf{x}_0')$ is bounded. Therefore $A(\mathbf{x}_0')$ is compact. Let $\mathbf{p}(\mathbf{x}) = \mathbf{x}'$. The transformation $\mathbf{p}$ is called a *projection* of $E^n$ onto $E^s$. Since $\mathbf{p}$ is continuous, the set $\mathbf{p}(A) = \{\mathbf{x}' : (\mathbf{x}', \mathbf{x}'') \in A$ for some $\mathbf{x}''\}$ is compact.

An important particular case of Theorem A–6 is obtained by taking $T \subset E^1$ as follows.

**Corollary.** *If $S$ is a compact space and $f$ is real valued and continuous on $S$, then $f$ has a maximum and a minimum value on $S$.*

*Proof.* Any compact subset of $E^1$ has a least and a greatest element (Problem 2). ▮

As an application of the corollary let us prove the following.

**Mean value theorem.** *Let $f$ be real valued and continuous on a closed interval $[a, b]$, and let the derivative $f'(x)$ exist for every $x \in (a, b)$. Then there exists $c \in (a, b)$ such that*

$$f(b) - f(a) = f'(c)(b - a).$$

*Proof.* Let $m = [f(b) - f(a)]/(b - a)$ and let $F(x) = f(b) - f(x) - m(b - x)$. Then $F$ is continuous on $[a, b]$ and $F'(x) = -f'(x) + m$ for $x \in (a, b)$. Since $[a, b]$ is compact, $F$ has a maximum and a minimum value on $[a, b]$. If the maximum value is positive, then since $F(a) = F(b) = 0$, the maximum must occur at some $x_1 \in (a, b)$. By elementary calculus $F'(x_1) = 0$ and we may take $c = x_1$. Similarly, if the minimum value is negative we may take $c = x_2$, where $F(x_2)$ is the minimum value. If neither of these possibilities occurs, then $F(x) = 0$ on $[a, b]$ and $c$ is arbitrary. ▮

The mean value theorem has the following generalization.

**Taylor's theorem with remainder.** *Let $f$ together with its derivatives $f', f'', \ldots, f^{(q-1)}$ be continuous on a closed interval $[a, b]$ and let the $q$th-order* *derivative* $f^{(q)}(x)$ *exist for every* $x \in (a, b)$. *Then there exists* $c \in (a, b)$ *such that*

$$f(b) - f(a) = f'(a)(b - a) + \frac{f''(a)}{2!}(b - a)^2 + \cdots + \frac{f^{(q-1)}(a)}{(q-1)!}(b - a)^{q-1} + R_q,$$

*where*

$$R_q = \frac{f^{(q)}(c)}{q!}(b - a)^q.$$

*Proof.* Let

$$G(x) = f(b) - f(x) - f'(x)(b - x) - \frac{f''(x)}{2!}(b - x)^2 \ldots - \frac{f^{(q-1}(x)}{(q-1)!}(b - x)^{q-1} - \frac{K}{q!}(b - x)^q,$$

where the number $K$ is so chosen that $G(a) = 0$. Then $G(b) = 0$ and, using the product rule,

$$G'(x) = \frac{(b - x)^{q-1}}{(q-1)!}[-f^{(q)}(x) + K].$$

Repeating the reasoning in the proof of the mean value theorem, there exists $c \in (a, b)$ such that $G'(c) = 0$. Then $f^{(q)}(c) = K$. ∎

The number $R_q$ is called the *remainder*. If $f$ has derivatives of every order $q$ and if $R_q \to 0$ as $q \to \infty$, then

$$f(b) = \sum_{q=0}^{\infty} \frac{f^{(q)}(a)}{q!}(b - a)^q.$$

This is called *Taylor's series* about $a$. We have set $f^{(0)} = f$, $0! = 1$. A *sufficient* condition that $f(b)$ be given by the Taylor series about $a$ is that there be a positive number $M$ such that $|f^{(q)}(x)| \leq M^q$ for every $x \in [a, b]$ and $q = 1, 2, \ldots$ For if $C = M(b - a)$, then

$$|R_q| \leq \frac{C^q}{q!},$$

which tends to 0 as $q \to \infty$.

We assumed that $a < b$, but the case $a > b$ is similar.

## PROBLEMS

1. A point $\mathbf{x}$ is an *isolated* point of $A$ if there is a neighborhood $U$ of $\mathbf{x}$ such that $A \cap U = \{\mathbf{x}\}$. Show that every point of cl $A$ is either an isolated point of $A$ or an accumulation point of $A$.
2. Let $S$ be a compact subset of $E^1$. Show that inf $S \in S$ and sup $S \in S$.

3. Show that $S$ is a compact subset of $S_0$ if and only if $S$ is a compact topological space in the relative topology. [*Hint:* If $\mathfrak{A}$ is an open covering of $S$, then the sets $S \cap A$, $A \in \mathfrak{A}$, form a covering by relatively open sets. Conversely, every covering by relatively open sets can be obtained from some such $\mathfrak{A}$.]
4. Let $A_1, A_2, \ldots$ be nonempty compact subsets of $E^n$ such that $A_1 \supset A_2 \supset \cdots$ Show that $\bigcap_{m=1}^{\infty} A_m$ is not empty. [*Hint:* For each $m$ choose $\mathbf{x}_m \in A_m$. Apply the Bolzano-Weierstrass theorem to the set $A = \{\mathbf{x}_1, \mathbf{x}_2, \ldots\}$.]
5. Let $A$ be a nonempty subset of $E^n$, and let $f(\mathbf{x}) = \inf \{|\mathbf{x} - \mathbf{y}| : \mathbf{y} \in A\}$. This is the *distance* from $\mathbf{x}$ to $A$. Show that:
   (a) $f(\mathbf{x}) = 0$ if and only if $\mathbf{x} \in \text{cl } A$.
   (b) $|f(\mathbf{x}_1) - f(\mathbf{x}_2)| \leq |\mathbf{x}_1 - \mathbf{x}_2|$ for every $\mathbf{x}_1, \mathbf{x}_2 \in E^n$; and consequently $f$ is a continuous function on $E^n$. [*Hint:* Triangle inequality.]
   (c) If $A$ is closed and $\mathbf{x} \notin A$, then there is a point $\mathbf{y} \in A$ nearest $\mathbf{x}$. [*Hint:* Let $g(\mathbf{y}) = |\mathbf{x} - \mathbf{y}|$. Apply the corollary to Theorem A–6 to show that $g$ has a minimum on $S = A \cap K_r$, where $K_r = \{\mathbf{y} : |\mathbf{x} - \mathbf{y}| \leq r\}$ and $r > f(\mathbf{x})$.]
6. *Uniform continuity.* A transformation $\mathbf{f}$ is *uniformly continuous* on $S \subset E^n$ if given $\epsilon > 0$ there exists $\delta > 0$ (depending only on $\epsilon$) such that $|\mathbf{f}(\mathbf{x}) - \mathbf{f}(\mathbf{y})| < \epsilon$ for every $\mathbf{x}, \mathbf{y} \in S$ with $|\mathbf{x} - \mathbf{y}| < \delta$. Show that if $S$ is compact then every $\mathbf{f}$ continuous on $S$ is uniformly continuous on $S$. [*Hint:* If not, then there exists $\epsilon > 0$ and for $m = 1, 2, \ldots \mathbf{x}_m, \mathbf{y}_m \in S$ such that $|\mathbf{f}(\mathbf{x}_m) - \mathbf{f}(\mathbf{y}_m)| \geq \epsilon$ and $|\mathbf{x}_m - \mathbf{y}_m| \leq 1/m$. Let $\mathbf{x}_0$ be an accumulation point of $\{\mathbf{x}_1, \mathbf{x}_2, \ldots\}$. Show that the continuity of $\mathbf{f}$ at $\mathbf{x}_0$ is contradicted.]
7. Let $A' \subset E^s$ and $A'' \subset E^{n-s}$ be compact. Show that $A' \times A''$ is compact. [*Note:* This is a very special case of Tykhonov's theorem, which states that the cartesian product of compact topological spaces is compact. See [16], p. 175.]
8. Let $S_0$ be a topological space.
   (a) Show that if $S_0$ is compact, then any closed set $B \subset S_0$ is compact. [*Hint:* Let $\mathfrak{A}$ be any open covering of $B$. To the collection $\mathfrak{A}$ add the open set $S_0 - B$.]
   (b) Suppose that $S_0$ has the following property: (H). For every $p, q \in S$, there exist a neighborhood $U$ of $p$ and a neighborhood $V$ of $q$ such that $U \cap V$ is empty. Show that any compact set $S \subset S_0$ is closed. [*Note:* A topological space with property (H) is called a *Hausdorff* space.]
   (c) Show that any metric space (p. 305) is a Hausdorff space.
   (d) Let $f$ be continuous and univalent from a compact space $S$ onto a Hausdorff space $T$. Show that $f^{-1}$ is continuous from $T$ onto $S$. [*Hint:* Let $B \subset S$ be closed. Show that $(f^{-1})^{-1}(B)$ is closed and use Proposition A–6.]

## A–9 REVIEW OF RIEMANN INTEGRATION

Let $f$ be real valued and continuous on an interval $[a, b]$. Then $f$ has an integral over $[a, b]$, denoted by $\int_a^b f(t)\,dt$. According to Riemann's definition of the integral, it is the limit of sums:

$$\int_a^b f(t)\,dt = \lim_{\mu \to 0} \sum_{j=1}^{m} f(s_j)(t_j - t_{j-1})$$

where

$$a = t_0 < t_1 < \cdots < t_{m-1} < t_m = b, \qquad t_{j-1} \le s_j \le t_j,$$

and

$$\mu = \max \{t_1 - t_0, t_2 - t_1, \ldots, t_m - t_{m-1}\}.$$

More generally, the Riemann integral exists for any bounded function with a finite number of discontinuities. It agrees with the integral in Lebesgue's sense, which is defined in Chapter 5 for a much wider class of functions.

**Fundamental theorem of calculus.** *Let $f$ be continuous on $[a, b]$ and let*

$$F(t) = \int_a^t f(s)\, ds, \qquad a \le t \le b.$$

*Then $F'(t) = f(t)$ for every $t \in [a, b]$.*

*Proof.* By elementary properties of the integral, if $h > 0$ and $t + h \le b$, then

$$\frac{F(t+h) - F(t)}{h} = \frac{1}{h} \int_t^{t+h} f(s)\, ds.$$

Since $f$ is continuous, given $\epsilon > 0$ there exists $\delta > 0$ such that $f(t) - \epsilon < f(s) < f(t) + \epsilon$ whenever $|s - t| < \delta$. Then if $h < \delta$,

$$h[f(t) - \epsilon] < \int_t^{t+h} f(s)\, ds < h[f(t) + \epsilon],$$

$$f(t) - \epsilon < \frac{F(t+h) - F(t)}{h} < f(t) + \epsilon.$$

Hence

$$f(t) = \lim_{h \to 0^+} \frac{F(t+h) - F(t)}{h}.$$

The right-hand side is the right-hand derivative of $F$ at $t$. Similarly, $f(t)$ equals the left-hand derivative of $f$ at $t$. ▮

In the theorem, $F'(a)$ means the right-hand derivative and $F'(b)$ means the left-hand derivative.

The fundamental theorem says that $F$ is an antiderivative of $f$. If $G$ is any antiderivative of $f$, then $G'(t) - F'(t) = 0$ for every $t \in [a, b]$, and by the mean value theorem $G(t) - F(t)$ is constant on $[a, b]$. Thus $G(t) - F(t) = G(a) - F(a) = G(a)$, and upon setting $t = b$ we obtain

$$G(b) - G(a) = \int_a^b f(s)\, ds.$$

**Change of variables in integrals.** Let $\phi$ be any real-valued function possessing a continuous derivative on some closed interval $[\alpha, \beta]$ such that

$$\phi'(\tau) \geq 0 \quad \text{for every } \tau \in [\alpha, \beta], \quad \phi(\alpha) = a, \quad \phi(\beta) = b.$$

Then $a \leq \phi(\tau) \leq b$ for every $\tau \in [\alpha, \beta]$.

If $U = F \circ \phi$, then

$$U'(\tau) = F'[\phi(\tau)]\phi'(\tau) = f[\phi(\tau)]\phi'(\tau)$$

for every $\tau \in [\alpha, \beta]$. Since

$$F(a) = U(\alpha), \qquad F(b) = U(\beta),$$

$$\int_a^b f(t)\, dt = \int_\alpha^\beta f[\phi(\tau)]\phi'(\tau)\, d\tau.$$

This is the formula for change of variables in integrals. If $\phi'(\tau) \leq 0$ for every $\tau \in [\alpha, \beta]$, then $\phi(\alpha) \geq \phi(\beta)$. The same formula holds if we agree that

$$\int_a^b = -\int_b^a.$$

## A–10 MONOTONE FUNCTIONS

Let $f$ be real valued with domain $S \subset E^1$.

**Definition.** If for every $x, y \in S$ such that $x < y$,

| | |
|---|---|
| $f(x) < f(y)$ | then $f$ is *increasing*. |
| $f(x) \leq f(y)$ | then $f$ is *nondecreasing*. |
| $f(x) > f(y)$ | then $f$ is *decreasing*. |
| $f(x) \geq f(y)$ | then $f$ is *nonincreasing*. |

If $f$ is either an increasing function or a decreasing function, then $f$ is called *strictly monotone*. If $f$ is either nondecreasing or nonincreasing, then $f$ is *monotone*. If the restriction of $f$ to $A$ is monotone, then $f$ is *monotone on* $A$.

A function $f$ is univalent if $f(x) \neq f(y)$ whenever $x \neq y$. Clearly, any strictly monotone function is univalent. If $S$ is an interval, then conversely any continuous univalent function must be strictly monotone. This can be proved from the intermediate value theorem.

Let $A$ be an interval and assume that the derivative $f'(x)$ exists for every $x \in A$. It is proved in elementary calculus that:

(a) *$f$ is nondecreasing on $A$ if and only if $f'(x) \geq 0$ for every $x \in A$.*

(b) *If $f'(x) > 0$ except at a finite number of points of $A$, then $f$ is increasing on $A$.*

If $f$ is increasing, then $f$ is univalent and consequently has an inverse $f^{-1}$. The derivative of the inverse is given by

$$f^{-1'}(t) = 1/f'(x), \qquad (*)$$

if $t = f(x)$ and $f'(x) \neq 0$. For proofs of these facts see, for instance [8].

Among the examples of strictly monotone functions from calculus are the exponential function exp, whose inverse is log. The restriction to $[-\pi/2\ \pi/2]$ of the function sin is strictly monotone. Its inverse is denoted by $\sin^{-1}$.

**Limits at $+\infty$.** We say that $f(x) \to y_0$ as $x \to +\infty$ if for every $\epsilon > 0$ there exists $b$ such that $|f(x) - y_0| < \epsilon$ for every $x > b$. By the same proof as for Theorem A–1, if $f$ is monotone and bounded on a semi-infinite interval $[a, \infty)$ then $f$ has a limit as $x \to +\infty$. Similarly, if $f$ is monotone and bounded on $(-\infty, a]$, then $f$ has a limit as $x \to -\infty$.

## PROBLEMS

1. Let us say that $f(x) \to +\infty$ as $x \to +\infty$ if for every $C > 0$ there exists $b$ such that $f(x) > C$ for every $x > b$. Show that if $f$ is nondecreasing and unbounded on $[a, \infty)$, then $f(x) \to +\infty$ as $x \to +\infty$.
2. (a) Give a precise definition, similar to that in Problem 1, for "$x_m \to +\infty$ as $m \to \infty$."

   (b) Let $f$ have domain $[a, \infty)$. Show that $f(x) \to y_0$ as $x \to +\infty$ if and only if $f(x_m) \to y_0$ for every nondecreasing sequence $[x_m]$ such that $x_m \geq a$ for $m = 1, 2, \ldots$ and $x_m \to +\infty$ as $m \to \infty$.

# Historical Notes

*Chapter 1.* The ideas of space of $n$-tuples and $n$-dimensional geometry go back at least to the middle of the nineteenth century. Many of the early contributions to the theory of convex sets were made by H. Minkowski around 1900. In particular, he defined supporting hyperplanes and gave one of the first proofs of Theorem 1. Convex functions were introduced by J. Jensen (1906). Further historical background about convexity may be found in *Inequalities,* by G. H. Hardy, J. E. Littlewood, and G. Polya, Cambridge Univ. Press, 1934, and in *Theorie der Konvexen Körper,* by T. Bonnesen and W. Fenchel, Springer, Berlin, 1934.

*Chapters 2, 3, 4.* The formal rules of differential calculus for functions of several variables were practically all known by the early nineteenth century. Developments of the nineteenth century showed clearly the necessity in calculus of admitting a quite general notion of function. It is not enough to consider merely that functions "define analytically" [for example, the elementary functions and those obtained implicitly from elementary functions by solving equations of the type $F(x, y) = 0$]. Precise statements of the rules of several variable calculus and sound proofs of them came considerably later.

The definition of differentiable function was first given by W. H. Young (1908) and by M. Fréchet (1911). Afterward Fréchet developed the idea of differential of a function $f$ from a normed vector space $\mathcal{V}$ into a normed vector space $\mathcal{W}$. The differential (often called today the Fréchet differential) of $f$ assigns at each $p \in \mathcal{V}$ a linear function from $\mathcal{V}$ into $\mathcal{W}$. In Chapter 4 we have taken $\mathcal{V}$ and $\mathcal{W}$ to be euclidean vector spaces, and in Chapter 2 we took $\mathcal{W} = E^1$. Some economy of thought is gained by developing differential calculus from the start for general $\mathcal{V}$ and $\mathcal{W}$; this is done, for instance, in [6].

The determinant bearing his name was introduced by C. Jacobi in 1841. However, for a long time afterward the inverse and implicit function theorems were stated in an imprecise way, which often led those applying them to overlook the local character of these theorems. The false result that a transformation with nonzero Jacobian is globally one-to-one has been too often quoted by mathematicians, both pure and applied.

*Chapter 5.* In an article on representation of functions by trigonometric series (1854), B. Riemann defined the integral of a function $f$ over an interval $[a, b]$ as a limit of sums. Upper and lower Riemann integrals were introduced by J. Darboux (1875). The theory of finitely additive measure, usually called today Jordan content (or Jordan measure), was discovered around 1890 by G. Peano and by C. Jordan. The crucial importance of requiring that measure be countably additive was realized by E. Borel (1898). Soon afterward (1902), H. Lebesgue's thesis appeared, which decisively changed the course of integration theory. The $L^p$-spaces were introduced by F. Riesz (1910), who was one of the pioneers in the development of functional analysis (this includes the study of infinite-dimensional normed vector spaces).

For a more detailed historical account of integration theory, see N. Bourbaki, *Éléments d'Histoire des Mathématiques*, Hermann, Paris, 1960.

*Chapters 6, 7.* The algebra of multivectors (exterior algebra) was invented by H. Grassmann (1862). For many years his work was not properly appreciated. Exterior differential forms were introduced by H. Poincaré and by E. Cartan (about 1900). Poincaré used differential forms in his theory of integral invariants in mechanics, while Cartan first applied them to Pfaffian systems of differential equations. Since that time, exterior differential forms have found many uses in differential geometry, topology, and mathematical physics. See, for instance, [9].

The adjoint operation $*$ for differential forms on a riemannian manifold is due to W. Hodge (see his book, *The Theory and Application of Harmonic Integrals*, Cambridge Univ. Press, 1941). As we have defined it, $*\boldsymbol{\alpha}$ may differ in sign from Hodge's definition.

For further historical information about exterior algebra and calculus see the Note Historique at the end of reference [4], or pp. 78–91 of *Éléments d'Histoire des Mathématiques* cited above.

The classical formulas 7–12, 7–11b to which the divergence theorem reduce when $n = 2, 3$, were employed in the theory of potential by G. Green (1828) and C. Gauss (1839). Despite the name Green's theorem when $n = 2$, this formula actually appeared earlier in the works of Gauss and Lagrange.

Some authors call "converse of Poincaré's lemma" what we have called (according to rather common practice) Poincaré's lemma. The result in question was actually first proved by V. Volterra. See [17, p. 98].

# References


1. T. M. APOSTOL, *Mathematical Analysis.* Reading, Mass.: Addison-Wesley (1957).
2. G. BIRKHOFF and S. MACLANE, *A Survey of Modern Algebra.* New York: Macmillan (1953).
3. M. BÔCHER, *Introduction to Higher Algebra.* New York: Macmillan (1929).
4. N. BOURBAKI, *Éléments de Mathématique, Livre II Algèbre, Chapitre 3, Algèbre Multilinéaire, Actualités Scientifiques et Industrielles,* No. 1044. Hermann, Paris (1958).
5. E. A. CODDINGTON and N. LEVINSON, *Theory of Ordinary Differential Equations.* New York: McGraw-Hill (1955).
6. J. DIEUDONNE, *Foundations of Modern Analysis.* New York: Academic Press (1960).
7. H. G. EGGLESTON, *Convexity.* New York: Cambridge University Press (1958).
8. H. FEDERER and B. JONSSON, *Analytic Geometry and Calculus.* New York: Ronald (1961).
9. H. FLANDERS, *Differential Forms with Applications to the Physical Sciences.* New York: Academic Press (1963).
10. D. GALE, *The Theory of Linear Economic Models.* New York: McGraw-Hill (1960).
11. P. R. HALMOS, *Naïve Set Theory.* Princeton: D. Van Nostrand (1960).
12. K. HOFFMAN and R. KUNZE, *Linear Algebra.* Englewood Cliffs, N. J.: Prentice-Hall (1961).
13. S. KARLIN, *Mathematical Methods and Theory in Games, Programming, and Economics.* Reading, Mass.: Addison-Wesley (1959).
14. O. D. KELLOGG, *Foundations of Potential Theory.* Berlin: Springer (1929).
15. E. J. MCSHANE and T. A. BOTTS, *Real Analysis.* Princeton: D. Van Nostrand (1959).
16. B. MENDELSON, *Introduction to Topology.* Boston: Allyn and Bacon (1962).
17. G. DE RHAM, *Variétés Différentiables, Actualités Scientifiques et Industrielles,* No. 1222, Hermann, Paris (1955).
18. F. M. STEWART, *Introduction to Linear Algebra.* Princeton: D. Van Nostrand (1963).

19. A. Taylor, *Introduction to Functional Analysis.* New York: Wiley (1958).
20. E. C. Titchmarsh, *The Theory of Functions.* London: Oxford University Press (1939).
21. H. Whitney, *Geometric Integration Theory.* Princeton: Princeton University Press (1957).
22. T. J. Willmore, *An Introduction to Differential Geometry.* London: Oxford University Press (1959).

# Answers to Problems

# ANSWERS TO PROBLEMS

**Section 1–1**

1. $4\mathbf{e}_1 - 2\mathbf{e}_2 + \mathbf{e}_3 + 3\mathbf{e}_4, \quad -2\mathbf{e}_1 - \mathbf{e}_3 + \mathbf{e}_4, \quad \sqrt{30}, \quad \sqrt{6}, \quad \sqrt{6}, \quad \sqrt{12}, \quad 6$

7. $\mathbf{v}_4 = \pm(\sqrt{2}/10)(4\mathbf{e}_1 + 3\mathbf{e}_2 - 3\mathbf{e}_3 + 4\mathbf{e}_4)$

**Section 1–3**

1. $\{\mathbf{x} : x^1 + x^2 + 4x^3 = 1\}$

2. (a) $\{\mathbf{x} : 3x^1 - 3x^2 - 3x^3 - x^4 = 0\}$ (b) $t = \frac{1}{7}$

**Section 1–4**

5. $t = \frac{5}{8}; \quad t^0 = \frac{1}{2}, \quad t^1 = \frac{1}{4}, \quad t^2 = \frac{1}{4}$

9. (b) The barycenter is at the intersection of the line segments which join the vertices with the barycenters of the opposite $(r - 1)$–dimensional faces.

**Section 1–5**

1. (a) Concave on $E^1$ (b) Convex on $E^1$
   (c) Concave on $(-\infty, -1]$ and on $[0, 1)$, convex on $(-1, 0]$ and on $(1, \infty)$
   (d) Concave on $(-\infty, -1]$ and on $[1, \infty)$, convex on $[-1, 1]$

2. (b) If $f(x) = a_0x^4 + a_1x^3 + a_2x^2 + a_3x + a_4$, then $a_0 > 0$, $24a_0a_2 \geq 9a_1^2$.

**Section 1–6**

1. (b) $n$-cubes

2. (a) $\|(x, y)\| = [x^2 + xy + 4y^2]^{1/2}$ (b) 2

**Section 2–1**

1. (a) $f_1(x, y) = 1 + \log(xy), \quad f_2(x, y) = x/y$
   (b) $f_1(x, y, z) = 6x(x^2 + 2y^2 + z)^2, \quad f_2(x, y, z) = 12y(x^2 + 2y^2 + z)^2,$
   $f_3(x, y, z) = 3(x^2 + 2y^2 + z)^2$
   (c) $f_i(\mathbf{x}) = 2x^i$

2. The derivative in direction $(\cos\theta, \sin\theta)$ is $-2(\cos\theta + \sin\theta)$.

5. The derivative is 0 in those directions for which $v^1 + v^2 + v^3 = 0$. There is no derivative in other directions.

**Section 2–2**

1. It has the equation $4x + 5y + z + 4 = 0$.

2. (a) $\sqrt{5}$ (b) $1/\sqrt{2e}$ (c) 0

3. (a) $[2x(x^2 + 2y + 1)^{-1} + \cos(x^2)]\mathbf{e}^1 + 2(x^2 + 2y + 1)^{-1}\mathbf{e}^2$
   (b) 0.09

4. (a) $\mathbf{x}_0$ (b) $|\mathbf{x}|^{-1}\mathbf{x}$ (c) $2(\mathbf{x}_0 \cdot \mathbf{x})\mathbf{x}_0$
5. (b) $\{(x, y) : x = y^2, x \neq 0\}$, $\{(x, y) : x = -y^2, x \neq 0\}$
   (c) The union of the sets in 5(b) and the $x$-axis, with (0, 0) excluded since $f$ is not differentiable there
   (d) $\{(x, y) : x = y^2(c^{-1} \pm \sqrt{c^{-2} - 1}), x \neq 0\}$ if $|c| \leq 1$, $c \neq 0$; the $x$- and $y$-axes if $c = 0$

**Section 2–3**

1. $xyz = -z + (y + 1)z - (x - 1)z + (x - 1)(y + 1)z$
6. (c) $f_{12}(0, 0) = -1$, $f_{21}(0, 0) = 1$
7. $\binom{n + q - 1}{q}$; $\binom{q - 1}{n - 1}$ if $n \leq q$, 0 if $n > q$

**Section 2–4**

1. (a) Neither (b) Concave, not strictly
   (c) Convex if $p \leq 0$ or $p \geq 1$. Concave if $0 \leq p \leq 1$. Not strictly
   (d) Strictly convex
   (e) Neither. However, $f$ is strictly convex on each half of $\{(x, y) : 2xy < -1\}$.
3. (a) $a = 1$ (b) $a^2$ satisfies the equation $\cot a^2 = 2a^2$, $a^2 < \pi/2$.

**Section 2–5**

1. (a) Maximum at $\frac{1}{2}\mathbf{e}_1$ (b) Saddle point at $-\mathbf{e}_1 + 2\mathbf{e}_2$
   (c) Maximum at each point where $xy = \pi/2 + 2m\pi$; minimum at each point where $xy = -\pi/2 + 2m\pi$, $m$ any integer. Saddle point at $\mathbf{0}$
   (d) Saddle points at $\mathbf{0}$ and at $\mathbf{e}_1$
2. (a) Maximum at $-\mathbf{e}_1 + \mathbf{e}_2$, saddle point at $\frac{1}{3}(-\mathbf{e}_1 + \mathbf{e}_2)$
   (b) Saddle points at $-\mathbf{e}_2$ and at $\mathbf{e}_1 + \mathbf{e}_2$
   (c) Saddle points at $m\pi\mathbf{e}_1$, $m$ any integer
5. $\mathbf{x} = (1/m)(\mathbf{x}_1 + \cdots + \mathbf{x}_m)$. The minimum value is
$$\frac{1}{m^2} \sum_{j=1}^{m} \left| \sum_{k=1}^{m} (\mathbf{x}_j - \mathbf{x}_k) \right|^2.$$
6. (a) $\frac{1}{4}$, 0 (b) $\sin \frac{1}{2}$, $-\sin \frac{1}{2}$

**Section 2–6**

2. $M_2 = N_1$, $N_3 = O_2$, $O_1 = M_3$
3. (a) $f(x, y) = \frac{1}{2}x^2y + c$ (b) Not exact (c) Not exact
   (d) $f(x, y) = x/y - y/x + \phi(x, y)$, where $\phi$ is constant on each of the four quadrants into which the coordinate axes divide $E^2$.

**Section 3–1**

1. $y = 2(x - \sqrt{2})$
2. $y - 1 = \frac{1}{2}(x - 1)$, $z - 1 = \frac{1}{3}(x - 1)$
3. $\sqrt{2}(-\mathbf{e}_1 + \mathbf{e}_2)$

**Section 3–2**

1. (a) Simple closed curve (b) Neither (c) Simple arc
2. (b) $\frac{2}{27}[(4+9b)^{3/2}-8]$
3. $\mathbf{G}(s) = \mathbf{g}[s/\sqrt{2}], \quad 0 \leq s \leq 2\sqrt{2}\pi$
4. $-\mathbf{e}_1 - 2\mathbf{e}_2$, $\mathbf{e}_1 - 2\mathbf{e}_2$, and any scalar multiples of these tangent vectors
5. (b) No, since $\mathbf{g}'(0) = \mathbf{0}$.

**Section 3–3**

1. (a) $\frac{1}{2}ac$ (b) $\pi ab$
2. (a) $\frac{11}{2}$ (c) $2, \frac{11}{6}$ (d) $-\frac{5}{6}$
5. $f(x, y, z) = \frac{1}{2}\phi(\rho^2)$, where $\phi(u) = \int_0^u \psi(v)\,dv$
7. $2\sqrt{6}$ 8. (a) $\pi\mathbf{e}_3$ (b) $\frac{2}{3}\sqrt{2}\pi^3 + 2\sqrt{2}\pi$

**Section 4–1**

1. (a) $[-1, \infty)$
   (b) $\{\mathbf{t} : |\mathbf{t}| \geq 1 + (c+1)^{1/2}\}$; if $c > 0$,
   $\{\mathbf{t} : |\,|\mathbf{t}| - 1| \geq (c+1)^{1/2}\}$ if $-1 < c \leq 0$; $E^r$ if $c \leq -1$
2. (a) The parabola $x = c^2 + y^2/4c^2$ if $c \neq 0$; the positive $x$-axis if $c = 0$
   (b) The lines $t = s(k \pm \sqrt{k^2 - 1})$ if $k = 1/m$, $m^2 < 1$; the line $t = s$ if $m = 1$; the line $t = -s$ if $m = -1$; $\{(0, 0)\}$ if $m^2 > 1$
   (c) $\{(x, y) \in Q : x \leq a^2\}$
3. $\mathbf{g}(E^2) = \{(x, y) : x \geq 0, y \geq 0\}$
   (a) The parts of the lines $x + y = 2|c|$, $y = x + 2|c|$, $y + 2|c| = x$ in $\mathbf{g}(E^2)$
   (b) The union of the lines $s + t = m(s - t)$ and $s + t = -m(s - t)$
   (c) $\{(x, y) : x^2 + y^2 \leq 2a^2, x \geq 0, y \geq 0\}$
4. (b) The part of the cone between the plane $z = 0$ and the vertex
   (c) The $s$-axis; $\{(m, 1) : m \text{ any integer}\}$
5. (a) $\mathbf{g}(\Delta) = \{(x, x^2) : x \geq \frac{2}{3}\}$
   (b) If $c \geq \frac{2}{3}$, the part of the ellipse $s^2 + st + t^2 = 1/c$ in $\Delta$; if $c < \frac{2}{3}$, the empty set

**Section 4–2**

1. $\begin{pmatrix} 1 & 1 & 5 \\ -2 & 0 & 1 \end{pmatrix}$. The rank is 2. The kernel consists of all scalar multiples of
$$\epsilon_1 - 11\epsilon_2 + 2\epsilon_3.$$
3. (a) The diagonal elements are $c^1, \ldots, c^n$; all other elements are 0.
   (b) $(\mathbf{L}^{-1})^i(\mathbf{x}) = (c^i)^{-1}x^i$ provided $c^i \neq 0$ for every $i$
5. (a) Reflection in the line $s = t$
   (b) They are rotations through angle $3\pi/2$, $\pi/2$ respectively.
6. $\mathbf{L}$ is not a rotation.
8. (b) If $\mathbf{g}(\mathbf{t}) = \mathbf{L}(\mathbf{t}) + \mathbf{x}_0$, then $\mathbf{L}$ must be nonsingular.

### Section 4-3

1. (a) Except where $s^2 = t^2$; everywhere in $E^2$; everywhere in $\Delta$
   (b) $\mathbf{g}_1 = \mathbf{e}_1 + \mathbf{e}_2$, $\mathbf{g}_2 = -\mathbf{e}_1 + \mathbf{e}_2$ in $Q_1 = \{(s, t) : s - t > 0, s + t > 0\}$,
   $\mathbf{g}_1 = -\mathbf{e}_1 + \mathbf{e}_2$, $\mathbf{g}_2 = \mathbf{e}_1 + \mathbf{e}_2$ in $Q_2 = \{(s, t) : s - t < 0, s + t > 0\}$,
   with similar expressions in the other two of the four quadrants $Q_3$, $Q_4$ into which the lines $s = \pm t$ divide $E^2$.
   $\mathbf{g}_1 = -2\pi t(\sin 2\pi s)\mathbf{e}_1 + 2\pi t(\cos 2\pi s)\mathbf{e}_2$,
   $\mathbf{g}_2 = (\cos 2\pi s)\mathbf{e}_1 + (\sin 2\pi s)\mathbf{e}_2 - \mathbf{e}_3$;
   $\mathbf{g}_1 = -(s^2 + st + t^2)^{-2}(2s + t)[\mathbf{e}_1 - 2(s^2 + st + t^2)^{-1}\mathbf{e}_2]$,
   $\mathbf{g}_2 = -(s^2 + st + t^2)^{-2}(s + 2t)[\mathbf{e}_1 - 2(s^2 + st + t^2)^{-1}\mathbf{e}_2]$.
   (c) 2; 2 unless $t = 0$, and 1 if $t = 0$; 1
   (d) 2 in $Q_1, Q_3$, $-2$ in $Q_2, Q_4$; not applicable; 0

### Section 4-4

1. $F_{12} = xf_{12} + xyf_{22} + f_2$, the partial derivatives of $f$ being evaluated at $(x, xy)$
2. $F_1 = f_1 + f_3 g_1$, $F_2 = f_2 + f_3 g_2$,
   $F_{11} = f_{11} + 2f_{13}g_1 + f_{33}(g_1)^2 + f_3 g_{11}$,
   $F_{12} = f_{12} + f_{13}g_2 + f_{32}g_1 + f_{33}g_1 g_2 + f_3 g_{12}$,
   $F_{22} = f_{22} + 2f_{23}g_2 + f_{33}(g_2)^2 + f_3 g_{22}$
3. (a) 162 (b) $-\phi'(\frac{3}{2})\phi'(\frac{1}{2})$
4. (b) $15\mathbf{E}_1 + 54\mathbf{E}_2$, $-3\mathbf{E}_1$

### Section 4-5

1. (a) Yes, $\mathbf{g}(E^n) = E^n$, $\mathbf{g}^{-1}(\mathbf{x}) = \mathbf{x} - \mathbf{x}_0$
   (b) Yes, $\mathbf{g}(E^2) = E^2$. $\mathbf{g}^{-1}(x, y) = \frac{1}{3}[(x + 2y)\boldsymbol{\epsilon}_1 + (x - y)\boldsymbol{\epsilon}_2]$
   (c) No, $\mathbf{g}(E^2)$ is the half-plane $4x \geq -9$.
   (d) Yes, $\mathbf{g}(\Delta) = \Delta$, $\mathbf{g}$ is not univalent since $\mathbf{g}(-s, -t) = \mathbf{g}(s, t)$.
   (e) Yes, $\mathbf{g}(\Delta) = \{(x, y): 0 < y < \frac{1}{2}\exp(-x)\}$, $\mathbf{g}^{-1}(x, y) = \frac{1}{2}[(a + b)\boldsymbol{\epsilon}_1 + (a - b)\boldsymbol{\epsilon}_2]$, where $a = (y^{-1} + 2e^x)^{1/2}$, $b = (y^{-1} - 2e^x)^{1/2}$.
2. $g^{-1}(x) = [(x + 1)^{1/2} - 1]^{1/2}$, $x > 0$
3. Its matrix is $\begin{pmatrix} -1 & 0 & 1 \\ 0 & 1 & 0 \\ 1 & 0 & 0 \end{pmatrix}$.
4. If $0 < \cos c < 1$, the image of the line $t = c$ is the right half of the hyperbola $x^2/\cos^2 c - y^2/\sin^2 c = 1$; and if $-1 < c < 0$ it is the left half. If $\cos c = 0$, it is the $y$-axis, if $\cos c = 1$ the right half of the $x$-axis; if $\cos c = -1$, the left half.
5. (b) $(\mathbf{g}|\tilde{\Delta})^{-1}(x, y) = \log R(x, y)\boldsymbol{\epsilon}_1 + \Theta(x, y)\boldsymbol{\epsilon}_2$, where $R(x, y) = (x^2 + y^2)^{1/2}$, $\Theta(x, y)$ is the angle from the positive $x$-axis to $(x, y)$.
   (c) $\mathbf{g}(E^2) = E^2 - \{(0, 0)\}$

### Section 4-6

1. $\phi' = -\Phi_1/\Phi_2$. $\phi'' = -[(\Phi_2)^2\Phi_{11} - 2\Phi_1\Phi_2\Phi_{12} + (\Phi_1)^2\Phi_{22}]/(\Phi_2)^3$
2. $\phi_{11} = -[(\Phi_2)^2\Phi_{11} - 2\Phi_1\Phi_2\Phi_{12} + (\Phi_1)^2\Phi_{22}]/(\Phi_1)^3$
3. $\phi_1 = -1$, $\psi_1 = 0$, $\phi_2 = 0$, $\psi_2 = 1$ at $(-1, 1)$
4. (b) Radius $3\sqrt{2}/2$ (c) Radius $\sqrt{21}$

**Section 4–7**

1. $\{(x, y) : F(x, y) = c\}$ is an ellipse if $\log c > 2$, is the one point set $\{(0, 0)\}$ if $\log c = 2$, and is empty if $\log c < 2$. Any ellipse is a 1-manifold.

2. (a) The cone is not a 2-manifold.
   (b) $2(x - 2) - (y + 1) + 4(z - 1) = 0$

7. No

**Section 4–8**

1. $\frac{3}{5}$
2. $|c|$ if $c \leq \frac{1}{2}$, $\sqrt{c - \frac{1}{4}}$ if $c \geq \frac{1}{2}$
3. $\sqrt{14/3}$
9. (a) $\lambda_1 = \lambda_2 = 1, \quad \lambda_3 = -1$

**Section 5–1**

2. $V(Y) = 4, \quad V(Z) = 12, \quad V(Y \cup Z) = 13, \quad V(Y \cap Z) = 3$
3. $V(I_1 \cup I_2) = \frac{19}{2}, \quad V(I_1 \cap I_2) = \frac{1}{2}$
4. $(e - 1) \exp\left(\frac{1}{m}\right) \dfrac{1/m}{\exp(1/m) - 1}$

**Section 5–2**

5. $239\pi/240$.

**Section 5–3**

1. (a) Unbounded; $(-\infty, 0]$
   (b) Bounded; $E^2$
   (c) Bounded; $E^2$
   (d) Bounded; $\{(x, y) : y^2 \geq x^2, |x| + |y| \leq 1\}$
3. 1

**Section 5–5**

1. (a) $\frac{9}{2}$, $(\frac{1}{2}, \frac{8}{5})$ (b) $1 + \pi/2$, $(\bar{x}, 0)$ where $\bar{x} = 2/(6 + 3\pi)$
2. $(1 - 3e^{-2})/4$
3. $$\int_{-2}^{2} dx \int_{-\sqrt{4-x^2}}^{\sqrt{4-x^2}} dz \left\{\int_{\sqrt{x^2+z^2}}^{\sqrt{8-x^2-z^2}} f\, dy + \int_{-\sqrt{8-x^2-z^2}}^{-\sqrt{x^2+z^2}} f\, dy\right\}$$
4. 8
5. $\frac{51}{15}$
6. (b) $(e - 1)^2$ (c) $2 - 2\pi$

**Section 5–6**

1. (a) Exists (b) Exists if $p < 1$; divergent if $p \geq 1$
   (c) Exists (d) Exists
   (e) Exists if $p < 1$, $p + q > 1$; divergent otherwise
5. (a) 0 (b) $\pi$ (c) 0

**Section 5–7**

1. $\frac{1}{6}$ 2. 7

**Section 5–8**

1. $\int_2^3 f(x)\,dx = \int_0^1 f[g(t)](2 - 2t)\,dt$, provided either integral exists.
2. $2 \log 2$
3. $\frac{165}{6}$

**Section 5–9**

1. $2a^5/15$ 2. $\frac{1}{6}$ 3. $\frac{1}{2}$
4. $\int_0^{\pi/2} d\theta \int_0^{[\cos\theta + \sin\theta]^{-1}} r\,dr \int_0^{g(r\cos\theta,\, r\sin\theta)} f[r\cos\theta, r\sin\theta, z]\,dz$
5. $\frac{4\pi}{3}(a^2 - b^2)^{3/2}$ 7. $\pi/2$ 9. $\pi^2/4$

10. (a) $\frac{1}{3}\Gamma(\frac{3}{2})\Gamma(\frac{1}{3})/\Gamma(\frac{11}{6})$ (b) $\Gamma(\frac{3}{4})\Gamma(\frac{1}{2})/\Gamma(\frac{5}{4})$
 (c) $\frac{1}{b}\Gamma\left(\frac{a+1}{b}\right)$ (d) $\left(\frac{-1}{d+1}\right)^{c+1}\Gamma(c+1)$
 (e) $\Gamma(k+1)/\Gamma(n+k+1)$
 (f) $a_1^{-(k+1)/2}\,\Gamma\left(\frac{k+1}{2}\right)(a_2 \ldots a_n)^{-1/2}\,\pi^{(n-1)/2}$

**Section 5–11**

1. (a) $2\tan^{-1}(1/t)$ (b) $\frac{1 + \exp(\pi t)}{t^2 + 1}$
3. $\phi(x) = (\sqrt{\pi}/2)\exp(-x^2/4)$
5. $t^{-1}[2\exp(t^4) - (1 + 1/\log t)\exp(t^2 \log^2 t)]$

**Section 6–1**

1. $-1,\ 0,\ 1,\ 0,\ 0$
2. $-1$

**Section 6–2**

1. $\mathbf{e}^1 \wedge \mathbf{e}^{234} = \mathbf{e}^3 \wedge \mathbf{e}^{124} = \mathbf{e}^{1234}$, $\mathbf{e}^2 \wedge \mathbf{e}^{134} = \mathbf{e}^4 \wedge \mathbf{e}^{123} = -\mathbf{e}^{1234}$
2. (a) $6\mathbf{e}^{12} + 2\mathbf{e}^{13} - \mathbf{e}^{23}$ (b) $\mathbf{0}$
 (c) $-3\mathbf{e}^{123}$ (d) $4\mathbf{e}^{123}$
3. (a) $-\mathbf{e}^{12345}$ (b) $\mathbf{e}^{1235} - \mathbf{e}^{1234} - \mathbf{e}^{1345}$

**Section 6–3**

1. (a) $-\mathbf{e}_{2345}$ (b) $\mathbf{0}$ (c) $-\mathbf{e}_{146}$
 (d) $2\mathbf{e}_{6'} + \mathbf{e}_{2'} - 2\mathbf{e}_{1'}$, where $i' = (1, \ldots, i-1, i+1, \ldots, 6)$
 (e) $2\mathbf{e}_{1\cdots 6}$
2. (a) 2 (b) 0 (c) $-1$ (d) $-3$
3. Negative 4. Yes 5. No 6. $\sqrt{3}/2$ 7. $\frac{1}{2}$

**Section 6–4**

1. (a) If $\mathbf{b} = \mathbf{L}^*(\mathbf{a})$, then $b_1 = a_1 - a_2 + 2a_3$, $b_2 = -2a_1 + 3a_3$
   (b) $c_{12}^{12} = -2$, $c_{12}^{13} = 7$, $c_{12}^{23} = -3$
   (c) If $\boldsymbol{\beta} = c\boldsymbol{\epsilon}_{12}$, then $\mathbf{L}_2(\boldsymbol{\beta}) = c\mathbf{v}_1 \wedge \mathbf{v}_2 = c(-2\mathbf{e}_{12} + 7\mathbf{e}_{13} - 3\mathbf{e}_{23})$, where $\mathbf{v}_1$ and $\mathbf{v}_2$ are the column vectors.
   (d) If $\boldsymbol{\omega} = \omega_{12}\mathbf{e}^{12} + \omega_{13}\mathbf{e}^{13} + \omega_{23}\mathbf{e}^{23}$, then $\mathbf{L}_2^*(\boldsymbol{\omega}) = (-2\omega_{12} + 7\omega_{13} - 3\omega_{23})\boldsymbol{\epsilon}^{12}$.
   (e) $\mathbf{0}$

**Section 6–5**

1. (a) $4xy\, dx \wedge dy$ (b) $2xy \sin(xy^2)\, dx \wedge dy \wedge dz$
   (c) $-f_2\, dx \wedge dz$ (d) $3\, dx \wedge dy \wedge dz$

3. (a) $\frac{1}{n} \sum_{i=1}^{n} (-1)^{i+1} x^i\, dx^i \wedge \cdots \wedge dx^{i-1} \wedge dx^{i+1} \wedge \cdots \wedge dx^n$

   (b) $\frac{1}{r} \sum_{k=1}^{r} (-1)^{k+1} x^{i_k} \mathbf{E}^{\lambda_k}$, where $\lambda_k = (i_1, \ldots, i_{k-1}, i_{k+1}, \ldots, i_r)$

5. (a) $0$ if $r$ is odd; $-2\, d\omega \wedge d\zeta$ if $r$ is even
   (b) $\mathbf{0}$

7. $\boldsymbol{\omega}^{\#} = M \circ \mathbf{g}\, dg^1 + N \circ \mathbf{g}\, dg^2$. $(d\boldsymbol{\omega})^{\#} = \left(\frac{\partial N}{\partial y} - \frac{\partial M}{\partial x}\right) \circ \mathbf{g} \frac{\partial(g^1, g^2)}{\partial(s, t)}\, ds \wedge dt$

8. (a) $f \circ g\, s\, ds \wedge dt \wedge du$ (b) $s \cos t \sin t\, ds \wedge du + s^2 \cos^2 t\, dt \wedge du$

**Section 6–7**

3. $\mathbf{e}_1 \times \mathbf{e}_2 = \mathbf{e}_3$, $\mathbf{e}_1 \times \mathbf{e}_3 = -\mathbf{e}_2$, $\mathbf{e}_2 \times \mathbf{e}_3 = \mathbf{e}_1$

**Section 7–1**

1. (a) $4\sqrt{3}$; the triangle with vertices $2\mathbf{e}_3$, $\mathbf{e}_1 + \mathbf{e}_2$, $\mathbf{e}_1 - 3\mathbf{e}_2 + 4\mathbf{e}_3$
   (b) $\rho \sin \alpha$; a solid cone from which points $(x, 0, z)$, $0 \leq x \leq z$, are deleted
   (c) $[1 + s^2 + t^2]^{1/2}$; the hyperboloid $x = yz$

2. (a) $T_N(\mathbf{t}) = \{\mathbf{k} : k^1 s + k^2 t + k^3 u = 0\}$,
   $T_M(\mathbf{x}) = \{\mathbf{h} : h^1 x/a^2 + h^2 y/b^2 + h^3 z/c^2 = 0\}$
   (b) $J\mathbf{g}(\mathbf{t}) = [a^2b^2u^2 + a^2c^2t^2 + b^2c^2s^2]^{1/2}$

3. $\mathbf{g}$ is not an open transformation.

**Section 7–2**

1. $\Delta = \{(x, y) : |x| < 1, |x| < y < (3 - x^2)/2\}$,
   $\tilde{\Delta} = \{(x, z) : |x| < 1, z > 0, z^2 < 3 - x^2 - 2|x|\}$,
   $\mathbf{g}(x, y) = x\mathbf{e}_1 + y\mathbf{e}_2 + (3 - x^2 - 2y)^{1/2}\mathbf{e}_3$,
   $\tilde{\mathbf{g}}(x, z) = x\mathbf{e}_1 + \frac{1}{2}(3 - x^2 - z^2)\mathbf{e}_2 + z\mathbf{e}_3$,
   $\phi(x, y) = (x, (3 - x^2 - 2y)^{1/2})$

2. $\mathbf{F}(M) = \{(s, t) : t < \exp s\}$

**Section 7–3**

1. $\frac{2\pi}{3}[2^{3/2} - 1]$

3. $\frac{\partial \mathbf{g}}{\partial \phi} \wedge \frac{\partial \mathbf{g}}{\partial \theta} = (\sin \phi \cos \phi)\mathbf{e}_{12} + (\sin^2 \phi \sin \theta)\mathbf{e}_{31} + (\sin^2 \phi \cos \theta)\mathbf{e}_{23}$

4. (a) $8\pi/3$ (b) $\sqrt{3}/6$
6. (b) $4\pi^2 r_1 r_2$

**Section 7–4**

2. (a) $-8\pi$ (b) $\pi(e^4 - 1)$
3. $\frac{1}{3}$
4. $\frac{1}{2}$
5. (a) $\mathbf{o}(\mathbf{x}) = [(-\sin s)\mathbf{e}_1 + (\cos s)\mathbf{e}_2] \wedge [(-\sin t)\mathbf{e}_3 + (\cos t)\mathbf{e}_4]$
   (b) $\pi^2$

**Section 7–5**

2. $\frac{1}{12}$
3. $\boldsymbol{\omega}$ is not of class $C^{(1)}$ on cl $D$.
4. (a) $-\dfrac{\pi}{3}$ (b) $-\dfrac{8\pi}{15}$

**Section 7–6**

1. $\pi$ 2. (a) 0 (b) $\sqrt{2}(1 - e^{-1})$ (c) 0

**Section A–1**

1. (a) 2, 1 (b) $\sqrt{2}$, no lower bound
   (c) $\sqrt{2}$, $-1$ (d) 0, $-e^{-1}$ (e) 1, $\frac{1}{2}$

**Section A–2**

1. One basis for $\mathcal{V}$ is $\{1, x, x^2, \ldots, x^m\}$.

**Section A–3**

1. (a) $\{\mathbf{x} : 0 < |\mathbf{x} - \mathbf{x}_0| < \delta\}$, $\{\mathbf{x} : |\mathbf{x}| = 0 \text{ or } \delta\}$, $\{\mathbf{x} : |\mathbf{x}| \leq \delta\}$
   (b) Empty set, $A$, $A$
   (c) $A$, the union of the half-lines $y = 0$, $y = x + 1$, $x \geq -1$, $\{(x, y) : 0 \leq y \leq x + 1, x \geq -1\}$
   (d) $A$, the union of the circle $x^2 + y^2 = 1$ and the line segment joining (0, 0) and (1, 0), the closed circular disk $x^2 + y^2 \leq 1$
   (e) Empty set, $E^2$, $E^2$
   (f) Empty set, $A$, $A$
   (g) Empty set, $A \cup \{0\}$, $A \cup \{0\}$
2. Open in (c), (d); closed in (b), (f)

**Section A–4**

1. (a) 0 (b) No limit (c) 0 (d) $e^2$ (e) 1
2. (a) $(-\frac{1}{2}, 0)$ (b) No limit (c) (1, 0)

**Section A–5**

1. (a) $\frac{1}{2}$ (b) No limit (c) $\frac{1}{2}$ (d) $(1, 5) = \mathbf{e}_1 + 5\mathbf{e}_2$ (e) No limit
   Continuity: In (a), (b), (e) except at (0, 0). In (c) except at 0. If we set $f(0) = \frac{1}{2}$, then $f$ is also continuous at 0. In (d) at every point of $E^1$
6. (a) 0 (b) No limit (c) No limit (d) 1

# Index

# INDEX

ABCDE698765